Nazi War Crimes, US Intelligence and Selective Prosecution at Nuremberg

Controversies regarding the role of the Office of Strategic Services

Nazi War Crimes, US Intelligence and Selective Prosecution at Nuremberg provides a balanced but critical discussion of the contribution of American intelligence officials to the Nuremberg war crimes trials process. It discusses the role of such officials in mobilising the unique resources of a modern intelligence agency in order to provide a range of important trial evidence and undertake controversial plea-bargaining negotiations. The book also reviews recently declassified US intelligence documents to provide new details of how senior Nazi war criminals, such as SS-General Karl Wolff, were provided with effective immunity deals, partly as a reward for their wartime cooperation with US intelligence officials, including Allen Dulles, former CIA Director. This historical case study suggests that both war crimes prosecutors and intelligence officials can engage in mutually beneficial collaborations. The proviso, Michael Salter argues, is that both sides need to recognise and appreciate the problems that may arise from the fact that these institutitions are required to operate according to different, and in some cases contradictory, agendas.

Michael Salter is Professor of Law at Lancashire Law School, UK.

Nazi War Crimes, US Intelligence and Selective Prosecution at Nuremberg

Controversies regarding the role of the Office of Strategic Services

Michael Salter

Routledge
Taylor & Francis Group
LONDON AND NEW YORK

First published 2007 by Cavendish Publishing

Published 2015
by Routledge
2 Park Square, Milton Park, Abingdon, Oxon, OX14 4RN

Simultaneously published in the USA and Canada
by Routledge
711 Third Avenue, New York, NY 10017

Routledge is an imprint of the Taylor & Francis Group, an informa business

Typeset in Times New Roman by
RefineCatch Limited, Bungay, Suffolk

British Library Cataloguing in Publication Data
A catalogue record for this book is available from the British Library

Library of Congress Cataloging-in-Publication Data
Salter, Michael, 1957–
Nazi war crimes, US intelligence and selective prosecution at Nuremburg : controversies regarding the role of the Office of Strategic Services / Michael Salter.
p. cm.
ISBN–13: 978–1–904385–81–3 (hardback)
ISBN–10: 1–904385–81–8 (hardback)
ISBN–13: 978–1–904385–80–6 (pbk.)
ISBN–10: 1–904385–80–X (pbk.)
1. Nuremberg Trial of Major German War Criminals, Nuremberg, Germany, 1945–1946. 2. Nuremberg War Crime Trials, Nuremberg, Germany, 1946–1949. 3. United States. Office of Strategic Services. 4. United States. Central Intelligence Agency. 5. World War, 1939–1945—Military intelligence—United States. 6. Evidence, Criminal—Germany—History—20th century. I. Title.
KZ1176.5.S25 2007
341.6′90268—dc22 2006036701

ISBN10: 1–904385–80–X (pbk)
ISBN10: 1–904385–81–8 (hbk)
ISBN10: 0–203–94510–7 (ebk)

ISBN13: 978–1–904385–80–6 (pbk)
ISBN13: 978–1–904385–81–3 (hbk)
ISBN13: 978–0–203–94510–0 (ebk)

I would like to thank those individuals and publishing collaborators too numerous to list for their professional inspiration and help, and – on a more personal and familial note – to dedicate this work to Charlie, Glen, John, Leslie, Martin, Naomi and Ray.

Contents

Chapter 1

Introducing the rationale, aims and methodology

> Intelligence work is by definition illegal. If it is very effective intelligence work it is very illegal.
>
> (David Whipple, former OSS official, who worked under Allen Dulles in wartime Bern)[1]

Introduction

This book addresses the various controversies and contradictions affecting the involvement of one US intelligence organisation, the wartime Office of Strategic Services ('OSS', 1942–45, precursor to the CIA, 1947–), within the Nuremberg war crimes trial programme. In particular it focuses upon the OSS's dual role as a source of incriminating trial evidence and possible immunity for war crimes suspects deemed to be valuable for future intelligence operations as informants or agents.

The OSS was created in 1942[2] as a complex wartime organisation. It had various sub-divisions, ranging from the scholarly Research and Analysis Branch (R&A) through to the espionage work and guerrilla warfare operations of the Secret Intelligence (SI) and Special Operations Branches (SO) respectively; it also included Foreign Nationalities, Visual Presentation and Field Photographic Branches.[3] The OSS was formally dissolved at the end of September 1945, but nearly all of its 130-plus war crimes staff remained at Nuremberg as employees of a re-branded organisation: the Strategic Services Unit (SSU) attached to the US War Department. It is true that gathering

1 Cited in A. Lebor, *Hitler's Secret Bankers* (London: Pocket Books, 1997), 215–16.

2 Originally titled the 'Office of the Coordinator of Information', headed by General William J. Donovan.

3 For general studies of the OSS, see also B. Smith, *The Shadow Warriors. OSS and the Origins of the CIA* (New York: Basic Books, 1983); A. Cave Brown, *The Last Hero, Wild Bill Donovan* (New York: Times Books, 1982); B. Katz, *Foreign Intelligence, Research and Analysis in the Office of Strategic Services, 1942–1945* (Cambridge, MA: Harvard University Press, 1989); and R. Winks, *Cloak and Gown, Scholars in the Secret War, 1939–1961* (New York: Morrow, 1987).

potential trial evidence and preparing prosecution strategies was hardly the main wartime aim of the OSS, and its activities on this front only began in earnest from November 1943. Nevertheless, it remained the case that, at the end of the war in May 1945, this organisation had still made greater progress with trial preparations than any other American or British government agency, including the legal departments of the Allied armies, or the understaffed United Nations War Crimes Commission.

Whilst the present book focuses mainly on the role of the OSS, this should not be taken to imply that OSS staff were the only intelligence officials who were active in this field. On the contrary, the American Army's Counter Intelligence Corps (CIC) were also deployed, albeit largely in the far narrower role of hunting down middle and lower level war crimes suspects.

This chapter will explain both the objectives of the present book and a number of the different contexts into which readers, and other researchers working within a range of different disciplines, could situate aspects of the detailed historical case studies that it contains. It is necessary to clarify the reasons why a distinctly interdisciplinary book of this kind is required to revise, and partly fill a gap within, the existing scholarship. Hence, this section also discusses the different ways in which war crimes prosecutors have collaborated with intelligence officials, and identifies the challenges such interaction poses to the apparently disconnected and independent academic sub-disciplines of international criminal law and intelligence studies. It will also indicate the specific criticisms of assumptions behind earlier scholarship and academic controversies to which the author seeks both to address through detailed historical case studies and, through reflection upon the implications of these case studies for existing debates, to carry forward into the future.

This book is deliberately empirical in nature, in that it seeks to 'reconstruct' from previously secret archival documents what happened when Nuremberg prosecutors entered into a temporary form of collaboration with aspects of the OSS. Yet, all empirical work including archival studies will, whether or not this is recognised, make a series of assumptions concerning the meaning, scope and implications of both the subject matter and the activity of conducting viable research. These assumptions cannot themselves be proven or falsified by reference to empirical facts. This is because they underpin the very activity of defining, identifying and gathering such data. Hence, it is reasonable for all researchers to try to state these assumptions as clearly as possible, without entering into the entirely different project of seeking to justify these through theoretical argumentation and conceptual analysis. For present purposes my assumptions are as follows:

- Few, if any, social phenomena are simple, lacking ambiguities, or internal or external contradictions.
- Events are rarely, if ever, explicable from a single standpoint that focuses on one type of causal explanation, such as economic interests.

- No single academic discipline, such as economics, philosophy or psychology, is capable by means of its own efforts and distinctive mode of analysis of providing a complete and self-sufficient account of any research topic.
- All research topics are subject to processes of historical change; and therefore it is important to consider issues of emergence, development and destruction over periods of time. Nothing is simply 'given'; everything is always in the process of becoming different from how it has been in the past and how it now is.
- There can be no ultimate perspective or explanation of any topic that is complete and sufficient to the point of being immune from future criticism and constructive development.
- Any research findings and their interpretation by researchers are necessarily provisional, contingent and open to future reinterpretation, particularly when new data or theoretical insights become available. All research builds upon and presupposes the work of past investigators, and will be built upon in various ways by later researchers in ways that cannot always be predicted or controlled.
- Even apparently straightforward events are likely to be defined, perceived and acted upon in different ways by various individuals and groups. Hence, it is necessary for researchers to appreciate and do justice to multiple accounts of the 'same' events.
- Conflicts, unnoticed gaps, contradictions and ambiguities are to be expected, perhaps even welcomed, both in the subject matter and in the process of conducting research into them.
- Detailed case studies of specific events can be as revealing of wider historical and institutional tendencies, as apparently broader sociological approaches that seek to capture and generalise about the entire field. Indeed, it is helpful if such broader approaches are based upon a series of in-depth case studies so that knowledge is developed 'from the bottom up' as it were.
- Apparent 'negatives' (such as the failure to prosecute a potential war crimes defendant) should be recognised as comprising a legitimate part of the research agenda, as are so-called 'positive' dimensions (e.g., the actual trial, conviction and punishment of such a defendant). Indeed, the 'positives' are perhaps better understood when grasped in the context of the so-called 'negatives'.

Based on the belief, stated above, that no 'single' and supposedly self-sufficient academic discipline can ever be adequate to any single research topic, it is necessary for this book to integrate aspects of at least two such disciplines.

In one sense, the following chapters aim to make a contribution to legal, as well as intelligence history, focusing mainly upon events within the Second

World War and the immediate post-war decade. On the other hand, the present work also addresses a cluster of issues, possibilities and dilemmas regarding the selective granting of legal immunity that resonate at least as strongly today as they did during the time in which they originally took place.

The present book makes a largely empirical contribution to the start of a wider project of developing a model of the conditions under which Western intelligence agencies consider trading legal immunity in return for the cooperation of leading figures within regimes responsible for mass human rights violations. One part focuses on the extent to which Karl Wolff, former Chief of Himmler's Personal Staff and joint second highest official within the entire SS,[4] was able to avoid legal accountability within the Nuremberg process for a range of war crimes, partly as a direct result of his wartime cooperation with a US intelligence agency.[5]

In earlier studies, the present writer has set out, and then refined, a programme of socio-legal research into newly declassified intelligence files.[6] This programme addresses the previously neglected topic of the close institutional relationships that have existed episodically during the last 60 years between war crimes prosecutors and Western intelligence agencies. One argument is that the perceived legitimacy of war crimes trials is governed by imperatives of transparency (including press reporting), reasoned justifications for decisions, independence from government control, and respect for standards associated with due process and the rule of law. By contrast, officials working for intelligence agencies necessarily have to work to, and under, a very different set of institutional imperatives. As secret arms of the executive concerned with the anticipation and thwarting of threats to a politically defined conception of 'national security', such officials cannot operate effectively according to the imperatives governing the legal response to past war crimes.

One purpose of the wider agenda behind this book is to encourage a series of detailed, empirical research projects into a number of proposed case studies regarding how the considerable logistical resources of modern intelligence agency can assist in the prosecution of those war criminals responsible for planning, ordering and committing large-scale human rights

4 R. Koehl, *The Black Corps* (Madison: University of Wisconsin Press, 1983), 113–20, 234–45.

5 We cannot discount the possibility that Wolff's immunity also arose to some extent as one of the unspoken conditions of his extensive post-war assistance to his interrogators within both Allied Military Intelligence and then the Nuremberg prosecutors, an important theme for later investigations.

6 I. Bryan and M. Salter, 'War Crimes Prosecutor and Intelligence Agencies: The Case for Assessing their Collaboration' (2001) 16 *Intelligence and National Security* 93–120; M. Salter, 'Unsettling Accounts: Methodological Issues Within the Reconstruction of the Role of a US Intelligence Agency Within the Nuremberg Trials' (2003) 56 *Current Legal Issues* 275–305.

violations and atrocities more generally.[7] Whilst this earlier programme still remains defensible, it also needs to be counter-balanced by a number of case studies that, from a liberal human rights perspective at least, highlight the 'negative' aspects of allowing close institutional collaboration between war crimes prosecutors and intelligence agencies, particularly the CIA. What is still needed is a close empirical reconstruction of the events recorded in the paper trail scattered across various archival collections in Britain, America and Germany in order to assess the extent to which the trenchant moral judgements regarding Wolff's alleged immunity from prosecution can now be supported by clear empirical evidence.

The events regarding the combination of immunity deals and a series of positive contributions to the preparing of the prosecution's case that characterises the historical record of intelligence officials with respect to the Nuremberg process continue to resonate. As Breitman *et al.* recognise, even today: 'the post-war fate of the perpetrators of wartime atrocities' remains 'controversial', and that during the 1980s, 'the international hunt for Josef Mengele and the trial of Klaus Barbie raised questions about how some Nazi war criminals managed to escape post-war justice, or at least postpone it for decades'.[8] Furthermore, the Barbie case highlighted the fact that part of the explanation for such evasions lay in the interventions of US Army Counter Intelligence officials.[9]

At this point it is, perhaps, useful to recall some basic historical facts that need to be understood before the more detailed material is discussed. The assessments regarding future war crimes policy produced by the OSS Research and Analysis (R&A) Branch intelligence officials were, until April 1945, largely speculative. This is because Allied war crimes policy was still undecided. Whilst the Western Allies had established a United Nations War Crimes Commission at the end of 1942, it remained unclear for a long time whether German military, diplomatic and political leaders would be dealt with in a summary fashion under military law, or by means of a costly and time-consuming international trial. Furthermore, American planning with

7 See C. Hulme and M. Salter, 'The Persecution of Religion as a War Crime: The OSS's Response within the Nuremberg Trials Process' (2001) 3 *Rutgers Journal of Law and Religion*, http://www.camlaw.rutgers.edu/publications/law-religion/v3n1.htm; M. Salter, 'The Prosecution of Nazi War Criminals and the OSS: The Need for a New Research Agenda' (2002) 2 *Journal of Intelligence History*, 77–119.

8 Breitman *et al.*, 2004, *op cit*, introduction.

9 *Ibid.* R. Wolfe, IWG Historian, 'Analysis of the Investigative Records Repository (IRR) File of Klaus Barbie *(Alias Klaus Altmann, Klaus Becker, Heinz Becker, Klaus Behrens, Heinz Behrens, Klaus Spier, Ernst Holzer)*', 19 September 2001: http://www.archives.gov/iwg/research-papers/barbie-irr-file.html.

respect to the related but more extensive programme of de-Nazification[10] did not begin to take shape until June to October 1944 during the debate on the 'Morgenthau Plan' for the de-industrialisation of post-war Germany. Even then it faced a variety of firm objections from War Department officials.[11] It was only in April 1945, virtually at the end of the war, that the Allied authorities issued an *Arrest Categories Handbook* containing a list of persons to be immediately arrested.

The Nuremberg programme began within weeks of the end of the Second World War, that is, in early May 1945. It was prompted largely by the appointment of Justice Jackson, a former Supreme Court Judge, as chief of the dominant American prosecution organisation, the Office of the Chief of Counsel (OCC). The charges contained in the extensive indictment, which Franz Neumann, *de facto* chief of the Central European sub-section of OSS–R&A based in Washington DC and later at Nuremberg,[12] helped draft, were presented to the defendants on 25 October 1945. These charges, known as Counts One through to Four, stemmed from the Nuremberg Charter, an international agreement negotiated between the Allied powers throughout the summer of 1945 which, on 8 August 1945, culminated in a signed agreement setting up both an International Military Tribunal and certain new criminal offences.

The offences contained in Article 6 of the Charter, included 'crimes against the peace' (Count Two of the indictment), e.g., 'planning, preparation, initiation and waging aggressive war', traditional war crimes against the 'laws and customs of war' (Count Three), such as the maltreatment of captured soldiers, and 'crimes against humanity' (charged under Count Four), including the 'persecution, enslavement, deportation and murder' of civilian populations 'before or during the war'. In addition, Count One of this indictment also created the new offence of formulating or participating in a 'conspiracy' or 'common plan' to commit the crimes defined in the Counts Two, Three and Four.[13]

The trials themselves opened on 20 November 1945 and lasted for over ten months. The lawyers' final presentation of evidence before the International Military Tribunal (IMT), which was comprised of eight judges, two each from France, America, Britain and the Soviet Union, occurred on 31 August

10 See 'Security-Classified "Civil Affairs Guides" and Correspondence Relating to Conditions and Institutions in Germany and German-Occupied Countries 1944–1945': US National Archives Modern Military Division (NA), Record Group (RG) 226, Entry 44, Boxes 3–8.

11 L. Niethammer, *Das Mitläuferfabrik: Die Entnazifizierung am Beispiel Bayern* (Berlin: Verlag, 1982), 52.

12 Neumann was, of course, a member of the radical Frankfurt School of Critical Social Theory, alongside Herbert Marcuse and Otto Kirchheimer.

13 For additional details, see *The Judgement of Nuremberg: 1946* (London: HMSO, 1999), 1–6.

1946. As an international trial of 'major war criminals', the 22 individual defendants who stood trial were drawn mainly from leadership positions within different sectors of the Nazi regime. Adolph Hitler as Head of State, SS Chief Heinrich Himmler and Nazi Labour Front leader Robert Ley had committed suicide, whilst Martin Bormann, Hitler's private secretary, was tried in his absence even though it has later been accepted that he died in Berlin in May 1945.[14] The other key defendants were drawn from the SS or secret police (Ernst Kaltenbrunner), Hitler youth leader (Jugendführer des Deutschen Reiches), Hitler's Foreign Minister (Joachim von Ribbentrop) and other leading Nazi diplomats (Konstantin von Neurath and Franz von Papen), the German Minister for Armaments and War Economy (Albert Speer), the German Army (Generals Jodl and Wilhelm Keitel), Navy (Admirals Erich Reader and Karl Doenitz) and Air Force (Hermann Göring) and colonial government (Hans Frank, Fritz Saukel). Nazi propagandists were also targeted as defendants, including radio broadcaster Hans Fritzsche and the anti-Semitic publisher Julius Streicher. Hitler's early finance minister, Hjalmar Schacht, was also a defendant, despite the fact that, from 1937 onwards, he was increasingly associated with the anti-Nazi opposition (which included acting as an informant to the OSS) and ended the war being detained in various concentration camps.

In addition to charges against specific individuals, six 'criminal organisations' were also prosecuted at Nuremberg: the Nazi Party, the SS (Internal Security Police), the Gestapo (political police which pre-existed the Nazis but was later subsumed into a sub-section of the SS after 1933), the SD (SS's overseas political intelligence agency), Hitler's Cabinet, the paramilitary SA (or 'brown shirts') and the Military High Commands (OKW). Ultimately, only three individual defendants were acquitted, Fritzsche, Schacht and von Papen, whilst of the organisational defendants, the High Command, Hitler's Cabinet and the SA were found not guilty.

Although a number of the defendants who were convicted were killed by hanging, with their bodily remains scattered so that there would be no symbolic site for fascist revivalists to return to, the sentences of the remainder were, in common with most other convicted Nazi war criminals, subjected to politically inspired commutations of sentence and early release in the early 1950s. Once again, these interventions, stemming from the need to retain Germany as a front-line state in the Cold War conflict against the Soviet empire, meant that few of the many thousand convicted Nazis, including

14 The OSS had told Jackson that its investigations suggested that Bormann had probably been killed in the final battle for Berlin in May 1945 but that there remained an outside possibility of him turning up alive. Hence, the file on Bormann remained open in the absence of conclusive intelligence, which finally arrived only as late as 1999, following DNA testing of a buried skull uncovered by building workers in Berlin. See N. Goda, 'Manhunts: The Official Search for Notorious Nazis', in Breitman *et al.*, 2004, ch. 15, 19–21.

those responsible for acts of genocide, were still in prison after 1953. Once again, highly contingent imperatives of political expediency clashed and overcame the supposed 'independence' and 'universality' of liberal standards of law and justice.

In order to discuss the OSS–Nuremberg trials relationship, this book focuses extensively upon the controversial work of Allen Dulles, who headed the OSS Bern Field Office between 1942 and 1945, and, to a lesser extent, Franz Neumann.[15] Throughout our analysis of different aspects of the relationship between OSS officials and the Nuremberg prosecutors, it will be necessary to focus on the wartime intelligence role of Dulles, including his interventions regarding the selective prosecution and non-prosecution of suspected war criminals. Dulles' dual role as an important source of *both* protection for Nazi war crimes suspects and incriminating documentary and witness evidence, expresses, in a microcosm, a series of the ambiguities, contradictions and dilemmas addressed by this work.

At a methodological level, the process of studying such complex relationships must avoid the danger of selectively focusing upon the issues from either the perspective of Jackson's organisation or exclusively from that of OSS officials more generally. It is equally important to reject the assumption that this topic must be understood either from the perspective of international criminal law (in isolation from intelligence studies) or *vice versa*. It is necessary for scholarly analysis to adjust itself to the object under investigation, not to discard essential elements simply because they fall outside the agenda of any specific and narrowly defined academic discipline, whether this is international criminal law or intelligence studies.

It is possible to summarise the main requirements for future research on the collaboration of intelligence agencies and war crimes prosecutors. First, this topic can be adequately reconstructed and analysed only if these events, negotiations and conflicts are understood in the wider context of the changing forms of interaction between the two relevant agencies as the preparations for the trials moved closer to completion. Secondly, the *relational aspect* needs to be addressed as an important topic in its own right. A third and related point is that such collaboration needs to be analysed from an *interdisciplinary approach* that has overcome such familiar practices of disciplinary insulation and resulting 'reductionism'.

A reductionist orientation, which perpetuates the self-insulation of the disciplines of intelligence studies and international criminal law, is only capable of analysing, say, the purely 'legal' themes as if these could be abstracted from other contextual factors. The overcoming of a reductionist approach is

15 On Neumann, see Katz, 1989, *op cit*, ch. 2; C. Hulme and M. Salter, 'The Nazis' Persecution of Religion as a War Crime: The OSS's Response within the Nuremberg Trials Process' (2002) 3 *Rutgers Journal of Law and Religion* http://www.lawandreligion.com.

needed because it results in an orientation that effectively excludes the most interesting part of the topic, the 'relational' aspects that transcend the competence of a single discipline. The antidote to reductionism lies in developing an *interdisciplinary*, as distinct from 'multi-disciplinary', approach to the study of institutional collaborations. This approach must aim to reconstruct and supplement the findings of relevant research, taking into account and integrating both of the two particular institutional contexts in question. It is the overcoming of entrenched 'reductionism' that distinguishes the proposed 'hybridisation' of parts of the two disciplines (or perhaps sub-disciplines) in question from, say, the colonisation and/or assimilation of one by the other.

A fourth requirement is for a comprehensive cross-referencing of how war crimes issues feature within the existing literature of intelligence studies and international criminal law. Participation within the Nuremberg process formed one of the many contexts in which the post-war OSS was operating, and *vice versa*. Hence, the programme of interdisciplinary research developed in the present work must extensively cross-reference and integrate these findings to ensure that this instance of inter-agency collaboration is understood from *both sides*. This programme requires researchers to produce a broader account of this collaboration so that the findings of research conducted in both relevant disciplines can then be re-assessed and, if need be, revised in the light of insights contained within the scholarship of the other.

The final requirement is to identify broader interdisciplinary conceptualisations of issues located within the overlap between 'intelligence studies' and 'international criminal law'. Such conceptualisations could provide additional momentum towards the reinterpretation of the relationship between the OSS and Allied war crimes prosecutors as this emerged and changed during the OSS's final months, and then continued under the auspices of its successor organisations, the Strategic Services Unit (SSU) of the US War Department and, from 1947, the CIA.

If these requirements can be met, the results of such research should contribute to the 'transcendence from within' of self-imposed disciplinary boundaries that, in the war crimes trials area at least, currently restrict the vision and possibilities of both intelligence studies and international criminal law. This, in turn, could allow for the fruitful expansion of the breadth of vision of these disciplines through both a process of cross-fertilisation of existing research findings, and by encouraging new empirical research projects precisely in those 'overlapping' topics that mainstream contributors to these disciplines might not otherwise envisage. The grounds for this are that they are 'too legal' for intelligence scholars, and excessively intelligence related for the tastes of international criminal law scholars.[16]

16 For example, 'cross-over' topics spanning the two disciplines could include a study of issues arising from the following: the admissibility and credibility as trial evidence of incriminating

Conclusion

This chapter has argued for the adoption of an interdisciplinary approach to study of the OSS's role at Nuremberg, which hybridises and supplements aspects of both Nuremberg and intelligence scholarship in a manner that gives equal weight to both sides of this evolving collaborative process. A major difficulty created by the adoption of an inquisitorial orientation is that it tends to preclude the very possibility of scholars being able to formulate an even-handed assessment of the ambiguities, contradictions and conflicts that characterise the OSS's interventions within the war crimes prosecution field generally. This has resulted in the neglect of important documentation that, to some extent at least, other strands of scholarship have succeeded in uncovering. As a corrective, it is necessary to study the relationship between intelligence agencies and war crimes agencies from a more nuanced and supple interdisciplinary perspective that is receptive to such ambiguities, contradictions and conflicts, and which transcends the false alternative of adopting either a prosecutorial or affirmative agenda.

Thus, one of the key aims of the present work is to provide a range of arguments, interventions within existing debates and detailed empirical analysis of specific case studies that could help develop a distinctly interdisciplinary agenda for the study of the institutional collaboration between modern war crimes prosecutors and Western intelligence agencies. This agenda suggests that the best way forward is to conduct archival research on recently declassified intelligence documentation in order to produce a series of particular case studies of specific instances where such collaboration has, in fact, taken place.

The next chapter begins the task of interdisciplinary analysis by considering evidence of the war criminality of the Wolff group.

materials contained in intelligence files; the potential legal accountability of the leadership of intelligence agencies before the emerging International Criminal Court for illegal acts committed directly or indirectly by their subordinates; the potential liability of such agencies in civil law for 'intelligence failures' to prevent terrorist atrocities; the potential legal liabilities of intelligence officers who publish their memoirs; the continuing obligation to protect covert 'sources' of intelligence whilst also cooperating with various law enforcement processes; issues arising under international human rights law regarding the partial accountability of the state for breaches of legal recognised 'privacy' rights through programmes of surveillance.

Chapter 2

Evidence of the war criminality of the Wolff group

It is inevitable, in view of the nature of my work in Switzerland, that defendants' counsel will from time to time try to drag my name into the [Nuremberg] proceedings.

(Allen Dulles)[1]

The crimes of the Third Reich were the product of specialisation and minute division of labor. Some people planned, some incited, some contributed money, and some were the 'trigger men'.

(Nuremberg prosecutor, Flick Case, 24 November 1947, transcript 10427)

It is we who have to pay for, we have to admit the bad treatment of the Jews . . . The twelve thousand charred bodies and skeletons they've found in the concentration camps naturally speak against us, and they are evidence that we will never be able to disprove . . . But I have to add that I too bear responsibility for the SS on my shoulders.

(Waffen-SS General Karl Wolff, secretly taped conversion between high-ranking German prisoners, 15 May 1945)[2]

He didn't act like a prisoner of war, which he was. At parade rest, his uniform immaculate, Wolff fixed his hazel eyes directly ahead. His features were tightly controlled, a training exercise he had mastered as No.1 aide to . . . Heinrich Himmler . . . 'I'm not a criminal' he said matter of factly. 'I did my duty as I saw it to my fatherland . . . I never had anything to do with the murders of Jews' he declared. The word 'Juden' brought a clench to the miserable fists of the human skeletons on the sidelines. How could Wolff have served for at least 10 years as chief of staff to Himmler and been innocent? 'My duties' Wolff replied 'involved many things not that' . . . His order, as other German prisoners told me and far more important people, was like getting it right from Himmler. Wolff even outranked Field

1 Dulles (Wall Street, New York) to Justice Jackson, 6 March 1946: Jackson Papers, Library of Congress, Washington D.C., Box 102.

2 CSDIC Report, CMF/X 166, Cornell Collection, Rare Books Room, Cornell Law Library, Cornell University, Ithaca NY (hereafter Cornell Collection), vol. xxx, 3–4.

> Marshall Albert Kesselring, Nazi commander in Italy. Kesselring was tried as a war criminal and convicted. Never Wolff.[3]

> The Lord Chancellor on his visit out here asked if there was any chance of Wolff being brought to justice, and it is because of this that I have interested myself in the case.
>
> (Cap't Somerhough, War Crimes Group)[4]

> Wolff is, as we know, a very slippery customer.
>
> (R. Shanshalf, JAG, London)[5]

Introduction

The following chapters focus upon the more legally and constitutionally problematic aspect of the involvement of US intelligence within the Nuremberg war crimes process. They address the policy of the OSS and other branches of US intelligence (such as the US Army's Counter Intelligence Corps) selectively to promise immunity for war crimes. On at least one occasion, which is addressed through an in-depth case study of the non-prosecution of the Karl Wolff group of senior SS officials, OSS/CIA officials effectively honoured such promises by making a series of interventions within the Nuremberg and related trial processes.

This chapter discusses the evidence of the war criminality of Karl Wolff and, to a lesser extent, Guido Zimmer and Eugen Dollmann, particularly evidence which was at that time available to the Nuremberg prosecutors and other legal officials responsible for war crimes/de-Nazification trials. It sets out the range of offences with which members of the Wolff group could have been prosecuted. It also explains the types of actions and levels of intent required by the relevant law.

Earlier studies from Simpson, Hirsch and others have claimed that the Wolff group directly benefited from the interventions of US intelligence as a reward for their cooperation within the OSS's, 'Operation Sunrise'.[6] However, these earlier works fail to make a compelling case. This is because the specifically legal basis for such claims in terms of the range of incriminating evidence establishing liability under the relevant headings of international criminal

3 See Cobentz and Freidin, 'Strange Story of SS General', *New York Herald Tribune*, 23 January 1962.

4 Censorship Intercepts, Internal Memorandum within the Legal Division of the Control Commission for Germany (British Element), 20 October 1947: PRO, WO 309/347.

5 Shanshalf (JAG, London): 'General Harster': PRO, WO 208/4671.

6 B. Hersch, *The Old Boys* (New York: Macmillan, 1992), 134–35; C. Simpson, *The Splendid Blond Beast: Money, Law and Genocide in the Twentieth Century* (Maine Monroe: Common Courage Press, 1995), 236–39.

law generally remains unspecified, or at least insufficiently articulated. Yet, if we cannot establish that the prosecutors possessed, or had readily available, sufficient incriminating evidence to merit prosecution, then it can hardly be claimed that the Wolff group were, in fact, the beneficiaries of a legal immunity deal brokered by the OSS's Allen Dulles. Unlike these earlier works, which typically adopt a one-sided partisan orientation of potential prosecutors and critics, this chapter provides the necessary background context to later discussions of legal immunity.

These later chapters discuss the specific military and geo-political context in which the promise of privileged treatment, including at least by implication legal immunity, first emerged as an integral part of the back and forth exchange of commitments that were integral to the OSS's Operation Sunrise. This operation involved a series of on/off 'negotiations' between Dulles and Wolff and their various intermediaries and subordinates, which culminated in the unofficial surrender of approximately one million German-led forces in Nazi-occupied northern Italy. Later chapters examine the range of promises exchanged between the two principal actors in this particular drama, Dulles and Wolff, of which promises of favourable post-war treatment for the Wolff group were only one part of a far wider series of negotiated terms and conditions. These suggest that it is important to appreciate that the broader military and policy context of negotiations, which involved an exchange of terms and conditions in circumstances where only an 'unconditional surrender' was officially permitted. Without such an appreciation of this wider context, which anticipated later Cold War conflicts, it is not possible to gain a comprehensive understanding of our topic: that is, how the legal immunity aspect initially arose, was sustained by the motivations and interests of the different parties immediately participating in Operation Sunrise, and then became increasingly controversial.

Intelligence agencies have, over the past seven decades, demonstrated an increasingly sophisticated ability to monitor acts of war criminality as they occur and to secure important information on the internal political and military command structure of regimes engaged in genocide. Both activities are able to produce incriminating types of potential trial evidence useful to war crimes prosecutors. However, at the same time, officials working for intelligence agencies have, on occasions, intervened within the legal processes related to the prosecution of war crimes, either by withholding evidence or by actively shielding suspects. This has occurred, for example, to protect actual or potential informants, agents or double-agents whose prosecution could damage perceived national security interests, or which would either jeopardise the retention of useful sources and methods, or undermine the careers of specific senior intelligence officials. The controversial involvement of Dulles provides a most promising case study of this wider tension.

As already noted, Dulles was a former senior US wartime intelligence official with the OSS, based in Berne, Switzerland (1942–45), and subsequent Director of the CIA (1953–61).[7] In March and April 1945, Dulles negotiated the early surrender of German and Axis forces in North Italy with Wolff, a mission codenamed 'Operation Sunrise' by American intelligence, and 'Operation Crossword' by Winston Churchill (as it remained a continuing puzzle for him). The controversy regarding Dulles' involvement with Wolff failed to impede Dulles' rapid promotion to head of the CIA during the Cold War era. In 1951, he returned to the intelligence field to hold the post of Deputy Director, and, from 1953 to 1961 (when Dulles was dismissed for the disastrous 'Bay of Pigs' fiasco), he held the post of overall CIA Director.[8] The fact that the individual at the centre of the controversy was promoted to such a senior position, and that his younger protégés also held, or perhaps still hold, senior posts, provides additional spice to the issue. As Breitman notes:

> Dulles' negotiations, codenamed 'Operation Sunrise,' saved some lives and certainly added lustre to his achievements as head of the OSS office in Switzerland . . . [publicity] about Dulles' wartime successes helped him later to become director of the CIA. Therefore, new evidence about the background of Operation Sunrise is historically quite significant.[9]

A close examination of Dulles' complex relationship to the Nazi war crimes prosecution process illustrates in microcosm many of the wider issues, dilemmas and contradictions already mentioned. As discussed, Dulles, OSS and US intelligence officials have been subjected to severe criticisms with respect to their interventions within aspects of the Nuremberg and related Allied war crimes trials and de-Nazification processes.

Relevant offences

The offences for which members of the Wolff group could have been prosecuted included not only those already discussed relating to crimes against the peace, crimes against the laws of war and crimes against humanity as set out in Article 6 of the Nuremberg Charter, but also 'organisational liability' or 'membership of criminal organisations' under Law No. 10 of the Allied Control Council for Germany, of 20 December 1945. The idea of the crime

7 R. Moseley, *Mussolini's Shadow: The Double Life of Count Galeazzo Ciano* (Cambridge, MA: Yale University Press, 1999), 154.

8 See B. F. Smith and E. Agarossi, *Operation Sunrise: The Secret Surrender* (New York: Basic Books, 1979), 187–88.

9 R. Breitman, 'Record Group 263: Records of the Central Intelligence Agency, Records of the Directorate of Operations: Analysis of the Name File of Guido Zimmer': http://www.archives.gov/iwg/declassified_records/rg_263_cia_records/rg_263_zimmer.html.

of membership originated in the United Nations War Crimes Commission; it later evolved in rules laid down by governments as part of contemporary international law and implemented by the IMT and other courts. At the time in which prosecution of Wolff, Zimmer and Dollmann was a real possibility, the only authoritative pronouncement on criminal groups or organisations on the basis of international law occurred during the Nuremberg Tribunal; it was based upon those specific provisions of the Charter that defined its jurisdiction and procedure. The Tribunal's interpretation of the meaning and scope of this membership was, to some extent, influenced by the prosecution's discussion. Both the Charter and the IMT's Judgment introduced a new way of responding to organised mass criminality that created a far-reaching judicial precedent for later local trials within national or local courts. The relevant provisions in the Nuremberg Charter:

Article 9

> At the trial of any individual member of any group or organisation the Tribunal may declare (in connection with any act of which the individual may be convicted) that the group or organisation of which the individual was a member was a criminal organisation.
>
> After receipt of the Indictment the Tribunal shall give such notice as it thinks fit that the prosecution intends to ask the Tribunal to make such declaration and any member of the organisation will be entitled to apply to the Tribunal for leave to be heard by the Tribunal upon the question of the criminal character of the organisation. The Tribunal shall have power to allow or reject the application. If the application is allowed, the Tribunal may direct in what manner the applicants shall be represented and heard.

Article 10

> In cases where a group or organisation is declared criminal by the Tribunal, the competent national authority of any Signatory shall have the right to bring individuals to trial for membership therein before national, military or occupation courts. In any such case the criminal nature of the group or organisation is considered proved and shall not be questioned.

Article 11

> Any person convicted by the Tribunal may be charged before a national military or occupation court, referred to in Article 10 of this Charter, with a crime other than of membership in a criminal group or organisation and such court may, after convicting him, impose upon him punishment independent of and additional to the punishment imposed by the

Tribunal for participation in the criminal activities of such group or organisation.[10]

The Nuremberg Charter did not, as a matter of law, define the meaning of either a 'group' or 'organisation', relying instead upon the International Military Tribunal to deal with these issues as questions of fact. The provisions set out above lay down the following rules or principles, which granted a measure of discretion to both the prosecuting authorities and local courts, whilst still removing any possibility for the defence lawyers challenging the criminal nature of any organisation declared to be such:

(a) A declaration of criminality in respect of a group or organisation can be made by the Tribunal on condition that any of the defendants before it is a member of such group or organisation.
(b) The declaration is an act within the discretionary power of the Tribunal, which is not bound to adjudicate on the issue if it does not deem it appropriate to do so.
(c) The declaration is confined to establishing the criminal nature of the group or organisation, and no punishment is pronounced against the individuals involved. This is left to the subsequent courts.
(d) Once a group or organisation is declared criminal by the Tribunal, the bringing of its members to trial is within the discretionary power of the Signatories to the Charter. The declaration does not bind them to prosecute such members.
(e) An individual brought to trial as a consequence of the declaration is prosecuted for the crime of 'membership' in the group or organisation. This is particularly emphasised in the wording of Art. 11.
(f) The legal effect of the declaration is that, during the subsequent proceedings of the court before which a member is brought to trial, the criminal nature of the group or organisation is considered already proved and cannot be questioned.[11]

A literal interpretation of the terms of (f), focusing purely upon the 'letter of the law', could suggest that simple proof of membership from September 1939 of, say, the SS or another organisation declared criminal would in itself be constituted proof of a crime. Hence, the very act of bringing a prosecution of a member of the SS based upon firm evidence that the person's name was recorded as a member of this criminal organisation would be a sufficient determination of guilt, irrespective of any pleas concerning the relevance of traditional defences in criminal law. This would reduce the role of the court to merely rubber-stamping this process before determining an appropriate

10 http://nizkor.com/ftp.py?imt/tgmwc/judgment/j-accused-organisations.01. 11 *Ibid.*

sentence, bearing in mind any mitigating factors. On the other hand, and as all first year law students within a common law jurisdiction should know, one cannot rely upon judges always giving a strictly literal interpretation to statutory measures, particularly when to do so would conflict with traditional conceptions of due process within criminal trials and the conventional presumption of statutory interpretation that measures extending criminal liability should be interpreted narrowly.

Hence, the provisions of the Charter were subject to a measure of ambiguity. This ambiguity allowed at least two possible bases for criminal guilt of individual members. As already noted, the first possibility was that the declaration made by the IMT created a rebuttable *presumption of guilt* against every member, such that all the prosecution is required to do is to establish that the accused was, as a matter of fact, a member of the organisation. This course was eventually prescribed for the de-Nazification courts in the United States zone of Germany. In this case, it had to be presumed, unless and until the defendant could establish with clear evidence proof to contrary, that the accused *personally knew* of the criminal purposes or acts of the organisation or that he or she *was personally implicated in the commission of crimes*. This would remain the case even if he or she did not join the organisation on a voluntary basis.

The second alternative interpretation was based, partly at least, on the traditional presumption against extending criminality liability in the absence of unambiguous statutory wording. This interpretation would hold that it was for subsequent courts to positively require the prosecution to prove not only that the accused was, as matter of established fact, a member of the organisation declared criminal, but also that he or she knew the relevant facts of its criminal purposes, and was personally implicated in the commission of crimes.

In practice, however, neither the Tribunal, nor the majority of the prosecutors interpreted the provisions in the first, literal manner. Justice Jackson argued that:

> there could be no such thing as automatic condemnations, because the authority given in the Charter is to bring persons to trial for membership. But the points could be raised by the defendant that he had defences, such as duress, force against his person, or threats of force, and would have to be tried.[12]

In other words, even the Nuremberg prosecutors interpreted the relevant provisions of the Charter in a manner that still allowed the possibility of a contested trial in which a person who was clearly a member of one of the

12 8 IMT, 103–4: http://www.nizkor.org/hweb/imt/tgmwc/tgmwc-08/tgmwc-08-71-07.shtml.

organisations declared criminal could ultimately be acquitted after having successfully raised one of a number of defences.

Jackson's interpretation appears, however, to place the onus upon a defendant to prove his or her innocence by reference to any one of the relevant defences. The Judgment of the IMT left open any decision regarding whether the Charter established a presumption of guilt or innocence. However, it held that, with the exception of cases where a member of the organisation in question was proved guilty of specific crimes, such as genocide, the tests of *voluntary* membership, and of *actual* or *reasonably presumed knowledge* represented the main issues upon which the subsequent courts had to decide each individual case. This did not clarify the question of whether it was for the prosecutors or the defence lawyers to prove their cases concerning these legal requirements.

The IMT made a general ruling that suggested that 'appropriate standards of justice', including perhaps a presumption of innocence until proven guilty and the avoidance of any procedures that resemble judicially sanctioned arbitrariness, would need to be applied in any contested trial, not least because of the possibility of a death sentence. The alternative of sentencing individual members to imprisonment and even death without consideration of any defence arguments or other traditional safeguards associated with the concept of a fair trial, would be a dangerously unacceptable violation of basic minimal standards of procedure and due process. The IMT stated that, under the Charter, there was a 'crime of membership' for individuals who belonged to organisations declared criminal:

> A member of an organisation which the Tribunal has declared to be criminal may be subsequently convicted of the crime of membership and be punished *for that crime* by death. This is not to assume that international or military courts which will try these individuals will not exercise appropriate standards of justice. This is a far-reaching and novel procedure. Its application, unless properly safeguarded, may produce great injustice.[13]

Hence, the Judgment of the IMT accepted US Chief Prosecutor Jackson's interpretation that neither the rules of the Charter, nor the category of collective or organisational criminality involved in any declaration of organisational criminality, would result in an unqualified or indiscriminate liability for each member. Such liability cannot be automatically applied to all members in a mechanical fashion at the expense of due process and judicial discretion to take into account the particular circumstances of each individual case. The

13 IMT Judgment, 66–68: http://nizkor.com/ftp.py?imt/tgmwc/judgment/j-accused-organisations.01.

involvement of judges, rather than an administrator, implied that decision-making had to conform with traditional objective norms governing issues of legitimacy within domestic criminal trials that rule out the arbitrary application of conceptions of *collective* guilt and punishment which are insensitive to the particular degrees of responsibility of specific individuals:

> This discretion is a judicial one and does not permit arbitrary action, but should be exercised in accordance with well settled legal principles, one of the most important of which is that criminal guilt is personal, and that mass punishment should be avoided. If satisfied of the criminal guilt of any organisation or group, this Tribunal should not hesitate to declare it to be criminal because the theory of 'group criminality' is new, or because it might be unjustly applied by some subsequent tribunals. On the other hand, the Tribunal should make such declaration of criminality so far as possible in a manner to insure that innocent persons will not be punished.[14]

Hence, the Tribunal rejected a literal interpretation of automatic guilt following proof of membership of the SS alone. Instead, it required *additional* proof of individual or personal guilt of its members before a conviction would be legally warranted. Arguably, these qualifications suggest, without firmly deciding the matter in a definitive fashion, that the onus of proof lay with the prosecution not the defence, otherwise it is difficult to see how innocent persons would avoid punishment. On the other hand, the IMT did not reject the prosecution's contention that initially there would be a presumption of guilt once a person had been proven to be a member of a criminal organisation but that the defence could rebut this by providing appropriate and compelling evidence to the contrary.

The Tribunal defined 'criminal organisations' and, whilst doing so, it fully accepted the tests submitted by the Nuremberg prosecutors which rejected the interpretation of the Charter that would allow conviction and sentencing for simple membership alone, irrespective of any need to establish criminal intent and knowledge of relevant circumstances:

> A criminal organisation is analogous to a criminal conspiracy in that the essence of both is co-operation for criminal purposes . . . Since the declaration with respect to the organisations and groups will, as has been pointed out, fix the criminality of its members, that definition should exclude persons who had *no knowledge* of the criminal purposes or acts of the organisation and those who were drafted by the State for membership, unless they were personally implicated in the commission

14 *Ibid*, 68.

> of acts declared criminal by Article 6 of the Charter as members of the organisation. Membership alone is not enough to come within the scope of these declarations.[15]

Clearly, the key points are that those members 'who had no knowledge of the criminal purpose or acts of the organisation' cannot be convicted; nor can those 'who were drafted by the State unless they were personally implicated in the commission' of specified criminal acts. This suggests that not only was there a requirement for prosecutors to present credible evidence of the *actus reus* (criminal deed) of this membership offence but also that they needed to do the same with respect to the accused's *mens rea* (criminal intent). Proof of *mens rea* alone was insufficient. In other words, persons who were compulsorily drafted into, say, the military Waffen-SS, even if they had prior knowledge of the criminal purpose of the organisation, were not to be held guilty unless they personally were also implicated in the commission of crimes.

These qualifications to a narrowly strictly interpretation of the Charter cast additional light on the question of whether, by implication at least, the onus of proof lay on the accused or the prosecution. Although, as already noted, the Tribunal failed to make a ruling on whether, when a member of a criminal organisation is tried, the defence or the prosecutors had to bear the onus of proof regarding tests of personal guilt; and, if so, whether this required 'proof beyond reasonable doubt'. However, the wording used by the Tribunal implied that, irrespective of the extent of the burden of proof, this either lay with the prosecution – who therefore positively had to make a case rather than merely cast doubt on the defence – or shifted at different points in the trial.

The Judgment of the IMT provided no guidance on the question of what type of evidence was needed to either prove or disprove individual guilt by the prosecution or the defence. This gave subsequent courts and tribunals considerable discretion in admitting *purely circumstantial evidence*, particularly with respect to the *mens rea* element. It allowed for a presumption of knowledge of the illegal acts and purposes of criminal organisations based upon the accused's rank and position, duties and assignments while serving in the organisation. With regard to the second requirement, concerning the implications of members who joined the criminal organisation on a non-voluntary basis, it appears that, once an accused established the compulsory nature of his or her enlistment, then the burden of proof that he or she has actually committed relevant crimes switches back to the prosecution.

In short, in the absence of express decision concerning the burden of proof generally or at particular points in the trial process, the IMT delegated decisions on this important point to the discretion of later competent

15 *Ibid.*

courts and tribunals. In later cases in the American-led Nuremberg Subsequent Proceedings, particularly the *Pohl* and *Flick* cases, judges explicitly reinstated the presumption of innocence placing the burden of proof upon the prosecution.[16]

The Allied de-Nazification laws were based largely on a codification of aspects of the IMT's Judgment. The crime of membership was set out in Art. II, para. 1 of Law No. 10: 'Each of the following acts is recognised as a crime: . . . . (d) Membership in categories of a criminal group or organisation declared criminal by the International Military Tribunal.' Article II, para. 1(d) reflects the declaration made by the IMT that the SS (Die. Schutzstaffeln der Nationalsocialistischen Deutschen Arbeiterpartie) was a criminal organisation. Hence, it is necessary to review this declaration, not least because it contains an additional qualification relevant to the time-scale of membership:

> The SS was utilised for purposes which were criminal under the Charter involving the persecution and extermination of the Jews, brutalities and killings in concentration camps, excesses in the administration of occupied territories, the administration of the slave labour programme and the mistreatment and murder of prisoners of war . . . In dealing with the SS the Tribunal includes all persons who had been officially accepted as members of the SS including the members of the SS-Verbände, members of the Waffen-SS, members of the SS-Totenkopfverbände and the members of any of the different police forces who were members of the SS . . . The Tribunal declares to be criminal within the meaning of the Charter the group composed of those persons who had been officially accepted as members of the SS as enumerated in the preceding paragraph who became or remained members of the organisation with knowledge that it was being used for the commission of acts declared criminal by Article 6 of the Charter, or who were personally implicated as members of the organisation in the commission of such crimes, excluding, however, those who were drafted into membership by the State in such a way as to give them no choice in the matter, and who had committed no such crimes. The basis of this finding is the participation of the organisation in war crimes and crimes against humanity connected with the war; this group declared criminal cannot include, therefore, persons who had ceased to belong to the organisation enumerated in the preceding paragraph prior to 1st September, 1939.

16 This is discussed in detail in 'Trial Of Ulrich Greifelt And Others' United States Military Tribunal, Nuremberg, 10 October 1947–10 March 1948: Law Reports of the Trials of War Criminals. United Nations War Crimes Commission. Vol. XIII (London: HMSO, 1949): http://www.ess.uwe.ac.uk/WCC/greifelt6.htm, 57–64.

This declaration included classes of members liable to prosecution for the crime of membership all persons who had been officially accepted as members of any of the branches of the SS, except the so-called Riding units. On the other hand, it excluded those members of the SS who were drafted by the State in an involuntary manner and who had not committed any crimes personally, as well as those who had ceased to be members before 1 September 1939 – the outbreak of the Secound World War.

The penalties generally prescribed for any crime under the law included the death penalty and imprisonment for life with or without hard labour. In the case of simple membership, that is, not aggravated by complicity in, for example, crimes against humanity, the rules concerning punishment were supplemented by the recommendations of the Nuremberg Tribunal, which later judges followed and applied.

In short, the legal test for the individual guilt that those considering the prosecution of the Wolff group needed to meet consisted in ascertaining whether Wolff, Zimmer and Dollmann 'became or remained members of the organisation *with knowledge* that it was being used for the commission of acts declared criminal by Article 6 of the Charter' (i.e., crimes against peace, war crimes, and crimes against humanity), or whether they were 'personally implicated as members of the organisation in the commission of the crimes'. In other words, to guarantee a conviction, a prosecutor would have had to present credible evidence that, being members of the SS, each of these three SS officials had the relevant knowledge of the criminal purposes of the SS and/or were personally implicated in the perpetration of crimes committed by this organisation. Since both Dollmann and Zimmer remained in the SS voluntarily throughout the war, no defence lawyer would be in a position to claim coercion. However, the prosecution may still have had to establish their actual knowledge of the fact that this organisation was being used by the Nazi leadership for the commission of acts declared criminal by Control Council Law No. 10. The exception might have been if there was evidence of personal involvement in specific crimes. In principle, it would have been possible to convict Dollmann and Zimmer on two different grounds: for example, to hold that Dollmann – as an SS-Standartenführer – possessed actual or, by virtue of his senior rank, imputed knowledge of the criminal purposes of the SS without any requirement to prove personal involvement in any criminal act; whilst the lower-ranking Zimmer could be convicted on the basis of factual evidence of his actual complicity in such acts of anti-Semitic persecution and looting, irrespective of proof of whether he possessed actual or imputed knowledge of these purposes. Dollmann's senior rank would have made him more vulnerable to the admission of circumstantial evidence deriving from his official position and duties, including his personal contacts with the SS leadership. This could have led to the presumption that he could not have been in ignorance of the general character of the SS. A court or tribunal could have reasonably inferred criminal intent from the fact that it would have been impossible for a man of his intelligence not to have known of the commission of the SS's crimes, at least in part.

These rather abstract legal questions need to be borne in mind when considering the details of evidence of the Wolff group's complicity in various war crimes discussed in the next section.

Evidence of the Wolff group's involvement in Nazi war crimes

It is not possible to provide a comprehensive assessment of the full significance and implications of the immunity issue regarding Wolff without first clarifying the full range of war crimes for which he could, in principle, have been prosecuted within the Nuremberg process.[17] As both Himmler's Chief of Staff (a senior SS administrator (in post 1936–43), Highest Police and SS Leader in Nazi-Occupied Northern Italy (1943–45), and General within the Waffen-SS (1944–45), Wolff certainly played a senior role within the policy-making and policy execution aspects of the Nazi regime. These positions were sufficient to implicate him in at least four of the offences successfully prosecuted during the Nuremberg process.[18]

Nearly all of the most incriminating evidence was available to the Nuremberg prosecutors who detained Wolff from August 1945 to mid-1948, and indirectly to Dulles through OSS channels. Justice Jackson, head American Nuremberg prosecutor, had previously identified Wolff as a possible defendant in the first Nuremberg trials of 'major' war criminals.[19] According to one of Jackson's representatives in the London negotiations from late June 1945, which selected the defendants, Dulles' colleague and OSS General Counsel, James Donovan, played a key role. He contributed to a process in which a list proposed by the Americans of 'something like 50 to 60' defendants, including the senior surviving members of 'five of the principal groups and organisations to which they belonged' (which would almost certainly have included Wolff as the most senior SS official in custody), was

17 The Allied authorities subjected Wolff only to a quasi-administrative de-Nazification proceeding in Hamburg in 1948–49. It was not until 1962–64 that the German authorities successfully prosecuted Wolff (see below).

18 Wolff's biography and official posts within the SS is summarised helpfully in *'Extracts From Testimony Of Defense Witness SS-General Karl Wolff', Trial of War Criminals before the Nuremberg Military Tribunal Under Control Council No. 10* (hereafter 'TWC') (Washington: US Government Printing Office, 1953), Vol. 5 (*Pohl* Case), p. 769.

19 See 'papers desired from R.H. Jackson Files', Jackson Files, *op cit*, Box 2; Salter and Ost, *op cit*. Jackson Papers, *op cit*, 29 May 1945 includes a memo, 'Meeting at the House of Lords, May 29, 1945, 2.00 pm', discussing potential defendants in which Wolff's name is misspelled 'Woolf'.

narrowed down to a provisional list of 24.[20] Even then, Wolff was included amongst a small group of 24 potential defendants on whom Dr Kempner, JAGD-WCO, prepared a dossier of 'evidence or definite leads' for Justice Jackson, the majority of whom were in fact later named as defendants.[21] Dulles purported to be unaware of Wolff's activities and potential liabilities as a war criminal during his wartime negotiations. However, OSS information files record that the General was the 'master of ceremonies' within Nazi-occupied Northern Italy with direct command responsibility second only to Himmler for Gestapo and SS actions there, including the rounding up and deportation of Italian Jews.[22]

How was it possible that clear documentary evidence demonstrating that, as high-level state official within Hitler's Germany, Wolff was complicit in the administration of genocide could result in prosecution processes that culminated in three vastly different legal outcomes? Yet this occurred when differently constituted prosecuting authorities and courts considered Wolff's complicity in the extermination of European Jewry. Following the suicide of Hitler and Himmler, he was the highest-ranking Nazi official to survive the war, and clearly outranked the majority of the defendants tried before the first International Trials at Nuremberg.

The Nuremberg international (IMT 1945–46) and subsequent trials (NMT, 1946–49) have clearly established that those members of the Nazi regime who played a decisive role in, for example, the organisation of concentration and extermination camps, slave labour and medical experiments on human beings can be successfully prosecuted and punished as war criminals. As is well known, the Nuremberg Charter, in effect the primary legislation for the Nuremberg trials, defined a number of offences:

> The following acts, or any of them, are crimes coming within the jurisdiction of the Tribunal for which there shall be individual responsibility:
>
> (a) Crimes against peace: . . .
> (b) War crimes: namely, violations of the laws or customs of war. Such violations shall include, but not be limited to, murder, ill-treatment or deportation to slave labor or for any other purpose of civilian population of or in occupied territory, murder or ill-treatment of prisoners of war or persons on the seas, killing of hostages, plunder

20 See S. Alderman, 'The London Negotiations for War Crimes Prosecutions' in Jackson Papers, *op cit*, Box 112, 18, 50–51 (published later in *Negotiating with the Russians* (New York: World Peace Foundation, 1951).

21 See Telford Taylor to Jackson, 'Kempner Assignment', 11 July 1945: NA, RG 238, Entry 51, Box 30, Folder 'defendants'.

22 'Industries and German Control', report TB-125, 21 April, 1944: NA, RG 226, Entry 16, Box 818.

of public or private property, wanton destruction of cities, towns or villages, or devastation not justified by military necessity;

(c) Crimes against humanity: namely, murder, extermination, enslavement, deportation, and other inhumane acts committed against any civilian population, before or during the war; or persecutions on political, racial or religious grounds in execution of or in connection with any crime within the jurisdiction of the Tribunal, whether or not in violation of the domestic law of the country where perpetrated.[23]

The Nuremberg Charter also made it clear that offences could be committed not only by those who personally killed or ill-treated individuals but also by those who were implicated in a senior capacity in the planning, organisation and administration of policies. This remained the case even if these individuals never left their desks, or issued orders that directly resulted in atrocities:

> Leaders, organizers, instigators and accomplices participating in the formulation or execution of a common plan or conspiracy to commit any of the foregoing crimes are responsible for all acts performed by any persons in execution of such plan.[24]

For present purposes, the offence of crimes against the peace (or 'waging aggressive war') is of little relevance. However, with respect to his role as Chief of Himmler's Personal Staff, Wolff could have been prosecuted for acts recognised as 'crimes against humanity' with respect to the 'deportation to slave labour' and ill-treatment of civilian population, and for 'extermination' under respect to the deportation of Jews to Treblinka and other death camps. It is arguable that his administrative involvement in so-called 'medical experiments' involving concentration camp inmates also represented a 'crime against humanity' as defined in Article 6 of the Nuremberg Charter. Certainly, correspondence cited in evidence early in the first international trial at Nuremberg indicated that Wolff was complicit in the administrative aspect of these experiments.[25]

Between 1945 and 1948, the Nuremberg prosecutors gathered three folders of evidence relevant to Wolff's administrative involvement in war crimes, including the extermination of European Jewry.[26] Such evidence was then

23 The full text of the Charter and offences are available online at: http://www.yale.edu/lawweb/avalon/imt/proc/imtconst.htm.

24 *Ibid.*, Art. 6.

25 See Nuremberg document 16I7-PS/Pros. Exhibit USA 266, Himmler to Milch, November 1942, referred to in: IMT 3, 164.

26 Karl Wolff, OCC, 14 August 1948 to Chief of Legal Division HQ CCG (BE), Berlin: PRO, FO 1030/424 forwarded to Inspector General, Central Legal Office, Hamburg on 27 April 1948.

transmitted to German prosecutors in Wolff's 1948–49 de-Nazification trials,[27] parts of which regarding the Treblinka transportations, later formed a key element of the prosecution's case in the German trials at Munich (1963–64). When later called as a defence witness in Wolff's domestic war crimes trial at Munich, Telford Taylor, former head prosecutor for the American-led Nuremberg Subsequent Proceedings trials, recalled that: 'As to the question who was prosecuted for what criminal offence, different reasons, and not only legal considerations, had been taken into account.'[28] Taylor's enigmatic statement conceals as much as it reveals. However, it is possible to think that extra-legal factors (including geo-political considerations and alleged promises of immunity from US intelligence officials) determined Wolff's non-prosecution. This conclusion is, however, not plausible unless and until it can be clearly established that the decision not to prosecute Wolff could not be justified in *purely legal terms*, that is, in terms of the lack of sufficient and credible admissible evidence.

Any thorough explanation of this apparent legal discrepancy within the three different criminal justice processes discussed above would need to both reconstruct and explain the various conflicts of interpretation that arose with respect to the nature and extent of Wolff's complicity in wartime genocide. Such a project would, however, require a work extending to at least monograph length. By contrast, the second part of the present chapter makes an initial, and necessarily limited, contribution to that wider research project. It does so by closely reviewing the nature and quality of evidence of Wolff's complicities in genocide obtained by the Nuremberg prosecutors between May 1945 and late 1948. The large quantity of evidence that came to light after 1948, when all possibility of including Wolff in the second round of Nuremberg trials had passed, will *not* be considered. The ultimate goal of this preliminary study is not to answer the question: 'What historical evidence has emerged over the last 60 years linking Wolff to war crimes?' Instead, it is to make an initial response to the far narrower question of: 'Given the quality of the evidence of Wolff's complicity in such criminality

27 The Nuremberg materials used in the 1948 trials were: 'exclusively documentary, consisting of captured letters, signed by Wolff or copies which had been passed to him. Generally Wolff denied recollection of the precise letters and in some cases tried to explain that his signature was a mere pro forma signature. In cases where he received copies, he alleged that such copies had not been sent on to him at the Führerhauptquartier, or if they had, he had no recollection of them.' Reportedly when questioned as to Jewish persecution, Wolff admitted knowledge of the rounding up and detention of Jews only because they were Jews from 1938 onwards, and their forcible deportation to the East. Yet he insisted he had helped specific individuals escape persecution, such as Garfin Gork, and that SS 'measures against the Jews were not part of his duties, and that he was glad he did not have to have any official connection with them'. Furthermore, his defence lawyer argued that Wolff acted 'under inescapable compulsion': Legal adviser's report on 'Trials of Karl Wolff, 9 November 1948', 2: PRO, FO 1030 /424.

28 Case Wolff, *op cit*, 51, a-112, 496.

that, at the time, was in their possession, why did the Nuremberg prosecutors decide not to charge Wolff with "crimes against humanity" under the Nuremberg Charter?' Given the restricted scope of the present research, it would be perverse to introduce material that, despite its inherently interesting nature for other, more widely defined research projects, was unavailable to senior Nuremberg prosecutors when they made their decisions not to prosecute Wolff for war crimes.[29]

Waffen-SS Major General Wolff, Himmler's former Chief of Staff (1936–43) and Highest SS Police and SS leader for Northern Italy (1943–45),[30] was vulnerable to being successfully prosecuted for 'crimes against humanity' under Article Six of the Nuremberg Charter of August 1945. This at least is suggested by a wide range of materials, including court transcripts, uncensored archival sources,[31] and relevant scholarship. Wolff's prosecution could have taken place in either the first or second Nuremberg war crimes trials, or as part of the British war crimes trials in Italy 1946–47.

On the other hand, it is necessary to acknowledge, at the outset, that the specifically 'legal' evidence discussed in later sections of this book amounts only to a *sub-set* of the total historical evidence to date. The latter expands with every successive release of, for example, formerly classified intelligence files relating to Nazi war crimes. The fact that this study is only concerned with a sub-set of the total available historical evidence means that the following incriminating documentary evidence will not be discussed in the present study:

29 On the other hand, although forming no part of the central argument, references to later material will, on occasions, be cited in footnotes in order to assist future researchers with different agendas to those of the present project.

30 R. Koehl, *The Black Corps* (Madison: University of Wisconsin Press, 1983), 113–20, 234–45. The discussion of Wolff's character is rather mixed in the original Sunrise cables and correspondence. See cable 538, 'Sunrise', Airey to AFHQ, no date: NA, RG 226, Entry 139, Box 60, Folder 554, noting Wolff was: 'a strong personality, active and intelligent – otherwise nothing much to recommend him above others of his kidney. Has crafty appearance . . .'

31 Previously unknown documentation exists in General Donovan's Nuremberg Files deposited in Cornell Law School, and, unlike the documentation stored in the US National Archives, Modern Military Division II, Washington DC, still remains 'unweeded' by the CIA. In collaboration with Dr Kerstin Von Lingen, the present writer has reviewed the full range of available archival evidence from the National Archives in Washington DC, the Public Records Office in London, the Institute of Historical Research (IFZ) at Munich and General Donovan's extensive Nuremberg files stored at Cornell Law School, Cornell University, Ithaca, NY. Each of these collections contains materials relevant to the immunity allegation that are not available in other collections. On the Cornell Collection, see M. Salter, 'Unsettling Accounts: Methodological Issues Within the Reconstruction of the Role of a U.S Intelligence Agency Within the Nuremberg Trials' (2003) 56 *Current Legal Issues* 275–305; 'Memorandum to General Donovan', 20 November 1945: Donovan Archive, Subdivision 11, Storm Troops, Gestapo, SS and SD, Vol. 53.107.

1 Wolff's correspondence with Chief of the German Administration in Serbia, i.e., 'Staatsrat' Harald Turner, over the use of mobile gas-wagons to kill Jews.[32]
2 A letter personally dictated by Wolff advising Himmler of a forthcoming meeting discussing the resettlement of ethnic Germans into the German occupied Crimean region in which Wolff notes in passing and without comment that the indigenous population would be subject to detention and 'liquidation by action squads'.[33]
3 The significant critique of Wolff's claims regarding the small number of SS officials involved in mass extermination that emerged during recent 'Holocaust denial' trials,[34] including expert historical testimony commission specifically for these trials.[35]
4 Documentary and witness testimony regarding Wolff's complicities that was presented during post-war domestic war crimes trials held after 1948.[36]
5 The results of researchers' archival discoveries from the early 1960s that were fed into Wolff's 1963–64 trials in Munich, Germany. This includes potentially key correspondence, dated 17 September 1942, from Chief of

32 For the relevant extract of this letter, see H. Friedlander and M. Sybil (eds.), *Archives of the Holocaust*, Vol. 11, Part 2, 1992, 284–86: http://www.holocaust-history.org/19420411-turner-wolff/. Sereny provides a fuller translation, *op cit*, 353, translating an original document available from the Institute of Historical Research, Munich. For more background information to these killing devices, see M. Beer, 'The Development of the Gas-van in the Murdering of the Jews', published online at http://www.nizkor.org/hweb/camps/chelmno/sonderdruck.html, and http://weber.ucsd.edu/~lzamosc/chelm10.htm. Breitman notes that, in mid-1940, Walter Rauff, who was later to become of Wolff's most trusted SS subordinates in North Italy, was involved in the design and testing of early gas-wagons, and that Wolff's link with Turner formed part of his wider trouble-shooting role administrative remit and SS liaison work with Nazi Foreign Minister Ribbentrop. See R. Breitman, *Himmler, The Architect of Genocide* (London: Grafton, 1992), 121, 197. Rauff's role was known to Nuremberg prosecutors. See Nuremberg document PS-501: 'Collection of four documents in execution by gas', 7 September 1945.

33 J. Von Lang (co-author: C. Sibyll), *Der Adjutant. Karl Wolff: Der Mann zwischen Hitler und Himmler* (Frankfurt/M., Berlin: Ullstein, 1989), 178 (all quotations are based on private translations carried out by Anja Becker).

34 *David Irving v Penguin Books and Deborah Lipstadt*, QBD, 1996 -I- 1113, 11 April 2000, Court 36, Royal Courts of Justice, judgment given by Mr Justice Gray, paras. 6.137–38. I am grateful to Davenports solicitors for providing me with a full transcript of this case.

35 Presented by the Evans Report commissioned by Davenports available from: http://www.holocaustdenialontrial.com/evidence/evans004.asp. The start of this lengthy and scholarly report from the Cambridge History Professor is published online at http://www.holocaustdenialontrial.com/evidence/evans001.asp.

36 See Rediess to Wolff, 7 November 1940, contained in the indictment of Wilhelm Koppe for his trial in Berlin in 1964, 8 Js 52/80, 188–89/T 175, Roll 60, Federal Records Centre, Alexandria microfilmed collection. NARA guide to German records.

Gestapo, Müller, to Wolff, regarding 'the solution of the Jewish question in the General district' [Generalgouvernement].[37]

6 Newly declassified intelligence intercepts of German communications relevant to Wolff's role in the rounding up of Italian Jews and their deportation to Auschwitz.[38]

7 Various post-war accounts in witness statements of Wolff's first-hand experience of witnessing SS killings of Jews at Minsk, capital of Byelorussia, where he and Himmler met with Arthur Nebe, commander of SS-Einsatzgruppe B, including those gathered for the Eichmann trial in 1960–61.[39]

8 Wolff's knowledge and limited involvement within the decision-making and policy execution processes associated with the early Reichskristallnacht persecution of German Jews on 9–10 November 1939, which saw over 20,000 Jews confined to concentration camps.[40]

37 Letter T. Friedmann to J. Streit (Attorney General of the GDR), 5 August 1964: Bundesarchiv Berlin, DY30/IV A 2/2.028, which copied documents from SS files in which Wolff was named as the main SS contact for IG Farben to liase with regarding Auschwitz Camp.

38 See Rome to Berlin, RSS 32/7/10/43, cable to Wolff, 6 October 1943: NA, RG 226, Entry 122, Box 1, Folder: Italian decodes (revealing that contrary to his post-war statements, Wolff both received advance warning of the rounding up of Italian Jews, and Kesselring's concerted opposition to this). For more detail and an analysis of the context, see R. Breitman, 'New Sources in the Holocaust in Italy' (2002) 16:3 *Holocaust and Genocide Studies* 2002, 404–5: based on Wolff (Rome) to Himmler, 18 September 1943: decode no. 6252, NA, RG 226, Entry 122, Box 1; Breitman and Naftali, 'Report to the IWG on Previously Classified OSS Records': http://www.archives.gov/iwg/report/report_on_previously_classified_oss.html; M. Dobbs, 'Allies Knew of Plan for Italy's Jews', *Washington Post*, 27 June 2000; 'Britain "could have saved Italian Jews",' *Guardian*, 27 June 2000. Non-classified documentation indicates that, although Wolff was effectively bypassed by Himmler and Hitler with respect to the rounding up of over 1,200 Italian Jews between late September and mid-October 1943, Wolff – as newly appointed Highest SS leader for North Italy – received direct reports on this persecution from SS-Obersturmbannführer Kappler. See Kappler to Wolff, IFZ/NO 24/27. This letter is dated 10 October 1943 and describes the deportation round up which started at 5.30 in the morning and ended at 2.00 in the afternoon. 1,259 Jews were arrested in their homes. After the release of the offspring of mixed marriages, 1,007 remained under arrest. Their deportation was fixed for 18 October. Mention is made of the resistance of an Italian fascist who faced the German search squad, dressed in his party's uniform, and tried to help the Jews. This document was also discussed in the Eichmann trial: http://www.nizkor.org/hweb/people/e/eichmann-adolf/transcripts/Sessions/Session-075-01.html.

39 For Erich von dem Bach-Zelewski's account of Himmler and Wolff's visit to Minsk, see *Aufbau* (New York) 23 August 1946, 1–2; http://www.nizkor.org/hweb/people/e/eichmann-adolf/transcripts/Testimony-Abroad/Erich_Von_Dem_Bach_Zelewski-02.html. Breitman also notes that, in January 1940, both Wolff and Himmler witnessed executions of civilians at Przemysl: Breitman, 1992 *op cit*, 95, 194–96.

40 Hilberg, *The Destruction of the European Jews* (New Haven: Yale University Press, 2003), 38, summarising Heydrich's police report from 11 November 1938, Nuremberg document PS-3058; Breitman reports that Wolff was aware and monitored this early atrocity in which 1,000 synagogues were destroyed and c. 100 German Jews killed, and reported Himmler's negative

9 Wolff administrative involvement in the seizure and exploitation of Jewish forced labour, including Silesian Jews in late 1940.[41]

Wolff's legally problematic actions included administrative responsibilities in relation to 'medical' experiments on concentration camp inmates, negotiating slave labour transactions involving concentration camp detainees and, to a lesser extent, occasional bureaucratic involvement in facilitating the extermination of European Jews.[42]

Medical experimentation

Between 1942 and 1943, during his period as Himmler's Chief of Staff, Wolff was implicated in, amongst other things, illegal and often fatal medical experiments on human subjects within Dachau concentration camp. This administrative involvement could have resulted in his prosecution as part of the famous Doctors' Trial held as the first of the 'Subsequent Proceedings' at Nuremberg that opened in late 1946.[43] In late November 1945, Justice Jackson's famous open speech at the major Nuremberg trials even referred to Wolff as one of the 'masterminds' responsible for facilitating and overseeing these gruesome experiments.[44] As one of the doctors centrally involved in these experiments, Dr Rascher, mentioned in his report to Himmler:

reaction, 1992, *op cit*, 53–55. Hoehn notes that Wolff's fury at this pogrom was not based on any element of compassion felt towards the Jewish victims but rather upon the fact that the initiative had been taken by Goebbels in an area of internal security and race policies that Wolff saw as the exclusive preserve of the SS. See H. Hoehn, *The Order of the Death's Head* (London: Penguin, 2000), 342–45.

41 Breitman, 1992, *op cit*, 137.

42 For further biographical details of Wolff and his institutional role as Himmler's Chief of Staff and Principal Liaison officer with Hitler's HQ, see Vol. 5 (*Pohl* Case), 769; M. Salter and S. Ost, 'War Crimes and Legal Immunities: The Complicities of Waffen-SS General Karl Wolff in Nazi medical experiments' (2004) 4 *Rutgers Journal of Law and Religion* 12–26: available at http://www.lawandreligion.com. Relevant documentation also includes Nuremberg documents 343-PS and 1617-PS published, in part, in *Nazi Conspiracy and Aggression* (hereafter NCA), Vol. III (Washington: USGPO 1946), 266 and Vol. II, 173, 237. More pertinent evidence appeared during subsequent trials at Nuremberg regarding Wolff's knowledge and administrative involvement in Nazi 'experiments'. See 'B) Freezing Experiments', in TWC, Vol. I, Case I ('Medical Case'), 41–43, 199. See Nuremberg documents No-284, Pros. Ex. 64, No-261, Pros. Ex. 63; No-1359, Pros. Ex. 493: NCA, Vol. III, 110, 266; TWC, Vol. I, 41–43, 95, 199.

43 The trial began on 9 December 1946. Extracts from the transcript of the Doctors' Trial are available at: http://www.law.umkc.edu/faculty/projects/ftrials/nuremberg/NurembergDoctorTrial.html#Indictments.

44 IMT 2, 129: published online at: http://www.yale.edu/lawweb/avalon/imt/proc/11-21-45.htm. Wolff's vulnerability is clear from comparing the charges with which defendant Milch was charged. See TWC, Vol. 5, 861: http://www.mazal.org/archive/nmt/02/NMT02-T0861.htm.

> For the following experiments Jewish professional criminals who had committed 'Rassenschande' (race pollution) were used; the question of the formation of embolism was investigated in 10 cases. Some of the VP's [participants] died during a continued high-altitude experiment; for instance, after one-half hour at a [simulated] height of 12 kilometres. After the skull had been opened under water an ample amount of air embolism was found in the brain vessels, and, in part, free air in brain ventricles . . . after relative recuperation . . . some VP's were then kept under water until they died . . . one VP was made to breathe pure oxygen for two and a half hours before the experiment started. After six minutes at a height of 20 kilometres he died and at dissection also showed ample air embolism as was the case in all other experiments.[45]

The Nuremberg judgment not only cited such experiments as examples of the persecution and ultimately extermination of the Jews, but also referred to these as part of the evidence that justified the conviction of the SS as a criminal organisation.[46] As Himmler's co-deputy until September 1943, Wolff was, of course, the most senior SS official to survive the war.

Funding concentration camps

In addition, Wolff was vulnerable to prosecution at Nuremberg for another 'crime against humanity': the exploitation of slave labour. Wolff had organised and participated in Himmler's 'circle of friends', comprising leading industrialists, financiers and bankers, including representatives from Siemens, AEG, IG Farben, Portland-Zement and Deutsche Bank.[47] Industrialist members of this circle gained considerable economic benefits from being able to exploit large-scale concentration camp slave labour, for which Wolff had negotiated the precise financial terms. Wolff's deal created an arrangement that, of course, left the workers themselves without either pay or safe working conditions.[48]

45 Quoted in *USA v Edmund Milch*, NMT Vol. 2, Case 2, 14 December 1947, 384–5: NA, RG 238, M-888, Roll 2, Frame 471ff.

46 IMT, *The Trial of Major German War Criminals*, (London: HMSO, 1946), Vol. 23, 63–64, 77–78: http://www.nizkor.org/hweb/imt/tgmwc/judgment/j-war-crimes-jews-02.html; http://www.nizkor.org/hweb/imt/tgmwc/judgment/j-accused-organisations-04-02.html.

47 See TWC, Vol. 6, p.430: http://www.mazal.org/archive/nmt/06/NMT06-T0430.htm.

48 See minutes of meeting between Wolff and Bütefisch, 27 March 1941, 374 cited as evidence within TWC, Vol. 8, 377–81; Nuremberg document, NG, IG Farben trial, Document Book of the Prosecution, No. 91, 23–24. See the critical examination of Wolff when he gave evidence on behalf of Pohl in: TWC, Vol. 5, 770–71, 788 and – more fully – the mimeographed transcript 3–5 June 1947, 2090–2206 available from the US National Archives, Washington DC.

The persecution and extermination of European Jews

In some measure, Wolff was vulnerable to being charged for permitting and administratively overseeing (as distinct from positively ordering) the rounding up of Italian Jews who were then deported to death camps.[49] Kaltenbrunner's interrogation report of 28 September 1945 suggests that Wolff was implicated in the rounding up and deportation of Italian Jews to concentration and death camps, although Kaltenbrunner – as head of the RSHA – had his own reasons for wanting to divert responsibilities in this matter.[50] Wolff's defence was that orders for the deportation of Italian Jews were sent directly from the RSHA to the commander of the local security police, who had full responsibility for their implementation. The Nuremberg prosecutors had a report from Kappler to Wolff that showed that the latter was certainly aware of the deportations of 1,007 Jews to Auschwitz on 19 October 1943.[51]

Wolff was in overall charge of a detention camp at Bolzano in the Alps, from which transportations to Auschwitz took place.[52] On the other hand, Wolff would no doubt have argued that, since this camp was under the direct control of the Political Intelligence Section of the SS (the SD), he was not informed as to the events that took place there despite its physical proximity to his own HQ. Certainly SS forces, particularly those of the Waffen-SS who were, at least with respect to discipline but not always operational matters, under Wolff's direct command, were directly involved in the extermination of Jews. For example, soldiers within Joachim Peiper's SS-Panzergrenadier Bataillon were belatedly prosecuted for the killing of various Italian Jews in towns alongside Lake Maggiore but the charges failed because of the prosecution had exceeded the relevant statute of limitation.[53]

When interrogated, Wolff claimed that, as Chief of Himmler's Personal Staff, he was administratively insulated from those sections of the SS (the RSHA and Order Police) who organised and carried out Himmler's extermination campaigns against European Jewry, and other groups. However, this claim is contradicted by a host of surviving evidence documentation. For example, it is clear that Wolff personally witnessed mass killings of Jews at Minsk by his SS subordinates.[54] During 1942, Wolff was also personally

49 Hilberg, 2003 *op cit*, 710–12.

50 Cornell Collection, Vol. 15, Pt. 1, 38.02.

51 Kappler to Wolff, 18 October 1943, Nuremberg Document NO-2427.

52 See J. Wetzel, 'Das Polizeidurchgangslager Bozen,' *Dachauer Hefte*, Vol. 5 (Munich 1994), 28–29.

53 See M. Reynolds, *The Devil's Adjutant* (Staplehurst, Kent: Spellmount, 2002), 31–32.

54 Nuremberg document NO-2207; Himmler to Pohl, Krüger, the RSHA and Wolff, 9 October 1942, NO-1611; Himmler to Krüger, copies to RSHA, Pohl and Wolff, 3 January 1943, NO-1882; R. Hilberg, *The Destruction of the European Jews* (New Haven: Yale University Press, 2003), 343, 555. For von dem Bach's account of Himmler and Wolff's visit to Minsk,

involved, albeit in a trouble-shooter capacity, in the administrative processes the Nazi regime created to transport Polish Jews to Treblinka concentration and death camp.[55] This remained the case even where they had possession of documentation that included Wolff's name within correspondence demonstrating the Nazi regime's increasing willingness to insist that the Italian authorities enforce anti-Semitic measures, including rounding up and interning Jews within those territories, such as parts of France, which they controlled.[56]

From September 1943, when Wolff took over the leadership of the SS in occupied Italy, his subordinates within the SS were partly responsible for atrocities committed against Italian civilians, including, of course, the deportation of Italian Jews to Auschwitz.[57] As Hilberg states: 'In the end, more than 7,500 Jews were deported from Italy . . . Some 800 of the deportees survived.'[58] Yet such persecution of civilians generally fell under the jurisdiction of British war crimes investigators preparing for trials outside the Nuremberg process. Hence, given that our present concern is with the reasons why Wolff escaped prosecution within the Nuremberg process, it would be problematic to give much weight to such evidence.[59] The Nuremberg prosecutors were entitled to rely on this division of labour.

Italian anti-partisan warfare

Finally, with respect to his period as Höhere SS-und Polizeiführer in Nazi-occupied Italy, Wolff had 'command responsibilities', that is, responsibility

see *Aufbau* (New York) 23 August 1946, 1–2. Other witness accounts are contained in Case Wolff, 10a Js 39/60, particularly Z-Prot II/vol.2; M. Linklater, I. Hilton and N. Ascherson, *The Fourth Reich* (London: Hodder and Stoughton, 1984), 331; M. Gilbert, *The Holocaust: The Jewish Tragedy* (London: Fontana, 1987), 190–91.

55 Rüter-Ehlermann/Rüter/Bauer/Bracher: Justiz und NS-Verbrechen. Sammlung deutscher Strafurteile wegen nationalsozialistischer Tötungsverbrechen 1945–1999, Amsterdam 1971, Vol. 20 (12.4.1964–20.3.1965), case No. 580, Karl Wolff, 380–504 at 458: letter from Wolff to Ing. Dr. Ganzenmüller, 13 August 1942; TWC, Vol. 5, 774–76.

56 OKW/WFSt/Qu via RSHA to Wolff and Ritter, 4 December 1942: Nuremberg document NO-1118.

57 For details of the three main camps at this location, one of which, Birkenau, became an extermination camp: M. Gilbert, *Auschwitz and the Allies* (London: M. Joseph and Rainbird, 1981); P. Levi, *Survival in Auschwitz* (New York: Collier, 1958); A. Menasche, *Birkenau* (New York: Saltiel, 1947); R. Höss, *Commandant of Auschwitz: The Autobiography of Rudolf Hoess* (London: Pan, 1974); R. Höss, *Death Dealer: The Memoirs of the SS Kommandant at Auschwitz*, S. Paskul (ed.), A. Pollinger (trans.) (New York: Da Capo, 1996); I. Gutman *et al* (eds.), *Anatomy of the Auschwitz Death Camp* (Bloomington: Indiana University Press, 1994).

58 Hilberg, 2003, *op cit*, 723.

59 Of course, those historians interested in the wider question of Wolff's involvement in wartime genocide, as distinct from evidence directly pertinent to his prosecution within the Nuremberg trials, would have to take this evidence particularly seriously.

as a commander for the actions of his subordinates, for a series of war crimes committed against civilians by his subordinates during anti-partisan operations. These including reprisal killings of approximately 9,200 Italian women and children.[60]

OSS archival sources contain references to Wolff suggesting that in the absence of *de facto* immunity he could and should have faced prosecution at Nuremberg.[61] Despite the firm conviction of Allied investigators that he was guilty of major war crimes against Italian civilians,[62] and therefore deserved to be prosecuted alongside German Field Marshal Albert Kesselring,[63] Wolff also managed to escape being prosecuted for his command responsibilities for these offences committed by his subordinates.[64] Given his overall command responsibility for atrocities committed by German forces conducting anti-partisan warfare in Italy, including reprisal killing of Italian civilians, he was extremely vulnerable to prosecution and a death sentence on this ground alone.[65]

The next section of this chapter concentrates upon the key details of Wolff's institutional position within the SS. This is followed by a close analysis of different strands of Wolff's denial of personal knowledge or involvement in genocide.

60 See the correspondence over Wolff at PRO, WO 310/127, particular that between JAG and War Crimes Group in the autumn of 1947; Cable from Wolff to Chiefs of General Staff via Lt. General Roettiger, 12 January 1945 (although the year is cited as 1944, this must be a mistake as the cable refers to events taking place in late 1944): NA, RG 226, Entry 92, Box 619, Folder 2; G. Schreiber, 'Partisanenkrieg und Kriegsverbrechen der Wehrmacht in Italien 1943 bis 1945', in *Repression und Kriegsverbrechen. Die Bekämpfung von Widerstands- und Partisanenbewegungen gegen die deutsche Besatzung in West- und Südeuropa* (Beiträge zur Nationalsozialistischen Gesundheits- und Sozialpolitik, Vol. 14) (Berlin: 1997), 93–129 at 93; R. Lamb, *War in Italy 1943–1945: A Brutal Story* (New York: St Martins, 1994), 73–4. With respect to the Bardine killings, see statements and affidavit of Padre Lino Delle Piane and John Baendale, PRO: WO 235/375.

61 See the list of potential defendants contained in 'Suggested Lines of Research for Prosecution of Nazi War Criminals', 11 July 1945, 13; and 'Prosecution of Major Nazi Criminals', appendix 'individuals': NA, RG 238, Entry 1, Box 8, pt. 2.

62 See Telford Taylor (OCCWC) to Robert Murphy, 24 October 1947: IFZ, Polad/33/18 'Interrogation of Wolff by Husmann and all correspondence' (with handwritten annotations from 15 November 1947).

63 JAG to War Crimes Group, 15 September 1947: PRO, WO 310/127.

64 See the correspondence over Wolff at PRO, WO 310/127, particularly that between JAG and War Crimes Group in the autumn of 1947.

65 See cable from Wolff to Chiefs of General Staff via Lt General Roettiger, 12 January 1945 (although the year is cited as 1944, this must be a mistake, as the cable refers to events taking place in late 1944): NA, RG 226, Entry 92, Box 619, Folder 2.

Wolff's institutional position

Wolff remains particularly notorious for his participation, albeit largely in an administrative capacity, within the Nazis' genocidal campaigns against Jews and other groups. Wolff's potential liabilities depended, in part, on the executive functions exercised by Himmler's immediate subordinates, including the scope they possessed for taking independent action.[66] For present purposes, the nature of both Wolff's involvement in genocide, and his defensive claims discussed in the next section, require a review of his institutional position as Himmler's Chief of Personal Staff from 1936 to September 1943, and its relationship to other, more specifically repressive, branches of the SS. Such institutional clarification is vital since the weaknesses of Wolff's defensive claims, which of course represented potential opportunities for the Nuremberg prosecutors, remain unintelligible until the institutional relationship between different branches of Himmler's SS has been clarified. Without such clarification, it would be impossible to properly assess Wolff's argument that the nature of his official role within this complex organisation (which combined relatively innocent functions with distinctly genocidal activities) meant that, despite his institutional seniority as second only to Himmler, he was effectively 'insulated' from the decision-making loop involved in the planning and execution of Nazi genocide.

Wolff's role as Chief of Himmler's Personal Staff from 1936 (which followed his appointment in May 1933 as an adjutant)[67] meant that he headed one of the 12 main departments of the SS's complex institutional hierarchy, which – in terms of holding the entire organisation together – possessed a unique status within this organisation. Formally, he held this key post until the end of the Second World War but, in practice, it largely terminated on 18 February 1943, following Wolff's hospitalisation and later re-assignment to Italy in September 1943. His section included a variety of functions including racist cultural policies involving preserving the 'heritage of the forefathers',[68] the 'Lebensborn' programme of encouraging 'racially pure' children, and the SS's 'chief of protocol'.[69] The most important question, for present purposes,

66 See D. Cameron Watt, 'The fantasy life of Hitler's hitman', *Sunday Times*, 24 June 1990, reviewing P. Padfield, *Himmler: Reichsführer, SS* (London: Macmillan, 1989).

67 *USA v Friedrich Flick et al*, *op cit*, transcript 10024.

68 In particular, the study group Ahnenerbe e.V. agency was, according to Kaltenbrunner, to: 'more intensely acquaint the people with its Germanic past and to prove to them that the life bound by tradition has many advantages. This was done chiefly by way of literature, illustrations etc. The Ahnenerbe later indulged in scientific research and experiments. This organisation was first directed by SS General Wolf [sic] in his capacity as Chief of the Personal staff . . . After Wolf had lost his position the Ahnenerbe came under Himmler's direct direction [sic] . . . it may have been directed by Dr Rudolf Brandt.' Summary of Interrogation of Kaltenbrunner, Nuremberg, 16 September 1946, no. 137, 4: RG 238, M-1019, Roll 82, Frame 348–351.

69 G. Mauz, 'Himmler nannte ihn "mein Wölffchen",' in *Der Spiegel* 30 (22 July 1964), 34.

was Wolff's relationship to the SS-Hauptamt or Main Office (headed by Wittje and then Berger but whose executive functions he gradually usurped) and the Reichssicherheits-Hauptamt (RSHA). The RSHA had initially been headed by Reinhard Heydrich and then, following his death in June 1942, Ernst Kaltenbrunner (who was to become an upstart rival to Wolff).[70] However, between April 1942 and Kaltenbrunner's appointment as Heydrich's successor as Chief of the Security Police and SD and Head of the RSHA, Himmler personally took control of this department.[71]

During his interrogations and witness testimony, Wolff insisted the RSHA was primarily and exclusively responsible for Gestapo (or Geheime Staatspolizei) repression and anti-Jewish measures, and that the chain of both information and command with respect to such measures bypassed his office altogether. This, he claimed, explains why he heard of the systematic extermination of Jews only in March 1945.[72]

The head of the RSHA (as with each other SS department) reported *directly* to Himmler without routing matters through Wolff's office of Chief of Personal Staff. As is well known, the RSHA was responsible for internal security, with its security police section divided between mundane criminal police (Kripo) and Gestapo (political police), who numbered between 40,000 and 45,000. The second division of the RSHA was the Sicherheitsdienst des Reichsführers SS or SD, which was responsible for gathering political intelligence and numbered only a few thousand.[73] The persecution and extermination of the Jews was carried out mainly under the control of the RSHA and the 'Order Police' controlled by the Main Office. This police force consisted both of technical services, such as fire fighters, and mobile killing squads, or 'Einsatzgruppen', comprising in total of c. 10,000 men. These 'Einsatzgruppen' squads were permanent formations that were ordered to move from region to region, and which had control over indigenous local police in occupied territories.

In his efforts to deflect accusations of complicity in the Nazi genocide against European Jews, Wolff made a series of interrelated and – he must have believed – mutually supporting defensive claims. They included giving a highly restrictive interpretation of the remit of his role as Himmler's Chief of

70 Hoehn records that Wolff and Kaltenbrunner exchanged allegations of abuse of official power for personal gain, *op cit*, 433. This is supported by a copy of Max Schellenberg's interrogation statement. Schellenberg notes that: 'Kaltenbrunner could not get on at all with Wolff, the Graf Westarp must have played some role in this respect. He therefore wanted Himmler to dismiss Wolff.' Statement by Schellenberg re Wolff, n.d., included in Allen Dulles' papers, Mudd Library, Princeton University, New Jersey, Box 59, Folder 10.

71 This opens the possibility that Wolff's post could have received reports from Gestapo head Müller regarding the extermination of Jews in the death camps unless Müller was expressly ordered to report exclusively to Himmler.

72 See Wolff's testimony in the Pohl Case: TWC, Vol. 5, 777.

73 R. Hilberg, 2003, *op cit*, 202.

Personal Staff, denying any knowledge of the details of concentration camp atrocities, and highlighting his alleged expulsion from Himmler's inner policy-making circle precisely at the time when the extermination campaigns were becoming systematic and intensified. However, Wolff's personal pride in his rapid promotion and higher institutional position meant that he made statements that also partially discredited his other claims not to be incriminated in any acts that were even indirectly related to war crimes. He explained his mental breakdown in spring 1947 as an understandable reaction of someone who was not only being deprived of the credit merited by his good deeds, including the Sunrise capitulation, but was kept imprisoned for suspicion of involvement in offences that were so distant from his specific role that he had not even known that they were taking place.

Wolff's defensive claims in the light of the Nuremberg evidence

Of course, it was one thing for Wolff to make the defensive claims discussed above concerning his lack of knowing involvement in genocide; it was quite another for Nuremberg prosecutors to accept these assertions. In particular, and as this section will demonstrate, the prosecutors possessed considerable firm evidence, largely documentary in nature, which, at the very least, called Wolff's assertions into question. This section will address the implications of such evidence for the credibility of Wolff's defensive claims.

The Nuremberg prosecutors would have known that Wolff's administrative position from 1936 to September 1943 could hardly be equated to the genocidal role within the SS played by Himmler, Heydrich, Kaltenbrunner or Eichmann.[74] Yet Wolff's claim to have been entirely insulated from RSHA and Order Police activities is partially contradicted by two surviving reports obtained by the Nuremberg prosecutors.

At least during January and February 1943, SS-Oberstgruppenführer Daluege (Chief of the Order Police (ORPO), whose forces committed mass killings of Jews within occupied Europe) *reported directly to Wolff*. Daluege's report provided extensive details of the statistical composition, internal organisation and regional distribution (into rural and urban areas, and over different territories) of the various branches of his forces.[75] It states that,

74 It may well, therefore, be an exaggeration to claim that: 'Armed with all special powers Wolff had a leading part in the so-called "final solution of the Jewish problem" ' as is stated in National Council of the National Front of Democratic Germany, *Brown Book: War and Nazi War Criminals in West Germany* (Berlin: 1980), 84.

75 'Report on the work of the Order Police during the year 1942' (reported dated 1 February 1942) sent with covering letter Daluege to Wolff, 28 February 1943, NO-2861, Exh: 802 VIII on 8 December 1947: NA, RG 238, Entry 174, Box 54; and file 7771 Document Centre Berlin File A3 SS-2925.

during the second half of 1942, the Order Police was being virtually trebled in number from three to six regiments, with almost half of these deployed for activities behind combat lines, supported by six additional battalions under the command of the regional SS leader.

Furthermore, Daluege's report indicated that the SS had recruited large number of indigenous groups, including Ukrainians, Baltic and White Russians, to assist in 'special operations' – standard SS euphemisms for murder.[76] The report claims responsibility for: 'cleaning up and clearing of isolated enemy units, combating criminal – especially political elements'.[77] Such activities, which appeared to link the extermination of civilians during 'special actions' with anti-partisan warfare, including the 'mopping up of the Warsaw Ghetto already performed'[78] – resulted in the killing of 30,000 'bandits' in battle and making 4,000 arrests, of which 3,000 were later executed as 'saboteurs and assistants to partisans'.[79] Daluege's forces claimed 'credit' for retaliatory strikes in the wake of the assassination of Heydrich, which led to the 'annihilation of innumerable political criminals'.[80] Given the extensive use of auxiliary locally recruited individuals in the rounding up and extermination of Jews within Eastern territories, the fact that the report states that such forces had been expanded tenfold from 30,000 in 1941–42 to 300,000 by the end of 1942, is particularly significant. Such forces were commended, 'since everywhere we experienced satisfying results with these auxiliaries'.[81]

In addition, this report linked the extermination of 'political elements of foreign races' resident in Marseilles, France, with the policy of making 'this area a clean city'. It also reported the use, in response to Allied air-raids, of concentration camp detainees 'for the removal of duds and bombs with delayed time fuses'.[82] The report finished by providing details of the support the Order Police had provided for the genocidal 'Germanisation' of occupied eastern territories, including the 'the resettlement of Ukranian Ethnic Germans'.[83]

Daluege's covering letter to Wolff asks him to continue to support the work of his Order Police:

> It is short and contains all the information about my work which you will need to accomplish your important tasks at the Fuehrer's HQ . . . I would like to ask you to continue to support my work at the Fuehrer and the office of the Fuehrer HQ.[84]

76 *Ibid.* The Nuremberg prosecutors pressed Wolff on his receipt of such reports from those responsible for mobile killing squads. See Interrogation of Wolff, 16 December 1946: National Archives, Modern Military II, Washington DC (hereafter NA), RG 238, Microfilm 1019, Roll 80, Frame 968.

77 *Ibid*, 6. 78 *Ibid*, 12. 79 *Ibid*, 7. 80 *Ibid*, 12. 81 *Ibid*, 11.

82 *Ibid*, 20. 83 *Ibid*, 32. 84 *Ibid*.

It is highly relevant to the credibility of Wolff's defensive claims that this report was sent direct to him, rather than to either Himmler, or to Kaltenbrunner as the newly appointed Chief of the RSHA Branch. The bulk of the 43-page report is devoted to summarising relatively unproblematic police, air-raid and fire-fighting activities. Nevertheless, it is significant that the Nuremberg official who analysed this report listed Wolff as amongst the persons 'implicated' by its contents, and indicated that it should be filed for later use under the headings 'persecution of the Jews' and 'atrocities against civilians'.[85]

A second incriminating document that also passed over Wolff's desk makes it clear that the SS were engaged in the wholesale and forcible 'deportations' of Rumanian Jews, presumably – given that such documentation was classified as 'Top Secret' – to concentration and death camps.[86] Certainly, those comparatively lower-ranking analysts amongst the Nuremberg prosecution organisation who initially sifted through and analysed such documentation listed Wolff as one of the persons directly 'implicated' by their contents.[87] In short, Wolff's repeated denials of personal knowledge or direct involvement in genocide are surely further eroded by the fact that the Nuremberg prosecutors had information that he had personally received at least two reports from those directly implicated in the logistics of racist mass extermination.

More generally, Wolff's defensive claims regarding the limited scope of his administrative remit within the SS are contradicted by other Nuremberg documentation confirming that, irrespective of his formal job title, he was included amongst the small circle of Himmler's senior staff making decisions regarding the persecution, exploitation, transportation and ultimate slaughter of Jews. Indeed, the Nuremberg prosecutors must have known that one of Wolff's key roles, which gave him disproportionate personal influence and power over other senior colleagues, was to act as a gatekeeper to, and a messenger from, Himmler.[88] It was precisely the seniority of Wolff's role within the Nazi regime that made him a particularly valued insider source for prosecutors seeking to clarify various organisational relationships. One relevant example was presented by Defendant Ohlendorf, former SD leader, during his testimony at Nuremberg NMT.

> *A* Heydrich sent me on an official trip with Himmler, and during its course disputes arose, the consequence of which was that in Warsaw he had me informed, through his chief adjutant Karl Wolff, that I

85 10 April 1947, *ibid.*

86 See Staff Evidence Analysis report of 13 June 1946 relating to a letter from an unnamed SS-Sturmbannführer to Wolff, 'Evacuation of Jews out of Rumania', 11 August 1943: Nuremberg document NO-023: http://www.mazal.org/NO-series/NO-0023-000.htm.

87 *Ibid.*

88 Breitman, 1992 *op cit*, 148 who refers to this role in the specific context of the Sonderkommando Kunsberg.

must leave his services, that agreement between us about the work was not possible.

Q What was the reason for this disagreement with Himmler?

A He reproached me that the members of the SD in Poland had not been able to carry out the treatment of the Jews in the form he wanted and that, he said, was the product of my training.[89]

As already noted, one of Wolff's defensive strategies was to shelter behind formal titles and related jurisdictional distinctions as recorded in organisational charts. Yet, the prosecutors would have rapidly appreciated that the SS, in common with other institutional aspects of Hitler's regime, was characterised by a chaotic division of labour with considerable overlap and duplication of functions. This tendency meant that insulation of information and function within any SS department was, in practice, far less hermetically sealed than Wolff tried to claim. In particular, the SS was an organisation where command responsibilities for security policing, intelligence gathering, internal repression and quasi-military actions were often confused by a series of overlapping and competing sections, which often worked against each other.[90] For example, Herbert Kappler, SS senior police official in Italy, was required to report unofficially to Berlin in additional to his official SS superior, Wolff.[91]

In short, Nuremberg prosecutors investigating the chaotic internal structure of the Nazi regime must have appreciated that, as Himmler's senior administrative trouble-shooter, Wolff had to deal with a number of interdepartmental disputes. These disputes must have included conflicts involving the repressive and genocidal sections of the SS.

Another example of Wolff's claim to have been administratively isolated from genocidal practices is the following statement by a Nuremberg prosecutor in relation to the interdepartmental character of one of Wolff's responsibilities, securing large-scale sponsorship from Himmler's 'circle of friends'. The prosecutor linked the membership of this circle to some of the gravest SS war crimes, of which members of that circle must have been aware:

89 http://www.mazal.org/archive/nmt/04/NMT04-T0233.htm.

90 For example, Kappler, a police attaché and one of Wolff's subordinates in Rome from 1943, noted that, on certain issues, Wolff's authority would be disputed by Kaltenbrunner, whose authority over the repressive aspects of the work of the SS overlapped with Wolff's policing and internal security remit. Kappler gives the example of Himmler issuing an order to both Kaltenbrunner and Wolff to establish sabotage operations against Allied forces and their supply lines. This resulted in Wolff appointing Kappler to this task; whilst Kaltenbrunner also appointed his own representative for Italy, a conflict that was ultimately settled in Wolff's favour. See 'Interrogation report SS Obersturmbannführer Kappler, Herbert': CSDIC/SC/15AG/SD 18: NA, R G226, Entry 194, Box 63, Folder 7.

91 *Ibid*; J. Staron, *Fosse Ardeantine und Marzabotto: Deutsche Kriegsverbrechen und* Resistenza (Paderborn/München/Wien/Zürich: Ferdinand Schöningh, 2002), 40, n. 52.

> In 1941, Farben made a contribution to the SS, through the 'Circle,' of 100,000 marks, and thereafter made similar annual contributions to the SS. The defendant Bütefisch was a member of the 'Keppler Circle,' subsequently known as the 'Friends of Himmler' and 'Freundeskreis' (Circle of Friends). This select group included the leading industrialists in Germany. Regular and frequent meetings were held at which Heinrich Himmler, Reichsfuehrer of the SS, presided. Its membership, in addition to leading German industrialists and bankers, included Karl Wolff, Himmler's adjutant; Oswald Pohl, Chief of all concentration camps; Otto Ohlendorf, a leading official of the SS who testified before the IMT that his SS Kommandos had killed 90,000 women, men, and children, mostly Jews, in Russia; and Wolfram Sievers, who directed the program of criminal medical experimentation on human beings. This 'Circle' made regular annual contributions of at least one million marks to Himmler to aid in financing the criminal activities of the SS. These activities consisted of the guarding and administration of concentration camps and the brutal treatment of their inmates; subjecting prisoners of war and concentration camp inmates to a series of experiments, including freezing to death and killing by poisoned bullets; shooting unarmed prisoners of war; extensive participation in the slave-labor program; murder and ill-treatment of the civilian population in occupied countries, including massacres such as at Lidice and the destruction of the Warsaw ghetto; and the persecution and extermination of millions of Jews and others deemed politically undesirable by the SS. The criminal programs of the SS were so widespread and conducted on such a gigantic scale that they were a matter of common knowledge throughout Germany and throughout the world.[92]

Here the Nuremberg prosecutor had little difficulty in establishing that members of this circle, including Wolff, were routinely informed by SS officials regarding different aspects and phases of the deportation and persecution of European Jews. Furthermore, it was clear at this time that Wolff was – as confirmed by Defendant Flick – a longstanding and key SS member of this circle who played a vital coordination role within it. This trial evidence should have been sufficient to undermine Wolff's defensive claim to have been ignorant of such actions.[93]

Both Wolff, and Otto Ohlendorf, an early section head of the RSHA,

92 Prosecution statement in the Flick trial (*USA v Friedrich Flick et al*, NMT case 5, 4 November 1947: NA, RG 238, M-891, Roll 11). See also further relevant documentation http://www.mazal.org/archive/nmt/07/NMT07-T0056.htm.

93 See Flick's testimony in his NMT trial: http://www.mazal.org/archive/nmt/06/NMT06-T0405.htm.

testified that the SS relied chiefly upon contributions from industrialists for its funds. The SS had no budget of its own, and practically no revenue from official state sources. Although the evidence just quoted was directed against Flick, the implication is that Wolff's assistance in first establishing, and then maintaining, such crucial funding was essential in securing the resources necessary for every aspect of the SS, including, of course, its massive genocidal operations.[94]

Indeed, the Nuremberg prosecutors must surely have been aware that the link between securing funding for the SS and the persecution of Jews clearly implicated Wolff, particularly his involvement in policies of confiscation of Jewish property. In 1939, Wolff was indirectly involved in aspects of the 'Ayranisation' of Jewish industries and other commercial organisations: that is, their forceful confiscation by German nationals or Nazi-related corporations, including the Göring Worke. For example, during a protracted and contested battle to take control of parts of the Rothschilds' extensive and international business empire, the SS intervened to arrest Baron Louis Rothschild in order to exert pressure upon his family.[95] It was Wolff who personally received the thanks of Rasche, employed by the grateful Dresdner Bank, for authorising this gangster-style intervention, whose effects had been to lower the price for which the stock could be purchased.[96] Rasche wrote to Wolff on 2 August 1939 confirming that:

> The negotiations with the Rothschild Group . . . the subject of which I discussed with you a few months ago . . . have now led to a satisfactory result. . . . You will remember that I pointed out at that time already how valuable the support of the Security Service, Special Command Prague and [illegible possibly Berne], has already been to me and my staff [and] resulted in the fact that the basic purchase price in foreign currency could be considerably reduced by using arguments which had to be recognised even by the opponents. I feel it necessary to thank you very much for this most valuable support . . .[97]

In addition, the Nuremberg prosecutors possessed a considerable amount of documentation indicating the close nature of Wolff's personal relationship to Himmler and his inner circle of advisers. This evidence challenged Wolff's defensive assertions that his relationship with Himmler was entirely formal and lacking any measure of personal intimacy of longstanding friendship that allowed communication across departmental barriers. The questionable

94 http://www.mazal.org/archive/nmt/06/NMT06-T0103.htm.
95 Hilberg, 2003, *op cit*, 105 and – more generally on Ayranisation – 92–137.
96 Rasche to Wolff, 2 August 1939, NI-13669: NA, RG 238 T301, Roll 111, Frame 1213.
97 *Ibid.*

character of Wolff's assertion is clear not only from the length of Wolff's service for Himmler from 1934 onwards, initially as his adjutant, but also from a personal reference Himmler supplied on Wolff's behalf to the Nazi Party's treasurer in April 1941. Whilst justifying a transfer to Wolff of 21,500 Reichsmark (itself a remarkable gesture of confidence), Himmler gave an apparently heartfelt expression of how he regarded Wolff as both an intimate friend and trusted colleague:

> I regard SS-Obergruppenführer Wolff as one of my most valuable associates whose pure and faultless character I have continuously noticed daily and hourly for 8 years, and whom I have come to love as a friend. In line with your proposal, I have decided to give 21,500 RM. to SS-Obergruppenführer Wolff from a special fund of at my disposal, part as an outright gift and part as a loan.[98]

Wolff's claim to have been permanently expelled from the inner circle of the SS leadership as a punishment for his remarriage in defiance of Himmler's specific orders, is also challenged by documentation uncovered during the Nuremberg process. According to Kaltenbrunner's post-war interrogation report held by the Nuremberg prosecutors, Wolff: 'had been very influential in the matter of SS appointments',[99] and 'his relations with Himmler eventually improved due largely to the efforts of Prof. Gebhard'.[100] Other documentary evidence in the possession of the Nuremberg prosecutors clearly implicates Wolff as one of a close circle of trusted individuals with whom Himmler discussed the ultimate destruction of European Jewry. For example, from early October 1942, Himmler sought to encourage Lublin's development as an industrial centre for SS manufacturing enterprises in Poland employing slave labour. He intended this policy to be a joint venture of the various organs of the SS and police. This explains why Wolff, together with other SS departmental heads, became parties to a chain of correspondence that challenges Wolff's defensive claims.[101] (Wolff had previously toured the larger Polish cities with Himmler in October 1939.)[102] In pursuit of the Lubin

98 'Himmler's opinion of SS-Obergruppenführer Wolff', 21 April 1941: Nuremberg document NO-0028, summarised in Staff Evidence Analysis report of 13 June 1946. The Berlin Documentation Center classified it as File No. XI A/18 from SS HQ files [I have modified the ungrammatical sentence structure of the English translation].

99 This remained the case even after Wolff's so-called 'banishment' to Italy, which actually represented a promotion in terms of ranking within the SS hierarchy.

100 Kaltenbrunner's 'Immediate Interrogation Report' of 28 June 1945 (itself part of the Nuremberg specific archive): Cornell Collection, Vol. 18, Annex 9: 'Remarks on SS Personalities' pt. 25, 34.

101 The others included: SS-Obergruppenführer Pohl, SS-Obergruppenführer Krüger, SS-Brigadeführer Odilo Globocnik, Reich Security Main Office (Reichssicherheits Hauptamt).

102 Breitman, 1992 *op cit*, 80.

project, Himmler ordered that the remaining Jews, who were then located at various sites within the General Government, had to be transported to workshops in concentration camps in Warsaw and Lublin. He further ordered that Jews employed by armaments firms be gradually isolated in 'a few large Jewish concentration camps' in the eastern area of the General Government. On 2 October 1942, Himmler wrote to Wolff, Pohl, Krüger and Globocnik regarding his determination to extract the Jews:

> With reference to the memorandum from the Commander of the Military District (Wehrkreisbefehlshaber) in the Government-General to the OKW [High Command of the Wehrmacht] concerning the replacement of Jewish labor by Poles, I have the following comments:
>
> 1. I have given orders that all so-called armament workers who are actually employed solely in tailoring, furrier and shoe-making workshops be collected in concentration camps on the spot, i.e., in Warsaw and Lublin, under the direction of SS-Obergruppenführer Krüger and SS-Obergruppenführer Pohl. The Wehrmacht will send its orders to us, and we guarantee the continuous delivery of the items of clothing required. I have issued instructions, however, that ruthless steps be taken against all those who consider they should oppose this move in the alleged interest of armaments needs, but who in reality only seek to support the Jews and their own businesses.
> 2. Jews in real war industries, i.e., armament workshops, vehicle workshops, etc., are to be withdrawn step by step. As a first stage they are to be concentrated in separate halls in the factories. In a second stage in this procedure the work teams in these separate halls will be combined, by means of exchange, into closed enterprises wherever this is possible, so that we will then have simply a few closed concentration-camp industries in the Government-General.
> 3. Our endeavor will then be to replace this Jewish labor force with Poles and to consolidate most of these Jewish concentration-camp enterprises into a small number of large Jewish concentration-camp enterprises – in the eastern part of the Government-General, if possible. But there, too, in accordance with the wish of the Führer, the Jews are some day to disappear. signed H. Himmler.[103]

Himmler's message was prompted by the possibility that German military authorities in Poland, who were heavily reliant upon Jewish slave labour for

103 Himmler to Pohl, Krüger, the RSHA and Wolff, 9 October 1942, NO-1611/Pros. Ex. 498, an English version is published in the Nuremberg 'Green Series', Vol. 5, 616–17; Response by Himmler to General von Gienanth (9 October 1942), Reichsfuehrer SS Field Command Journal No. AR 31/22/42 9 October 1942.

arms production and distribution, might attempt to 'protect' Jews. His concern was that Jews who were working in industries that could, on a broad definition of the term, be classified as related to armaments, would escape anti-Semitic measures.[104] The notorious final sentence of Himmler's letter referring to the disappearance of the Jews, deployed standard SS euphemisms for extermination ('evacuation', 'disappearance', 'special measures' etc.). As such, it also challenges Wolff's additional assertion that Himmler's extermination programmes lacked Hitler's authorisation. In this context, it is also worth recalling that the distinction between slave labour and summary extermination was not always clear. Indeed, the conditions to which the Nazi regime subjected Jewish labour often amounted to little more than a delayed form of killing, a form of working to death.[105]

Other related parts of this chain of correspondence should have indicated to Wolff that Himmler's reference to the 'disappearance' of Polish Jews was no empty threat. This was because he had ordered that Jews be singled out, even where this was detrimental to the economic aspect of the German war effort. In the same period, Globocnik wrote to Wolff on 22 July 1942, the day deportations began from the Warsaw ghetto to Treblinka, stating:

> The Reichsführer SS . . . has given us so much new work that with it now all our most secret wishes are to be fulfilled. I am so very thankful to him for this, and he can be sure of one thing, that these things he wishes will be fulfilled in the shortest time.[106]

It is arguable that, taken as whole, Wolff was party to a chain of documentation that clearly foreshadowed Stroop's brutal military attack on the Warsaw ghetto between 19 April and 16 May 1943.[107] For example, in January 1943, three months before the violent evacuation programme was launched by Stroop, Wolff also received copies of other correspondence. This expressed Himmler's irritation that an owner of a factory in the Warsaw Jewish ghetto had become wealthy as a direct result of SS policies. Himmler insisted that the number of Jews in Warsaw who, contrary to his earlier directives, were still being 'protected', must be sharply reduced.[108] In the same month, Wolff was also included within the correspondence loop for a letter Himmler wrote to Krüger complaining that his 'evacuation programme' was being carried out too slowly, and ordering the immediate transfer of 16,000

104 Hilberg, 2003 *op cit*, 555. 105 Breitman, 1992 *op cit*, 234.

106 See Nuremberg document NO-2207; Globocnik SS file, Berlin Document Center.

107 This documentation was discussed in this context by prosecutors during the Pohl trial: http://www.mazal.org/archive/nmt/05/NMT05-T1174.htm.

108 Himmler to Krüger, copies to RSHA, Pohl and Wolff, 2 January 1943: Nuremberg document NO-1882/Pros. Ex. 499.

Jews to a concentration camp at Lublin.[109] It is difficult to accept that, having read these ominous documents, Wolff could have failed to appreciate that Himmler was intensifying a process of singling out Jews for persecution in a manner that was already paving the way for their mass extermination. Here, we must remember that Wolff was undoubtedly intelligent and attuned (albeit in an opportunistic manner) to his organisation's policy nuances, a key factor behind his rapid promotion.

Under interrogation, Kaltenbrunner claimed that, during the internal 'turf wars' between senior SS department heads, Wolff had been extremely successful in expanding the scope of his own department's functions over personnel and organisational matters at the expense for example, of Gottlob Berger's SS-Hauptamt. The latter was originally supposed to function as Himmler's own executive 'directing agency' for the entire SS. Kaltenbrunner explained this partly by the fact that Wolff: 'had a strong influence over Himmler. Thus, Berger's SS Main Office lost all prestige in personnel matters . . . Wolff also succeeded in considerably weakening Berger's personal influence [over Himmler and] Berger's office became more and more a place of mere [formal] representation.'[110]

Furthermore, in early October 1943, Himmler made a very public endorsement of Wolff during his notorious Posen speech to the entire leadership strata of the SS.[111] Himmler reminded the other SS-Obergruppenführer that Wolff was *the only* member of the SS leadership whose contribution merited the award of a new, and specially created, rank of Höhere SS-und Polizeiführer.[112] This effectively meant that, within the SS hierarchy, Wolff outranked all other Obergruppenfuehrers; whilst Wolff himself was subordinate only to Himmler (and Hitler). During this speech, Himmler singled out Wolff for particular praise, referring to him as:

> One of my closest and oldest associates, SS-Obergruppenführer Wolff, after a severe illness which seriously endangered his life (operation for kidney stone) has, thank God, gotten well again, and is now – it is the first time anyone has held this position – the Höhere SS-und Polizeiführer for all of occupied Italy. He is therefore responsible for a region with 25 to 30 million inhabitants. SS-Gruppenführer Globocnik . . . as well as several other SS and Police Leaders, will be subordinate to him.[113]

109 Kaltenbrunner's 'Immediate Interrogation Report' of 28 June 1945: Cornell Collection, Vol. 18, Annex 9: 'Remarks on SS Personalities' pt. 25, 34.

110 Summary of Interrogation of Kaltenbrunner, Nuremberg, 16 September 1946, No. 137, 2: NA, RG 238, M-1019, Roll 82, Frame 348–51.

111 More generally, see Breitman, 1992 *op cit*, 242–43.

112 There were a number of Höhere SS-und Polizeiführer, such as SS-Obergruppenführer Hans-Adolf Prützmann.

113 Himmler, Posen, 4 October 1943: Nuremberg document PS-1919.

As already noted, Wolff claimed to have possessed no knowledge of mass extermination within death camps until he heard of this in March 1945. Wolff was one of the few amongst the SS leadership who was absent from audience of Himmler's Posen speech in which the Reichsführer made a rare public acknowledgement of *the centrality of the racist extermination of European Jewry to the mission of the SS*. At Posen, Himmler praised the unflinching orientation of SS officials involved in the killing of Jews.[114] It is, perhaps, just possible that, at this time, Wolff still considered himself expelled from Himmler's inner circle, and remained unaware of the contents of this speech. However, Lang suggests that, on the basis of captured correspondence between Himmler and Wolff, the Nuremberg prosecutors would have had reason to question this:

> If Wolff had ever fallen out of favor with Himmler in the way and intensity in which Wolff claimed, it was not long before their relationship returned to one of friendly benevolence. In a speech in Posen on 4 October 1943 . . . The entire highest leadership of the SS listened to this with the exception of Wolff. He was working in Italy, but the speech he probably read a few days thereafter in Himmler's camp, because in this speech Himmler celebrated him as one of his 'closest and oldest' associates. . . . Himmler's letters to Wolff had resumed addressing him in intimate and personal terms as 'dear little wolf.'[115]

If the Nuremberg prosecutors had believed that Wolff had become aware of the contents of the Posen speech, which is likely because Wolff is specifically named as one of the individuals 'implicated' in the extermination of Jews by the Nuremberg Staff Evidence Analysis summary of this speech,[116] then the following extract would have proved interesting. It would have been particularly damaging to Wolff's assertion that only a small number of SS officials, 'probably 70', were directly involved in organising mass extermination:

> I also want to speak to you here, in complete frankness, of a really grave chapter. Amongst ourselves, for once, it shall be said quite openly, but all the same we will never speak about it in public. . . . I am referring here to the evacuation of the Jews, the extermination of the Jewish people. This is one of the things that is easily said: 'The Jewish people are going to be exterminated,' that's what every Party member says, 'sure, it's in our program, elimination of the Jews, extermination – it'll be done.' And then they all come along, the 80 million worthy Germans, and each one has his one decent Jew. Of course, the others are swine, but this one, he is

114 *Ibid.* 115 Von Lang, *op cit*, 219.
116 See SEA, PS-1919 in Cornell Collection, Vol. 20, Pt. 1.

> a first-rate Jew. Of all those who talk like that, not one has seen it happen, not one has had to go through with it. Most of you men know what it is like to see 100 corpses side-by-side, or 500 or 1,000. To have stood fast through this and – except for cases of human weakness – to have stayed decent, that has made us hard. This is an unwritten and never-to-be-written page of glory in our history, for we know how difficult it would be for us if today – under bombing raids and the hardships and deprivations of war – if we were still to have the Jews in every city as secret saboteurs, agitators, and inciters. If the Jews were still lodged in the body of the German nation, we would probably by now have reached the stage of 1916–17. . . . We had the moral right, we had the duty towards our people, to destroy this people that wanted to destroy us. But we do not have the right to enrich ourselves by so much as a fur, as a watch, by one Mark or a cigarette or anything else. We do not want, in the end, because we destroyed a bacillus, to be infected by this bacillus and to die . . . All in all, however, we can say that we have carried out this most difficult of tasks in a spirit of love for our people. And we have suffered no harm to our inner being, our soul, our character . . .[117]

This extract from Himmler's speech possibly adds limited support to Wolff's assertion that the SS leadership were hardly publicly advertising their extermination programmes, and regarded the frank discussion of this topic as generally 'off-limits', even within internal SS documentation and discussion. On the other hand, it also indicates that Wolff's claim to have been expelled permanently from the inner core of Himmler's decision-making loop responsible for genocide was little more than an exaggeration made for tactical purposes. A hostile interpretation would suggest that this claim represented little more than an excuse based on the dubious suggestion that he lacked both knowledge of, and personal involvement in, any policy-making or application aspects of SS policies relating to systematic atrocities.

Wolff's defensive and clearly self-serving claim that 'probably only 70' SS officials were directly involved in the extermination of European Jewry is challenged not only by the admissions contained in Himmler's Posen speech already cited but also by one of its own self-contradictory implications. Ironically, Wolff's contention can only be judged credible if it was supported by evidence that Wolff was privy to the relevant discussions between Hitler and Himmler regarding the extermination of European Jewry. However, Wolff repeatedly denied this. Indeed, if Himmler had *not* been acting on Hitler's direct, if purely verbal, orders, then this would suggest that the potential legal and organisational liability of the SS leadership for mass murder was, if anything, greater. This was because Himmler,

117 Himmler, 4 October 1943, *op cit*.

Kaltenbrunner and, to a lesser extent, Wolff had clearly been acting beyond their authority.

Wolff may have recognised this contradiction in his defensive position. If so, then it would certainly explain why he insisted that his supposedly more complete record of this exchange with Himmler, which he deposited in Institut für Zeitgeschichte in Munich (IfZ), could not be made public during his life-time.[118] During his life, historians could only cite this document as 'Wolff uncitable'! Lang suggests that Wolff's remarkably full recollection of this conversation with Himmler, which contrasts markedly with his supposedly poor recollection of more incriminating details, stems from the fact that it 'serves him as an alibi'. Hence, Lang asks rhetorically, is Wolff really suggesting that the origins of the Jewish genocide lay in a mere misunderstanding between Hitler and Himmler?[119]

Lang also rightly raises the question of whether the Nuremberg prosecutors, who had closely studied the actions and orientation of leading SS officials (including those lauded in Himmler's Posen speech), could possibly accept Wolff's claims that he had been shielded from knowledge of SS atrocities:

> But such concern for sensitive souls was not the common custom of the men's society of the SS; in fact, the men of the higher ranks were proud of the fact that they were so manly as to take all the horrible atrocities without being touched in any notable way. Even if the group leader Karl Wolff – 'among all the SS-leaders the closest to the Reichsführer,' (as a colleague named Berger in late 1941 wrote to Himmler) – indeed had been excluded

118 With respect to the credibility of Wolff's story, the court's judgment in the David Irving libel case (in which the full account was subjected to strong criticism from expert witnesses), noted: 'Irving accepted that SS-General Wolff, one of whose roles was to act as a conduit between Himmler and Hitler, would have told Hitler about the transports of Jews to the death camps. But he relied on the post-war recollection of Wolff (dismissed by Longerich as self-serving) that he was certain that Hitler did not know what was going on. Irving produced an extract made in manuscript from a document contained in the Munich archive in which Wolff is recorded as having said in 1952 that only 70-odd people ranging from Himmler to Hess (whose association went back to the 1920s) were involved in the extermination of the Jews. When the complete document was obtained, it became apparent that Wolff had said that "probably" (*wohl*) only those 70 had been involved. Wolff is also recorded as having said that Bormann and Himmler were the real culprits; they had taken the view that the Jewish problem had to be dealt with without Hitler "getting his fingers dirty". Himmler is said by Wolff to have taken the whole burden on his own shoulders for the sake of the German people and their Fuehrer. Irving relied heavily on this document, emanating from someone close to both Himmler and Hitler, as convincing evidence that Hitler was not implicated in or even aware of the killing in the death camps.' *David Irving v Penguin Books and Deborah Lipstadt*, QBD, 1996 -I- 1113, 11 April 2000, Court 36, Royal Courts of Justice, judgment given by Mr Justice Gray, para. 6.137. I am grateful to Davenports solicitors for providing me with a full transcript of this case.

119 Von Lang, *op cit*, 311.

> from the circles of those who knew about the crimes, the duration and the permanent contact with those who knew should have made him suspicious, especially as the 'General-what's-the-news' [Wolff's nickname amongst disrespectful subordinates] was a very attentive observer.[120]

Wolff's claims not to have been directly implicated in the execution of policies regarding the extermination of European Jews is contradicted by other hard documentary evidence that he positively lobbied for extra railway transportation to Treblinka concentration/death camp, notwithstanding competing demands from the German Army.[121] One document, cited during the Nuremberg war crimes trials (although often falsely described as only coming to light in the early 1960s), includes Wolff's highly incriminating reply to a secret letter dated 28 July 1942 from Dr Albert Ganzenmüller, Staatssekretär im Reichsverkehrsministerium and Reichsbahn-Generaldirektor.[122] Himmler had verbally ordered Wolff to see to it that 'Sonderzüge' (special trains), which had been used in the rapid transportation of Polish Jews to various concentration camps, including Sobibor, Belzec and – from June 1942 – Treblinka, were rapidly re-established. On 16 July 1942 Wolff telephoned Ganzenmüller from Hitler's HQ (where Wolff had additional responsibilities as Himmler's Principal Liaison Officer), seeking help in finding a solution to this suspension of transportation.[123] As already noted, the Nazis often referred to this transportation euphemistically in coded terms as an 'evacuation' or 'population movement'.[124] At this time, the transportation of Jews had been given priority second only to the needs of the German Army. Yet in mid-summer 1942, the Nazi authorities suspended 'evacuation' of the Polish ghettos because of the transportation needs of the Wehrmacht who were preparing for an attack against Krakow.

In response to Wolff's intervention, Ganzenmüller then investigated the reasons behind the various delays, and discovered that the problems had largely been resolved locally by diverting trains to Treblinka, which had originally been scheduled to take several hundred thousand Jews to the Sobibor death camp.[125] On 28 July 1942, Ganzenmüller, who was later unsuccessfully

120 *Ibid*, 175.

121 See Simpson, 1995 *op cit*, 202.

122 Ganzenmüller was the Staatssekretär im Reichsverkehrsministerium in charge of arranging the transport of Jews to Polish death camps. His agency was paid by the SS for each transportation completed on the basis of contracts that established third class group fares for 'Umsiedlungssonderzüge' (special trains for resettlement) at 4.0 Reichspfennig per kilometre. Children under 10 years old travelled at half fare, with no charge for children under 4 years. At the collection points, Reichsbahn officials counted the number of Jews loaded into each boxcar, and a bill was forwarded to the RSHA (Reichssicherheits-Hauptamt) Department based in Berlin.

123 Breitman, 1992 *op cit*, 238–39.

124 Sereny, *op cit.*, 351.

125 Hilberg, *op cit*, 512.

prosecuted by German authorities as a war criminal,[126] wrote to Wolff stating:

> With reference to our telephone conversation of 16 July, I wish to pass on to you the following report from my General Directorate of the Eastern Railways at Krakow for your information: 'Since 22 July one train per day with 5,000 Jews goes from Warsaw via Malkinia to Treblinka, as well as two trains per week with 5,000 Jews each, from Przemysl to Belzec. Bedob is in constant touch with the SD at Krakow. The latter agrees that transports from Warsaw to Sobibor, near Lublin, should be interrupted only as long as building on this route makes these transports impossible.'[127]

Wolff's reply from Hitler's headquarters, dated 13 August 1942, included the following incriminating statement, again using one of the standard euphemisms for extermination:

> I sincerely thank you for your letter of July 28, 1942, also in the name of the Reichsführer-SS. I was especially pleased to receive the information that, for the last 14 days, a train has been leaving daily for Treblinka with 5,000 members of the chosen people, and that in this way we are in a position to carry out this population movement at an accelerated tempo. I myself have made contact with the offices involved, so that smooth accomplishment of the entire measure appears to be guaranteed. I thank you again for your efforts in this matter and, at the same time, I would be grateful if you would give to these things your continued personal attention.[128]

This incriminating exchange would never have entered into the Nuremberg

126 In 1973 Ganzenmüller, then aged 68, was prosecuted with arranging transportation for well over one million Jews to the death camps in Treblinka, Belzec, Sobibor, Auschwitz and Lublin. The destruction of incriminating RVM documents at the end of the war meant that the prosecutor's case depended largely on the testimony of 119 eyewitnesses, among them two of Ganzenmüller's former secretaries. This meant that the letters exchanged with Wolff represented one of the few hard documentary pieces of evidence. Three weeks into his trial, Ganzenmüller suffered a massive heart attack resulting in the postponement for six months of his trial, which was further delayed over the next four years due to Ganzenmüller's deteriorating health. This resulted in his case being officially closed on 2 March 1977 and he died shortly afterwards in Stuttgart.

127 Nuremberg document NO-2207. For additional details, see Pohl Case, TWC 279; G. Reitlinger, *The Final Solution* (London: Valentine, Mitchel & Co, 1953), 252–53.

128 Nuremberg IMT document NO-2207(2). For the full document, see Bundesarchiv, Berlin, 29 July 1941 (Telefonnotizen, NS 19/1439). This exchange of letter is discussed more fully in: H. Arendt, *Eichmann in Jerusalem: A Report on the Banality of Evil*, 2nd edn (Harmondsworth: Penguin Books, 1994), 15; K. Feig, *Hitler's Death Camps: The Sanity of Madness* (New York: 1981), 36; Hilberg, *op cit*, 512.

evidence had it not been for Ganzenmüller's bureaucratic thoroughness in confirming, in precise written form, the details of this telephone conversation. When transportations from Warsaw and its surrounding district ended in early October 1943, Fischer, the district governor, reported that a total of 400,000 Jews had been deported.[129]

The Nuremberg prosecutors were fully aware of the fate of the Jews transported to Treblinka at this period. Rudolph Höss had described this graphically:

> *Q* What did you see there [in Treblinka]?
> *A* At that time the action in connection with the Warsaw Ghetto was in progress, and I watched the procedure.
> *Q* How was it done there?
> *A* They had chambers for about 200 people. Into these chambers the fumes from an exhaust machine came in. These motors had been taken from captured enemy equipment such as tanks, trucks and had been installed next to the gas chambers. They were run by gas, and those victims were supposed to be suffocated by the fumes.
> *Q* How many chambers were there, and how many people were killed?
> *A* I do not know the exact figure, but there may have been about ten chambers. It was built next to a ramp and the train drove right up to it. The people were unloaded right into the chambers, and this procedure was necessary because the motors did not always work right.
> *Q* Weren't the people first registered or interrogated?
> *A* No.
> *Q* They were put directly into the chambers from the trains?
> *A* Yes.
> *Q* And what happened to their clothing?
> *A* They had to undress before they were put into the chambers. . . .
> *Q* Did the train loads consist of women, men and children all together?
> *A* All together.
> *Q* We are now talking about the train in Treblinka?
> *A* Yes, the one in Treblinka.
> *Q* Were there babies, real small children and very old people also?
> *A* All kinds, if they were evacuated from Warsaw . . .[130]

It is important, however, to resist the temptation, armed with the benefit of hindsight, to over-interpret this exchange of letters as if it proved that Wolff was *centrally* involved in such transportation to death camps, as if he was a

129 See C. R. Browning, 'Evidence for the Implementation of the Final Solution', Part 4, 2000: published online at http://www.ess.uwe.ac.uk/genocide/browning4.htm.

130 Höss interrogation report, 1 April 1946, 27–29 also at: www.holocaust-history.org/operation-reinhard/final-destination-treblinka.

'chief sponsor' of the Treblinka camp, and to imply that the quoted exchange was somehow typical of scores of other such interventions.[131] This would amount to an exaggeration for which there is little documentary or other evidence. On the contrary, surviving documentation indicates that, whenever such transportation problems arose later requiring the interventions of the SS leadership, it was Himmler, rather than Wolff, who negotiated directly with Ganzenmüller.[132] Thus, Himmler certainly had not delegated the role of intervening to remedy *ad hoc* transportation difficulties to Wolff generally. Furthermore, Wolff's *ad hoc* interventions on behalf of specific Jews had infuriated Adolf Eichmann who – reportedly – considered such interventions, from an official without direct 'line management' responsibilities for such affairs, and the underlying attitude they displayed, a clear impediment to his work.[133] Several hundred Jews were interned at Bozen under Wolff's direct command. However, this was not a death camp, and Wolff sought to exploit

131 Eichmann's lawyers attempted to argue, in appeal, that: 'The exchange of letters between State Secretary Ganzenmüller and Wolff, the head of Himmler's personal staff, shows clearly that the transports to the Generalgouvernement as mentioned could definitely be carried out without involving the Accused's Section': http://www.nizkor.org/hweb/people/e/eichmann-adolf/transcripts/Appeal/Appeal-Pleading-02-05.html. The court's judgment cited this correspondence but gave it less significance that Eichmann's lawyer sought to have placed upon it as evidence of the direct involvement of Himmler and Wolff in the extermination of Jews in a manner that bypassed Eichmann's department: http://www.nizkor.org/hweb/people/e/eichmann-adolf/transcripts/Judgment/Judgment-043.html.

132 When a second interruption occurred in December 1942, Himmler personally intervened by writing directly to Ganzenmüller claiming that transportation difficulties stemmed from the actions of Jewish partisans, whereas poor weather, a shortage of trains and supplying the German army at Stalingrad were the real reasons. Nevertheless, on 20 January 1943, Ganzenmüller fully restored the transports to the death camps at full pace. Hilberg, *op cit*, 194.

133 'Sassen Interview', during which he characterised Himmler's former Chief of Staff as one of the 'Salon officers' who wished to keep their hands in white gloves and did not want to hear anything about the 'solution' of the Jewish problem. This episode was addressed in the Eichmann judgment as follows: 'In the first extract (p. 1 of T/1393/a) the Accused relates an incident which occurred between himself and Wolff, Himmler's adjutant, who held the rank of general (Obergruppenführer). Wolff requested that a certain person not be deported, and the Accused refused to comply. Wolff became angry and remarked that the Accused was only an Obersturmbannführer, whereas he himself was an Obergruppenführer. To this the Accused replied: "Yes, Obergruppenführer, I know that, but may I be permitted to reply that you are now speaking to the State Secret Police and to the Referent of the Secret Police Office, Obersturmbannführer Eichmann.' " (See *Jerusalem Post*, 21 June 1961, for Eichmann's disparaging comments on Wolff's role and attitude made during his with this request.) Apparently Wolff considered himself to be in a position to issue orders to Eichmann owing to his superior rank, whereas Eichmann considered Müller his superior, and complained to this official regarding Wolff's interference: http://www.nizkor.org/hweb/people/e/eichmann-adolf/transcripts/Judgment/Judgment-056.html; http://www.nizkor.org/hweb/people/e/eichmann-adolf/transcripts/Appeal/Appeal-Pleading-02-06.html. Ironically, the court in his 1963–64 trials accepted that Eichmann was right because, with respect to the

this group as part of his bargaining with the OSS for an 'unofficial' military capitulation.[134]

In short, and whilst recognising that his official position did not specifically include responsibility for extermination programmes within concentration camps, both Wolff's senior role as Himmler's Chief of Staff and personal confidant, and a series of incriminating documents, contradict his assertion that he remained entirely unaware of, and insulated from, both their existence and genocidal function. Our review of the evidence available to the Nuremberg prosecutors supports Lang's conclusion:

> What then could Wolff have known, what must he have known about the mass murder? He must have realized that, in the first six months of 1942, Hitler threatened Jews more than ever with violence and death – in no less than six public speeches and announcements and at least eight times during the so-called dinner-talks in the Führerhauptquartier. In retrospect, this attitude may be explained by the fact that at the time the mass extermination in the death camps had just begun. Wolff must have noticed, because he was an acute observer, and that was actually his task.[135]

Although Wolff was clearly not a major figure in the planning and execution of genocide, given their familiarity with the correspondence discussed above, the prosecutors must have known that he was, on specific occasions at least, included within the loop that both made and implemented genocidal policies.[136] The documents held by the Nuremberg prosecutors indicates that Wolff was implicated in knowing involvement in war criminality to the point where his post-war denials stretch credibility virtually to breaking point.

The complicities of Guido Zimmer

Having previously examined evidence of Wolff's complicity in war crimes, the next task is to complete the picture of the war criminality of the Wolff group

persecution of and measures of extermination against Jews, Wolff had no institutional responsibilities for any specific task, and certainly lacked command responsibilities, that is, the right to issue orders on his own authority to the offices, organisations, and leaders whose tasks included the elimination of Jews. Wolff case, *op cit*, 53. a-113/a-114, S. 497–98.

134 Untitled Sunrise folder compiled by T. S. Ryan, 'Narrative on Sunrise', 14: NA, RG 226, Entry 110, Box 711, Folder 11a; Cable 9 March, 1945, Dulles to Glavin, Donovan and Forgan: NA, RG 226, Entry 110, Box 711; Smith and Agarossi, *op cit*, 82; A. Dulles, *The Secret Surrender* (New York: Harper and Row, 1966), 99.

135 Lang, *op cit* 220.

136 One example is the recall of the Nazis' Jewish expert from Romania, whose efforts were being frustrated to the point where the only effect of retaining this official would be that: 'We are going to be accused of something.' Himmler to Müller (copy to Wolff), 20 January 1943, Himmler Files, Folder 8, LOC MSS division, cited in Hilberg, *op cit*, 847.

more generally by briefly reviewing similar evidence with respect to Wolff's key collaborators within Operation Sunrise: SS-Hauptsturmführer Guido Zimmer and SS-Standartenführer Eugen Dollmann.

It must be recalled that the SS was one of the institutions of the Nazi state that was charged and convicted at the Nuremberg war crimes trials with being a 'criminal organisation', the voluntary membership of which was itself deemed to constitute a war crime for which fines and imprisonment could be ordered by a de-Nazification tribunal. Indeed, one of the key tasks of the large group of OSS officials, who were seconded to the Nuremberg prosecutors, was to build up the case against these criminal organisations.[137] For present purposes, however, such 'organisational criminality' is of less interest than Dollmann and Zimmer's specific activities as middle-ranking SS officials based in Italy. Zimmer worked under the soon-to-be notorious SS-Obersturmbannführer Walter Rauff. Dollmann's role was largely as Himmler's personal representative in Rome, and official intermediary and translator whenever Hitler or Himmler met Mussolini in either Italy or Germany. The details of their roles and actions will now be discussed individually.

From 1940 to 1945, Zimmer[138] worked for the political intelligence division (SD) of Himmler's SS. Following his relocation to Italy in early 1944,[139] Zimmer worked within the Abt. 6, a political intelligence department of the SS's Milan office immediately under Rauff, who had headed this office since September 1943.[140] Zimmer had previously been based in both Genoa,[141] and in Rome[142] – where he learned and refined his trade by working as a case officer under SS-Obersturmbannführer Kappler. (Kappler was later prosecuted for being directly involved in the Ardeatine Caves massacre of 335 Italian civilians in Rome (including 75 Jews) on 24 March 1944, none of whom were involved in the earlier ambush of German forces.) This atrocity was ordered as a reprisal for a successful partisan attack that killed 33 South Tyrolean police (Polizeirregiment Bozen), soldiers and Italian bystanders.[143]

137 See Hulme and Salter, 'The Nazis' Persecution of Religion as a War Crime: The OSS's Response within the Nuremberg Trials Process', (2002) 3 *Rutgers Journal of Law and Religion* www.lawandreligion.com.

138 Born 18 November 1911 and therefore in his early thirties during the Second World War.

139 The relevant intelligence reports in Zimmer's CIA Name File give different months, ranging from February to November 1944: NA, RG 263.

140 Abt VI was located within the German regional HQ in 39 Via Corvo Milan, headed by Captain Haug. See 'File traces on Zimmer', Zipper Desk (nd), #11 report from Miodrag Yevremovic (sanitised copy), 29 August 1945: NA, CIA Name Files, Guido Zimmer: *op cit.*

141 Interrogation report on Egon Schönpflug, XX 8386, 19 June 1945, *ibid.*

142 Zimmer used journalistic cover in Rome, certainly from July 1941 to his recall to Berlin in October 1941. See 'File traces on Zimmer', Zipper Desk (nd), #12 interrogation report of Rosa Cappelli [Zimmer's maid], sanitised copy 3 September 1945, *ibid.*

143 Kappler was later prosecuted and convicted because the SS killed not 330 hostages (in keeping with the state ratio of 1 to 10) but 335. The reprisal killing of these five extra

Whilst working on espionage affairs under diplomatic cover in Rome from 1940, Zimmer had blundered in his dealings with an Italian source, supplied by the American diplomatic attaché. This source had revealed details of a plot to kill Mussolini. Zimmer's direct transmission of this threat to diplomatic sources compromised both the source and diplomatic relations between Germany and Fascist Italy, who, as Allies, had agreed not to spy upon each other.[144] This 'embarrassing incident' resulted in Zimmer's superiors deciding to recall him to Berlin in 1942, where he was re-assigned to an Italian desk working under Dr Wilhelm Höttl.[145] (In a later section we will see how this incident was used by OSS/SSU officials as one of the grounds for opposing Zimmer's recruitment and protection.)

One intelligence official characterised Zimmer as follows: 'There is something hard in his manner that indicates a possible police background.'[146] It would, however, be grossly inaccurate to characterise Zimmer's actions and orientation as those of a stereotypically brutal SS officer engaged full-time in the organisation and execution of genocidal activities. It would be equally misleading entirely to accept the unduly positive and self-serving account of Zimmer provided by Dulles in his book on Operation Sunrise:

> Zimmer, despite his membership of the SS, was a devout Catholic . . . Zimmer was deeply troubled by the possibility that the SS might be ordered by the SS in Berlin to scorch the Italian earth. Zimmer, somewhat of an aesthete and an intellectual, was moved by a desire to save the art and religious treasures of Italy. Parilli was convinced of Zimmer's sincerity because Zimmer had on occasion protected Italians whom the Gestapo had orders to arrest . . . Zimmer seemed to be a misfit in the SS . . . He was good looking, clean-cut, not the way one pictures the typical SS officer.[147]

The reality was far more complex than either the stereotype of the brutal qualities SS officers in general, or Dulles' rhetorical attempt to portray Zimmer as possessing qualities diametrically opposed to those of an SS war criminal.

people took the matter beyond any recognised defence in military law. See G. Steinacher, *Südtirol im Dritten Reich. NS-Herrschaft im Norden Italiens 1943–1945* (Munich/Vienna, Studienverlag, 2003). Kappler stated directly in his trial that, contrary to the claims of the Italian authorities, Dollmann was not involved in any respects with this massacre.

144 Agent BBS to Saint Amzon, 'Zimmer Guido', November 1945 (partly illegible), Zimmer Name File, Vol.1, *ibid.*

145 'Guido Zimmer', Chief Foreign Division M to Chief of Station, Karlsruhe, 28 March 1951, ref: 7381: *ibid.*

146 The desk was within the SS's security office, RSHA Amt VI/B Loose document, (NWC-001223), *ibid*, Vol. 3.

147 Dulles, 1966 *op cit*, 72–76.

Some elements of his overall work involved actions that could be interpreted as, for example, anti-Semitic 'war crimes', but these comprised only a small fraction of his work. Furthermore, these were, in some measure, counter-balanced by positive interventions on behalf of individuals who would otherwise have become victims of Nazi war criminality. Information concerning Zimmer's wartime record included clear evidence that he was involved in committing war crimes both personally and indirectly through his supervision of SD subordinates. Evidence of this can be found in numerous US intelligence documents. This information only emerged during the months immediately after the end of the Second World War, following the interrogations of his SS colleagues and associates, during which time it appears that Zimmer, his agents and network sub-agents were being actively investigated by Allied counter-intelligence officials.[148]

Before we examine the details of the possibly unlawful elements of his work, it is first necessary to provide some wider background context. The interrogation of Rauff suggested that: 'Abt.VI was first set up in Milan in Feb 44, under Zimmer, with the task of building up a post-occupational network and procuring political information from abroad.'[149] Other interrogations noted that Zimmer had been storing away valuables 'to form a 5th Column'.[150] Indeed, one report claimed that Zimmer's principal function was: 'the preparation of a Fifth Column and a self-styled clandestine patriotic committee manoeuvred by the Germans in opposition to the C.L.N. [Italian Partisan resistance committee]'.[151] Zimmer undertook this role using the 'Team Textile Firm' as 'cover'. Apparently, his proposed post-occupational network of approximately five agents had, he discovered, become known to the Allies, and was dropped without realising his plan to establish a viable replacement.[152]

Whilst the bulk of Zimmer's political intelligence operations did not involve committing recognised war crimes, certain aspects of his work certainly overlapped with recognised offences within the scope of war crimes prosecutors. Some reports from US intelligence officials described Zimmer as one of a group of: 'notorious SS and SD officials' based in Italy, including Dollmann, Kappler, Engel and Hugel.[153] It soon became clear to Allied investigators that, before the war, Zimmer had been a member of both the SD[154] in Dusseldorf (1936–37) and the Gestapo-Hauptampt in Berlin (1937–39).[155] His work with

148 JHX 1509, 20 June 1945, *ibid.*

149 JHX 1000, 'Interrogation report on Walter Rauff', 8 June 1945, *ibid.*

150 JHX 1913, 6 August 1945, *ibid.*

151 XX-1482, 20 October 1944, Files Traces on Zimmer/Zipper Desk, (nd), *ibid.*

152 Files Traces on Zimmer/Interrogation Report of Walther Rauf, JRX-1000 CSDIC/SC/15AG/SD11, 29 May 1945, *ibid.*

153 JXX 4032, 10 September 1945, *ibid.*

154 The SD carried out part of the SS's role in internal surveillance and repression.

155 JZX-5519, 21 September 1945; cable LWX-010-926, 26 September 1945, SCI Weekly Operations Report: both Zimmer Name File, *op cit.*

the SS in Genoa had reportedly 'consisted of spying on and tracking down Jews'.[156] When he was transferred to become head of the SS Abt.VI in Milan in May 1944, he took charge of a pre-existing group of SS subordinates based, from September 1944 at least, in an office at Via Marengo. This group of Zimmer's new colleagues were 'connected with the persecution of Jews and the sequestration of their property'.[157]

Allied authorities later arrested three of these surviving subordinates: Koch, Timm and Saevecke.[158] This group of Zimmer's new colleagues was responsible for the arrest of many Jews and their families in Milan and its environs and for the sequestration of their property and that of the partisans. Their villa was filled with loot, which was brought from every part of the country: works of art, jewels and silverware (even that taken from synagogues). In collaboration with two other SS members, Zimmer had these items regularly sent to Germany as one part of his wider trafficking in looted goods. He made sufficient money through such trafficking to fund a highly luxurious life-style in Milan. Zimmer's various activities allowed him to extract considerable personal wealth from entering into 'private deals' with various Italians. These were individuals who were either trafficking in black market and looted goods, or members of wealthy families who had been interned in Germany for various reasons and who now sought to be repatriated. US intelligence officials based in Italy soon discovered that Zimmer was associated with 'trafficking in stolen goods'.[159] One intelligence report states that: 'this partnership came to an end in January 1945, probably as a result of Zimmer's first efforts at saving his skin by contacting Partisans and even American elements'.[160]

Zimmer appears to have largely delegated oversight of the day-to-day persecution of Jews in Milan to SS Saevecke.[161] Instead, he preferred to concentrate upon those internal political aspects of what could be loosely described as 'intelligence work'.[162] Nevertheless, as their commanding officer, it is arguable that Zimmer could have been held legally responsible for the actions of SD subordinates in Milan. Zimmer could, it seems, personally arrange for

156 JZX-4039, BBS to DHA [partly illegible], 11 September 1945; J. Angelton, CO SCI/Z Units Italy, 'The Case of Guido Zimmer, SS Feldpost No. 02059,' JFX-4039, (nd), para. 5.

157 *Ibid*, para. 1.

158 File traces on Zimmer, Zipper Desk, (nd), # 13 extract from 'Guido Zimmer', JZX-4039, 11 September 1945, BBS to DHZ: Zimmer Name File, *op cit.*

159 J. Angelton, CO SCI/Z Units Italy, 'The Case of Guido Zimmer, SS Feldpost No. 02059,' JFX-4039, (nd); also summarised in 'File traces on Zimmer,' Zipper Desk, (nd), # 13, *ibid.*

160 *Ibid.*

161 For statements on such persecution, see 'The Zimmer Notebooks,' BBS to JJS, JRX-3746, 28 June 1946, ref no. 57, note 4: 130, note 2; 137 note 2, *ibid.* On Saevecke role, see CSDIC/SMF/SD30, Second detailed interrogation report on SS Hptatbf Saevecke, Theodor.

162 This reported that Zimmer's political intelligence and espionage role meant that his work: 'had little connection with the other [SS] sections in Milan'. File traces on Zimmer, Zipper Desk (nd), # 3 (this extract from May 1945), sanitised copy, *ibid.*

an individual's arrest and transfer to a concentration camp, although this was not central to how he operated.[163] It is equally clear that he also had the power to intervene *to shield* individuals from arrest, torture and detention by the Gestapo, particularly where this would interfere with one of his Abt.6 operations. This was a power he exercised sparingly only when strictly needed, and not, it seems, for humanitarian reasons. Relevant intelligence files contain very few, and then only incidental, references to Zimmer having any dealings with the concentration camp system.[164] For example, when replying to a request from Mussolini to confirm whether a new SS concentration camp was to be built in Pavia, Italy, Zimmer had to consult Saevecke before he was able to answer this in the negative.[165]

Only occasionally was Zimmer involved in taking actions with respect to Italian Jews in Milan, and then only when this was deemed necessary as part of some wider political intelligence mission.[166] For example, he complained in his notebooks that one informant, who had protected a local Italian Jew from being rounded up, had later been arrested by the Gestapo. This arrest, he argued, was counter-productive. It reduced political intelligence opportunities. In addition, arresting this individual, as distinct from keeping him under close surveillance, only lessened the possibility of the escaped Jew being detained whenever he resumed contact with his rescuer.[167] On the other hand, Zimmer intervened to protect one Jew who was being threatened with loss of her Italian citizenship. This intervention was not, however, based on humanitarian considerations. Rather, she was about to marry someone with whom Zimmer wanted to remain on positive terms because he possessed vital technical expertise and knowledge.[168] A similarly instrumental orientation is clear from Zimmer's reaction to the detention within a Turin jail of Gabbai, a Jewish radio technician whose services remained relevant to his ongoing political espionage activities. In response, Zimmer ordered that: 'all technical publications and necessary equipment be placed at his disposal in his private cell so that he may continue his work in jail'.[169]

Zimmer's notebooks suggest that, possibly through his subordinates' anti-Semitic measures, he was at least acquainted with the numbers of Jews hiding in Turin and the methods through which they protected themselves, including

163 *Ibid*, 50, ref. 47/paras. 163–64; also 56, ref. 53/para. 191.

164 *Ibid*, 68/ref. 234. On one occasion, he intervened to have a group of Italian workers, arrested and deported for striking, who had been sent to Mauthausen death camp when he had intended them only to be sent to Germany for labour, *ibid* 97/ref. 110, paras 339–40.

165 Zimmer Notebook, *op cit*, 102/ref. 119, paras. 361–62.

166 *Ibid*, 58/ref. 57, paras. 201–02. Other occasional references to the persecution of Jews are located at ref. 130/note. 2, ref. 134/note 1 and ref. 137/note 2.

167 *Ibid*, 58/ref. 57, para. 202.

168 *Ibid*, 112/ref. 130; cf. refs. 57/note 4, ref. 134/note 1 and ref. 137/note 2.

169 *Ibid*, 115–16/ref. 134, paras. 413–15.

the obtaining of false Italian identity papers.[170] However, there is no evidence of Zimmer's direct involvement in countering this. There are few other references to Zimmer taking direct measures against Jews in his notebooks. Instead, these are dominated by various intelligence-gathering operations, including industrial espionage.[171]

Zimmer, for example, initiated various missions attempting to penetrate the communications and contacts of the Spanish consulate (Operation Guitar),[172] and bribe sympathetic members of the Catholic Church, such as Cardinal Schuster.[173] Apparently, he succeeded in obtaining reports from the Spanish Consul General in Milan from 'Chantal'.[174] (It is possible that Zimmer was preparing an escape route for himself to Spain, an option that, as reports in his name file make clear, was used by other former members of the SS to evade capture.)[175] Another aspect of work involved monitoring a range of Italian individuals who were defeatist,[176] or whose loyalty was deemed questionable, possibly because they had maintained contacts with Allied officials in Switzerland and elsewhere,[177] and receiving and acting upon the results of 'petty informing'.[178]

It was characteristic of his distinctly political intelligence role that, whilst his immediate subordinates persecuted and extorted Jews, Zimmer himself was willing to hire at least one Jewish agent, a well-known Hungarian sportsman, Andreas Zolygany.[179] Zolygany's mission was to penetrate a local communist 'cell' with 26 members:

> amongst whom is a big shot who fought in Spain and is a member of the Red Faculty . . . the purpose is . . . to have an alibi for playing a role in the communist party tomorrow . . . He wants to prepare them for future propaganda work and sabotage . . . for this work I urge you to send soon the necessary dynamite and fuses . . . During September '44 Zolygany began transporting sabotage materials for this 'communist' movement.[180]

Zolygany's communist group, of which he was chief and: 'with Zimmer [acting] as the liaison between it and Dr Hegeus, would be only a portion of the large scale "Cypresse" network of Hegeus'.[181] Zimmer's notebooks also refer to one other Jewish agent of the SS, Prager from Vienna, who was employed by

170 *Ibid*, 117/ref. 137, para. 418.
171 *Ibid*, 100/ref. 351–52, also refs. 116–18, 126–30.
172 *Ibid*, 42/ref. 38, 84/ref. 90, para. 289, note.1
173 *Ibid*, 92/ref 101, para. 319. Schuster was later to claim excessive credit for the success of Operation Sunrise, and to pressurise Dollmann formally to acknowledge this.
174 JZX-1509, 20 June 1945, File traces on Zimmer/Zipper Desk (nd), *ibid.*
175 Berne 422, 31 October 1946, *ibid.*
176 Zimmer Notebooks, *op cit*, p. 119/ref. 141, para. 424.
177 *Ibid*, 101/ref. 118, para. 356.
178 *Ibid*, para. 142, also note 1/130.
179 *Ibid*, 162–63/ref. 16, note 11.
180 *Ibid*, paras. 479–82.
181 *Ibid*, 133, note 2.

the Gestapo.[182] On a broader front, he expressed concern that, 'by destroying [anti-communist, albeit socialist] elements' within the Partisan movement, 'we are consequently indirectly helping to achieve the aims of Moscow'.[183]

Another side of Zimmer's political intelligence role was to deploy agents and intermediaries to spread division amongst the Allies by, for example, suggesting to those in contact with the British that it was questionable 'why the British are still fighting in Germany when they should be preparing for their fight against the communists who are the only true rivals of Germany'.[184] This theme, that the Allies were allowing themselves to be driven up 'a blind alley' at the expense of both Germany and their own interests, but in favour of those of the Soviets, occurs on a number of occasions in Zimmer's notebooks.[185] It also informed Zimmer's attempts to find: 'thoughtful persons [such as Parilli] who have a sufficient number of personal contacts with leading personalities in the opposite camp at their disposal, in order to find out how the opposite camp judges the political world situation and possibly in order to engage in politics'.[186] It is likely that his geo-political orientation underpinned aspects of Operation Sunrise/Wool, in ways that will be explored more fully in later sections. Indeed, initially Zimmer hoped to exploit Parilli's personal contacts with a series of influential Englishmen, including Lord Jones (Sheffield), Jack Robinson (MP) and Gimmes (a personal friend of Winston Churchill).[187] The later contact with Dulles may have represented a 'second best' option for Zimmer.

At the same time, Zimmer made contact with non-communist and anti-communist factions within the Italian resistance. His idea was to encourage internal divisions at the expense of the communist elements.[188]

It was, perhaps, because Zimmer could offer access to agents who had already penetrated Italian communist cells which later made his services particularly attractive to some but not all American intelligence officials, who were concerned to combat the spread of communism during the immediate post-war years.

Zimmer's notebooks also revealed other indications of an underlying anti-Soviet agenda behind SS attempts to deploy Parilli (pretending to be a neutral intermediary) to contact influential Allied officials in Switzerland and elsewhere. Parilli was instructed to:

> further intimate that Zimmer, without the knowledge of his office, belongs to some circles of influential people who are pursuing a definite political course that is of importance to Englishmen, providing that the decision

182 *Ibid*, 93/321, para. 323.
183 *Ibid*, 74/ref. 76, para. 257.
184 *Ibid*, 54/ref. 49, para. 175.
185 *Ibid*, 78/ref. 80, para. 271.
186 *Ibid*, 79/ref. 82, para. 274.
187 *Ibid*, 79/ref. 82, paras. 276–77.
188 *Ibid*, paras. 141–43.

> has not already been settled to destroy Germany at any cost and leave the field open for Russia.[189]

In addition, and perhaps as a prelude to the Sunrise deal, Zimmer had little scruples regarding 'playing on both sides of the street' by courting Italian partisans involved in the anti-fascist resistance.[190] For example, at the end of 1943, he had intervened to save a partisan leader, Colonel Minetti, from the Gruppo D'Annunzio, from death at the hands of the Gestapo.[191] He was to later emphasise this intervention (and others in favour of Minetti's wife, an Italian Jew, Ursula Altmann, his action against the notorious Koch group of Italian fascists and, of course, his participation in Operation Sunrise) in order to curry favour with US intelligence officials.[192] Minetti then became a trusted contact through which he could initiate 'illegal relations with the British and the Americans'.[193]

During the last year of the war, Zimmer was in contact with various other individuals who were proposing peace feelers to the Allies, long before the Sunrise/Wool initiative took shape.[194] Indeed, entries in Zimmer's notebook suggest that he was seeking to send agents to Switzerland to 'penetrate Allied intelligence circles there'.[195] It was Dulles who insisted that such contacts be made only with the Americans to the exclusion of the rival British intelligence services in Switzerland.[196]

On 14 April 1945, Zimmer left Italy in an expensive sports car and then took temporary refuge in neutral Switzerland, a border crossing that was possibly assisted by his contacts with Swiss intelligence who had participated in the Sunrise negotiations.[197] Zimmer may have left his detailed notebooks (albeit with some pages removed)[198] behind for discovery by Allied counter-intelligence officials almost as an advert, or CV, to demonstrate his potential post-war utility as the gatekeeper to various anti-communist networks.[199] Certainly, those US intelligence officials reviewing and translating these

189 'Baron Parilli's Swiss Journey', Zimmer Notebooks, *op cit*, para. 113.

190 LWI-010-926, 'SCI weekly Operations Report,' 'Operations under consideration', 26 September 1945.

191 ZZX 5519, 21 September 1945; J. Angelton, CO SCI/Z Units Italy, 'The Case of Guido Zimmer, SS Feldpost No. 02059,' JFX-4039, (nd), *ibid.*

192 'Translation of excepts from statement by Guido Zimmer', (nd) para. 4, but transmitted 26 August 1946, *ibid.*

193 *Ibid.*

194 JHX 475, 9 June 1945, *ibid.*

195 Notebooks, *op cit*, note 2, ref. 42/p. 47.

196 *Ibid*, 154(3).

197 J. Angleton, CO SCI/Z Units Italy, 'The Case of Guido Zimmer, SS Feldpost No. 02059,' JFX-4039, (nd), *ibid.*

198 Zimmer Notebooks, *op cit*, p. 51/ref. 49.

199 This value was recognised by those reviewing the notebooks whose daily accounts of activities contradicted the denials of suspected SD agents such as the lawyer Vinatzer: 'Zimmer's above jotting would seem to settle the matter of V's complicity', Zimmer Notebooks, *op cit*, note 2, p. 39/ref. 33.

notebooks noted that they: 'are of great operational importance here in due course'.[200] Zimmer left the task of destroying other (and perhaps more incriminating) documentation at his SS office to one of his subordinates, who duly obliged between 23 and 24 April. This took place barely a week before inrushing Allied forces, including war crimes investigators, would have been in a position to secure and exploit such material.[201] At this time, OSS officials were actively monitoring his whereabouts, noting, for example, that he was still located in this country on 26 April 1945.[202] They also interviewed his maid regarding the nature of his work and personal contacts, including various embassy officials, industrialists and SS-Obersturmbannführer Kappler.[203]

In short, although hardly a major criminal or someone whose everyday work was intrinsically linked to war criminality, Zimmer's actions and orientation, particularly regarding extortion and looting, were certainly those of 'an active Nazi' within the ambit of relevant Allied de-Nazification measures and possibly local Italian war crimes investigations. At the end of the war, this made him vulnerable to prosecution, conviction and imprisonment, assuming of course he was not shielded by elements within the post-war Allied authorities.

The complicities of Eugen Dollmann

In one sense, SS-Standartenführer Eugen Dollmann's record as a potential war crimes suspect and de-Nazification trial defendant is more complex than that of Zimmer. The major accusations of complicity in war criminality he faced stemmed not from Anglo-American authorities but from their Italian counterparts, and these related to the Fosse Ardeatine reprisal killings already discussed. It is possible that the desire amongst the Italian legal and political authorities to have Dollmann stand trial as a war crimes suspect stemmed less from their knowledge of his actual conduct and role than from the fact that he had become almost a symbol of Nazi occupation of Italy. Dollmann's role as a high-profile symbol of Nazism within Rome was driven partly by his appearance at numerous fashionable events within Rome's high society. These included those of the secular and Catholic aristocracy, courtiers, Fascist Party leaders and diplomatic circles, many of which were extensively photographed by the media.[204] He was courted by these circles as someone of supposedly mysterious influence and secrets, and who could, perhaps, exercise influence to provide them with various material favours.[205]

200 Para. 4, loose untitled document, Zimmer Name File, Vol. 1, *op cit*. 201 *Ibid*.
202 Cable XZ 9249, 'Dept VI order of battle' 16 September 1945 and interrogation report of Klaus Hügel, 5 June 1945, noting he was living in Erlangen, Zimmer Name File, Vol. 1, *op cit*.
203 Interrogation Report of Cappelli, 28 August 1945, JRX-601 [partly illegible], *ibid*.
204 *Ibid*, 139. 205 *Ibid*, 143.

Given that Dollmann was later to be sought by the post-war Italian authorities as both a witness and potential defendant in the trial of those SS officials responsible for, or associated in any way with, the massacre of Italian civilians, it is worthwhile to describe his own account. Dollmann claims that these reprisal killings were 'not only excessive but also politically inept'. Responsibility rested not with himself or even Kesselring but: 'a direct order from Hitler himself'.[206] By contrast, the Italian leftist press, aware of his high profile public contacts, repeatedly alleged that Dollmann was a fugitive war criminal implicated in the Ardeatine massacre and unjustifiably protected by the Americans. This reputation was to dog him throughout his post-war life.[207] Whilst detained immediately after the war at the Cine Città camp, located outside Rome, Dollmann's interrogator, Major Bridge, who was charged with investigating his possible complicity the Ardeatine Caves massacre, told him that British intelligence had been closely studying his wartime actions and orientation. They had build up a detailed picture which even included his gastronomic preferences at diplomatic dinners. Bridge wanted to hear his account of the role, if any, that Dollmann had played in:

> [the] execution of the hostages in the Ardeatine Caves. Of course we know that you had nothing directly to do with that affair, but you must understand that there are certain inquiries we have to make. 'Yes' I said. 'I understand that of course but I really had nothing to with it directly or indirectly.'[208]

Major Bridge also told Dollmann that Kappler's trial testimony had just exonerated him from any, even indirect, personal involvement in the Ardeatine Caves atrocity.

Furthermore, the British authorities responsible for mounting war crimes trials now accepted his innocence, and were willing to arrange his release, providing that the Allied War Crimes Commission knew of no other possible charges against him:

> By the way, you can set your mind at rest about the shooting of those hostages. Kappler himself has declared that you had nothing whatsoever to do with it. 'I said that in the beginning' I replied . . . 'We knew it already', he said, 'but we have our instructions to carry out just the same as you had.' . . . 'All right' he said. 'All that remains is for you to be cleared by the Allied Commission.'[209]

206 *Ibid*, 295.

207 Wolfe, 'Coddling a Nazi Turncoat' in Breitman *et al*, 2004, *op cit*, 328, noting that Italian journalists had misdescribed him as the 'tyrant of the fascist ministry of the interior'.

208 *Ibid*, 31.

209 *Ibid*, 33.

Dollmann (and Wolff) appeared before the Allied Commission of Inquiry into war criminality in Italy which acquitted him 'of all charges in connections with executions, atrocities and so on'.[210] However, he remained concerned that the 'general atmosphere did not encourage me in the belief that all was now forgiven and forgotten'.[211] In short, although investigated by British authorities for any possible involvement in the atrocity for which he had been accused by the Italian media and others, Dollmann was cleared. This allows the present study to examine the more interesting questions of his borderline complicities relative to liabilities under Allied Control Council Law No. 10.

It is arguable that Dollmann's close liaison with the leadership of both the Italian Fascist and Nazi Party rendered him vulnerable to punishment less as a major war criminal responsible, under the Nuremberg Charter, for crimes against the peace, traditional violations of the laws of war (war crimes in the narrow sense) or crimes against humanity, than as an 'active Nazi' under Allied de-Nazification laws. These offences still permitted substantial periods of imprisonment and even death. A possible defence was that his involvement was not voluntary, or that he was acting as an Allied double-agent, carrying out sabotage from within.

The remainder of this chapter will consider the arguments for and against his prosecution on this ground, and the viability of any such legal defences. The first issue is to consider the circumstances of Dollmann's decision to join first the Nazi Party and then the SS, with particular attention to the question of whether he was, in any sense, coerced in participation within these institutions.

Dollmann's decision to join the Nazi Party and the SS

Should the Allies have categorised and prosecuted Dollmann as an 'active Nazi', who voluntarily joined the Party and its elite SS knowing of their complicities in atrocities for which there was likely to be legal accountability? If this charge could have been made out, then Dollmann would have faced at least ten years' imprisonment, together with severe future restrictions in employment and public service.

Dollmann, who was born in 1900 to an English mother and German father, was raised in Bavaria before spending parts of his youth and doctoral and post-doctoral studies in Italy.[212] Reportedly, he joined both the Nazi Party and the SS: 'early in the Nazi regime, and by 1937 was a rising SS

210 *Ibid*, 43. 211 *Ibid*, 43.

212 Memorandum, Assistant Chief of Staff, G2 to CIA, Eugen Dollmann, 17 November 1951, #2, Dollmann Name File, *op cit*.

official and a protégé of . . . Himmler'.[213] Other intelligence reports note that Dollmann had been appointed 'Himmler's personal envoy' to Italy as early as 1933.[214] In fact, his frank, if selective and partial, memoirs record that he joined the party in February 1934, becoming the press leader of the Roman party chapter the following year. He successfully applied to join the SS in November 1937, becoming attached to Himmler's personal staff. The internally competitive and brutal internal politics within the SS, and Nazi organisations more generally, meant that even Himmler sought to bypass chains of command. Since SS-Obersturmbannführer Herbert Kappler was close to, and a favourite of, both the fearsome Heydrich and then Ernst Kaltenbrunner, Himmler wanted someone to be his own 'eyes and ears' in Rome outside the official hierarchy of the RSHA.[215] From 1937, Dollmann then achieved a steady series of almost yearly promotions reaching, in 1943, an SS rank broadly equivalent of Colonel.[216]

Certainly, Dollmann played a role the combined diplomatic emissary with translator. He was, for example, introduced to Ricci, Mussolini's Minister for Youth. Ricci in turn sought to exploit Dollmann's knowledge of Germany with respect to his preparation for a forthcoming visit from Nazi Youth Leader, and future Nuremberg defendant, Baldur von Schirach. Dollmann played a similar quasi-diplomatic and advisory function when Karl Wolff and other senior Nazi leaders were seeking to prepare for visits from prominent Italians, such as Balbo (who, like Italian Foreign Minister Ciano, expected diplomatic trips to be accompanied by more erotic pursuits).[217]

Having met the expectations of these members of the Italian fascist leadership, Dollmann then obtained part-time employment as a translator for a German Nazi Youth organisation in Rome. This assignment 'absolved' Dollmann 'from further contact with the party in Rome', which had been taken over by a German he regarded as a petty sadist. Dollmann was then brought in to translate between Ricci and Schirach when the former visited Berlin in April 1937. He later translated on various exchanges between Italian and German youth groups, including during official receptions with von Neurath and Goebbels, two other future Nuremberg defendants, during a diplomatic event in which Himmler participated in May.[218] It was only by accident that Dollmann was summoned on 28 October 1937 to a meeting between Arturo and Himmler and other European police chiefs in a context where the Italian authorities had forgotten to deploy their own official translator.[219]

In early November of 1937, Dollmann made what was later to appear to many, including Italian legal authorities, as his fateful decision to join the SS.

213 *Ibid.* 214 'Dollmann, Standarienfuehrer Dr Eugen', *ibid.*
215 Dollmann, 1967, *op cit*, 241. 216 Wolfe, 1994, *op cit*, 318.
217 Dollmann, 1967, *op cit*, 124–25, 132, 159–60, 162. 218 *Ibid*, 69–70, 74–75.
219 *Ibid*, 73.

This was a commitment to sign up with the forces of cultural barbarism posing as national renewal that perplexed those who knew of his intensely academic, artistic and cultural talents and sensitivities.[220] Dollmann accepted a measure of personal responsibility for this decision but sought to exonerate himself from its implications, as will be discussed in a later section.

Dollmann's activities as a translator and diplomatic emissary

Dollmann's responsibilities as an SS emissary attached to the German embassy in Rome were extensive. They included acting as liaison officer with the Vatican and the Royal Italian Government, and official interpreter in summit meetings between Hitler and Mussolini.[221] During 1938, Dollmann rapidly became a 'star translator' for the German and Italian fascist regimes. He was brought in to facilitate better communications between the political, security and military leaders of Fascist Italy and Nazi Germany, particularly on special occasions such as Axis summit meetings and official state visits. Dollmann's services as a translator were highly regarded by Hitler, and Himmler on the one hand, and Mussolini, Italian Foreign Minister Ciano,[222] and Air Marshall Balbo on the other.[223] As a result: 'I spent the two years between autumn 1938 and Italy's entry into the war in June 1940 shuttling back and forth between Rome and Berlin.'[224] For example, he translated during Hitler's state visit to Rome in May 1938,[225] Mussolini's trip to Berlin in the autumn of the same year,[226] the fateful Munich Peace conference of September 1938,[227] Himmler's trip to Italian occupied Tripoli in November 1938,[228] Reinhard Heydrich's trip to Rome in October 1938, numerous official engagements by the German ambassador to Italy von Mackensen[229] and during meetings between Balbo and Hitler at Obersalzberg in 1939.[230]

At this time, he was ordered to carry out this important function at meetings taking place in both Germany and Italy between other senior officials and

220 B. Berenson, *Rumor and Reflection* (New York: Simon and Schuster, 1952), 11; G. Reitlinger, *The SS: Alibi of a Nation* (London: Heinemann, 1956), 192.

221 R. Trevelyan, *Rome 1944: The Battle for the Eternal City* (London: Book Club Associates, 1981), 12–13; R. Wolfe, 2004, *op cit*, 318.

222 Dollmann interpreted for Ciano during his state visits to Berlin in 21–23 May 1939, where he met with Hitler, Göring, Bormann, Ley, Himmler and Speer, and helped solidify the military alliance. *Ibid*, 157.

223 E. Dollmann, *The Interpreter* (London: Hutchinson, 1967), 122–24 (re Balbo's meeting with Hitler in August 1938). The meetings between Hitler and Ribbentrop on the German side and Ciano representing Italy on the other in Berlin 1938 are verified in contemporary photographs including Dollmann with these parties located between pp. 224 and 225 of these memoirs.

224 *Ibid*, 144. 225 *Ibid*, 100. 226 *Ibid*. 227 *Ibid*, 127.

228 *Ibid*, 119–20. 229 *Ibid*, 102. 230 *Ibid*.

government officials of these two nations. This included Italian minister Ricci's visit to Germany (where he met with Hitler's Propaganda Minister Goebbels and Nazi Youth leader Schirach) and at the funeral in Rome of Arturo Bocchini, the Italian Chief of Police in November 1940, attended by Himmler, Karl Wolff and Heydrich.[231]

One G2 report notes that, 'during the early phases of the war', Dollmann 'became a trusted personal representative of Hitler in Italy, and organised intelligence networks all over Italy'.[232] His HQ was in the German embassy in Rome.[233] This report was accurate only if one distorts the definition of 'organising intelligence networks' to mean picking up gossip from attending an endless parade of high society parties, dinners and formal occasions.

It must have helped his status that the Nazi leadership generally perceived Dollmann as Germany's most well-informed diplomatic emissary, who fully understood the otherwise obscure mindset of the Italian leadership. Furthermore, he was regarded by the Italian fascist leadership as an unusually sympathetic and pro-Italian German who, in private, lacked reverence for the ideology and protocols of the fascist leadership.[234] Within Italian circles, he was regarded as having 'gone native', following over a decade of residence in Rome, and was pleased to be known as 'Eugenio', rather than the Germanic Eugen, a matter noted and replicated even by Karl Wolff.[235] Certainly, he managed to play this part of being 'everybody's man' by successfully concealing his personal contempt for many of those he had to translate for, not least Ciano, Mussolini, Hitler, Himmler and Heydrich.[236]

This increasingly high-level work as a translator meant that he was soon able to avoid having to translate for the influx of lower status Italian and German delegations that became fashionable during the honeymoon phase of the German-Italian alliance.[237] His function as a translator and intermediary was important because few of these leaders spoke the language of their counterparts in the other regime. Dollmann, by contrast, was fluent in both Italian and, of course, his native German language. As an intelligent, cultured and highly educated man, Dollmann's translations were also better able to identify and convey nuances and shades of meaning, the tone of what

231 *Ibid*, verified in contemporary photographs located between 256–57.

232 Memorandum, Ass't Chief of Staff, G2 to CIA, 'Eugen Dollmann', 17 November 1951. As was typical of the duplication of functions in the National Socialist regime, these intelligence functions were specific to the SS and thus independent of the 'official' military intelligence activities conducted under Admiral Canaris, head of the German Intelligence Service [Abwehr].

233 For additional sources of Dollmann's pre-war role, see his SS officer's file, NA-BDC, RG 242, SSO, Roll 159 and Toland, *The Last Hundred Days* (New York: Random House, 1965), 238–44, 475–76, 483, 486.

234 Dollmann, 1967, *op cit*, 183, 216, 249.

235 *Ibid*, 126.

236 *Ibid*, 121.

237 *Ibid*, 121.

was said, than more literal or mechanical forms.[238] This positive view of Dollmann's abilities as a linguist was apparently shared by Hitler.[239]

It is even likely that, during his translations of the exchanges of the fascist leaderships, he exercised a suitably 'diplomatic' form of censorship that minimised the scope for unintended conflict and avoidable misunderstandings. Certainly, Dollmann himself has recognised the responsibilities, influence and even hidden power of translators in contexts where political leaders have had to rely upon their services.[240] With respect to Axis summit meetings, he even admitted to having 'judiciously slanted my translations so as to steer discussion into calmer waters'.[241] (Of course, this very quality of 'managing' appearances for the sake of the immediate audience's interests means that we have to be careful not to place too much faith in Dollmann's own accounts and memoirs where these are not independently corroborated by other sources.)[242] Given the often tactless, arrogant and insensitive nature of many of these fascist leaders,[243] not least contemptuous German attitudes towards the Italian monarchy and the Vatican,[244] combined with Ciano's repeated displays of contempt for von Ribbentrop, Hitler's foreign minister,[245] Dollmann's diplomatic function may have helped smooth interstate relations within the Axis. This became vital as the Axis prepared to launch aggressive war(s) in a coordinated manner. As a result, he could be accused of knowingly contributing, admittedly in a comparatively minor way, to the developing catastrophe of world war, albeit in a manner that probably fell outside the requirements of liability for 'crimes against the peace' under Article 6 of the Nuremberg Charter.

Dollmann's work as a translator became more arduous following his recruitment by the SS. This was particularly with respect to numerous meetings between Himmler and his associates and their Italian counterparts under Bocchini.[246] Dollmann certainly translated for a number of Nazi officials whose seniority meant that they later became Nuremberg defendants. In that respect, he can certainly be accused of having facilitated aspects of their work and of sharing, by voluntary association, in their complicity in war criminality. Furthermore, in the post-war context he expressed some sympathy for some of these defendants, such as Schirach, based on his earlier personal contacts.[247] From October 1943, Dollmann became a high-level personal

238 *Ibid*, 144. 239 *Ibid*, 144. 240 *Ibid*, 69–70, 197. 241 *Ibid*, 245.

242 To be fair, most of what Dollmann has claimed during in the post-war years concerning his role in the SS has been corroborated by other sources, and, compared with the memoirs of his SS colleagues, Dollmann is not especially self-exonerating. Katz's review of OSS files on Dollmann and the Ardeatine massacre concludes that Dollmann's various accounts in his memoirs and interviews were factually correct: *Robert Katz's History of Modern Italy*: http://www.theboot.it/mar_intros.html#and15.

243 Dollmann, 1967, *op cit*, 195, 209. 244 *Ibid*, 196. 245 *Ibid*, 108, 137, 165.

246 *Ibid*, 79. 247 *Ibid*, 69.

liaison officer to General Wolff and Generalfeldmarschall Albert Kesselring in their dealings with the Italians (Field Marschal Graziani, Minister of the Interior, Bocchini and others).[248] At this time, Dollmann thus 'resolved to place my official services and knowledge of Italy at Kesselring's disposal'. He frankly admitted that this decision, as with so many others, was determined by his overwhelming desire to 'stay in Rome as long as possible', where he had carved out an agreeable social life, and to optimise his personal freedom and independence.[249] Kesselring accepted Dollmann's services as a well-informed political adviser and liaison officer with the Italian authorities (albeit without incorporating him into the military hierarchy). Dollmann's translation and liaison work with Kesselring brought him into direct association with other military leaders who were later to become Nuremberg defendants. These included Field Marshal Keitel and General Jodl, and Italian fascist Minister for War Graziana, a future war crimes defendant in domestic Italian trials.[250]

In short, Dollmann's work as an translator and emissary for the Nazi leadership brought him into close association with many of the key participants in the 'conspiracy' that was later to be criminalised within the Nuremberg trials process. He could be accused of helping, albeit in a small way, the formation of the Axis, whilst knowing from his translation of the words of Hitler, Mussolini, Ciano and Ribbentrop that this alliance was bent on a process of global conquest. Before rushing to any judgement, it is necessary to evaluate critically a series of potential defence arguments that Dollmann could have made had he stood trial. This task is facilitated by many of Dollmann's own post-war statements under interrogation, sympathetic assessments from certain US intelligence officials, and his memoirs.

Potential defence argument 1: an accidental Nazi?

If one of the main purposes behind de-Nazification prosecutions was to identify and imprison hard core and still ideologically committed Nazis who would remain a security risk by exploiting the opportunities of post-war democracy to re-establish a fascist dictatorship, then the case of Dollmann would have been distinctly borderline. Unlike his SS superior from September 1943, General Karl Wolff, there is little evidence that Dollmann's decision to join the Nazi Party on 1 February 1934 was motivated by any idealism or firm political or ideological commitment to any aspect of this party's programme, least of all its rabid anti-Semitism or militarism. Instead, he claimed that this decision was a vaguely conformist and self-interested attempt to follow the example of others by aligning himself opportunistically with elite German

248 Memorandum, Ass't Chief of Staff, G2 to CIA, Eugen Dollmann, 17 November 1951, #2: Dollmann Name File, *op cit*.

249 Dollmann, 1967, *op cit*, 266, 280, 306.

250 *Ibid*, 282–84.

circles within Rome. He believed that some of these elites, such as the German ambassador von Hassell, might, perhaps, be able to facilitate his continuing, if sporadic, post-doctoral studies into a sixteenth-century cardinal. Whilst he apparently thought that his academic background as a sixteenth-century Italian art historian was barely relevant to the Nazi Party's activities, they still might find some use for him that would secure his relatively comfortable existence.[251]

The fact that Dollmann was not entirely able to conceal his more cynical, agnostic and self-serving motivations, which marked him out as an atypical Nazi, became rapidly apparent to more 'committed' fascists he had to work with. For example, both the Rome SS-Obersturmbannführer Herbert Kappler, and the Italian Fascist leader, Ciano, bitterly resented him for his lack of zeal, reluctance to wear the SS uniform and engage in other displays of public devotion to 'the cause'.[252] There is little evidence that, at the initial stage of his involvement with fascism, Dollmann was either being sought out by the Nazi leadership because of any distinctly Nazi characteristics or associations. Instead, he was valued and exploited as a translator pure and simple.

Indeed, Dollmann has claimed with factual justification that his involvement with the SS stemmed from the near accident that it was the Italian police chief who initially hired his services as a translator for certain of his contacts with Himmler, rather than other ministers of less problematic departments within the Italian state, such as agriculture. Dollmann has also maintained that he lacked any criminal intent, claiming that his private motivation was to use his membership of the SS as a way of remaining in Rome to continue his agreeable life-style and post-doctoral studies. In mitigation, he has further argued that, given that he had not lived in Germany since 1927, he was far from acquainted with the true nature and role of Himmler's organisation, which at that time had yet to embark on systematic atrocities and genocide. In other words, he was both ill-informed and naïve.

Ironically, Dollmann's involvement with Himmler's notorious SS did not stem from any particular affinity or contacts with the German leadership. Instead, it emerged from an assignment in late summer 1936 which he accepted from the Italian Police Chief, Arturo Boccini. Boccini was about to be sent to Germany by Mussolini, and had been impressed with how Dollmann had, over the past decade, become 'very Italianised' in manner and even appearance,[253] as well as his skills as an expert translator. Hence, Boccini consulted Dollmann to help prepare himself for this high profile meeting with

251 *Ibid*, 46. His membership number was 3,402,541, suggesting that he was something of a latecomer to the Nazi movement.

252 *Ibid*, 237.

253 Dollmann cultivated this to distinguish himself from more typical SS RSHA types, *ibid*, 239 (re Skorzeny).

the Nazi leadership. This assignment offered Dollmann a measure of welcome protection as a foreigner in the unstable atmosphere of pre-war fascist Italy.[254] Boccini wrongly assumed that, as an SS-Standartenführer, Dollmann knew both Himmler and Hitler personally. Despite this disappointment, Dollmann was able to brief him about certain features of the Germans and their typical sensitivities so that Boccini could avoid diplomatic blunders and cultural insensitivities.[255] Similarly, Dollmann helped Balbo prepare for his visit to Hitler in August 1938.[256] Through his successful completion of these *ad hoc* assignments, Dollmann soon became seen in Italian Fascist government and diplomatic circles as a something of a rarity, an untypical Nazi and a German official one could do business with, almost as 'their German'.

In short, Dollmann's military rank of SS-Colonel was, in one respect at least, more formal than substantive, as he lacked any military, police or security background, inclinations or even talents.[257] Indeed, this 'failing' was widely known and even commented upon by the Axis leadership.[258] On the other hand, even if Dollmann was able to convince a post-war de-Nazification court that his SS rank was a pure formality to dress up what was in substance a purely diplomatic role, this may not have amounted to a complete defence. Here we must bear in mind that both von Ribbentrop and von Papen were prosecuted and convicted at the Nuremberg trials for their diplomatic service to Hitler. Since within these trials there was no post-war immunity for those active Nazis who served their movement only through *diplomatic channels*, it is debatable whether a de-Nazification tribunal would have adopted a more sympathetic stance.

Potential defence argument 2: Dollmann as a saboteur?

Allied de-Nazification laws specifically allowed defendants to plead as a complete defence that they had been covertly acting as a saboteur. Arguably, this required something more active than a degree of defeatism, disengagement or lack of personal zeal.

Dollmann's frank memoirs certainly record consistent distain for Himmler as a faintly ridiculous figure in terms of his manner, dogmatic beliefs and appearance. They also express an 'instinctive dread' for Heydrich, the Gestapo chief and Himmler's 'evil genius' with a Jewish grandmother, whom Dollmann believed would have had both Hitler and Himmler killed in the final year of the war had he lived to see it.[259] Dollmann also claims to have been personally and institutionally far closer to the comparatively benign Italian police chief Bocchini, than with Himmler. As evidence, he points to his involvement in

254 *Ibid*, 53. 255 *Ibid*, 53–55. 256 *Ibid*, 123. 257 *Ibid*, 212–13.
258 *Ibid*, 111–12. 259 *Ibid*, 71, 81–84, 92–97.

minor conspiracies with the Italian at the expense of the SS leader,[260] and almost acting as an advocate for the Italians with respect to the Nazis' attack on Christianity and the Italian monarchy.[261]

Dollmann certainly took some risks in associating and socialising with anti-Nazi Germans resident in, or visiting, Rome, many of whom were being watched by Kappler's Gestapo. At least some of these dissidents had good reason to trust in Dollmann's discretion.[262]

To be fair to Dollmann, or rather the 'case for his defence', he claimed to have tried to use his limited influence behind the scenes to keep Italy out of the European war, not least by reporting upon and emphasising the lack of preparedness of the Italian military forces.[263] Yet, when challenged during British interrogation in Rome in 1945:

> why I had not prevented Italy from entering the Second World War, I endeavoured to explain that any such intervention would have far exceeded the scope and potential of an interpreter. . . . He [Mussolini] only credited me with political influence when things began to go badly for him. Dictators do not listen to their advisers until they are at their wits' end.[264]

With respect to the Nazi leadership, making any such pacifist intervention would, Dollmann claimed, have amounted to a 'suicide attempt'.[265]

Dollmann was a self-serving opportunist who had prostituted himself to fascism (as he might equally have done for democracy or even communism). Yet, from a Nazi war crimes and de-Nazification prosecution standpoint, his war record contains many mitigating factors relevant to the claim that he had acted as an opponent of Hitler's regime. In the various intrigues that Dollmann launched and participated in, he tended to support more moderate, diplomatic elements within the German and Italian authorities, and thereby worked against the overtly repressive and genocidal elements of the SS. For example, during the autumn of 1943, he met Möllhausen with whom he rapidly established a friendly, loyal and cooperative relationship. In his diplomatic role as Consul-General and Deputy German Ambassador to

260 *Ibid*, 125, 194. Dollmann enjoyed exploiting his translation role to engage in minor conspiracies and deceptions on behalf of those Italians with whom he felt closest to, even at the expense of Himmler, *ibid*. Cf Dollmann, 1956, *op cit*, 99–100.

261 *Ibid*, 87, 91, 138. Dollmann could indeed be accused of serving two masters.

262 For example, with respect to the Prince and Princess Bismark, Carl Clemm, Felix Kersten, and von Gaevernitz and even Mussolini's anti-Nazi wife: *ibid*, 173–78, 219–21.

263 *Ibid*, 139–40, 185–87. Eventually he gave up his 'private peace talks' claiming not only was it impractical but also that it was up to the Italian authorities to extricate themselves from their self-created difficulties with Hitler's regime, *ibid*, 187.

264 *Ibid*, 185. 265 *Ibid*.

Italy, Möllhausen actively sought to limit Nazi atrocities against Roman Jews and others, and took great personal risks in opposing the orders of Himmler, Kaltenbrunner and Kappler.[266] Möllhausen and Dollmann worked together and with Kesselring to save Rome from the threat of destruction following the Allied invasions in 1943–44.[267]

Even if we accept that Dollmann was a cynical opportunist unimpeded by moral principles other than self-interest, it is still necessary to recognise that he was a pioneer of unofficial, even 'treacherous', peace moves regarding Italy. This took place in a context where few others were willing to rise to this challenge, or to take the associated risks of being arrested and killed for defying Hitler's orders. Dollmann is recorded as having been at the forefront of moves to initiative contacts with Dulles. It was Dollmann who initially set up a meeting between Wolff and the Pope in May 1944, which he knew would result in pressure upon Wolff to work towards an early and unofficial capitulation that put the lives of all participants and their families at risk from retribution by Himmler and particularly Kaltenbrunner.[268] He first raised the issue with the German Kommandierender General der Luftwaffe von Pohl as early as July 1944,[269] before discussing the idea to Wolff later in December of the same year and then, on Wolff's behalf, with Italian partisan resistance, Cardinal Schuster and indirectly with Mussolini.[270] Dollmann's liaison with Vatican and German diplomatic officials, such as Rahn, and with von Pohl,[271] thus helped prepare the ground for Wolff's later peace initiative. By contrast, Zimmer took the initiative through his agent Baron Parilli at the end of 1944 *only after* hearing Dollmann urge attempted peace feelers with the Allies.

Dollmann also played a prominent part in the later stages of Operation Sunrise by bringing Allen Dulles into contact with Wolff during March 1945, and keeping these fraught negotiations on track towards their ultimately successful conclusion in late April 1945.[272] In other words, Dollmann undoubtedly must be credited with being one of the main 'behind the scenes' players seeking to bring about peace feelers with the Allies in defiance of Himmler and Kaltenbrunner; and therefore at a measure of personal risk.

266 R. Katz, 'The Möllhausen Telegram, The Kappler Decodes, and The Deportation of the Jews of Rome: The New CIA-OSS Documents, 2000–2002,' in J. Zimmerman (ed.), *The Jews of Italy Under Fascist and Nazi Rule, 1922–1945* (Cambridge: Cambridge University Press, 2005); E. F. Möllhausen, *La carta perdente. Memorie diplomatiche 25 luglio 1943–2 maggio 1945* (Rome, 1948).

267 Dollmann, 1967, *op cit*, 296, 305.

268 *Ibid*, 298, 300–2. Also Dollmann 1957, *op cit*, 90.

269 Dulles, 1966, *op cit*, 79–80.

270 'Eugen Dollmann and Eugen Wenner', ND, Dollmann Name File, *op cit*.

271 Dollmann, 1967, *op cit*, 312–13.

272 *Ibid*, 306–8, 343–46.

Potential defence argument 3: Dollmann's lack of knowledge of SS war criminality?

Had Dollmann been able to convince a de-Nazification court that, whilst he actively performed a senior role within the SS in Italy, he lacked any real knowledge or criminal intent, then this may have reduced his sentence, or even served as a complete defence. It is doubtful, however, whether he could have succeeded in this task. Dollmann remained personally close to Mussolini, and enjoyed a series of private audiences with him, including a few days before the Duce was lynched in April 1945.[273] His work as a translator took him into the inner sanctums of the Nazi leadership, including Hitler's private apartment and study[274] and the Obersalzberg,[275] as well as his other offices and headquarters. Knowing of ongoing Nazi atrocities and diplomatic duplicities linked to waging war (later criminalised by the Nuremberg Charter of August 1945 as 'crimes against the peace'), Dollmann continued to smooth the course of German-Italian relations by carrying out numerous translation assignments. For example, between 23 and 30 August 1941, he translated for Hitler and Mussolini on their joint expedition to occupied Russia.[276] In January 1943, he performed this role for an Italian delegation visiting Hitler,[277] and for meetings between Herman Göring and Italian General Ambrosio in April 1943,[278] and at Mussolini's meeting with German Generalfeldmarschall Albert Kesselring in August 1944.[279]

Arguably, Dollmann's decision to continue his translation work after hostilities began, and even after it became clear to him that the Nazi leadership, particularly Himmler's SS, were engaged in systematic repression and war criminality which could result in post-war legal accountability for all senior SS officials, rendered him particularly vulnerable to post-war retribution.

Dollmann would not have been able to claim that he was surprised that senior SS officers would, following Germany's military defeat, be subjected to war crimes proceedings. His memoir recalls that, in 1941, he was warned of this by the German Ambassadress to Rome who noted that: 'all of us who had served the Third Reich in any capacity would be hauled from one tribunal to the next. Even she failed to guess that the first victim of this persecution would be her own father, Neurath [former German Foreign Minister].'[280] In short, Dollmann's close contacts as a trusted translator in Axis summit and other high-level meetings meant that he would have had extreme difficulties in either denying that he had knowledge of the purposes of the Nazi leaders, or rebutting any legal presumption which imputed such knowledge to

273 *Ibid*, 227–28. Apparently, Dollmann also enjoyed the confidence of the Italian king, who expressed frank views of on the personalities and pathologies of some of the Nazi leadership, particularly Ribbentrop (Hitler's 'evil genius') and Heydrich: *ibid*, 134.

274 *Ibid*, 165.

275 *Ibid*, 164.

276 *Ibid*, 188–89.

277 *Ibid*, 115, 118.

278 *Ibid*, 199.

279 *Ibid*.

280 *Ibid*, 107.

him based on his senior rank within the SS. Indeed, his well-known personal dread of leading figures within the SS, such as Heydrich, was based on an all-too-precise awareness of their complicity in individual and mass murders.

Potential defence argument 4: his lack of any policy-making role

If Dollmann could have established that the comparative seniority implied by his rank of SS-Standartenführer was illusionary in practice because he had no subordinates or role in any decision-making within the inner sanctum of the Nazi leadership, then this may have assisted his defence, at least with respect to mitigating his sentence. Dollmann had close personal relationships with the Nazi leadership relevant to the formation or execution of policy, other than perhaps with Karl Wolff from September 1943.[281] There is no evidence that, although he was present at many key and even fateful Axis meetings, that anyone sought his advice on matters of substantive policy relevant to war crimes charges,[282] even assuming that he had anything useful to contribute to affairs of state outside the realm of protocol between the Axis partners.[283]

On the other hand, Dollmann could hardly deny being an emissary for Himmler and, in this capacity, giving him advice. Certainly, for Himmler, Dollmann was a source of diplomatic protocol and cross-cultural guidance. Yet there is no evidence that this role ever extended to decision-making with respect to Nazi policy or its execution, least of all with respect to state security issues related even indirectly to war crimes. Instead, Dollmann has claimed that his role with respect to Himmler was to provide him with:

> detailed lectures on the Italian world which was so alien to him, briefing himself for every meeting with Italians, like a schoolboy preparing for a lesson . . . I cannot say he ever disgraced me . . . he followed my hints and suggestions like an apt pupil – at least in Italy. It was not my job to discuss German questions with him, and the police sphere was happily *tabu* when I was concerned.[284]

In short, although Dollmann possessed knowledge of, and was indirectly involved in, high-level diplomatic intrigues between the Italian and German leadership,[285] he never exercised a policy-making role relevant to war crimes criminalised in the Nuremberg Charter or Law No. 10. Unlike Ribbentrop and the pre-war diplomat Franz von Papen, Dollmann could not be accused

281 *Ibid*, 129.

282 *Ibid*, for example, concerning whether Italy should go to war with the Allies despite the opposition of many sectors of Italian society, *ibid* 170.

283 *Ibid*, 132.

284 *Ibid*, 83.

285 Wolfe, *op cit*, 318–20.

of direct participation in the various diplomatic deceptions and policy-making activities that were relevant to the Nuremberg charge of 'waging aggressive war' in violation of one of the new and retrospectively applied criminal offences used by the Nuremberg prosecutors.

Potential defence argument 5: lack of involvement in the unlawful activities of the SS

Whilst Himmler's SS is rightly notorious for its creation and organisation of concentration and death camps, as well as for its secret police sub-divisions the RSHA and Gestapo, not all branches of this organisation were directly involved in war criminality. In his defence, Dollmann would have almost certainly argued that his work for the SS was as disconnected from the death camps and internal repression through secret police activities as it was possible to be. In particular, he would have distanced himself from SS-Standartenführer Kappler who oversaw such operations within Rome. Contrary to Simpson's claims that he was 'instrumental in the killing programmes directed against Italian Jews',[286] there is little evidence of his complicity in either the rounding up and deportation of Jews, or concerning the 'organisation' of the 'German reign of terror' more generally alleged by Wiskemann,[287] which fell under different branches of the SS in Italy.[288]

Dollmann knew his limitations. This explains why he deliberately avoided any assignments that overlapped with SS police or security work even in the slightest ways.[289] This reluctance included resisting pressure from Heydrich to monitor Felix Kersten, Himmler's Finnish masseur who, in early 1940, had been assigned to carry on his quasi-medical work with the Italian fascist leaders, whom the Gestapo leader strongly suspected of Allied espionage.[290] For obvious reasons, Dollmann's post-war statements emphasised that he had always minimised his contacts with both Kappler and Heydrich as representatives of the most terrifying, repressive and ultimately genocidal aspects of the SS.[291] He notes, for instance, that:

> From 1938 onwards, police liaison work between Rome and Berlin was handled by two police attachés of whom the German in Rome

286 Simpson, 1998, *op cit*, fn 93; 1995, *op cit*, 236.

287 E. Wiskemann, *The Rome-Berlin Axis: A History of the Relations between Hitler and Mussolini* (Oxford: Oxford University Press, 1949), 325–26.

288 J. Toland, *The Last 100 Days* (New York: Random House, 1975, *op cit*); Wolfe, 2004, *op cit*, 328. Most of the better researched accounts suggest he played a largely diplomatic and political role and was not implicated directly in committing or ordering Nazi atrocities.

289 *Ibid*, 222.

290 *Ibid*, 178–80. Apparently, Dollmann told him to take the matter up with Himmler knowing this would cause difficulties for both men.

291 *Ibid*, 181.

> was Herbert Kappler, an avowed favourite of the chief of Central State Security Bureau, Heydrich, and thus a secret but unmistakable foe of mine. I only learned later that Heydrich would have liked to incorporate me into his own organisation, and his subsequent campaign against me through Kappler may have been attributable to the fact that Himmler's personal chief of staff . . . Karl Wolff, had firmly opposed any such transfer. I had taken out additional insurance against this by enlisting the support of Bocchini, who saw no reason to accommodate Heydrich in any way.[292]

Dollmann claimed that even his friend Bocchini, the Italian fascist chief of police, had difficulties with Kappler's orientation and actions, and in effect both Dollmann and this Italian official resisted the SS leader's activities in some respects at least.[293] Hence, Dollmann claimed that he translated for Heydrich only twice (in April 1938 when checking Italian security arrangements for Hitler's later state visit to Italy, and October 1939, when Heydrich represented Germany on an international police day held in Italy). Even these assignments were of an interim nature because Kappler had not yet mastered sufficient Italian to be able to fulfil this function for his RSHA superior.[294] Dollmann claimed to have only telephoned Himmler once, and that was at the insistence of the Italian authorities who wished to canvass opinions on the appointment of a new police chief.[295] Dollmann worked with Kappler only on a single occasion, a joint effort to save Rome from a bloodbath by means of a political plan agreed with Karl Wolff to declare it an open city.[296]

Furthermore, Dollmann's work with Kesselring from autumn of 1943 to the end of the war gave him a measure of respect and status, and hence protection, in relation to Kappler.[297] Yet, Dollmann claimed that his largely diplomatic role was barely tolerated by Kappler: 'a man who had no executive staff or armed men at his disposal could never mean more to him, for all of Kesselring's patronage, than a drawing room soldier. In that capacity he was prepared to tolerate me.'[298] Trevelyan's impressively researched work on Italy during this period, which is sensitive to the chaotic and internally competitive nature of Nazi institutions and internal institutional politics, argues that Dollmann's reputation has suffered from being 'muddled with Kappler's, especially in books published just after the war'.[299]

SS-Obersturmbannführer Herbert Kappler was the actual representative

292 *Ibid*, 92.

293 *Ibid*, 78. He later characterised Kappler: 'as narrow-minded as his supreme Chief, Himmler. He was incorruptible as Robespierre and professional as it was possible to be. Nothing escaped his steely blue eyes.' *Ibid*, 285–86.

294 *Ibid*, 92. 295 *Ibid*, 98. 296 *Ibid*, 237, 241–42. 297 *Ibid*, 286.

298 *Ibid*. 299 Trevelyn, 1981, *op cit*, 116.

of the SS's repressive secret police apparatus within Rome, and was centrally concerned with arrests, torture and deportations. Dulles, for his own reasons, has contrasted Dollmann's activities and orientation to that of Kappler and Harster, arguing that he was a most untypical Nazi, of 'a quite different cut', who never attended SS training schools or rarely wore the SS uniform, for example, and whose rise to prominence owed more to accident than design. Dulles argues that it was precisely because of his atypical role and qualities that explains why he was amongst the first to press for peace feelers with the OSS in Berne, and then to guide Wolff towards Dulles, partly through his Vatican contacts.[300] Dulles further argues that although he initially knew of Dollmann (and Wolff) as mere names in a chain of command of the SS who shared in the 'black reputation' of the SS more generally held for good reasons by OSS-supported Italian partisans, closer investigation and personal contacts revealed just how misleading this stereotype was.[301] Kappler was, in fact, one of Dollmann's enemies. Dollmann sometimes worked against him to assist detained Italians, not least by exploiting the fact that he was a favourite of Karl Wolff, both men's SS superior in Italy. As Trevelyan rightly notes:

> Kappler disliked Dollmann, whom he regarded as a drawing room soldier, with nebulous duties that were 'clear to neither himself nor anybody else.... The animosity between him and Kappler ... was indeed very deep. Kappler ... affected to despise him, and probably was jealous, not only of Dollmann's better education [he held a doctorate] but because he was the favourite of General Karl Wolff, the head of the SS in Italy.'[302]

Furthermore, Dollmann returned the animosity towards an individual he contemptuously regarded as an unquestioning Nazi zealot. For Dollmann, Kappler was a stereotypical police official who treated superior orders to commit war crimes, including the rounding up of Italian Jews, that could have been partly avoided, or at least delayed, as strictly and completely binding.[303] Indeed, Trevelyan even doubts whether Dollmann passed on information regarding defeatist or anti-German comments he gathered from his contacts with Italian 'high society' to Kappler.[304]

It appears that Dollmann's orientation was far closer to that of the German consul Möllhausen, who secretly assisted Italian Jews, than to Kappler's subordinates within the repressive part of the SS apparatus responsible for war crimes.[305] Furthermore, one would search in vain in the many hundred books devoted to the Nazi holocaust and war criminality more generally to find any references to Dollmann's personal or direct participation. In

300 Dulles, 1966, *op cit*, 55–56, 61, 79. 301 *Ibid*, 66.
302 Trevelyn, 1981, *op cit*, 12–13, 116–17. 303 Dollmann, 1967, *op cit*, 217.
304 Trevelyn, 1981, *op cit*, 13. 305 *Ibid*.

short, Dollmann's activities and orientation within the SS were located at the opposite end of the spectrum from those war crimes for which this organisation became notorious, and this was even recognised, as a criticism, by Kappler and others.

Potential defence argument 6: Dollmann's humanitarian interventions

Although lacking any particular sympathy for the fate of entire groups who were victimised by the SS sufficient to motivate principled opposition and resignation, at an individual and interpersonal level there is evidence of a measure of humanitarianism. By temperament, Dollmann showed considerably fondness for Rome and the Italians more generally than for many of his fellow Germans, which partly explains his occasional acts of assistance for high society Italians arrested by Kappler's subordinates, providing they were not, like partisan General Simoni, too heavily implicated in military attacks.[306] As already indicated, Dollmann also frequently boasted at having helped arrange for Rome to be declared an 'open city', and therefore off-bounds to fighting in the Second World War.[307]

Dollmann certainly, on occasions, used his influence with the Italian Ministry of the Interior, Karl Wolff and Kesselring in a humanitarian fashion. For example, he intervened to assist those connected with his Italian friends to avoid military conscription, and protected individuals accused of defeatist or anti-fascist sentiments who were at risk of arrest and torture from Kappler's secret police.[308] Dollmann also used his contacts with Wolff to intervene successfully on behalf of Count Calvi, who, as a member of the Italian monarchy that had switched to the Allies' side, had been imprisoned by the German authorities. As a result of this intervention, Calvi was then granted house arrest, rather than detention and probable death in a concentration camp, as befell his sister-in-law, Princess Mafalda.[309] Dollmann assisted Count Cini, who had been detained in Dachau concentration camp but, following pressure from Wolff upon the Berlin RSHA authorities, was later released to Switzerland.[310] Dollmann also intervened with Kesselring to have notorious Italian fascist torture chambers located in Polazzo Braschi, Regio Emilia and Villa Roncina closed down.[311] He also assisted the Ciano family to escape from an Italian house arrest.[312] On Dollmann's initiative, Kesselring sought, with ultimate success, to preserve Rome as an open city, off-limits from destructive military conflict.[313]

306 *Ibid*, 117. 307 *Ibid*, 113 308 *Ibid*, 142. 309 *Ibid*, 278.

310 *Ibid*, 288–99; cf. Dollmann 1956, *op cit*, 99–100.

311 *Ibid*, 287, 331, 336–37, cf. 309 regarding the closure of something similar in Florence for which church officials thanked Dollmann. See also Dollmann, 1956, *op cit*, 72–73.

312 Dollmann, 1967, *op cit*, 291–94. 313 *Ibid*, 266–67.

Once again, during 1943–45, there was additional evidence of Dollmann's sporadic humanitarianism. Dollmann engaged in some prisoner exchanges on Kesselring's behalf, which the Field Marshal acknowledged in his memoirs, and assisted in the prevention of a scorched-earth policy by retreating German troops during the last year of the war.[314] OSS reports summarising Operation Sunrise note that Dollmann was best characterised as Himmler's personal envoy in Italy, a fluent Italian speaker and exercising considerable beneficial influence largely from his base in Rome:

> Reports had it that Dollmann was exceedingly influential in Rome prior to its liberation and that he had apparently claimed credit for having saved Rome from destruction. Reputedly he had built up a considerable fortune in connection with the ransoming of important individuals and generally, though sometimes for a price, had shown some sympathy for Italians.[315]

In short, had Dollmann been tried and convicted under Law No. 10, then he could have raised a number of arguments suggesting that, with respect to sentencing, his offence should be recognised as falling at the least grave end of the spectrum owing to his various humanitarian interventions which reduced his criminal intent.

Problems with these defence arguments

Few, if any, of Dollmann's potential defence arguments can be considered decisive or compelling. For example, his decision to minimise contact, or any working relationship, with the overtly repressive and genocidal wing of the SS within Italy was not based upon any obvious concern for particular categories of their victims. Instead, he realised how restricting and dangerous any association with such men could become. Dollmann discovered that even senior military governors, such as General Mältzer, German Governor of Nazi-occupied Rome, had good reason to fear Kappler and his SS superiors.[316]

Had Dollmann possessed any real anti-fascist tendencies and commitments, then he could have used his powerful position to secretly augment, rather than minimise, the scope for misunderstanding, conflict and mistrust both within and between the leadership of this unstable Axis. These fault-lines were epitomised by Ciano's repeated leaking of Axis decisions to friends known to

314 Cited in *ibid*, 338, 343.

315 Untitled Sunrise folder, narrative on Sunrise, compiled by T. S. Ryan, 5: NA, RG 226, Entry 110, Box 711, Folder 11a.

316 Dollmann, 1967, *op cit*, 285.

be in direct contact with the British authorities.[317] Yet, in fact, and by his own admission, Dollmann achieved the opposite,[318] even when posing as a disengaged and irreverent onlooker to the all-too-human personal foibles of the Axis leadership and the 'snake pit' of internal politics within both fascist regimes.[319] Certainly, Dollmann translated for Ciano at vital periods in the formation and development of the Axis and its later preparation for war.[320]

In one sense, Dollmann could be accused of being closer to the activities, diplomatic intrigue and high-level policies of the worse Nazi war criminals, such as Hitler and Himmler. Dollmann was certainly Himmler's trusted liaison officer with Mussolini, and participated personally, albeit as a translator, in many high-level contacts between Mussolini and both Himmler and Hitler. Höttl has recalled that:

> [T]he German government was badly served by its diplomatic reports from Rome . . . Himmler's delegate to Italy, SS Colonel Dollmann, was equally unsuccessful in gaining any insight into the secret machinations of Italian politics. His talent was more for conspiracy than for serious politics, and he owed his appointment to the fact that Himmler regarded Kappler, the Police Attaché, as a mere creature of Heydrich and was most anxious to have in Rome his own man whom he could trust.[321]

Despite these acts of disengagement and ultimate betrayal in the closing months of the war, it is doubtful whether it would have been possible for Dollmann to rely upon a defence of acting as a saboteur engaged in internal subversion of the kind required by post-war de-Nazification laws to qualify as a complete defence. The time period of active defiance with respect to the capitulation was, perhaps, too short and the other evidence insufficient to amount to sabotage at all. With respect to the Nazi faith, Dollmann's overall record more closely resembles that of an agnostic, then a subversive atheist undermining Hitler's regime from within.

Undoubtedly, Dollmann's role in Italy was located at the opposite end of the spectrum of SS activity involving the Gestapo repression and concentration and death camps. Hence, any charge would have had to be confined to a simple membership offence. However, it is difficult to believe that he lacked

317 *Ibid*, 168, 201. Dollmann certainly did not assist Ciano's later efforts to sabotage this pact, not least through reporting back to the British: *ibid*, 168–70, 185.

318 *Ibid*, 236. (Dollmann appears to have taken a professional pride in his talents at translation that aided communication across cultural as well as linguistic divides, even in contexts where the parties themselves were attempting to deceive one another as to their attitudes, intentions and plans.)

319 *Ibid*, 137, 232.

320 *Ibid*, 155, 165–67.

321 W. Höttl, *The Secret Service* (New York: Praeger, 1954), 222–23.

relevant *mens rea* because he was not aware of his organisation's genocidal actions and orientation and still chose, for purely selfish reasons, to continue to serve it at a senior level and in the way that he was best qualified to do so. As Trevelyan notes: 'He must have known of the equally dreadful things that happened in the Gestapo interrogation centre at Via Tasso, run by Kappler, the real terror of Rome.'[322] Given Dollmann's close working contacts with these leading figures, any typical legal defence claim that he only remained in the employment of the SS because of his continued ignorance of either its repressive role, or the character and objectives of the fascist leadership, would be difficult to sustain. If he had ever possessed doubts regarding the genocidal orientation of key aspects of Himmler's organisation, which as a member of Himmler's personal staff is highly unlikely, then the Ardeatine Massacre and the deportation of Italian Jews to death camps in October 1943 would surely have resolved these.

Whilst Dollmann could, and often did, intervene to shield high-society Italians from Kappler's officers, there were also limits to this. For instance, Dollmann personally ordered the house arrest of the blatantly pro-Allied Duchess of Sermoneta.[323] Furthermore, there is no record of Dollmann taking any measures between 1934 and 1943 that could, in any sense, be described as generally subversive of SS policies, activities or ideologies. It was only in early 1944, once it had become obvious that Germany was losing the war, with potentially dire consequences in terms of war crimes prosecution or possibly mass execution for SS officers as a group, perhaps at the hands of the Soviets, that Dollmann was prompted to act more independently in terms of making unofficial peace contacts.

Knowing of ongoing Nazi atrocities and diplomatic duplicities linked to waging war (later criminalised by Article 6 of the Nuremberg Charter of August 1945 as 'crimes against the peace'), Dollmann continued to smooth the course of German-Italian relations by carrying out numerous translation assignments. For example, between 23 and 30 August 1941 he translated for Hitler and Mussolini on their joint expedition to occupied Russia.[324] In January 1943, he performed this role for an Italian delegation visiting Hitler,[325] and for meetings between Herman Göring and Italian General Ambrosio in April 1943,[326] and at Mussolini's meeting with German Generalfeldmarschall Albert Kesselring in August 1944.[327] Arguably, Dollmann's decision to continue his translation work after hostilities began, and even after it became clear to him that the Nazi leadership, particularly Himmler's SS, were engaged in systematic repression and war criminality which could result in post-war legal accountability for all senior SS officials, rendered him particularly vulnerable to post-war prosecution. Dollmann cannot claim to be

322 Trevelyan, 1981, *op cit*, 13. 323 *Ibid*, 63. 324 *Ibid*, 188–89.
325 *Ibid*, 115, 118. 326 *Ibid*, 199. 327 *Ibid*.

surprised that senior SS officers would, following Germany's military defeat, be subjected to war crimes proceedings.

Faced with the prospect of prosecution for war crimes under the Nuremberg Charter with respect to the 'conspiracy' charge, or at least de-Nazification measures, Dollmann could not have argued in his defence that he was positively *coerced* into supporting the Nazi movement, and therefore lack criminal intent and motivation. On the contrary, as a German citizen resident in Italy, he could have avoided any form of military or related service to Hitler's regime. He could have remained aloof and relied upon income from translation assignments of a more literary nature than the interchanges between Hitler and Mussolini and their immediate political and military subordinates. Indeed, Dollmann's assignments in Italy before the war included freelance translating of Italian books into German. This included works by an Italian diplomat concerning his role between 1914 and 1919, Donna Vittoria, an Italian duchess with strong anti-Nazi views, on her recollections of royal Italian life, and another by his personal friend Pietro Badoglio, Marshall of Italy, entitled *The Abyssinian War*.[328]

In short, most of the defence arguments cannot be considered to be compelling in terms of providing a complete defence sufficient to warrant an acquittal. On the other hand, many of these arguments could have been pleaded in mitigation to reduce the sentence to somewhere close to the lowest possible level.

Conclusion

Relative to many other senior SS officials, Dollmann's qualifications as a potential war crimes defendant were far from clear or unambiguous. His 'career', actions and orientation as a Nazi SS official, was not as benign as suggested by Dulles' book, *Secret Surrender*. However, nor were these as complicit in war criminality and genocide as claimed by Italian press reports of the mid to late 1940s and the allegations of both Wiskemann and Simpson. On the one hand, Dollmann was not directly complicit in ordering or personally committing atrocities sufficient to justify classification as even a middle-ranking war criminal. On the other, as a senior SS officer aware of his organisation's genocidal policies, he may well have faced severe punishment, including imprisonment, as an 'active Nazi' and a voluntary member of a criminal organisation if he was ever brought before a German de-Nazification court.

Furthermore, had he stood trial before an Italian court in the punitive atmosphere of the immediate post-war years, then, as both he and Allied

328 *Ibid*, 50–51. This author went on to lead the revolt against Italian fascism in July 1943, replacing Mussolini as Italian leader and realigning Italy with the Allies, to the horror of the Nazi leadership.

intelligence officials were well aware, he would have been at serious risk of both conviction and execution simply for being part of the local SS leadership in Rome at the time of the Ardeatine massacre. Those Allied officials reviewing Dollmann's wartime record came to a similar conclusion, at least with respect to probable liability before a German de-Nazification hearing:

> Persons of the category of Dollmann and Wenner could normally expect rather stiff sentences as having been fully conscious of their acts, and could only expect a mitigation of the sentence if they were able prove that they had actively opposed the Nazis . . . Activity on behalf of the Allies would be given consideration but . . . I don't see how these men could allege anti-Nazi activity. On the contrary, both received Iron Crosses as late as 1945. Their first known act unfavourable (let alone opposed) to the Nazi regime was their engagement in the negotiations under Operation Sunrise . . . a time when even an imbecile could have seen that the German cause was hopelessly lost. It can be assumed from the nature of the alleged 'promises' that their real motive . . . was to seek protection from expected punishment.[329]

In short, and despite the clear differences between their functions and the level at which they operated within the SS hierarchy, both Zimmer and Dollmann were certainly vulnerable to being prosecuted and sentenced as 'active Nazis' before an Allied de-Nazification tribunal. It is understandable to assume that individuals who rose to a comparatively senior position within an organisation as centrally implicated in genocide, concentration camp atrocities and brutal repression as Himmler's SS (which included the feared Gestapo) must have been directly implicated in some type of war criminality. However, it is arguable that the wartime records of Dollmann and Zimmer was never so grave as to render these SS officials vulnerable to being treated by the Nuremberg prosecutors at least as *major* war criminals on a par with the defendants in the first round of Nuremberg trials, including Göring and Kaltenbrunner. Nor is it certain, at least once Dollmann's lack of involvement in the Ardeatine Caves atrocity was eventually established, that either man was substantially involved in making or executing policies directly linked to Nazi atrocities. Hence, and bracketing out the attitude of the Italian authorities, it remains arguable that neither man merited prosecution by the Allies as mid-ranking Nazi war criminals during the subsequent hearings at Nuremberg from 1947 to 1949 or in British-led war crimes trials in Italy.

Zimmer may have been vulnerable to prosecution for overseeing extortion in Italian domestic war crimes trials. Certainly, Zimmer's Milan office was involved in financial extortion from Italian Jews; yet this policy hardly

329 *Ibid.*

originated with Zimmer, nor was he centrally involved with its practical enforcement. Dollmann's Nazi credentials were described dismissively by Höttl as those of a 'drawing room hero'.[330] In short, the wartime record of both Dollmann and especially Zimmer made these officials vulnerable to prosecution in domestic war crimes trials and certainly to being convicted and punished in post-war de-Nazification hearings established by the Allies. However, there is only limited and partial evidence that either man was sufficiently complicit in offences of such gravity as to merit prosecution as either major or even middle-ranking war criminals.

If this analysis is correct, then it follows that, insofar as US intelligence sought to protect Zimmer and Dollmann from prosecution as part of a wider package of 'privileged treatment', this subversion of the rule of law cannot be considered to be on a par with that which took place with respect to SS-General Wolff, who – once Dulles resigned as head of the CIA – was eventually prosecuted in 1962 for complicity in the extermination of 300,000 Jews the SS deported to the Treblinka death camp.

The present chapter has, in many respects, confined the scope of the evidence considered in ways that may appear unduly generous to Wolff and other members of his SS group based in Northern Italy. Yet, even after having narrowed down the range of source materials considerably, there is no doubt that the Nuremberg prosecutors possessed a considerable array of documentary evidence indicating that, contrary to his strategies of denial, Wolff at least was aware of at least certain aspects of Himmler's policy of exterminating European Jews and that, on a limited number of occasions at least, he participated in an administrative capacity in the *ad hoc* coordination of their execution. On the basis of the documentary evidence that he was complicit in 'crimes against humanity', including being knowingly involved in the persecution and extermination of civilian populations, Wolff must be considered to have been particularly vulnerable to prosecution, if not in the first international trials as co-defendant with Kaltenbrunner (who he had outranked) then certainly before the Subsequent Proceedings at Nuremberg.

The implications of the findings of this initial project are clear. Given the incriminating nature of the documentary evidence then available, and given the likely inability of Wolff's defensive claims to withstand cross-examination, we must now address the question of how, given the evidence, it was possible for the Nuremberg prosecutors to allow Wolff to escape from being charged with 'crimes against humanity'. Of course, it is always necessary to be cautious about using the benefits of hindsight to criticise prosecutors and their links with influential intelligence officials seconded to the Nuremberg process without a full appreciation of the pressures and policy imperatives under which they were working at the time. Yet, had the prosecutors decided to

330 Höttl, *op cit*, 223.

charge Wolff, then, through active investigation, they could have surely expanded the nature and scope of incriminating evidence considerably. For example, some simple cross-referencing of documents and follow-up interrogations of incriminated individuals would have been sufficient to have placed Wolff in Minsk, which had become a killing centre for German Jews, precisely at the time when Himmler's party witnessed a grim demonstration of SS execution techniques there.[331]

The senior prosecutors re-assigned from OSS certainly had access to secretly taped CSDIC reports consisting of transcripts of Wolff's conversations with fellow detainees during the immediate post-war months in which he made it clear that, during the war, he was aware that Himmler had a bad conscience over the concentration camps atrocities.[332] Indeed, more than half of the documentary materials mentioned in the introduction as falling outside the scope of the present study because they had not formed part of the Nuremberg evidence were in fact *potentially available*. Therefore, the explanation of Wolff's non-prosecution cannot lie in either the paucity of documentary evidence, or the robust nature of Wolff's defensive strategies. We must identify other factors to explain this remarkable decision not to prosecute.

This conclusion opens up an agenda of questions addressed later in this book: was Wolff's non-prosecution influenced by the interventions of American intelligence and military officials, primarily Allen Dulles, involved in wartime capitulation negotiations codenamed Operation Sunrise?[333] Was Wolff rewarded by the Nuremberg prosecutors for his conditional form of cooperation with his interrogators, which included giving trial testimony in relation to his former colleagues with the Nazi leadership, to the point where he effectively 'worked his passage' to freedom? If it was the case that Wolff was of more assistance to the Nuremberg prosecutors as a cooperative informant and witness than as a defendant, especially following periods of apparent mental instability,[334] then can this pragmatic, utilitarian argument really be held to justify his non-prosecution in the second round of Nuremberg trials

331 NA, RG 238, PS 1138. 332 CSDIC Report, *op cit*, 12.

333 In February 1961, Gaevernitz cabled Dulles reporting with concern that Wolff's arrest had generated considerable publicity through an interview in a February 1961 edition of *Der Spiegel*, highlighting the role of Wolff and Dulles in the Sunrise Operation, which stated that 'negotiator Wolff was left unmolested' after the war 'as he had stipulated in his discussions with Dulles and returned to his profession'.

334 Wolff became prone to outbursts claiming he was being persecuted by Jewish demons, and was detained in an asylum during February 1947. Lang reports that he compared his conditions of solitary detention in a dark cell unfavourably to the Nazis' treatment of Jews: 'a Jew was killed in a gas chamber within a few seconds without him knowing or even suspecting anything. Myself and my comrades in the course of the past 21 months were left dying each night anew. That is by far more inhuman than the extermination applied to the Jews. And a lot of things have been exaggerated big time.' Lang, *op cit*, 308–9.

held after he had been thoroughly debriefed? What influence, if any, was played by geo-political factors, including the threat that, if prosecuted during the Cold War period, Wolff could make embarrassing claims regarding the anti-Soviet sub-text to the wartime capitulation negotiations with US intelligence? To what extent can these questions be answered by surveying the contents of recently declassified US intelligence files documenting the internally contested, yet repeated, interventions of CIA officials on behalf of other members of Wolff's senior SS group who had assisted Wolff in Operation Sunrise?[335]

335 In particular, the CIA 'Name Files' on Wolff's assistants Eugen Dollmann and Guido Zimmer: NA, RG 263 Boxes 5 and 8 respectively.

Chapter 3

The geo-political context of peace negotiations surrounding the OSS's Operation Sunrise

> In the abstract, geopolitics traditionally indicates the links and causal relationships between political power and geographic space; in concrete terms it is often seen as a body of thought assaying specific strategic prescriptions based on the relative importance of land power and sea power in world history . . . The geopolitical tradition had some consistent concerns, like the geopolitical correlates of power in world politics, the identification of international core areas, and the relationships between naval and terrestrial capabilities.
>
> (Oyvind Osterud)[1]

> Nevertheless, one cannot be sure that, at some level, Wolff may not have been given some inducements by agents of the O.S.S. . . . my experience of the workings of the occult services lead me to conclude that it would be wise to assume they were.
>
> (British Major General Terrence Airey, Chief of Intelligence for British Field Marshall Alexander)[2]

Introduction

This book is at least as much about the operation of specific geo-political factors within, and upon, the prosecution process within the Nuremberg trials as the trial process itself considered abstractly as an event within legal doctrine. How are we to define geo-political factors? As one of the two opening quotes suggests, geo-politics refers to the relationship between political power, widely defined, and zones of geographical space. Such space can extend, in some cases, beyond formal state borders to the exertion of zones of control and powerful influence over entire continents, such as that exerted

1 'The Uses and Abuses of Geopolitics', (1988) 2 *Journal of Peace Research* 191.

2 General Brian Robertson (HQ, Control Commission Germany, British Element (hereafter CCG(BE) Berlin) to William Strang (Secretary for State, Foreign Office, London), 4 September 1948: PRO, FO 371/70652.

until 1989 by the Soviet Union over subordinated Eastern European states.[3] During a wartime military alliance between two major powers (or potential superpowers) against a third major power, it is likely that considerations relating to comparative gains and losses in the future peace, a balance of power during a future post-war territorial 'carve up' amongst the military victors, will influence the conduct of the war itself, especially when military victory is almost assured. This was certainly the case with the Alliance against Nazi Germany and Japan between the Anglo-Americans, on the one hand, and the Soviet Union on the other. Indeed, the official policy of 'unconditional surrender' was, in part, designed to avoid suspicions that, for example, regional surrenders could be privately agreed with elements of the Nazi regime by, say, the Americans to benefit their specific geo-political interests at the expense of the Soviets, whether as a defensive or offensive measure. The official policy insisted that any surrender must be to the Allies as a whole, and without private negotiations over terms and conditions with any of the Allied powers. Hence, geo-political factors shaped the creation of this Allied policy, not least because it attempted to forestall attempts by the Nazis to break up this Alliance by playing one side against the other, possibly by exploiting fears of a communist dominated Eastern and Central Europe. On the Allied side, there were suspicions that Wolff's peace feelers were intended by the Nazi leadership to stir up mistrust between the Anglo-Americans and the Soviets. At this time the Soviets were, for geo-political reasons that Dulles appreciated,[4] naturally suspicious. There was the risk that, by allowing such divisions to emerge under the guise of peace contacts, the war itself (and its resulting casualties) could even be prolonged.[5]

Allen Dulles' role in Operation Sunrise bent, if not entirely violated, the geo-politically determined policy of unconditional surrender, which he came to strongly oppose.[6] The reasons for this were themselves geo-political in nature. One reason was the desire to forestall the advance by Red Army or Tito's communist partisans into parts of Central and Eastern Europe, not least Northern Italy and Austria, which had a particular strategic importance in post-war power politics between rival Western and Soviet dominated 'blocs'.[7]

3 C. S. Gray and G. R. Sloan, *Geopolitics, Geography, and Strategy* (Portland: Frank Cass, 1999).

4 These related to the strategic importance of the port of Trieste within any post-war geopolitical settlement. *Ibid.*

5 Cable 7589, Dulles to Washington, 24 March 1945: NA, RG 226, Entry 134 (speculating on whether Himmler was 'pulling the strings' behind apparently independent peace feelers from von Epp and Kaltenbrunner); Cable 575(9), Nicholson [Lemnitzer] and McNeely for SGS, undated; Cable, 640(9) MacNeely to Dulles, 14 April 1945: both at NA, RG 226, Entry 139, Box 60, Folder 554.

6 See N. Petersen, 'From Hitler's Doorstep' in Chalou, 1992, *op cit*, 276.

7 President Truman's memoir paints a more jaundiced view of the upshot of the Dulles-Wolff contacts. In *1945: Year of Decisions*, Truman notes that: 'Nothing ever came of these parleys [between Dulles and Wolff] except to make the Russians highly suspicious of our motives.

It makes sense, therefore, to analyse geo-political aspects of Operation Sunrise, as these provided the context in which promises of legal immunity for the Wolff group were originally made and later justified. Later, it will become clear that the British authorities were especially sensitive to any war crimes trial of Wolff. In particular, they were concerned that such a trial could give him a public forum to allege that Stalin was right to allege that, through Dulles' 'negotiations' with Wolff, the Anglo-Americans had violated the agreed policy of unconditional surrender. Such an exposure of wartime duplicity during the early phases of the Cold War, which the Western powers had angrily denied at the time, would of course have represented an ideological victory for the Soviet side of this growing conflict. This, in turn, could have been variously exploited, not least to add weight to propaganda claims regarding the West's recruitment of named Nazi war criminals as part of a wider anti-Soviet agenda.

The first section explores Dulles' reaction of various 'peace feelers' by senior SS officials, many of which sought explicit guarantees of legal immunity for war crimes in return for such cooperation. The fact that Dulles was willing to entertain some but not all of these proposals suggests that certain individuals, such as SS-RSHA Chief Ernst Kaltenbrunner, were so implicated in war criminality as to be deemed beyond the pale of such deals. By contrast, others proposals, such as Wolff, could be seen as falling the other side of this rather fuzzy line, particularly if there was no precondition for the terms and conditions, including any promises of legal immunity for war crimes, to be expressed in writing. Terms and conditions that were embodied in purely verbal agreements could of course be denied if the Soviets challenged them as violations of the agreed prohibition on regional, conditional surrenders. The second section describes the emergence, during a process of back and forth exchanges, of a series of agreements on proposed terms and conditions taking place against an undercurrent of geo-political tension with the Soviets. This undercurrent meant that these terms and conditions (and the process of negotiation through which they were proposed and modified) had to be misrepresented as something other than what they really were: clear attempts to negotiate a conditional surrender of German military and para-military forces in Northern Italy and hopefully beyond. Any fulsome

Molotov wrote to the Ambassador Harriman in Moscow demanding that the negotiations with the Germans be broken off. President Roosevelt cabled Stalin that the Russians were misinformed . . . This did not satisfy Stalin, who answered that the Germans had tricked the Allies and had profited by moving three divisions from the Italian front to the Russian front . . . It was not a good situation. Any break with the Russians at this time would have interfered with our advances into Germany . . . Wolff's approach to the Americans and British made them suspect that we were trying to get the German forces in the West to surrender to us while they still continued to fight on the Russian front. The Russians also appeared to be afraid that we would occupy all Germany and leave them on the other side of the Polish border.' (New York: Da Capo Press (reprint of 1955 original), 1988), 200–1.

interpretation of the meaning of at least some of these terms and conditions, the need for the process of negotiation to be misrepresented, and the sources of Soviet distrust all require some grasp of the geo-political context dimension.

Introducing specific contexts shaping Dulles' wartime role regarding SS peace feelers 1944–45

Between 1944 and 1945, Dulles' Bern Field Office was at the centre of numerous 'peace contacts' from various SS and other senior Nazis.[8] With the exception of Karl Wolff, a number of Nazi officials, including Nuremberg defendant and SS deputy leader Ernst Kaltenbrunner, had used intermediaries to seek explicit and written guarantees of legal immunity. They sought such guarantees in return for their cooperation with the OSS, and Allied authorities more generally, in bringing about the overthrow of Hitler, sometimes promising to redirect German forces towards the Eastern Front to stiffen resistance to the rapid advance of Soviet forces.

Dulles was charged with compiling lists of prominent Germans, divided into anti-Nazis, on 'white lists', and active Nazis, placed in 'black lists'. These distinctions informed Dulles' policy regarding how to respond during the closing months of the war to apparent peace feelers from SS and other senior Nazi officials, including Nuremberg defendant Ernst Kaltenbrunner.[9] Through Wilhelm Höttl, his senior subordinate, who was later recruited as an OSS agent despite Dulles previously noting his 'bad record',[10] Kaltenbrunner contacted Dulles and sought to play the 'Austrian card'.[11] The Bavarian Nazi

8 A. LeBor, *Hitler's Secret Bankers: The Myth of Swiss Neutrality During the Holocaust* (Secaucus, NJ: Carol Publishing Group, 1997), 213–14.

9 Cable 7959, Dulles to Glavin, 29 April 1945, reporting that: 'Kaltenbrunner, who is most powerful figure in this area, has taken over leadership in this capitulation move [from Höttl] and desires come to Swiss frontier to discuss matter.' Dulles describes Höttl as a: 'contact handled very discreetly through cut out [deniable intermediary]', *ibid.* See also Cable 6829, 12 March 1945, Dulles to Glavin, 12 March 1945: NA, RG 226, Entry 134 reporting on Kaltenbrunner's attempt to hijack Wolff's leadership of peace feelers to Dulles, and Cable 7037, 15 March 1945: NA, RG 226, Entry 134 in which Kaltenbrunner offered the release of prisoners and other concessions.

10 Cable 7959, Dulles to Glavin, 29 April 1945, *ibid*; Cable 8619, Dulles to Washington, 13 April 1945: NA, RG 226, Entry 134 (reporting that Höttl was prepared for his own reasons to defy Himmler and Kaltenbrunner by acting as an OSS double-agent (codenamed Alpberg reporting on military developments) sabotaging the alleged 'national redoubt' plans. On Dulles' view of Höttel's complicity and hence his need to try to 'save his own skin', plus details of his reports back to Dulles regarding the 'reduit' (mountain fortress), see Cable 9099, 21 April 1945: NA, RG 226, Entry 134.

11 Kaltenbrunner may have known that Dulles had already cultivated Austrian nationalists, such as Fritz Molden (codename K-28) as intermediaries to senior regional leaders including Hofer, and as both informants and double-agents: Cable 6477, Dulles to Washington (for Climax and Jolis), 7 March 1945: NA, RG 226, Entry 134.

leader von Epp adopted a similar strategy.[12] Many such officials sought explicit guarantees of future legal immunity to 'save their skins'[13] and to obtain related 'alibis' in return for their wartime cooperation with the OSS and the Allied authorities more generally.[14] Such contacts rapidly took on an anti-communist geo-political dimension, including defeating Stalin's threatened expansion to seize the important port of Trieste.[15]

Not surprisingly, Dulles exploited these contacts for intelligence-gathering purposes. However, certain Nuremberg defence lawyers and defendants attempted, for their own ends, to capitalise upon such contacts.[16] For example, Dulles had been forewarned that Kaltenbrunner was, as part of his defence case, seeking to capitalise upon his indirect wartime contacts with Dulles. This defendant was suggesting that, from at least 1943 onwards, he had being trying to negotiate an end of the war. One cable from the Nuremberg prosecutors noted:

> Defendant Kaltenbrunner calling Doctor Wilhelm Höttl . . . as witness to testify 'That Kaltenbrunner took steps to induce Himmler to release people from concentration camps, that since May 1943 Kaltenbrunner pursued a policy designed to bring about peace and that for this reason he established contact between the witness, Doctor Höttl, and Mr Dulles, the confidential representative of the late President Roosevelt, in order to work toward that end.' . . . Essential we have background data if contact did take place. Request Dulles be queried and fullest information, including dates, forwarded by earliest cable or airmail.[17]

12 On von Epp as the centre of a conservative and catholic faction based in Bavaria pressing for a peace deal, see Cable 7569, 23 March 1945 (asking whether despite Dulles' knowledge of his 'bad record' whether 'man like von Epp is beyond pale' as a negotiating partner): NA, RG 226, Entry 134; Cable 647, Dulles to Glavin, 9 April 1945: RG 226, Entry 139, Box 60, Folder 554; Cable 8759, 7 April 1945: NA, RG 226, Entry 134 (reporting that it was a 'good gamble' to come to terms with von Epp to accept his offer of turning against Hitler in Bavaria and sabotaging reduit efforts. See N. Petersen, 'From Hitler's Doorstep', in Chalou, 1992, *op cit*, 284.

13 'Kaltenbrunner is now attempting to save his skin.' *Ibid.* See also Cable 2487, Dulles to Washington, 26 December 1944: RG 226, Entry 134; Cable 7589, Dulles to Washington, 24 March 1945: NA, RG 226, Entry 134.

14 Dulles reacted negatively to von Epp approach. *Ibid.* The Kaltenbruner approach, brokered by Wilhelm Hötll, is discussed in the latter's memoirs, which are published in English as *The Secret Front: The Story of Nazi Political Espionage* (London: Weidenfeld & Nicholson, 1953).

15 Cable 6647, Dulles to Washington via Paris, 8 March 1945: NA, RG 226, Entry 134; Cable 7589, Dulles to Washington, 24 March 1945, and Cable 710, Dulles to Caserta, 18 April 1945: NA, RG 226, Entry 134.

16 'Intermediate Interrogation Report (IIR), Prisoner: O-Gruf Kaltenbrunner, Ernst' (Secret), Headquarters 12th Army Group Interrogation Center, 28 June 1945: Cornell Collection, Subdivision 38.

17 Cable, SSU, 5 March 1946, Office of US Chief of Counsel Nuremberg Germany, to Griggs Washington: Project: 857146: NA, RG 226, Entry 146, Box 47.

At the time of the Nuremberg trials, this tactic seriously embarrassed Dulles. Dulles' sensitivity is, for example, clear from a letter he wrote to the US chief Nuremberg prosecutor Justice Jackson to the effect that, through a sworn affidavit, he wanted to set the record straight regarding:

> [A] false and misleading statement by [Ernst] Kaltenbrunner's counsel, in which he refers to me [March 3 1946 reported the following day]. It is inevitable, in view of the nature of my work in Switzerland, that defendants' counsel will from time to time try to drag my name into the proceedings, and I shall naturally do what I can to prevent any improper use being made of my name by the defense.[18]

Dulles has also been strongly criticised for intervening within the Nuremberg trial and related processes for the benefit of Karl Wolff who escaped prosecution at both rounds of the Nuremberg trials. As already noted, this evasion was despite being implicated, as Himmler's effective co-deputy, in various war crimes.[19] Not surprisingly, Dulles' alleged interventions on behalf of Wolff, the most senior SS official to survive the war and remain at liberty in the immediate post-war period, has prompted considerable controversy, including polemical writing from both left- and right-wing critics.[20] The left-wing contributions harmonised with aspects at least of the East German propaganda campaign. This had been developed in conjunction with this former state's intelligence service, and emphasised substantial continuities in personnel between the Nazi regime and later post-war West Germany, which contradicted its claims to have been rebuilt as a true democracy unlike the communist controlled East Germany. The central allegation is that the non-prosecution of Wolff represented a major example of the granting of *de facto* legal immunity as a reward for cooperation with senior intelligence officials.[21] This allegation, which both refers to geo-politically determined actions and itself contributes to strategies of contestation of power, has even featured within a recent 'Holocaust denial' defamation trial.[22]

Allegedly, Dulles' behind-the-scenes interventions driven by an anti-Soviet

18 Dulles (Wall Street, New York) to Justice Jackson, 6 March 1946: Jackson Papers, Library of Congress, Washington DC, Box 102.

19 B. Hersh, *The Old Boys: The American Elite and the Origins of the CIA* (New York: Charles Shribner's Sons, 1992), 125–33.

20 C. Simpson, *The Splendid Blond Beast: Money, Law and Genocide in the Twentieth Century* (Maine Monroe: Common Courage Press, 1995), 13, 199, 201–5, 236–42; Hersh, *op cit*, 125–33; and the highly polemical M. Aarons and J. Loftus, *The Secret War Against the Jews* (New York: St Martin's Press, 1994), 71–80.

21 Salter, 2002, *op cit*; Bryan and Salter, 2002, *op cit*.

22 This was *Irving v Penguin Books*, and involved an exhange between Irving and Professor Evans: P-32 Day 19: http://www.david-irving.de/docs/proc/irving-day19.pdf.

agenda, also protected Wolff's middle-ranking SS staff based in Northern Italy, including Guido Zimmer, Eugen Dollmann, SS-Standartenführer Eugen Wenner (Wolff's adjutant) and, possibly, SS-Standartenführer Walter Rauff (who helped design the infamous Black Raven gas wagons).[23] There are some indications that OSS's James Angleton (later head of CIA counter-intelligence) and Dulles were involved in securing the services of Rauff as an informant once he was released by his CIC interrogators to OSS Unit S Force, Verona.[24] As already noted, each of these SS officials were vulnerable to custodial punishment following their prosecution either for war crimes, or as 'active Nazis' within Allied de-Nazification tribunal hearings.[25]

Dulles' critics rely upon statements within recently declassified documentation revealing that his assistants and subordinates within US intelligence, acting in conjunction with various intermediaries such as Max Husmann, made a series of interventions on behalf of the Wolff group to secure *de facto* immunity from prosecution.[26] These interventions allegedly exploited the fact that the former Director of the OSS, General William Donovan, had recently been appointed Deputy Head Prosecutor within the dominant American Nuremberg prosecution agency, the Office of Chief of Counsel, headed by Justice Jackson.[27] This gave Dulles an entry point to influence prosecution decisions in favour of his own geo-political agenda, which increasingly took on an anti-communist dimension. Critics of Dulles also highlight how his senior aide, Gero von Gaevernitz, also provided strong personal testimony on Wolff's behalf, which helped him secure only a token conviction in a later de-Nazification trial held by the British in 1949, which meant he was the highest ranking officer in the SS to remain at large. Dulles' critics attribute the fact that Wolff received only a token sentence, which allowed his release within weeks of conviction, largely to the impact of these direct and indirect interventions prompted by geo-political factors.[28]

A key allegation against Dulles is that Wolff's protection stemmed from an unwritten agreement which formed an integral part of OSS's Operation

23 See R. Winks, *Cloak and Gown* (New York: Morrow, 1987), 350; Aarons and Loftus, 1991, *op cit*, 339, n. 1.

24 R. Winks, 1987, *op cit*, 350; Aarons and Loftus, 1991, *op cit*, 339, n. 1; Simpson, 1998, *op cit*, 13.

25 See Simpson, 1995, *op cit*, 12–13, 20–2, 55–6, 121–4, 156–7, 189–91, 199–205, 217–19, 240–4, 267, 272–4, 276; and Aarons and Loftus, *The Secret War Against the Jews* (New York: St Martin's Press, 1994), 21–2, 38–41, 46, 55–92, 100–2, 109–12, 133–44, 151–2, 217–25, 230, 239–40, 252.

26 Simpson, 1995, *op cit*, 13.

27 M. Salter and M. Eastwood, 'Negotiating Nolle Prosequi at Nuremberg: The Case of Captain Zimmer', (2005) 3 *Journal of International Criminal Justice* 649–65.

28 Hersh, *op cit*, 135.

Sunrise. This operation was the secretly organised military capitulation Wolff negotiated with Dulles that resulted in the early surrender of over one million regular, SS and fascist militia forces at the end of April 1945.[29] For good reasons, the Allied authorities remained suspicious of what lay behind Wolff's approach, fearing that it could form part of the Nazi leadership's desperate attempt to divide the Soviets from the Anglo-Americans, perhaps in pursuit of a new anti-Communist alliance that could remove the threat of the dissolution of Germany as a separate state. In this sense, geo-political questions included the issue of whether Central Europe was to be controlled by the capitalist West or the socialist East. To understand this allegation requires us first to analyse the context of the wider pattern of negotiations which, after many delays, culminated in this surrender process.

Negotiating the conditions of an 'unconditional' surrender

This section will address the context of negotiating terms and conditions for an early surrender which culminated in a series of agreed terms and conditions, including a promise of legal immunity. The latter, which is clearly the most important aspect for present purposes, will be discussed more fully in the next section.

In December 1944, President Roosevelt firmly rejected General Donovan's request to be allowed to offer immunity deals to specific Nazis in return for their cooperation in separate peace deals with the Anglo-Americans.[30] At the start of 1945, Dulles had been told that OSS negotiations with 'any officials of the German government'[31] were strictly prohibited, not least because they could lead to serious internal conflicts with the Soviets. Those immediately involved in Sunrise had no objection to Soviet participation as observers and made positive suggestions along these lines which were rejected by their superiors.[32] Indeed, Dulles received permission to meet with Wolff's

29 This occurred a few days before the final surrender by the remainder of German forces. See B. F. Smith and E. Agarossi, *Operation Sunrise: The Secret Surrender* (New York: Basic Books, 1979), ch. 7.

30 'Memos for the Secretary', 'Memos for the President', in Edward Stettinius Papers, University of Virginia, US, Box 733.

31 Cable 29479, 31 January 1945, Glavin to Dulles and Donovan: Donovan Files, Churchill College, Cambridge (hereafter CCC), Box 12, Reel 76.

32 Cable 208, Sunrise, 14 March 1945, Dulles to Washington: NA, RG 226, Entry 139, Box 60, Folder 554; Cable 3 'Sunrise,' Lemnitzer to SGS, 18 March; Cable 633(9) Nicholson [Lemnitzer] to Dulles, 13 April; Cable 640(9) MacNeely to Dulles, 14 April 1945: all at NA, RG 226, Entry 139, Box 60, Folder 554. On the acrimony at leadership level generated by Dulles' action between the Anglo-Americans and the Soviets, see J. Persico, *Roosevelt's Secret War* (Westminster, MD: Random House, 2001), 425–9; Roosevelt-Stalin telegrams March–April 1945, Franklin D. Roosevelt Library, Map Room Files, Box 28; I. Bishop,

representatives Eugen Dollmann[33] and Guido Zimmer[34] on 8 March 1945 only if he could do so 'without entering [into] any negotiations or without promising any further talks' in order to 'secure what information' he could.[35] In other words, recognising that 'negotiations' (in the normal sense of this term as involving a process of haggling over proposed terms and conditions with a view to arriving at a compromise agreement) remained strictly prohibited, Dulles was later forced to claim that these contacts were no more than intelligence-gathering exercises, with any implicit incentive for the Nazi partners acting as little more than bait in a carefully prepared trap.

Early internal OSS communications between Dulles and Washington emphasised that Dulles was primarily interested in securing promises of military capitulation that: 'bear upon [the] future disposition of German forces in north Italy'. He claimed that his contacts would involve a minimum possible number of verbal (and hence 'deniable')[36] terms and implicit understandings as to the future treatment of these Nazis, simply to act as false incentives, as distinct from binding commitments.[37] Furthermore, it became clear that, during the last year of the war, Wolff had been 'shopping around' for the best possible 'deal' from British and other secret services.[38] That is: 'making fairly

FDR's Last Year (New York: Morrow, 1974), 505 ff. More generally, see T. Fleming, *The New Dealers' War* (New York: Basic Books, 2001).

33 Dollmann was consistently involved with Sunrise: see Cable 647, Dulles to Glavin, 9 April 1945: NA, RG 226, Entry 139, Box 60, Folder 554.

34 Captain Zimmer was described as Wolff's 'aide who is a party to critic's [Wolff's] plan and who travels between Chiasso frontier and Milan'. For this and additional details on Zimmer's role in maintaining contact with Dulles, see Cable 574, Nicholson [Lemnitzer] to SGS, AFHQ, 26 March 1945: Cable 540(9), 'Sunrise', Lemnitzer to SGS, 20 March 1945: NA, RG 226, Entry 139, Box 60, Folder 554.

35 Cable 6716, Glavin to Dulles, 8 March 1945: CCC, Box 12, Reel 76. Glavin continued: 'AFHQ considers reliability of parties and verification of who they represent as important items. Information on Kesselring-Himmler relationship also desired.' Dulles had reported early contacts with Dollmann and Zimmer as surprising and emerging through Swiss and Italian intermediaries (Husmann and Parrili) and colleagues within Swiss intelligence (Max Waibal): Cable 6329, 5 March 1945: NA, RG 226, Entry 134. He reported Wolff's arrival at Lugano, Switzerland as being 'allegedly prepared to talk definitely' recapitulation: Cable 1146, 8 March 1945: NA, RG 226, Entry 134.

36 Cable 662, Dulles to Nicholson [Lemnitzer], 10 April 1945; Cable 6719 Dulles to Nicholson [Lemnitzer], 12 April 1945: both at NA, RG 226, Entry 139, Box 60, Folder 554: the former noting: 'they have never received anything in writing from us'; whilst in the latter Dulles reassures his superiors that 'nothing in writing has been or will be given'.

37 Cable 6342, 5 March 1945, Dulles to Washington. Dulles also reported that Paul Blum did not give his or any OSS associates' name to the German party but that: 'Presumably, however, intermediaries told Dollmann that he was associated with me.' NA, RG 226, Entry 139, Box 60, Folder 554.

38 Cable 693(9) 679 to Dulles or Gamble, 15 April 1945, reported that the British SOE were intervening with Wolff citing Dulles name: NA, RG 226, Entry 139, Box 60, Folder 554.

free contacts with such Allied secret agencies with which he could get in touch'.[39]

As the process of 'negotiation' intensified during March and early April 1945, Dulles emphasised in all official communications, even those internal to the OSS, that Wolff's proposed regional surrender would indeed *appear* 'unconditional'.[40] Furthermore, he claimed that this capitulation could begin a process culminating in a total military collapse of the Axis forces, and thereby save many thousand Allied lives.[41] In reporting back to OSS-Washington, Dulles had every reason to be cautious in how he described his 'negotiations'. He was a well-known opponent of the official policy of strictly 'unconditional surrender', agreed in 1943 at the Allied Summit meeting in Casablanca, and this may have made him doubly cautious in such communications.[42] For example, when first reporting on his initial contacts with Wolff's subordinates,[43] and then transmitting Wolff's terms to his superiors, Dulles was anxious to reinterpret such conditions as 'some palliative, not perhaps of substance as concerns the unconditional character of the surrender but rather as regards the military status of those surrendering'.[44] After their initial meetings in mid-March and early April 1945, Dulles emphasised that he had made no commitments to Wolff and had 'engaged in no negotiations, merely listened to his presentation and stated, with no refutation Wolff's part, that unconditional surrender only possible course'.[45] Dulles took pains to ridicule the idea that 'at this stage, and with Germans thoroughly beaten, we would stoop to negotiations is in itself ludicrous'.[46] He needed to do this because the military and OSS leadership doubted whether Dulles' 'negotiations' fully conformed to the agreed unconditional surrender policy.[47] This concern and sensitivity became intensified following Stalin's vehement objections to Dulles' secret negotiations, after he had presumably discovered

39 Cable 640(9), MacNeely to Dulles, 14 April 1945: NA, RG 226, Entry 139, Box 60, Folder 554.

40 Cable 6342, Dulles to Washington, 5 March 1945 (emphasising the 'negotiations' encouraged by Swiss intelligence officials).

41 Cable 7419, Dulles to Caserta, 22 April 1945: NA, RG 226, Entry 134, reporting that 'immediate unconditional surrender' was 'the only objective we had in mind'.

42 N. Petersen, *From Hitler's Doorstep: The Wartime Intelligence Reports of Allen Dulles* (Pennsylvania: Pennsylvania State University Press, 1996), 10–11, 17; Telegram 1023, Dulles to Washington, 9 November 1943: NA, RG 226, Entry 134.

43 Cable 6329, 5 March 1945: NA, RG 226, Entry 134: 'If Dollmann returns I shall arrange to ascertain what he has to say. If this should be of a nature to facilitate unconditional surrender of German forces [in] North Italy, it might be desirable to arrange that Military contact takes place on Swiss side of frontier.'

44 Cable 647, Dulles to Glavin, 9 April 1945: NA, RG 226, Entry 139, Box 60, Folder 554.

45 *Ibid.*

46 Cable 6689, Dulles to Caserta, 11 April 1945: NA, RG 226, Entry 134.

47 Cable 9419, 27 April 1945 referring to Donovan's OUT 77855, in which he had been told to comply in a strict and literal way to the instructions of the Allied Joint Chiefs of Staff's decision to resume Sunrise without any negotiations or 'conferences' between OSS and Wolff.

details through the NKGB's (Soviet intelligence) penetration of the OSS and its ciphers. These objections had culminated in the temporary cancellation of Sunrise.[48]

A close analysis of recently declassified OSS files recording the exchange of promises between Dulles and Wolff rebuts Dulles' official designations of them as 'confidence building measures' or signs of 'good faith', or Wolff's 'ability to demonstrate authority'.[49] This record contradicts Dulles' claim that these were merely preliminary contacts taking place *prior to* a 'negotiation stage' that was supposed to culminate in a strictly *unconditional* form of surrender.[50] Instead, the following terms and conditions emerged during the pre-surrender negotiations, each of which will now be discussed in turn:[51] (a) safe passage; (b) prisoner exchange; (c) the Wolff group to break with the Nazi leadership; (d) the safeguarding of unique Italian artworks and public utilities; (e) the Wolff group to receive privileged treatment including legal impunity. This last condition is, for present purposes, the most important and will be discussed in greater detail in the next section.

A major condition of their agreement was the promise by the Americans to use their sponsorship and partial control of Italian partisan forces, partly handled through the intermediary of the Catholic Church in Italy,[52] to ensure that German forces could safely retreat and surrender without military harassment from these resistance forces. In return, Wolff promised 'discontinuing active warfare against Italian partisans, merely keeping up necessary pretence pending the execution of the plan'.[53] In return, the partisan forces would have to cease all acts of sabotage and aggression to the German armed forces, and agree to allow Wolff and the Germans to withdraw from

48 Cable 9119, Dulles to Washington, 21 April 1945: NA, RG 226, Entry 134.

49 These were the terms in which Dulles reinterpreted the exchange of Parri: Cable 1146, Dulles to Glavin, 8 March 1945: NA, RG 226, Entry 134.

50 Cable 211, 'Sunrise' 15 March 1945: NA, RG 226, Entry 139, Box 60, Folder 554. Dulles even promised that the 'potentialities of these developments so far-reaching . . . if Wolff [is] really working with Kesselring, these two might pull off unconditional surrender . . .': Cable 1146, Dulles to Glavin, 8 March 1945: NA, RG 226, Entry 134.

51 These are summarised in Parilli's memo of a meeting with Wolff, Glazier, Vietinghoff and Roettieger regarding the terms of agreement protecting prisoners, preventing destruction, limiting action against partisans and passing over representatives: RG 226, Entry 139, Box 60, Folder 553, 10–11.

52 The Church of course had its own interests in avoiding the militantly atheistic and secular consequences of any communist takeover of Italy.

53 Cable 6689, Dulles to Glavin, 9 March 1945: NA, RG 226, Entry 134; Cable 648, Dulles to Glavin for Nicholson [Lemnitzer], 9 April 1945: NA, RG 226, Entry 139, Box 60, Folder 554; Cable 6689, Dulles to Glavin, Donovan and Forgan, 9 March 1945: NA, RG 226, Entry 90, File 64; Smith and Agarossi, *op cit*, 82; Dulles, 1966, *op cit*, 99. Dulles had previously reported that Wolff's earlier efforts to secure a partial 'armistice for Piedmont' in October 1944 had been rejected, prompting threats of an 'immediate clean up': Telegram 10, Dulles to Washington, 29 October 1945: NA, RG 226, Entry 134.

Italy without attack.[54] Wolff had nearly been killed when Allied aircraft strafed his car with bullets,[55] and sought and received a commitment that his SS base at Bolzano would be exempted from Allied attack during the Sunrise negotiations.[56] This condition of the Dulles/Wolff bargain was directly tested, and honoured by the OSS side, after OSS officials had to rescue Wolff, who had came under direct personal threat from partisan forces.[57]

The second condition agreed between Dulles and Wolff related to the *exchange of prisoners and hostages*.[58] A number of Nazi groups approached Dulles claiming to have intervened for humanitarian reasons to safeguard prisoners from imminent, or continuing, persecution at the hands of the SS, and offering to intensify such interventions in return for various concessions.[59] One part of this deal was that Wolff would release Ferruccio Parri (the Italian partisan leader),[60] two Allied agents (Antonio Usmiani, a former OSS agent who ran a spy network in Milan),[61] and another from the British SOE (Tucker/Mullaby).[62] In addition, Wolff would free an unnamed 'radio man' and a priest.[63] The OSS had specifically requested the release of these prisoners[64] as 'earnest of ability [to] produce',[65] and as an important 'contribution for the continuation of the talks in the amicable spirit in which they

54 NA, RG 226, Entry 190C, Box 9, File Dulles Files – Sunrise Reports, 4–5; and RG 226, Entry 190C, Box 8, Dulles Files 10; Dulles, 1966, *op cit*, 47.

55 Cable 211, 'Sunrise' 15 March 1945: NA, RG 226, Entry 139, Box 60, Folder 554.

56 Cable 773(9), Dulles to Glavin, 27 April 1945: NA, RG 226, Entry 139, Box 60, Folder 554.

57 NA, RG 226, Entry 190C, Box 9, Dulles Files – Sunrise Reports, 11; NA, RG 226, Entry 190C, Box 8, Dulles Files , 15.

58 Cable 648, Dulles to Glavin for Nicholson [Lemnitzer], 9 April 1945: NA, RG 226, Entry 139, Box 60, Folder 554.

59 *Ibid.*

60 Cable 6679, Dulles to Glavin, 9 March 1945: NA, RG 226, Entry 134.

61 See Cable 6709, Dulles to Glavin, 9 March 1945: NA, RG 226, Entry 134; also 'Sunrise Reports', RG 226, Entry 110, Box 2, File 15, 2 – reporting on the dilemmas and logistical difficulties associated with this exchange, including the need to make Parri's release appear to be a relatively uncontentious exchange in order to provide internal cover for Wolff.

62 Wolff exchanged prisoners Parri and Major Usmani for German generals: NA, RG 226, Entry 190C, Box 8, Dulles Files, 10; NA, RG 226, Entry 110, Box 2, File 15, 2 regarding the details of the efforts to secure Parri's release and that of British agent 'Ducker'. Later memorandum confirmed that the exchange of Parri had taken place outside of normal channels of prisoner exchange of comparable ranks: Cable 588, Nicholson [Lemnitzer] and McNeely to SGS, 29 March 1945: NA, RG 226, Entry 139, Box 60, Folder 554.

63 Cable 211, 'Sunrise', 15 March 1945: NA, RG 226, Entry 139, Box 60, Folder 554.

64 This condition was agreed when Wolff's representatives Dollman, Zimmer, and Parilli met for a preliminary meeting with one of Dulles' officials: Sunrise Report, NA, RG 226, Entry 190C, Box 9, Dulles Files, 6. The Americans would later support Parri as a post-war political leader and prime minister of Italy. He had been a leader of one of the Italian partisan groups, which, although largely socialist, was not directly subordinated to the communists.

65 Cable 6342, 5 March 1945, Dulles to Washington: NA, RG 226, Entry 134.

were then proceeding'.[66] Dulles claimed Parri (who was soon to become the first post-war Italian Prime Minister) and the other prisoner were 'delivered to me in Zurich unconditionally and even prior to any indication that I would see Wolff'.[67] There are indications that, although a prisoner, Parri had been in contact with Zimmer.[68] Yet, for reasons already discussed, Dulles needed to gloss over the fact that, in return, Wolff had insisted on prisoner releases from the Allies, including Hitler's favourite adjutant Wuensche. Dulles' claims that Wolff had provided an unconditional sign of good faith and institutional authority meant that he had to reinterpret his side of this bargain as no more than providing Wolff with a 'cover' for his supposedly 'unconditional' release of the Allied hostages.[69] Wolff was later to try to capitalise on the release of Parri in his immediate post-war contacts with the Allied authorities.[70]

In addition, Wolff controlled a detention camp at Pragser Wildsee (in the Dobbiaco region) that contained 160 prominent hostages, including relatives of Churchill and the Soviet Foreign Minister, Molotov,[71] and Wolff's promise to secure their personal safety also became part of the overall deal with Dulles. Indeed, following the meeting on 8 March 1945, Wolff agreed to a number of wider-ranging OSS 'conditions' involving:

2. releasing to Switzerland several hundred Jews interned at Bolzano . . .
3. assuming full responsibility for the safety and good treatment of 350 British and American prisoners at Mantua, of whom 150 are in the hospital and 200 on the southern outskirts: Wolff claims that these are all the British-American prisoners [which are] held in North Italy . . .
4. . . . releasing to Switzerland Sogno Franci, a well-known Italian patriot working with CLNAI and the British: the release is particularly desired by Parri.

66 Cable 6329, 5 March 1945: NA, RG 226, Entry 134; Sunrise Report: NA, RG 226, Entry 109, Box 40, tab 3, Project 877190. The report informs us that: 'a slip of paper was handed to Source [Dollmann] bearing the name PARRI: it was explained that it was Mr. Dulles' urgent desire to have this man released from prison in Milan as soon as possible and brought to Switzerland'. Dulles, 1966, *op cit*, 77 noted that the slip of paper given to Blum had the names of two prisoners on it, not only Parri but a Major Usmiani also. Major Usmiani ran one of the OSS Secret Intelligence Branch chains in Milan, where he had been imprisoned. See Cable 6864, Dulles to Caserta, Glavin and Donovan, 9 March 1945: CCC, Box 12, Reel 76.

67 Cable 6709, Dulles to Glavin, 9 March 1945: NA, RG 226, Entry 134.

68 Zimmer Notebooks, op cit, 90/ref. 99, para. 341, and *ibid*, ref. 18/note 1.

69 Cable 6829, Dulles to Glavin, 12 March 1945: NA, RG 226, Entry 134; Cable 648, Dulles to Glavin for Nicholson [Lemnitzer], 9 April 1945: NA, RG 226, Entry 139, Box 60, Folder 554.

70 Livermore to Glavin and Dulles, 8 May 1945: NA, RG 226, Entry 139, Box 60, Folder 555.

71 Cable 43, Wolff to Alexander via Wally, 4 May 1945: NA, RG 226, Entry 139, Box 60, Folder 555.

5. facilitating as much as possible the return to North Italy of Italian officers presently held in Germany who might be useful in the post-hostilities period.[72]

No doubt for his own reasons, Wolff chose to honour his side of these agreements, often through direct personal interventions and orders to subordinates.[73]

Dulles' claim that the release of Parri, and other prisoners, was strictly and entirely 'unconditional', does not withstand close examination. For example, Dulles was deceived into treating Baron Luigi Parilli as a neutral intermediary and honest broker.[74] Yet Parilli, an Italian industrialist, was being blackmailed by Zimmer, and hence in a state of being 'bound hand and foot' to him,[75] but concealed this fact from Dulles who was therefore deceived into treating him as an neutral intermediary and honest broker.[76] Parilli asked Dulles to try to find a high-ranking German prisoner held by the Allies who could be released to use as an alibi for releasing Parri and Usmiani.[77] Dulles continued to treat Parilli as his trusted intermediary even when he endorsed Wolff's ability and willingness to 'deliver north Italy on a silver platter'.[78] In addition, OSS Berne had made it clear to the Wolff group that their *very access to Dulles* depended upon them complying with Dulles' request for the prisoner release. Whilst still insisting that Parri had been released

72 Cable 6689, 9 March 1945, Dulles to Glavin, Donovan and Forgan: NA, RG 226, Entry 134 also Entry 90, File 64; Cable 9169, Dulles to London, 3 April 1945: NA, RG 226, Entry 134 (forcefully reminding Wolff of these undertakings). Smith and Agarossi, *op cit*, 82; Dulles, 1966, *op cit*, 99; Cable 647, Dulles to Glavin, 9 April 1945: NA, RG 226, Entry 139, Box 60, Folder 554.

73 On 8 March 1945, Max Waibel, from Swiss intelligence, had called Dulles' senior assistant von Gaevernitz and asked him to inform Dulles that the two prisoners, Parri and Usmiani, had been released: Cable 6709, Dulles to Glavin, Donovan and Forgan, 9 March 1945: NA, RG 226, Entry 134.

74 See Cable 647, Dulles to Glavin, 9 April 1945; Cable 662, Dulles to Nicholson [Lemnitzer], 10 April 1945: NA, RG 226, Entry 139, Box 60, Folder 554, noting Parilli: 'took notes in own handwriting'.

75 Parilli was vulnerable because he had been forced to assist the Italian Partisans with foodstuffs: Zimmer Notebooks, 90/ref. 99, para. 313.

76 Cable 9119, Dulles to Washington, 21 April 1945: NA, RG 226, Entry 134 (mis-describing Parilli as 'anti-fascist Italian intermediary'). On the blackmail efforts, see Zimmer Notebooks, 76/ref. 79, para. 265, CIA Name File, Guido Zimmer: NA, RG 263.

77 Cable, Dulles to Glavin, Information for Donovan, Forgan, Armour, 12 March 1945: NA, RG 226, Entry 134: 'For Forgan: Please ascertain location Wuensche. Advise whether he USA PW and whether he could be made available and how soon . . . Wolff is having some difficulty explaining to underlings the disappearance of Parri and might wish to dress him up as an exchange. If so, Wuensche, if available and you consider likely to be trustworthy, could be used to kill two birds with one stone.'

78 Cable 647, Dulles to Glavin, 9 April 1945: NA, RG 226, Entry 139, Box 60, Folder 554.

'unconditionally', Dulles confirmed this reciprocal element of the bargain to Washington through a cable of 9 March 1945:

> Parri was delivered to me in Zurich unconditionally and even prior any indication I would see Wolff. Saw him last night in good health. Does not know how released and important this be kept secret. Purpose hint that this was an exchange when his presence here becomes known . . . Wolff apparently controls all police and border forces on entire Swiss Italian Frontier and believe we now have means of quick contact with top German personalities north Italy.[79]

Furthermore, by insisting that Wolff had immediately to release Parri, 'his most important hostage',[80] knowing that this would cause the SS general real difficulties with Mussolini and the Nazi leadership, Dulles was drawing the Wolff group further into adopting an oppositional stance, another part of their overall bargain.

Dulles' claim that Wolff's release of Parri and other prisoners was unconditional is highly debatable, since it represented one of a number of clearly interrelated exchanges of promise between the two sides, many of which opened up further bargaining opportunities. Indeed, Dulles had demanded the release of Parri and Usmiani as the condition for Wolff gaining the access he desired to high Allied military authority for contact to be made in neutral Switzerland.

A third element of their overall bargain was Wolff agreeing to Dulles' request that he 'act alone' if need be.[81] This meant Wolff agreeing to surrender his extensive SS and associated para-military forces independently of not only Himmler and Hitler but also German Army leaders.[82] Dulles even expected Wolff to reveal the full details of his forces,[83] their planned deployment and capacity to temporarily resist other Germans military forces prior to the capitulation, 'if principal army commanders do not cooperate', that is, to kill their German comrades.[84] The fact that Italy had become virtually cut

79 Cable 6679, London to OSS, 9 March 1945, NA, RG 226, Entry 134.

80 Cable 6864, Dulles to Caserta, Glavin and Donovan, 9 March 1945: CCC, Box 12, Reel 76; Dulles, 1966, *op cit*, 77; Smith and Agarossi, *op cit*, 73; Grose, 1994, *op cit*, 227.

81 Cable 211, 'Sunrise' 15 March 1945: NA, RG 226, Entry 139, Box 60, Folder 554.

82 Sunrise Report: NA, RG 226, Entry 190C, Box 8, Dulles Files, 15: reporting that Wolff stated he will refuse orders from Himmler to stop dealings with the OSS. See also Cable 495(9), Sunrise, Dulles to Glavin, 12 March 1945 (pressing Wolff on his reaction if he is ordered to return to Berlin, and asking what areas could his SS forces control temporarily in the event of a capitulation unsupported); Cable 693(9), 679 to Dulles/Gamble, 15 April 1945: all at NA, RG 226, Entry 139, Box 60, Folder 554.

83 Cable 7329, Dulles to Washington, 20 March 1945: NA, RG 226, Entry 134.

84 Cable 6969, Dulles to Paris, 12 March 1945: NA, RG 226, Entry 134.

off from Germany meant that 'Hitler and Himmler would be powerless to take effective counter measures' or reprisals against his capitulation.[85]

Allied officials, including Dulles,[86] were not initially convinced that Wolff was acting independently or, despite his denials, that 'the risks he would otherwise be taking indicate that the plot might even go as high as Himmler'.[87] Dulles, however, soon became convinced that Wolff was in fact acting in good faith.

When acting independently, Dulles expected Wolff to try to 'redouble precautions against premature disclosures' and take into account not only the German leadership, particularly Himmler, but also demands for explanation from Mussolini, the Italian dictator. Mussolini rightly suspected he was being excluded from negotiations relating to the fate of Italy.[88] The condition Dulles' negotiated was that Wolff's group would, in effect, take instructions from Dulles by actively negotiating on behalf of the Allies with Generalfeldmarschall Albert Kesselring,[89] and other German military leaders.[90] In this way, Wolff agreed to betray the Nazi and Italian leadership to the Allies.[91] This agreement also meant Wolff had to defy Hitler's official policies and military orders, and even report on the physical whereabouts of Mussolini, Himmler and Hitler, which of course meant that they became vulnerable to

85 Cable 6689, Dulles to Glavin, 9 March 1945: NA, RG 226, Entry 134.

86 Dulles interpreted early peace feelers from Neurath as driven by Himmler, as having 'a special mission from Himmler', with Wolff acting as more than Himmler's 'subordinate' and intermediary: Cable 1757, Dulles to Washington, 5 December 1944: NA, RG 226, Entry 134. Dulles' suspicions persisted even after initial contacts in early March 1945 but then evaporated: Cable 1146, Dulles to Glavin, 8 March 1945: NA, RG 226, Entry 134 (asking: 'Question is how much does Himmler known about this [contact by Wolff].') See also Cable 6679, Dulles to Glavin, 9 March 1945: NA, RG 226, Entry 134, in which Dulles claimed: 'Wolff claims Himmler unaware of his activities. This may or may not be correct.' *Ibid.*

87 Cable 588, Nicholson [Lemnitzer] and McNeely to SGS, 29 March 1945: NA, RG 226, Entry 139, Box 60, Folder 554.

88 Cable 647, Dulles to Glavin, 9 April 1945: NA, RG 226, Entry 139, Box 60, Folder 554.

89 Cable 6679, Dulles to Glavin, 9 March 1945: NA, RG 226, Entry 134 (reporting Wolff's agreement to proceed 'immediately to Kesselring to endeavour [to] sell program to him').

90 Cable 747(9), Dulles to Glavin, 23 April 1945; Cable 778(9), Dulles to Glavin, 27 April 1945; Cable 575(9), Nicholson [Lemnitzer] and McNeely for SGS, undated, all at NA, RG 226, Entry 139, Box 60, Folder 554. Through assorted 15,000 German soldiers, 20,000 Cossacks and other irregulars Russian forces, 10,000 Serb, 10,000 Slovenes, 5,000 Czechs, Indian Legion and 100,000 Italian fascists, including militia, Black Shirts and 'X' Mas, 10,000 SS, and 55,000 German administrative troops. Cable 7329, Dulles to Donovan and Forgan, 20 March 1945: NA, RG 226, Entry 134; Cable 538, 'Sunrise', Airey to SGS, no date: NA, RG 226, Entry 139, Box 60, Folder 554. Wolff controlled the 'rear areas' located behind the front lines, whilst Kesselring was surrounded by SS officials loyal to Himmler not Wolff: Cable 610, undated, Dulles to Caserta: NA, RG 226, Entry 139, Box 60, Folder 554. In fact, Vietinghoff was to take over from Kesselring, and would, according to Wolff, be harder to win over to surrender idea.

91 Wolff reported to Dulles on Mussolini's current mental state, influences and orientation: Cable 538, 'Sunrise', Airey to SGS, AFHQ no date: NA, RG 226, Entry 139, Box 60, Folder 554.

assassination.[92] This term of the Wolff–Dulles bargain clearly overlapped with related terms and conditions regarding Wolff's willingness to defy any orders to engage in a scorched-earth policy, which will be discussed in more detail later.[93] Wolff accepted Dulles' terms and, in return, promised Dulles that if Himmler did not approve of his plans for an independent surrender, then he would personally disassociate himself from his former SS leader.[94]

One institutional impediment to an early surrender by German military leaders was a real fear of Gestapo reprisals against anyone involved in the proposed capitulation, and even members of their families.[95] By agreeing to Dulles' terms, Wolff risked his own life[96] and that of his family,[97] a risk that,

92 Cable 939(9), Dulles to Glavin, 'Sunrise', undated (re Hitler); Cable 770 Dulles to Glavin, [illegible] April 1945 (re Mussolini, who was later killed by OSS supplied partisans); and Cable 693(9) 679 to Dulles or Gamble, 15 April 1945 (re Himmler's location): all at NA, RG 226, Entry 139, Box 60, Folder 554. See also telegram, 1 April 1945, which Zimmer sent through Wolff to OSS in which Wolff presented a 'plan' to Emperor [Kesselring], who approved it in principle, but stated he cannot go along in practice at that time: NA, RG 226, Entry 110, Box 2, File 15. Dulles wrote in correspondence on 9 March 1945, that Wolff had stated: 'that the time had come when some German with power to act should lead Germany out of the war to end useless material and human destruction'. Wolff stated that, in order to achieve an unconditional surrender, the commanders of the German armed forces would need to be won over. Dulles thought the fact Wolff purported to have considerable influence over Kesselring and Rahn would be of great value, Wolff declared that he felt he could 'persuade Kesselring to cooperate, and that the two control the situation in North Italy'. See Cable, 9 March 1945, Dulles to Glavin, Donovan and Forgan, CCC, Box 12, Reel 76; NA, RG 226, Entry 190C, Box 8, Dulles Files, 12 (noting that Himmler was suspicious of surrender plan, and that was Wolff acting without his support).

93 NA, RG 226, Entry 110, Box 2, File 16 (reporting on a conversation between Wolff and Dulles regarding 'the available of considerable food supplies and industrial resource in North Italy).

94 Cable 693(9) 679 to Dulles or Gamble, 15 April 1945: NA, RG 226, Entry 139, Box 60, Folder 554.

95 Cable 9119, Dulles to London, 1 April 1945 (reporting that Kesselring was 'half a prisoner' of the Gestapo): NA, RG 226, Entry 134; Cable 575(9), Nicholson [Lemnitzer] and McNeely for SGS, undated; Cable 640(9), MacNeely to Dulles, 14 April 1945: both at NA, RG 226, Entry 139, Box 60, Folder 554; Cable 2487, Dulles to Washington, 26 December 1944: RG 226, Entry 134 (reporting the arrest of General Speidel, one of Kesselring's subordinates and potential intermediary for unauthorised surrender contacts); Cable 6329, 5 March 1945: NA, RG 226, Entry 134 (noting how Kesselring was surrounded by 'fanatical Nazis' who would report any such contacts to Himmler).

96 Allied participants anticipated that Wolff may 'fall a victim to [the] hazards of his enterprise': Cable 575(9), Nicholson [Lemnitzer] and McNeely for SGS, undated: NA, RG 226, Entry 139, Box 60, Folder 554.

97 Indeed, Himmler was later to threaten Wolff's wife and seven children once he became aware of Wolff's contacts with Dulles: NA RG 226, Entry 190C, Box 9, Dulles Files – Sunrise Reports, 7–9. See also Cable 9119, Dulles to London, 1 April 1945: NA, RG 226, Entry 134 (in which Himmler asked Wolff to explain his surrender of British agent 'Tucker' prompting Wolff to make excuses and to claim he was acting on Hitler's secret orders); Cable 9169, Dulles to London, 3 April 1945: NA, RG 226, Entry 134 (reporting that Wolff's family were now in effect Himmler's hostages).

in April 1945, appeared distinctly ominous.[98] This was particularly true at the end of that month, when Wolff personally ordered surrender of SS-controlled forces, which led to attempts to have Wolff arrested.[99] Bizarrely, this threat of arrest prompted Wolff to request the Allied military authorities for 'relief by parachute and/ or armoured troops' to protect his headquarters from his 'own' German military forces.[100]

Wolff was, in effect, accepting a role which resembled that of an OSS double-agent. In this role, Wolff agreed not only to risk his own life by reporting security and military developments frankly to Dulles but also to accept a secret OSS radio operator ('Little Wally') at his Bolzano HQ.[101] This operator used his fluency in German to rapidly transmit crucial information direct to OSS Berne and Allied HQ at Caserta Italy, including the 'movements of intermediaries' and the arrangement of 'parliamentarians' authorised to sign a surrender.[102] This allowed 'Wally' to report on the precise location of Vietinghoff's military HQ, which Allies planes then bombed.[103] This bombing gave additional support to Wolff's efforts to exert pressure upon Vietinghoff and other military leaders to finally accept the 'futility' of refusing to become a party to Wolff's planned capitulation.[104]

During the Sunrise negotiations, Wolff committed himself to attempting to build agreement with German Generalfeldmarschall Kesselring, and any successor, prior to declaring a capitulation. However, he also promised Dulles to surrender the various SS and SS-controlled Italian forces under his personal command, even if other German military leaders refused his overtures.[105] Wolff also confirmed that he would not betray the details of the

98 NA, RG 226, Entry 190C, Box 9 Dulles Files – Sunrise Reports, 11; NA, RG 226, Entry 190C, Box 8 Dulles Files, 15.

99 Cable 22949, Dulles to Glavin, 18 April 1945: NA, RG 226, Entry 134 (anticipating Himmler's 'elimination' of Wolff); Gilbert to Boots, 26 March 1945 (noting that Wolff needed to take precautions re the Gestapo). Sunrise Report: NA, RG 226, Entry 110, Box 2, File 15 (reporting that Himmler had ordered Wolff's arrest).

100 Cable 21, Wolff to Dulles, 2 May 1945: NA, RG 226, Entry 139, Box 60, Folder 555; Cable 19, Wolff to Alexander, 2 May 1945: NA, RG 226, Entry 110, Box 2, Folder 11 (both withdrawing the request for military assistance against Wolff's German 'comrades').

101 Cable 540(9), 'Sunrise', Lemnitzer to SGS, 20 March 1945; Cable 662, Dulles to Nicholson [Lemnitzer], 10 April 1945: both at NA, RG 226, Entry 139, Box 60, Folder 554: Cable 6859, Dulles to Caserta, 13 April 1945: NA, RG 226, Entry 134.

102 Cable 211, 'Sunrise', 15 March 1945 and Cable 6859, Dulles to Glavin, 13 April 1945: both at NA, RG 226, Entry 139, Box 60, Folder 554. See also Sunrise Report: NA, RG 226, Entry 190C, Box 8, File – Dulles Files, 13; Cable 788(9), Dulles to Glavin and Nicholson [Lemnitzer] undated, reporting on an alternative, if Wally's mission failed, of infiltrating Dulles' agent Tracey Barnes directly into Bolzano: NA, RG 226, Entry 139, Box 60, Folder 554.

103 Cable 696(9), Dulles to Glavin, 16 April 1945: RG 226, Entry 139, Box 60, Folder 554.

104 NA, RG 226, Entry 190C, Box 9, File Dulles Files – Sunrise Reports, 10.

105 *Ibid*, 12.

secret negotiations, which at a time of war were treasonable, to either Himmler or Hitler.

The fourth condition of the Dulles/Wolff agreement related to Wolff's promise that, during hostilities, he would safeguard and hand over to the Allies various works of art and cultural treasures which he controlled. His forces would avoid the unnecessary destruction of Italian industry. They would also disobey Hitler's policy of scorched earth, which would of course destroy all remaining public services and installations within Northern Italy.[106] According to Dulles' account, Guido Zimmer anticipated that Hitler or Himmler would order the SS to carry out Hitler's scorched-earth policy,[107] and he wanted to save the Italian art and religious treasures from being destroyed.[108] Wolff largely honoured his promises, again by personal interventions.[109] Under this peace initiative, Wolff instructed each regional commander within his jurisdiction that he would 'hold each responsible in his own territory for preventing destruction'.[110] Once the capitulation took place, OSS both claimed and received substantial credit for allowing vital industrial and infrastructure installations in Italy and Austria to remain intact.[111]

The next chapter will describe how, during Wolff's 1948–49 trial proceedings, his lawyers skilfully used the threat of exposing how his Sunrise negotiations had been underpinned by an 'an active Anglo-American-German understanding' of the threat of communism, as a powerful bargaining chip.[112] This threat facilitated the occupation authorities, allowing Wolff's lawyers to obtain and use supportive affidavits from British and American military and civilian intelligence officials. Wolff also claimed that Captain Tucker, a captured SOE agent, had approached him allegedly with a message from Field Marshal Alexander suggesting the need for a form of capitulation prompted by a joint Anglo-American and Nazi interest in forestalling the 'spread of

106 Cable 648, Dulles to Glavin for Nicholson [Lemnitzer], 9 April 1945: NA, RG 226, Entry 139, Box 60, Folder 554; Cable 8927, Dulles to Washington, 19 April 1945: NA, RG 226, Entry 134 (reporting that Dulles' subordinates (and British intelligence officials from SOE) were reinforcing this imperative by making separate 'private deals' with the Italian Partisans, Wolff's forces and private companies that the partisans would honour).

107 Wolff could not, however, promise that Italian Marines, who remained under the command of Admiral Doenitz, would obey his orders to avoid destruction: Cable 8499, Dulles to Washington, 9 April 1945: NA, RG 226, Entry 134.

108 Cable 648, Dulles to Glavin for Nicholson [Lemnitzer], 9 April 1945: NA, RG 226, Entry 139, Box 60, Folder 554.

109 Cable, 9389, Dulles to Washington, 26 April 1945: NA, RG 226, Entry 134.

110 Cable 647, Dulles to Glavin, 9 April 1945: NA, RG 226, Entry 139, Box 60, Folder 554.

111 RG 226, Entry 190C, Box 8, Dulles Files, 10 (recording how Wolff met Dulles and discussed the urgent necessity of ending the war soon to 'save lives'). The OSS, which was fighting for its post-war existence, sought to make considerable propaganda capital from the 'success' of Sunrise: Glavin, 'release of Sunrise material', 19 June 1945: NA, RG 226, Entry 139, Box 60, Folder 553.

112 CSDIC report, *op cit*, 8.

communism' in Italy, which would have followed in the wake of mass unemployment created by a German scorched-earth policy. Furthermore, Wolff claimed that American intelligence had approached him via Kesselring: 'They warned me against the communist danger which might rear its head here [Italy] – so near to the Balkans – at any moment.' Wolff claimed that the unofficial negotiations were predicated on the assumption that the Anglo-Americans could gain a distinct geo-political advantage from a surrender in the south-west, including control of Trieste, only providing the Red Army had not advanced too far.[113] It is possible, however, that Wolff was fooled by Tucker in order to secure the latter's release from captivity. Dulles himself received correspondence in the wake of the publication of his *Secret Surrender* book on Operation Sunrise, which valorises Wolff's role, confirming the Anglo-Americans were anxious to secure Trieste and Venetia Giulia against Tito's advancing communist partisan forces, and praising Dulles' role in 'getting our own troops on the ground in the agreed Austrian occupation zones head of the Russians'.[114]

Conclusion

In short, contrary to the requirements of the agreed policy of unconditional surrender, which meant that the Axis powers had to surrender to the Allies as a whole, Dulles and Wolff entered into negotiations and agreed a series of mutually beneficial terms and conditions. Stalin knew of this violation, presumably through his secret service's penetration of the OSS codes and security. The Western powers, presumably acting in good faith, rejected Stalin's allegations. As the Cold War intensified during the immediate post-war decade, these wartime denials became an embarrassment, which any war crimes trial of Karl Wolff could threaten to expose, not least because he could testify to a specifically anti-Soviet dimension. Of the agreed terms and conditions, perhaps the most controversial was Dulles' oral promise to protect and help rehabilitate Wolff and his immediate SS group associated with Operation Sunrise.

113 *Ibid*, 6–7.
114 Col. G. A. Lincoln to Dulles, 27 December 1966: Dulles Papers, Box 59, Folder 10.

Chapter 4

Intervening on behalf of Karl Wolff

> In the last months of WWII . . . their one hope was to be able to surrender to the Americans rather than the Soviets. It is unthinkable that these criminals should have been merely released from captivity.
>
> (Allen Dulles, 1968)[1]

> As to the question who was prosecuted for what criminal offence, different reasons, and not only legal considerations, had been taken into account.
>
> (Telford Taylor, former head prosecutor for the American-led Nuremberg Subsequent Proceedings trials, giving evidence in Wolff's 1964 trial)[2]

> Between you and me [Karl Wolff] doesn't realise what a lucky man he is not to be spending the rest of his days in jail, and his wisest policy would be keep fairly quiet about the loss of a bit of underwear, etc. He might easily have lost more than his shirt.
>
> (Allen Dulles, OSS Bern/CIA Director)[3]

> It looks as if Mr Wolff will get a pretty stiff sentence unless we do something about it.
>
> (British Military Governor for Germany, 1947)[4]

Introduction

Wolff knew that, given the likelihood of an Allied victory, he was vulnerable to prosecution not only for his command responsibility for SS atrocities committed in Italy from September 1943 to April 1945, but also for administrative

1 A. Dulles, preface to R. Storey, *Final Judgement: Pearl Habor to Nuremberg* (San Antonio: Naylor Co., 1968).

2 *Case for the prosecution against Karl Wolff for participation in mass murder*, Public Prosecutor's Office, Provincial Court Munich II, Ref. Ioa JS 39/60 at 51, a-112, 496.

3 Dulles to Max Waibel (Swiss Intelligence official), 12 June 1950: Dulles Collection, Mudd Library, Princeton University, USA ('Dulles Papers'), Box 59, Folder 10.

4 Chief Legal Division, OCC (Nuremberg) to Office of Military Governor Berlin, 14 August 1948: PRO, FO 1030/424.

complicities in a range of other earlier SS war crimes. As Lamb notes, Wolff: 'realised in the Autumn of that year [1944] that Hitler had irretrievably lost the war. He was acutely conscious that he might be tried as a war criminal, and was anxious to work his passage with the Allies.'[5] This chapter will summarise the still incomplete archival evidence on the immunity aspect of Operation Sunrise.[6] The substance of the allegation against Dulles is that, as wartime Chief of OSS Field Office in Bern, he had unrestricted access to secret intelligence information regarding the war criminality of Wolff and other Nazi participants in Operation Sunrise, including Dollmann, Zimmer and SS-Standartenführer Walter Rauff.[7] However, in pursuit of a high-profile intelligence triumph, Dulles both ignored (or turned the proverbial blind eye to) this evidence and, later, during the immediate post-war years, sought to suppress details of his direct and indirect interventions on Wolff's behalf within the prosecution process. The reasons for protecting the Wolff group were mixed and may have varied from case to case and from situation to situation. At different times, they included some element of moral obligation for those who had risked their lives in a joint effort to bring about an early capitulation, a sense of having to honour commitments of rehabilitation and immunity made, without express authorisation, by his sunrise 'intermediaries' Husmann and Parilli, and gratitude for all those who contributed to a mission that resulted in great plaudits from the OSS leadership, positive media coverage and perhaps even to Dulles' reputation as a supreme spymaster deserving rapid promotion.[8]

During the last year of the Second World War, Dulles deployed the promise of legal immunity as the bait to lure senior Nazis into capitulation negotiations. This is clear from his reaction to German Generalfeldmarschall Kesselring's attempt to secure legal immunity as part of the unauthorised surrender of the military forces under his command in Northern Italy.[9]

5 R. Lamb, *War in Italy 1943–1945: A Brutal Story* (New York: St Martins Press, 1994), 9.

6 The implications of certain aspects of recently declassified material is discussed in greater detail elsewhere in K. von Lingen and M. Salter, 'Contrasting Strategies within the War Crimes Trials of Kesselring and Wolff' (2005), 25 *Liverpool Law Review* 225–66. The remainder of the present section will concentrate mainly on evidence that has not previously been discussed by Dulles' critics.

7 Rauff helped designed the Black Raven gas wagons that predated the gas chambers as a means of mass killing of Jews. Although his role is clear from the cables, it is understated in later accounts, including that of Dulles: Cable 22949 Dulles to Glavin 18 April 1945: NA, RG 226, Entry 134 describing Rauff as: 'second in command of SS in Italy under Critic [Wolff] now wholly with Critic'. See also Cable 699(9), Dulles to Glavin: NA, RG 226, Entry 139, Box 60, Folder 554, reporting further on Rauff's involvement with Parilli.

8 R. Wolfe, 'Coddling a Nazi Turncoat', in Breitman *et al*, 2004, *op cit*, 326.

9 Dulles to OSS Washington, 24 February 1945: Cambridge College Cambridge (CCC), Reel 76, Box 12; T. S. Ryan, 'Narrative on Sunrise', *op cit*, 2. This claim was also reported by Charles Clark, Berne correspondent for the London *Daily Dispatch* on 24 February 1945, who may have been briefed by Dulles as a way of applying pressure on Allied authorities.

Whilst Dulles, and General Donovan, head of OSS, sought to exploit such offers of 'conditional' surrender, this was firmly rejected their superiors.[10] For example, Allied Military Commanders (AFHQ) cabled Dulles on 24 February 1945 re-affirming that they would not depart from the demand that only a strictly 'unconditional surrender' was acceptable. They emphasised:

> . . . AFHQ certainly would not recommend to combined chiefs any modification unconditional surrender such as would be involved in promises, commitments or bargaining. Indeed, we believe it extremely doubtful that any modification would be made although undoubtedly Kesselring would be given the customary privileges of his rank as a prisoner of war.[11]

Thus, the precondition for any leading Nazi figures within Northern Italy to gain immunity was their willingness to negotiate with an Allied official, such as Dulles, who was willing to either bypass, or at least bend to near breaking point, the requirements of official policy by entering into a private, oral agreement. The explicit character of Kesselring's demand had proved counterproductive. In practice, it had removed the possibility of any covert grant of legal immunity because it would have made Dulles immediately vulnerable to allegations that there was indisputable evidence that he had subverted official Allied policy.

Compared with Kesselring, Wolff was altogether subtler in accommodating himself to Dulles' 'flexible' orientation towards these Allied policy demands. Obviously, any immunity agreement requires *both* parties to seek, and then come to, an agreement regarding the precise terms and conditions on which legal immunity would be granted. For reasons already discussed, Dulles' communications with his superiors emphasised that he had not given any commitment to Wolff and that, in his early meetings in March 1945, he wished it 'clearly understood I have engaged in no negotiations, merely listened to his presentation and stated, with no refutation [on] Wolff's part, that unconditional surrender [is the] only possible course'.[12] Dulles' later book on Operation Sunrise continued to insist that:

> Neither at this [opening] meeting nor later did Wolff suggest that his action would be contingent upon any promise of immunity for himself.

10 General Donovan made a request in December 1944 to President Roosevelt to be allowed to offer immunity to specific Nazis in return for their cooperation in peace deals: 'Memos for the Secretary' located in Box 733, 'Memos for the President', in Edward Stettinius Papers, University of Virginia, US.

11 Cable 5527 (in reply to Dulles, 24 February 1945): CCC, Reel 76 Box 12.

12 'Operation Sunrise', 2677th Regiment OSS (Provisional), (nd): NA, RG 226, Entry 139, Box 60, Folder 553, 3–4.

> He did say that he did not consider himself a war criminal and was willing to stand on his record.[13]

Whilst both Wolff and Dulles insisted, and indeed for their own reasons needed to insist, that neither of them had been party to an immunity agreement, there is, however, clear evidence that Dulles had made a private undertaking of this kind to the Wolff group. This is confirmed by numerous sources, including the voluntary statements of SS-Sturmbannführer Heinrich Andergassen, one of Wolff's subordinates. These pointed out that the Wolff group, then based at Palazzo Pistoia at Bozen (Bolzano), were relying upon an agreement assuring Wolff and his immediate SS subordinates that they would escape legal accountability, at least for war crimes committed against Italians:

> [From Palazzo Pistoia] came the information that the Americans on one side and Wolff on the other side stipulated in their surrender conditions that all cases referring to Italian citizens in connection with fighting the enemy handled by the Sicherheitspolizei will not be further investigated.[14]

From the start of his contacts with Dulles, Wolff was probably made aware that to expressly demand personal immunity both in writing, and as an explicit precondition for a military capitulation, would have been counterproductive. This contention receives support from his interrogation reports. These indicate that, during a wartime meeting on 19 March 1945, Wolff intended to discuss the granting of favourable treatment for his SS subordinates, even though Professor Max Husmann, a Swiss intermediary, persuaded him not to raise this matter formally with Dulles:

> During the discussion, Wolff asked Husmann whether he could not obtain at least a written assurance of decent and honourable treatment for his assistants . . . Husmann advised against discussing this question with the British and American representatives and added that a promise made would be honoured by the Allies even if given only in oral form . . . Wolff repeats that Husmann promised as a matter of course, the same honourable and decent treatment for Wolff and his friends that Dulles had personally indicated as certain. Informant adds that, owing to the tension which prevailed during these days, he was possessed only of one idea, namely, to bring about the capitulation. Therefore, he neglected details and did not even consider legal aspects. The whole plan . . . was

13 Dulles, 1966, *op cit*, 98.
14 *Ibid.*

> built on a basis of good faith and he is well aware of the weakness of the legal side of the arrangements.[15]

Nevertheless, Wolff was convinced that Dulles had made him an unsolicited promise of 'honourable treatment' that, in his specific context, at least implied a measure of legal immunity. During Wolff's post-war interview with Husmann at the Nuremberg Place of Justice, he reported that, during the early stages of the Sunrise negotiations on 19 March, Dulles had made a point of flattering Wolff. Dulles had commented positively on the fact that he was the only German official putting out peace feelers who was not obviously motivated by self-interest:

> Mr Dulles mentioned of his own volition that President Roosevelt had expressed his supreme satisfaction over the fact that, for the first time during this war, a prominent German personality had negotiated for peace or surrender without having made any personal or material demands on his own behalf . . . Dulles said: 'Even though you have not made any personal demands, and no requests had been made regarding your future services in Germany, I hope that I can count on your tried cooperation and cooperation of your most valuable comrades.[16]

If this statement is accurate, it confirms our earlier view that the most effective wartime strategy for Wolff (and other Nazis vulnerable to prosecution as war criminals who fell outside the category of the most obviously incriminated types such as Himmler and Kaltenbrunner) towards achieving legal immunity was not to make this an explicit demand. Instead, their best policy was to allow this question to arise as an apparently unsolicited promise from Dulles, or other senior OSS officials, dressed up as a request for their post-war cooperation within German reconstruction. It would then become clear to both sides that this could only take place if the Allies were willing to spare them from prosecution and imprisonment as war criminals. It appears that, amongst those seeking to contact Dulles 'to save their own skins', Wolff alone was aware of, and willing to exploit, this opportunity in a suitably flexible and accommodating manner. Hence, Wolff accepted that Dulles' interventions to secure his immunity would remain dependent upon his continued silence about the politically embarrassing and damaging secret that Dulles had flouted the unconditional surrender policy. In one sense, by providing promises of future assistance, Dulles had trapped himself into a situation of vulnerability on this point.

15 'Summary', 10, transmitted by W. Rapp to Telford Taylor, 16 October 1947, in reply to a request of 16 September 1947: Institute for Historical Research (IFZ), Munich, Polad/33/18.

16 Husmann–Wolff interview transcript, July 1947, 6: IFZ, Munich, Polad/33/18.

In addition to meeting one of Dulles' requirements for gaining his post-war protection, Wolff realised that maintaining the impression that he had not actively sought legal immunity could prove beneficial more generally, particularly in supporting his contention that he was innocent of any war crimes. Wolff was anxious to emphasise that at no time had he actively sought or demanded any promises of legal immunity from Dulles. He sought to rely on the fact that, on one interpretation at least, Wolff's reluctance suggested that his wartime record was such that he had *no reason* to fear prosecution before any impartial legal court. By contrast, the fact that Kaltenbrunner, Kesselring and other senior figures in the Nazi regime had actively sought out such immunity reflected an unintentional confession that without such unofficial assistance they would almost certainly be convicted and possibly executed for their war crimes. Although after the war Wolff frequently reminded Allied officials that they should reward him for his key role in Operation Sunrise, he often insisted that the only explicit discussions of future legal immunity that arose as part of that project related to: 'the sparing of my subordinate Kappler'.[17] According to Wolff then, his unique willingness to allow his wartime record to 'speak for itself' provided further proof that he 'had an absolutely clear conscience'.[18] During his interrogation as a possible witness and source of information at Nuremberg, Wolff continued this strategy:

> Wolff again emphasises that it was not his intention to gain any advantage for himself and he adds that he therefore did not examine the developments as to their material consequences. He adds that he placed his life as well as that of his family at stake by working on the capitulation, believing that this deed, like any other noble deed, would one day be appreciated.[19]

It is possible that Wolff realised, either by himself or as a result of a briefing by Dulles or his staff, that *if* his words and actions suggested to Allied officials that he was yet another leading Nazi who, like Kaltenbrunner and Kesselring, had every reason to seek legal immunity as the price the Allies were expected to pay for any cooperation, then this would have proved counterproductive. Such an approach amounted to an unintended confession of their war guilt sufficient *to increase their prospects of being prosecuted.*

If this appreciation of the subtleties of avoiding prosecution was the

17 CSDIC/CMF/X 167, 5: Cornell Collection 148/Vol. 108.

18 'Voluntary statement by KW', 8, LD 1470, 'Low Pressure and Low Temperature Experiments in Concentration Camps', report No: WCIU/LDC/1436 (a) – APS/HC, PRO, WO 208/4372.

19 'Summary', 4, transmitted by W. Rapp to Telford Taylor, 16 October 1947, in reply to a request of 16 September 1947: IFZ, Munich, Polad/33/18.

rationale behind Wolff's strategy, then he was relying upon an assessment of Allied policies and attitudes that was probably correct. Certainly, during the closing months of the Second World War Dulles had felt it necessary to rebuff other leading Nazis, including Kaltenbrunner and the von Epp group of Bavarian Nazis, because their apparent peace feelers were clearly driven by an underlying desire to 'save their own skins'.[20] Wolff may also have learned the lesson from Kesselring's earlier counterproductive attempt to exchange military capitulation on the Italian front for an explicit guarantee from the Allies that they would afford him legal immunity from war crimes.

As already discussed in the previous chapter, Wolff's prospects for legal immunity stemmed from the agreement through which he, acting as Höhere SS-und Polizeiführer of Northern Italy, brought about an unofficial military capitulation at the end of April 1945.[21] The success of this joint operation, which Dulles arranged whilst he was chief of OSS field station in Berne, helped secure Dulles' reputation as a supreme spymaster. Dulles' enhanced reputation certainly helped his rapid rise in America's post-war Central Intelligence Agency (CIA) during the most dangerous phases of the Cold War.[22]

On the other hand, Dulles had purchased this 'intelligence triumph' at a high price. There was a short-term gain available but one which could only be achieved at the cost of longer-term difficulties. Throughout the post-war years, Dulles had to conceal the fact that he had bent, if not entirely broken, the official Allied unconditional surrender policies which, as already noted, strictly prohibited 'negotiations' with leading Nazis. Chief amongst the prohibited negotiations, perhaps, were those which required promises of legal immunity in return for military or other concessions. Furthermore, and contrary to those who demonise intelligence officials as uniformly lawless and anti-constitutional, Dulles' support for Wolff was controversial within the OSS and its successor organisations (SSU and CIA). This was because a large number of his colleagues within different branches of the OSS and its two successor organisations[23] devoted considerable resources to supporting the Nuremberg and related war crimes processes.[24] Others had worked with

20 Regarding Dulles' attempts to negotiate with von Epp group, see Telegram 7569, 12 March 1945: NA, RG 226, Entry 110, Box 2.

21 On 2 May, and following many false starts, protests from Stalin and both a formal cancellation and subsequent reactivation, this much-vaunted covert operation culminated in the early surrender of approximately one million German and Italian fascist soldiers in Northern Italy. This occurred a few days before the final surrender by the remainder of German forces. See B. Smith and E. Agarossi, *Operation Sunrise: The Secret Surrender* (New York: Basic Books, 1979), ch. 7.

22 Smith and Agarossi, *op cit*, 187.

23 That is the Strategic Services Unit and – from 1947 – the CIA.

24 In the immediate post-war months, OSS officers were given instructions to give a high priority to war crimes investigative work, a point discussed in detail during later chapters.

agents and informants who had been brutally tortured by SS and Italian fascist forces who were under Wolff's command.[25]

Dulles' alleged motivation for this secret intervention stemmed from recognising that any post-war trial would disclose additional details of Wolff's war criminality. This, in turn, would make Dulles' verbal promises of immunity appear even more problematic. Such revelations would indicate that he had defied express orders from the OSS leadership and had violated the Allied policy of 'unconditional surrender' agreed at the Casablanca Conference in 1943.[26]

Worse still for Dulles if Wolff was prosecuted, there would have been the risk of Wolff's defence lawyers producing documentary evidence that, contrary to Roosevelt's indignant denials, would confirm that Stalin was essentially correct when he charged the Western Allies with double-dealing over partial surrender in the Western front in pursuit of their own geopolitical interests.[27] Any such revelation would have undermined the consciously slanted and self-glorifying account of the OSS's involvement in Operation Sunrise, which this organisation leaked to the press as part of its unsuccessful attempt to counter the growing threat of its dissolution.[28] There were also more personal factors at work. In large part, Dulles' rapid promotion within the CIA depended upon the credibility of his wartime achievements, and Operation Sunrise was certainly the best known.

The previous chapter identified four distinct but related terms and conditions which Wolff and Dulles eventually agreed. However, the fifth, and for present purposes most important, condition related to the promise of favourable treatment to SS forces under Wolff's command, particularly his immediate entourage of Dollmann, Zimmer and Wenner, and his subordinate Harster.[29]

There is considerable documentary evidence that the OSS were, if authorised by the relevant military and political authorities, willing to engage in surrender negotiations with the leading figures of the Nazi regime. This remained the case even where the possibility of immunity from war crimes prosecution was clearly one of the terms of the overall agreement. For example, the OSS leadership, including both Colonel Glavin and General Donovan, made it clear to Dulles that the question of whether he should embrace the Wolff group partly depended *on the degree to which Wolff was implicated in war crimes*. It was assumed that senior SS officials would, to a greater or lesser extent, be implicated in war crimes; and only those at the

25 Hesch, *op cit*, 133.

26 On this aspects of Sunrise, see M. Waibel, *Kapitulation in Norditalien 1945* (Originalbericht des Vermittlers, Basel: 1981), 30.

27 Smith and Agarossi, *op cit*, 101–6.

28 Cable 15389 from Paris, 6 May 1945: NA, RG 226, Entry 134.

29 M. Salter and M. Eastwood, 'Negotiating Nolle Prosequi at Nuremberg: The Case of Captain Zimmer' (2005), 3 *Journal of International Criminal Justice* 649–65.

lesser end of the spectrum could be dealt with. In response, Dulles received from Max Husmann (his Swiss intermediary) a folder filled with papers, rather like a curriculum vitae, containing glowing references and character witnesses for Wolff.[30]

During the Sunrise negotiations, issues of possible legal immunity for war crimes arose during the series of back and forth 'negotiations' over the future treatment of Wolff's German SS and Army forces including the Waffen-SS under Wolff's overall command in German-occupied North Italy. Dulles rejected only some of Wolff's proposed terms as 'untenable propositions'.[31] Insofar as immunity issues were concerned, the overall terms that the two men finally agreed had two connected strands. The first related to the immediate treatment of SS forces generally. The second strand comprised of a promise that elements of the leadership of the SS, including of course the Wolff group, could in principle form part of a new post-war elite contributing to the rebuilding of Germany.[32] Here, we must recall that Dulles was also responsible at this time for preparing 'white lists' of reliable Germans for such post-war reconstruction work.

Dulles realised that 'selling' the proposed deal with Wolff, as Himmler's deputy, would not be straightforward, especially as evidence of concentration camp atrocities created a particularly hostile context for any proposals for rewarding SS officials. Nevertheless, once Dulles became convinced of the far-reaching potential (for himself, his organisation and the Allies more generally) of the proposed capitulation, he began to reinterpret and portray Wolff to his superiors in particularly positive terms. Wolff was no longer presented as an SS regional governor (1943–45) in charge of Gestapo forces responsible, as his OSS colleagues were painfully aware, for various atrocities and the torture of OSS agents, and Himmler's overall trouble-shooter (1935–43). Instead, Dulles portrayed Wolff as the representative of the 'more moderate element in Waffen-SS, with mixture of romanticism . . . Probably most dynamic personality [in] North Italy.'[33] Dulles also reinterpreted the implications of the military developments in mid-March 1945 in terms that favoured immunity for the Wolff group, particularly with respect to the prospects of continuing mountain warfare. That is, as posing 'the awful alternative of either renouncing punishment of the Nazi leaders, or jeopardizing the lives of millions of decent human beings'.[34] Indeed, Dulles claimed

30 Grose, 1994, *op cit*, 230.

31 Dulles to Glavin, 9 April 1945: NA, RG 226, Entry 139, Box 60, Folder 554.

32 The promise here was: 'their personnel when repatriated would go back to Germany and form nucleus of some future German military revival'. See Nicholson [Lemnitzer] and McNeely to SGS, 29 March 1945: NA, RG 226, Entry 139, Box 60, Folder 554.

33 Cable 6689, Dulles to Glavin, 9 March 1945: NA, RG 226, Entry 134.

34 Radiotelephone Transmission, No. 287, Dulles to Washington, 14 March 1945: NA, RG 226, Entry 134.

that Wolff's promises of unofficial regional surrender represented an opportunity to create and intensify internal divisions within SS ranks. This opportunity could, in turn, be used to 'defeat' the threat of a 'national reduit' located high in Alpine mountain strongholds from which guerrilla warfare could be continued indefinitely.[35]

For reasons that may induce a degree of scepticism, Dulles expressly endorsed Wolff's view that, having an exemplary war record, he had *no need* to seek immunity, claiming that: 'throughout the whole meeting critic [Wolff's codename] made no reference to any conditions of surrender and did not attempt to bargain'.[36] During official reports to his superiors, Dulles was anxious to claim that: 'Wolff made no request re personal safety or privileged treatment from war criminal viewpoint.'[37]

There is, however, a clear discrepancy between Dulles' claims, on the one hand, and the implications of recently declassified files on the other. These reveal that other Allied military participants in Operation Sunrise expressed a far more sceptical view, noting that: 'Critic [Wolff] hopes to have it both ways in that meanwhile he and other . . . [Sunrise] personalities feel they are insuring themselves.'[38] Furthermore, at the start of the negotiations, Dulles' Swiss intermediary, Max Husmann, promised Wolff that: 'while the surrender must be unconditional, certain privileges might be accorded to German troops in Italy'.[39] This included exempting Wolff's base at Bolzano from allied air attack, which was partly but not entirely honoured.[40] In discussions with Wolff, Husmann recalled that leading Italian fascists, including Marshall Badoglio, Mannerheim, and Grandi, had already obtained immunity because of their earlier assistance in shortening the war.[41] During the early part of the negotiations, Wolff had sought to 'extract guarantees from Dulles that the "idealistic" and "decent" men of the army, party, and SS would be able to play an: "active part in the reconstruction" '.[42] In response, Dulles' subordinates and agents made promises to the Wolff group that certain privileged members of the SS leadership would play an influential post-war role as a government elite in charge of reconstruction.[43] Presumably, Wolff included

35 Cable 7699, Dulles to Glavin, 28 March 1945: NA, RG 226, Entry 134.

36 Cable 540(9), 'Sunrise', Lemnitzer to SGS, 20 March 1945: NA, RG 226, Entry 139, Box 60, Folder 554.

37 Cable 6689, Dulles to Glavin, 9 March 1945: NA, RG 226, Entry 134.

38 Cable, 640(9), McNeely to Dulles, 14 April 1945: NA, RG 226, Entry 139, Box 60, Folder 554.

39 Project 877190: NA, RG 226, Entry 109, Box 40, tab 3.

40 Cables 2 and 8, undated but probably late April 1945 (complaining 'repeated night bombings' and, 'in spite of promise' of another 'attack . . . from low flying planes'): NA, RG 226, Entry 139, Box 60, Folder 555.

41 Max Waibel, *op cit*, 38–9.

42 Smith and Agarossi, *op cit*, 138.

43 Husmann–Wolff interview transcript, July 1947, 6: Institute for Historical Research (*IFZ*), Munich, Polad/33/18; Cable 6329, 5 March 1945: NA, RG 226, Entry 134; Dulles, 1966, *op cit*, 73–76.

himself within this potential new elite, the prosecution of which would have been both unwarranted and impractical.

Wolff later relied on this commitment promising the SS forces under his command that, notwithstanding the notoriety of the SS generally and their involvement in atrocities against civilians and captured partisans within Italy, they could still anticipate the Allied authorities easing the strictness of their unconditional surrender policy. This would involve them receiving a range of specific concessions and forms of privileges that were entirely incompatible with the treatment of suspected war criminals. These included a promise of return to Germany to work, under Allied supervision, as security police. This was supposed to take place almost immediately after the end of hostilities delayed only by a short period of purely token detention for these SS officials.[44] In justifying making these commitments, Dulles resorted to hair-splitting semantic arguments beloved of lawyers. He insisted to his superiors that, although such concessions were being presented as preconditions for honouring their commitments to the OSS, this still did not violate official Allied policy. This was because: 'principle of unconditional surrender not questioned'.[45] The material already discussed in earlier parts of this chapter should be sufficient to cast more than a little doubt on Dulles' claim, however.

Furthermore, immediately after the capitulation, Dulles' senior aide, Gero von Gaevernitz, honoured his promise to recommend that Allied authorities should give favourable treatment to reward the Wolff group,[46] a promise Wolff relied upon. In secretly taped conversations, Wolff stated: 'Certain promises were made and certain hopes aroused during the talks which took place before the actual surrender . . . at the moment it is wiser not to mention these things or to make too much of them.'[47] In response to Dulles' verbal promises, Wolff sought guarantees from General Alexander immediately

44 Under interrogation after the war, Wolff noted that: 'We were not to become prisoners. There might have to be a short period of internment, and then back to Germany. The SS Police were to be made responsible for law and order in Germany': 'Karl Wolff interrogation', undated report, 7; Dulles Collection, Princeton University, Box 59, Folder 9. On another occasion, Wolff attempted to safeguard his personal war booty (including three million shares in Italian companies). Wolff also sought symbolic concessions, such as the retention of 'belts and bayonets', as well as SS forces being allowed to: 'do some useful work such as repairing roads and railways in Italy'. Cable 8499, Dulles to Washington, 9 April 1945: NA, RG 226, Entry 134; Cable 647, Dulles to Glavin, 9 April 1945: RG 226, Entry 139, Box 60, Folder 554.

45 *Ibid* (Cable 8499).

46 Sunrise Report: RG 226, Entry 110C, Box 9, Folder 121 – Dulles Files; RG 226, Entry 110C, Box 9, Folder 121 – Dulles Files, Para. 3. Vietinghoff and Roettiger suggested that surrendered troops were in a position to repair the (Brenner) railway line quickly – contributing to solving Allied supplies problems in Austria, para. 7; Gaevernitz recommends favourable treatment to those German commanders who helped bring about the surrender.

47 Smith and Agarossi, *op cit*, 76.

after the final capitulation on 4 and 5 May 1945 that, despite their complicity in war crimes against Italian civilians, including reprisal killings, his former SS forces would now receive equal treatment with regular German soldiers who were being sent back to Germany.[48] Relying upon the advice from Gaevernitz, Wolff insisted that the Allied authorities recognise in writing 'the irreproachable behaviour' of his SS forces in North Italy, 'in contrast to that of other commands'.[49] For obvious reasons, this demand generated concern amongst Dulles and other Sunrise participants because 'it is clear from this that he is trying to collect ammunition which might produce far-reaching consequences at a later date'.[50] Dulles was even warned to: 'drop the entire question of giving Critic [Wolff] any message of encouragement or commendation on his behaviour during recent weeks'.[51]

The 88th Division of US Army Military Intelligence (G2) arrested Wolff during his birthday party on 13 May 1945.[52] He reacted by writing a letter of protest suggesting that there must have been confusion in the US circles. He pointed out that Dulles 'had promised' him 'honorable treatment'.[53]

Smith and Agarossi note that, at this time during the summer of 1945, Dulles must have recognised that it would need a concerted effort to halt, or at least delay, Allied efforts to prosecute Wolff at the first international trial at Nuremberg:

> As soon as the pursuit of Nazi war criminals assumed the central place in Allied policy, Wolff's dreams of immediately playing an independent political role were doomed. His rank, position, and previous services to the party and the SS guaranteed that he would be in the front rank of those accused. After ten days of post-war quasi-freedom in Bolzano, he

48 See Wolff's reply to Alexander thanking him for the 'equal' treatment of his SS troops: to which Alexander responded by denying any such commitment had ever been made: Cable 50, Alexander to Wolff, 6 May 1945: NA, RG 226, Entry 110, Box 2, File 11 and RG 226, Entry 139, Box 60, Folder 555, respectively.

49 *Ibid.*

50 See Cable 1215/768, Nicholson [Lemnitzer] to Dulles, 6 May 1945: NA, RG 226, Entry 139, Box 60, Folder 555: On this occasion at least Wolff did not appear to appreciate that such *de facto* conditions to a supposedly 'unconditional surrender', which had been negotiated secretly with intelligence officials, could not even be referred to publicly in writing – let alone treated as if they had contractual force. He was told, in no uncertain terms, not to make such requests through these formal military channels, as these would prove to be counterproductive for all involved. *Ibid.*

51 *Ibid.* 52 Smith and Agarossi, *op cit*, 189.

53 Karl Wolff to US General Kendall in Bolzano, 13 May 1945 (SECRET): NA, RG 338 (Fifth Army Records/Liaison section Italy Box 3, F X. At first, Wolff was interned in Italy in order from the fall of 1945 to give testimony as a witness in the Nuremberg war criminal trials. G. Steinacher, *Südtirol und die Geheimdienste 1943–1945* (Insbruck/Wien/München: Studien-Verlag, 2000), 266–67. Wolff is discussed under the sub-heading 'The Escape of War Criminals – Case Studies'.

was taken in custody on his birthday (13 May) by members of the American Eighty-Eighth Division.[54]

Despite his arrest, von Lang, his biographer, notes that Wolff remained confidant that the expected period of detention following his arrest would be little more than a temporary concession to public opinion and the formal Allied policy of 'unconditional surrender'. Furthermore, under this plan, Wolff would shortly become Minister of Education in the new post-war Germany:

> Everyone who in Bolzano was wearing a German uniform was taken to a prison camp in the South . . . But he [Wolff] held back his anger because he remembered what his guest Gaevernitz, after all a member of the US secret service, had announced to him only days before: the victors necessarily would have to arrest the Höhere SS-und Polizeiführer of Italy, because the entire world expected them to do so, but after several days or a few weeks at most he would be sent back to Germany and into liberty, so that he could be entrusted there with the kind of tasks that had been talked about during the capitulation negotiations.[55]

For his part, Dulles always insisted that he had made no explicit or implicit promises of immunity or privileged treatment as part of Operation Sunrise. Instead, he insisted that any such questions of immunity and related protection for the Wolff group arose only later from a 'moral obligation'. He claimed that this obligation extended into the post-war years and required him to emphasise the more favourable aspects of Wolff's wartime record.

Whilst remaining sceptical of this clearly self-serving claim, the rest of this chapter will chart how Dulles, and his assistants, intervened at various crucial stages to protect Wolff and other SS officials involved in Operation Sunrise.

Dulles' interventions on behalf of Wolff with respect to the International Military Tribunal at Nuremberg

Previous studies, many of which are intended to be powerful critiques of Dulles and the CIA, have tried but failed to establish any *direct relationship* between his promise to protect the Wolff group and any direct interventions by US intelligence officials on Wolff's behalf within the quasi-independent Nuremberg process.[56] The failure to date of Dulles' critics to provide any firm empirical evidence on this key point surely represents a serious weakness in their overall case. Breitman acknowledges that Dulles was generally willing to

54 Smith and Agarossi, *op cit*, 189. 55 Lang, *op cit*, 298–99.

56 The link is implied but not fully substantiated in Simpson, 1995, *op cit*, 236–37.

intervene in support of Wolff.[57] However, unlike Simpson and other critics, he does not suggest that Wolff's comparatively favourable treatment in avoiding being prosecuted during the first round of the Nuremberg trials was based *directly and exclusively* upon Dulles' interventions. On the contrary, and consistent with earlier findings, he implies that factors other than an alleged wartime immunity agreement must have explained the prosecutor's decision not to bring Wolff to trial before the IMT.[58]

This poses the question of why precisely Wolff was 'passed over' by the Nuremberg prosecutors. Another related question concerns the possible link between the 'distinct advantages' Wolff received from his relationship to Dulles (and other Allied participants within Operation Sunrise), and the Nuremberg prosecutors' decision not to charge Wolff in the first round of the international trials. Did his immunity with respect to the American-dominated Nuremberg trials stem largely from the added factor of direct interventions from US intelligence officials, particularly Allen Dulles?

Immediately after the war, Dulles started a goodwill campaign for Wolff, stressing the services he rendered for the interests of the United States.[59] The OSS's own Operation Sunrise files indicate that he insisted that Wolff's 'conduct' should justify him receiving an 'early hearing' to clarify where he stood with respect to the Allied authorities.[60] The internal correspondence between Dulles and other participants in Sunrise, particularly military officials, such as Generals Airey (AFGQ intelligence chief) and Lemnitzer (Field Marshall Alexander's deputy at AFHQ), makes it clear that Dulles reacted with real concern at the implications of Wolff's internment and listing by the Allied authorities as a war criminal.[61] Generals Airey and Lemnitzer, the two Allied military officials directly involved in the later stages of the Sunrise Mission, took divergent positions regarding Dulles' policy of protecting Wolff and his immediate SS associates. Hence, it is reasonable to assume that their correspondence will refer directly to the current status of such efforts. Indeed, this correspondence indicates that, between mid-1945 and 1948, Dulles had not betrayed and abandoned Wolff, as the latter apparently believed. On the contrary, Dulles continued to take a pro-active interest in Wolff's

57 R. Breitman, 'New Sources in the Holocaust in Italy', (2002) 16(3) *Holocaust and Genocide Studies* 410: 'Wolff had the distinct advantage of having helped to arrange an early surrender . . . Although Dulles had made no promise of immunity to Wolff, he had been impressed with the man and spoke up for him afterwards. Wolff nevertheless had a number of post-war difficulties. In a climate where world opinion was shocked by photos of corpses and survivors from concentration and extermination camps, there was no way for Himmler's former chief of staff – one of the highest ranking SS officers to survive – to escape imprisonment. Wolff was moved from one internment camp to another and regularly interrogated. He almost was named as one of the major defendants at the International Military Tribunal at Nuremberg, but was ultimately passed over.'

58 *Ibid.* 59 Breitman, 2002, *op cit*, 410.

60 Sunrise Files: NA, RG 226, Entry 110, Box 2, File L1. 61 *Ibid.*

post-war fate, and actively sought to protect him from prosecution and punishment.

Recently declassified intelligence documentation also provides direct evidence of Dulles' interventions within the Nuremberg process. The most general is a statement contained in a letter Dulles wrote to Lemnitzer on 4 July 1945, in which he acknowledges receipt of an earlier letter from June: 'about Critic [Wolff's codename] and other matters'. Dulles then notes that he had been using his intelligence and military contacts to monitor Wolff's statements and orientation whilst in detention. He may have been concerned that Wolff might, on his own initiative, renege on their earlier understanding that he was not to seek to exploit the promises of immunity.

General Lemnitzer's letters indicate that Dulles had asked the General to inform him regarding any developments in Wolff's treatment, location and likelihood of being granted special treatment in view of his contribution to Operation Sunrise. Lemnitzer, however, expressly warned Dulles that his continuing efforts to protect Wolff – still referred to as 'Critic' – from prosecution could lead to unfortunate repercussions. Ironically, it was Lemnitzer, a military officer, who sought to give Dulles, the former international commercial lawyer, a lesson in the importance of respecting the rule of law. The general gently criticised Dulles for seeking to pre-empt and subvert the standard legal process for officially listed war criminals:

> In my recent message to you I referred to Critic's indignation at being arrested. He is still in the interrogation center in Rome, where he will remain for some time. With his being placed on the war criminal list, there was no alternative as the Combined Chiefs of Staff insist that anyone on that list be treated as a prisoner of war without regard to any extenuating circumstances involved. In many respects I believe that it is better that this should happen because it will tend to suppress any recriminations or criticisms regarding any favouritism in his case. I do not know what exact war crimes charges which will be placed against him, but whatever court handles the case, they will have to weigh his good deeds against the bad and make their decision accordingly.[62]

Certainly, OSS officials based in Italy were also aware of the negative implication of Wolff's arrest and listing as a war criminal for their plans to lend support to Wolff and his family.[63] This came as a particularly unwelcome surprise to OSS officials involved in Operation Sunrise. For

62 Lemnitzer to Dulles, 1 June 1945, Dulles Files – Sunrise – Lemnitzer: NA, RG 226, Entry 190C, Box 9.

63 Wolff featured as No. 346 on 'list 7' of UN War Crimes Commission's list of accused persons detained by the Allied Forces HQ, Mediterranean theatre, together with General Vietinghoff and Lt General Wilhelm Harster: UNWCC, C. 135, 16 July 1945: PRO, WO 219/3585.

instance, OSS Caserta noted that: 'With recent receipt of instructions from Allied Governments placing him on a list of war criminals, it has now been necessary to abandon those arrangements and plans.'[64] For reasons beyond their control, OSS officials could no longer honour Dulles' promises of favourable treatment for Wolff and his family. This was a fact that had to be kept from Wolff (and Dulles' various intermediaries) for as long as possible, to delay a predictably negative reaction arising from feelings of betrayal by Dulles.

Knowing of his protective attitude to Wolff, Lemnitzer had unofficially forewarned Dulles of Wolff's impending listing as a war criminal:

> [I]nstructions from CCS [Combined Chiefs of Staff] prescribe rigidly procedures to be followed in such cases. In accordance with those instructions, Critic will henceforth be treated as [a] prisoner of war and like other German general officers who are prisoners his family will not be permitted to join him . . . I consider it essential that you and 476 [Gaevernitz] have this information so you will understand [the] situation in case mention of critic's treatment is made by your Swiss or German contacts. However, it is of utmost importance that information of Critic's being on war criminal list does not pass beyond 476 and yourself.[65]

There was, therefore, official concern that Husmann, or the Italian intermediary Count Parilli could react negatively to Wolff's listing as a war criminal and reassignment to Nuremberg. In turn, this expression of concern indicates that Allied authorities were aware that it was *these individuals*, rather than Dulles or his immediate staff, who had conveyed Dulles' promise that the Wolff group would receive legal immunity. Hence, these intermediaries could be tempted to react to news that Wolff had been transferred to Nuremberg by making politically embarrassing statements regarding how the Allied authorities had betrayed such promises of immunity, the validity of which they had guaranteed as a matter of their personal honour.

During the early summer of 1945, Dulles was actively intervening on Wolff's behalf, not only with military intelligence officials as one would expect, but also with senior Nuremberg prosecutors:

> I am keeping in close touch with the top people handling the War Criminal matter and I trust that Critic's case will take a favourable turn unless, of course, we turn up some evidence against him. So far I have seen nothing serious except his long SS service, unless of course every SS atrocity in Italy is laid at his door.[66]

64 See Nicholson to Dulles (Berne), 27 May 1945: NA, RG 226, Entry 139, Box 60, Folder 553.
65 *Ibid.* 66 *Ibid.*

It is likely that Dulles' main source of influence was none other than former OSS leader William Donovan. Indeed, Dulles had discussed with Donovan the possibility of Wolff's potential prosecution at the international Nuremberg trials as a threat to OSS's interests. This occurred in written correspondence prior to a provisional decision to remove Wolff from the list of likely major defendants. It also took place verbally as the two men were crossing the Atlantic together in September 1945, when Donovan showed his OSS subordinate the CSDIC transcript (that is the record of a secretly taped conversation involving Wolff and other detainees).[67]

One of the means through which Dulles was 'keeping in touch with the top people' was through redeploying one of his wartime anti-Nazi German contacts, Fabian von Schlabrendorff, to General Donovan's personal staff amongst the Nuremberg prosecutors. This occurred during the period from June to December 1945 when Donovan, former director of the OSS, remained an influential deputy to Justice Jackson within the dominant American Nuremberg prosecution agency, the Office of the Chief of Counsel (OCC). Donovan used Schlabrendorff to handle a number of sensitive issues connected with the case, which he did not want to be handled through official channels, or to form part of the bureaucratic record of Jackson's organisation.[68]

Furthermore, at this time, Donovan was also developing a controversial plan to allow Schacht, and even Göring, to benefit from a type of plea bargaining 'deal' under which they would improve their legal position by giving dramatic evidence against former colleagues within the Nazi leadership circles.[69] If Dulles was aware of this, then it may have supported the conclusion that Donovan was hardly averse to the broad principle underpinning Dulles' suggestion. In August 1945, Donovan's organisation was fighting for its institutional life. Hence, its public relations office was using the 'success' of Operation Sunrise as part of its media campaign to offset this threat of dissolution. In this context, it is reasonable to assume that Donovan would have, as far as possible, acted on Dulles' suggestion. The last thing Donovan needed was for a war crimes trial, which – as already noted – the OSS had actively supported, to hear a high-profile case involving testimony that was highly damaging to the reputation of this intelligence agency, and – by implication – to that of Donovan himself.

Unfortunately, but not really surprisingly, the extent to which General Donovan intervened personally to exert pressure on US Chief Prosecutor

67 Dulles to Roman, 7 February 1966, Dulles Papers, Box 59, Folder 10.

68 This may explain why Donovan retained his personal set of Nuremberg papers and had these locked away in his law firm's safe, where they were only recently discovered and gifted to Cornell Law School.

69 This led to the heated Donovan–Jackson dispute, culminating in Donovan's forced resignation in December 1945. See Storey, *op cit*, 97–99, and later chapters of the present book.

Justice Jackson to exempt Wolff is not recorded in archival records that the CIA have presently declassified. Had Donovan refused Dulles' request, then it is possible that there would have been an accessible chain of declassified correspondence giving his reasons. It is most likely that Donovan was the person Dulles was referring to amongst 'the top people' monitoring developments regarding Wolff on Dulles' behalf. Given this hard evidence of Donovan's cooperation, there is no obvious reason why he would not have extended such assistance further by exerting pressure on Jackson to exclude Wolff from the international trials.[70] Certainly, there is no evidence that Donovan ever withdrew this support, or had any overriding reason to do so.

Dulles sought to mobilise his extensive range of military and legal contacts to intervene on Wolff's behalf and those of other Nazis involved in Operation Sunrise, such as Zimmer and Dollmann.[71] Dulles had asked General Lemnitzer to inform him regarding any developments in Wolff's treatment, location and likelihood of being granted special treatment in view of his contribution to Operation Sunrise. Such was the vigour of Dulles' interventions in favour of granting immunity that these even prompted reproaches from the military participants in Sunrise as being contrary to the rule of law.[72] Dulles also personally made representations with General Donovan to protect Wolff, Zimmer and other SS officials associated with Sunrise who, immediately after the war, were being arrested as war criminals by US counter-intelligence.[73] General Donovan cooperated with Dulles by writing directly to Brigadier General Betts, head of US JAG (US Army Legal Department) by, for instance, making special pleadings on Zimmer's behalf.[74]

The existing historical literature clearly establishes that, even during the immediate post-war months when public anger at SS concentration camp atrocities was at its height, Dulles, Gaevernitz and US military officials who were key Allied participants in Operation Sunrise, sought to assist and protect Wolff. Wolff was hidden away in a quiet internees camp in Austria, and even

70 Donovan was not a party to the decisive meeting itself, however, as the American side was represented by Justice Jackson and his son.

71 With respect to interventions on behalf of Zimmer whilst Dulles was Chief of OSS Mission for Germany, see Dulles to Major Lewis, 30 September 1945: 'Zimmer rendered very real services in the Sunrise operation and I am glad that he is safely at home. If any further difficulty arises with regard to Zimmer, I would appreciate being informed thereof': Dulles Files – Sunrise letters re Wolff-Zimmer: NA, RG 226, Entry 190C, Box 8.

72 Lemnitzer to Dulles, 1 June 1945, Dulles Files – Sunrise – Lemnitzer: NA, RG 226, Entry 190C, Box 9: 'I believe that it is better that this [impartial treatment] should happen because it will tend to suppress any recriminations or criticisms regarding any favouritism in his case.'

73 Cable 9719, 2 May 1945: NA, RG 226, Entry 134 relating to 'unfortunate' arrests in Milan.

74 Donovan to Betts, 23 November 1945: Cornell Collection, Vol. 17, Pt. 1.

given the opportunity to live with his wife and children and to sail his own yacht on Lake Gmunden.[75] Smith and Agarossi note that:

> Dulles, Lemnitzer, and the others [Allied participants in Operation Sunrise] were prepared to let bygones be bygones and to treat Wolff like a regular fellow as a reward for his surrender services. But the wishes of both Wolff and the western sunrise people were thwarted by the great rush of popular anti-Nazi feeling, as well as the horror generated by the revelations regarding German atrocities [which in the spring of 1945 led to] a stringent and comprehensive action against alleged war criminals.[76]

This dispenses with any suggestion, based upon a number of Dulles' wartime cables, that any promises of immunity made by Dulles were little more than a tactic within a wartime 'double cross' operation. Already during the war, Dulles had noted that:

> [C]ertain other high SS officials might not go along with die-hard fanatics and might try to gain some immunity by serving as 'uebergangs' [supervisory] regime between Hitler and occupation forces . . . Naturally, persons of Himmler, Kaltenbrunner type can gain no immunity from us, but as long as they believe this is possible it might give us an opportunity to drive a wedge in SD [Himmler's SS political intelligence section] and thus reduce effectiveness of German reduit plans. This seems to be a matter well worth handling by clandestine methods as I feel one need have no scruples in double crossing types such as Himmler, Kaltenbrunner *et al.*[77]

Dulles was willing to hold to his promise of post-war assistance. Dulles and Donovan also intervened on behalf of Wolff by suppressing (or at least not drawing attention to) an incriminating report on Wolff's record by the OSS branch.[78]

Assuming that Donovan did, in fact, successfully intervene with Jackson on Wolff's behalf, then it is likely that the American and British (given their close working relationship between Jackson and with the British prosecutors) would have formally opposed Wolff's inclusion in the decisive meeting in London of the four chief prosecutors on 23 August 1945. The formal minutes of this meeting stored in PRO gloss over the details of any disagreements in silence, and simply record that:

75 G. Cobentz and S. Freidin, 'Strange Story of SS General', *New York Herald Tribune*, 23 January 1962.

76 Smith and Agarossi, *op cit*, 188.

77 Berne to Washington, Telegram 6209, 2 March 1945: NA, RG 226, Entry 90, Box 6.

78 Cornell Collection, Vol. 87: R&A Report No. 3133.7, 'Principal Nazi Organisations involved in the Commission of War Crimes: Part Four: The Nazi Party', 10 September 1945, draft, 107.

> after considerable discussion a shorter list excluding Wolff would be announced and that further names could be added later . . . Various other names were considered, but it was agreed that list was now quite long enough and that other possibilities, such as . . . Wolff . . . could be dealt with later if necessary.[79]

Smith and Agarossi's account adds some important additional elements:

> In August he [Wolff] narrowly missed being included on the defendant list for the main Nuremberg trial. With both Himmler and Heydrich dead, Ernst Kaltenbrunner had been designated the major defendant for the SS and the Gestapo, but in the light of the enormity of the accusations against these two organisations, they were underrepresented, and other prominent SS men could have been placed in the dock. During one of the final preparatory meetings of the Chief Prosecutors . . . an effort was made to expand the list of defendants, but after a lively discussion, the Allied prosecutors decided to hold the list of the accused at two dozen, and to go after other top Nazis in a second trial. Of those deemed most worthy of inclusion as defendants in such a follow-up proceeding against major Nazi war criminals, four individuals were named, and one of them was Karl Wolff.[80]

Although useful, this account glosses over one of the most important issues as far as the present study is concerned: was it the case that Jackson and his deputy, General Donovan, supported the exclusion of Wolff? If Dulles' interventions within the Nuremberg process on behalf of Wolff had succeeded, then surely he would have needed to bring Jackson on board as well as Donovan?

Simpson, who has provided the fullest account to date, notes that this may have been the case. He claims that, notwithstanding the clearly expressed desire of both the French and Soviet chief prosecutors to expand the list of defendants to include Wolff, an Anglo-American alliance on the relevant committee vetoed this:

> Allied war crimes prosecutors identified Wolff almost immediately as one of the most powerful members of the Nazi inner circle to survive the war. The French and Soviet governments favoured prosecuting Wolff before the first international tribunal at Nuremberg – an 'honour' of sorts, as

79 PRO, FO 1019/86.

80 Smith and Agarossi, *op cit*, 189. They cite PRO, FO371/50486/U6602. Unfortunately, however, this is no longer a valid PRO citation (the relevant file refers to shipping issues!), and the minutes are found at PRO, FO 1019/86. Also Simpson claims the meeting took place on the 24th (the day the minutes were prepared for a meeting that occurred on the previous day).

> this trial was reserved for the highest-ranking Nazi criminals in custody. Had Wolff been tried there, he almost certainly would have been hung. But the U.S. and British representatives on the Nuremberg planning committee demurred. There were too many high-ranking Nazis to try at the first tribunal, they contended. Only one SS officer should be prosecuted there; the others would certainly get their turn later. The case against the Gestapo's Chief Ernst Kaltenbrunner would be easier to make than that against Wolff, the U.S. contended, even though Wolff probably had more power in the SS as a whole. After much debate, the tribunal's planning committee decided to prosecute Kaltenbrunner first in the autumn of 1945. They slated Wolff to be the Chief SS defendant at second international tribunal, scheduled to open sometime in 1946.[81]

At this time, Dulles was intervening on Wolff's behalf not only with military intelligence officials as one would expect but also with senior Nuremberg prosecutors.[82] On 23 August 1945, Dulles sent a personal cable to Donovan pleading for Wolff to be exempted from inclusion in the first international trial at Nuremberg.[83] This recorded Dulles' concerns regarding the credibility of the embattled OSS if Wolff was tried and allowed to present 'his version of Sunrise as part of his defense'. With respect to Wolff, Dulles suggested to Donovan that 'he not be included in the first batch' of defendants, that is, be exempted from the trial of major war criminals at Nuremberg.[84]

Dulles sent Donovan this urgent telegram on the very day when senior prosecutors were meeting in London and taking decisions over the identification of defendants for the first international trial of 'major' war criminals.[85] Amongst the topics for discussion was whether Wolff should be included as a defendant. As the writers Tusa and Tusa note:

> [T]he Chief Prosecutors met in London on 23 August . . . It seemed worth indicting Bormann and 22 others. Many extra names were canvassed – military commanders such as Rundstedt, Milch, Wolff and Brauchitsch . . . but although it was felt that strong cases could be made

81 Simpson, 1995, *op cit*, 236–37. Simpson is presumably basing this elaboration on interviews with, or memoirs from, at least one of the chief prosecutors but unfortunately the details are specified in his book, which cites only Smith and Agarossi, *op cit*, 189 quoted in full above.

82 Dulles to SSU Chief, General John Magruder, 27 December 1945: NA, RG 226 Director's Office, Roll 44, Frame 0518.

83 Dulles to Donovan only, Cable 5024, 23 August 1945: NA, RG 226, Entry 90, Box 6, Folder 64.

84 Cable 5024, Dulles to Donovan, 23 August 1945: NA, RG 226, Entry 90, Box 6, File 64.

85 Tusa, and Tusa, *The Nuremberg Trials* (London: BBC Books, 1995), 93, citing BWCE N/10; Smith and Agarossi, *op cit*, 189–90.

> against them they in fact duplicated other, even stronger candidates for inclusion.[86]

Given that Donovan, and his former senior lawyer James Donovan, were both involved in the decision-making regarding the selection of defendants, this cable represents the first piece of hard evidence that has emerged to date that *directly* links Dulles' well-known interventions on behalf of Wolff to the decision-making processes concerning the selection of Nuremberg defendants. This cable also explains and corroborates a recorded interview with Wolff by one of Dulles' intermediary in the Sunrise negotiations, Max Husmann in which this intervention took place:

> It was due to Dulles that you did not get on the first list [to stand trial at the International Military Tribunal at Nuremberg] because he immediately said at Nuremberg: 'Let some time pass before you take this man. Perhaps we will be able to help him.'[87]

Lang's biography of Wolff strongly supports Husmann's claims. This well-researched work independently confirms that Dulles intervened to prevent Wolff standing trial as one of the two most senior SS officials. It also confirms that Dulles' intervention had succeeded in blocking plans to prosecute Wolff during the first international trials:

> The victors initially had planned in the first trial instead of Himmler, who had poisoned himself during his arrest, to place the former Chief of his Personal Staff [Wolff] in the dock . . . But Allen Dulles in the background had put in the veto of the secret service. For his partner of the capitulation, however, he now was out of reach. When Wolff sent him outraged calls for help, he pretended to be deaf. But he still wanted to spare him from prosecution because he knew how it would end. When in those days Husmann once again travelled to Berne as Wolff's intercessor, he [Dulles] said: 'Let time pass over this man. Maybe we'll be able to help him later on.'[88]

Wolff was, as already discussed, considered as a likely candidate for being tried as major war criminal during the first Nuremberg trials as one of the symbolic embodiments of the SS. In short, and possibly as a direct result of Dulles' interventions, Wolff appeared in the Nuremberg trials dressed in a Waffen-SS general's uniform only as a *prosecution* witness. This followed his

86 See also the minutes of this meeting recording the decision to defer Wolff's prosecution: PRO, FO 1019/86; Smith and Agarossi, *op cit*, 189.

87 'Husmann–Wolff interview': 15 April 1947, 7: IFZ, Munich, Polad/33/18.

88 Lang, *op cit*, 301.

thorough cooperation with the interrogators and war crimes prosecutors, with some of whom he built up a cordial relationship, including Telford Taylor (who went on to head the subsequent proceedings at Nuremberg (1947–49)).

Intervening to protect Wolff from the second round of Nuremberg trials

It is, perhaps, just arguable that the borderline decision not to prosecute Wolff at Nuremberg could be legally justified if, but only if, he was regarded as a prime candidate for trial at either the British-led Italian trials or the American-led subsequent proceedings at Nuremberg. Certainly, the decision not to name him as a defendant in the international trial, possibly stemming from Dulles' interventions already discussed, certainly did not remove him from any risk of later trial, conviction and possible execution in these follow-up hearings. This section will discuss how Dulles appreciated and reacted to this risk by continuing to protect Wolff from the threat of prosecution.

It is likely that, following the dismissal of General Donovan in December 1945 from his post as deputy to Justice Jackson for reasons discussed in a later chapter, Wolff's protection at Nuremberg temporarily evaporated. This deterioration meant that Wolff's name was more likely to go forward to be included amongst a list of possible defendants for the second round of war crimes trials, the 'subsequent proceedings'. Under Telford Taylor's leadership, these American trials energetically prosecuted over 180 middle-ranking Nazi officials ranging from four SS officials, doctors involved in SS-sponsored medical experimentation within Himmler's concentration camps, to industrialists who formed part of Himmler's 'circle of friends'.

During 1946 and 1947, Dulles was playing a double game, both covertly protecting Wolff, whilst – at the same time – concealing this intervention from Wolff. Presumably, Dulles believed that this former leading SS official might seek to further exploit the promises of favourable treatment made as part of the Sunrise negotiations. The object of this double game was to ensure that Wolff, whose period of being a 'model prisoner' had clearly ended during the opening months of 1947, remained safely out of circulation. However, it remained important to Dulles that Wolff was not given the public forum of a high-profile war crimes trial at either Nuremberg or Rome to publicise his politically embarrassing claim that Dulles had betrayed earlier, unauthorised promises of legal immunity and had engaged in negotiations to disadvantage the Soviet forces on the Eastern Front. At this delicate stage of both his own career and the Cold War, Dulles needed to delay making any explicit assistance until circumstances changed.

As late as May 1946, the question of whether Wolff merited trial before the second round of Nuremberg trials remained undecided. This is clear from a request from the Nuremberg prosecutors regarding Wolff's involvement in atrocities committed by the Waffen-SS in Italy.[89] Furthermore, on 9 July 1946, possibly in preparation for the Subsequent Proceedings at Nuremberg, Justice Jackson signed a request to the Document Center controlled by G–2 (US Army intelligence division). This note was following up an earlier telephone enquiry from Rigney (a Nuremberg prosecutor preparing the SS criminal organisation case). Jackson's note stated that he 'would appreciate information by T.M.X. if your HQ has any documents concerning Wolff or forced labour program or Anti-partisan activities by Germans in Italy'.[90] This request may indicate that the head of the US Nuremberg prosecutors for the first round of the international war crimes trials considered the non-prosecution of Wolff, not as a complete vindication of his innocence (as he was later to allege during his war crimes trial in 1964) but merely a delay motivated by tactical considerations.[91]

As already noted, those drawing up the list of Nuremberg defendants classified Wolff as one of the most clear-cut defendants for the subsequent proceedings, and 'since Wolff was in American hands, one might suppose that he would have been caught in this net'.[92] However, as Simpson points out, Wolff was saved again:

> But Karl Wolff again succeeded in wriggling off the hook, despite the fact that he was personally implicated in one way or another in almost half of the cases brought to trial in the subsequent proceedings series.[93]

In other words, his responsibilities overlapped with the offences with which senior Nazi bureaucrats, doctors involved in unlawful 'medical experiments' and industrialists who sponsored and benefited from slave labour within concentration and death camps. Simpson claims that, although Dulles was unable to directly order Taylor not to prosecute Wolff: 'Dulles and the emerging CIA could nevertheless make their influence felt both directly and indirectly.'[94] Smith and Agarossi also recognise the continuing relevance of immunity promises made during the Sunrise negotiations: 'in addition, the prosecutors were not certain how to deal with his [Wolff's] sunrise experiences'.[95]

Acting on Wolff's behalf, Gaevernitz (Dulles' senior aide and personal friend) wrote a letter to former OSS-consultant Robert Kempner. Kempner was the only German national the Americans employed as a trial counsel

89 Telegram Nuremberg to JAG CMF, 22 May 1946 and, in reply, telegram, 23 May 1946 supplying the requested material: PRO, WO 310/123.

90 Hekking (signed Jackson), OCC, Nurnberg, to Col. G. Smith, Document Center: PRO WO 204/12804, 106173.

91 See Jonathan Bush's account of Telford Taylor's recollections http://www.bard.edu/hrp/atrocities/panelone.htm.

92 Smith and Agarossi, *op cit*, 189.

93 *Ibid*, 238.

94 Simpson, 1995, *op cit*, 238.

95 *Ibid*, 190.

at Nuremberg who had stayed on to become Deputy Chief of Counsel for War Crimes at Nuremberg under Telford Taylor. Gaevernitz's letter pleaded that Wolff had 'rendered outstanding support at great personal risk to the success of operations "Sunrise-Crossword" '.[96] Kempner made enquiries on Gaevernitz's behalf and provided helpful insider information on future plans for Wolff.[97]

In addition to complications regarding the alleged promises of immunity, Wolff's sudden bout of apparent mental instability was another complicating factor. Taylor's attitude seemed to be that, whilst Wolff may have merited prosecution (at least at this stage), he would be glad if another group of prosecutors could play this role. As Smith and Agarossi summarise their own correspondence with Telford Taylor: 'Thus when the British asked that Wolff be turned over to them so that he could be prosecuted together with Generalfeldmarschall Kesselring for crimes committed during the Italian campaign, the American Chief Prosecutor General Telford Taylor agreed with alacrity.'[98]

British cooperation with the US authorities at Nuremberg was particularly good.[99] It extended to the point that the Americans offered to include German generals wanted for war crimes in Italy in the American-led Nuremberg subsequent proceedings. Counsel Edward G. Rigney, who was preparing the case against the SS personnel at Nuremberg, had provided: 'secret documents concerning . . . General Wolff'.[100] Furthermore, in return for British investigation files about German atrocities in Italy, General Taylor invited the Chief of JAG/CMF, Major Field-Fisher, urgently to Nuremberg to discuss: 'matters of mutual interest concerning [the] prosecution of German War Criminals'.[101] This meeting was the first signal that there was a possibility that Wolff could ultimately escape prosecution in the British trial programme for Italy, as well as that within the American-led Nuremberg process.[102] Later, on

96 This is partly quoted in the reply from James Riddleberger, deputy to Ambassador Robert Murphy, to whom Kempner had wisely forwarded the letter. Riddleberger (OMGUS, Berlin) to Gaevernitz, 23 January 1948: Dulles Papers, Box 59, Folder 9.

97 *Ibid.* 98 *Ibid.*

99 Correspondence between British and US JAG over, e.g., Heinrich Andergassen, is found in PRO, WO 310/123.

100 Telegram, 3 July 1946: PRO, WO 310/127. In return, Rigney visited the JAG CMF at Naples in July 1946 for information available about German atrocities in Italy. See message Chief of Counsel Nuremberg to JAG CMF, 18 July 1946 and 25 July 1946: PRO, WO 310/123.

101 Message Chief of Counsel Nuremberg to JAG CMF, 21 August 1946: PRO, WO 310/123.

102 The War Crimes Branch of the British HQ had initially planned to hold their own trial of Wolff immediately following that of Kesselring PRO, WO 310/127, Telegram GHQ to JAG London, 10 January 1947. Both trials were expected to last no longer than the end of February. Special trial instructions, 7 February 1947: PRO, WO, 310/129.

27 April 1948, the Chief of the Legal Division of the American Nuremberg prosecutors had:

> dispatched three folders containing material on Wolff, which had been made available to me by the U.S. war crimes authorities here [in Berlin]. I understand that these documents were forwarded to the Inspector General, Central Legal Office, Hamburg, for the use of the German prosecution . . . against Wolff.[103]

Once it became clear to Wolff that he was not going to be prosecuted at Nuremberg as a major war criminal, which occurred during late 1947, he quickly revised his previously cooperative attitude with the Nuremberg prosecutors. He now insisted that the time had now come for Dulles' earlier promises of favourable treatment in recognition of his contribution to Operation Sunrise to be honoured in full.[104] By this act, Wolff was finally playing his ace card. However, at this time he was clearly exhausted, depressed and frustrated, and was suddenly viewed as suffering from some kind of 'mental illness'. Although closer to extreme stress and exhaustion, Dulles could always subsequently argue, if need be, that Wolff's 'mental condition' discredited any inconvenient testimony regarding promises of immunity or an anti-Soviet dimension to Operation Sunrise.[105]

By November 1947, the Nuremberg prosecutors agreed to return Wolff to British custody.[106] This was not convenient to Dulles because it took the case outside the scope of his direct influence and meant that his interventions on Wolff's behalf had to take place through another layer of intermediaries. However, at the end of December, US Ambassador Robert Murphy, a personal friend of Dulles and leading American player in the Allied administration of Germany, requested his subordinates to 'prepare a suitable note to the British about the case of SS-General Wolff'. Here, Dulles made a positive case for giving Wolff privileged treatment as a reward for his role in Operation Sunrise. Dulles' position was, as we shall see in the next section, ultimately accepted as British policy as well.[107]

103 Chief, Legal Division HQ to Private Office of the Military Governor, 14 August 1948: PRO, FO 1030/424.

104 Lang, *op cit*, 308–9; Wolff to Teich, 15 April 1947: IFZ, Munich, Polad/33/18, 'Interrogation of Wolff by Husmann'.

105 Rapp to Taylor (Nuremberg), 16 October 1947: IFZ,Munich, Polad/33/18.

106 *Ibid.*

107 Laukhuff to Murphy, 30 December 1947: IFZ, Polad/33/18. '[F]or my part, I conclude from the evidence that this is a border line case but that Wolff's activities were sufficiently risky, and sufficiently valuable to us in lives and material to warrant recommending to the British that he be paroled and not turned over to any other power for trial . . . I hope that we will not emulate General Walsh [from US Military Intelligence in Germany] and adopt this hideous police-state term of protective custody.'

Wolff's escape from prosecution by the British authorities[108]

There is some, albeit limited, evidence that, at least during the period 1945–47, the umbrella of American protection stemming from Sunrise was fully recognised and endorsed by the British authorities preparing war crimes trials to be staged in Italy with respect to atrocities committed in this country. During the summer of 1945, when the British prosecutors were planning to put on trial the senior German officers responsible for the reprisals against civilians in Italy, the consensus was to try: 'all those from Kesselring and Wolff downwards whom it is considered undesirable to hand over to the Italians'.[109] Initially, the plan was to hold trials in Britain.[110]

One difficulty was that, although Italian-based British officials remained committed to trying Wolff, their enthusiasm was not fully shared by civil servants in the War Office and Foreign Office located in London, particularly during the summer of 1947. Hence, although these legal officials made repeated efforts to prosecute Wolff for his overall command responsibility for SS atrocities committed during anti-partisan warfare, this was ultimately vetoed. Political decisions from JAG London, supported by the British War Office, frustrated their efforts. This was despite the Foreign Office retaining its general commitment that Nazi war crimes had to be punished severely. It is possible that the increasing pragmatism of the War Office in the emerging Cold War context meant that they privately considered German generals as potential future comrades in the next world war.

Despite the clear intention to prosecute Wolff for war crimes in Italy, the preparation of evidence proved difficult. For example, Wolff had proved skilful at evading his interrogators' attempts to secure a confession providing fresh information or confirming existing suspicions: 'He gave information only after being convinced by lengthy discussions of actual orders in our hands and of the investigations we had carried out, that we knew so much that it was useless to evade the points.'[111] Wolff was particularly careful to excuse himself with respect to SS atrocities: 'He was . . . most careful to stress his own dislike of severe reprisal measures and was obviously greatly concerned lest he himself should be held responsible for what had occurred.'[112] Therefore, the British prosecutors had to try to make a case against Wolff by means other than his own confession or even partial admissions.

108 Nearly all the archival work cited in this section was originally obtained by Kerstin von Lingen, which I gratefully acknowledge, and which is in part used in Von Lingen and Salter, 2005, *op cit*.

109 Handwritten letter King to Passingham, 14 August 1945: PRO, WO 310/123.

110 *Ibid.*

111 Memorandum JAG, 13 January 1946, 7; PRO, WO 310/127; report on trial, 22: PRO, WO 311/28.

112 *Ibid.*

Despite a discouraging lack of cooperation from Wolff's former SS subordinates, British investigators gathered a limited range of evidence sufficient to merit further examination of the case against Wolff. An escaped British POW, Captain Ballentyne, who had fought with Italian partisans, had witnessed a massacre by SS troops at Bardi in central Italy, which was then under Wolff's command.[113] Allied investigators also managed to secure a statement from SS-Sturmbannführer Heinrich Andergassen. Andergassen was the only SS man willing to clarify the inner organisation of the SS in Italy.[114] Unfortunately, he worked at Bozen/Bolzano with the SD (the political intelligence branch of the SS). This meant that he could provide first-hand evidence only against Wolff's SS subordinates, Harster, Kranebitter, Thyrolf and Brunner, but not against Wolff personally.

By January 1946, British officials based in London came to the conclusion that, providing the facts were 'completely clear' and there was evidence that at least two atrocities involved (to counter any defence argument that an atrocity was a single isolated incident), they would start the proposed trials of Wolff and Kesselring as soon as investigations were completed.[115] The Judge Advocate General (JAG) defined British policy in a manner that threatened the interests of Wolff as well as Kesselring: 'It has been decided that as many as possible of these high-ranking German officers shall be tried as war criminals under the Royal Warrant.' London hoped that if Wolff, Kesselring and others were convicted, these trials would be politically beneficial in calming the difficult situation emerging within British-occupied Italy:[116]

> As one of the primary objects of this trial is presumably to benefit Anglo-Italian relations by the effect it will have on Italian public opinion, it is considered that Italian Government should be asked as to where the trial should be held at Rome, Milan or some other city . . . It is strongly represented that this case should not be brought to trial unless we are certain of securing a majority of convictions as otherwise the effort will not be worthwhile.[117]

Certainly, by April 1946, British officials were optimistic that they could successfully prosecute against not only Wolff but also his collaborators in

113 JAG noted with respect to Ballantyne's report of 27 November 1945: 'It is believed that at this time, the area under discussion was under command of the Supreme head SS and Police SS-General Wolff': PRO, WO 310/123.

114 Statement of SS-Sturmbannführer Heinrich Andergassen, 21 February 1946: PRO, WO 310/123.

115 Memorandum JAG, 13 January 1946, 5: PRO, WO 310/127.

116 Letter of Shapcott, JAG London, to AG3 (War Crimes Branch, CMF), 15 March 1946: PRO, WO 310/123.

117 Letter of Napier, War Crimes Commission CMF to War Office, 9 April 1946: PRO, WO 310/123.

Operation Sunrise, namely SS-Standartenführer Eugen Dollmann, SS-Major Eugen Wenner and Lt Guido Zimmer.[118] The preparations of the case against Wolff had, however, become increasingly difficult. In addition to the problems of tracing German generals or obtaining valuable and admissible evidence against them, the prosecutors were constantly short of investigative personnel, available transportation and time.[119]

The first British-led trial was that of General von Mackensen and General Mältzer at Rome in November 1946. This trial was supposed to serve as a test run for the larger-scale trials of Wolff and Kesselring.[120] Even in January 1947, there remained a clear intention to prosecute Wolff. The War Crimes Branch of the British HQ planned: 'to start the Kesselring trial at Venice on February 10th 1947, followed immediately by a Wolff trial'.[121] Despite this continuing desire to prosecute Wolff, it was becoming increasingly obvious that, in a changing policy context where retribution for Nazi war crimes had slipped down the Anglo-American agenda in response to Cold War tensions, there would be problems with implementing this plan. JAG's increasingly pragmatic approach restricted trial preparations against SS personnel. A shortage of British investigation personnel combined with delays with SS crimes investigations meant that the case against Wolff (and his SS subordinate, Harster) had not been developed to the point where it could be confidently predicted that a conviction was guaranteed in advance. If there was even a small chance of Wolff being acquitted, then, from the perspective of Foreign Office officials based in London, this could have proved counterproductive for Anglo-Italian relations.

Compared with the caution of their London colleagues, the Allied War Crimes Group based in Italy retained a more idealistic and committed approach to prosecuting *all* SS high-ranking officials who they considered guilty of war crimes, including of course Wolff. Despite the changed policy context reflecting altered Cold War priorities, this group made one final effort to prosecute Wolff and Harster in connection with SS atrocities committed in the Fossoli concentration camp in Northern Italy, which was under Wolff's personal command.[122] Evidence of supposedly retaliatory killings of 63 Italian political prisoners in this SS-controlled camp had reached

118 Telegram, 21 April 1946: PRO, WO 310/123.

119 War Crimes Group to JAG, 1 October 1947: PRO, WO 310/127.

120 The Rome trial raised considerable security issues, including the problem of maintaining discipline in the courtroom amongst the Italians in the public gallery.

121 Telegram GHQ to JAG London, 10 January 1947: PRO, WO 310/127. Both trials were expected to last no longer than the end of February: 'Special trial instructions', 7 February 1947: PRO, WO, 310/129. These trials were to be held under severe security measures permitting mainly journalists or British officers' wives in the public gallery.

122 War Crimes Group to Major Marshal, JAG, 9 September 1947: PRO, WO 310/127. For details of the role Fossoli played in wider atrocities against Italian Jews and others, see Lamb, *op cit*, 50; Primo Levi, *If This Is a Man* (London: Abacus, 1991), 22–25.

Mussolini.[123] Between November 1943 and the end of 1944, at least 3,198 Jews and political opponents of the regime passed through Fossoli, the vast majority en route to the extermination camps in Germany and Poland.[124] Hence, the Allied War Crimes Group sought to use Wolff's command responsibility for this camp as grounds for bringing a prosecution. At this late stage, prosecutors even secured new evidence that implicated Wolff's SS forces concerning 'the murder of 70 Italians as a reprisal at Fossoli in 1944'.[125] However, officials based in London rejected this request fearing that there still remained some possibility of Wolff being found not guilty. Meanwhile, the JAG welcomed the Dutch authorities decision to prosecute Harster in the Netherlands for having ordered the murder of Dutch Jews. This decision was based on evidence that was far stronger than that which had been obtained with respect to his command responsibility for complicity in Italian atrocities committed by Wolff's SS subordinates. Regarding Wolff, JAG continued to question whether the quality of the evidence and Wolff's proven ability to evade self-incrimination would allow a successfully prosecution:

> With so little evidence to go upon there is no doubt whatever that he would deny all knowledge of the incident. As you know, Wolff was fully interrogated both in C.M.F. (= Central Mediterranean Forces) and later at London district cage concerning atrocities in Italy but it was found impossible to obtain any incriminating admissions of any kind from him.[126]

It appears that the British decision definitely not to prosecute Wolff took place sometime in the late summer and early autumn of 1947. Telford Taylor wrote that the British originally requested Wolff's return from the Americans for the specific purpose:

> [T]hat they could prosecute him as a war criminal in Italy . . . and the British were informed we would grant that request [but] some months

123 Lamb, *op cit*, 274.

124 Rail transports containing primarily Jewish Italians were sent chiefly to Auschwitz or Bergen-Belsen. Political prisoners were sent to their death mainly to Mauthausen. The first major shipment comprising mainly Jews left Fossoli on 22 January 1944: http://www.istrianet.org/istria/history/camps/fossoli.htm. For an eye-witness description of executions by firing squad of 68 deportees (and anti-fascists) on 12 July there, see Alba Valech Capozzi, *A 24029*, originally published by Soc. An Poligrafica, Siena in 1946, and reprinted in 1995 by the Historic Institute of the Siennese Resistance for the presses of Nuova Immagine Editrice, Sienna. Extracts are published at http://www.deportati.it/campi/fossoli/valech70_1.htm.

125 Lt-Col. Barrat (partly illegible signature), JAG (London) to War Crimes Group, N.W.E., HQ British Army of the Rhine, 31 October 1947: PRO, WO 309/347.

126 JAG to War Crimes Group, 15 September 1947: PRO, WO 310/127.

> have passed since that time [Winter 1946], but the British have not recently shown any further interest in the matter.[127]

This request was not acted upon until November.[128] Taylor noted that:

> Somerhough advises me that the British would now like to have Wolff return to British custody in the British Zone of Occupation [within Germany]. He further advises me that a) the British do not themselves intend to try Wolff. b) that they do wish to interrogate him in connection with certain matters, and c) that they plan thereafter to turn him over to one of the formerly occupied counties (possibly Czechoslovakia), several of which have requested Wolff's extradition as a war criminal.[129]

Officially, JAG made one final attempt to obtain an incriminating statement against Wolff from With, his former adjutant, but again without producing any useful results.[130] This attempt came too late, since both Wolff and With had already been transported to Germany (in Wolff's case he had been returned to American custody at Nuremberg) and supposedly could not be traced.[131]

In short, and for reasons that the available documentation fails to clarify, sometime between September and December 1947, the British authorities changed their policy towards Wolff by reversing their previously agreed plan to prosecute him for his role in SS atrocities in Italy. There is little evidence of successful pressure being exerted by Dulles or other American intelligence officials. This was not to remain the case, however, as the remainder of this section will make clear.

Initially, British officials had no particular interest in protecting Wolff from extradition, even to the questionable legal systems of Soviet satellite regimes. On the contrary, they were pro-active in re-opening the possibility of extradition with the Czechoslovakian authorities. For example, during the autumn of 1947, officials from the Czechoslovakian War Crimes Commission based in Germany were contacted by a military officer of the British War Crimes Group, Group Captain Somerhough. With respect to Wolff, he stated:

127 Telford Taylor to Robert Murphy, 6 September 1947, 'Interrogation of Wolff by Husmann and all correspondence': IFZ, Polad/33/18.

128 *Ibid.*

129 Taylor (OCCWC) to Robert Murphy, 24 October 1947: IFZ, Polad/33/18 'Interrogation of Wolff by Husmann and all correspondence'. With handwritten annotations from 15 November 1947.

130 JAG to War Crimes Group, 28 October 1947: PRO, WO 310/127.

131 JAG to War Crimes Group, 31 October 1947: PRO, WO 310/127.

> It is understood that you are interested in the above mentioned. He appears in the UNWCC List No 6 No 393 as being wanted by Czechoslovakia. He also appears in Lists 8 and 16 Nos 55 and 162 respectively as being wanted by Belgium. Finally he appears in List 7 No 246 as a German war criminal holding a key position. If you are interested in this man I will arrange for him to be brought to Tomato [Allied transit detention camp]. Will you consider in conjunction with the Belgians whether you wish to apply for his extradition with a view to avoiding if possible a clash from both countries which would have to be adjudicated upon in Berlin. I would be glad to know your proposed course of action in this case.[132]

Weeks later, however, the situation was complicated by a final attempt by British prosecutors (officials of the Judge Advocate General's office assigned to Italy) to prepare a case against Wolff regarding Fossoli. Previously, Wolff had escaped prosecution within the British war crimes programme for Italy not because the investigators regarded him as innocent but rather because, as a 'slippery customer', he had proved particularly adept at avoiding incriminating himself with respect to 'any particular crimes'.[133] In the light of the new evidence regarding atrocities in Fossoli concentration camp 'a number of witnesses are to be interrogated at the London District Cage but until this has been done it is not intended to apply for Wolf [sic] to be transferred to the London District Cage'.[134] Although this final attempt by the prosecutors to mount a trial also proved unsuccessful, it may have initially delayed, and then ultimately stalled, the possibility of Wolff being extradited.

The Belgium authorities kept open this option by replying to earlier contacts by British officials similar, presumably, to that sent to Czechoslovakia's war crimes commission. The Belgium Ministry of Justice stated (inaccurately) that, given that Wolff's alleged offences were confined to atrocities committed at Auschwitz and Dachau concentration camps, that is, to locations outside Belgium: 'The Belgium government has no intention of asking for the extradition of this subject.' However, these authorities still reserved the right to renew a request if: 'neither the British not the Czech Authorities, undertake to try the subject . . . so that this War Criminal shall not escape his due punishment. In view, thereof, my Commission would be very glad to be informed of Wolff's eventual trial, and of the verdict pronounced in due time.'[135]

With respect to the extradition issue, the attitude of the Americans who intervened in this case was, compared with that of the British, aggressively

132 Captain A. G. Somerhough, War Crimes Group (NWE) to Czechoslovakian War Crimes Commission, 20 October 1949: PRO, WO 309/347.

133 *Ibid.* 134 *Ibid.*

135 Major M. G. Fontaine, Head of Mission, Belgium War Crimes Liaison Group, to Somerhough (Bad Oeynhausen, Germany), 28 October 1947: PRO, WO 309/347.

protective of Wolff's interests. In January 1948, Telford Taylor,[136] decided to release Wolff from US custody at Nuremberg, where he had been a prosecution witness, to the War Crimes Section of the British Army of the Rhine, from whom he had been 'borrowed'. In response, Robert Murphy, who headed the Political Adviser Division of the Military Government of the American zone of Allied-occupied Germany,[137] sought to exert pressure on Wolff's behalf. At the end of January 1948, Murphy, or one of his subordinates, contacted the British Political Division of the Control Commission for Germany in Berlin 'with a request for our views on the probable future of SS-General Karl Wolff'. According to British officials, the reason Murphy gave for making this contact was that they:

> [U]nderstand that Wolff is soon to be returned to 'War Crimes Section' B.A.O.A. for further interrogation and for [a] decision regarding further disposition to be made of him [drawing attention] to the possibility of his being subsequently extradited to Czechoslovakia as a War Criminal and . . . inviting us to consider certain services he rendered to the Allied cause in Italy. The US statement of these services is impressive . . . [These are listed in a later quotation set out below]. We should be grateful for a statement of the legal position as it affects Wolff and for an indication as to what, in the normal course of events, would be his fate. In particular we would be glad to learn of any application which may have been made concerning the possible extradition of Wolff to Czechoslavakia or to any other power.[138]

The War Crimes Group replied in early March 1948 that they had forwarded this letter to JAG HQ in London who: 'in due course . . . cleared the above named of British War Crimes interest'.[139]

In January 1948, Robert Murphy also wrote to Kit Steel, British President of the Governmental Sub-Commission, Control Commission for Germany (Berlin), in similar terms. He expressed concern that, with respect to Wolff, the relevant British authority 'will give consideration to extraditing him to Czechoslovakia, or to some other country, which has requested his

136 Taylor was, as already noted, the Head Prosecutor in the American-led 'Subsequent Proceedings' at Nuremberg.

137 Referred to as 'OMGUS'. The correspondence between Murphy and Dulles over Wolff showed that these two men were on personal 'Bob and Allen' terms.

138 J. P. Davies for Chief, Political Division, HQ CCG (BE), Berlin to War Crimes Group (NWE), HQ, B. A.O.R.1, 30 January 1948: PRO, WO 309/347.

139 Somerhough to Political Division, CCG, Berlin, 3 March 1948. It also noted that Wolff was accordingly transferred to No. 2 War Criminals Holding Centre in Fischbeck for onwards transfer to No. 6 Civilian internment camp at Neuengamme: PRO, WO 309/347.

extradition as a possible war criminal'.[140] Murphy then made a series of points that he wanted the British to consider 'before determining whether or not to extradite Wolff'.[141] These partisan 'arguments for the defense' were identical to the 'impressive' list already mentioned in passing. They focused largely upon: 'his various activities as leader of the German group negotiating "Operation Sunrise–Crossword" which tended to accelerate the surrender in North Italy'. Murphy's letter then cited and paraphrased Dulles' earlier letter to General Clay (of 20 November 1947), which had noted:

> [T]hat all evidence at his [Dulles'] disposal indicates that from March 1945 onwards, Wolff, at considerable personal risk, exerted himself to the utmost to bring about the unconditional surrender of the German and Fascist forces in North Italy; that during the period in question Wolff exerted himself to prevent wanton destruction in North Italy; to protect prisoners and hostages held by the Germans; to limit last minute German reprisals and operations against the Italian partisans and to protect priceless art treasures from destruction; that Wolff liberated from the Verona dungeon Ferrucio Parri, an outstanding leader of the Italian resistance and later Prime Minister of Italy and delivered him to Dulles in Switzerland on 8 March 1945; finally, that although it was obvious that total German defeat was only a matter of weeks, the great majority of German Wehrmacht generals and others allowed the carnage to proceed, whereas Wolff tried to stop it.[142]

Subsequent sections of this chapter will discuss how Gaevernitz, and Generals Lemnitzer and Airey endorsed Dulles' pleas of mitigation. Murphy then strengthened the arguments derived from Dulles' earlier letter by revealing, 'in confidence', that 'on 7 January, 1948 American Military Government suspended further extradition to Czechoslavakia'. This was because the Czechoslovak Government had: 'by surrendering two individuals to the Soviet authorities violated its written agreement to return to US custody those individuals who had been earlier extradited to Czechoslovakia'.[143] Murphy finished his letter by stating that: 'I will greatly appreciate learning from you the disposition finally made of ex-General Wolff by the British authorities.'[144]

On 30 January 1948, Steel responded favourably to such American pressure by seeking to intervene on Wolff's behalf with the British Foreign Office, who, of course, retained an interest in any ex-SS general held in British custody. However, Dean, from the Foreign Office's German section, gave Steel a less than enthusiastic response to his representations on behalf of Dulles,

140 Murphy (Berlin) to Steel (Berlin), 'secret', 7 January 1948: PRO, FO 371/70652.
141 *Ibid.* 142 *Ibid.* 143 *Ibid.* 144 *Ibid.*

Lemnitzer and Murphy. Indeed, Dean reminded Steel that, whatever the attitude of leading American officials towards Wolff, the United Nations War Commission had previously alleged that Wolff was responsible for 'the following war crimes: medical experiments on prisoners, illegal arrest, deportation, ill-treatment of internees, mass murder and torture'.[145] He was sought for extradition not only by Belgium but also by Czechoslovakia. Hence, whilst noting his positive contribution to Sunrise–Crossword:

> [I]f there is reliable evidence that he committed some of the wide selections of crimes alleged against him, and if Czechoslovakia or Belgium can produce a strong *prima facie* case, then I think we shall have to hand him over. Indeed we will be putting ourselves in an indefensible position if we did not, and should let ourselves in for a great deal of trouble.[146]

The handwritten drafts of this correspondence suggest that Dean had received internal Foreign Office advice that: 'we cannot act otherwise in a war crimes case'.[147]

Dean was, however, willing to offer Steel (who had in effect become a mouthpiece for Dulles) the crumb of comfort that the military governor in the British zone of occupied Germany was setting up a 'special tribunal' to hear such extradition cases. This procedure would give Wolff an opportunity for stating his own case and 'bringing forward evidence in his favour'. Yet, whilst such a tribunal would, in mitigation, certainly take account of Wolff's 'behaviour in the closing stages of the war as evidence of his good character . . . I doubt whether any court could refuse his extradition on this account if there is a good *prima facie* case that he committed the crimes of which he is charged'.[148] Dean also reminded Steel that, whilst 'the Americans have suspended extradition to Czechoslovakia, I do not imagine that this is the case as far as we are concerned.'[149]

In short, between 1947 and 1948, Dulles and his Sunrise associates continued to exert pressure upon the British authorities responsible for the treatment of Wolff, including this possible extradition, to ensure that he received privileged treatment in rewards for his contribution to Operation Sunrise.

Indeed, Gaevernitz's correspondence with Dulles during February 1948 indicates that both men remained concerned to protect Wolff from extradition. They were particularly anxious to protect Wolff from a trial in a foreign regime over whom the US authorities could exert no influence, and which

145 P. Dean (London) to Steel (Berlin), 9 February 1948: PRO, FO 371/70652 referring to UNWCC List No. 7.

146 *Ibid.*

147 These notes indicate that Dean had received advice to this effect from P. Fraser on 7 January: PRO, FO 371/70652.

148 Dean (London) to Steel (Berlin), 9 February 1948: PRO, FO 371/70652.

149 *Ibid.*

would permit Wolff to use any trial to embarrass Dulles over the anti-Communist dimension to Operation Sunrise. In February 1948, Gaevernitz stated that wanted his next face-to-face meeting with Dulles to discuss 'the case of General Wolff', with a view to frustrating his proposed extradition to face war crimes charges.[150] Gaevernitz had also copied to Dulles the reply to a letter he had sent to former OSS consultant Robert Kempner. Gaevernitz's original letter had engaged in special pleading not only on behalf of Wolff but also for German General Roettiger (one of Wolff's German collaborators in Sunrise–Crossword).[151] According to Gaevernitz, these two individuals had 'rendered outstanding support at great personal risk to the success of operations "Sunrise-Crossword" '. Riddleberger's reply was that, in return for cooperating with US Army's Historical Project at Neustadt, Germany: 'his [Roettiger's] name has been removed from all war criminal wanted lists and there are no requests for his extradition'.[152] Furthermore:

> Concerning General Karl Wolff, he is now in the custody of the U.S. Chief of Counsel for war crimes at Nuremberg. It is my understanding that he will be returned very soon to the war crimes section of the British Army of the Rhine from which he had been borrowed. I have been told that the British War Crimes Section wishes to interrogate Wolff on certain matters, after which it will give consideration to extraditing him to Czechoslovakia or some other country which has requested his extradition as a possible war criminal.[153]

Gaevernitz was clearly alarmed at the implications of these developments. In a letter to Dulles, he suggested that, over and above their shared 'moral commitment' towards Wolff: 'I believe it would be a grave political error if he had to be extradited to Czecho Slavakia [sic] – for very obvious reasons.'[154] Unsurprisingly, during a period of escalating Cold War tensions, in which war crimes issues had become one element within an increasingly strident exchange of ideological criticisms between East and West, Dulles agreed with his former senior assistant. He suggested resorting to the already well-proven strategy of exploiting the good offices of those senior military contacts amongst the Allies whom had previously been involved in Operation Sunrise:

> The thing to do would be to drop a line to Field Marshal Alexander. It is one thing for Wolff to be tried by American or British justice but to have

150 Gaevernitz to Dulles, 7 February 1948: Dulles Papers, Box 59, Folder 9.

151 This is partly quoted in the reply from James Riddleberger, deputy to Ambassador Robert Murphy, to whom Kempner had wisely forwarded the letter.

152 Riddleberger (OMGUS, Berlin) to Gaevernitz, 23 January 1948: Dulles Papers, Box 59, Folder 9.

153 *Ibid.*

154 Gaevernitz to Dulles, 7 February 1948: Dulles Papers, Box 59, Folder 9.

> him turned over to the Czechs or by them to the Russians would be unconscionable.[155]

Later internal Military Government correspondence, presumably copied to Dulles (as he had copies in his personal files), is instructive. It indicates that Robert Murphy had renewed his request for Kit Steel to disclose any developments in the Wolff case, including any possibility of extradition. On 9 March 1948, Steel reported back that:

> War Crimes Group British Army of the Rhine inform me that Wolff has been cleared by them and has now been transferred to No.2 War Criminals Holding Centre in Fischbeck, from where he will move to No.6 Civilian Internment Camp at Neuengamme to appear before a German denazification panel. Although there does appear to have been some talk about Wolff's possible extradition to Italy and Czechoslovia, nothing seems to have come of it and . . . no formal application for his extradition has been received from a foreign Government.[156]

Meanwhile, British legal and war crimes officials based in Germany noted that, since Wolff had been released from his Nuremberg cell on 30 January, they had been subjected to pressure from 'on high', following the Americans' interventions. 'British and American attention on high level' had focused on how the British planned to dispose of Wolff, with particular concern relating to the possibility of his extradition. One middle-ranking army lawyer recorded, possibly with a degree of scepticism in the face of these American interventions, that: 'The interest from on high centres round the fact that from March 1945 onwards he apparently turned 100% pro-Ally and did everything he could to bring about the final collapse in North Italy.'[157] This contention was, of course, almost identical to the central claims of the Dulles group. In the event of *both* Belgium and Czechoslovakia requesting his extradition, this British official noted: 'it is presumed the procedure laid down by Control Council No. 10 will be followed and the matter referred to the Legal Directorate, to decide the priorities'.[158] In order to 'determine what action is proper to take' in these circumstances, this official asked to receive 'advance information on this' from any of the different branches of Military Government with jurisdiction over Wolff's possible extradition.[159]

The British authorities, who had received Clay's letter including Dulles'

155 Dulles to Gaevernitz, 9 February 1948: *ibid*, Box 59, Folder 9.

156 Steel to Murphy, 9 March 1948: *ibid*, Box 59, Folder 9.

157 N. H. Moller, Deputy Chief, Zonal Executive Office, CCG, BAOR to War Crimes Group (NWE), BAOR, 28 February 1948: Dulles Papers, Box 59, Folder 9.

158 *Ibid*. 159 *Ibid*.

statements of support for Wolff, had, at this stage, just abandoned their plans to prosecute Wolff for war crimes against Italian civilians. Instead, and possibly to pre-empt Wolff's extradition, British officials decided to prosecute Wolff before a German de-Nazification court/tribunal. This 'resolved' the difficult issues raised by contested extradition proceedings that had already aroused the forceful interventions of Dulles' various high-ranking military and political contacts.

Having successfully intervened to fend off the possibility of extradition, Dulles and other Anglo-American participants in Operation Sunrise renewed their support for Wolff's legal defence in the forthcoming de-Nazification trial in Germany.

The 'Old Lace' de-Nazification trials

The British authorities charged Wolff under Military Government Ordinance No. 69 with: 'being or remaining a member of an organisation declared to be criminal by the Nuremberg judgement with knowledge of the criminal acts and purposes of the organisation'. Lemnitzer, whom Dulles had asked to support Wolff, intervened repeatedly. He did so in a manner that needed to be discussed and approved at the highest levels of administration. These involved the Military Governor personally in the decision-making loop. There is an interesting anonymous handwritten comment on a document regarding Wolff held by the Private Office of the Military Governor. (This earlier correspondence reveals that Nuremberg prosecutors had provided the British with three entire files of incriminating evidence on Wolff.) The annotation, possibly from the Military Governor himself, expresses concern that: 'It looks as if Mr Wolff will get a pretty stiff sentence unless we do something about it.'[160]

It is widely noted that Dulles and one of his senior aides even supplied Wolff's lawyers with an affidavit, dated 21 May 1949, for use during his appeal hearing before the German-organised Old Lace Court in Hamburg. This stated that: 'In my opinion, General Wolff's action during the period March–May 1945 materially contributed to bringing about the end of the war in Italy and thereby hastened the end of general hostilities.'[161] Gaevernitz and Generals Lemnitzer and Airey each lent their strong personal support to Wolff by providing sworn affidavits for his defence lawyers. On 4 September 1948, Lemnitzer personally visited General Brian Robertson whilst the latter was in London and, according to Robertson, was:

160 Chief Legal Division, OCC (Nuremberg) to Office of Military Governor Berlin, 14 August 1948: PRO, FO 1030/424.

161 Cited in the second feature article on Wolff in the German weekly magazine *Revue*, No. 19, 13 May 1950.

> [G]reatly concerned about the Wolff case. He feels very strongly that Wolff's action in regard to these [Sunrise] negotiations should be held to compensate for any past misdeeds. He is going to send me a statement which he wishes to put into the trial. He also suggested that I should get in touch with Airey [a British Military official involved in Sunrise].[162]

Robertson, who at this time was clearly a key player in the British element of the Allied Military Government of Germany, reacted positively to such American pressure. He sought and obtained a supportive affidavit from General Airey. Robertson then forwarded Airey's sworn affidavit to William Strang, Secretary of State in the British Foreign Office.[163] Of particular interest for present purposes is Airey's understanding of the precise *reasons why these particular American officials* (all of whom were directly associated with Dulles' Operation Sunrise) were so anxious to protect Wolff:

> I should add that Wolff had stated that assurances were given to him at the time [of the wartime negotiations] about his future treatment. Airey tells me quite positively that no such assurances were given to his knowledge, but he adds the following: 'Nevertheless, one cannot be sure that, at some level, Wolff may not have been given some inducements by agents of the O.S.S. . . . my experience of the workings of the occult services lead me to conclude that it would be wise to assume they were.'[164]

Although previous research has recognised the fact that Airey and Lemnitzer presented affidavits for use by Wolff's defence lawyers, the impact of geo-political factors in shaping these interventions has not, to date, been clarified. First, it needs to be recognised that the very idea of a high-ranking American general providing such public support to one of Himmler's two most senior SS officials raised questions of a distinctly political and diplomatic character. One issue posed by Lemnitzer's proposed intervention was:

> whether an affidavit by U.S. General Lemnitzer testifying to the great saving in lives on both sides by the action taken by General Wolff . . . would do more harm than good, if tendered in evidence on behalf of Wolff before the special German Tribunal which is to try him.[165]

The Military Governor referred this novel question to the 'Office of the Legal Adviser of the British Element' (also based in Berlin). Remarkably, this

162 Robertson (Berlin) to William Strang (Secretary for State, Foreign Office, London), 4 September 1948: PRO, FO 371/70652.

163 *Ibid.* 164 *Ibid.*

165 Re Karl Wolff, Office of Legal Adviser Berlin (N. Macaskie) to Personal Staff of Military Governor, 18 August 1948: PRO, FO 1030/424.

official provided some informed advice as to how Lemnitzer's affidavit should be worded in order to exert the optimal rhetorical effect upon the tribunal hearing Wolff's case. The willingness to offer such advice meant that the American and British authorities were, in effect, providing substantial 'insider' assistance to Wolff's legal team, albeit indirectly. This is all the more remarkable when we consider that, in effect, these lawyers were preparing a *defence case* against a charge brought under their own government's de-Nazification laws. Furthermore, Wolff's case was going to be decided by a tribunal, and within a wider prosecution system, that the Anglo-American authorities *had themselves established precisely to punish and deter former Nazis, virtually all of whom were of lower rank with Hitler's regime than Wolff.* If a case involving Himmler's former Chief of Staff was not considered to fall at the most severe end of the spectrum deserving of the most rigorous and committed prosecution before such de-Nazification proceedings, then it is difficult to imagine a case that would so qualify.

The British legal adviser's opinion on Lemnitzer's proposed affidavit was both detailed and designed to provide the most effective form of intervention, even to the point of falsification:

> [S]uch an affidavit would be regarded by the tribunal as a mitigating circumstance in reduction of punishment, particularly if it emphasises the fact that further resistance was hopeless and that General Wolff's actions resulted in the saving of very many German lives and if it were combined with evidence of the fact: (a) that neither the Americans nor ourselves have found any ground for charging him with the commission of a war crime, (b) that, although he held high rank in the SS, his services were rendered as a fighting general in areas where he had little or no opportunity of acquiring knowledge of the criminal acts or purposes of the organisation of which he was a member, and (c) that he had been in detention ever since the end of hostilities either in the hands of the Americans or in our hands.[166]

Arguably, this advice as to how best 'construct' this element of trial evidence misrepresented the nature of Wolff's role as leading administrator within the SS and Himmler's trusted adviser. It also drew highly questionable conclusions from the fact that he had (following earlier interventions by Dulles and Gaevernitz) escaped prosecution both at Nuremberg and within the British war crimes programme in Italy. Indeed, the false claim that Wolff had been 'a fighting general' in Italy, and therefore distant from either active participation within, or insight into, SS atrocities, had been specifically corrected in earlier correspondence. This had informed the British Foreign Office that Wolff had

166 *Ibid.*

been: 'head of the SS and Police in Italy and not a member of the German fighting services'.[167] The legal adviser not only offered this expert advice but also promised to intervene indirectly through the Ministry of Justice Control Branch. This intervention was to take place with the 'German heads of the Central Legal Office, who are responsible for the "Old Lace" [de-Nazification Tribunal] operation, to get their reaction to the use of such an affidavit before a German Tribunal'.[168]

Lemnitzer ultimately produced two affidavits. The first, which was originally intended to be the sole version, included a series of statements clearly designed to support Wolff but without considering the geo-political imperative to re-affirm earlier American and British interpretations of Dulles' role in Operation Sunrise. The implications of this first affidavit generated controversy leading to a flurry of diplomatic 'top secret' correspondence between the American and British authorities, which in itself merits close review. Airey's affidavit was also originally transmitted from Berlin to London as the final draft but subject to the proviso that: 'if there is anything in Airey's affidavit which gives the wrong impression owing to the way it is drafted I have no doubt that I could get Airey to submit a fresh affidavit'.[169]

Wolff certainly recognised and exploited the potential embarrassment for the OSS generally, and for Dulles in particular, of himself being given a public forum within a war crimes trial. Prior to his de-Nazification hearing, Wolff's lawyers threatened to exploit the Anglo-American vulnerability concerning the distinctly (but arguably justifiably) anti-Soviet aspect of Operation Sunrise. In the words of the British authorities, Wolff's lawyers showed that they: 'were clearly aware of our [Anglo-American] desire that the evidence. . . about Wolff's part in the Armistice arrangements. . . should not be used'.[170] Wolff's lawyers threatened to expose the allegation: 'that we are concealing evidence of our having made arrangements with the Germans at the expense of the Soviet forces'.[171] Allowing Wolff to testify on this particularly sensitive aspect of his negotiations with Dulles could have resulted in the defence lawyers making highly sensitive and embarrassing revelations with distinct geo-political ramifications at a time of escalating East/West tensions.

Not surprisingly, the thought of Wolff's lawyers making embarrassing

167 Lt. Col. Gidd, WCG, Legal Division, 2 February 1948, Memo in relation to Col. Barratt obtaining: 'a Foreign Office ruling as to the disposal of Wolff . . . meanwhile he would remain in Tomato as a potential war criminal': PRO, WO 309/347.

168 *Ibid.*

169 Robertson (Berlin, HQ CCG(BE)) to Kirkpatrick (London), marked 'Personal and Confidential', 17 September 1948: PRO, FO 371/70652.

170 Brownjohn to General Robertson, Telegram 419, 2 October 1948 (also distributed to Military Governor, Chief of Staff and Political Adviser): PRO, FO 1030/424.

171 *Ibid.*

political revelations generated considerable anxiety amongst senior Anglo-American diplomatic, intelligence and military circles. Understandably fearful of allowing legal proceedings to provide the Soviets with a propaganda coup, senior British officials within the Allied 'Office of the Military Governor' for Germany made plans to 'pressurise' Wolff. Their counter-strategy was to threaten to withhold affidavits from Airey, Lemnitzer, Gaevernitz and others useful to Wolff's defence if he, or his lawyers, ever made such revelations in open court before both national and international media. As General Robertson noted:

> I would have thought that ways would be found for conveying to Wolff's counsel the impression that any attempt by him or his client to show that negotiations with Wolff were aimed at arresting the advance of communist forces would . . . hinder Allied officers who might otherwise be able to produce evidence as to the true and useful part actually played by Wolff . . . I cannot allow affidavits from [Generals] Airey and Lemnitzer to be handed to Wolff's counsel unless he gives some undertaking that he will drop the anti-Communist story.[172]

Amongst these senior governmental circles, it was also appreciated, however, that such threats to his German lawyers could not, in any event, have prevented Wolff from having 'his say' in open court. Furthermore, if these interventions became exposed as an example of improper governmental pressure upon the supposedly independent judicial process to 'suppress the evidence', then they would have 'looked very bad'. Hence, as a fallback position, these officials developed a counter-propaganda line to combat the threat of Soviet ideological exploitation of this potential embarrassment.[173] Robertson wrote to Kirkpatrick, Assistant Under-Secretary of State in the British Foreign Office, drawing attention to the decidedly geo-political dimensions of Wolff's trial. However, Robertson confirmed that he had already taken action to suppress the most potentially damaging aspect of Wolff's threat to re-kindle controversy with the Soviets concerning Operation Sunrise:

> I would be grateful for authority to hand the two Affidavits to the defence Counsel. In this connection the Secretary of State might like to know that I received a report to the effect that Wolff's counsel intended to take the line that negotiations with Wolff were aimed at arresting the advance of the Communist forces of the U.S.S.R. and Yugoslavia. On receiving this report I arranged for unofficial contact to be made with

172 Robertson (Foreign Office) to Brownjohn, 'Trial of Obergruppenführer Wolff', 'Top Secret', Telegram 327, 3 October 1948: PRO, FO, 1030/424.

173 *Ibid.*

> Wolff's Counsel in order to advise him that if he took that line he must expect to find allied officers rebutting it and giving evidence prejudicial to Wolff's case. Wolff's counsel immediately accepted this advice and has given assurances that he will not take this line. I hope that the Secretary of State will find it possible to give me the requisite authority because General Lemnitzer has taken a strong personal interest in this case.[174]

In other words, part of this 'shotgun agreement' was that, in return for receiving supportive affidavits from Lemnitzer and Airey, Wolff's lawyers agreed to suppress evidence of an anti-Communist dimension to Operation Sunrise. As already noted, such trial evidence would have embarrassed both Dulles and the Anglo-US authorities more generally, precisely at a time of heightening tension and ideological conflict with the Soviet empire.

Under these intensely political circumstances it is, perhaps, not surprising that the British authorities in London also asked Lemnitzer to revise his affidavit, which he was willing to do.[175] The reasons necessitating this revision were considered highly sensitive by all parties. As a result, the correspondence relating to this was originally classified as 'top secret'. Lemnitzer was also anxious to avoid copies of the original version becoming public as this could be compared with the revised copy to reveal the extent to which he had changed his evidence for geo-political reasons. Presumably, he was concerned that this would expose the fact that, in a sworn affidavit intended as hard documentary evidence within a criminal trial, he had amended his first-hand account of 'the facts' in order to comply with specific geo-political and diplomatic factors:

> General Lemnitzer has again requested us to ask you to be sure, when sending his new affidavit on to General Robertson, [British Administrator in Berlin] to recover from the latter for return to Lemnitzer all three copies of the original affidavit which Lemnitzer provided.[176]

A hand-written annotation suggests that the British were willing to comply with Lemnitzer's attempts to 'cover his tracks', and no copy of the original affidavit has apparently survived.

Presumably, he destroyed the origin draft once it was returned to him as he requested. However, the remainder of the declassified correspondence provides sufficient detail to allow us to reconstruct precisely which sections of the original affidavit Lemnitzer subsequently removed and altered.

174 Robertson to Kirkpatrick (Personal and Secret), 8 October 1948: PRO, FO 371/70652.

175 The original request was in a Foreign Office Telegram No. 11188 of 11 October 1948, cited in Allen (British Embassy Washington) to Sir Ivone Kirkpatrick (London), 13 October 1948 (enclosing in a sealed envelope a copy of the revised affidavit): PRO, FO 371/70652.

176 *Ibid.*

This correspondence also provides additional clues as to why the authorities deemed this necessary. The British diplomatic authorities, specifically Sir Ivone Kirkpatrick,[177] considered the original affidavit to raise such sensitive political and geo-political issues that it required immediate consultation with the US State Department (broadly speaking, the American equivalent to the British Foreign Office). In turn, this consultation resulted in a telephone call to Hickerson, an American diplomat:

> In view of the political issues involved, we thought it best to consult the State Department in the first place rather than to approach General Lemnitzer either direct or through the Joint Staff Mission . . . Hickerson quite appreciated the position and at once telephoned to Lemnitzer. From what I could hear of the conversation Lemnitzer seemed equally to understand the situation and to be perfectly prepared to fall in with your suggestion . . . I understand that Lemnitzer is quite ready to redraft his affidavit as you suggested. He will, however, have to have an entirely fresh complete text typed out and sworn before a public notary.[178]

Kirkpatrick had sent two telegrams to Miller, from which he produced a memorandum for Lemnitzer to use as the basis for revising his affidavit to ensure that the new version of 'the facts' would better match shared Anglo-American diplomatic and geo-political sensitivities.

The precise nature of the British sensitivities regarding the contents of the two affidavits becomes clearer if we consider both the historical background and the flurry of correspondence over the affidavits. General Robertson's letter to Strang indicates that he was willing to facilitate Lemnitzer and Airey providing affidavits for Wolff in a legal proceeding in the British zone of Allied-occupied Germany. However, this raised one particularly delicate question of East–West relations, the 'Bern Episode'. (Some writers have traced the start of escalating Cold War tensions between Stalin on the one side and the Anglo-Americans on the other to the row that erupted over Dulles' 'negotiations' with Wolff in Bern during March–April 1945, from which the Soviets were excluded.)[179] Robertson reminded Foreign Secretary Strang:

> [T]hat Stalin took very particular exception to these negotiations. I do not feel that this fact should prevent me from taking the course I propose [re the two affidavits]. Certain statements and explanations were however

177 Undersecretary for State the Foreign Office and the latter's subordinate Hoyer Miller from the British embassy in Washington.

178 Hoyer Miller to Kirkpatrick, 12 October 1948: PRO, FO 371/70652.

179 A. Beevor, *The Fall of Berlin* (New York: Viking Press, 1992), 78. In fact, the Soviets had been invited to be present at the signing of the surrender in Italy.

> given to the Russians at that time and it would be unfortunate if Airey's affidavit contradicted what had been said previously. In the present state of our relations with the Russians I imagine that there is no reason to be unduly tender about their feelings but of course we must not do anything to falsify the position which we took when those events occurred. As the trial is due to take place shortly I should be grateful for an early reply.[180]

Kirkpatrick replied that Strang 'who remembers the whole question in the Cabinet, is slightly uneasy at reviving these unpleasant memories'.[181] Kirkpatrick then engaged in a classic example of bureaucratic 'double-speak'. He insisted, on the one hand, that 'there is no real inconsistency between General Airey's affidavit and what we told Stalin because we told Stalin the truth'. However, on the other hand:

> The Secretary of State [Strang] fastened on the first sentence of paragraph six of the affidavit, which is perhaps unfortunately worded. He says that this sentence represents that the surrender was negotiated with Karl Wolff but according to our own [earlier] account . . . surrender was negotiated at Caserta [Italy, where the official signatures were given by SS Col. Eugen Wenner, Wolff's representative] . . . The Secretary of State is afraid that the wording of the opening sentence of paragraph six will give the Russians the impression that the real surrender was negotiated in Italy with Karl Wolff, whilst proceedings in Caserta were merely a blind [deception]. He has asked me to go into the matter again without prejudice to his final decision. I shall continue to do my best to get you an early and satisfactory reply.[182]

Robertson then cabled Kirkpatrick in London an extract of the text of Lemnitzer's original affidavit, also copied to the legal and intelligence divisions of the British authorities in Berlin. Kirkpatrick (or possibly Strang) annotated this telegram.[183] Kirkpatrick's earlier telegram from London to the British embassy in Washington, which was itself classified as 'of particular secrecy', reveals that General Robertson had indicated that Lemnitzer's affidavit 'would be acceptable to the Secretary of State if amended'. The proposed amendments related to the need to remove references to the fact that, contrary to the wartime reassurances given to placate Stalin, Dulles had

180 Robertson (Berlin) to William Strang (Secretary for State, Foreign Office, London), 4 September 1948: PRO, FO 371/70652.

181 Kirkpatrick to Robertson (Personal and Confidential), 14 September 1948: PRO, FO 371/70652.

182 *Ibid.*

183 Cable 4483, Robertson via Lubbecke to Kirkpatrick, Foreign Office (London, German Section), 10 October 1948: PRO, FO 371/70652.

engaged in mutually beneficial 'negotiations' with Wolff. Hence, the following statements contained in Airey's first affidavit were marked for deletion:

> negotiations were prolonged ... my instructions were to negotiate ... the standpoint he [Wolff] adopted in negotiations ... as a result of these negotiations ... the surrender of the German armies in Italy was negotiated, therefore, with Karl Wolff.[184]

In response to Robertson's concerns, Kirkpatrick noted that Lemnitzer and Airey were part of the Allied team in Operation Sunrise–Crossword that, officially at least, was supposed to strictly comply with the prohibition on secret negotiations with the Nazis:

> The Russians were not allowed to participate and this led to a major row between Stalin and ourselves. The United States President and Mr Churchill gave Stalin categorical assurances that there had been no negotiations in Switzerland even for a military surrender of the German Armies. All that had been done was to arrange for the dispatch of German emissaries to Caserta where the surrender would be negotiated in the presence of Russian officers. General Airey and General Lemnitzer in the interest of justice have made affidavits describing the course of events ... But if we are to avoid a revival of the row with Stalin it is essential that the affidavit should not contradict the categorical assurances of the President and Mr Churchill.[185]

In other words, in order to placate Stalin, the Anglo-American political leaders had provided one interpretation of 'the facts' to the Soviet leadership. This was given in response to Stalin's allegation that, contrary to wartime policy of unconditional surrender agreed at the Casablanca conference in 1943,[186] the Anglo-Americans were, in private, negotiating a mutually beneficial surrender deal with Wolff in Switzerland. This arrangement operated in effect to exclude both the representatives and wider interests of the Soviets by making it less likely that Red Army forces or communist partisans would ever advance to the point of seizing control of Austria and the strategically important port of Trieste.

British sensitivities on this point were understandable because it would have been acutely embarrassing for them if one of the Anglo-American parties with first-hand experience of these 'negotiations' with Wolff made a sworn

184 *Ibid.*

185 Kirkpatrick to Hoyer Millar, Cable 11188, 11 October 1948: PRO, FO 371/70652.

186 As already noted, this policy insisted that a German surrender had to be entirely 'unconditional' and given to the Allies as a whole.

statement, read out in open court, that blatantly contradicted the earlier Anglo-American's reassurances to Stalin. In short, it was now clear to senior British diplomats that both Lemnitzer and Airey's original affidavits needed amendment because they contained references that unintentionally lent support to Stalin's earlier complaints, and thereby falsified the official version of Dulles' wartime contacts with Wolff.

The two options for the British diplomatic authorities were either to admit that these wartime reassurances to Stalin were false, either in whole or in part, or to ask Lemnitzer and Airey to alter their account of 'the facts' to better match the earlier reassurances given to Stalin. The British decision was in favour of the second option. The discussion over Airey's affidavit had even reached the level of the British Secretary of State, William Strang.[187] Given that Airey was still a British officer, he was required to alter his affidavit. In this respect, his military superiors noted: 'We have seen to this with regards to General Airey's affidavit.'[188]

This, however, still left the question of whether the interpretation of 'the facts' contained in Lemnitzer's affidavit also needed amending to better match those of the official version. Kirkpatrick's opinion was that such amendment was vital:

> But unfortunately General Lemnitzer's affidavit . . . is not entirely watertight in that he states that at the conference in Switzerland the means and methods for ending the war in Italy were discussed in considerable detail. He also speaks of representatives proceeding to Caserta to 'complete' final arrangements for the termination of hostilities. The [British] Secretary of State attaches considerable importance to ensuring that the affidavits are in line with our assurances to Stalin.[189]

The problem, of course, was that if it had been true that 'no negotiations of any kind' had taken place between Wolff, Dulles and the two generals, then there could have been no question of 'completing' arrangements, but rather merely establishing a system for making contact. If the wartime official reassurances had been entirely accurate, there would have been no 'discussion' of the 'means and methods for ending the war' because the only officially permitted option was for an entirely 'unconditional' form of surrender. The latter prohibited processes of discussion amounting to negotiations over terms and conditions. Hence, Kirkpatrick stated:

187 Kirkpatrick, to Secretary of State: 'the case of General Wolff', 9 September 1948 (annotated: 'I agree, W. Strang. 10/9'): PRO, FO 371/70652.

188 *Ibid.*

189 Kirkpatrick to Hoyer Millar, Cable 11188, 11 October 1948: PRO, FO 371/70652.

> We accordingly suggest the following amendments to the affidavit. Delete the words 'the means and methods for ending the war in Italy were discussed in considerable detail. In addition' and in same sentence substitute the words 'make arrangements' for 'complete arrangements'. Please show this telegram to general Lemnitzer and ask if in the circumstances described he would be good enough to amend the affidavit as suggested. If as we hope he will be ready to do so we should be grateful if he would send it direct to General Robertson. The matter is urgent in view of the imminence of the trial.[190]

On 13 October 1948, Lemnitzer redrafted his affidavit in the exact way that the British authorities had suggested. The remainder of the affidavit was based largely on information supplied by Gaevernitz's highly favourable report on his immediate post-war visit to Wolff at his luxurious Bozen HQ. Lemnitzer reinterpreted this friendly and supportive visit as an 'investigation of events' immediately prior to, and during, the surrender period that he, Lemnitzer, had personally commissioned Gaevernitz to provide.

Lemnitzer's revised and 'sanitised' affidavit emphasised Wolff's willingness to risk his life in the cause of peace, and the decisive role he had played in the Italian capitulation:

> Much of the success in implementing the terms of the surrender agreement and in terminating the hostilities in Italy was due to General Wolff's determined action and his insistence on carrying out the terms of the surrender agreement. It is my opinion that General Wolff's actions in this regard resulted in the saving of many lives and much property and contributed materially toward expediting the end of the war in Europe.[191]

General Airey's affidavit claimed that, from his experience of working with Dulles in Operation Sunrise:

> It was clear to me that Wolff's object was to save further bloodshed and destruction and fighting a hopeless defensive battle in the 'National Redoubt' [Alpine fortress locations]. The standpoint he adopted ... made this quite clear to me at the time. On this basis we included demands that the Germans should avoid all further destruction in Italy and among other things specifically that the hydro-electric power stations should be preserved ... Wolff had personally intervened and ordered that the surrender take place on his own responsibility, an act entailing great personal risk ... His action led to the abandonment of the fighting withdrawal through the remainder of Italy into Austria and must

190 *Ibid.* 191 Sworn affidavit of General Lemnitzer, 13 October 1948: PRO, FO 1030/424.

> necessarily have saved the lives of a large number of German soldiers, Austrian and Italian civilians, and avoided further useless destruction not only on the battlefield but from bombing which would have continued had the campaign been further prolonged. The surrender of such a large part of the German forces cannot have been without its effect on the German High Command in Germany itself and may well have hastened the end of resistance by the Nazi forces in that country. I must make it clear that, as a direct result . . . Italian industry and property, and the important power stations of North Italy, were saved from destruction.[192]

Although misleading when taken as the whole truth, Lemnitzer's statement is not entirely inaccurate. Its misleading quality stems from a combination of exaggeration and the omission of countervailing factors, not least the fact that Wolff's contributions emerged as part of the 'give and take' of a wider deal with Dulles. By omitting to mention the various advantages that Wolff obtained in return for these contributions, including the promise of favourable post-war treatment, Lemnitzer's affidavit created a distinctly false impression of Wolff's actions and intentions without actually stating anything that was factually untrue.

In short, and following a process of geo-politically determined amendment to trial evidence, both Lemnitzer and Airey provided favourable affidavits. These argued that, within any future legal hearings, Wolff needed to be given considerable credit for brokering a peace deal that had saved numerous lives on both sides, hastened the end of the war and preserved key industrial plants and public utilities from destruction as required by Hitler's scorched-earth policy.[193] Such factors should be treated as more than compensating for any past complicity in war crimes.

Wolff's case was heard between 3 and 7 November 1948 by a de-Nazification tribunal, in this case known as 'Old Lace' trial, located at Bergedorf, Hamburg. Although deliberately low-key, it was observed and reported upon by the German Court's Inspectorate of the Ministry of Justice Control Branch. It was deemed a case of particular interest because of Wolff's seniority as 'Himmler's adjutant of many years . . . [who] had in 1945 negotiated the surrender of the German Armies'. The affidavits of Lemnitzer and Airey were read out in open court. The report records the significance the court attached to Wolff's role in the surrender negotiations, his period of interrogation and detention at Nuremberg and London and that 'no

192 Sworn affidavit of Major General T. S. Airey, 27 August 1948: PRO, FO 1030/424. The references to 'negotiations' were removed from the copy read out in the trial but that revised version could not be located within the relevant archival records.

193 *Ibid.*

proceedings on charges of committing War Crimes were, however, commenced against him'.[194]

In addition to the help provided by the affidavits from the two generals involved in Operation Sunrise, Dulles' interests in protecting Wolff during the initial hearing were also well served by the oral testimony of his former associate within this operation, Professor Husmann. Husmann claimed that:

> It was largely due to Wolff's initiative and courage that the negotiations did not fail. It was also due to Wolff's courageous act of returning to the German HQ on 28 April 1945, and personally supervising the implementation of the surrender terms that the actual surrender was carried through without incident.[195]

As it transpired, Wolff's lawyers appear to have honoured their covert agreement not to highlight, or even mention, the distinctly anti-Soviet aspect of Operation Sunrise. The prosecution willingly accepted nearly all the demands of Wolff's defence lawyers, with the sole exception of insisting that Wolff still be convicted on the charge of 'voluntary membership of the SS with knowledge of its involvements in criminal acts'. This was an offence that Wolff, as Himmler's former top administrator, could barely deny. Hence, the authors of the inspectors' report on the trial (who must have been briefed on the geo-political dimension) reassured the authorities that, although the public and press were well represented, 'Dr Husman [sic] did not touch on the scope or content of the negotiations, nor was Wolff examined thereon.'[196] The affidavits of Lemnitzer and Airey recording Wolff's positive role 'in bringing the negotiations to a successful conclusion, and thereby saving North Italian industry and considerable number of human lives' were also noted approvingly.[197]

On 8 November 1948, the Tribunal found Wolff guilty of an organisational membership offence under Ordinance No. 69. This meant that, although convicted of 'membership of a criminal organisation', unlike many of those of his subordinates who had been convicted and executed for carrying out his orders, Wolff avoided being personally charged with committing individual war crimes. He was sentenced to five years' imprisonment. However, the court discounted two years from this sentence in recognition of his period of prior internment. The Tribunal's judgment was that, despite Wolff's seniority in what was the 'most criminal' of the 'criminal organisations', the SS, his

194 Deputy Legal Adviser (signature illegible), Zonal Office of the Legal Adviser Germany, to Foreign Office (2) German Section, London/Office of the Legal Adviser, HQ, CCG (BE), Operation 'Old Lace' – Reports on trials of Karl Wolff before Spruchgericht Bergedorf, 9 November 1948: PRO, FO1030/424.

195 *Ibid.* 196 *Ibid.* 197 *Ibid.*

cooperation with Dulles (as portrayed in entirely positive terms by Dulles' intermediaries and associates) amounted to *a substantial mitigating factor*:

> On the one hand . . . Wolff's guilt was very considerable, because he had held a very high rank for a long time, and had very extensive knowledge of the criminal concentration camps, persecution of the Jews, forced labour and Germanisation activities. On the other hand, the mitigating circumstances were also considerable, for he had not had any hand in any criminal activity and had tried to prevent excesses as far as he could, though this did not amount to sabotage. Furthermore, he had the courage to bring about the North Italian capitulations, at the risk of his own life.[198]

The British authorities based in Berlin were clearly cooperating closely with the Americans involved in Operation Sunrise over Wolff's trial. For example, Macaskie, a senior official in the Office of the Legal Adviser British Element, wrote directly to British General Brian Robertson, who in turn liaised with Lemnitzer. The tone of the correspondence, together with the fact that such senior officials were involved in Wolff's case at all, makes it clear that the senior players actively sought either a lenient sentence, or an acquittal, to minimise the potential geo-political ramifications. Macaskie, who clearly recognised the pressure from 'on high', noted to General Robertson:

> Bearing in mind the fact that for a number of years he acted as Himmler's Chief of Staff and must have been well aware of the enormities perpetrated by the SS, of which Himmler was the head, I think you will agree the sentence is a very lenient one. I have called for a full report on the case and . . . I will send it to you.[199]

Dulles had clearly successfully lobbied his former senior military contacts and received an interesting letter from Lemnitzer updating him on the Wolff case. Lemnitzer enthusiastically records the contents of a letter he had received from General Robertson:

> General Robertson informs me that he considered the sentence a very lenient one. He believes that the affidavits signed by Airey and myself undoubtedly influenced the Court favourably in reaching its decision.[200]

This letter confirms that, over three years after the culmination of Operation Sunrise and the dissolution of the OSS, Dulles and senior intelligence and

198 *Ibid.* 199 Macaskie (Berlin) to Robertson, 9 November 1948: PRO, FO 1030/424.
200 Lemnitzer to Dulles, 23 November 1948: Dulles Papers, Box 59, Folder 9.

military figures associated with this operation continued to support Wolff. Possibly, if Airey's suspicions based on previous experience with Dulles were correct, this stemmed from a felt obligation to honour earlier and private commitments, probably made through intermediaries during the capitulation negotiations. Furthermore, it provides evidence that the British officials in overall charge of organising the prosecutions considered such interventions to have been highly successful, particularly given that they clearly realised that the evidence merited a far 'stiffer' sentence.

The interventions into the legal process by Dulles and Gaevernitz continued into 1949. In April of that year, Gaevernitz wrote to Dulles indicating that he had used family contacts within Germany to keep in contact with Wolff and his lawyers preparing an appeal against the earlier conviction and sentence. He informed Dulles that he, and other Sunrise participants, had already supplied additional, supportive affidavits for the defence, and asked him to intervene yet again within legal proceedings on Wolff's behalf, not as a private citizen but specifically in his capacity as a former OSS official:

> My brother in law, Edmund H. Stinnes, conferred recently in Germany with Karl Wolff's attorney, Dr Behn. I am enclosing copy of a recent letter from Dr Behn to Edmund. The appeal of Wolff's case will come before a German court during the first days of May [1949]. In this connection it will be of the greatest importance that an affidavit from you, describing in detail Wolff's accomplishments, should be available. As you know, both General Lemnitzer and General Airey as well as I, have given such affidavits, and you will understand that the German authorities are anxious to have an affidavit from you as the principal American participant. Dr Behn feels that the outcome of the appeal will largely depend on the fact whether such an affidavit from you will be available. Personally I feel that Wolff deserves such an affidavit. He has been in prison for almost four years, as a result of which his health has been severely affected. This seems particularly unjust in view of the fact that many arch-Nazis have by now been released . . . [who had] never done anything to assist the Allied war effort. Dear Allen, I feel that it would be most helpful if you would send an affidavit as soon as possible, as the matter is urgent.[201]

Gaevernitz's letter is remarkable in that it suggests that the Tribunal was not entirely independent from the 'German authorities' who, at this time, were still operating under Allied supervision, and that these 'authorities' were to base their decision partly in the basis of Dulles' affidavit.

Lemnitzer continued to be one of the main channels through which Dulles

201 Gaevernitz to Dulles, 9 April 1949: Box 27, Folder 4.

supported Wolff. Despite having been congratulated on contributing to Wolff's 'very lenient sentence', Lemnitzer, now promoted to a senior position in Office of the Secretary of Defense in Washington, challenged the fairness of the original conviction and sentence. His critique was that it was 'incredible' that Wolff had received a sentencing 'discount' only for the two years he had spent in British custody but no such 'credit' for the similar period he had spent in American custody at Nuremberg. Lemnitzer also claimed to have heard a rumour that the sentence was 'well known in advance of the trial' and that, if true, this 'would cause a frightful reaction in our press'.

Curiously, he even attempted to challenge the legal basis of the conviction, notwithstanding the fact the criminal organisation charge was a distinctly American innovation (derived from anti-syndicate measures). Lemnitzer claimed: 'some doubt was raised by various Americans regarding a man being convicted on the basis of "what he knew" rather than for some act which he committed'. Lemmitzer also queried how the British could possibly justify a five-year sentence given that Walter Schellenberg, supposedly 'Hitler's Chief Intelligence Officer' (an exaggeration in fact), and other German generals who, unlike Wolff, 'did not turn a hand or take a single risk', had received sentences subject to longer periods of discount for periods spent in prior confinement. He ended his letter in a bombastic manner by expressing a high degree of exasperation with the British response: 'So much for the Wolff affair. I hope the damn thing will get settled once and for all.'[202]

The British occupation authorities, namely General Robertson, replied to Lemnitzer's critique. Robertson reaffirmed their continued willingness to respond to his ongoing concerns, which included 'watching the case closely' and asking legal specialists to respond in detail to his critical points. Nevertheless, they reminded Lemnitzer that they lacked any *direct* power to intervene as fully as he demanded in what were supposed to be entirely 'German' legal proceedings. Robertson claimed, rather defensively, that a two-year discount for time served was hardly harsh, 'given the circumstances of the case', and – with respect to the legal point regarding basing a conviction on knowledge not deed – he 'sympathised in many ways with this view'. However, this was the law already laid down authoritatively at Nuremberg by the International Military Tribunal. Robertson noted that the German courts and de-Nazification tribunals had little option but to enforce it consistently in every case. He also minimised the apparent discrepancy with Schellenberg's sentence as within the bounds of normal variation. Robertson concluded by reminding Lemnitzer that:

> [T]he court had no alternative but to give Wolff a substantial sentence. He could not deny having had a very extensive knowledge of what the SS

202 Lemnitzer to Robertson, 5 May 1949: PRO, FO 1030/424.

> did and why – the organisation and administration of concentration camps, persecution of the Jews and forced labour, and so on. Indeed he admitted it himself. It will be interesting to see what happens at the rehearing. It would hardly be possible for the court greatly to reduce the sentence on the evidence available.[203]

Between 31 May and 3 June 1949, Wolff appeared once again before the de-Nazification Tribunal at Bergedorf, Hamburg, in a rehearing on 'all issues of fact and law'. This followed Wolff's successful action in the Court of Appeal at Hamm on grounds of procedural irregularities in the first hearing. Although the prosecution revisited the same 'evidence of knowledge of criminal activity' as before, it appeared to have lost the will to fight when confronted with such high-level support from Allied personnel. Dulles supplied Wolff's lawyers with an affidavit, dated 21 May 1949, for use during his appeal hearing before the Old Lace court in Hamburg. This stated that: 'In my opinion, General Wolff's action during the period March–May 1945 materially contributed to bringing about the end of the war in Italy and thereby hastened the end of general hostilities.'[204] According to an official report sent to Lemnitzer, the prosecution refused to challenge the defense evidence of these senior Allied officials and willingly 'admitted the services Wolff had rendered' through his involvement with Dulles and Operation Sunrise 'in bringing the capitulation negotiations to a successful conclusion'.[205] The prosecutor now 'asked for a sentence of five years imprisonment, the whole period spent in internment to be considered part thereof'. In effect, and possibly under direct or indirect pressure from the British authorities, the prosecutor's concession accepted Lemnitzer's critique of the first sentence. The official report of the appeal case stated that the emphasis the defence placed on the Sunrise aspect was particularly effective: 'The defence concentrated on leading evidence as to Wolff's activities in Northern Italy from 1943 to 1945 and further evidence as to his part in the negotiation the surrender of German forces in Italy.' Wolff's lawyers had called on additional witnesses, including Rahn, former German Ambassador to Italy, to confirm the defendant's role in obstructing Hitler's scorched-earth policy.

At this rehearing, Dulles' senior aide Gaevernitz gave testimony in person for the defence. He emphasised Wolff's key role in the Sunrise Mission, the fact that Wolff had 'taken the initiative' in approaching Dulles and 'when so requested, given proof of his good faith by returning the head of the partisan movement from SS imprisonment'. Gaevernitz's testimony also emphasised

203 Robertson to Lemnitzer, 9 June 1949: PRO, FO 1030/424.

204 Cited in the second feature article on Wolff in the German weekly *Revue*, No. 19, 13 May 1950.

205 General Robertson to Lemnitzer, 18 June 1949: PRO, FO 1030/424.

that: 'Wolff had kept strictly all the promises he had made to the Allies, and had taken such risks that it was considered a miracle by the Allied authorities that Wolff was not shot by his own people.' Reportedly, the testimony of Dulles' senior aide proved decisive, even more influential than that of Dulles' intermediary, Professor Husmann, in the first trials: 'the evidence of von Gaevernitz, who had fought the war on the Allied side, told even more in favour of Wolff with the court, as Husmann had been a neutral and an intermediary only'.[206] The tribunal was moved by Gaevernitz's additional evidence to the point of accepting, remarkably, that once Wolff entered into negotiations with Dulles, he was in effect 'sabotaging' the SS: 'He was held to have sabotaged the criminal organisation after he had started negotiations with the Allies.'[207]

Such testimony, combined with the affidavits of Dulles and the other Allied representatives from Operation Sunrise, proved effective. Wolff was given additional credit for his actions that 'culminated in negotiations for surrender'.[208] The affidavits of Lemnitzer and Airey were also read and made part of the case record. As Smith and Agarossi note:

> All his major Anglo-American Sunrise associates now came forward to assist him. . . . In the face of a half-hearted effort by the prosecution, this high-level endorsement of Wolff's activities in the cause of peace and the interest of the Western world was enough.[209]

Remarkably, for someone who had been Himmler's deputy and the highest SS official to survive the war, Wolff was now convicted of falling within the *least serious* classification of active Nazis, that of an 'opportunist fellow-traveller'. Hence, Wolff faced no restriction on his occupation or future activities other than a restriction on employment within the public sector. Had the Tribunal classified him as falling within any of the higher categories of 'active Nazi', then he would have faced far greater restrictions on his future activities. Furthermore, Wolff's already 'very lenient' sentence was reduced from five to four years' imprisonment but with *full allowance* given for the period he had previously been 'detained'. This meant that Wolff was released

206 H. G. Wills, Office of the Legal Adviser, Berlin to Foreign Office, German Section, London, 9 June 1949: PRO, FO 1030/424.

207 *Ibid.* 208 *Ibid.*

209 Smith and Agarossi, *op cit*, 190. They wrongly claim that Wolff was acquitted. In fact he was convicted of voluntary membership of a criminal organisation. See Deputy Legal Adviser (signature illegible), Zonal Office of the Legal Adviser Germany, to Foreign Office (2) German Section, London/Office of the Legal Adviser, HQ, CCG (BE), Operation 'Old Lace – Reports on trials of Karl Wolff before Spruchgericht Bergedorf, 9 November 1948: PRO, FO1030/424; H. G. Wills, Office of the Legal Adviser, Berlin to Foreign Office, German Section, London, 9 June 1949: PRO, FO 1030/424.

within eight days of this token 'conviction' on the scarcely appropriate, and in that sense, 'reduced' charge of membership of a criminal organisation, the SS.[210]

According to the court, this increased sentencing discount was justified on the ground that 'the time Wolff had served in Allied internment since the war had been punishment enough'.[211] Hilberg notes that: 'Informed by the presiding judge that he could leave "in clean and unstained dress", he walked out of the courtroom with a radiant face, while his lawyer angrily demanded exoneration.'[212] It appears that, although convicted, Wolff's minimal sentence operated in effect as an acquittal. This, in turn, allowed Wolff to act as if he had, in fact, been legally exonerated, and that his involvement in the leadership of the SS was no cause for shame, or restricted employment or travel.[213]

The British authorities received a report of this rehearing, which was copied not only to Lemnitzer and the Nuremberg prosecutors but also British Military Intelligence Division. It noted, with apparent approval, that Wolff had once again not carried out his threat to expose the allegedly anti-Soviet dimension to Operation Sunrise, and that 'none of the witnesses dealt with the scope of content of the capitulation negotiations'.[214] This report concluded by noting 'so the whole affair if now satisfactorily concluded'. The British authorities reassured Lemnitzer that his earlier critique of the first trial and its sentence had been taken on board because the prosecutors had only 'asked for a sentence of five years imprisonment, of which the whole period spent in internment [was] to be considered as part'.[215]

It might be thought that Wolff's release in 1949 would see the end of his attempts to cash in on the promises he had received from Dulles through intermediaries. This was not the case. Although generally supportive, Dulles, on occasions, expressed annoyance that Wolff repeatedly sought to exploit his involvement with the Sunrise Mission to gain a series of post-war advantages. Wolff even sought to claim compensation for loss of personal effects that American soldiers had looted from his residence. Dulles had to respond to Waibel's reminder of the need to continue to honour their gentleman's agreement: 'I feel – as you certainly also do – that we should help out General Wolff if there is any possibility to do so.' Waibel described this issue as 'the last phase of our sunrise game' before immediately adding that 'Just between us . . . I doubt whether this game will ever finish!'[216] Dulles' reply to Waibel is telling because it clearly indicates that Dulles personally considered Wolff to

210 Smith and Agarossi, *op cit*, 206, n. 108. 211 Von Lang, *op cit*, 321.

212 Hilberg, *op cit*, 1168. Hilberg himself cites Telford Taylor's 'Final Report', 78 and 'Sie gehen mit fleckenlosem Kleid' *Aufbau* (New York), 1 July 1949, 4.

213 Smith and Agarossi, *op cit*, 206, n. 108.

214 H. G. Wills, Office of the Legal Adviser, Berlin to Foreign Office, German Section, London, 9 June 1949: PRO, FO 1030/424.

215 *Ibid.* 216 Waibel to Dulles, 7 June 1950: Dulles Papers, Box 59, Folder 10.

be a major war criminal who had escaped his just deserts in that there was sufficient incriminating evidence to merit his conviction and life-time imprisonment: 'Between you and me KW doesn't realise what a lucky man he is not to be spending the rest of his days in jail, and his wisest policy would be to keep fairly quiet about the loss of a bit of underwear, etc. He might easily have lost more than his shirt.'[217]

From 1950, Wolff worked in Germany in the public relations, publishing and advertising fields and became involved in the murky European arms trade.[218] Wolff also worked as a solicitor and estate agent. He became sufficiently wealthy during the 1950s to buy a luxury lakeside villa at the small town of Kempfenhausen, near Munich and overlooking Lake Starnberger, north of the Bavarian Alps.[219] As a former Waffen-SS general in the German Army, he even received a monthly pension from the German Federal Republic. Wolff had maintained personal contact not only with Telford Taylor, the lead US prosecutor in the subsequent proceedings at Nuremberg but also with unrepentant Nazis, such as Leon Degrelle,[220] and even the fugitive Walter Rauff, who Wolff visited whilst in Chile. Rauff had been a Gestapo chief in Tunis, and later in Italy, and had cooperated with Wolff in the Sunrise Operation, even accompanying Zimmer to an early meeting with Max Husmann and Swiss SI official Major Waibel.[221]

During the 1950s, Wolff's confidence that he had now become almost fully rehabilitated appeared to be well founded. Wolff's biographer notes that, notwithstanding continued official investigation of Nazi war crimes, the 1950s held little threat of full legal accountability for Wolff:

> In the post-war years in Stuttgart a 'central office' was opened in order to collect and put into order all materials about Nazi crimes. This had become necessary because the courts of the individual federal states were unable to get more complete pictures about these crimes; victims and aggressors of one case generally were spread all over the Federal Republic. As a result, some facts were checked out twice and some interrelations were only discovered when all materials were centralized in one place. In this way, quite late, more and more guilty persons were

217 Dulles to Waibel, 12 June 1950: *ibid.*

218 Simpson 1995, *op cit*, 236, 345, n. 42 (citing 'Memorandum for file: subj: Grombach, John, V.,' 21 December 1952, Naval Intelligence Command Files, Document no. 62/77/306, with attachments obtained through FOIA).

219 G. Cobentz and S. Freidin, 'Strange Story of SS General', *New York Herald Tribune*, 23 January 1962.

220 M. Linklater, I. Hilton and N. Ascherson *The Fourth Reich, Klaus Barbie and the Neo-Fascist Connection* (London: Hodder and Stoughton, 1985), 203.

221 'Rauff, Walther', JRX- 1005, Zimmer Name File: NA, RG 263; J. Tagliabue, 'Trail Of Hitler "Diaries" Leads To Former Nazis', *New York Times*, 7 May 1983.

> discovered and put on trial . . . Yet no one in the legal system had yet voiced the idea to press charges against Wolff for his mere presence when the murders were committed.[222]

This remarkable period of Wolff's post-war existence protected under the umbrella of American-sponsored legal immunity was, however, soon brought to an end in the early 1960s, the details of which will be discussed in the next section.

1962–64: Wolff's arrest and German trials

The 1950s had undoubtedly treated Wolff far better than many of his immediate subordinates in the SS. However, this state of affairs was not to continue undisturbed into the next decade. This section will discuss whether the decisive factor was a change not in the state of the law or available evidence, but rather various political factors. For present purposes it is interesting to note that the decision by the German authorities to prosecute Wolff for war crimes was not based upon the sudden discovery of new, and more incriminating, evidence that had not previously been available to the Nuremberg prosecutors. On the contrary, the German prosecutors relied heavily upon the same evidence that the Nuremberg prosecutors held regarding how Wolff had 'supported and guaranteed' transportation of Polish Jews from Poland to Treblinka death camp.

In 1958, the German Federal Republic began to search for Nazi war criminals on a larger scale than had taken place previously. During the following year, Wolff received some unwelcome publicity when 'his name came up in the testimony at the Ulm mass murder trial', and – partly as a result – 'West German investigators quietly began a closer look at his past'.[223] Under changed geo-political circumstances, in which the influence of American intelligence and military authorities in German domestic affairs had been sharply eroded, Wolff was investigated as a possible war crimes defendant.[224]

This followed international pressure triggered by disclosures at the Adolf Eichmann trials in 1960–61. At Eichmann's trial in Jerusalem, Wolff's

222 Lang, *op cit*, 325. 223 *Time*, 9 October 1964, 32.

224 G. Cobentz and S. Freidin, 'Strange Story of SS General', *New York Herald Tribune*, 23 January 1962, summarising Wolff's contribution to a *Der Stern* article published in the autumn of 1961. Wolff's name was discussed in the Eichmann trial in terms of the deportation of Italian Jews through the deposition of Herbert Kappler, police attaché to the German embassy in Rome, which largely exonerated Wolff from playing an active role, and allocated policy-making responsibility to Himmler and Müller, whilst policy execution was delegated to a subordinate sent specially for this task, Theodor Dannecker: http://www.nizkor.org/hweb/people/e/eichmann-adolf/transcripts/Testimony-Abroad/Herbert_Kappler-01.html.

name was cited with reference to SS orders (albeit stemming from Himmler) deporting Italian Jews.[225] Furthermore, during the trial of SS-Obergruppenführer Bach-Zelewski, who – in the spring of 1961 – was sentenced at Nuremberg for the execution of an Eastern Prussian land owner, Wolff was called upon to give evidence as a witness. He stated that his responsibilities had been 'merely to prepare business trips of the Reichsführer and to deal with police-related things'.[226] In every case, he claimed, responsibility for deciding upon executions fell to Himmler and Heydrich, and their discussions always took place behind closed doors.

On 18 January 1962, Wolff was arrested at his luxurious Munich Lakeside villa by two plain-clothes police officers. These officers were acting on instructions from the central offices in Ludwigsburg, which had been established to investigate Nazi crimes. The Munich district attorney had been involved in the investigation and planned prosecution of this case for several months, and a special official had been appointed to take charge of further investigations.[227] His arrest was prompted, in part, by the controversy stirred by a polemical article from Uri Dan, an Israeli journalist, published in *Der Spern* in May 1961. In other words, another factor that began to threaten Wolff's continued immunity may have been the publication of 'an angry article about his post-war comfort by an Israeli reporter who recently visited West Germany'.[228] This article was based upon an interview with Wolff that Dan conducted at his luxurious villa near Lake Starnberger. During this interview, Wolff claimed that he had only accidentally found out about the SS death camps in March 1945. During this interview, Wolff further maintained that, although he was administratively involved in organising the transportation of thousands of Jews to Treblinka in Poland, he had also helped many Jews during the Second World War, and had maintained personal friendships with many Jews in later years. By contrast, other SS members of Operation Sunrise had kept a far lower public profile.[229] This interview generated negative publicity and controversy, including furious correspondence both for and against Wolff, with many contributors making anti-Semitic comments.

At the time of his arrest, the Bavarian justice minister reportedly stated little more than that Wolff 'was suspected of complicity in the mass murder of Jews in Nazi-occupied Europe'.[230] The basis given for his arrest was that, in the summer of 1942, some 20 years previously, Himmler had instructed him

225 On the 108th session, see http://www.nizkor.org/hweb/people/e/eichmann-adolf/transcripts/Sessions/Session-108-03.html

226 *Westfälische Rundschau*, Dortmund, 23 January 1962.

227 See *Westfälische Rundschau*, Dortmund, 23 January 1962.

228 See Cobentz and Freidin, *op cit*.

229 Simpson, 1995 *op cit*, 242; Smith and Agarossi *op cit*, 189–90.

230 See Cobentz and Freidin, *op cit*.

to contact Under-secretary Ganzenmüller, Chief of the Nazis' Transportation Ministry, regarding negotiations about the availability of trains for the 'resettlement of the Jews'. The under-secretary agreed in writing to have a train ready for that purpose. Wolff was later charged with both 'aiding and abetting murder in at least 300,000 instances' and personal participation in the murder of at least 100 others at Minsk in Nazi-occupied Belorussia.

At a preliminary hearing, Alfred Seidl, Wolff's lawyer, sought to obtain Wolff's release but his client was refused bail.[231] According to his lawyer, Wolff had answered Ganzenmüller with a letter that was, in fact, dictated by a subordinate, a lowly SS-Unterführer, but which he had personally signed purely as a matter of protocol. Seidl initially complained that, back in 1947, Wolff had already been interrogated with respect to this exchange of correspondence with Ganzenmüller during his testimony when he appeared as a witness at Nuremberg. At this time, neither the prosecution nor the judges inferred that Wolff should be tried for any offence. The implication of his defence argument was that, if the judges and prosecutors who were members of recently victorious alliance could not attribute criminality to Wolff based on their interpretation of the Ganzenmüller/Wolff correspondence, then it was absurd for fellow Germans reviewing the matter some 17 years later to interpret it as such. Meanwhile, according to Seidl, this correspondence had been published in a number of books without arousing any particular outrage, or prompting demands for Wolff's immediate prosecution as a war criminal.

Seidl's arguments in this preliminary hearing proved ineffective. As a result, Wolff had to spend the next two and a half years (1962–64) imprisoned whilst awaiting trial. During this period, his health deteriorated, and he suffered a heart attack. Between July and September 1964, Wolff was belatedly tried in Munich, this time before a regular German criminal court. He was charged for his part in the deportation and murder of Jews to the Treblinka concentration camp in 1942, reprisal killings against Italians and other crimes already discussed.[232]

Lang notes that, even now, Wolff still believed he could rely upon the extended umbrella of assistance stemming from his Operation Sunrise associates within US intelligence:

> Wolff hoped to get some first aid from a party that in fact was in no position to say anything about the crimes he was charged with – his American friend Gero von Gaevernitz, who indeed already in February

231 *Bonner Rundschau*, Bonn, 10 February 1962: 'SS-General Wolff is planning to file complaint about his arrest. Inquiries are based on an exchange of letter with the Transportation Ministry of the Reich – trials not before Summer', *Die Welt*, Berlin, 23 February 1962.

232 See 'SS-General Wolff gestorben', *Franfurter Allgemeine, Zeitung*, 17 July 1984.

> agreed to speak with the prosecution in Munich. He could not help the accused at all, yet the fact that Wolff had resorted to calling on this particular friend suggests that he counted on making use of his involvement in the capitulation activities in order to be acquitted of all his sins from his Nazi past.[233]

Breitman supports the view that, even at this late stage, Wolff continued to receive assistance from Dulles and his assistant:

> After the Eichmann trial West German prosecutors turned up evidence that Wolff had helped to speed deportations of Jews to Treblinka. . . . Although Allen Dulles' former assistant Gaevernitz came to the National Archives to try to find evidence that would help Wolff, he was convicted. OSS officials long before had turned up evidence in German records that Wolff was responsible for reprisal killings in Italy – evidence which had never been used against him.[234]

Media reports of his 1964 trial before the Munich 'Landgericht', or 'Palace of Justice', noted that Wolff represented: 'The most prominent figure among the Third Reich leaders who has ever had to answer for their crimes to a German court.'[235] During his 11-week trial the prosecution argued that he had supported and guaranteed the Nazis' plans to exterminate the Jews. Key to the prosecution's case was the claim that Wolff was complicit with Himmler and other senior SS officials in the organisation and execution of the notorious 'final solution' of the so-called 'Jewish problem' within German-occupied Europe, which Hitler ordered in early summer 1941. This systematic murder had been organised by Heinrich Himmler and high-ranking leading officials of the SS, the police, and the Nazi Party. It had been carried out: 'by means of mass killings, fatal forced labour, gassings and executions by different types of action squads'.[236]

The prosecution claimed that Wolff, in his various senior positions and with conscious intent, cooperated with others involved in the planning, organisation and execution of 'the final solution of the Jewish question as an informing, advising, representative, and shaping participant'.[237] The key piece of evidence the prosecution relied upon in the trial was documentation showing that, between July and September 1942, Wolff had facilitated the supply

233 Lang, *op cit*, 331.

234 R. Breitman, 'CIA Name Files: Analysis of the Name Filer of Guido Zimmer': http://www.archives.gov/iwg/declassified-records/rg–263-cia-records/rg–263-zimmer.html.

235 *Ibid*, 13.

236 'Die Anklage lautet: Massenmord', *Süddeutsche Zeitung*, 14 July 1964, 13–14.

237 *Ibid*, 13.

of the boxcars that transported 300,000 Jews from the Warsaw ghettos to various death camps.[238]

With respect to the first charge relating to Wolff's participation in the shooting of almost exclusively Jewish, Russian inhabitants of Minsk, the prosecution accused him of having accompanied Himmler's inspection of the 'Action Squad B'. This defendant's very presence had served to implicitly authorise the killings by the officer and the troops of the 8th squad. Wolff's presence with this group as Himmler's Head of Staff acted to legitimise 'their intention to obediently execute an illegal shooting'.[239]

With respect to the second charge of aiding and abetting the murder of 'at least 300,000' individuals, the prosecution continued to rely upon Wolff's liaison with Dr Ganzenmüller in the transportation of Polish Jews to Treblinka during the second half of 1942. They claimed that, through his intervention with the general management of the eastern railroad in Krakau, Wolff was instrumental in having the state rail service provide a sufficient number of trains for the deportation of hundreds of thousands of Jews living in 'Jewish residential areas' to the death camps of Treblinka, Belzec and Sobibor. According to the prosecutors, by facilitating this transportation Wolff had acted to ensure and advance the wider programme of murderous activity taking place within the general administrative district. On this basis, Wolff should, they claimed, be considered responsible for the deaths of at least 300,000 of the Jews who, between 22 July 1942 and late September 1942, were transported from the Warsaw ghettos to these death camps.

In response to these charges, Wolff pleaded not guilty. When giving evidence for his own defence, Wolff claimed to have had no knowledge of ongoing extermination programmes. This was despite the fact that the prosecution has shown that Wolff had escorted Himmler to Auschwitz in 1942, had witnessed at first-hand executions at Minsk that had made Himmler faint,[240] and was implicated in gruesome and illegal medical 'experiments' carried out at Dachau concentration camp.[241] Wolff's trial strategy was boldly to deny any knowledge of, or personal involvement in, acts of genocide. He continued to exploit the fact that the dominant American Nuremberg

238 *Time*, 9 October, 1964, 32.

239 Wolfgang Wehner, *op cit*, 13.

240 On Wolff, Himmler and the Einsatzgruppen killing squads, see the Nuremberg materials presented at http://www2.ca.nizkor.org/ftp.cgi/orgs/german/ einsatzgruppen /esg.nuremberg.

241 For Nuremberg documentation on Wolff's involvement in altitude experiments on concentration camp detainees, see http://www.yale.edu/lawweb/avalon/imt/proc/12-20-45.htm. Other documentation includes Nuremberg documents 343-PS and 1617-PS published, in part, in *Nazi Conspiracy and Aggression*, Vol. II (USGPO, Washington, 1946), 173–237, available online at: http://www.ess.uwe.ac.uk/genocide/ssnur4.htm. For German documentation demonstrating Wolff's knowledge of, and involvement in, early extermination programmes involving gas wagons, see http://www.nizkor.org/hweb/camps/chelmno/sonderdruck.html.

prosecutors had decided not to prosecute him during the immediate post-war years as if this escape from prosecution was based on purely legal reasoning regarding the state of the evidence. During a recent symposium on the legacy of Nuremberg, Jonathan Bush, a colleague and close associate of Telford Taylor, recalled that:

> In the early '60s, a German defense lawyer asked Taylor to be a defense witness at the trial of Karl Wolff . . . And without batting an eyelash, he called Taylor as a witness. Now Wolff's legal theory was harebrained, it was basically that, 'If I can get the Americans to testify that they had cleared me, or not tried me for good reason, this will be a powerful exculpatory argument.' . . . I think the shamelessness of Wolff's claim illustrates the focus on the economy, the sense that we're moving on, Germany has some things we needn't talk about, and so on.[242]

When called as a defence witness, Telford Taylor, former head prosecutor for the American-led Nuremberg Subsequent Proceedings trials, recalled that: 'As to the question who was prosecuted for what criminal offence, different reasons, and not only legal considerations, had been taken into account.'[243] Taylor's enigmatic statement conceals as much as it reveals. It is possible to conclude that extra-legal factors (including geo-political considerations and alleged promises of immunity from US intelligence officials) had been influential in the decision not to prosecute Wolff.

On grounds of his health and age, Wolff requested that he be allowed to remain seated throughout the trial. In his actions before the court, Wolff took the opportunity to emphasise those circumstances and actions that placed him in the best possible light, and which contradicted public stereotypes regarding the nature of senior SS officials. He therefore presented himself to the court as a jovial, polite and good-natured person, and repeatedly emphasised his military service and sense of patriotic duty, even using this as his justification for joining the Nazi Party and the supposedly 'elite' SS.[244] Wolff claimed that:

> Back then I believed I could transfer the two-hundred-year tradition of my glorious guard regiment to the guard of the movement. I claim to be an idealist and I always tried to be true to this ideal. That afterwards it was abused terribly is a different story.[245]

Wolff justified his decision to join the SS in October 1931 by reference to the combined effect of the recruitment by a former war comrade, and his belief

242 http://www.bard.edu/hrp/atrocities/panelone.htm.
243 Case Wolff, *op cit*, 51, a-112, 496.
244 Wehner, *op cit*, 13.
245 Quoted in *ibid.*

that, during the economic depression and political polarisations of the late 1920s and early 1930s, Germany faced the stark choice of adopting Communism or National Socialism. Wolff claimed that, at the time, there was no ethical dilemma in joining the SS because Hitler, before his takeover of power, had told the young SS leaders who were taking their oath that he would never ask them to do anything either illegal or contrary to their conscience.[246]

Wolff's defence included a serious effort to 'cash in' on his contribution to Operation Sunrise by presenting himself as a far-sighted peacemaker who, in late 1942, realised that a German military victory had become impossible. By the summer of 1944, Wolff claimed that he knew that the war was already lost. This realisation explained his decision, in May 1944, to have a secret audience with Pope Pius XII, who was then encouraging peace talks with the Western Allies.[247] Wolff then claimed to have risked his life in defiance of Himmler and Kaltenbrunner by taking the initiative in contacting Dulles: 'brother of the future US Secretary of State, a move which led to successful negotiations regarding the capitulation in Italy'.[248]

This was a clever rhetorical strategy as it relied upon pre-existing negative evaluations of the war criminality of Himmler and Kaltenbrunner, the heroic defiance of whom indicated that Wolff was a quite different character. Wolff testified that:

> During a visit in the Führer HQ, in the course of which I reported to him about the negotiations, he gave me a penetrating look, and if I had not faced this look because of my good conscience, I would have ended on the gallows as a little later did Hermann Fegelein.[249]

Wolff claimed prime responsibility for the ultimate success of the difficult capitulation negotiations of 29 April 1945, and suggested that his positive contribution was recognised even by senior military Allied commanders:

> Field Marshall Alexander, commander of the Allies in Italy, told me himself that I saved the lives of tens of thousands of German and Allied soldiers, and I also deserve merit for the fact that Hitler's strategy of burnt earth was not executed in Italy.[250]

During this trial, Wolff sought once again to rely upon the apparently objective evidence of Gaevernitz regarding his various benevolent acts, including the capitulation agreement. Yet this strategy was no longer underpinned by the authority of an occupying power. In his personal testimony for the defence, Gaevernitz stated that Wolff was a Nazi 'who began to see the light

246 *Ibid.* 247 *Ibid*, 14. 248 *Ibid*, 13. 249 *Ibid*, 14. 250 *Ibid.*

in 1943, and tried not to extricate himself but to extricate the nation from the impending disaster to which Hitler's policy was clearly leading'.[251]

Following his testimony, the court asked Wolff to reconcile the interpretation he has presented of his own motivations and actions with the charges and evidence supplied by the prosecution. Once again, Wolff's response was to present himself as a dutiful, if perhaps naïve, idealist: 'I joined the NSDAP because of my ideals. I was deceived and betrayed. But I had nothing to do with the things of which I am accused today.'[252]

With respect to his own attitude to Nazi anti-Semitism, Wolff attempted to present himself as someone whose actions were motivated by factors other than outright prejudice. He testified that he had 'never taken seriously the Jew paragraph in the party program'. Wolff claimed he had had joined the Nazi Party, because, in his view, before 1933 the Jewish influence in the Germany of the Weimar Republic had become far too strong. Hence, this group had to be pushed back to a point where it corresponded to their proportion of the population. He maintained that the Jews had quite often ousted 'Germans' with questionable methods.[253] Perhaps contrary to his intentions, Wolff's testimony on this point betrayed a deep-seated form of racism that singles out German Jews as 'foreigners', irrespective of how members of this group actually defined their own identity, and in a historical context where the overwhelming majority of German Jews (as with other faith groups) considered themselves 'good Germans'.

Wolff's denials of knowledge of systematic genocide and reliance on his role in Operation Sunrise failed to impress the court, particularly when their credibility was contradicted both by fellow ex-members of the SS and German participants in Operation Sunrise, such as Rahn. As Lang notes:

> Unsurprisingly, [in court] he had all those appear who could confirm his benevolent activities. Gero von Gaevernitz was among that crowd again, and he too insisted that, with the capitulation, Wolff had saved the lives of many a person who thus escaped the so-called heroic death. Yet the chairman did not allow for such speculation. After all, the trial was not about the number of lives Wolff had saved but the number of those who had lost their lives because of Wolff's involvement. He thus would be found guilty if the court could be convinced that he had known about the purpose of the transportations, about the 'final solution.' The witness Ganzenmüller, who had organized the train, avoided giving the impression that he had even known or even suspected where the Jews were to be sent . . . The entire operation, Ganzenmüller claimed, had sort of passed

251 Warburg to Dulles, 8 September 1963: Dulles Papers, Box 59, Folder 10. The testimony itself is reported in *Die Welt*, 8 September 1964: copied in *ibid.*

252 Quoted in *ibid*, 14.

253 Lang, *op cit*, 115.

> him by – a phrase that Wolff used as well whenever a written piece of evidence proved him wrong. In the course of the trial, this happened frequently, but the more the sentence was uttered, the more inclined was the court not to believe it. Even Rudolf Rahn, Wolff's diplomatic aide during the capitulation, stated as a witness: 'the shooting of Jews could hardly have escaped Wolff's attention.' And Wolff's close friend SS-Obergruppenführer Erich von den Bach-Zelewski, who had been sentenced to imprisonment for life for mass murders, said in court: 'it is absolutely impossible that today someone who'd been in such a leading position claims he hadn't known about anything.'[254]

On 24 July 1964, Bach-Zelewski testified that 'Hitler knew nothing of the mass destruction of the Jews' and that 'the entire thing began with Himmler'. Yet the prosecution presented evidence that rebutted Wolff's claims that he had never been personally committed to Himmler's racist agenda. This included a letter Wolff had written in February 1939 to his first wife, Frieda, while he was in Sicily. This stated:

> . . . destiny has placed me as the closest associate of a unique man, the Reichsführer-SS, whom I not only admire immeasurably for his extraordinary qualities, but in whose historic message I deeply believe. Our mutual, to me infinitely satisfactory work . . . is rooted in the racial thought. My entire being and ambition is geared toward the SS and its distant goals.[255]

Wolff was also confronted by verbal testimony from a witness, supported by documentary evidence in the form of a diary, suggesting that he had accompanied Himmler to the Warsaw ghetto. This was a fact which he had previously denied. Wolff also testified he had been specifically ordered, presumably by Himmler himself, to attend the execution of the 100 partisans and Jews at Minsk but that he took no personal part in the actual killings. He repeated his earlier claim that he was unaware of the fate of Jews sent to concentration camps.[256]

The West German court did not accept Wolff's various defence arguments. On 30 September 1964, Wolff was convicted of responsibility for murdering 300,000 persons, mainly Jews, and overseeing the SS's involvement in slave labour programmes for IG Farben and numerous other companies.[257] The chief trial judge, Emil Mannhart, concluded that Wolff had been 'continuously engaged and was deeply entangled in guilt', and characterised Wolff as Himmler's 'bureaucrat of death'.[258] The court stated that Wolff was guilty

254 *Ibid*, 336. 255 Lang, *op cit*, 193. 256 *Ibid*, 183–84.
257 Simpson, 1988, *op cit*, 94. 258 *Time*, 9 October 1964, 32.

of 'abetment in a crime that in the history of mankind was without precedent'.[259]

> When deliberating the sentence, the court had to take into account that the defendant abetted in a crime which in extent and monstrosity is unsurpassed, and which caused unspeakable harm and suffering to the victims, unutterable grief to the few surviving relatives, and profound horror, abhorrence, and disgust to all human beings with a sense of justice in this world.[260]

Wolff was sentenced to 15 years' imprisonment combined with ten years' loss of civil rights. This sentence was later confirmed on appeal.[261] However, in 1971 and following a heart attack, Wolff was released on health grounds and for 'good behaviour'. This meant that he served only seven years' imprisonment.[262] Aarons and Loftus bitterly claim that Wolff's much delayed and ultimately brief period of imprisonment represented one year for every 50,000 of the civilian deaths for which he was responsible.[263]

In short, when Wolff finally had to face a case prepared by committed prosecutors who were not subject to pressure and influence from US intelligence and military officials, and where the legal process was allowed to run its normal course, he was tried, convicted and received a long prison sentence. This was despite his age and the long period of time that had elapsed since his original crimes. Neither of the these last two factors would have applied had Wolff been tried in either of the two rounds of war crimes trials held at Nuremberg during the 1940s. It is reasonable to conclude that, in the absence of the influential interventions by Dulles and his associates, Wolff would not have received any lesser sentence had he faced trial in either of the two rounds of Nuremberg trials. Indeed, there was every likelihood that, in the more punitive climate of 1945–47, he would have shared the fate of his fellow co-deputy to Himmler, Kaltenbrunner, that is, death by hanging. If this conclusion is correct, then it would be reasonable to claim that Wolff owed his life to Dulles, and that the non-prosecution of Karl Wolff is one of the most significant case studies of intelligence officials 'successfully' intervening in the war crimes process to afford comparatively privileged treatment to a potential defendant in return for 'services rendered'. Indeed, Dulles kept in touch with

259 'Auge und Ohr Himmler's,' *Frankfurter Allgemeine Zeitung*, 1 October 1964, 7–8.

260 W. Wehner, '15 Jahre Zuchthaus für Wolff', *Süddeutsche Zeitung*, 1 October 1964, 1, 9–10.

261 Smith and Agarossi, *op cit*, 190–91; I. Sagel-Grande, H. H. Fuchs and C. Folder Rüter (eds) ['Seminarium voor Strafrecht en Strafrechtspleging Van Hamel', Universität Amsterdam], *Justiz und NS-Verbrechen. Sammlung Deutscher Strafurteile wegen Nationalsozialistischer Tötungsverbrechen 1945–1966*, Vol. XX (Amsterdam: University Press Amsterdam BV, 1979).

262 Bower, 1995, *op cit*, 398, 412.

263 Aarons and Loftus, *op cit*, 534, n. 61.

the Wolff case as late as 1968, when Gaevernitz made sustained and ultimately successful interventions with the Secretary of Justice for Bavaria to have Wolff granted early release on health grounds.[264]

Conclusion

The existing historical literature indicates that Dulles and Wolff entered into a wartime agreement, expressed in the form of a gentleman's agreement (albeit guaranteed by Swiss intermediaries such as Husmann), to violate official Allied wartime policy of demanding a strictly unconditional form of surrender. Although not expressed in writing, one of the negotiated 'conditions' of this surrender deal was that Wolff and a number of his immediate SS subordinates associated with Operation Sunrise would receive privileged treatment during the post-war period, including legal immunity. General Wolff's late cooperation with Dulles and American intelligence in Operation Sunrise – Crossword was certainly well rewarded. Dulles and his subordinates intervened directly and indirectly to help influence the decision not to prosecute Wolff before the International Military Tribunal at Nuremberg, and once again to support his non-prosecution in the second round of American-led trials at Nuremberg, the Subsequent Proceedings. This meant that he was left facing the possibility of being tried for his command responsibility for war crimes committed by SS forces whilst he was Highest Police and SS Leader in Nazi-occupied Northern Italy between September 1943 and April 1945. However, this was in a context where the British prosecutors located in Italy, who were convinced of his guilt, faced real difficulties establishing firm proof sufficient to convince their increasingly sceptical superiors based in London. Although Dulles appears to have exercised little influence concerning Wolff's escape from justice with respect to these trials, he certainly exerted influence, both directly and through intermediaries such as Husmann and Lemnitzer, to protect this potential war crimes defendant from extradition to Eastern Europe. When faced with this threat of extradition and almost certain conviction and execution, Wolff received sustained and highly effective support from Dulles, Gaevernitz and Lemnitzer in successfully resisting extradition and trial abroad.

When, in 1948, Wolff finally faced a formally independent de-Nazification trial concerning his voluntary membership of the SS, a prescribed criminal organisation, he also received considerable support from Dulles and others involved in Operation Sunrise. The written support of Dulles, Generals Airey and Lemnitzer, combined with the oral testimony of both Husmann and Gaevernitz, helped ensure that Wolff received – in the view of the British authorities – a 'very lenient' sentence, both initially and even more so on

264 See Gaevernitz to Dulles, 23 April 1968, Dulles Papers, Box 59, Folder 10.

appeal. This meant that, following his partially successful appeal in 1949, he was released within eight days, despite the original conviction being re-affirmed.

The issue regarding the amendments to the two affidavits for Wolff are not entirely semantic. Instead, they involved a substantial conflict as to the truth of what had taken place during these 'negotiations' (which officially were supposed to have involved no process of negotiating). The Soviet version was, in all likelihood, based on electronic intercepts of communications supplemented with reports from its wartime intelligence services, which had penetrated the OSS at the highest levels. This version of events insisted that negotiations, which eased the terms for Wolff at the expense of the Soviets, had indeed taken place. The Anglo-American official interpretation of the same events was to deny this 'offensive' suggestion, and to express righteous indignation at the very idea that they would even contemplate such a betrayal. Yet the first-hand testimony the two generals gave in the *original versions* of both affidavits appeared to give more support to the Soviet's version of 'the facts' than those presented as true by Roosevelt and Churchill. At this time, that is 1948, the British and Americans were in conflict with the Soviet's newly won Eastern European empire over a variety of geo-political conflicts and East–West rivalries, which threatened to escalate into a third world war.

By the early 1960s, Germany had almost become an independent sovereign state in its own right. Hence, the influence of American intelligence had declined. This meant that the umbrella of protection that Dulles and others had previously used to shield Wolff was no longer as effective as it once had been. Nevertheless, it is clear that, through Gaevernitz, Dulles continued to try to protect Wolff and this, according to Katz, was well known to both war crimes investigators and Jewish groups. In 1966, Dulles' book on Operation Sunrise attracted mixed and critical reviews, particularly with respect to his portrayal of Wolff's complicity and the 1964 trial. Robert Katz, a specialist in the wartime Nazi occupation of Northern Italy under Wolff, argued:

> After glossing over the true nature of the case and avoiding the fact that the SS general lived under American protection for many years after the war, Dulles tells us that his aide Gaevernitz 'followed the Wolff trial closely' and reported to the German court about the accused's part in the surrender talks ([Secret Surrender] p. 253). In truth some other kind of participation took place. Some months ago I learned from a high West German official, who was directly involved in this case in a principal role, that 'very influential American circles' sought to prevent the prosecution of Karl Wolff. It is a well known 'secret' among West German and Jewish war crimes investigators that both Wolff and Colonel Dollmann, another key figure in the surrender, had made a deal with the

> Americans and would never be tried by the Allies. And, of course, they never were.[265]

Throughout this chapter, Katz's anecdotal statement, which was made before the relevant secret intelligence documentation was declassified, has received considerable confirmation precisely by reference to the content of such documentation.

265 R. Katz, 'The Good Nazis' (letter), *New York Review of Books*, 19 March 1967.

Chapter 5

Protecting the wider Sunrise group: Zimmer, Dollmann and Wenner

Introduction

This chapter will extend the analysis of its predecessors by considering the extent to which the protection Dulles and his colleagues afforded to Wolff also allowed his SS subordinates, who participated centrally in Operation Sunrise, to shelter under a broad umbrella of full or partial immunity from post-war prosecution. In addition, certain details contained in recently declassified 'CIA Name Files' on Zimmer and Dollmann will be shown to reveal new light concerning Dulles' orientation towards the Nazi participants in Sunrise as a whole, including, of course, Wolff. Hence, this and the previous chapter need to be taken together because each casts new light upon aspects of the other. Indeed, some of the more interesting suggestions that the Wolff group may have received an offer of immunity as part of a wider oral agreement with Dulles guaranteed by a Swiss intelligence official and various intermediaries is contained in intelligence files relating not to Wolff but rather to SS officials SS-Hauptsturmführer Guido Zimmer, SS-Sturmbannführer Eugen Wenner and Colonel Eugen Dollmann. In other words, amongst the sources of potentially relevant evidence regarding Wolff's alleged immunity are the various intelligence records relating to Wolff's collaborators within Operation Sunrise, particularly Dollmann, Zimmer and Wenner (and possibly Wolff's immediate SS subordinate in Italy, the soon to be notorious Walter Rauff).

Immediately after the war, US intelligence officials discovered incriminating correspondence between Becker and Rauff. This suggested that, whilst Rauff was head of Abt II D of the RSHA in Berlin, 'There are indications that this Abt. was responsible for [the] operation of mobile gas execution chambers on the eastern front. Rauff was questioned in this connection.'[1]

If Dulles had made a clear promise of legal immunity as a direct reward for participation in an early military capitulation, then it is likely that the scope

1 'Rauff, Walther', Cable 16573, 10 July 1945 [partly illegible], and II, 7357, 2 June 1945, Zimmer Name File, Vol. 1: NA, RG 263.

of such immunity would have to be extended at least as far as these SS officials as they formed the inner core of the Nazis' side of Operation Sunrise. It is arguable that, if researchers could uncover hard evidence that these officials were aware of having received a promise of legal immunity and had then sought to rely upon it during the post-war period, then this would represent an important finding with clear implications for the debate over Wolff. It would be particularly important to discover whether or not such claims to be entitled to immunity were then accepted by independent military, legal and diplomatic Allied authorities as binding with respect to ongoing war crimes investigations.[2] It is important, therefore, to review declassified documentation relating to Wolff's SS subordinates which suggests that, amongst officials working for the various successor organisations to the OSS,[3] many appreciated that immunity remained a live issue.

Zimmer's post-war recruitment and deployment as a US intelligence asset

In March 1945, as the end of the war appeared close at hand and issues over future Allied occupation policies came to the fore, OSS Secret Intelligence Branch officials based in London were preparing strategies for the post-war penetration of 'what may remain of the Nazi Party or of movements which may arise from its remnants'. William Casey, later to rise to become Director of the CIA under President Reagan, argued that the OSS should be willing to put aside sympathy for anti-Nazi Germans as potential agents. This was because such individuals would have difficulty penetrating the target organisation. Instead, the OSS should follow 'the old truism that it takes a thief to catch a thief' and either recruit 'former minor Nazi informants and stool pigeons against the party itself, [or] . . . Nazi Party members now held in the US as POW's who may be willing to work for us after reparation'. Casey argued that, based upon the nature of work and contacts as counter-intelligence officials, members of OSS X-2 Branch could supply their OSS-SI Branch colleagues with 'a list of several thousand such people' who would be 'more "pliable" than the more important Nazis, are trained in "dirty" undercover work, have the makings of an excellent cover story, and if unsatisfactory can be dealt with in a summary fashion'.[4] Such individuals would, according to Casey, need to be subject to vigorous control (the 'use of brutality

2 Of course, it is arguable that Wolff's subordinates could have received promises of legal immunity that, for contingent reasons, Dulles did not extended to Wolff, but this would surely have been most unlikely given that he alone was in a position to bring about the early surrender.

3 That is, the Strategic Services Unit (SSU), Central Intelligence Group (CIG), and then – from 1947 – the CIA.

4 Casey to Callisen, 24 March 1945: NA, RG 190, Box 134, Folder 345.

where necessary') and have their information double-checked. However, even so, this proposed intelligence strategy could provide the best means of penetrating, and hopefully thwarting, post-war Nazi groups.[5] In some respects, and in certain contexts at least, Casey's suggestions appear to have been adopted at the end of the Second World War.

Unlike many other middle-ranking SS officials implicated in war crimes against civilians, such as looting and other acts of persecution, Zimmer apparently was confident that, during the last month of the war, he had already won sufficient favour from the Allied authorities to have 'saved his skin'. Therefore, he had no reason to become a fugitive from justice at the end of hostilities. As a result of his involvement within Operation Sunrise, possibly confirmed by Dulles or his subordinates in OSS Germany field office,[6] Zimmer appeared to believe that he would be granted privileged treatment, including even recruitment as a US intelligence agent involved in counter-intelligence work. Indeed, one OSS cable based on the interrogation of his SD superior, Dr Klaus Hügel, specifically confirms that Zimmer would be particularly useful because of his 'detailed knowledge of post-occupation agents in Milan'.[7] This would explain why, at the end of August 1945, Zimmer left Salzburg and returned to Italy, where he made contact, through the Allied military police, with US counter-intelligence officials belonging to 'SCI Erlanger'.[8]

Declassified files on Zimmer state that:

> After checking with X-2/OSS Mission to Germany, subject [Zimmer] cleared with local CIC [counter-intelligence] and MG [Military Government],[9] Zimmer was given necessary paperwork, such as ration cards.[10]

Presumably, these checks re-affirmed his perceived entitlement to privileged status. By, at the latest, the third week of September 1945, Zimmer had accepted the role of an American agent that Dulles had previously offered him in his capacity as head of OSS espionage operations within occupied Germany. A cryptic note from OSS Germany contains a description of Zimmer's physical appearance and the statement that Zimmer was 'Working

5 *Ibid.*

6 Dulles had taken over OSS Germany in July 1945, after being forced to clear up matters in Bern. See N. Petersen, 'From Hitler's Doorstep' in Chalou, 1992, *op cit*, 287.

7 Cable JRX 002-507, 7 May 1945, CIA Name File, Guido Zimmer: NA, RG 263 (most references in this section are to materials stored in this newly declassified source).

8 LWX-010-915a, 21 September 1945, *ibid.*

9 OSS Germany, 'Guido Zimmer', LWX-002-820 (X-3208), nd [but clearly late September 1945], summarising Cable LWZ-010-915a, dated 21 September 1945, *ibid.*

10 LWX 010-915a, 8 October 1945, two semi-monthly reports covering period stated (15 Aug–15 Sept): source Capt. Scivener, *ibid.*

for Mr Dulles – cleared through CIB.' This note also indicates that OSS Washington 'had been in contact with subject interested in him as X2 [OSS counter-intelligence] agent'.[11]

Zimmer's protection included provision of a false cover story. Within OSS-SSU intelligence files of this immediate post-war period, Zimmer is frequently characterised in glowing but inaccurate terms as a 'high level OSS agent in early 1945', who also assisted the Italian partisan resistance to the fascist government.[12] After the war, US intelligence reports began to describe Zimmer as 'a high level agent for the OSS' who had 'cooperated with the Italians in the resistance movement'.[13] Within OSS files from the autumn of 1945, the story of his cooperation with the Italian resistance appears to have been further exaggerated, with statements claiming that he had 'cooperated throughout his service with the Italian resistance movement'.[14] In fact, his contacts were sporadic and self-interested, and often made in pursuit of covert penetration or disruption operations.

Nevertheless, one OSS report states that US intelligence officials were interested in him for counterintelligence work.[15] Furthermore, Dulles' German Mission decided:

> to use subject [Zimmer] in connection with the Freikorps Adolph Hitler . . . Subject['s] immediate task will be the penetration of a resistance movement know as the Freikorps Adolph Hitler, which is alleged to have 16,000 members. Penetration project in preparation.[16]

This indigenous German organisation targeted by OSS officials was an extreme right-wing paramilitary group that had become prominent immediately after Germany's military defeat in the First World War; it had contributed to the rise of Nazism in the decade before Hitler's initial seizure of power. It is likely that, in May 1945, US intelligence officials were concerned to pre-empt this organisation from repeating its earlier role during the months and years following Germany's second military collapse. Zimmer promptly accepted this assignment, even though it meant appearing to abandon his past Nazi allegiances ('the cause', as he refers to his SS work in the Notebooks) and even adopting American insignia as his own. Reportedly,

11 OSS Germany, 'Guido Zimmer', LWX-002-820 (X-3208), 20 September 1945, summarising cable sent from OSS-Rome 1716.7, *ibid.*

12 'Progress report on X-2 penetration cases run in the American Occupied Zone Germany, Sept 1945', 1 October 1945, LWX-01001001, *ibid.*

13 Telex 010-926/TS-1715, 26 September 1945, *ibid.*

14 LWX-101-1001, 1 October 1945, 'Progress Report on X-2 penetration cases: Run in the American Occupied Zone in Germany September 1945', *ibid.*

15 Cable 1716.7, 10 September 1945, *ibid.*

16 See Cable LWX-010-926, 26 September 1945, SCI Weekly Operations Report, *ibid.*

the phrase 'turncoat' took on a literal, as well as metaphorical, pertinence: 'in the summer of 1945 he returned to Milan wearing an American uniform'.[17]

As Cold War tensions began to escalate during the autumn of 1945, with a resulting shift in the political definition of national security threats and priorities, OSS/SSU officials later employed Zimmer in a specifically anti-communist role. His mission was to tap into the 'impressions of persons just returned from [the] Russian-occupied zone – also [report on] information they have'.[18] Another report notes that Zimmer was given responsibility for making contact with:

> intellectuals of Erlangen and gives us coverage of what they are thinking about. He has made contact with a few persons who have just returned from Russian occupied Zone and is preparing a report on their impressions and what information they have on the Russian zone.[19]

Later sections will discuss in greater detail the internal controversy generated by Dulles' successors' attempts to continue Zimmer's employment following his return to Italy in February 1946. American intelligence officials continued to monitor his whereabouts and contacts, even after it had dropped him as an agent from February 1946 onwards.[20] Nevertheless, as a one-time OSS/SSU agent, Zimmer continued to enjoy protection throughout the 1940s and 50s. For reasons discussed in a later part of this book, this protection was one factor in explaining why he was never subjected to either Allied de-Nazification hearings, or put on trial for his command responsibility for war crimes committed by his SD subordinates in Milan, including the persecution of Italian Jews. Any such trial would provide Zimmer with the opportunity of pleading that his wartime contacts with OSS officials and intermediaries should be recognised as a mitigating factor. Furthermore, it would have allowed him to reveal details of his post-war endorsement and recruitment as an intelligence source as part of an effort to claim that authorities had already granted him at least partial exoneration. These possibilities were not interpreted as being in the interests of US intelligence during the immediate post-war years.

17 'Zimmer' (nd), *ibid*, Vol. 3.

18 LWX 010-915a, 8 October 1945, two semi-monthly reports covering period stated (15 Aug–15 Sept): source Capt. Scivener: CIA Name File Guido Zimmer, *op cit*. This report is summarised in an untitled OSS/SSU document summarising various cables relating to Zimmer, possibly a continuation and update of OSS Germany, 'Guido Zimmer', LWX-002-820 (X-3208), September 1945, *ibid*.

19 LWX 010-915a, 8 October 1945, two semi-monthly reports covering period stated (15 Aug–15 Sept): source Capt. Scivener, *ibid*.

20 Cable Bern 422, 31 October 1946, *ibid* (noting that 'Zimmer stated to be with [George] Sessler . . .').

Dollmann's post-war detention, recruitment and deployment as a US intelligence asset

It is not possible to recount a smooth and straightforward chronological narrative concerning Dollmann's post-war treatment, including his protection and recruitment as an intelligence asset, without jumbling together a series of topics and issues which, for analytical purposes, need to be tackled separately. For example, the question of how he was treated in various periods of detention from 1945 to 1948 is important to the charge that he was pampered by US intelligence officials. The related question of his recruitment by US intelligence officials, and the narrative that emerges from his CIA Name File, requires analysis in a separate sub-heading, even though this breaks the chronology. A similar point applies to the controversy created within US intelligence, diplomatic and government circles more generally by the allegations that Dollmann and Wenner were receiving an unwarranted form of special treatment and *de facto* immunity from prosecution. In short, any attempt to bring together the details recounted in the following distinct sub-headings into a single chronological narrative would create an unwieldy and confusing account of issues that, although obviously interrelated, still require separate analysis under different sub-headings.

During the late 1940s, Dollmann was still being sought by the Italian authorities for his alleged complicity in the Ardeatine Caves massacre. Furthermore, others (admittedly more senior Nazis involved in various diplomatic intrigues outside of the context of the SS) were, during 1945–46, facing trials at Nuremberg. The threat of Allied and Italian prosecution on war crimes charges, and later prosecution in Germany before a de-Nazification court, hung over Dollmann's head at least until the late 1940s.

Unlike Zimmer, Dollmann received comparatively punitive treatment between 1945 and 1947, which disappointed earlier hopes that his active engagement in Operation Sunrise would, as promised, be rewarded. During the days immediately after the capitulation, there was little sense for either Dollmann or Wolff that the promises of honourable treatment and special concessions would not be fully honoured. Indeed, these men were allowed to remain in their luxurious conditions of a Royal Villa at Bolzano with their families and a fleet of 20 cars. They were treated almost as hosts and equals by the Allied forces, who even shared their champagne and protected them from Italian partisans bent on reprisals.[21] Based on previous discussions, Dollmann and Wolff expected that they would be subjected to a purely notional form of arrest, short detention and debriefing at Allied HQ at Caserta, followed by an invitation to participate in a new post-war government. This fools' paradise was rudely interrupted by their less than

21 E. Dollmann, *Call me Coward* (London: Kimber and Co, 1956), 11–14.

gentle arrest and looting of their property by American military police on 13 May 1945.[22]

During the post-war decade, Dollmann's hopes of receiving privileged treatment in recognition of his assistance with the Sunrise capitulation were not fully or consistently realised. Indeed, he recalls that he served periods of detention in no less than 13 different prisons controlled by the Allied authorities.[23] After a brief detention in Bolzano town prison, Dollmann and Wolff were sent to Modena detention camp, where they and others suffered grim living conditions at a mosquito-infested and generally unsanitary site. Dollmann and Wolff feared that other German POWs would kill them for defaulting on their promises of securing honourable treatment at the hands of the Allies, a threat supported by the remarks of their former German 'comrades' in German military intelligence.[24] Even now, both Wolff and Dollmann apparently consoled each other that their signing of the capitulation, which saved Italy from further destruction, would provide them with a measure of protection.

Both men were soon transferred from the grim conditions of Modena to the British intelligence CSDIC interrogation and detention camp located outside Rome in an old film studio, Cine Città, where former SS officers, Marshal Grazioni and Italian intelligence officers were also being detained.[25] Here, British intelligence officers interrogated Dollmann regarding his knowledge of Himmler and the SS leadership, and especially the possible complicity of his wife in SS war crimes, as she was a fellow detainee.[26] At CSDIC, Major Bridge invited him to inspect a copy of the 'Diary of Count Ciano', later to be used as trial evidence at Nuremberg, which he claimed was at least partly fabricated, even though the style was generally convincing: 'Whoever had "edited" this diary of Ciano must have had some of Ciano's material at his disposal but it was quite certain that half the stuff I had just read had not come from Ciano at all. In secret I was rather impressed.'[27]

Whilst in detention in Rome, Dollmann and Wolff still tried to cash in aspects of the capital they assumed they had acquired with the Allies and others with respect to Operation Sunrise. They attempted to exert influence upon Parri, whom they had released as one of the negotiated terms of Operation Sunrise, suggesting that he return the compliment. Dulles had seen Parri as 'the future strong man of Italy'. They received no reply.[28]

Despite being cleared of involvement in the Ardeatine Caves massacre in July 1945, Dollmann was not immediately released. Instead, British intelligence officials employed him to write a 'highly confidential' report on 'the Duce's visit to Rastenburg just after the attempt on Hitler's life on July 20th [1944]'.[29] In this report, copies of which may have been of interest to the

22 *Ibid*, 14. 23 *Ibid*, 16. 24 *Ibid*, 18–19. 25 *Ibid*, 21. 26 *Ibid*, 28–29.
27 *Ibid*, 33. 28 *Ibid*, 43. 29 *Ibid*, 35.

Nuremberg prosecutors, Dollmann discussed the duplicities of Ribbentrop and the role of the SS leadership in the preparing for a brutal mass purge of suspected German opposition figures, particularly within the Army.[30]

Dollmann rightly suspected that Wolff's removal from this camp in August 1945 was not, as the SS general believed, the start of his freedom, but rather the beginning of a new period of detention, this time at a Nuremberg prison cell attached to the Palace of Justice. Later, Bridge, the British intelligence official responsible for Dollmann, told him that 'between you and me he'll wish himself back in Cine Città before he is much older'.[31] Although Dollmann was anxious that he would also be transferred to Nuremberg, this intelligence official reassured him that this was not planned. However, he also stated that, by October 1945, his authority over Dollmann would come to an end, and that the latter's next place of detention would be the Ascona camp.

This transfer took place and he had to sleep in tents located on the side of a hill, and endure unpleasant living conditions more generally.[32] Dollmann was, however, soon transferred to a larger detention camp at Rimini, in which 'hundreds of SS, Intelligence, Security Service and Party leaders' were still being detained.[33] SS-Standarterführer Walter Rauf, Kappler's counterpart in Milan and 'one of my most disagreeable acquaintances', had been made camp supervisor of the Rimini camp. Kappler was also detained there, and Dollmann believed that: 'In my opinion, he was quite certainly due for the high jump when they got round to him.'[34]

Dollmann escaped from Rimini camp with the assistance of an NCO who had somehow 'acquired' – possibly through Rauff – a pair of wire cutters, and made his way to Milan, where he sought assistance from Cardinal Schuster, whom Dollmann had known 'quite well'.[35] Dollmann had collaborated with Schuster during the war, and recognised that the Cardinal was one of only three senior churchmen who had, through Dollmann and Kesselring, influenced the German High Command to save 'Florence, Bologna, Milan and the whole of the Po plateau' from the threat of destruction and German scorched-earth policies.[36]

In December 1945, Schuster and an Italian military intelligence (SIM) official, Captain Ghissetti, arranged for Dollmann, who at this time had little more than the fugitive status of an escaped prisoner of war, to be accommodated at the Cardinal Ferrari Institute, located outside Milan. This was an asylum for drug addicts and mental patients, which was under Schuster's personal patronage.[37] Here, he was blackmailed with promises of money and a legitimate passport into agreeing to write his memoirs that could then be

30 *Ibid*, 35–42. A copy of Dollmann's report was given to Dulles, who made extensive use of it without acknowledgement in his 1947 book, *Germany's Underground. Ibid*, 42.

31 Dollmann, 1956 *op cit.* 32 *Ibid*, 44–45. 33 *Ibid*, 48. 34 *Ibid*, 48.

35 *Ibid*, 58–62. 36 *Ibid*, 61–64. 37 *Ibid*, 65.

freely 'edited' to support Schuster's Vatican-slanted account of the Sunrise capitulation: 'they wanted to exploit my as yet unwritten memoirs in some way or other as yet unknown to me. However, the thought of the passport and the money was tempting.'[38]

At this time, Dollmann was also contacted by letter by Baron Parilli, whom he knew to be well connected to the Americans, as well as the Vatican's Order of Malta, informing him that he had told the American intelligence authorities his whereabouts, who promptly acted upon this information:[39]

> The next day a huge Buick with a US army pennant drew up in front of my private lunatic asylum and I was invited to take seat in it . . . The Negro chauffeur then drove us off to Rome and on the way we were respectfully greeted by all the Carabinieri we came across. On our arrival in Rome, I was deposited in this flat . . . Two types then came in who looked like a music-hall turn: Mutt and Jeff, or the long and the short of it. They introduced themselves to me as Jim [Angleton] and Joe of the OSS [actually SSU] and shook my hand as though we were long-lost friends. 'We are very glad to have found you, Mr Dollmann' they assured me . . . They inquired solicitously about my 'journey', expressed regret that I had been so bothered and assured me that they were very glad to be able to do something for me.[40]

Angleton told Dollmann that they wished to use his services as part of an anti-communist operation, for which his past complicities and Italian claims concerning his involvement in war crimes were of no relevance:

> Well, you see, for us of the American Secret Service the struggle against Communism is only just beginning . . . and so we thought of sending you to Germany on a secret mission . . . you would have to take a six weeks' course, and after that you would be able to build up a really good espionage organisation against the Russians. I have already informed my superiors in Washington about what I intend to do with you, and the G.2. General in Caserta has already confirmed the plan . . . even before you came here Baron Parilli discussed the whole matter with General Morgan, our Commander in Chief at Caserta, and that they came to a satisfactory agreement about your future . . . You can stay here for a while perhaps . . . but in view of the nature of the struggle we aren't particularly interested in the Mediterranean. Our new frontier lies in Germany.[41]

Dollmann's objection that with 'with my name and my reputation I can hardly . . .' was met with firm rejection by these intelligence officials, who

38 *Ibid*, 76.   39 *Ibid*, 82–83.   40 *Ibid*, 83–84.   41 *Ibid*, 84.

noted that: 'We're the masters of the world no one can touch you.'[42] Dollmann was reluctant to accept the terms of this recruitment pitch. Yet he still accepted the 'sweetener' of a bundle of currency, and a false identify document in the name of Alfredo Casani, stating that he was an employee of the American government. US intelligence officials in Italy also provided Dollmann with a large and relatively luxurious apartment in Parioli, a residential area of Rome. It was fully equipped with a library, chauffeur and even a maid.

This encouraged him to believe that certain of the promises made as part of the Sunrise affair were finally being honoured: 'I felt that the Americans had installed me here . . . perhaps in recollection of my services at the time of the capitulation.'[43] Dollmann certainly exploited his new-found American protection, even, he claimed, announcing 'his special protection' to the astonishment of his former Italian contacts, who assumed he still remained a fugitive from Anglo-American justice.[44] Dollmann's memoir recalls that he was well aware that his freedom in 1946 'was only by the grace of Jim and Joe of the OSS that I was here at all. Without their false papers I should have been in a far less pleasant place. Thanks to the secret police of the New World.'[45]

This short period of comparative freedom was, however, soon to take a turn for the worse as far as Dollmann was concerned. Whilst in Rome attending the cinema, he was arrested by an Italian detective who recognised him and rejected his false identity papers in the name of Casani. Senior Italian police were, however, willing to release him if the Americans agents were willing to 'send an officer to vouch for you'. However, local US intelligence officials sent only a GI chauffeur to retrieve him, which 'stiffened the Italians' attitude' and gave Dollmann the impression that 'the Americans seemed to attach very little importance to me'.[46] Eventually Angleton, and his colleague, 'Joe', personally visited Police President Polito to retrieve Dollmann, and succeeded in gaining 'a personal victory over the Italian police' by having him released to their custody.[47]

This was to be a short-lived victory, however, in that it brought trouble down upon both Dollmann and the OSS officials involved. Perhaps to take revenge upon these agents, the Italian police briefed the media of Dollmann's presence in Rome and his *de facto* protection by the Americans. This, in turn, led to a storm of protest from local communist politicians, denouncement by Radio Moscow of the 'notorious Colonel Dollmann' and even the involvement of the US State Department. Within days, Angleton announced that it was no longer going to be possible to keep Dollmann at liberty in Rome, and he was told that 'they were pulling out of the whole affair and leaving me

42 *Ibid*, 84. 43 *Ibid*, 82. 44 *Ibid*, 93. 45 *Ibid*, 102. 46 *Ibid*, 109.
47 *Ibid*, 114.

to the mercies of someone else'.[48] This unnamed person turned out to be Major Pagnotta, the deputy chief of US CIC in Rome, who 'treated me as though I were a pretty low sort of criminal'.[49] Supposedly on Pagnotta's 'word of honour', Dollmann was then relocated for one night only to the grim, dark and unsanitary conditions of a cell in a military prison.[50] Although personally visited by General Lee, who possessed overall command responsibility for US armed forces in the Mediterranean, and referred to him as the 'Capitulation Colonel', Dollmann was still detained for many months. During this period of extended detention, he developed kidney problems.[51] He was also asked to write a report on Kesselring, who was, at this time, facing trial for war crimes.[52]

Just before Ash Wednesday 1947, Dollmann was visited again by Angleton and 'Joe'. Both men reportedly 'looked a little sheepish' when they saw at first-hand the squalid conditions in which he had been detained over the previous months. They gave him 500 Swiss francs but no immediate release and his detention continued over the Easter period. A week before Whitsun 1947, he received a second personal visit from General Lee, who was appalled at his conditions; and within a few days he was removed from this prison on a stretcher. This was perceived as necessary not because of his ill-health but to protect him from being identified by communists, who continued to create controversy over his presence in Rome under American protection. Dollmann was taken to a plane which flew him from Italy to the Rhine-Main airfield in Frankfurt, Germany.[53] From here he was sent initially to a juvenile prison and then on to the more comfortable and freer conditions of a large guest house in which the American occupation authorities detained 'outstanding cases' prior to their ultimate disposal or permanent release. Amongst these was Otto Skorzeny, Hitler's famous commando, who had previously organised the 'liberation' of Mussolini from Allied captivity, and Franz Hofer, former Gauleiter of Tirol and a minor figure in Operation Sunrise.[54]

Dollmann remained resident in this building until he decided to return unlawfully to Italy via Austria in November 1947 with the assistance of a former Offizier der Luftwaffe.[55] The purpose of this trip was to hunt down a supposed arms cache controlled by former Nazi regional leader Franz Hofer (Gauleiter of the Tyrol-Vorarlberg and, after September 1943, High Commissioner of the Bolzano-Trento region). This adventure involved Dollmann illegally crossing from Italy to Austria, which was still controlled by French occupation authorities, who soon arrested him. He served a short period of imprisonment. Dollmann's links with US intelligence came to his aid once again in the form of CIC liaison officer Captain Bell, and then Irving Ross

48 *Ibid*, 116.
49 *Ibid*, 117.
50 *Ibid*, 117.
51 *Ibid*, 123.
52 *Ibid*, 120.
53 *Ibid*, 126.
54 *Ibid*, 126–36.
55 *Ibid*, 138–40.

from the CIA. The latter, whose intelligence status gave him the privileges of a diplomatic passport, took Dollmann across the Italian border through the Brenner Pass in the boot of his Cadillac.[56]

In short, a close review of Dollmann's post-war treatment at the hands of the American authorities contradicts the idea that he received particularly privileged treatment. On the contrary, he was repeatedly detained until grim and unsanitary conditions not because of any belief that he was even a middle-ranking war criminal but because of a desire to exercise control over him.

There is considerable evidence that, once it became clear he was not facing credible charges with respect to the Ardeatine Caves atrocity, US intelligence officers hired Dollmann as a part-time intelligence agent. Indeed, certain intelligence officials who 'handled' the Dollmann case were, when he was confronted with an intelligence issue, able to experience at first-hand his more impressive analytical and strategic skills, which contrasted with his other, negative qualities.[57] This confirms the point that, once an actual or potential agent has been put on trial for war crimes, for example, or even appears as a named witness, then he or she may be effectively 'blown' as a future intelligence 'asset', so that the recruitment of a war crimes suspect may have to be delayed until a decision is made that they are not going to have to appear in court.

Between 1947 and 1948, Dollmann worked for SSU/CIA in Rome and then Frankfurt in Germany. Indeed, it is difficult to reconstruct his movements between Germany, Austria, Italy and Switzerland with any precision in the immediate post-war decade. In January 1948, following his illegal border crossing, the American intelligence officials based in Innsbruch who had secured his release from French custody[58] warned Dollmann that it was not safe for him to remain in Austria, and facilitated his return to Italy. One report states that,[59] in post-war Italy, Dollmann also maintained links with unspecified Italian 'intelligence officials . . . In part because of his previous acquaintance with these individuals.'[60] Indeed, the CIA had questionned G2 (US Army Military Intelligence Division) as to Dollmann's role as an intermediary between German experts on rocket-propelled missiles, one of whom was resident in the Soviet zone, and the Italian Navy.[61] Dollmann's anonymous American handler stated that this agent had exploited his contacts in Rome with highly influential 'behind the scenes' figures to secure

56 *Ibid*, 153–56. 57 Anon, diary extract, 21 July 1950, Zimmer Name File, *op cit*.

58 Extracted from a report, whose title is withheld, dated 21 July 1950, #15; *ibid*.

59 In the typed copy of the sanitised release, the word Italian is deleted but the CIA official charged with sanitising this document prior to its public release failed to delete the same word in the handwritten copy of the same document!

60 Memorandum, Ass't Chief of Staff, G2 to CIA [details deleted], Eugen Dollmann, 17 November 1951, #5, Dollmann Name File, NA, R6236.

61 *Ibid*, #6.

introductions for US agents, who presumably wanted to tap into any information or intrigues in which these figures were engaged.[62]

In January 1948, Dollmann moved temporarily to Venice and Milan, and then, with the help of a priest and female Italian partisan, he crossed illegally into Lugano, Switzerland,[63] where he lived 'like a king', possibly enjoying the patronage of former OSS official Donald Jones.[64] One document from this period, a cover note to one of Dollmann's reports forwarded to the CIA, includes the revealing comment, from an Italian-based CIC official, that: 'Your people are probably supporting Dollmann in Switzerland so I think you should read this. I don't know why he writes reports for us.'[65] This CIC official forwarded this document to the CIA 'in view of its possible specific interest by reason of its origin'. In other words, the report was worth highlighting for the CIA less for its detailed intelligence content than for what it revealed concerning Dollmann's recent activities and contacts.

The report itself is clearly slanted to create or strengthen certain beliefs that could work to Dollmann's own advantage, not least with respect to war crimes issues. It includes details of how Soviet intelligence efforts within Germany concentrated less upon advancing the position of the German Communist Party than in making contacts with German military technicians, especially those with specialist knowledge of tanks and aircraft.[66] Dollmann records that 'a skilfully organised arms trafficking was taking place between Italy and Germany . . . with a view to the next war', one of whose major beneficiaries was the Soviet Union.[67] Dollmann's report argued that the Western powers had alienated many German ex-Army officials. These powers had achieved this unfortunate outcome by altering the line of military defence in the event of a military conflict with the Soviets. The result of making Germany into a front-line state with respect to a future world war was that 'each German is trying to work out an arrangement with the East or with the West depending on which side is thought most likely to gain control of their particular area of Germany'.[68] It noted that ex-Waffen SS General Steiner [? partly illegible] was 'extremely influential in extreme Right circles' and – particularly interesting for present proposes – that 'Ex-SS and police General for Italy, Karl Wolff currently free and active, allegedly under Anglo-American patronage.' Dollmann's exact words were actually more controversial than the CIC's own précis just quoted:

62 Extracted from a report, whose title is withheld, dated 21 July 1950, #34, *ibid.*

63 Dollmann 1956 *op cit*, 165–68. 64 *Ibid*, 156.

65 'Forwarded Italian-Slanted report on Eugen Dollmann', 8 February 1950, Dollmann Name File, *op cit*.

66 *Ibid*, # 3.

67 *Ibid*, # 26 – Dollmann blames 'German capitalists, principally Jews who took refuge in Switzerland with their wealth.'

68 *Ibid*.

> Thanks to the energetic intervention of his collaborators of 2 May 1945 (Baron Parilli, the American Gero von Gaevernitz and the Swiss professor Max Husmann), Wolff now enjoys complete freedom although German authorities had earlier condemned him to 10 years imprisonment as Himmler's ex-chief of Staff. Today Wolff lives near Munich and is building a new life under patronage which can easily be imagined. On the occasion of a visit to Kesselring, who was then imprisoned in one of the Rhine provinces, Wolff reminded him that if he had taken a more active part in the surrender negotiations, he too would undoubtedly be free. This observation was not kindly received by Kesselring.[69]

For the purposes of this book, this statement adds weight to the contention that Wolff himself had not attributed his immediate freedom to his lack of involvement in war criminality. Instead, he attributed this to his ability to shield behind the umbrella of protection from US intelligence officials forming part of the terms and conditions he negotiated with Dulles during Operation Sunrise.

Dollmann's report also addressed the private orientation and plans of another German associated with Operation Sunrise – Rahn, former 'Hitler-Ribbentrop representative to Mussolini'. Rahn was seeking influence in Italy. He was doing this by pushing forward his protégé Möllhausen, former German consul in Rome. In another clearly self-interested statement, Dollmann's report further addressed the counter-productive effects for the Allied authorities of continuing Nazi war crimes trials under changed geopolitical circumstances: 'After five years when the entire situation has changed.' Dollmann was referring to the American mistreatment and trial of ex-Waffen-SS-Standarterführer Peiper.[70]

He further claimed that the Vatican's own Order of Malta, in which both Zimmer and Parilli were involved: 'is a rich intelligence field whose "possibilities" could usefully be "exploited" by the Americans'.[71] Dollmann reported on the situation in the Eastern Soviet-controlled zone of Germany, as indicated by his contacts with a German industrialist, and former Germany Army officer, whom Dollmann suspected of acting as a Russian spy.[72] This report also notes how certain former generals, including Westphal and Haldar, had been 'promised facilitation of their de-Nazification proceedings' in return for cooperation with Allied authorities in writing a 'war history'.[73] Presumably, Dollmann chose to highlight this type of traded immunity because it could be interpreted as a relevant precedent with respect to his own claims for protection.

69 *Ibid*, # 7. 70 *Ibid*, # 32–33. 71 *Ibid*, # 14–15. 72 *Ibid*, # 18.
73 *Ibid*, # 4.

Later, CIA officials received several reports dated June and September 1948 from an Italian source. These stated that Dollmann was living in the vicinity of Milan and in the employ of CIC (US Counter Intelligence Corps). This document within Dollmann's Name File justified recording such details because 'we are interested in determining whether Dollmann and possibly Wenner, have an Odeum [Order of Knights of Malta] connection', and sought verification from one of the CIA's German Field Offices that these reports were indeed accurate.[74] As already noted, when arrested by French authorities in Austria in 1949, Dollmann was able to secure his release through the intervention of US CIC officials.[75]

Senior CIA officials, namely the Chiefs of the Italian and German Field Offices, continued to monitor Dollmann's activities and whereabouts. This even included monitoring the serialisation in July 1949 of his memoirs within a leading Italian newspaper, *Il Tempo*. A similar concern was evident with respect to other publications addressing aspects of Operation Sunrise.[76] These proposed publications contained embarrassing details of how Dollmann had been shielded from the Italian authorities in an American-controlled safe house in Rome before, on 7 November 1946, being recognised on the way to the theatre by his former chauffeur, a communist ex-partisan. Allegedly, he was released 'by order of Caserta' [Allied Military and Intelligence base in Southern Italy], and was then immediately 'interned'.[77] The CIA also secured and recorded details of how the newspaper came to acquire these memoirs via their lawyer, who had negotiated with Dollmann in Lugano, Switzerland.[78] The active monitoring of Dollmann's movements, activities and contacts was probably linked to the concern within US intelligence circles that the Nazi partners of Operation Sunrise might publish accounts of events that flatly contradicted the self-serving official interpretation of this 'intelligence triumph', not least the anti-Soviet geo-political aspects and violation of the policy of unconditional surrender.

By late 1950, Dollmann had returned to Lugano, Switzerland, where the US CIC continued to employ Dollmann to write reports on developments within Germany. Whilst resident in Switzerland, Parilli, still a prominent and influential person in the Vatican's Sovereign Order of Malta, visited Dollmann. He had persuaded the Italian Chief of Police in Rome, Polito, personally to issue Dollmann with a 'genuine, valid and authentic passport in

74 *Ibid.*

75 Extracted from a report, whose title other than MSGA–169, is withheld, dated 21 July 1950, # 33–34, *ibid.*

76 'Milan Newspaper publication of activities of OSS Switzerland', JRX 4800, 24 September 1946; 'Present whereabouts of Eugen Dollmann', 9 May 1952, both *ibid.*

77 'Operational, Dollmann Memoirs', 25 July 1949, *ibid.*

78 The CIA also monitored press coverage of Dollmann, for example, a series of articles appearing in *Unita*. See 'Forwarding of Dollmann clipping', 12 September 1950, *ibid.*

my own name' as a birthday present.[79] On his return to Italy following his expulsion by the Swiss, Dollmann used the assumed surname 'von Amonn'. This false identity was confirmed by forged Italian identity papers that the Italian Navy had issued him in consideration for the 'valuable services' he had performed. However, 'When Dollmann could no longer be utilised by the Italians, the Italian Counter Espionage Service was requested to pick up Dollmann's passport on the pretence of renewing it.'[80] But, as a precaution, Dollmann had photographed the passport before releasing it. This meant that, following his expulsion from Switzerland, the Italian authorities were forced to honour Dollmann's copy as 'proof' of his right to residence in Italy:[81]

> He refused to return to Germany for fear that he might be assassinated by ex-Nazis who regarded him as a traitor. Concomitantly he was advised that should he return to Italy he should be arrested and tried for what the Italian press described as 'acts of violence and murder committed against Italian hostages', e.g., the Ardeatine caves episode.[82]

There is evidence that, during the summer of 1950, US intelligence officials continued to use Dollmann for intelligence purposes. One factor was that, when dealing with individuals other than Allied officials, who put him on edge because they knew too much about his background and failings, he was still capable of effective action based on a logical analysis of the situation in hand and the ramifications of various options.[83] In addition, he retained a wide network of influential and, for the Anglo-Americans, potentially troublesome contacts within Rome.[84] On the other hand, by this time Dollmann had become increasingly notorious for using some of these strategic thinking skills to exert pressure on US intelligence officials to extort funding, not least by threatening to write articles and memoirs that exposed their actions, identities, sources and methods in relation to his own previous contacts with them. In other words, whilst his CIA handlers could exploit Dollmann's dire financial plight to their own advantage, he was more than capable to returning such pressure by threatening to 'blow' their cover and sources and methods.[85]

CIA officials gave Dollmann the mission of infiltrating diehard Nazi groups who were funding their underground movement through gunrunning and drug importation.[86] In particular, the CIA employed him to monitor the

79 Dollmann, 1956, *op cit*, 173–74.

80 'Eugen Dollmann', Memorandum for Ass't Director for Special Operations, CIA, 8 September 1952, *ibid.*

81 *Ibid.*

82 'Germans in Spain, Eugen Dollmann', (nd), *ibid.*

83 MSGA-169, 21 July 1950, *op cit*, # 11, *ibid.*

84 *Ibid*, # 33–34.

85 *Ibid*, # 15.

86 There is a clear analogy here to the deployment of Zimmer as a penetration agent against a similar clandestine group.

activities of ex-Nazis, such as Hofer, the former Gauleiter of the Bolzano area (the base of Wolff's former SS HQ).[87] Hofer was the centre of an extreme right-wing movement involved in arms dealing, which was centred in the Austrian Tyrol area around Innsbruck. Hofer had been on the fringes of the Sunrise Operation, although he later betrayed Wolff to Kaltenbrunner once his own political demands to remain a regional governor of both Austrian and the Italian South Tyrol (to be retained as a unified region) had been rejected by all parties as absurd. One note states:

> As Dollmann is about the only person left of the higher Nazi circles, he is probably the only one who could contact these people and talk to them, [deleted] agreed to send Dollmann on this trip [to Innsbruck on the 12 July 1950].[88]

Dollmann's mission was to participate in a 'sting' operation by posing as an agent for a secret arms purchaser claiming to be acting on behalf of more senior neo-Nazi groups, by implication perhaps association with Karl Wolff.[89] Apparently, there was a 'considerable' cache of arms derived from the Brandenburg Regiment buried in a cave in South Tyrol, and controlled by Hofer, and Dollmann extracted 150,000 lire from US intelligence personnel to penetrate this group.[90] Allegedly, Dollmann's efforts failed to provide useful intelligence. In turn, this resulted in the judgement that: 'the subject is completely finished as far as intelligence possibilities are concerned, and [we] will not spend any more money on him'.[91]

On the other hand, it appears, from reports reaching CIA Rome, that at least some Italian military/Naval intelligence officials, who enjoyed close relations with Angleton,[92] took the view that he remained a 'salvageable intelligence asset' to the extent that they consistently defended him and provided him with false passports in return for 'valuable services'.[93] This protection from Italian military and counter-intelligence officials effectively shielded Dollmann from investigation from Italian war crimes prosecutors.[94]

During the early 1950s, Dollmann's poor financial state, worsened by his chronic inability to manage his personal finances successfully, led him to attempt to sell his memoirs both as a whole and as various extracts in newspaper articles. These contained a series of scandalous claims concerning the sexual activity of both the Italian monarchy (the House of Savoy) and the American ambassador to Italy, the exposure of which continued to be monitored by intelligence officials.[95] He also attempted to peddle German

87 MSGA-169, 21 July 1950, # 9, *op cit*. 88 *Ibid*, # 33. 89 *Ibid*, # 32–33.
90 'Eugen Dollmann', PIMA 1130, 11 February 1952, *ibid*. 91 *Ibid*, # 9.
92 Naftali, 1992, *op cit*, 225. 93 'Eugen Dollmann', 8 September 1952, *ibid*.
94 'Dollmann, Eugen', 20 March 1952, *ibid*. 95 PIR-10103, 12 July 1951, *ibid*.

wartime documents[96] (including the whereabouts of a cache of Hitler's personal effects), films and intelligence information.[97] Dollmann even approached American intelligence officials based in Italy with a veiled offer to sell them a cache of potentially embarrassing wartime documents hidden in Austria, including documentation of Hitler/Stalin peace talks, so that these could be either suppressed or exploited as anti-Soviet propaganda.[98] Although local CIA personnel did not believe this story, they regarded paying a moderate degree of financial sponsorship, 200,000 lire, as a 'long-term investment in Dollmann through a good channel which we can hope to control'.[99]

His arrangement of the recruitment by the Italian Navy of German scientists with expertise in guided missile technology attracted the attention of the CIA and G-2,[100] whose agents had wrongly suggested they were nuclear scientists.[101] One report from this period confirmed that Dollmann had: 'from time to time [been] in contact with Italian intelligence officials in post-war Italy, in part because of his previous [wartime] acquaintances with these individuals'.[102] At the same time, CIA documents alleged that Donald Jones, identified as an American intelligence agent based in Lugano Switzerland, had close and possibly sexual relations with Dollmann.[103] However, the two men had reportedly become estranged, possibly over money or jealousy:

96 'Eugen Dollmann' 27 August 1951, *ibid.*

97 On Dollmann's efforts in the summer of 1952 to sell to *Life* magazine for one million lire a buried cache of Hitler's documents, which allegedly contained a letter from Stalin to Hitler proposing a separate peace, see 'Activities of Eugen Dollmann', 10 November 1952, # 7, *ibid.* In what could have been an exaggerated sales pitch, Dollmann claimed that this cache of documents contained materials of various secret diplomatic intrigues involving Hitler of sufficient duplicity to bring about the collapse of several European governments, and that the Russian intelligence services sought to protect Stalin's reputation from embarrassment by taking Dollmann out of circulation. See, 'in re: Col. Eugen Dollmann', 3 December 1953 – a translation of a long newspaper interview Dollmann published in the Italian paper *Epoco*: Memorandum, Ass't Chief of Staff, G2 to CIA [details deleted] Eugen Dollmann, 17 November 1951, #2, *ibid.*

98 PIMA, 10 September 1951 (referring to a 'rash of Dollmann approaches' and noting the: 'guarded approaches to the subject of the joint exploitation of Dollmann advanced regularly in the past. . . .'; Daily Intelligence Summary, 6 August 1951, both *ibid.*

99 Chief of Station Rome to Foreign Division F, 16 November 1951, *ibid.*

100 Angleton had penetrated Italian Naval intelligence: Naftali, 1992, *op cit*, 225.

101 Daily Intelligence Summary, 6 August 1951; 'Eugen Dollmann', 4 October 1951 (G-2); 'Dollmann, Eugen' 27 November 1951; Memorandum, Ass't Chief of Staff, G2 to CIA, Eugen Dollmann, 17 November 1951 (correcting the nuclear/'heavy water' story and providing additional details: all CIA Name File, *op cit*. The German scientists were Hermann Oberth (a rocket propulsion expert) and Gottfried Koch (chemist).

102 Memorandum, Ass't Chief of Staff, G2 to CIA, 'Eugen Dollmann', 17 November 1951, *ibid.*

103 For additional linkages between Jones, officially described as 'Counsellor of Embassy', and Dollmann, see 'Eugen Dollmann': Chief WE to Chief, 23 July 1954, *ibid.*

'both are suspected of being sexual perverts'.[104] If this story is true, then it adds an additional interpersonal element to the motivations behind Dollmann's internally controversial deployment and protection by at least one US intelligence official.

Certainly, the same report confirms that, as late as 1952 and despite all the potentially compromising information already known about Dollmann, he was still being considered for additional temporary employment as both an informant and sub-agent. This was mainly because of his claims to be part of various influential networks concerning whom he could reveal inside information:

> As to the present value of Dollmann as an agent or informer, the following can be said. Dollmann is in great need of money. His value is uncertain; however, he is not the man he was in 1940–45. Dollmann claims to have the support and confidence of 'certain high German personalities'.[105]

In 1951, Dollmann left Germany to reside in Lugano, Switzerland, where he had various contacts and friends. However, on 8 February 1952, Dollmann was expelled from his Swiss residence. He was deported to Italy following a scandal involving his homosexual relationship with a Swiss police official and his possession of a false passport under the name 'Ammon'.[106] This scandal generated unfortunate press coverage, which continued to refer to him as a Nazi war criminal. Such media coverage probably blew his credibility within far-right circles, and hence his continued usefulness as a future US intelligence informant targeting such circles. Nevertheless, in return for his past services, the CIA continued to assist Dollmann by, for example, meeting him at the Swiss border and arranging for his transport to a Franciscan monastery[107] to shelter him temporarily before he returned to the Milan area, where the CIA paid him visits 'to keep him quiet'.[108] It appears that a number of senior CIA officials, possibly including Allen Dulles,[109] were especially concerned about the possible ramifications of this particular situation.

For his part, Dollmann feared that he would be deported to Germany and

104 'Dollmann, Eugene', 27 November 1951, *ibid.*

105 *Ibid.* These included former Generalfeldmarschall Albert Kesselring, and various elite Italian groups in Rome and Milan: 'Present whereabouts of Eugen Dollmann', 9 May 1952, *ibid.*

106 'Memorandum for Ass't Chief of Staff G2, 'Eugen Dollmann', (nd), *ibid.*

107 It is doubtful that the CIA actually arranged his trip to Spain, however: 'Subject was apparently aided in reaching Spain through Italy by Italian monks with whom he has been friendly since wartime days. Subject arrived in Spain in early March 1952 accompanied by a monk, and was temporarily lodged in a monastery in Madrid.' Memorandum for Ass't Chief of Staff G2, Eugen Dollmann, (nd), *ibid.*

108 'Eugen Dollmann', 24 February 1952, *ibid.*

109 *Ibid.* The names of the officials are deleted from the sanitised release.

had prepared to commit suicide through a vial of cyanide, that is arrange 'a Nazi death'. He also expressed a desire to emigrate to either Franco's Spain (where he had relatives and offers of help and accommodation from monasteries), or Latin America – a traditional refuge of fugitive Nazis.[110] The Catholic Church in Milan, which was highly cooperative with the CIA, had arranged counterfeit travel documentation to Spain and accommodation in a monastery. During the last days of February 1952, Dollmann, who – in common with his travelling companion – was 'dressed in the habit of a Fransican monk',[111] departed for Madrid. He was using an assumed name supported by a false Italian passport.[112]

In Madrid, where he arrived in early March, an unnamed CIA official, who also employed a former Nazi military intelligence sub-agent, took part responsibility for Dollmann. Once settled in this city, Dollmann was soon 'taken under the wing of' the 'notorious' Nazi commando leader Otto Skorzeny.[113] By securing Skorzeny's protection, Dollmann could function even in the absence of Spanish identity papers.[114] Skorzeny, who used the alias Otto Steinbauer,[115] not only headed the Odessa organisation (the ex-SS mutual support group), but was also suspected as working as an agent for the AIS (Austrian Intelligence Service). He was reported to be 'quite well set up in a commercial office which obviously does little commerce'. Indeed, Skorzeny was using his ownership of an import-export business in Madrid as a front for his European intelligence and pro-Nazi activities, which maintained direct contacts with the Spanish fascist party leadership.[116]

Dollmann's new protector provided him with accommodation owned by a German, and enjoyed patronage from a number of powerful individuals, including a senior Catholic Church official who was reportedly close to Franco.[117] Later, during the autumn of 1952, Dollmann was made 'Skorzeny's confidential agent in Italy'. In this capacity, on 7 October of that year, he attempted to re-enter Germany with false Italian papers obtained by a former fascist associate to make contact with German youth groups.[118]

During the early 1950s, CIA's Munich Field Office noted that Dollmann had continued his contacts with far right-wing movements. These included those 'extreme Nazi groups' based in Egypt and North Africa: 'connected with the grand Mufti and the former SS-Führer Lauterbacher. The center of

110 *Ibid.* 111 'Germans in Spain, Eugen Dollmann,' 23 April 1952, *ibid.*

112 'Eugen Dollmann', 24 February 1952, # 8, *ibid.*

113 'Eugen Dollmann', Memorandum for Ass't Chief of Staff G2, (nd), *ibid.*

114 'Eugen Dollmann', Memorandum for Ass't Director for Special Operations, CIA, 8 September 1952, *ibid.*

115 'Activities of Eugen Dollmann', 10 November 1952, # 7, *ibid.* 116 *Ibid.*

117 'Security information', (nd), but clearly from March 1952; *ibid*; 'Memorandum for Ass't Chief of Staff G2, Eugen Dollmann', (nd), *ibid.*

118 'Further data on Eugen Dollmann', 17 October 1952, *ibid.*

this group is in Italy, probably in Rome.'[119] At this time, CIA officials obtained reports on Dollmann from other intelligence agencies in a clandestine manner, which suggests he was still being regarded as an important target.[120] There is also evidence that, during 1952, Dollmann returned to Rome where, on one occasion, he was 'noticed by certain Communist elements in Rome whilst attending the cinema and was rescued by the police from a threatening mob. He was thereafter given an Italian passport and escorted to the Austrian frontier.'[121]

During the spring of 1952, CIA officials in Washington told their Madrid-based colleagues that 'headquarters would appreciate being informed on subject's activities'.[122] However, this internal CIA correspondence between, presumably, the German or Italian field offices[123] and their colleagues based in Spain, expressed caution 'against [the] operational use of Dollmann during his stay in Spain because he had already been involved with several intelligence organisations in Western Europe since 1945; his reputation for blackmail, subterfuge and double-dealing is infamous; he is homosexual'.[124] Part of this note refers presumably to Dollmann's involvement with AIS through Skorzeny, his links with Italian military intelligence (including acting as an intermediary between the Italian Navy and German scientists) and, of course, his sporadic employment by both the CIA and the US Army's CIC. There is also a record stating that Dollmann had been denounced to the Spanish authorities 'by the dirty French as a British spy', which – if true – indicates that Dollmann's employment record as a freelance informant or sub-agent included yet another Western intelligence agency.

On the other hand, whilst in Spain Dollmann certainly maintained contact with the CIA and possible American Military Intelligence (G.2), and reportedly acted in the belief, encouraged by the CIA, that:

> if he got in any trouble he could call on [deleted] head of US intelligence in Spain. This identification [of the name of the official who held this senior post] according to [illegible] had been given him by Lt Col. Luis Garcia.[125]

It is possible, but perhaps unwise, to further speculate which senior CIA official was continuing to offer Dollmann such protection during a period

119 'Dr Eugen Dollmann', Munich, 25 January 1952, *ibid.*

120 PIRM-2337 [partly illegible], 2 February 1952, *ibid* (referring to an earlier report of November 1951).

121 'Activities of Eugen Dollmann', 10 November 1952, # 3, *ibid.*

122 The parties are deleted from the sanitised release, *ibid.* 'Germans in Spain, Eugen Dollmann', 23 April 1952, *ibid.*

123 *Ibid.* 124 *Ibid.* 125 Chief WE to Chief, 'Eugen Dollmann', 23 July 1954, *ibid.*

when Allen Dulles was, of course, the Deputy Director and then Director of the CIA.

As with Zimmer, it is conceivable that Dollmann was playing all sides against each other in pursuit of his own personal interests. If this was the case, then it is highly likely that he would have offered his services to one of his many other contacts within rival European intelligence agencies and neo-fascist networks. He was certainly reporting on the activities, membership and plans of Nazi groups for different branches of US civilian, military and counter-intelligence agencies. Yet, Dollmann was also receiving payment and support from these same groups, living on gifts of money from former Nazis in Austria and Germany, who may, in turn, have relied upon him to perform the role of a penetration agent into American intelligence.

Dollmann's CIA Name File contains later documentation which discusses his further potential to penetrate 'neo-Nazi groups' in Austria, particularly Vienna, who 'financed their activities from proceeds from the sale of cocaine'.[126] This assistance with a 'narcotics investigation' was an assignment that Dollmann, whose finances were in a dire state, offered to perform for the CIA. Given that a significant number of former Nazi fugitives from Allied justice had found sanctuary in many of the Latin American countries that have traditionally supplied the raw ingredients for cocaine, Dollmann's claims may have appeared credible. There is indirect evidence that the CIA took Dollmann's offer seriously enough to recommend, or at least forward on, this offer to the Commissioner of the American Narcotic Bureau. In turn, this bureau's Rome office sent newspaper coverage of Dollmann, which appeared in early December 1952, to both his superiors and the CIA, presumably as such coverage could be prejudicial to his future usefulness as a penetration agent.[127]

It appears that, although during the mid-1950s, and at the request of senior operation colleagues, CIA officials continued to monitor Dollmann's orientation, contacts and actions, sometimes even through requests to the Gehlen Organisation and contacts within other friendly intelligence services, nothing of operational significance emerged from 1953 onwards.[128] One partly illegible CIA report from 1953 notes that Dollmann was still willing to cooperate with the recovery of other Second World War arms caches, and discusses Karl Wolff, presumably in connection with such arms trafficking.[129]

According to recently declassified CIA files, by 1955 Dollmann was no longer employed by US intelligence, even in a freelance capacity. He made

126 'Activities of Eugen Dollmann', 10 November 1952, *ibid.*

127 'Activities of Eugen Dollmann', 17 December 1952, *ibid.*

128 Dulles to SR Net Pullachl . . . [partly illegible] 14 July 1954; Chief NE to Senior [illegible] 'Eugen Dollmann' 20 July 1954 (containing 11 different 'traces' or references to Dollmann in assorted intelligence reports from 1952, Zimmer Name File, *op cit.*

129 'Dollmann, Eugen', September 1953 (originally from 201 folder), *ibid.*

attempts to resume contact via officials in the American consulate in Munich, not only touting the potential services of a possible sub-agent with free access to East Germany but also to discuss any deletions (presumably for a price in his characteristic blackmailing fashion) from his memoirs if these proved offensive to the US authorities. This rash of contacts met with no positive response.[130] This snub was despite his name-dropping reference to his 'great friend [Dulles] with whom he allegedly had contact during WWII', and his sending of draft copies of these memoirs to Mr Eisenhower.[131] Dollmann pestered American authorities for a decision on which parts might require modification to avoid compromising agents, such as BB008 (aka Major O'Brien but actually James Angleton),[132] but apparently he received no satisfactory reply, other than a holding letter.[133] Dollmann then stated he would ask the publishers to print the book regardless, as he had now discharged his obligations to the US authorities, a statement regarded as a possible 'threat' in a communication with Dulles.[134] Whilst Dollmann's espionage offer and a file on him was passed on to 'operational' colleagues involved in spying for possible exploitation (subject to the caveat that the touted sub-agent may be a 'plant' secretly employed by the Russians), there is no record in currently declassified records of the matter being taken up any further.[135] Intelligence officials suggested that Dollmann's motivation for making this offer was 'seeking what he deemed to be the relative safety of US protection' in far-flung Spain, 'which he could tap at will'. Certainly, one official decided to 'take no action' because he was 'not anxious to deal through as controversial figure as Dollmann'.[136] If the matter was to be pursued further, it would preferably have to take place through a direct approach 'without using Dollmann or [illegible] as middlemen'.[137] Dollmann died in Munich in 1985, some 30 years after the last recorded entry for him appears in declassified US intelligence files.

In short, there were understandable reasons why, in the Cold War context, OSS/SSU/CIA officials perceived that there were vital national security interests requiring Dollmann to be kept quiet. Nevertheless, we can still question, at many different levels, the wisdom of intelligence personnel shielding Dollmann from Italian war crimes investigators. On the other hand,

130 These were published in Milan, Italy, during mid-summer 1955 under the title *The Cowardly Hero* (*Der Feige Held*). The CIA may have regretted this, given that, when they were published, they contained embarrassing details of the homosexual activities taking place in parties allegedly organised by Mr Alexander, the US ambassador to pre-war Italy, which prompted a CIA memorandum. See 'Allegations of SS Col. Dollmann', 11 April 1955, *ibid.*

131 'Dr Eugen Dollmann', 22 March 1955, *ibid.*

132 Naftali, 1992 *op cit*, 235, n. 3.

133 Chief of Staff, Pullach [Zipper/Gehlen HQ] to Chief [illegible], 4 August 1954 [partly illegible]; Director/Dulles from Pullach, 17 March 1955; both *ibid.*

134 *Ibid.*

135 'Eugen Dollmann case', 18 August 1954, *ibid.*

136 *Ibid.*

137 *Ibid.*

Dollmann's CIA Name File and related declassified documentation suggest that there was no overarching, centrally organised and uniform right-wing conspiracy by intelligence agencies to subvert legality with respect to war crimes trials. These *ad hoc* interventions to create a never entirely reliable umbrella of protection raised considerable uncertainty and internal controversy. Indeed, the treatment of Dollmann and Zimmer reveals a degree of episodic reactions by senior intelligence officials to a series of largely unpredicted events. There is no evidence that, at least once it was known that he was in US custody, had Dollmann's alleged complicity in the Ardeatine Caves massacre ever been firmly established, he would have been fully protected from later prosecution. On the contrary, US intelligence officials specifically held him in Italy in case this eventuality materialised, and only resumed protection once he had been vindicated. These factors contradict the widely held assumption that Anglo-American intelligence were operating on the basis of a pre-planned and centrally directed conspiracy to hire and protect selected Nazi war criminals, or otherwise to grant unconditional legal immunity to those Nazi officials who assisted Dulles in Operation Sunrise.

The internal controversy regarding the 'privileged treatment' of the Wolff group

One aspect of the wider internal conflict regarding Zimmer's receiving immunity and other comparative privileges occurred between Dulles (and his subordinates and successors in OSS/SSU/CIA German mission) and other branches of OSS and Allied authorities, especially James Angleton's counter-intelligence, or X2 section, of OSS based within Rome. This unit, SCI/Z,[138] comprising approximately 20 British and American staff, was charged with identifying and arresting the SD's 'stay behind agents' and their informants who could threaten Allied interests in Italy and beyond, not least by acting as 'line crossers' supplying order of battle information during the final months of the war.[139] These and other intelligence officials questioned the post-war usefulness of Zimmer by emphasising that, as recorded in an earlier cable, the 'subject thoroughly blown by satevpost' [*Saturday Evening Post*].[140] This American newspaper had printed an OSS-leaked and augmented story concerning its triumphant role in the so-called 'secret surrender' negotiations as part of General Donovan's desperate propaganda attempt to forestall

138 Naftali, 1992, *op cit*, 235, n. 3.

139 T. Mangold, *Cold Warrior: James Jesus Angleton* (London: Simon and Schuster, 1991), 20–21; T. Naftali, 'Artifice: James Angleton and X-2 Operations in Europe', in Chalou, 1992 *op cit*, 218, 218–19. Angleton, then under 30 years old, still rose from head of X-2 in Rome in 1944 to Chief of OSS operations in the whole of Italy by 1945.

140 Cable 1701.7, 10 September 1945, summarised in 'Guido Zimmer', Zimmer Name File, Vol. 1.

impending dissolution.[141] Later, OSS/SSU officials received reports that Zimmer's name featured prominently in the coverage of Sunrise in a Milan newspaper, which would have further compromised his potential usefulness as an agent within Italy.[142] It should be emphasised that OSS/SCI-Z Italy under Angleton was not in principle averse to shielding individuals wanted by legal authorities who had been or could become useful to them.[143] By contrast, Dulles and his immediate subordinates in OSS Germany continued to try to protect Zimmer. They provided him with a misleading cover story that he had been operating as an undercover OSS agent who, as such, merited privileged treatment, and could usefully continue such work during the post-war period.

Neither this cover story nor its attempted justification met with universal acceptance within the OSS/SSU, however. Angleton's X-2/SCI-Z staff had been targeting Zimmer's SD operation in Milan during the last year of the war as a potential centre for post-hostilities resistance and Nazi espionage, and later mounted missions to recover looted treasures.[144] Ultimately, Angleton was given a medal for apprehending over 1,000 enemy agents and sub-agents in Italy, establishing over 50 secret informants, and successfully penetrating seven different foreign intelligence services, including Tito's communists and different branches of Italian military and civilian intelligence. His post-war work involved developing expertise, through surveillance and other methods, in the personnel and methods of foreign intelligence agents, including SD agents, and seeking to convert such agents into double-agents who could be controlled. The underlying framework was that, in the post-war context, espionage had become the way in which states confronted one another, hence counter-espionage which restricted, eliminated or controlled the covert gathering of intelligence by foreign powers became a vital aspect of national security. This involved monitoring the whereabouts of those such as Zimmer, Wenner and Dollmann, who were perhaps still

141 To be fair, British intelligence were making similar claims regarding the early capitulation with far less justification than the OSS. In a cable from Forgan to Glavin on 15 May 1945, Forgan discussed a news report of London *Daily Telegraph* dated 7 May 1945 which gave 'quite [an] accurate account of [the] whole sunrise operation' but the 'Chief inaccuracy is that all credit is given to British Agents and British Secret Service . . . In our business we cannot expect to receive public acknowledgement of our work. On the other hand it is extremely annoying to have credit for success of this operation handed over to the British in the Press.' Cable, Forgan to Glavin, 15 May 1945, CCC, Donovan Collection, Reel 75.

142 'Milan newspaper publication of Activities of OSS Switzerland,' JRX 4800, 24 September 1946; 'La Carta Perdente Diplomatic Memories of E. F. Moellhansen,' 26 November 1949; CIA Name File, 'Guido Zimmer', *op cit*.

143 Indeed, Angleton protected the Italian fascist Borghese, who had created a stay-behind network despite demands for his prosecution from the Italian government; JJA to Titolo, 6 November 1945, NA, RG 226, Entry 108A, Box 260; Naftali, 1992, *op cit*, 226.

144 Mangold, 1991, *op cit*, 21.

capable of causing security problems. It also required building up as complete a picture as possible of the names, aliases, capabilities and areas of work of foreign agents and their local contacts – precisely the sort of information alluded to but not entirely resolved by Zimmer's notebooks.[145] This is one of the contexts that explains Angleton's anger at being denied access to Zimmer whilst, as will be discussed later, showing greater willingness to assist Dollmann.

One side of this internal debate, represented by Angleton, who had emerged from the war with heightened prestige,[146] rejected the manner in which the umbrella of legal immunity and wider protections was being extended even as far as the Italian Baron Parilli, the supposedly 'neutral' intermediary between OSS and the Wolff group. Dulles had mis-described Parilli as 'not a German emissary but anti-fascist Italian intermediary'.[147] OSS/SSU officials based in Italy complained that their senior colleagues were, unfortunately, still accepting Dulles' rosy interpretation of Parilli. This was despite clear evidence that, during the war, Parilli had operated as an SS double-agent controlled by Zimmer. Angleton's staff were searching not only for 'lingering fascist but more importantly for him, nascent communist networks'.[148] Parilli was clearly incriminated by the contents of Zimmer's notebooks and related attachments. The Italian-based side of the internal debate within US intelligence maintained that this misinterpretation needed to be reversed through the direct and unambiguous intervention of the OSS leadership based in Washington.

The immediate cause of the controversy was that Parilli was still being afforded privileged treatment by senior Allied officials, that is 'the benefits of neutral protection'.[149] The tone, as well as the contents, of the following memorandum clearly reveals the frustration that OSS/SSU field teams in Italy were concerned about the protection granted to Sunrise participants:

> The attitude of this Unit regarding Parilli from the moment he was signalled as a German collaborator and agent by OSS SI field teams, has been that at the minimum he must provide a full and detailed account of the contacts he had long before the armistice negotiations . . . No interrogation of GIS [German intelligence service] personnel received or conducted in this theatre has indicated other than that Parilli was a double agent working for the GIS. Several of Subject's [Zimmer's] memos, attached, state this both explicitly and implicitly.[150]

145 Naftali, 1992, *op cit*, 219–21. 146 *Ibid*, 218–23.

147 Telegram 9119, 21 April: NA, RG 226, Entry 90, Box 7.

148 Mangold, 1991, *op cit*, 20.

149 See 'Guido Zimmer, re: Your X–3377': OSS BB8/Angleton to OSS Washington, 28 November 1945, JZX–5519, Zimmer Name File, *op cit*.

150 *Ibid*.

It might be thought that, following Dulles' return to private legal practice at the end of 1945, the source of Dollmann and Zimmer's protection would rapidly evaporate. Dulles, however, maintained realistic ambitions to return to a leading role within US intelligence (which, of course, he realised in the 1950s when he became the longest ever serving director of the CIA). As one intelligence report makes clear, Dulles had no intention of letting his self-serving and highly selective interpretation of Operation Sunrise unravel to his detriment. He sought to secure the continuing protection of Dollmann and Zimmer by promoting the idea that Zimmer, at least, could be exploited as a post-war intelligence asset:

> Re Guido Zimmer. Before return USA. 110 [OSS codename for Dulles] asked us to assist return to Rome subject and family . . . with Cap't George Shiever, Rome. Zimmer sure aid contacts Rome enable him subsist without help if you do not wish to interrogate or put to work.[151]

In other words, one of Dulles' subordinates informed his counter-intelligence branch colleagues in Rome that 'in compliance with wishes of Mr Dulles it is desired to return SS-Hauptsturmführer Guido Zimmer, wife, Kathie, and children Klaus Luigi and Luisa to Rome'.[152] However, during the winter and spring of 1946, the continuing efforts of certain US intelligence circles to reward Zimmer, not least by facilitating and sponsoring his repatriation, was proving too much for the Commanding Officer of OSS/SSU Rome, Capt. James Angleton.[153] Through a signed memo, Angleton bitterly complained:

> In the past, Subject has enjoyed privileged treatment at the hands of non-CI agencies in this theatre because of his role in the Sunrise operation. This fact makes it difficult for this Unit, under present circumstances, to take a position with reference to the above request. It is this Unit's opinion that Subject at the outset was deserving of no better treatment than that afforded persons of much greater importance to the success of Sunrise than he, namely General Wolff and [Eugen] Dollmann. The time that has elapsed and the evident condoning treatment afforded subject, raises some doubt whether at this stage Subject should still be handled in accordance to the directives laid down for the treatment of GIS [German intelligence service] personnel in April 1945.

151 Amzo 3416, archives 32339, 4 February 1946, *ibid.*

152 JXX 6113 [partly illegible], SCI/Z to AC SO2 CI, AFHQ, 11 February 1946, *ibid.*

153 Angleton used the cover name of 'Major O'Brien' in his dealings with Dollmann. He had served with the OSS/SSU/CIG in Italy during 1944–47, and became CIA Chief of Counter-intelligence 1954–74: T. Naftali, 'Artifice: James Angleton and X-2 operations in Italy', in G. Chalou, 1992, *op cit*, 218–45.

> It is in any case certain that once in Rome, this Unit will desire to interrogate Subject in detail.[154]

Angleton's effort to scupper the continuing 'condoning' and rehabilitation of Zimmer, particularly his transfer to Rome, was largely effective. Allied Forward HQ (AFHQ) rejected the request from Dulles' successors by insisting that Zimmer be 'treated as any other GIS officer' and noted the 'later necessity to intern and repatriate him'.[155]

Dulles' successors attempted to exert pressure to have this decision reversed. They made a complaint concerning how they had received little more than 'nominal support from Angleton vis-à-vis AFHQ'. These attempts proved unsuccessful. However, for present purposes, these follow-up memoranda are important because they reveal greater details of Zimmer's services, the measures of protection he received, partly as a result of Dulles' strong personal support:[156]

> Guido Zimmer [was an] important figure [in] sunrise operation, was SCI agent Germany after May 45 . . . 110 [Dulles] left instructions [to] give all possible aid [in] recognition [of] his services.[157]

Dulles' successors in SSU/CIA received little support from Washington SSU in their attempt to 'pull a flanker' via the US War Department. This was largely because of 'AFHQ's hostility to subjects [Zimmer and his family] going to Italy'. Indeed, in the spring of 1946, Washington's position appeared to harden against Zimmer following the continued complaints from Angleton and others. After 'a review of this entire matter', it was concluded that 'Zimmer is not entitled to any such preferential treatment'. Indeed, this memo prohibited any further attempts to shield Zimmer without prior permission from the US War Department, Washington.[158]

In response to this rebuff, senior officials in SSU Germany continued the controversy, demanding to know: 'What steps have you taken to reverse AFHQ decision re Zimmer. Amzon anxious to aid Zimmer and family return basis sunrise and SCI services and instructions 110 [Dulles].'[159] OSS Germany received no support in this attempt. Hence, Dulles' personal secretary and close friend, Gero von Gaevernitz, supplied additional information in support

154 JXX 6113 [partly illegible], SCI/Z to AC SO2 CI, AFHQ, 11 February 1946, Dollmann Name File, *op cit.*

155 Amzo 2167, archives 33190, 22 February 1946; also summarised in 'File traces on Zimmer,' Zipper Desk, (nd), # 15 extract, both *ibid.*

156 Amzo 5107 archives 3328, 25 February 1946, *ibid.*

157 *Ibid.*

158 Memo to SSU AB . . . JRX 11 . . . [partly illegible], 10 April 1946 (declassified only in a sanitised form), *ibid.*

159 MASE 159957, 28 February 1946, *ibid.*

of Zimmer's case for continuing to receive 'preferential treatment', including American-financed health care in Switzerland for his two children.[160] He argued that Zimmer had given 'outstanding help' to Operation Sunrise, both as one of its 'principal originators' and in acting as a go-between with respect to the senior parties. Zimmer's assistance, which included numerous clandestine visits to Switzerland, was provided notwithstanding 'great personal risk', in that it occurred 'right under the nose of the Gestapo'. Gaevernitz further claimed that Colonel Waibel of Swiss intelligence, who had been a fellow participant in the Sunrise operation, not only endorsed this request but would also facilitate the necessary travel arrangements of Zimmer's family on the Swiss side of the border.[161]

During the late summer and autumn of 1945, the problem faced by lower-level officials seeking to counteract the immunities and preferential treatment US intelligence afforded to Zimmer and Parilli was that OSS Washington was seeking to capitalise on the organisation's wartime successes as a way of staving off threatened closure. Advancing favourable media publicity concerning the role of OSS officials in Operation Sunrise played a significant role in this propaganda. In this context, any indication that Dulles had been largely duped by Zimmer, Parilli, Dollmann, Rauff and Wolff, or that these Axis participants in this operation should now be reclassified as defendants in war crimes trials, would have been far from welcome. It would have been particularly embarrassing if this alternative interpretation proved, in fact, to be closer to the mark than the account provided by the official OSS propaganda which was then being serialised in American popular magazines, such as the *Saturday Evening Post*.[162]

Remarkably, Angleton attacked the OSS inspired media portrayal of the roles Zimmer and Parilli played in Operation Sunrise as an 'unfortunate exaggeration'.[163] Presumably, this official considered that such exaggeration was 'unfortunate', largely because it was still impeding his colleagues' efforts to mount an honest and open investigation into Zimmer's wartime record (with possible legal ramifications), and to assess any post-war potential he possessed as an intelligence asset.

In addition, Angleton's memorandum sought actively to undermine the rationale being used to grant immunities to Zimmer and Parilli. It supplied Washington with documentation from Zimmer's notebooks selected to contradict Dulles' interpretation of Zimmer's status as an Allied double-agent by suggesting that his: '[E]ffective contribution to Italian resistance activities was negligible and insofar as they existed at all were predicted upon the fact

160 Edward Green, Deputy Chief SSU Germany, to SSU operations att'n Mr Gilpatric, 'Zimmer Children', 12 April 1946, *ibid.*

161 *Ibid.* 162 On 22 and 29 September 1945.

163 See 'Guido Zimmer, re: Your X-3377': OSS BBS to OSS Washington, 28 November 1945, JZX-5519, Zimmer Name File, *op cit.*

that as an Abt VI officer he looked at things in a slightly more subtle way that Abt IV.'[164] In other words, Zimmer's contact with the partisans cannot be considered to reflect his personal and heroic attachment to the anti-fascist or Allied cause, which now merited a positive reward. Instead, such contacts merely formed part of the political brief of an SS intelligence officer which distinguished this role from the overtly repressive and secret police techniques of, for example, the Gestapo.

Angleton also noted that the ability of Zimmer and Parilli to cite examples in which they 'aided' anti-fascist partisans and Allied intelligence (the use of the sceptical quotation marks is contained in the original documentation) was, in reality, misleading. Indeed, he claimed that these examples were more than counter-balanced by their more questionable actions which, for obvious reasons, they now preferred to conceal. These actions included their joint failure is intervene to assist captured OSS agents, including Professor Ziccardi Zucca, 'head of the important OSS Zucca mission', when the latter was 'picked up by Abt IV [Gestapo] in Milan in the fall of [August] 1944'. One of Zimmer's colleagues, Count Thun, enjoyed considerable success in counter-intelligence work against Allied intelligence service operations mounted from Switzerland, particularly through the interception and decoding of communications. This lead to '25 arrests from mid-December 1944 through Feb. 1945'.[165] Indeed, Angleton's memo emphasises the fact that, when arrested by SS officials, Zucca held a photograph of Zimmer supplied by Parilli. It appears that Zucca's OSS successor, Ricciulli O Mare, had been cooperating with Parilli, even to the point of securing false Italian identity cards for Zimmer.[166]

By underlining this point (literally in fact), Angleton and other US intelligence officials in Italy presumably meant to convey a negative impression of Zimmer to Washington, including the view that, in their opinion as highly successful, professional counter-espionage officials, he remained an incompetent intelligence agent.[167] This implied that he was recognised as undeserving of recruitment (as indicated by a variety of other sources). Angleton forwarded on a local assessment which noted that 'possibly conditioned by this episode [the blunder in Rome] considered subject as an incompetent intelligence officer. In our opinion, the episode is not without interest in appraising subject's capabilities.'[168] Alternatively, these officials

164 *Ibid.*

165 'Rauff, Walther', German CI activity in Milan, February 1945, Zimmer Name File, *op cit.*

166 'The Zimmer Notebooks,' BBS to JJS, JRX-3746, 28 June 1946, # 418, citing p. 77/ref. 79, n. 4; and ref. 137, *ibid.*

167 BBS made reference to Zimmer's blunder in Rome and emphasised that 'it was only due to the intervention of an influential uncle of his that he was not sacked completely'. Agent BBS to Saint Amzon, 'Zimmer Guido', November 1945 [partly illegible], *ibid.*

168 *Ibid.*

could have been trying to suggest that, via Parilli, Zimmer was personally responsible for betraying the OSS Zucca Mission and their subsequent mistreatment at the hands of Abt. IV. The implication of this alternative interpretation was that he should, perhaps, be deprived of special protection and face prosecution as a war criminal.[169]

By contrast, the Zimmer Name File contains documentation summarising the contents of secret cables recording that OSS officials in Rome were 'eager to get full [interrogation] of subject'. Yet, at least initially, OSS Washington were willing to override critics of the preferential treatment Zimmer was being afforded. They were more interested in securing for themselves (and thereby Dulles' OSS intelligence operations in Germany) 'the benefit [of] your info' on Zimmer that OSS Rome possessed than in making him immediately available for interrogation by their colleagues based in Rome.[170]

The same OSS-Germany file on Zimmer suggests that, by mid-October 1945, the controversy had intensified, with OSS officials based in Rome claiming that 'Sub[ject] receiving better treatment than any Abt VI official in Italy', whilst recording, presumably by way of explanation, that '4 sets [of] Zimmer's shorthand correspondence [are] in processing'.[171] It was argued that he should not receive any better treatment than General Wolff: 'who was placed at the disposition of CSDIC and thoroughly exploited'.[172]

Other recently declassified documentation reveals, in very frank terms, the further development of what was fast becoming a heated controversy. Consider, for instance, the following complaint contained in Angleton's internal OSS report:

> Zimmer had become the CI [counter-intelligence] 'ghost' of this theatre, just escaping our Unit's net in Milan and having equal success in Rome. He is evidently receiving protection from some high AFHQ [Allied Forward Military HQ] quarter on the basis of his contribution to the Sunrise operation. SCI/Z Milan has been considerably exercised by the sloppiness with which the case has been handled and the apparent 'clamming up' which takes place when straight questions are asked. We . . . see no particular reason why Zimmer should be treated any differently from General Wolff, who as you know was placed at the disposition of CSDIC [an Allied intelligence body that used covert methods of recording supposedly private conversations of senior Nazi figures] here

169 For evidence in favour of the second interpretation, see 'The Zimmer Notebooks', BBS to JJS, JRX-3746, 28 June 1946, ref 79, n. 4, *ibid.*

170 IX 26476, 16 October 1945; OSS Germany, 'Guido Zimmer', LWX-002-820 (X-3208), 20 September 1945, summarising a cable sent by OSS Washington, *ibid.*

171 *Ibid.*

172 See undated summary of JZX-5519, 23 November 1945, which reiterates the points quoted immediately below; see also JXX-4039, 11 September 1945, *ibid.*

> and thoroughly exploited before being moved to Nuremberg for the War Crimes trials. Zimmer . . . should be given at least a complete tactical interrogation on Abt VI activities in the Milan area, details of which, from all available evidence, he knows thoroughly. . . . [The] OSS liaison officer to AFHQ, is being asked to clarify the whole affair at Caserta.[173]

Given Angleton's success at detecting over 1,000 other fascist agents and networks of sub-agents across Italy, it was not understandable that the network at one of the most strategically important parts of Italy, the industrialised region around Milan, would remain protected.[174] Other parts of this document that indicate cross-referencing to other individuals and documents (perhaps internal OSS/CIA files on Dulles and/or Wolff?) were 'blanked out' from the 'sanitised' version of this declassified document.

The Zimmer controversy rumbled on sporadically during the spring of 1946. Former OSS staff linked administratively to Operation Sunrise, including F. J. Shelden, wrote supportive memos to the American military authorities. These reiterated Dulles' interpretation of Zimmer's heroism and indispensable role, and his close work with 'Wally', that is, the OSS agent and radio operator whom, in the service of US intelligence, Zimmer smuggled into German-occupied Milan at considerable personal risk. Shelden emphasised those aspects of Dulles' official report on Operation Sunrise that clearly supported the pro-Zimmer position. He maintained that, although no express promises of immunity had ever been sought or offered during the course of the negotiations:

> [F]rom various conversations on the Sunrise Operation I seem to remember that it was repeatedly mentioned that Zimmer should be given every possible consideration by the Allied authorities for the part he played in the surrender negotiations . . . personally I could not see any objection to grant him small favors.[175]

OSS/SSU Berne continued to pressurise American military authorities on Zimmer's behalf, emphasising the importance of respecting Dulles' opinion that the Allies owed Zimmer a 'moral obligation'. These notes confirmed that Zimmer had, so far, evaded continuing attempts by US counter-intelligence officials in Italy who, even after a year following the surrender, still 'very much desire to interrogate him'.[176] Indeed, US intelligence's belated interrogation

173 JZX-4039, BBS to Saint DNI, 'Guido Zimmer, CO Abt VI, ANO Milan', 11 September 1945, *ibid.*

174 Mangold, 1991, *op cit*, 21–22.

175 Zimmer, Stelden to Mr Horton, 3 April 1946, Zimmer Name File, *op cit.*

176 Cable Berne 388 to, presumably, SSU Washington, 9 April 1946, archive in 35548, *ibid.*

of Parilli in May 1946 included a wide range of questions seeking 'full details on subject's relationship with Zimmer'. These included the latter's activity in securing false identity papers for various Italians on both sides of the wartime conflict, his contacts with various Italian agents and double-agents and role in proposing 'peace negotiations'.[177] During this interrogation, Parilli made a number of claims that contradicted Dulles' version of events. Not least of these was his admission of various close collaborations with the Nazis, his state of being 'bound hand and foot' stemming from Zimmer's coercion and threats.[178] During the relevant period, Parilli was both subject to Gestapo surveillance and related threats of search and arrest, and deployed by Zimmer as a penetration agent directed against Dulles' Berne operation, a contradictory state of affairs recognised by Zimmer himself.[179]

One difficulty for those who accept Dulles' story is that these rebuttal statements were accepted by US intelligence as, at least partly, substantiated by relevant parts of Zimmer's own notebooks.[180] These and other intelligence sources confirmed that Parilli was:

> One of Abt. VI's prominent double-agents bound hand and foot to Abt. VI and the plans which Zimmer and his superiors dictate. In connection with [the] surrender negotiations Zimmer built up Baron Parilli from his first social contacts following P's qualms about having aided the partisans under duress in August 1944.[181]

In other words, far from acting as a neutral intermediary between Dulles and Wolff, Parilli had been acting as one of Zimmer and Rauff's double-agents, and this mission was expressly approved by SS-General Harster. Zimmer had possibly used Parilli both to entrap a Lt. Cramer,[182] who was serving with Allied intelligence as a radio operator,[183] and to exercise discretion, possibly extortion, with respect to the capture and release of various wealthy Italians vulnerable to the potentially deadly attentions of the SS.[184] It appears that, far

177 'Baron Luigi Parilli, Questionnaire on subject's D/A career', 7 May 1946, JZX 8024, *ibid.*

178 'Rauff, Walther', German CI activity in Milan, February 1945, and the 'Zimmer Notebooks', June 1945 [partly illegible], *ibid.*

179 Zimmer complained it was 'not proper that three different sections should each handle the same case in its own way', not least because he 'is planning to send the Baron to Switzerland on an important political mission'. Zimmer Notebooks, *op cit*, 75/ref. 77, para. 262 and 'Rauff, Walther', June 1945 [partly illegible]: *ibid.*

180 'Zimmer Notebooks,' BBS to JJS, JRX-3746, 28 June 1946, *ibid.*

181 'Rauff, Walther', the 'Zimmer Notebooks', JRX-June 1945 [partly illegible], *ibid.*

182 Zimmer Notebooks, ref. 31/p.36, Zimmer to Parilli; 'Zimmer Notebooks,' BBS to JJS, JRX-3746, 28 June 1946: both *ibid.*

183 'Zimmer Notebooks,' refs. 12, 31 (Feb–Mar 1945): BBS to JJS, JRX-3746, 28 June 1946, *ibid.*

184 JRX 3423, 5 June 1946, *ibid.*

from being an OSS mission, Operation Sunrise had in fact been planned by Zimmer and his superiors in Abt. 6. At: 'a Abt.6 conference in Verona in November 1944 . . . Zimmer suggested that a certain Baron Parilli should be sent to Switzerland to open contact with Allied circles. This plan was given the code-name "Operation Wool".'[185] The intelligence officer editing Zimmer's notebooks noted:

> This Zimmer letter [to Parilli] should constitute another interesting obstacle for Baron Parilli to hurdle in the course of his repeated [claims] . . . that he was an utterly pro-Allied individual in German-occupied Italy.[186]

A related point is that Frau Hildegard Beetz, one of the SS employees involved in Dulles' recovery of the Ciano Diaries,[187] later used as prosecution evidence at Nuremberg trials,[188] was also previously employed by Zimmer as a translator during the summer and autumn of 1941. She was later recruited by the OSS following vetting which disclosed her link with Zimmer.[189]

OSS officials noted that, as well as working for OSS Germany, Zimmer was, by the mid-summer of 1945, also 'secretary to Parilli and a paid agent of ODEUM [the Vatican's Sovereign Order of Malta]':[190]

> on his first visit to Germany after the end of the war Parilli re-established contact with Zimmer, made him his private secretary for matters pertaining to the Sovereign Order of Malta and placed considerable sums of money at his disposal.[191]

Other reports confirmed that 'Parilli is now active [in the] Order of Malta, Zimmer is his secretary.'[192] In short, OSS/SSU officials based in Italy made a series of statements challenging the basis on which Zimmer and his agent

185 XX 8568, 14 August 1945, Interrogation Report of Dr Klaus Hügel. See also CSDIC/CMF/SD25, 21 June 1945, both *ibid.*

186 Zimmer Notebooks, *op cit*, n. 8, p. 37/ref. 31.

187 See Salter and Charlesworth, 'The Ciano Diaries at the Nuremberg Trial', *Journal International Criminal Justice*, 2006 4(1), 103–27. For details of how Dulles secured this evidence through a process of negotiation, espionage and pressure, see Charlesworth and Salter, 'Ensuring The After-Life Of The Ciano Diaries: Allen Dulles' Provision Of Nuremberg Trial Evidence', *Intelligence and National Security*, 2006 in press.

188 *Ibid*, 110/n. 3 noting that her: 'major assignment during this period was the recovery and translation of the Ciano documents'.

189 'Interrogation report Frau Hildegard Beetz', 9 July 1945, LWX 002-7096; Vetting of Hildegarde Beetz, 30 August 1945, both Zimmer Name File, *op cit*.

190 'Rauff, Walther', JRX-1005, 5 June 1945, *ibid.*

191 'Guido Zimmer', Chief Foreign Division M to Chief of Station, Karlsruhe, 28 March 1951, *ibid.*

192 'Zipper Desk', (nd), NWC-00-1197, *ibid.*

Parilli were continuing to receive privileged treatment, arguing that, far from meriting a reward for cooperating with Dulles' plans for capitulation, both men had in effect penetrated OSS security and played the Americans in pursuit of their own preconceived political intelligence agenda codenamed Operation Wool.

Regarding Zimmer's movements, it appears that:

> In February 1946 he was returned to Italy with the idea of exploiting him further there; Allied Forces Headquarters was uncooperative, and contact with him has dropped. He has not been used since.[193]

However, Zimmer's activities from the second half of 1946 continued to attract the interest of SSU officials in Italy and Switzerland. This included his possible links with illegal groups of SS veterans and the MI6/GIS double-agent George Sessler, who had identified Zimmer as a Abt.VI colleague to whom he had transferred 'line-crossing' agents.[194] Sessler had given evidence in the war crimes case regarding captured and executed OSS personnel of Operation Ginny, which led to the conviction and execution of General Anton Dostler.

OSS/SSU officials mined Zimmer's notebooks for operational purposes, particularly the identification of potential agents including chains of 'stay behind' agents, potentially hostile to Allied interests, and technical espionage material, such as plans for improved radio transmitters.[195] This included having another, and presumably former SS official, codenamed Daybit, read over these notebooks, and to offer both comments and supplementation of specific details regarding operational matters.[196]

In July 1946, the US State Department took an interest in both Parilli and his contacts with Zimmer.[197] The latter gave American intelligence officials a detailed voluntary statement, including additional information concerning Parilli and a number of other agents and sub-agents, which were deemed to be of interest to Milan and Genoa fields stations 'for follow up'.[198] Through Parilli, Zimmer was also in contact with the Gehlen Organisation, codenamed 'Zipper', in pursuit of a closer liaison with the Order of Malta, and had to apply for a travel pass:[199]

193 'Guido Zimmer', 9 January 1951, *ibid.*

194 'Interrogation Report on Sessler, George' (with reference to agent Miscati), *ibid.*

195 Cable 271, 17 December 1946, *ibid*, noting: 'Zimmer has all details of inventions and how handled German side. Is available for detailed interrogation at Amzon.' Clearly, as of December 1946, US intelligence officials still regarded him as both available and cooperative.

196 'Daybit comments on the Zimmer Notebooks', *ibid.*

197 Extract, Zimmer Name File, *op cit*, 31 July 1946 (no other identification given).

198 'Statement by Guido Zimmer', JRX 4384, 26 August 1946, *ibid.*

199 On 17 January 1949, see 'Application for temporary travel document . . .', *ibid.*

> In January 1949 when negotiations were under way for a working agreement between Zipper and the Sovereign Order of Malta Parilli received from Zipper a temporary travel document for Zimmer which was to be used in connection with the planned working arrangement; it developed, however, that this agreement never materialised. Zimmer's limited relationship with Zipper ended when the latter terminated its contact with Parilli.[200]

From this time onwards, US intelligence received only occasional reports of Zimmer's later activities, including his attendance at a reunion in June 1949 of Sunrise participants from the German, Swiss and possibly American sides of the 'intelligence community'.[201] There are indications at least that Zimmer maintained occasional contacts with the Gehlen Organisation in March 1951, but no details have yet been released.[202]

For present purposes, it is noteworthy that later intelligence reports are far less flattering as to Zimmer's character and political orientation than those stemming from Dulles and his subordinates which emphasised his supposedly anti-Nazi credentials. For example, one report from spring 1950 noted that:

> Parilli is frequently seen in connection with former SS groups. Zimmer . . . is probably acting as liaison to the above-mentioned circles. However, he personally is unimportant and not of sufficient stature to take the initiative and thus become dangerous.[203]

Another report from this period contains a fitting epitaph for present purposes: 'Zimmer was believed to be involved constantly in double dealings.'[204]

In short, it was widely recognised by both sides of the internal debate amongst US intelligence officials that Zimmer had been provided with special treatment, including protection from arrest, as a direct result of his role within Operation Sunrise. German-based American intelligence officials sought to continue his protection, whereas their colleagues located in Italy opposed this special treatment most forcefully, and, by the spring of 1948, were ultimately successful in preventing its continuation through their repeated interventions to OSS/SSU Washington and the War Department.

200 'Guido Zimmer', Chief Foreign Division M to Chief of Station, Karlsruhe, 28 March 1951, *ibid.*

201 One name is blanked out in the relevant sanitised document, but – given the potential for political embarrassment – it may have been that of Dulles, or less likely, Gaevernitz. See Cable 35287, 23 June 1949: Dollmann Name Files, *op cit.*

202 'Zimmer, Lt', (nd), *ibid*, Vol. 3.

203 'Activity of Military Circles in Western Germany', 4 April 1950, *ibid.*

204 'Guido Zimmer', Chief Foreign Division M to Chief of Station, Karlsruhe, 28 March 1951, *ibid.*

From that time onwards, Zimmer was reclassified as a former enemy intelligence official who had retained contact with more senior Nazis, and who merited *ad hoc* surveillance as a potential security threat.

Questions of legal immunity in the light of Dollmann's CIA Name File

At this point, it is useful to compare the generally preferential treatment of Zimmer from 1945 onwards, with the haphazard manner in which US intelligence officials handled Eugen Dollmann, Zimmer's colleague and co-participant with the Sunrise affair. When compared with Rauff, Wolff and Zimmer, Dollmann's wartime record as a quasi-diplomatic emissary, liaison officer and high-level translator meant that he was perhaps the *least likely* of the Wolff group involved in Operation Sunrise to be found guilty of personal involvement in war crimes. It is reasonable to assume that any offers of legal immunity, or other privileged treatment, US intelligence and Allied authorities made to Dollmann as a reward for his contributions to Operation Sunrise would have applied equally to Zimmer, whose contribution was of no less importance.

As already discussed it is clear, however, that Dollmann received *far less* favourable treatment from the Allied authorities than Zimmer. Dollmann and Wenner surrendered to British forces in Bolzano, Wolff's base, on 13 May 1945. Over the next 18 months, Dollmann was then detained, often under grim physical and psychological conditions, and apparently lived in fear of violence from a variety of different groups, including former Nazis who believed he had betrayed their cause. Ironically, it was *precisely because* US intelligence officials afforded him inferior treatment that discussion was generated within various internal memorandum of whether they had been defaulting on alleged earlier promises of privileged treatment. In other words, the question of granting full, or partial, legal immunities for the Nazi participants in Operation Sunrise came more sharply in focus with respect to Dollmann because of his comparatively inferior treatment.

Unlike Zimmer, who witnessed the end of the war from the comparative safety of Switzerland, Dollmann and Wenner (Wolff's senior adjutant, military adviser and Sunrise participant) were subjected to arrest, detention and interrogation at various Allied internment camps. Both men were initially detained in a POW cage in Modena until 7 October 1945, when they were re-assigned to a low security British compound at Ancona where Dollmann allegedly received 'rough treatment'.[205] Following some unspecified measure of 'intrigue' by external parties, Dollmann and Wenner eventually 'escaped' from Allied detention on 20 December 1946. There are indications that, in

205 Memo, 20 November 1945, Dollmann Name File, *op cit.*

conjunction with members of SIM (Italian military intelligence), US intelligence officials pre-arranged and assisted this escape from the low security camp.[206] Certainly, SIM officials, who were largely controlled by Allied intelligence,[207] issued both men with false identity papers, with Dollmann assuming the identity of 'Cassani'.[208] Dollmann was protected in an Italian lunatic asylum, and then, following his attempted blackmail by SIM and Schuster (discussed later), he was rescued or, more precisely, 'kidnapped' by SSU officials in August 1946. As already discussed, he was detained under a qualified form of house arrest in Rome awaiting arrangements for protection in a monastery, but was arrested by Italian police in early November and rescued again by SSU officials, who then had him locked away in a US military jail.[209] During this later period of detention under grim conditions his health deteriorated, which resulted in Dollmann having not only problems with his kidneys but also a severe ear infection.[210]

The immunity issue arose in a particularly dramatic way regarding Dollmann because, rightly or wrongly, he was identified as one of the senior SS officers based in Rome who were involved in the decision to order the execution of Italian civilians at the Ardeatine Caves. Dollmann, together with Kappler, Priebke and Shuttz, was being sought, partly on political grounds, by Italian war crimes prosecutors for his alleged involvement in this reprisal massacre. Eventually, on 14 January 1947 and as part of the preparations for German Generalfeldmarschall Kesselring's trial, the Italian authorities issued arrest warrants for these four men.[211]

Angleton, who opposed giving Zimmer protection, was more sympathetic to Dollmann, possibly because of his potential for use in active or passive (damage limitation) anti-communist missions which became an urgent priority for him even as the war was ending.[212] On 13 November 1946, he wrote to G-2 HQ explaining the reasons why he and his colleagues had to date deemed it important to protect Dollmann, in which he justified his actions as dictation by 'military honor': 'Military honor dictated that we should honor the promises made to these men'. Dollmann and Wenner had acted in a way that had given US military real benefits that had assisted with America's vital

206 The phrase 'escape' is placed in quotation marks by the author of *Race for Rome*, who interviewed Dollmann; whilst intelligence sources have alluded to 'the intrigue' surrounding Wenner and Dollmann's escape: 'Eugen Dollmann and Eugen Wenner', 7 November 1947, Dollmann Name File, *op cit*.

207 Naftali, 1992, *op cit*, 224.

208 Angleton to Chief of Station Heidelberg, 'Dollmann and Wenner', July 1947, Dollmann Name File, *op cit*.

209 Telex, 20 November 1946, *ibid*.

210 Leghorn to Secretary of State, 15 May 1947: NA, RG 59, Box 3622, *ibid*.

211 Angleton to G-2, 13 November 1946: NA, RG 319, IRR Entry 134B, Box 40, 'Eugen Dollmann'.

212 Mangold, 1991, *op cit*, 22, 26–27.

national security interests in restricting post-war Soviet territorial gains. Sunrise had nipped various threats in the bud, including 'a redoubt in Austria, which may have resulted in a Tito or Russian occupation of parts of the Venezia Giulia as well as much of the present Allied zones in Austria'.[213]

In attempting to assist Dollmann, US intelligence officials had to shield him not only from the Italian legal authorities but also those of the British, who, as the occupying power, were planning to hold war crimes trials for senior SS and German army officials. Once it became known that the Americans held Dollmann, there was considerable pressure not to be publicly seen as subverting such British trials. It was because of pressure from military headquarters in Italy (AFHQ) that OSS officials had to delay 'shipping out' Dollmann from Italy to the American-controlled zone of Germany, at least until the end of the Fosse Ardeatine massacre trial, which remained 'a vital issue in the case'.[214] Fortunately for both Dollmann and SSU intelligence officials shielding him, on 18 November 1946 the prosecution testimony of SS-Obersturmbannführer Herbert Kappler, who had directly organised the killings, established Dollmann's lack of direct or even indirect involvement in these reprisal killings.[215] This was credible evidence, as Kappler was certainly no friend or admirer of Dollmann, and the two men had repeatedly clashed.[216]

In addition, it was clear to British authorities that, in the words of one British Foreign Office cable to Rome, Dollmann was 'under some form of Allied protection thanks to services rendered in the past. [His] case is said to be sensational news in [the] Italian Press. We should be grateful for a report with your comments . . .'[217] The report that was returned from Rome, re-affirmed the clear impression that Dollmann was, in practice, being shielded under the umbrella of unofficial legal immunity:

> Dollmann . . . was interned in Ascona until he escaped on December 20th 1945. He was subsequently sheltered by Italian of the Right Wing in a lunatic asylum near Milan until August 1946, when he again escaped . . . effected with the help of the OSS who were under the impression that Dollmann had been promised some immunity for the part he allegedly played in the surrender negotiations . . . He is now held in United States

213 Angleton to G-2, 13 November 1946: NA, RG 319, IRR Entry 134B, Box 40, 'Eugen Dollmann' (containing a copy of the arrest warrant naming Dollmann).

214 Leghorn to Secretary of State, 15 May 1947: NA, RG 59, Box 3622, 9, Dollmann Name File, *op cit.*

215 Anon. [sanitised] to Special Operations, 20 November 1946, # 11, *ibid.*

216 Angleton to Chief of Station Heidelberg, July 1947, 'Dollmann and Wenner', Dollmann Name File, *op cit*. Also cited in Chase to Taylor, 20 November 1947: IFZ, Munich, Polad/33/18.

217 Foreign Office to Rome, 21 November, 1946: PRO: FO 371/57557, AIR 2/28897. (Also citing in handwriting U.7946/126/73 OWL file.)

> custody in Rome area whilst arrangements are being made for his transfer back to Ancona [sic]. Meanwhile he is available as a witness at Adeatine [sic] Murders Trial should the court decide to call him and the Court has been so informed.[218]

This report wrongly stated that Dollmann had not, in fact, played a role in Operation Sunrise, and thus 'was given no promise of special immunity by anyone having authority to do so'. It noted that AFHQ had 'put out a press statement to this effect'.[219] It appears that media reporting was a notable feature of this case with the British complaining that Dollmann's name 'has had quite a lot of publicity already in *Colliers* Magazine and other transatlantic periodicals are wont to regale the public with their personal reminiscences'. The report concluded on a downbeat note: 'If the Ardeatine Trials do not lead to conviction and if Dollmann is not called I fear we may hear more of this story for Left Wing press claim that he is a most important witness.'[220] The reply from London indicated a need to place the best possible spin on the situation by releasing a press statement that the 'court was informed that Dollmann was available as a witness'.[221]

The British authorities seriously considered prosecuting Dollmann on war crimes charges once the main trials of German officials who organised the Ardeatine Caves massacre were completed. One British official noted that the death penalty in the main trial had satisfied popular sentiment but that it was now being asked: 'Why Dollmann was not present? And I suggested that AFHQ should announce whether he is to be tried.'[222] Gardner, of the Italian Section of the British Foreign Office, noted: 'Now that we have dealt with the two big shots – General von Mackensen and General Mältzer – I think we might consider allowing the Italians to deal with Dollmann and others concerned in the massacre.' His main concern was not that there was insufficient evidence to convict Dollmann but rather that the Italian authorities might not be trusted to conduct a trial in an appropriately 'dignified and proper way'.[223] This statement was a response to earlier exchanges with British officials based in Rome who had strongly supported the suggestion to 'announce very soon whether Dollmann is to be tried (e.g., with . . . Kappler) the S.S. man who carried out the Ardeatine Massacre if so by whom and when.

218 Office of the Political Adviser to Supreme Allied Commander, Mediterranean to Foreign Office (London), 26 November 1946, U. 8096, *ibid.* (Also citing in handwriting U.7946/126/73 OWL file.)

219 *Ibid.* 220 *Ibid.*

221 Foreign Office (London) to Office of the Political Adviser to Supreme Allied Commander, Mediterranean, No. 1206, 2 December 1946, U 9096/126/75: PRO, AIR 2/8897.

222 Telegram from Ward (Rome) to Gardner, Foreign Office (London), No. 1789 summarised in U 8145, 6 December 1946: PRO, AIR 2/8897.

223 *Ibid.*

Italians rightly or wrongly consider Dollmann to be a very big criminal and they will certainly not forget about him.'[224]

Later in December 1946, British officials in Rome emphasised that they thought it inadvisable to hold any more British-led trials of those, such as Kappler, responsible for the Ardeatine massacres as anything other than a death sentence could promote anti-British riots. It was noted, however, that whatever option was decided upon: 'the question of Dollmann . . . will come up. I understand that he is regarded as still being an American responsibility at present and that sympathy is still felt for him in certain American quarters.'[225] The conclusion was to consult with the Americans before making any commitments to the Italians re Kappler and Dollmann.

Dollmann ultimately benefited from the changed British policy over future war crimes trials in Italy in favour of allowing the Italian authorities to deal with middle-ranking offenders. He was also fortunate that he was being physically detained in American custody, which – after internal debate – led to him being reclassified from a war crimes suspect to 'an accepted American rather than an Allied responsibility'. A cable from British diplomats in Rome to London reported that American pressure for his continued protection remained an important, if not necessarily decisive, factor:

> After prolonged debate within the H.Q. of the MTOUSA [senior U.S. military command for the Mediterranean region], General Lee has today telegraphed to the United States War Department announcing the following intention. Since neither the British courts which conducted the Ardeatine massacre trial nor the Italian government have asked for Dollmann it is proposed to repatriate him to the United States zone in Germany through United States channels with arrangements for his return should he be required. The Italian government is being notified of the action taken and informed that 'should he be required he can be made available.' The United States authorities are unwilling to make any more positive offer to the Italian Government. Neither the British nor the United States authorities, after careful investigation, can find sufficient evidence of Dollmann's complicity in the Ardeatine massacres on which it would be possible to base a prima facie case against him and the Americans wish to avoid putting the matter to the Italian Government in such a way that would pre-judge Dollmann's guilt . . .[226]

This quotation refers to 'prolonged debate'. As with the Zimmer case, already

224 Rome (Ward) to Foreign Office, 4 December 1946: PRO, FO 371/57557 (handwritten reference to U 8096/126/D).

225 Sir N. Charles, Rome to Foreign Office, No. 1890: PRO, FO 371/57557.

226 Bendall (Caserta) to Foreign Office (London), No. 776, 28 December 1946, *ibid.*

discussed, attempts to give Dollmann favoured treatment, including protection from war crimes and de-Nazification prosecution, now need to be discussed in detail, as does evidence that these met with a degree of resistance that would surprise many critics of the actions of intelligence officials in this area.

Intervening to ensure protection

This section will retrace the different ways in which US intelligence officials intervened in different circumstances to shield Dollmann from the Italian, British and German authorities, who, in the immediate post-war years at least, were considering prosecuting him for alleged war crimes. A former head of one sub-branch of US intelligence (probably Dulles), asked Angleton 'whether we were interested in running Dollmann [as an agent or informant] whom he could contact'.[227] Angleton's response was not enthusiastic because he feared Dollmann was already too closely associated with British intelligence and he could become: 'particularly dangerous if [the] Communists took them over'.[228] On the other hand, Angleton was aware that certain of his colleagues felt under an obligation to protect Dollmann in return for his role in Sunrise. He reported that Parilli had made a 'statement that, on behalf of sunrise both he and [Max] Husmann made definite commitments to rehabilitate them. This substantiated by Parilli spending 150,000 lire of [his] own money to make up for harm done.'[229] Certainly, Dollmann was provided with a 'safe house', false papers and offered employment as an intelligence agent by OSS's James Angleton, which he initially rejected.[230]

It is useful at this point to cite parts of Dollmann's memoirs, which have been corroborated by other sources, that discuss promises of immunity. Dollmann confirms that Dulles and his agents had promised Dollmann, Wolff and others involved in Sunrise a 'share in the rebuilding of Europe'.[231] He confirms that, at an initial meeting with Husmann and Dulles' official, Paul Blum, in March 1945, he was made specific, if unofficial, promises. He was told that, although the surrender had to appear unconditional, 'concessions in the sense of honourable terms' were still possible.[232] Blum reiterated this stating that:

> officially and formally the capitulation would have to be unconditional, but that did not exclude the possibility of honourable special terms and personal facilities arrived at by a gentleman's agreement. [He] even found a hopeful word or two for the German parties in the capitulation negotiations and their future prospects.[233]

227 *Ibid.* 228 *Ibid.* 229 *Ibid.* 230 *Ibid.* 231 *Ibid*, 172.
232 *Ibid*, 178. 233 *Ibid.*

Dollmann further claims that Blum stated that the Allies could make good use of all men of good will in the rebuilding of Europe; and that those who brought the war to an early end would be treated as such. He also notes that verbal promises were made by Husmann directly to Wolff, suggesting 'more generous and elastic arrangements whose fulfilment could be guaranteed by Swiss and Italian personalities: Husmann and Parilli, and a prominent Swiss [Intelligence official Max Waibel]'.[234] Husmann had even suggested that Wolff could be appointed Minister of German education in a post-war government.[235] Dulles also asked for their cooperation in staffing a future Allied controlled government of Germany.[236] Dollmann noted sarcastically that in his case, and perhaps even in that of Wolff's, these promises of rehabilitation and implied immunity from any war crimes and de-Nazification hearings had been dishonoured: 'No mean prophetic gift would have been necessary to divine behind these fine words . . . the treatment that actually awaited us.'[237]

During 1946, Dollmann became embroiled in a complicated right-wing and Vatican plot to destabilise the immediate post-war Anglo-American occupation of Italy, not least by whipping up nationalistic sentiment. Wolff notes that:

> This was probably an attempt to prop up Pius XII's justification for remaining neutral, purportedly because he was on the verge of securing designation of Rome as an open city. That way he could avoid the calamity of an 'atheistic Communist' takeover of Rome, his very own bishopric.[238]

Cardinal Schuster was heavily involved in this plot, and sought to minimise the significance of OSS's Operation Sunrise by personally claiming much of the credit for saving Northern Italy from Hitler's scorched-earth policies.[239] Dollmann and Wenner, who were detained in an Italian insane asylum in Milan under church 'protection', were blackmailed into signing false affidavits. These supposedly 'confirmed' Schuster's contentious re-interpretation of the capitulation of Wolff's forces.[240] They signed these affidavits in return for Bishop Schuster's promises of protecting them within an Italian Jesuit convent from Italian war crimes investigators.[241]

Once they became aware of this plot in August 1946, SSU counter-intelligence officials in Italy intervened to rescue them. Angleton stated that

234 *Ibid*, 187–88, 194, re Waibel as neutral guarantor of verbal promises. 235 *Ibid*, 190.
236 *Ibid*, 191. 237 *Ibid*, 179. 238 Wolfe, *op cit*, 335/n. 41.
239 Anon [sanitised] to Special Operations, 20 November 1946; Angleton to Chief of Station Heidelberg, 'Dollmann and Wenner', July 1947, Dollmann Name File, *op cit*.
240 Angleton to Chief of Station Heidelberg, 'Dollmann and Wenner', July 1947, *ibid*.
241 *Ibid*.

he arranged for Dollmann and Wenner to be 'kidnapped'.[242] This action was designed partly to prevent these former Nazi officials from becoming vulnerable to further blackmail and even forced defection to the communists, a prospect which, for geo-political reasons already discussed, horrified the American authorities:[243]

> [B]oth were taken in hand by us and brought to Rome . . . Plan was to keep them quiet with proposal that US government publish white book [overt propaganda material] with full particulars [of] Operation Sunrise to offset Schuster's publication. This particularly necessary for historical developments in German armistice.[244]

At this stage, intelligence officials were concerned that the Vatican/SIM scandal involving Schuster already discussed 'could break'. In turn, this could upset the desired outcome of upcoming Italian general elections by providing unwelcome propaganda ammunition for the Italian Communist Party.[245] Another factor was that there was a perceived need to protect the OSS's own interpretation of Operation Sunrise as an intelligence triumph, supposedly a spectacular example of the value of covert intelligence operations. During 1946–47, this self-serving interpretation was under threat from both the political right, through Schuster's group, and the vocal communist left and associated newspapers. The last thing that US intelligence officials needed was to have Dollmann and Wenner endorse these alternative interpretations of what was behind the Sunrise process, or develop yet another account of what had happened to further contradict the OSS's story. Hence, by protecting Dollmann and Wenner by having them affirm in writing a supportive 'insider' interpretation of Sunrise, US intelligence officials were seeking to achieve two objectives at once.

This concern that Dollmann might publish memoirs that, for various reasons already discussed, could embarrass US intelligence officials (not least perhaps with respect to the anti-Soviet dimension of Sunrise and Baron Parilli's status as a Gestapo agent) was to remain a perennial threat. This is clear from later intelligence files from 1948 and 1949. Indeed, Dollmann's later attempts to sell extracts of his memoirs to *Colliers* magazine were frustrated by the intervention of British intelligence officials who simply removed the draft manuscripts from Dollmann's publishers before a copy could be made.[246] However, during the mid-summer of 1949, Dollmann eventually succeeded in publishing extracts from his memoirs in the Italian newspaper

242 Angleton to G-2, 13 November 1946: NA, RG 319, IRR Entry 134B, Box 40; 'Eugen Dollmann', (nd), Dollmann Name File, *op cit.*

243 Angleton to Chief of Station Heidelberg, 'Dollmann and Wenner', July 1947, *ibid.*

244 *Ibid.* 245 *Ibid.* 246 'Dr Eugen Dollmann', 23 December 1948, *ibid.*

Il Tempo, an event carefully monitored by US intelligence officials, who noted that their author had recently moved to Lugano in Switzerland.

Returning to our main narrative of developments concerning legal immunity taking place between 1946 and 1947, Dollmann, who was using the cover name of Cassani, was arrested by the Italian police, with news of his arrest creating a stir in the communist press. This prompted interventions by SSU officials. Notwithstanding media attacks from both left- and right-wing Italian sources, OSS officials mobilised their 'colleagues' within G2 (US military intelligence). They exploited the uncertainty of the Italian authorities over Dollmann's true identity to seize him.[247] In justifying their demands for his return to US custody, OSS officials claimed that, as an escaped prisoner of war and enemy intelligence agent, Dollmann fell outside the jurisdiction of the Italian national police and legal system. Instead, he remained the responsibility of Anglo-American occupation authorities.[248] US intelligence officials issued Dollmann with false Allied identity papers, again in the name of Cassani.[249]

The internal controversy concerning Dollmann's protection

As with Zimmer, a number of officials within US intelligence, diplomatic and military circles engaged in an internal debate concerning the justification, if any, for shielding Dollmann (and Wenner) from prosecution either before a full war crimes trial or a de-Nazification hearing. As Wolfe notes, the prosecution of Dollmann for war crimes, or even his court appearance as a witness, concentrated minds within Allied leadership circles: 'An inter-Allied debate ensued whether under such an invidious spotlight it was prudent to protect him in appreciation for his role in Operation Sunrise.'[250] During the final months of 1946, the participants in this debate included the US embassy in Rome, the US State Department (which involved personal interventions of the US Secretary of State), two American generals (Lemnitzer and Vandenberg) and AFHQ in Caserta. Only one part of the intelligence faction in this debate supported privileged treatment. By contrast, Italian-based OSS/SSU officials insisted that Dollmann's protection must be:

> [P]redicated on [the] result of [the] trial which should (and so far has) establish[ed] his innocence. . . . In view of impending Fosse Ardeatine trial which was a vital issue in case, telephoned to Hartman that original

247 *Ibid*, #7, #8. The next paragraph in the documentation within Dollmann's Name File, which presumably discusses further developments, is blanked out in the sanitised release.

248 *Ibid.*

249 Angleton to Chief of Station Heidelberg, 'Dollmann and Wenner', July 1947, *ibid.*

250 Wolfe, 1994, *op cit*, 328.

> request to [General] Lee that we trip [partly illegible] Dollmann out of the country is predicated on result of trial. Hartman replied that Lee had approved our memo (which justified our action on the basis that D and Wenner were Operation Sunrise obligations which must be liquidated whilst we still maintained the power to do so) and that we were to stand pat.[251]

Another remarkable document has been declassified, which is prefaced by the clichéd instruction that it must be 'immediately burned after you have read it and no reference should [ever] be made to it'. This provides additional details of the fraught internal debate taking place over Dollmann and Wenner during November 1946. Officials based in Caserta maintained that they: '[C]ould not assume responsibility for protecting a former SS-Standarterführer from being called to testify in the Ardeatine trial if [the] court asks.' The US State Department took a similar stance stating that: 'They did not feel that this government could go along with the protection of the two individuals [Dollmann and Wenner].'[252] However, this department did not object to a craftily worded statement to the effect that the controversy over Dollmann and Wenner, particularly the 'representations of the Italians' concerning Dollmann's alleged complicity in the Ardeatine massacre, amounted to an 'attempt to undermine the Allied position in Italy'.[253] In other words, intelligence officials relied on the standard tactic of asserting, without necessarily justifying, the importance of higher national security interests. They claimed that if the two former SS men who had cooperated with US intelligence were seen to receive 'unjust treatment', then this would undermine US national security interests. It would have severe 'repercussions' on 'the future long-range United States intelligence activities in Italy'. It was, therefore, in America's national security interests for AFHQ to 'show these individuals appropriate consideration in presenting these circumstances [of their involvement in Sunrise]'.[254]

The response to these claims concerning the justification of Dollmann's protection as a Sunrise obligation from senior military circles in AFHQ was decidedly formal and defensive. It emphasised that every aspect of the involvement of Generals Airey and Lemnitzer in the latter stages of Sunrise had strictly complied with the formal Allied demand of 'unconditional surrender'. Hence, they had not been involved in any promises of favourable treatment, including legal immunity, made to members of the Wolff group in

251 Angleton to Chief of Station Heidelberg, July 1947, 'Dollmann and Wenner', Dollmann Name File, *op cit*. Also cited in Chase to Taylor, 20 November 1947: IFZ, Munich, Polad/33/18.

252 'Dollmann and Wenner', HH to BBS Only (top secret), 5 December 1946, # 4, Dollmann Name File, *op cit*.

253 From General Vandenberg to General Lee, *ibid*.

254 *Ibid*.

return for the early capitulation of German and fascist military forces.[255] Hence: 'If any promises or undertakings of special treatment were made, they were made by persons not authorised by Supreme Allied commander to do so and are completely contrary to strictest instructions.'[256]

The already complicated dispute was made even more complex by Major Airey.[257] He stated that he had 'personally participated in the Sunrise negotiations and that D[ollmann] had nothing to do with [the] negotiations'.[258] This factually incorrect statement may indicate that Airey had not checked his own records, or that the OSS had not been entirely frank with these authorities regarding the role it had played during the earlier 'secret intelligence phases' of Operation Sunrise prior to Airey's involvement. Alternatively, it may simply reflect a more general failure to share information that was (and apparently continues to remain) endemic amongst US intelligence, counter-intelligence and military institutions. In response to Airey's statement and subsequent press release, Angleton passed to General Lee the

> complete D story together with the British CSDIC [Combined Services Detailed Interrogation Centre] interrogation of Dollmann which clearly indicates whether authorised or not D was made promises by both Husmann and Parilli . . . It was precisely because of these promises made by Husmann and Parilli during the negotiations that both contacted D and W during their incarceration by SIM in Milan[259]

Airey's statement was not helpful to intelligence officials because it unintentionally undermined their case for protecting Dollmann, and apparently they sought to rebut it. Certainly, Dollmann's CIA Name File includes an undated and unsigned memo emanating from OSS/SSU Washington, but actually written in conjunction with Dulles.[260] This memo corrects Airey's statement by confirming the positive role that both Wenner and Dollmann played: 'at no small risk' in different phases of the Sunrise negotiations. It also responds to the question of whether promises were made by Dulles or his representatives. In effect, this defensively worded statement, which cites Dulles as a key source, attempted to shift the terms of the debate. It neither confirmed nor denied the key issue of whether promises of immunity had, in fact, been made. Instead, it argued that Dollmann should be assisted for other reasons:

255 *Ibid*, # 5. 256 *Ibid*.

257 *Ibid*. The actual name is deleted but unintentionally revealed in a later section!

258 *Ibid*, # 5; Angleton to Chief of Station Heidelberg, July 1947, 'Dollmann and Wenner', Dollmann Name File, *op cit*.

259 *Ibid*. 260 *Ibid*.

> We have no information that Mr Dulles made any promises or commitments to Dollmann or Wenner, nor do we have any information regarding whether or not Husmann or Parilli made any such commitments. Husmann was connected with Mr Dulles in some of the connections in Switzerland. Parilli of course would have no authority to have made any commitments binding on the Allies. Whether or not binding commitments were made it seems that we owe some consideration to these men. It has just been ascertained that Mr Dulles made no promises or commitments to Dollmann or Wenner, nor did he authorise any other persons to make such commitments. He confirmed however that these men did participate in the negotiations and his feeling is that if they are in trouble that some effort should be made to help them.[261]

In response to hostile media coverage in left-wing Italian press, Allied AFHQ made an unintentionally false press statement without prior consultation with OSS/SSU. This statement admitted that Dollmann: 'was in Allied hands' but – based on Airey's mistaken claim – asserted that 'he had nothing to do with Sunrise',[262] and that, even if he had 'he would not have been given any special immunity'.[263] OSS/SSU[264] were then forced to release to AFHQ the full text of Dollmann's interrogation:

> [W]hich clearly indicates whether authorised or not D[ollmann] was made promises by both Husmann and Parilli and that he clearly participated in the secret I.S. [intelligence service] phase of negotiations. . . . [sanitised deletion] it was precisely because of these promises made by Parilli and Husmann during the negotiations that both contacted D[ollmann] and W[enner] during their incarceration by SIM [Italian Military Intelligence] in Milan.[265]

As this debate continued during the last two months of 1946 through a flurry of memorandum, Dollmann himself remained imprisoned in grim conditions in a US military police jail, without even the benefit of basic toilet facilities. He was imprisoned whilst the high profile trial of 'his mortal enemy Kappler', who exonerated Dollmann on the first day of his testimony, continued in late November.[266] Military authorities at AFHQ Caserta insisted that, notwithstanding any alleged promises of legal immunity offered by OSS officials or sub-agents, it:

261 Anon, 'Eugen Dollmann and Eugene Wenner', (nd), *ibid.*

262 Anon [sanitised] to Special Operations, 20 November 1946, #9, *ibid.*

263 'Dollmann and Wenner', HH to HS5 Only, (top secret), 5 December 1946, # 5, *ibid.*

264 *Ibid.* 265 Anon [sanitised] to Special Operations, 20 November 1946, # 11, *ibid.*

266 *Ibid*, # 12.

> [H]as already informed [the] court holding [the Ardeatine] trial in Rome that Dollmann will be made available as [a] witness if [the] court so requests. If [the] Italians hold [a] further trial to pass justice on lesser German officials implicated in the Ardeatine Caves murders, Italian court may well request Dollmann as [a] witness, and efforts to implicate him may be taken by [the] Italian prosecution . . . Since it is now known that Dollmann is held in United States custody, it would place AFHQ in [an] untenable position morally should it refuse request from [an] Italian court that Dollmann [should] testify.[267]

The handling of the Dollmann case by US intelligence became further complicated by the intervention of General Hartman from G-2. This official 'took the case in hand'. US intelligence officials noted that General Hartman had offered to 'cover for us at Caserta' (Allied Military Headquarters).[268] Yet, for the US intelligence officials concerned with this matter, this positive support from a senior military intelligence official was double edged. In practice, it limited the scope for action of OSS/SSU officials, and even their awareness of relevant decisions and events. OSS/SSU officials were then 'told privately' by Hartman that:

> [I]f War department [who had responsibility for the retained espionage aspects of OSS/SSU from October 1945] would send urgent cable . . . stating in effect that D and W participated in negotiations during their I.S. phase and were made promises of rehabilitation by American OSS agents Husmann and Parilli, he will consider whole matter most favourably. This act would re-establish our position and resolve present conflict. . . . Feel that no other interpretation can be placed on the D interrogation which was scientifically conducted by the British.'[269]

For the purposes of this part of the present book, this statement is particularly interesting. It is one of the few official statements recognising that, as a matter of fact, credible promises of rehabilitation and legal immunity had been made, albeit through Dulles' intermediaries, to members of the Wolff group. It contradicts the claims by Breitman and Wolfe that no such promises were ever made, even by intermediaries.[270]

US intelligence had been placed in a difficult position. On the one hand, it was in their interests to deny that Husmann or Parilli had any authority from Dulles to make any promises. Yet, any such denial would prevent them resuming their influential position with respect to the future treatment of Wenner

267 'Dollmann and Wenner', HH to HS5 Only (top secret), 5 December 1946, # 5, *ibid.*
268 Anon [sanitised] to Special Operations, 20 November 1946, # 13, # 14, *ibid.*
269 *Ibid.* 270 Wolfe, 2004, *op cit*, 329.

and Dollmann. Furthermore, Hartman had let slip to the British, who were responsible for holding high-level war crimes trials, that the Americans were holding both Dollmann and Wenner, a fact stated in a 'top secret control document'.[271] In response, senior US intelligence and military officials (Lt General Vandenberg and Lt General Lee at AFHQ) developed a rather vague, and therefore highly permissive and discretion-granting, formulae, which was apparently also accepted by the US State Department.[272] This formulae stated that, once it was firmly established that Dollmann and Wenner were, in fact, key participants within Operation Sunrise, then 'these persons should receive such consideration as might be appropriate in the present circumstances'.[273]

In releasing only a 'sanitised' version of the relevant document, the CIA 'censors' have blanked out the sentence in this paragraph where any more specific immunity would have been discussed. This blanked-out section immediately follows references to the 'repercussions and results' of allowing a trial. The perceived need for such selective declassification, even over fifty years after the events themselves, helps create the impression that, for interesting reasons, the issue of Dollmann's *ad hoc* immunity remains a politically sensitive topic.[274]

In April 1947, it seems that, in recognition of their role in Sunrise, senior US intelligence officials and their counterparts in US military intelligence sought permission from the State Department to transfer Dollmann (and Wenner) from Italy, where he was still held in American custody, to the US-controlled zone of Germany.[275] One reason they provided in support of this request was that: 'Both G-2 and CIG [Central Intelligence Group, precursor to the CIA] believe these men [to be] of continuing intelligence value.' These officials noted that the situation had become urgent because 'Italians formally asked military to hand Dollmann over to them in January [1947] and have recently repeated request but no answer given yet.'[276] When seeking

271 Angleton to Chief of Station Heidelberg, July 1947, 'Dollmann and Wenner', Dollmann Name File, *op cit*.

272 See Marshall to Leghorn, 24 May, 1947, 740.00116, EW/5–1547, A/CWB: NA, RG 59 decimal files (1945–49), Box 3622. This note from the State Department notes that: 'Department concurs [with the] action of General Lee (May 15) . . . should [the] Italian Government request surrender [of] Dollmann as war criminal [from US custody] through diplomatic channels, [this] matter will be reviewed in light [of the nature of] the accusations.'

273 *Ibid.*

274 See 'former SS-Standarterführer Dollmann', Robert Joyce to Walter Dowling, 1 December 1945, 740.00116 EW/12–146; NA RG 59, Entry Decimal Files (1945–49), Box 3620. With respect to this and related correspondence, it is difficult to explain what 'national security' ground could still exist for any withholding of information, other than embarrassment over the involvement of a former director of the CIA in granting legal immunity to SS officials.

275 Leghorn to Secretary of State, No. 53, 12 April 1947: Dollmann Name File, *op cit*. Indeed, these requests had been made previously in November 1946 and January 1947, *ibid*.

276 *Ibid.*

guidance from Washington, an Italian-based US diplomat (Leghorn) initially was only willing to give partial support to these intelligence officials' request for the 'repatriation' of Dollmann and Wenner to protect Dollmann from prosecution by the Italian authorities. He would support this 'only if overriding requirements of military intelligence exist', and left a decision on that point to Washington. If the answer came back as a positive, then Leghorn proposed a suitably 'diplomatic' statement:

> on his transfer Italians be notified that he will remain in American custody and any application for his return to Italy will be given every possible consideration after his detention by American authorities [is] no longer required. Wenner being checked on UNWCC [UN War Crimes Commission] lists; if not listed suggest informing military authorities no objection [to] his repatriation.[277]

Here we can see a balancing of supposedly overriding intelligence and national security factors with specific legal considerations, the perceived requirement to make Dollmann and perhaps Wenner available for a war crimes trial.

During the first two weeks of May 1947, Leghorn became subject to increasing pressure, particularly as he received no immediate reply from Washington, despite his chasing telegram. Officials from both US military and civilian intelligence (CIG) continued to argue that there was an overriding intelligence imperative that must be respected: 'understand long-range intelligence interest (including CIG) in Dollmann hinges on likelihood that if he is abandoned to Italian jurisdiction other agents will doubt American ability to protect them'.[278] As Wolfe notes:

> Failure to protect Dollmann . . . could deter more skilled Nazi intelligence sources from trusting US spymasters' promises of unending protection . . . CIG feared Axis intelligence sources would dry up unless some protection were offered to Germans who had risked their lives in making a separate peace.[279]

In effect, Leghorn was pressurised into giving initial and qualified local State Department permission for the transfer these two men to Germany.[280] Indeed, Leghorn (and/or his colleague Greene) came to positively support his transfer to Germany, not least because of the 'security threats inherent in moving [this] prisoner and in [view of the] possibility [that] he may have

277 *Ibid.* 278 Leghorn to Secretary for State, No. 78, 15 May 1947, *ibid.*
279 Wolfe, 1994, *op cit*, 317, 329 respectively.
280 Leghorn to Secretary of State, No. 73, 8 May 1947, Dollmann Name Files, *op cit.*

to be hospitalised as well as [the] imminent derequisitioning of Rome jail, Dollmann [should] be moved soonest'.[281] One result of this pressure was that, during mid-May 1947, the US military authorities finally sanctioned, at the highest local level, the transfer of Dollmann to detention in Germany where he could receive a form of 'protective custody'. This was to shield him from the possibility of having to stand trial in Italy. The reservations of the State Department concerning the provision of official protection for an indicted war criminal were overcome because 'General Lee . . . could not any longer run risk of keeping Dollmann in view of all the present circumstances . . . Dollmann and Wenner will be removed to Germany under security arrangements as EUCOM confirms they will accept them.'[282] Because State Department officials had not refuted the security considerations raised by their colleagues in US civilian and military intelligence, 'which for them are decisive', Leghorn's initial caution was soon modified in favour of the intelligence argument.

Between 17 and 19 May 1947, Dollmann and Wenner were finally transferred by CIC agents from Rome to the custody of the Director of Intelligence, EUCOM (G-2/CI).[283] They were transferred together with a 'complete brief of [their] past histories'.[284] The Heidelberg CIG officials who received them were told by their Italian-based colleagues that these officials were to continue an earlier policy of shielding the two men, even from the British authorities who were responsible for organising trials of senior German officials for major Nazi war crimes in Italy:

> [D]uring this period [1945–May 1947] we made every effort to prevent a/. Turnover of Dollmann to Italians b/. Return of Wenner and Dollmann to British custody, and to obtain their removal from this theater [Italy]. With Washington backing, this finally carried out. . . . Both have information which would place present Italian political regime in bad light if published. We solicit your aid in assuring expeditious rehabilitation and preferential treatment within sep[arate] regulations now in force. Desire, if possible they be informed directly or our part in achievement of program outlined . . .[285]

Now it becomes clear from this internal CIG memo that one previously unacknowledged factor motivating their protection was that Dollmann and

281 Leghorn to Secretary of State, No. 78, 15 May 1947, *ibid.* 282 *Ibid.*

283 It appears that Angleton supervised this operation even if CIC agents actually executed it: Angleton, 10 December 1951, NA, RG 319, IRR Entry 134B, Box 40, 'Eugen Dollmann'.

284 Leghorn to Secretary for State, No. 78, 15 May 1947; Leghorn to CIG, 28 May 1947; CIG memo (Heidelberg), 'special operations', PIR 1266, 7 July 1947, Dollmann Name File, *op cit.*

285 *Ibid.*

Wenner's involvement in Sunrise meant that they had acquired potentially embarrassing details, possibly relating to the Italian Prime Minister, Parri, whose release was one of the terms and conditions of that mission. It is possible that they were aware of Parri's alleged collaboration with the Nazis after his wartime capture, which had ensured his survival rather than immediate torture and execution. If such details had been widely exposed and believed, it would have devastated his popularity as a former socialist partisan leader. American intelligence may have been anxious to support Parri as a popular left of centre, anti-communist during a period in which the Italian Communist Party threatened to come to power through democratic means. If this was the case, then Parri presumably remained indebted to US intelligence officials and generally compliant with their wishes, not least because of their knowledge of this particular skeleton in his cupboard. Robert Wolfe has suggested: 'For US intelligence, failure to shield would risk embarrassing public disclosure of continued covert anti-leftist operations by the United States in postwar Italy.'[286] If this scenario was accurate, then it would also help explain why US intelligence officials remained anxious to monitor all memoirs or other publicly reported statements from the Nazi participants within Sunrise, and to seek to ensure that they were aware of (and grateful to) the source of their post-war protection.[287]

From June through to August 1947, senior American intelligence officials within Germany engaged in internal correspondence and exchanges concerning Dollmann and Wenner, with related Allied governmental officials in Germany, particularly with the Office of Political Affairs. Because of the political embarrassment that would be created if its details ever became public, this correspondence was originally classified as 'top secret'.[288] Relevant officials, whose identities are still withheld, were conscious that CIG/CIA officials in Heidelberg would be taking considerable risks in attempting to ensure 'the complete rehabilitation of these two men', not least because: 'a great many questions are likely to come up which Heidelberg is not probably in a position to answer.'[289] In particular, there were likely to be questions asked regarding the exchange of promises during the wartime negotiations with Dulles; that is: 'any developments that may have taken place prior to 1946.'[290]

At this time, that is the summer of 1947, American military intelligence officials (G-2) in Frankfurt held Dollmann and Wenner. These intelligence officials were proposing 'to discharge them as PWs [Prisoners of War],

286 R. Wolfe, 'Coddling a Nazi Turncoat', in Breitman *et al*, 2004, *op cit*, 317. For evidence of continuing CIA covert operations in Italy, see Mangold, 1991, *op cit*, 26–27.

287 Leghorn to CIG, 28 May 1947; CIG memo (Heidelberg), 'special operations', PIR 1266, 7 July 1947, Dollmann Name File, *op cit*.

288 Memo Dollmann and Wenner, from Anon to BSB, 14 July 1947, *ibid*.

289 *Ibid*.

290 *Ibid*.

exempt them from Denazification and provide them with domicile and certain facilities at and near Munich'.[291] Part of this correspondence, including a letter from Colonel Blunda to Colonel Fritzsche, made it clear that:

> It would be appreciated if both Dollmann and Wenner 'could be buried in the long list of people who are to appear before Denazification boards' and that the 'longer their names do not appear in any official records and public press the better'.[292]

Other related correspondence from intelligence officials reminded the Director of Military Government for Bavaria, Germany, whose officials had challenged this proposed immunity, that there were specific provisions for the exemption of: 'certain German nationals charged or prosecuted under German Denazification Law'. The latter had been designed to shield German double-agents who had secretly provided information to the Allies. Furthermore, senior American intelligence officials claimed that 'the pardon of these individuals is deemed advisable and appropriate on the basis of the valuable service which they have rendered to the U.S. Government and for reasons of security'.[293] Indeed, rather than have Dollmann and Wenner subjected to a public de-Nazification hearing, as the prevailing Allied law required, these officials directed that Wolff's former SS colleagues should be provided with housing and food rations and possibly even employment.

The practical implementation of this planned special treatment was not to prove straightforward. One reason was that such treatment required securing the active cooperation and coordination of a number of senior administrators within Military Government.[294] The effort to secure privileged treatment for these former SS officers continued to be classified as top secret.[295] These considerations meant that 'this case [must] be handled with the utmost

291 *Ibid.*

292 Cited in Chase to Mr Ambassador, Mr Heath: 're Proposal to "rehabilitate" SS Colonel Eugen Dollmann and SS Major Eugen Wenner', 15 July 1947: *I.F.Z*, AGTS/53/4, file 'Exemption from Denazification: Dollmann/Wenner'.

293 Col. Garde to Director of Military Government for Bavaria, 'Exemption of certain German Nationals from Denazification', 7 August 1947: (IFZ), Munich, AGTS/53/4: file, 'Exemption from Denazification: Dollmann/Wenner'.

294 These included the Deputy Chief of the Public Safety Branch, the Director of OMG in Bavaria, the Deputy Chief of the Food and Agriculture Branch, Economics Division, and the Deputy Director of the Manpower Division. See Colonel Peter Rodes, Director of Intelligence, to Chief of Intelligence, Office of Mil. Government for Bavaria, 7 August 1947, Exemption from Denazification: Dollmann/Wenner: (*IFZ*), Munich, AGTS/53/4.

295 The continuing intelligence dimension was to be handled by Colonel Garvey (Commanding Officer of Region IV of the US Counter Intelligence Corps).

possible discretion'.[296] Hence, all correspondence leaving a potentially embarrassing paper trail had to be returned 'because of the political and security considerations involved'. In other words, there was a concerted effort by these intelligence officials, who were aware of the politically sensitive and controversial nature of granting exemption to Dollmann and Wenner, to 'cover their tracks'.

During the summer of 1947, the requests for assistance regarding Dollmann and Wenner received a sympathetic reception from, for example, the Deputy Military Governor of Germany based in Berlin. This official directed that both Dollmann and Wenner complete the standard de-Nazification questionnaire (itself ironically created by OSS's Franz Neumann in 1944). The original policy was that:

> In order to comply with the wishes of the originators . . . the deputy Military Governor has directed that . . . entry amnesty under the Law for Liberation by order of Major General Frank A. Keating, and that the appropriate public prosecutor in each case be advised that this has been done because of the person's service in the interests of his own people. It is therefore desired that you carry out [this] as expeditiously as possible . . . Report of accomplishment of this action will be submitted to this Headquarters, Attention: Director of Intelligence, immediately upon its completion.[297]

During July and August 1947, the Office of the Director of Political Affairs of US Military Government, OMGUS, headed by Ambassador Robert Murphy, had to consider whether it had any political objection to the immunity proposals. Lockling, Beam and Chase addressed this issue, and seriously questioned just how far such privileged treatment should extend. In response, they were told:

> The main thing was to postpone public action on these cases as long as possible and that beyond that it would be desirable to give these individuals the most favourable possible status that could be done on the basis of their records.[298]

It appears that W. M. Chase, a senior official, had questioned the legal basis for any such exemption. He therefore had to be reminded of the 'secret

296 Lindjord to Rodes, 'Eugen Dollman and Eugen Wenner, 28 July 1947, 'Exemption from Denazification: Dollmann/Wenner': IFZ, Munich, AGTS/53/4.

297 *Ibid.*

298 Haakon Lindjord (Chief of Counter-Intelligence section) to Colonel Rodes: 'Eugen Dollman and Eugen Wenner', File 'Exemption from Denazification: Dollmann/Wenner,' July 1947 (date partly illegible), IFZ, Munich, AGTS/53/4.

directive' allowing Military Governors to grant amnesties: 'to individuals inculpated under the Law for Liberation'.[299] This did not, however, satisfy his objections. Indeed, Chase directly confronted one of the central questions addressed by the present book: had the Wolff group been promised immunity in a way that was now binding upon Military Government. His review of the evidence laid before him by comparatively senior US intelligence officials, which was provided mainly during the mid-summer period by Colonel Fritzsche, was highly sceptical. He questioned Fritzsche's claims that: 'certain promises as to their future treatment have evidently been made'. And claims that the relevant documentation reveals little more than a 'vague commitment' to 'rehabilitate them later in exchange for ... their active participation in Operation Sunrise ... and the hoped-for surrender of the German Armies'.[300] Chase interprets some of the documentation as implying that:

> One of the promises might have been to provide Dollmann and Wenner with 'necessary papers to leave Italy for South Africa'; it is said that the provision of the men with such papers will 'effectively discharge the American obligation which should have been discharged following the CSDIC period'.[301]

(This was the escape route used by Walter Rauff, a major war criminal who was Wolff's second in command in the SS in Northern Italy.)

Chase also strategically misinterpreted Gaevernitz's articles, published in 1946 by the *Saturday Evening Post*, as suggesting that the Wolff group had not in fact brought about an early surrender at all. Chase, who clearly was looking for reasons to obstruct any confirmation of legal immunity upon Wenner and Dollmann, emphasised that this policy had proved controversial *even within US intelligence circles*. He noted that:

> Although OSS Capt Angleton [later head of CIA counter-intelligence] wired Washington HQ, requesting proof of any promises made to Dollmann ... the only reply apparently received was made by General Vandenberg on 29 November 1946, in a telegram to General Lee that ... it was 'to the best interests of the Allies and future long-range US intelligence activities to show appropriate consideration to Dollmann.' ... Thus the 'promises', if any, remain unclarified.[302]

299 Frederick Hess (Chief CI Section) to Colonel Rodes, 29 July 1947, Exemption from Denazification: Dollmann/Wenner': IFZ, Munich, AGTS/53/4.

300 Chase to Mr Ambassador, Mr Heath: re Proposal to 'rehabilitate' SS Colonel Eugen Dollmann and SS Major Eugen Wenner, 15 July 1947, *ibid.*

301 *Ibid.* 302 *Ibid.*

Chase went on to recognise that Dollmann and Wenner (who, unlike Dollmann, was listed at the time as a possible suspect on the Allied CROWCASS listing of Nazi war criminals) were not major offenders. However, the more important point, he argued, was that their wartime record and voluntary membership of the SS was sufficient to render them likely to face conviction and severe punishment by a de-Nazification trial, irrespective of their involvement with the OSS. Indeed, his own advisers had informed Chase that the very fact that Dollmann and Wenner had sought to curry favour with Dulles could be taken as an unintentional acknowledgement of the vulnerability of these SS officers to arrest and punishment:

> Persons of the category of Dollmann and Wenner could normally expect rather stiff sentences as having been fully conscious of their acts, and could only expect a mitigation of the sentence if they were able prove that they had actively opposed the Nazis . . . Activity on behalf of the Allies would be given consideration but . . . I don't see how these men could allege anti-Nazi activity. On the contrary, both received Iron Crosses as late as 1945. Their first known act unfavourable (let alone opposed) to the Nazi regime was their engagement in the negotiations under Operation Sunrise . . . a time when even an imbecile could have seen that the German cause was hopelessly lost. It can be assumed from the nature of the alleged 'promises' that their real motive . . . was to seek protection from expected punishment.[303]

Chase also opposed the suggested use in this case of the secret directive from the Military Governor allowing German nationals to be exempted from de-Nazification who have: 'rendered US intelligence valuable information the disclosure of which services might be embarrassing'.[304] Indeed, he noted that this provision for effective pardon 'has *not* yet been used' and that 'I do not feel that the Dollmann and Wenner cases are analogous to that of Schulte' (a prior case where the intelligence exception was used to grant *de facto* immunity to one of Dulles' contacts and informants within German industry[305]).

The most powerful objection that Chase raised was the familiar constitutional argument that, even in difficult cases, it remained vital to respect the rule of law. This principle should be respected not only for its own sake but also because the exercise of discretion to selectively grant immunity necessarily makes unjustified distinctions between analogous cases. As such, this practice undermines the democratic credentials of any system of government based on the rule of law which insists on equal rights. Such exemption violates the basic principle of making government decisions on the basis

303 *Ibid.* 304 *Ibid.*
305 See N. Petersen, 'From Hitler's Doorstep', in Chalou, 1992, *op cit*, 277, 285.

that like cases should, on principle, always be treated alike. It also conflicts with the equally key constitutional principle that responsible governmental decision-making should avoid capricious exercises of unregulated discretion, a mode of government the German people had become all too familiar with under the Nazis:

> General Wolff, the former Chief of Dollmann and Wenner, now sits at Nuremberg, awaiting trial. I do not see how Dollmann and Wenner can escape the Denazification procedure if they remain in Germany. The road to 'rehabilitation' is through the Spruchkammer [Denazification Tribunal hearing]. I think we would be taking our responsibilities very lightly were we to advise ODI [Office of the Director of Intelligence] here and at Frankfurt otherwise. I cannot see how, regardless of whatever promises certain agents of OSS may have at one time made to both Dollmann and Wenner, Military Government could sanction their exemption from the procedure prescribed by German law for such cases.[306]

Chase reinforced this high-minded constitutional point, which assumes the validity of classic liberal democratic assumptions regarding the sources of governmental legitimacy, with a number of pragmatic arguments. These practical objections were clearly designed to appeal to the instrumental orientation towards national security interests that is, of necessity, one of the characteristics of the required mind-set of most intelligence officials:

> The release of these men in the US zone will *not* remain a secret, and G-2 Eucom is only cherishing illusions in that regard. A discovery that these two men have been 'protected' from the application of the German law would at the very least serve substantially to undermine what little respect remains in German minds for the Denazification procedure. Provision of Austrian or any other papers to these men to escape to South Africa is also a most undesirable solution and would surely ultimately have very painful political repercussions.[307]

Not surprisingly, given Chase's clear opposition to the proposed immunity proposal that resonates throughout his analysis, he recommended that Wenner and Dollmann 'be brought to as early trial as is feasible in order that they be given the benefits of whatever mitigating circumstances there are in their favor'.[308]

By contrast, other senior officials within Allied Military Government, particularly John Beam, opposed Chase's position by claiming that:

306 *Ibid.* 307 *Ibid.* 308 *Ibid.*

> It would appear that a moral obligation exists with respect to these SS officers who made an effort to bring about a German surrender in Italy. Quite apart from their moral character, they seemed to risk their lives in our interests . . . this question would seem to require a decision by the highest authorities here [in Berlin].[309]

Senior authorities appear to have accepted Beam's argument because it was simply restated as policy by Heath, the Director of the Office of the Director of Intelligence for the American-occupied zone of Germany. Beam then forwarded to Ambassador Robert Murphy a written statement from Wolff that:

> [I]ndicates . . . that certain commitments were made to him and his associates by Mr Dulles and von Gaevernitz. These now come up in connection with the proposal to obtain a pardon for Wolff's assistants Dollmann and Wenner.[310]

At this stage Chase appeared to be fighting a losing battle. He had been confronted with the implications of the Husmann–Wolff interview, which the Nuremberg prosecutors had forwarded. This interview contradicted Chase's argument that no definite or binding promises had been made by individuals authorised to bind the US government; and that, even if this had occurred, it would still be wrong in principle, and disastrous in practice, ever to grant legal immunity. In fact, during his Nuremberg interview with Husmann, Wolff had claimed that:

> I distinctly remember that Major Waibel, when we conferred in Zurich on March 8 and 9 1945, not only confirmed, as a whole, Dr Husmann's statements and views, but also added his own assertion that he, too, as a Swiss guarantor, vouched for the fulfilment of the oral American promises . . . In the presence of myself and Wenner, Major Waibel made it clear once more that, under the prevailing circumstances, such a written verification could not possibly be obtained. We Germans would just have to depend on the loyalty of the Allies and on the additional guarantee of the neutrals who were trusted on both sides. Major Waibel added that he, as a Major in the Swiss General Staff, vouched for the validity of the guarantee he had given with his officer's honor.[311]

309 J. D. Beam to Donald Heath, file 'Exemption from Denazification: Dollmann/Wenner', 21 July 1947: IFZ, AGTS/53/4.

310 Beam to Murphy, 8 August 1947: 'Exemption from Denazification: Dollmann/Wenner': IFZ, AGTS/53/4.

311 Husmann–Wolff interview: April 1947, 8: IFZ, Munich, Polad/33/18.

However, given the force of this internal dispute between Chase and US intelligence officials, and Chase's argument that both Dulles and Gaevernitz had retained a strategic silence on the whole affair, Beam recommended double-checking Wolff's claims stated immediately above. He asked for these to be confirmed not only with former OSS staff most closely involved in Operation Sunrise but also with Major Waibel, from Swiss intelligence. Waibel was another of Dulles' intermediaries in this operation whom Husmann had presented to Wolff as a neutral 'guarantor' of the verbal commitments of post-war rehabilitation and immunity:

> Waibel was present during a part of the surrender negotiations and vouched for the validity of the guarantee of immunity given by the U.S. negotiators . . . it is suggested that the U.S. military attaché in Bern might be requested to get in touch with Major Waibel to ascertain discreetly whether any such guarantees were in effect granted. An independent approach might also be made to Mr Allen Dulles respecting the same question.[312]

Beam considered such double-checking to be necessary before his Office of Political Affairs could comply with the urgent requests of US intelligence officials to recommend a pardon to General Clay, the overall Military Governor for occupied Germany. Beam's own view was that such inquiries were not disciplinary investigations of Dulles' wartime conduct, but merely to clear up factual disputes. Indeed, he suggested to Murphy that:

> [T]he German surrender in Italy was a tremendous advantage to us and hastened the surrender of the Central German Forces a few days later. There would, therefore, be nothing improper in any promise of immunity and if such an obligation exists, even morally, I believe it should be honoured.[313]

From a handwritten addition to Beam's correspondence, it appears that Beam's view was gaining ground, and he was asked to draft the required cables.[314] By early August 1947, Chase's objections had clearly been overruled by higher authorities in Military Government, as the Director of Intelligence had requested the Military Governor to issue a pardon to Dollmann and

312 Beam to Murphy, 8 August 1947, 'Exemption from Denazification: Dollmann/Wenner', IFZ, AGTS/53/4.

313 *Ibid.*

314 *Ibid.* The cable (No. 1915), sent on 11 August 1947 was entitled 'Alleged Promises to Gen. Wolff and adjutants by von Gaevernitz and Dulles', and a handwritten note indicates that a reply was received on 17 September 1947, Cable 1886: *ibid.*

Wenner citing an earlier precedent, and had presented it to him 'for urgent action'.[315]

Chase remained undeterred by this latest setback. He drafted a memorandum that cited aspects of the Husmann–Wolff interview, which, on the face of it, had answered some of his own criticism regarding the lack of evidence of promises, to emphasise that: 'there were no *written* promises, at least to Wolff'. He also sought to embarrass senior intelligence officials by noting that:

> I am perplexed by the nearly total silence of the high OSS (Dulles, von Gaevernitz etc) with regard to Wolff group and the alleged 'promises' to it . . . The promises thus appear to have been more a personal commitment by von Gaevernitz than a binding obligation on the U.S. Government . . . I believe that we should recommend to the Military Governor that he should postpone making any decision regarding the cases of Wenner and Dollmann until he has obtained from Dulles and von Gaevernitz clarification of the nature of any promises which they made to Wenner and Dollmann placing obligations on the U.S. Government in their regard. Secondly, I believe that we should invite the attention of the Military Governor to the possible effect of a pardon to Wenner and Dollmann on the status of Wolff. Might Wolff not, with some right, later claim that a pardon to his subordinates for their part in Operation Sunrise created an obligation to give him, the chief German figure in that Operation, comparable consideration. Is the case against Wolff such that the Military Governor could afford to mitigate in the manner of a possible punishment for Wolff?[316]

Chase's Department of Political Affairs then attempted to outflank the intelligence officials pressing for Dollmann and Wenner to be given privileged treatment by telegraphing the US Department of State twice in August 1947: '[A]sking that clarification of alleged promises to the Wolff group be made by certain Americans who were closely involved in the negotiations.' There was no reply, which effectively stalled matters and frustrated the intelligence officials. In response, the overall Director of Intelligence for US Military Government of Germany threatened to act unilaterally. He 'intended to take independent action regarding Dollmann and Wenner if no reply was received [by September 12] . . . no reply has been received to date [16 September]'.[317]

This internal conflict was further complicated by Telford Taylor, Head Prosecutor of the US-led Subsequent Proceedings at Nuremberg, forwarding

315 Chase to the Ambassador, Mr Bean, re 'SS Officers Dollmann and Wenner', 'Exemption from Denazification: Dollmann/Wenner', 8 August 1947, IFZ, AGTS/53/4.

316 *Ibid.*

317 Chase to Col. Rodes, 16 September 1947, *ibid.*

to Ambassador Murphy 'transcripts of several interrogations in June and July with Karl Wolff by Judge Musmanno, formal Naval Aide to General Clark'.[318] Chase still attempted to reinterpret this new evidence regarding Wolff's continued reporting back to Hitler and Himmler in a manner that opposed the granting of immunity. However, he now changed the ground of his opposition by claiming that:

> the information obtained by Wolff's answers to Judge Musmanno's questions raises a fundamental point: whether and to what extent the Wolff group actually endangered their lives by engaging in the Operation Sunrise negotiations ... Thus, on the basis of the information now on hand, it does not seem possible to say definitely that the Wolff group endangered their lives at any time during the negotiations ... Moreover the entire question of the alleged promises still remains obscure. Whatever they were, they were apparently made to Wolff and only through him to his aides. Until the facts regarding these matters are fully known, the Office of Political Affairs does not feel qualified to deliver an opinion regarding the recommendation made for special treatment of Dollmann and Wenner.[319]

At this time, Chase claimed that the *partially authorised* character of Wolff's negotiations, that is, Hitler's knowledge of his plans, contradicted the claim that this group were ever under direct personal threat. He also noted that Dulles continued to deny that he had authorised promises of legal immunity. The conclusion he sought to draw from both these points was that there was not even a *moral obligation* to give special treatment to members of the Wolff group.

This controversy within the occupation authorities continued into September 1947. The State Department eventually replied to Chase's queries, which had been designed presumably to embarrass Dulles and his successors. These replies informed his department that they had contacted Dulles, who continued to claim that Dollmann and Wenner merited privileged treatment not because of any promises made to them but because of the nature of their actions:

> [T]he officials concerned with Operation Sunrise have reported that *no* promises were made regarding personal immunity for Wolff and his assistants, in particular Dollmann and Wenner. However the officials concerned believe that, when weighing any war crimes with which the members of the Wolff group might be charged, definite consideration

318 *Ibid*; Memo, 10 December 1951, NA, RG 319, IRR Entry Box 40, 'Eugen Dollmann'.
319 Chase to Col. Rodes, 16 September 1947, *ibid.*

> should be given to the doctrine that the Allies have some moral obligation in return for aid performed and risks taken rather than to deal with the case on the basis of promises.[320]

Still undeterred, Chase continued to resist the immunity deal and forwarded copies of the Wolff testimony derived from Judge Musmanno's interrogation to the State Department, presumably because it clearly contradicted the claims of Dulles and Gaevernitz. In October 1947, Telford Taylor intervened again by forwarding on to Ambassador Robert Murphy additional correspondence he had received from Husmann challenging the continued detention of Wolff.[321]

Chase's persistence was at least partially successful. It appears that, following consideration of the implications of the Judge Musmanno interrogations that Chase had forwarded on to Washington:

> The deputy military Governor subsequently rejected the formal recommendations, made ... by General Heath, the Director of Intelligence, that special treatment be accorded Dollmann and Wenner because of their part in Operation Sunrise.[322]

Chase wrote to Taylor returning the Musmanno interrogation transcripts, reasserting his scepticism regarding the 'partiality of Wolff's unsubstantiated allegations that promises were made to him both of immunity for his group and himself . . . Wolff alleges not only that such promises were made but that they have not since be honoured'.[323] By the end of November 1947, this controversy appears to have died down, partly because Wolff had, following clearance by Chase's office on or around 25 November, been returned to British custody: 'from whom he had been borrowed'.[324]

The overall situation had, back in October 1947, become subject to an additional complication in that Dollmann and Wenner were seeking to leave Germany, where Dollmann feared for his life, and return to Italy. This generated a firm cable from Richard Helms (later to become CIA Director) of the

320 Cited in Chase to Major Hess, 18 September 1947, 'Exemption from Denazification: Dollmann/Wenner', IFZ, AGTS/53/4.

321 See Taylor (Nuremberg) to Murphy, 3 October 1947 (with handwritten annotations from 15 November 1947 re Wolff's possible extradition: IFZ, AGTS/53/4, file 'Exemption from Denazification: Dollmann/Wenner'.

322 James Riddleberger (Charge d'Affairs) to Secretary for State (Washington), 10 November, 1947: IFZ, AGTS/53/4, file 'Exemption from Denazification: Dollmann/Wenner.'

323 Chase to Taylor, 20 November 1947: IFZ, Munich, Polad/33/18.

324 *Ibid.* See also Riddleberger (Berlin) to Secretary for State (Washington), Cable 11300, 17 November 1947: Return of General Wolff to the war crimes section of the British Army of the Rhine (citing the 25 November date for the planned return of Wolff): IFZ, Munich, Polad/33/18.

CIG's 'special operations' division. This insisted that, although he approved funds for their 'rehabilitation in Germany', the two men:

> must not proceed to Italy now or foreseeable future. If they go to Italy they will be arrested, interrogated, exposed and possible tried as war criminals. Highly preferable they remain in Amzone Germany. If they go to Italy, we will *not* intercede [on] their behalf to get them out again.[325]

This attempt to prevent their return to Italy and instead shield Dollmann and Wenner in the US-controlled zone of Germany became controversial within the wider military occupation authorities. General Hayes, for example, specifically disapproved attempts to assist individuals who were 'possible war criminals or war profiteers'. Hayes claimed that: 'to grant amnesty to these men would be to condone their crimes without proper examination'.[326] This reaction alarmed the leadership of US intelligence, namely the Office of the Deputy Director of Intelligence (ODDI), Colonel Wentworth. He complained that even raising the issue with Hayes had made 'the final disposal twice as difficult as it was originally'. Wentworth also suggested it was unrealistic to block these men's return to Italy: 'since Italy is probably the only place in Europe where they can survive'. Intelligence officials contested this, arguing that: 'Dollmann and Wenner are regarded as war criminals in Italy and that their return to Italy would be embarrassing to us and dangerous to them.'[327] Wentworth was eventually prevailed upon to accept a compromise of allowing Dollmann and Wenner:

> [T]o go on leave for a period of two weeks . . . it is presumed that Dollmann and Wenner will not return after their leave and it is expected that they will not be heard of in the future. When their failure to return is noted in ODDI they will be entered in the rogues' gallery and if they are picked up in Germany they will be consigned to a civilian internment enclosure to await spruchkammer [de-Nazification] trial . . . had this case been purely and simply ours, I should have been inclined to consign Dollmann and Wenner to a civilian internment enclosure and to have helped them with their trial. . . . complete responsibility . . . rests with ODDI. They realise this and also realise the risk they are taking in attempting to shield Dollmann and Wenner from the spruchkammer trial.[328]

325 Helms to Heidelberg, Cable 2026, 22 October 1947, Dollmann Name File, *op cit.*
326 'Eugen Dollmann and Eugen Wenner', 7 November 1947, *ibid.*
327 *Ibid.* 328 *Ibid.*

It appears that the final outcome of this internal debate was that Dollmann and Wenner were not given formal immunity from de-Nazification or prosecution but that neither man had to face a formal hearing. Dollmann had to complete the standard de-Nazification questionnaire, *Fragebogen*, only.[329] Indeed, it is likely that their cases were, in fact, buried at the bottom of a long list of names to the point where they effectively escaped any form of legal accountability in a context where lower-ranking SS officials, who had already been officially classified as 'active Nazis', received substantial punishment, including imprisonment, fines and disqualifications from public sector employment. In June 1947, Dollmann was formally discharged from the SS but detained for debriefing purposes until 24 October 1947 at Oberursel and for intelligence debriefing at EURCOM CIC, regarding Italian political factions. He was then given some $450 worth of Swiss francs and residence papers for the American-occupied zone of Germany. He had to report weekly to CIC Munich.[330] The details regarding Wenner are sketchy. Apparently, he did avail himself of the offers of intelligence officials to provide him with safe passage to Latin America.[331]

Conclusion

At this point it is noteworthy that officials employed by Western intelligence agencies have frequently been subject to an absurdly prejudicial 'demonisation' by their radical critics. Such officials have been portrayed almost as the personification of evil during a critique that often makes reference to the alleged involvement of these agencies in the covert recruitment, protection and exploitation of Nazis who more properly belonged to a list of defendants in a war crimes trial. Such critiques are often both one-sided and simplistic. As already noted, they typically not only ignore the positive contributions of American and British intelligence agencies to the investigation and prosecution of war criminality (discussed in detail in later chapters of this book), but also focus exclusively upon cases of former Nazis who were able to trade intelligence contacts and expertise in return for immunity from prosecution as war criminals as if this was a consistent, if hidden, agreed policy concerning all former Nazi officials.[332] Fortunately, the CIA's recent release in 2000 and more fully in 2005 of its Name Files on Zimmer and Dollmann, with only a comparatively small (but simultaneously frustrating and intriguing) number of withheld parts, provides a number of documents that can now function as a timely corrective to such one-sided critiques. In place of a

329 For a copy see NA, RG 319 IRR Entry 134B, Box 40 'Eugen Dollmann'.

330 *Ibid*; Wolf, *op cit*, 330.

331 Dulles, 1966, *op cit*, 252. Dulles ignores totally the assistance he was offered and probably provided by his former CIA colleagues and subordinates.

332 For additional details, see Bryan and Salter, 2001, *op cit*; and see Chapter 2 above.

one-dimensional critique of the OSS and related intelligence agencies as generally supportive of former Nazis, these documents reveal the emergence of a *heated internal controversy*. This controversy related to claims that Zimmer and Dollmann were, as a result of their contributions to Operation Sunrise and immediate post-war contacts with Dulles, receiving comparatively privileged treatment.

Even this brief comparison of the contrasting treatment that Wolff, Zimmer and Dollmann received at the hands of the Allied authorities refutes the idea that there was a centrally organised and widely supported plot that was consistently applied by all relevant OSS/SSU officials to protect the German participants in Operation Sunrise both generally and from any threat of legal proceedings with respect to war crimes. Indeed, Dollmann's CIA Name File indicates that any promises of immunity were made not by Dulles personally but rather during the pre-negotiation phase of the contacts in which Zimmer, Parilli and Dollmann discussed the possibility of surrender with Major Waibel and Max Husmann: 'definite Parilli statement that on behalf of Sunrise both he and Husmann made definite commitments to rehabilitate them. This substantiated by Parilli spending 181,000 lire of own money to make up for harm done.'[333]

My point is there is little evidence of a consistent policy being either applied or implemented with respect to the former Sunrise participants. On the contrary, there were striking differences in their treatment with respect to legal immunities. Arguably, these divergences are largely explicable in terms of the various *ad hoc* institutional reactions to the repercussions of a series of contingent and changing events. At decisive points, each received and benefited from some measure of credit for their participation in the Sunrise negotiations. Yet, the individual who received least credit with respect to the threat of being tried and executed was Eugen Dollmann.

Compared with the complicity of Rauff and – to a lesser extent – Wolff in the planned extermination of Jewish civilians, Dollmann – whose main role was that of an interpreter and diplomatic intermediary between Himmler and Mussolini – was the *least likely* candidate for any successful war crimes trial. Arguably, in a hypothetical world of rational institutional and international responses to war criminality, Rauff would have had to stand trial at the subsequent Nuremberg proceedings. Indeed, the German authorities in Bonn belatedly sought his extradition for trial in 1963; yet in mid-May 1984, Zimmer's superior officer in Milan managed to die peacefully in his luxury villa in Chile, unmolested by any realistic threat of legal proceedings. Whilst the involvement of US intelligence hinted at the orchestrated 'escape' of Dollmann, Wenner and Rauff from low security Allied POW camps in Italy, there is little evidence to date that his *de facto* immunity owed anything else to

333 Anon [sanitised] to Special Operations, 20 November 1946, # 3, *ibid.*

the influence of US intelligence.[334] Indeed, one of the few common factors in these case studies is that a number of intelligence officials recognised that the active involvement by Wolff's subordinates in Operation Sunrise could be taken as sufficient grounds to justify positive interventions to secure immunity for each of the individuals involved.[335] Moreover, certain of the internal correspondence suggests that one of the main problematic issues related to the technical question of identifying precisely who was sufficiently closely involved in the capitulation process to be covered by the potential umbrella of legal immunity.

With respect to the evidence discussed throughout this book, taken in conjunction with earlier studies of Dulles' role within the Nuremberg process, it is unreasonable to accept the conclusion suggested by his critics that this intelligence official's record with respect to the prosecution of Nazi war criminals was entirely unambiguous. The criticisms that his work in this area was in general or even largely subversive of attempts by Nuremberg and related processes both to re-establish and extend liberal principles of legal accountability as an integral aspect of the rule of law are surely one-sided and misleading. Such accusations, which, as this chapter has shown, possess a measure of qualified support from recently declassified intelligence documentation, must at this stage be considered proven only in a strictly qualified sense. Their validity would require the failure of an attempt to falsify them through a close inspection of the Nuremberg record which suggests that there is no 'other side' to this particular story. That is, no counter-evidence that Dulles and other senior US intelligence officials provided substantial assistance to the Nuremberg prosecutors. Indeed, it is precisely the *double-edged* and *highly selective* aspect of the contributions of many senior intelligence agencies and officials to the prosecution of war criminals which makes this a particularly interesting area for interdisciplinary research.[336] At this stage of the present book, it is only possible to claim that the standard criticism may well be misleading. It is one of the tasks of the remaining chapters to survey a considerable quantity of detailed archival material to see if it contains evidence to substantiate a credible counter-argument that critics of the OSS typically pass over in silence. The guiding idea of this survey is to delay any 'rush to judgement' based on a handful of immunity cases by seeking out evidence whose implications could potentially counter-balance and nuance the standard critique of the role of US intelligence officials in the Nuremberg and related war crimes trials.

334 Simpson, 1988, *op cit.*

335 See US Political Adviser to Military Government, 'Role of the Wolff group in Operation Sunrise', Top Secret, No. 11265, 11 November 1947, State Department Decimal Files, 740.00116EW/11-1047 A/VS, 1–2: NA, RG 59 Decimal Files (1945–49), Box 3622.

336 Bryan and Salter, 2001, *op cit.*

Chapter 6

The contribution of OSS officials to the prosecution of Nazi war crimes

The next three chapters seek to contribute to existing debates over the role of US intelligence, particularly OSS and its successor organisations, SSU and, from 1947, the CIA, in the war crimes prosecution field by providing a more nuanced and balanced interpretation. This chapter reviews a wide range of different types of contribution that OSS officials made not only to the monitoring of Nazi war criminality as this was taking place, but also to the post-war investigation and gathering of trial evidence concerning such criminality[1] and the whereabouts of perpetrators.[2]

The overall goal of the remaining chapters of this book is to analyse a series of contributions that counter-balance the unhelpful tendencies within the current literature towards an entirely one-sided form of blanket condemnation, which previous chapters noted.[3] Any properly balanced historical

1 For recently declassified files on OSS officials monitoring and reaction to Nazi war crimes, see 'Records of the Europe-Africa Division Security-Classified Correspondence of the Division Chief 1942–1945': NA, RG 226, Entry 37, Box 5; 'Collecting War Crimes Evidence', February 1943: NA, RG 226, Entry 92, Box 247, Folder 22; 'OSS, MIS Collecting evidence of German violations of Geneva Convention for war crimes trials, 1944': NA, RG 226, Entry 92, Box 563, Folder 12.

2 Details of OSS's interest in suspected arch-Nazi war criminal Henrich Müller, Chief of the Gestapo, is clear from various documentation available from the US National Archive. See 'War Room Publication, G. I. S. Priorities for Interrogation,' 27 May 1945: NA, RG 226, Entry 119A, Folder 621, Box 22, and 21 May 1945, Entry 119A, Box 22, Folder 621, *ibid*; W. R. C.3, 'Fortnightly Report for the Period Ending 18th June, 1945,' Entry 119A, Folder 639, Box 25, *ibid*; 'Progress Report,' X-2 Branch, 1 June–30 June 1945, attached to Saint (London) to Saint (Stockholm), 13 July 1945, Entry 125A, Folder 76, Box 7, *ibid*. War Room Monthly Summary No. 4, 23 July 1945, Entry 119A, Folder 629, Box 24, *ibid*; 'Arrest Target List-Revision Note, 1 November 1945,' Entry 122, tab 6, Box 1, *ibid*. This interest was not related exclusively to planned war crimes prosecution but included a concern that Müller could be organising guerrilla movements that posed a security threat to Allied Military Government officials.

3 C. Simpson, *The Splendid Blond Beast: Money, Law and Genocide in the Twentieth Century* (Maine Monroe: Common Courage Press, 1995), 13; B. Hersh, *The Old Boys: The American Elite and the Origins of the CIA* (New York: Charles Shribner's Sons, 1992), 125–33.

reconstruction and assessment of the role of US intelligence organisations within the Nuremberg process must take into account the nature, extent and implications of the support that, for example, Dulles, and his assistant Gero von Gaevernitz, a German-born but naturalised American citizen of a Jewish family background, provided for the Nuremberg prosecutors.

The implications of the various interventions of these and other intelligence officials, however, need to be understood in the specific wartime intelligence contexts in which they originally took place. Dulles, as potential OSS leader for Germany (and he hoped continental Europe more generally), was responsible for making preparations, in conjunction with William Casey,[4] to exploit post-war intelligence and strategic opportunities as these became clearer from the onward march of Allied military forces during 1944–45.

These preparations included securing for the Western powers the much-needed German expertise of industrialists, scientists and engineers, who, if not provided a safe refuge via Switzerland, might otherwise turn to Russia as their only alternative haven.[5] Dulles was possibly conscious of having to face accusations concerning his recruitment of such experts of 'probable utility'. This accusation would involve the Allied authorities turning a blind eye to any complicity in war criminality of the kind that was later to bedevil the Nazi rocket scientists employed by America. The 'science' of these men had involved systematic use of the grossly abused concentration camp labourers detained in the Dora camp.[6] Dulles' vulnerability on this point may explain why he felt it necessary to reassure his subordinate Casey (who went on to head the CIA). He told Casey that prior screening of the motives and value of specific individuals in these groups would be impossible. However, if OSS officials ensured they were singled out for special protection following their initial recruitment, this could only be of a temporary and provisional nature. Furthermore, such recruitment would require making 'no commitments as to [future] treatment'.[7] For reasons already discussed, it is equally important to counter-balance the welter of strong, but one-sided, criticism directed at Dulles. This section will achieve this goal by focusing upon the generally untold details of how Dulles, once in post as head of OSS's immediate

4 Dulles' OSS Secret Intelligence (SI) Branch colleague in London from 1943–45, and later CIA director 1981–87.

5 Mosley, *op cit*, 229.

6 During the early Cold War period, the falsification by US military intelligence officials of the wartime record of Nazi rocket scientists in order to gain their services for the American space and military programmes is a noteworthy example. Some of these individuals were vulnerable to, and therefore – from a 'national security' perspective – needed protection from, prosecution within Allied de-Nazification and war crimes hearings. Such protection formed an integral part of 'Operation Paperclip'.

7 See Dulles to Casey, Telegram 3317, 12 January 1945: NA, RG 226, Box 192, Entry 234 (document 5–6 in N. Petersen, *From Hitler's Doorstep: The Wartime Intelligence Reports of Allen Dulles* (Pennsylvania: Pennsylvania State University Press, 1996).

post-war Field Office in Wiesbaden, Germany, from June to December 1945, provided a range of different types of support for the Nuremberg prosecutors. These prosecutors recognised a number of these contributions of trial evidence as having proved especially helpful, particularly against defendant von Ribbentrop.[8]

Mosely, one of Dulles' biographers, notes that Dulles did not adopt a negative or obstructive position with respect to the search for fugitive Nazi war criminals or the proceeds of their crimes. On the contrary, Dulles and his subordinates at Wiesbaden defined these and related operations as a key part of their immediate post-war role, at least until they were given good reason to prioritise competing anti-communist imperatives:

> When Allen Dulles first moved into Germany [May 1945] he saw as his principal mission something which, he believed, might well bring the Western Allies and the Russians together in common cause now that the war was over: the rounding up of the big Nazis who had gone into hiding, the chasing down of hidden Nazi funds, the uncovering of stolen treasures which the Nazis' had plundered from occupied Europe.[9]

William Casey worked under Dulles in OSS Wiesbaden. Casey recalls that their OSS Germany office was called upon to provide considerable help on war crimes related issues. These included providing support for the various OSS officials investigating works of art looted by Göring and other Nuremberg defendants, such as Rosenberg. Dulles and Casey were also supportive of the Nuremberg process by responding to the frequent requests made by the head of the OSS, General Donovan, regarding locating and taking statements from possible witnesses based in Austria Germany or Allied POW camps further afield.[10] The support provided by Dulles' operation in Germany was based on access to wartime intelligence sources and contacts that, in all likelihood, would not otherwise have found their way into the hands of these prosecutors.[11] In an earlier study, the present author has addressed the crucial importance to the Nuremberg prosecutors of the services performed by two of Dulles' informants and agents within the anti-Hitler German opposition: Fabian von Schlabrendorff (a former German Army lawyer and later judge in West Germany) and Hans Gisevius (former Gestapo

8 This was in connection with the Ciano diaries obtained by Dulles and used as vital evidence against this Nuremberg defendant.

9 Mosely, *op cit*, 227.

10 Casey recalls: '[S]ome of these [immediate post-war OSS] activities demanded a fair amount of my attention. One of these was the War Crimes Trials.' W. Casey, *The Secret War Against Hitler* (Washington, Regnery, 1988), 218.

11 A similar point can be made with respect to the OSS's Document Research Unit headed by Walter Rothchild, based in London.

official and OSS double-agent).[12] Dulles gathered together a collection of native German nationals at his Wiesbaden base, who, through their role as informants and active members of the internal resistance to the Nazi regime, had been of considerable service to American intelligence. During mid-May 1945, Dulles' superior within the OSS, General Donovan, first revealed to Justice Jackson, chief of the dominant US prosecution agency at Nuremberg, that he had taken under his wing a number of anti-Nazi German members of the internal opposition. He maintained that some of these individuals could serve as particularly useful witnesses for the prosecution, including an early organiser of the Gestapo, Hans Gisevius.[13]

On 7 July 1945, Jackson and Donovan visited Wiesbaden to meet with Dulles. At this meeting, Dulles provided a collection of captured German documents that Jackson was later to single out as 'of importance to the case'.[14] The two most important contributions Dulles made related to obtaining the Ciano diaries and providing a stream of Foreign Office papers from his agent codenamed George Wood.[15] The recollections of Robert Storey, a Nuremberg prosecutor, include the following remarkable tribute to Dulles with respect to these and other sources of documentation:

> Periodic reports from the German foreign office were brought to Bern by Mr Gisevius, who was available to us through the good offices of Allen Dulles . . . We shall be ever grateful to him and his staff for the major role they played in connection with assembling and processing the voluminous evidence that was introduced at the trial.[16]

Persico notes that Gisevius helped the Nuremberg prosecutors rebut claims from some actual and potential defendants that they had in fact been working undercover for the anti-Nazi resistance:

> After the war, Hans Bernd Gisevius performed his final service for his fellow conspirators, an obligation he felt he owed to those who had lost their lives. At the war crimes trials, it began to appear that the web of conspirators was far wider than anyone had expected. One Nazi defendant after another sought to link himself to the anti-Hitler resistance.

12 M. Salter, 'Intelligence Agencies And War Crimes Prosecution: Allen Dulles' Involvement In Witness Testimony At Nuremberg', (2004) 2 *Journal of International Criminal Justice* 826–854.

13 Jackson Diary, 15 May 1945: Library of Congress, Manuscript Division, R. H. Jackson Papers, Washington DC.

14 R. Jackson, *Report of the United States' Representative to the International Conference on Military Tribunals* (Washington: Department of State, 1949), preface.

15 Breitman *et al*, 2004, *op cit*, preface.

16 R. Storey, *The Final Judgement: Pearl Habor to Nuremberg* (San Antonio: Naylor Co, 1968), 97.

> Hans Gisevius spent days on the stand . . . identifying those who had and had not been actual parties to the plot. It was a fairly simple issue, as Gisevius well knew. Virtually all of the true conspirators were dead.[17]

Another of Dulles' agents, Fritz Kolbe, sought to give evidence and help the prosecutors in the war crimes trial of his former Foreign Office chief, Karl Ritter.[18]

In January 1945, Dulles also made efforts to include three of his 'trusted German' staff, including Hans Gisevius, in one of the OSS's T-Force teams entering newly conquered areas of Germany, particularly Berlin. Their mission was to take control of important scientific and technical information and both material and human resources. He maintained that Gisevius would be able to take control of original Nazi documentation, 'securing important documents through personal contacts . . . the successful penetration [of] Nazi records', and other technical resources. He specifically sought files from Gestapo HQ and Military Intelligence (Abwehr), a proportion of which were later regarded as useful by the Nuremberg prosecutors.[19] Dulles also helped locate a mass of potentially incriminating evidence stored in an old fortress in Hohen Salzberg and the Salzberg region more generally.[20] These included a store of relocated German military and Foreign Office files and archives, which later provided damning evidence against Nuremberg defendant von Ribbentrop, Hitler's Foreign Minister.

At the end of the Second World War, and notwithstanding the urgings of right-wing subordinates such as Frank Wisner, Dulles did not initially give priority to anti-communist espionage over war crimes related projects. This prioritisation began only during the last weeks of his tenure as head of the OSS German Field Office in late 1945. Dulles modified his stance partly owing to the obstruction, and even physical attacks, by Russian forces on his agents and officials whenever they sought fugitive Nazi war criminals located in the Soviet-controlled sector of Germany:[21]

17 Persico, 1979, *op cit*, 327.

18 *Ibid.*

19 Telegram 5377, Bern to London, 30 January 1945: NA, RG 226, Entry 90, Box 6. More generally, records relating to OSS plans for Germany are located at NA, RG 226, Entry 190, Boxes 25, 32. The available records do not indicate whether Dulles was entirely successful in including these particular émigrés within these OSS teams but the fact that Dulles' staff unearthed the documentation already discussed perhaps indicate that his efforts were not entirely unsuccessful.

20 Nuremberg Trials transcript/IMT, Vol 6, 122 (which confirms this fortress as a storage place for all manner of looted cultural and artistic items as well as documentation). OSS's John English discovered '10 tons of damning records behind the bricked-up walls of the castle dungeon'. Dunlop, 1982, *op cit*, 536.

21 Mosely, *op cit*, 228.

> Once Wisner announced that they had found a German general who was wanted for war crimes, and a team was sent to bring him in. It was ambushed on the way back, the Americans battered with rifle butts, the general snatched by the reds. As a result of this and other incidents, all allied forces were banned from the Russian zone, though Red Army officers continued to move freely in the Allied zones where they picked up Germans they claimed were wanted Nazis. Allied officers suspected they were simply hunting down left-wingers who happened to be anti-communist.[22]

Richard Helms, another of Dulles' subordinates who was later appointed as CIA Director, has suggested to Persico that, as the OSS German Office initially headed by Dulles: 'helped prepare evidence for the war crimes trials, they were already keeping one eye on the Soviets'. Helms has recalled that Dulles was pro-active in 'striking a bargain' with German General Reinhard Gehlen as part of this early phase of the emerging Cold War.[23] In other words, certain of Dulles' interventions on behalf of specific individuals potentially vulnerable to war crimes prosecution, such as Gehlen and Wolff, probably did not reflect any pro-Nazi sympathies on his part. Instead, his interventions on their behalf probably stemmed from either his sense of moral obligation in response to their prior intelligence cooperation in, for example Operation Sunrise, combined with an understandable disillusionment that, from 1945 onwards, the Soviets were increasingly exploiting the Nazi war crimes issue for ulterior political reasons hostile to the national security interests of the West.

Having focused on a number of Dulles' contributions to the Nuremberg process, it is now necessary to widen the focus of this chapter. This will be achieved by examining how OSS officials carried out investigations into looted art, and gathered documentary and visual evidence, including atrocity film and organisational charts.[24] These will provide the headings under which this chapter will discuss the details of the OSS's contribution.

It would be equally possible, however, for us to examine a range of other contributions under different headings. These alternative headings could include the preparation and transfer of biographical records on specific atrocities and war crimes suspects[25] and monitoring and participation in the

22 *Ibid.* 23 Persico, 1978, *op cit*, 335.

24 These charts were later presented in a courtroom that OSS officials had adapted to facilitate the prosecution's deployment of novel types of visual evidence, including films.

25 'Gathering information on Nazi Criminal Acts, July 1943': NA, RG 226, Entry 92, Box 330, Folder 3: 'List of War Criminals,' 4 July 1945: NA, RG 226, Entry 215, Box 1.

formulation of trial strategy,[26] including earlier Soviets trials.[27] Other possible headings include Donovan's assignment to Jackson numerous OSS legal, research and technical staff;[28] the preparation of lists of potential defendants (including SS officials, industrialists and Nazi organisations);[29] and potential trial witnesses.[30] Additional themes could include how OSS officials conducted interrogations with both Nuremberg defendants, including Göring, Funk, and Ley,[31] and those who were thought to have incriminating information,[32] and monitoring the whereabouts of suspected war criminals, including any escape routes to Latin America.[33] Finally, it would possible to address the extensive role OSS–R&A and OSS–SI officials played in both securing affidavits from anti-Nazi Germans for the Nuremberg prosecutors, and helping with the detection and arrest of fugitive war crimes suspects.

According to Persico, German agents of the OSS were apparently far more effective in searching and arresting fugitive Nazi war crimes suspects than other intelligence officials drafted in from Britain and the US: 'The rounding up of key Nazis and their replacement by decent democratic leaders proceeded far more effectively where OSS agents had operated than where Allied military governments lacked reliable, first-hand knowledge of local personalities.'[34] Former OSS–R&A official Stuart Hughes has recalled how, in the immediate post-war months, his colleagues based in Salzburg Austria had to: 'flush out the local Gauleiter [regional Nazi Party leader] who had taken to the hills . . . shortly after my arrival I saw him led in, obviously struggling

26 'United States Plans for Post War Trials of War Criminals, 1943': NA, RG 226, Entry 92, Box 357, Folder 51. James Donovan also assisted Jackson's staff, particularly Murray Bernays, with the preparation of a formal trial planning agreement in May 1945, whilst General Donovan served on Jackson's high-level preparation committee during the mid-summer of 1945.

27 R&A Report 1988, 'Russian Intentions to Punish War Criminals', 27 June 1944: NA, RG 226, Entry 194, Box 126, Folder 495.

28 For examples of staff involvement generally and regarding evidence-gathering see: 'War Crimes Information 1945–1946': NA, RG 226, Entry 92, Box 596, Folders 18–20; 'Channelling of war crimes materials May–August 1945': NA, RG 226, Entry 92, Box 614, Folder 42.

29 Re I. G. Farben and Nazi organisations responsible for war crimes, see: NA, RG 226, Entry 146, Box 36, Folders 459 and 467 respectively; 'Czechoslovakia, list of war criminals, March 1943': NA, RG 226, Entry 92, Box 269, Folder 15.

30 'German Personalities': NA, RG 226, Entry 146, Box 35, Folders 451, 453.

31 NA, RG 226, Entry 146, Box 217, Folder 3011.

32 For examples of interrogations, see NA, RG 226, Entry 146, Box 35, Folders 451, 453; NA, RG 226, Entry 146, Box 36, Folders 457. Details of these wider contributions are clear from various OSS war crimes memorandum: NA, RG 226, Entry 146, Box 192, Folders 2714–14; RG, 226, Entry 146, Box 2865, and are discussed in more detail in our next chapters examining the persecution and extermination of the Jews, which in one sense can be taken as a case study illustrating such wider participation.

33 'OSS Intelligence Liaison Office Memos' 1944–46, which include details on the locations and identities of German war criminals: NA, RG 226, Entry 92, Box 255, Folders 1–3.

34 Persico, 1978, *op cit*, 334.

to conceal his fright . . . I left him stewing in his fear.'[35] Furthermore, certain OSS officials were active in arranging for the identification and arrest for war crimes committed against agents involved in specific OSS missions, such as the Dupont/Dawes and Ginny operations.[36]

Although for purposes of exposition the topics to which entire chapters and sub-sections have been devoted will be discussed separately, they are, in one sense, interrelated. For example, although a discussion of the contribution of OSS officials to the redesign of the Nuremberg Palace of Justice may initially appear irrelevant to evidence regarding atrocities, the team involved were specifically instructed to include provision for the screening of atrocity film evidence in a manner that was consistent with the 'majesty' of formal court proceedings. Equally, the overlapping, internally contested and confused jurisdictions within the repressive arms of the Nazi state, including the German Order Police,[37] and the Waffen-SS, meant that the legal determination of lines of command (and hence potential legal responsibility for atrocities against civilians) would have been difficult to demonstrate without the OSS's organisational charts displayed in specially adapted panels. Hence, this section will examine how OSS officials contributed their expertise on design and visual presentations of complicated data to the task of reconstructing the Nuremberg Palace of Justice. OSS officials also redesigned and rebuilt this courtroom in a manner that would facilitate the display of a series of large organisational charts and the screening of films produced by their colleagues within other branches of the same organisation.

Designing the courtroom as a stage for a media event

During the preparation for the Nuremberg trials during the early summer of 1945, a contingent from the OSS Field Presentation Branch was assigned to the task of redesigning the Nuremberg courtroom so that films and organisational charts of different sectors of the Nazi regime, including the SS and Gestapo, could be more readily grasped.[38] These large-scale organisational charts clarified the complex and changing chains of command and lines of responsibility within various Nazi organisations. If, during the trials, this information had been articulated in a purely verbal manner, then it would soon have confused and bored the world media, not to mention the assorted lawyers. Under Donovan's command, the OSS had developed a particular

35 S. Hughes, *Gentleman Rebel* (New York: Ticknor and Fields, 1990), 169–70.

36 Persico, 1978, *op cit*, 334.

37 Amongst these forces were locally recruited paramilitary killing units.

38 'Presentation History': NA, RG 266, Entry 99, Box 76, File 44a; 'History of Presentation in OSS' (Preliminary Draft): NA, RG 226, Entry 99, Box 102, File 105.

expertise in the creation and deployment of such presentational devices. As Katz notes:

> Donovan had, in his civilian law practice, frequently supported his arguments with arresting visual devices. Behind the battle cry, 'One picture is worth a thousand words,' he vigorously promoted these practices . . . he allocated a remarkable 24.9 percent of his first annual budget toward the design of visual presentations. How could the latest techniques be applied so as to enable the President to absorb, in a one- or two-hour, multi-media briefing session, masses of intelligence data that, in written form, might take months to assimilate?[39]

Katz then suggests that Donovan's emphasis upon visual presentation was put to good effect with respect to the Nuremberg and other post-war projects:

> Through their pioneering experiments in the visual display of information in the propaganda war, in service of the War Crimes trials at Nuremberg and, finally, in the waning months of the organization, in preparation for the founding conference of the United Nations in San Francisco; they left a small but indelible mark on history.[40]

Katz's statement is a fair generalisation as far it goes. However, for the purposes of this book at least, it needs more detailed supplementation and further substantiation. In May 1945, the office of the OSS's Chief Counsel, James Donovan, circulated a memorandum to his colleagues outlining a comprehensive programme 'to demonstrate Nazi guilt clearly to the world'. This noted that:

> The role of the Presentation Branch . . . includes the collection of evidence; the preparation of graphic materials for use in the trial briefs and during the proceedings; and the architect planning and layout of the courtroom itself . . . with the legitimacy of the tribunal at stake, the designers were now challenged to solve a barrage of technical problems in ways that did not compromise its dignity, its dominance, or its authenticity.[41]

Dan Kiley was an important part of the OSS's operation in this area. Kiley's secret instructions were that the Palace of Justice should be redesigned in

39 B. Katz, 'The Arts of War: "Visual Presentation" and National Intelligence', (1996) 12 *Design Issues* 1–23 at 3.

40 *Ibid*, 5.

41 C. P. Kantianis to Lt James Donovan; 'Staging of Trials. The Courtroom of the International Tribunal', 12 June 1945: NA, RG 226, Entry 85, Box 42, File 687.

order to be: 'Unified, orderly, and dignified . . . to reflect the scales of justice.' In an important interview, Kiley states:[42]

> Our office made the charts showing the Nazi organisation and the culprits and everything. [showing photos] I had charts up on here, and the movie screens. That's a screen that goes up, and then there's a place where I could pull several charts out and show them from there. You see, that's the prisoners there, and that's where I was leaning against. The courtroom is sort of like this [sketches]. There's a balcony like this above. This is where the charts are shown. I had beautiful green drapes along the windows, like this. I wanted a neutral kind of soft colour. It wasn't jazzy but it was nice.[43]

In short, Kiley's task was to incorporate novel presentation devices and facilities into the very structure of the redesigned Palace of Justice at Nuremberg to enable the display of OSS trial evidence, particularly film and large charts. These modifications had to be incorporated in a way that avoided diminishing the formality and aura of this courtroom. The next section will further develop this theme.

Facilitating media coverage: controversies and logistical support

The extent to which the Nuremberg trials were to be organised as media events, or 'show trials', became one of the bones of contention between Jackson and General Donovan. If the trials were to become such a memorable historic event, which drew a line under the human rights atrocities committed systematically by the Nazi dictatorship, they needed to both attract and sustain a protracted form of media coverage, which Jackson's preferred trial strategy would, according to Donovan and others, jeopardise.

In pursuit of Donovan's wider agenda, OSS propaganda specialists had developed ample wartime experience of managing and manipulating media coverage. If Jackson was to succeed with his ambitious goal of creating a historic precedent designed to re-assert the rule of law and to outlaw 'waging aggressive war', then it was important that the trial be widely reported. This, in turn, required that the courtroom had to be redesigned to provide ample space, material and facilities for the world press and various 'newsfilm' agencies, which had to be given special access to the output of the custom- built sound recording system. However, this had to be incorporated in a manner that avoided turning the entire proceedings into a 'media spectacle', which

42 Kiley, 1998, *op cit*, 15. 43 *Ibid.*

would risk trivialising both the gravity of the proceedings and the important issues at stake.

As a result, OSS's Dan Kiley designed a special room built for journalists covering the trials, with a large glass window through which they could view proceedings without drawing attention to themselves, whilst also following the verbal exchanges through a specially 'piped in' sound system. Kiley's recollections, which quote his original R&A Branch instructions, give further details of OSS's contribution, aspects of which were apparently completed only at the very last moment:

> The floor below the courtroom was the pressroom, and I designed all the tables and stuff. They had to have lots of layout tables because documents were released, and the different newsmen picked up their documents and so forth there. 'Responsibility for the collection of visual evidence was assigned to the Field Photographic Branch, but the established machinery of Presentation Branch has been co-ordinated into this effort, and also into the work of the War Crimes Office, JAG [Judge Advocate General]. Presentation Branch is using its established contacts with newsreel company libraries the foreign information services and the Signal Corps in Astoria, as well as its European agent . . . Motion picture film when located . . .' – that's Research & Analysis Department of OSS. . . . Some German woman worked all night sewing carpets down; [they] finished the morning of the trial. Göring came in first, sat, then Hess, and the whole business lined up, while I was leaning against here. And I was that close to Göring. . . . Then up above there was an attic, and William L. Shirer was here, Kaltenbaum was here, and I made sealed glass windows, so they could do radio from there. And there were photographers; also, there were more here-writers – and Associated Press, and all that. So that's the diagram of the whole courtroom right there you see. We made a model of it. You see, this is the balcony here. This is for VIPs. This is for most of the staff, and all the different lawyers involved.[44]

The OSS's manipulation of the media was double-edged. There is evidence that, during May 1945, the OSS encouraged early trials of lesser war criminals in order to counter media criticism of undue delay that was likely to place 'a great deal of heat' upon the prosecutors. Jackson accepted this suggested strategy for deflecting such pressure by expediting 'the trial by normal military tribunals of a number of cases which were violations of ordinary laws of war and sort of things military tribunals ordinarily clean up very promptly'.[45] This role was positively encouraged by Jackson, who was

44 Kiley, 1998, *op cit*, 16–17.

45 See Jackson's Diary Entries for 17 May 1945, *Jackson Papers*, LCO, Box 95.

interested in exploiting the media so that these trials could realise his aim of becoming publicly regarded as a historical event in themselves.[46] As preparations for the major trials came to fruition during the late summer of 1945, the OSS's specialists in creating 'newsworthy stories' (including film images of the Nazis' atrocities) became increasingly important contributors.

On the other hand, during this pre-trial period the potential conflict between the institutional imperatives governing intelligence agencies and war crimes prosecutors came to a head regarding the OSS's attempts to apply its familiar tactics of media manipulation and psychological warfare to the forthcoming Nuremberg trials in a way that exceeded Jackson's rather more legalistic agenda. The OSS's specialists in manipulating media coverage under the guise of 'public relations' became important through their ability to construct favourable press releases and to stage-manage news conferences in support of the interests shared by the prosecutors and the OSS itself. For example, the assignments for the vital 'London phase' of the pre-trial preparations included not only the OSS's leaders, General Donovan as the most senior member of the ten persons who comprised Jackson's 'Board of Strategy, but also Gordon Dean, this agency's expert in journalistic affairs. Dean was to 'be kept advised on all phases of the work and will handle all contacts with press, radio, or other communications and supervise any activities directed to the public information'. This OSS official was responsible, with two assistants, for all aspects of press and public relations for the trial.[47]

Organisational charts

Another important part of the Visual Presentation Branch's contribution was to try to simplify, in a graphic form, the complex internal structure of the various Nazi organisations. To achieve this goal, slides had to be prepared from large paper charts, and facilities designed and built to allow for their projection. The charts themselves had to be of a kind that explained this organisational structure in a manner that would not only help interrogators focus their questions but also help with the organisation of trial briefs. Furthermore, prosecutors deployed 'blow up' versions of these charts within the trial itself to help clarify lines of command responsibility, institutional

46 Once the relationship between Jackson's office and OSS was formalised in May 1945, OSS support on strategic questions varied from providing propaganda assistance from OSS staff who had previously worked as journalists regarding the preparation of press releases and the 'stage management' of press conferences to strategic planning regarding the entire trial. Jackson was well aware of the importance of media management, describing Lord Beaverbrook (as distinct from any political or industrial leader) as 'probably the most powerful man in Britain by reason of his newspaper control'. Jackson had personally met with Beaverbrook.

47 See 'Assignments for London phase of the work', 28 June 1945, LOC, Jackson Papers, Box 106.

hierarchies and hence degrees of potential legal responsibility and accountability for the issuing of orders to commit unlawful acts. Once again, OSS officials had to design these unprecedented facilities in a manner that did not appear to be too conspicuous to avoid subverting the formality of the courtroom more generally. A memorandum from Taylor to Donovan indicates that the question of the most appropriate deployment of 'visual presentation devices (charts, graphs, models) to dramatise particular proof' was still being discussed during early November 1945:

> The subject matter of these proceedings is rather frighteningly broad and every legitimate device for simplification and emphasis must be used. Charts, graphs etc will be most useful in this connection, and they should be used freely in presenting the case. They will be particularly useful in presenting the evidence with respect to the criminal organisations and groups.[48]

One of the design team, Dan Kiley, has recalled in suitably vivid and dramatic terms, some of the contacts that had to be made in preparing for the trials, and the wider range of the Presentation Branch's mission in this field:

> I didn't have any direction. I had to do it myself. But our office in Washington – OSS – had a directive report that outlined what the purpose of the trials was. It's the document that got me started. Well, let me just quickly read part of it. 'Presentation Branch Work on War Crimes Project. June 14, 1945.' 'Work of the Presentation Branch has five main parts. (1) Participation and collection of evidence.' Our OSS people were on the road. As a matter of fact, I met two. They were like G-men, gangsters; you know, mobster-types. I met them in Paris, and they had captured these films. They had guns on both sides. They were little, kind of rubber-soled people, you know, like Edward G. Robinson. (2) Preparation of materials, especially charts for inclusion in trial briefs. (3) Preparation of materials, charts, exhibits, etc. for trial. First for the trial briefs and then for the trial. (4) Planning and layout of courtroom, its facilities and its mechanical operation. (5) Production of public relations material and consultation on public relations program.'[49]

Providing documentary and eye-witness evidence

OSS staff contributed to the production of documentary evidence and reports addressing or at least including different aspects of Nazi war criminality that

48 Taylor to Jackson, 3 November 1945, LOC, Jackson Papers, Box 111, 2.
49 1998, *op cit*, 26–27.

were fed into the Nuremberg process. The most important were the extensive series of R&A reports that OSS research analysts, particularly the Neumann group, produced both during the war and immediately afterwards, a group of which were specifically commissioned by Justice Jackson.[50] Other reports and investigative work, particularly Neumann's research on the persecution of Christian Churches, were controversial within Jackson's organisation. However, this was not due to the inadequacy of Neumann's investigations and report but rather because, within continental Europe, Neumann had 'been examining people about religious matters' in a way that appeared excessively independent of central control by either Amen or Storey, both of whom sought to appropriate his group's expertise to their own sub-sections.[51] (Neumann denied acting outside his instructions or 'using Jackson's name without authority'.)[52]

Senior prosecutors who had reviewed the OSS R&A reports commented that they were most useful background studies which, although not always directly evidentiary, in the manner of a prosecution brief against an individual defendant, they did contain 'a considerable amount of evidence buried in them, as [Murray] Bernays suggested and [Telford] Taylor agreed'.[53] At a prosecutors' pre-trial planning meeting of 11 August 1945, the senior prosecutors noted that Neumann should: 'stay here [London] in the capacity of a consultant to the lawyers who are analysing the R&A studies and trying to put them into evidentiary form'.[54] Jackson specifically requested that Neumann's expertise was vital to his senior prosecutors. Hence, he was to 'act in an advisory capacity explaining [R&A] studies etc'.[55] Partly with reference to these R&A reports, Jackson noted that: 'OSS did excellent work of laying foundation [for the case] and there is still room for valuable OSS contribution.'[56]

These R&A reports were also useful as guides for members of the Interrogation Division of Jackson's organisation, headed by Colonel Amen. Indeed, internal OCC correspondence indicates that 'Colonel Amen' had appointed 'a group of men scrutinising the [R&A] studies to get out of them what will be useful to interrogators'.[57] By mid-August 1945, and with the future of the OSS itself in doubt, Justice decided against commissioning any fresh reports and to concentrate on their supplementation with additional documentary and other eye-witness evidence from continental Europe.[58]

50 See minutes of prosecutors meeting 11 August 1945, noting that full-time OSS staff were to work under either colonels Storey or Amen, and 'work on projects to make studies and furnish us with the end results'. LOC, Jackson Papers, Box 107.

51 *Ibid.*

52 535 [Neumann] to Whitney, 15 August, 1945 – replying Whitney to Neumann 14 August 1945: Jackson Papers, *op cit*, Box 111.

53 Minutes of prosecutors' meeting, 11 August 1945, *ibid.*

54 *Ibid.*

55 Whitney to Neumann, 14 August 1945: Jackson Papers, *op cit*, Box 111.

56 *Ibid.*

57 Minutes of prosecutors' meeting, 11 August 1945, *op cit.*

58 *Ibid.*

Producing the *Nazi Concentration Camps* film

Cinematic evidence of Nazi atrocities was produced by an OSS team of Hollywood producers and technicians, which included John Ford, George Stevens and Budd Schulberg, operating under the overall administrative supervision of James Donovan's 'special projects' sub-division of the US prosecution organisation. The film was still being edited in the fortnight before it was finally shown on 29 November 1945.[59]

> We have just completed its final revision and it is now in the Berlin laboratories, which are working in three eight-hour shifts of German civilians. The principal changes are [page 4] (a) the dropping of two weak PW camps sequences, and (b) the adding of some new – and excellent – Mauthausen coverage, in which formerly we had only the shots of Lt. Jack Taylor. This film is due back here on 23 November, which should give us ample time to present it.[60]

This cinematic documentation of war criminality by using graphic film of atrocities as proof of criminal wrongdoing was first shown at Nuremberg and then replayed to numerous cinema audiences across the world; even as the Nuremberg trials were still in progress. This marked a wholly new legal method of developing a prosecution case. It will become clear that the OSS's film detailing atrocities exerted a powerful psychological effect upon both the world's journalistic media and the Nuremberg defendants themselves, and – had the OSS survived as a peacetime agency – would have represented a triumph for its wider media strategy. On the other hand, this controversy was more than offset by a more general pattern of well-received cooperation between OSS presentation staff and the Nuremberg prosecutors, a process of liaison that had started relatively early in the pre-trial phase. The review document produced from Colonel Bernays by Kaplan and Farr on 9 June 1945 confirms this, providing a concise summary of early liaisons between Jackson's office and the Presentation Branch of OSS:

> On 6 June we also conferred for about 2 hours with Mr. Hugh Barton of the Presentation Branch of OSS. Apart from its concern with such

59 See James Donovan 'Memorandum to the Planning Committee' 19 November 1945: Cornell Collection, Vol. 103, 56.03. This memo describes how the evidentiary charts, trial exhibits, and atrocity films (3–6) have been made and the manner in which they will be presented. This memorandum includes Donovan's account of how and when he was proposing to use these films in court. It also reveals that the OSS had tracked down SS films of a concentration camp (8 mm, about 90 seconds) and the Warsaw Ghetto (both of which were edited by the SS to delete all incriminating appearances of SS personnel).

60 *Ibid.*

> projects as preparing films of the trial and making arrangements for staging the trial, Preparation Branch has two functions in connection with the preparation of the case, (1) it is presently cataloguing the film which is now being collected and reviewed by the Field Photographic Branch and which may serve as evidence at the trial, so that it will be able to dig up on request all the film on any particular subject, such as all pictures of Göring, or all shots of concentration camps; (2) it will work with R&A in preparing charts, graphs, and other visual types of presentation of the material being prepared by R&A. It cannot, of course, do much to accomplish its second function until some trial briefs are at least in draft form.[61]

During early June 1945, members of Jackson's team were also making contact with the Field Photographic Branch of OSS in order to assess what contribution this branch could make to the proposed trial:

> On 7 June we conferred with Lt. English of the Field Photographic Branch. That Branch is charged with the responsibility for collecting and screening all film that may be useful as evidence in the case. It has already collected in Washington about 25,000 feet and is now screening in New York about 20,000 feet. The film available in this country is limited pretty much to German newsreels and propaganda film. OSS is also currently screening in Europe captured German film and is searching for German films in neutral countries. We offered to assist both Presentation and Field Photographic Branches in any way possible and told Mr. Barton and Lt. English to call on us at any time. They both indicated that our assistance will be welcome and will be called for.[62]

During the war, General Donovan had employed a number of film-makers, including John Ford,[63] and Kanin.[64] These cinematic talents were also mobilised for the production of atrocity and other films for the Nuremberg trials. As Kiley notes:

61 Memorandum to Bernays, 9 June 1945, Jackson Papers, Box 85, LOC. 62 *Ibid.*

63 In 1942, the Office of Strategic Services commissioned director John Ford to produce a film detailing the surprise Japanese attack on Pearl Harbor that precipitated US entry into The Second World War. The result was an 83-minute film, *December 7th*, named after the date of the attack in 1941. Even before the US was at war, in 1940 Ford had assembled film crew (a 'private army of Hollywood technicians'), and was lobbying Washington to support his group. When war broke out in December 1941 his film unit was formed into the OSS's Field Photographic Branch.

64 For example, after being posted to the London office of OSS, Kanin co-directed, with Carol Reed, *The True Glory*, a film based upon military footage; it was named best film of 1945 by the National Board of Review and later won an Oscar for best documentary. See 'Garson Kanin', *Daily Telegraph*, Obituaries Section, 20 March 1999.

> Besides designing the facilities, OSS Presentation Branch had to document Nazi organisations by way of charts, document the atrocities by way of film, etc. Budd Schulberg, [who] wrote the books *What Makes Sammy Run?* and *The Harder They Fall*, was in charge of that unit. John Ford was in charge of the photography unit of OSS. We had the top people in the country.[65]

Members of Neumann's war crimes group, including his deputy, Dr Kellerman, successfully sought out film evidence of the destruction of the Warsaw ghettos later shown in the trial itself.[66]

When introducing the film, James Donovan stated: 'These motion pictures speak for themselves in evidencing life and death in Nazi concentration camps . . .'[67] Laurence Douglas, a legal academic, interprets Donovan's claim as involving the suggestion that moving images could capture aspects of the unprecedented atrocities in ways that would not otherwise have been possible to represent through, for example, documentary or even eye-witness testimony:

> The filmic witness could offer pictures where speech failed; it could produce visual knowledge of atrocities that resisted summary in the words of eyewitness testimonials. Such a view echoed an understanding that both saw documentary film as capable of offering a more complete and transparent window upon the 'real,' and anticipated the crisis of representation that has come to characterize efforts to find an idiom capable of capturing the Holocaust's central horror. The representational problems raised by Nazi genocide are familiar to Holocaust scholars.[68]

Indeed, the formidable OSS expertise in film was mobilised for one of the most dramatic, and rhetorically powerful, pieces of evidence against the defendants at Nuremberg: the concentration camp atrocity film. The highly partisan and one-sided critique directed against the OSS by various 'revisionist' accounts of the Nuremberg trial could, in part, stem from their role in providing the most graphic and damning evidence of concentration camp atrocities, which stand out as widely circulated counter-evidence to Holocaust denial. One difficulty that Jackson faced was the prospect that some of the evidence of atrocities was so extreme, that the Nazis' themselves recognised that even the testimony of eye-witnesses would appear incredible to others. Furthermore, the fact that spreading false stories of atrocities had often formed part of Allied wartime propaganda, dating back at least to the First World War, did not assist Jackson's task. As Douglas notes:

65 1998, *op cit*, 22. 66 Kellerman, 1997, *op cit*, 346–48.
67 Recorded at 2 *IMT, supra*, at 433. 68 1995, *op cit*, 451–52.

> The Nazis themselves had recognized that the incredible nature of their atrocities would cast long shadows of doubt upon any allegedly eyewitness reports. Primo Levi describes how inmates at concentration camps heard the frequent taunt from their captors that should they survive, their stories would not be believed: 'And even if some proof should remain and some of you survive, people will say that the events you describe are too monstrous to be believed: they will say that they are the exaggerations of Allied propaganda and will believe us, who will deny everything, and not you.'[69,70]

The film itself was entered into evidence as Document No. 2430-PS; it is still available commercially. Nineteen pages of documentation associated with its production, including affidavits attesting to the truth of the film. The complete text of the film's narration, and the interview with OSS Jack Taylor, remain available from the Donovan Collection at Cornell Law School.[71] Given the key and controversial role this film played at Nuremberg and in subsequent Nazi war crimes trials and 'Holocaust denial' proceedings, it is worthwhile to describe in detail how the prosecution deployed this evidence before the IMT.

The film was screened almost at the start of the trial on the afternoon of 29 November 1945. On one insider's account, that of former OSS official Bernard Meltzer, the overall evidence about concentration camps presented later in the trials had been redrafted from original Army and other sources very much 'at the last moment', and that – largely for strategic reasons – it had been decided to show the film 'out of sequence' from such documentary evidence:

> . . . [H]orrible and vivid evidence regarding the camps had already been introduced out of order so as to meet the perceived need to add drama, emotion, and excitement to a primarily documentary case. That evidence consisted of films taken by American and British troops when they had liberated Dachau, Buchenwald and Belsen just about fifty years ago today. Those films were literally sickening, even for the tough combat-weary troops. The films showed living skeletons and frightful conditions. They also showed the naked bodies of the dead stacked in large burial

69 Douglas is citing Primo Levi, *The Drowned and the Saved*, R. Rosenthal (trans.) (New York: Vintage International, 1989), 11–12, paraphrasing Simon Wiesenthal, *The Murderers Among Us*, J. Wechsberg (ed.) (Columbus, OH: McGraw-Hill, 1967).

70 L. Douglas, 'Film as Witness', (1995) *Yale Law Journal* 450–51.

71 Cornell Collection, Vol. 9, Subdivision 16.03: 'Prisoners of War and Concentration Camps'.

> pits or sometimes sprawled on the ground. Some of these defendants found those films very hard to stomach indeed.[72]

Sydney Alderman, associate trial counsel, was given the task of preparing the IMT for the presentation of what was widely recognised as the prosecution's most dramatic evidence of the Nazi atrocities. The court transcript indicates that the prosecutors were almost apologetic for asking to show the OSS film on 29 November 1945, not least because the earlier evidence on the different phases of Nazi aggression had followed a logical order:

> Logically, if the Tribunal please, we should proceed at this point with the story about Czechoslovakia . . . We have had to change our plans somewhat from a strictly logical order, and the plan at present is that on Monday I shall go forward with the Czechoslovakian part of the aggressive war case. At this point it is planned by our staff to show a motion picture, and it will take some few minutes to make physical arrangements in the courtroom, so that if the Court should feel like recessing those arrangements could be made.[73]

After a brief recess the prosecution resumed, with Storey reiterating how the screening of the film represented an 'adjustment' to their 'presentation to some extent'. Another US prosecutor, Thomas Dodds, then attempted to 'frame' the suggested 'meaning' of the film that the prosecution intended the IMT to gain from this evidence:

> The film this afternoon, at the request of the defendants' counsel, made in writing to the Court, was exhibited to defendants' counsel the day before yesterday evening in this courtroom. I personally requested Dr. Dix to convey the invitation to defence counsel to witness the film. Eight of them came. Dr. Dix advised me kindly that he would not come unless he were forced to come. I now present Mr. Dodd, who will have charge of the presentation.
>
> MR. DODD: If it please the Tribunal, the prosecution for the United States will at this time present to the Tribunal, with its permission, a documentary film on concentration camps. This is by no means the entire proof which the prosecution will offer with respect to the subject of concentration camps, but this film which we offer represents in a brief

72 Bernard Meltzer, in the Nuremberg symposium: 'The Fifth Annual Ernst C. Steifel Symposium: 1945–1995: Critical Perspectives On The Nuremberg Trials And State Accountability: Panel I: Telford Taylor Panel: Critical Perspectives On The Nuremberg Trials', published in (1995) 12 *New York Law School Journal of Human Rights* 453, 513.

73 http://www.vex.net/~nizkor/hweb/imt/tgmwc/tgmwc-01/tgmwc-01-08-06.shtml.

> and unforgettable form an explanation of what the words 'concentration camp' imply.[74]

Dodd then proceeded to try to rationalise the screening of the film out of any logical sequence. He argued that evidence regarding the 'planning and preparation for aggressive war', which had previously been presented, was somehow bound up with evidence of the impact of concentration camp atrocities largely discovered at the end of war. Aspects of Neumann's argument that Nazi racist terrorism was not only an end in itself but also a means to a wider end, also resonate in this account:

> This subject arises appropriately in the narrative of events leading up to the actual outbreak of aggressive war, which, as Mr. Alderman's presentation shows, was planned and prepared by the Nazi conspirators. We propose to show that concentration camps were not an end in themselves but, rather, they were an integral part of the Nazi system of government. As we shall show, the black-shirted guards of the S.S. and the Gestapo stood ranged behind the official pages of the Reichsgesetzblatt. We intend to prove that each and every one of these defendants knew of the existence of these concentration camps; that fear and terror and nameless horror of the concentration camps were instruments by which the defendants retained power and suppressed the opposition to any of their policies, including, of course, their plans for aggressive war. By this means they enforced the controls imposed upon the German people, as required to execute these plans, and obliterated freedom in Germany and in the countries invaded and occupied by the armies of the Third Reich. Finally, we ask the Tribunal in viewing this film to bear in mind the fact that the proof to be offered at a later stage of this trial will show that on some of the organisations charged in this indictment lies the responsibility for the origin, the control and the maintenance of the whole concentration camp system. On the S.S., the S.D. – a part of the S.S. which tracked down the victims – upon the Gestapo, which committed the victims to the camps, and upon other branches of the S.S. which were in charge of the atrocities committed therein.[75]

Immediately after this presentation, Dodd announced that he was handing over the formal introduction of the film to James Donovan, who had of course organised and supervised its production. Donovan's main role was to offer evidence of the veracity and source of the film images and the narration (supposedly based on notes taken by the photographers themselves). Donovan

74 *Ibid*, 266.
75 *Ibid*.

sought such verification partly by reference to the sworn affidavits of those responsible for the film's technical production: affidavits that were also part of the opening images of the film itself.

Although not mentioned in the transcript, the film contained images derived mainly, but not exclusively, from the US Army Signal Corps of the impact of ill-treatment from the following concentration camps: Leipzig, Penig, Ohrdruf, Hadamar, Breendonck, Hannover, Arnstadt, Nordhausen, Mauthausen, Buchenwald, Dachau and Bergen-Belsen. It includes images of gas chambers and references to various atrocities, including mass murder, torture and so-called medical experiments. The transcript's only account following the material on the affidavits was to record in brackets, 'The film was then shown', with Storey stating, perhaps unnecessarily, that: 'That concludes the presentation.' It then states: 'The Tribunal adjourned until 30th November, 1945, at 1000 hours.'

One potential legal difficulty with the film as a piece of trial evidence is that it does not depict the war crimes of specific defendants as these were actually taking place because it was taken shortly after the liberation of the camps. In one sense, it represented 'hearsay evidence' that could, in principle, have been excluded under rules of evidence that apply within domestic criminal trials. The Charter establishing the International Military Tribunal at Nuremberg did not, however, prohibit such hearsay evidence, probably because James Donovan was heavily involved in drafting these rules in anticipation of OSS film evidence.[76]

Jackson referred to the atrocities film during his opening statement as providing evidence of the shocking nature of Nazi genocide:

> We will show you these concentration camps in motion pictures, just as the Allied armies found them when they arrived . . . Our proof will be disgusting and you will say I have robbed you of your sleep . . . I am one who received during this war most atrocity tales with suspicion and scepticism. But the proof here will be so overwhelming that I venture to predict not one word I have spoken will be denied.[77]

James Donovan certainly appeared to regard the film evidence of atrocities committed in Nazi concentration camps contained in the OSS film of the same name as 'the most significant in the case'.[78] He also noted: 'My main

76 Its rules were highly permissive admitting all evidence deemed to be of 'probative value' by the IMT. On the other hand, the fact that there was no jury to be prejudiced by dubious evidence meant that one of the usual justifications for the 'hearsay rule' had little relevance in the particular content of the IMT.

77 IMT 2, 130.

78 Donovan to Mary Donovan, undated but early November 1945: James Donovan Collection, Hoover Institute, Box 34, Folder 20.

job is on photographic evidence (movies of concentration camps, speeches by the defendant since 1928, etc.) It's fascinating work because you really re-live the whole period.'[79] Donovan was assisted in his film production work by Lt Budd Schulberg,[80] and later by Ray Kellogg. Donovan appeared to have been sufficiently impressed by the OSS film evidence that he offered General Donovan and Ambassador Murphy previews of the films.[81] In addition, James Donovan went from Nuremberg to Paris in his ultimately successful efforts to track down film evidence of SS concentration camp guards beating and otherwise maltreating their inmates.[82] Donovan 'had the FBI locate the film in the U.S. and had it shipped here to Paris. Now I'm trying to get it made up into regular movie size, etc.'[83] At the start of October 1945, he also liaised closely in Paris with the Army Signal Corps in gathering and refining additional scenes of atrocities.[84] Donovan himself appears to have been proud of the positive media coverage that his Nazi concentration camp film attracted once it was shown on 29 November 1945. Its screening was brought forward from its planned sequence in order to break the monotony created by the dry recitation of documentary evidence.[85] He wrote to his wife stating that one of the purposes of the film evidence was to bring home to the defendants the horrors of the concentration camps, and to have their reaction to these displayed to the court and indirectly to the world media:

> My first films were a tremendous success. Perhaps you read about them. Up to then the defendants had been taking the case very lightly. You should have seen the expression on their faces during the showing. We had little lights sets up so that we could watch them during the showing.[86]

For present purposes, it is worth emphasising the role played within the film of OSS Lt Jack Taylor, since he features as one of the victims of Nazi concentration camps giving cinematic evidence of the nature and extent of atrocities at the Mauthausen death camp.[87] As an inmate of this camp at the time of his liberation, Taylor's account in the film has a particular

79 *Ibid*, Friday letter, undated.

80 A Hollywood writer who wrote a best-seller entitled *What Makes Sammy Run*.

81 *Ibid*, Tuesday letter, undated. 82 *Ibid*, Tuesday undated letter. 83 *Ibid*.

84 *Ibid*, 2 October, Paris.

85 *Ibid*, 7 November 1945: 'I hear that my presentation of the evidence on concentration camps got quite a play in the NY "Times" the other day.'

86 *Ibid*, Monday undated but early to mid-November 1945.

87 On Taylor and other American POWs detained in Mauthausen camp, see M. G. Bard, *Forgotten Victims: The Abandonment of Americans in Hitler's Camps* (Boulder, CO: Westview Press, 1994).

authenticity and resonance.[88] Immediately after his liberation, Taylor opted to remain at Mauthausen in order to gather further incriminating evidence for the proposed war crimes trial of the camp staff. During this period, he also wrote a detailed account of the activities of the *Totenkopf* ('Death's Head') SS staff based at Mauthausen.

Taylor gave indirect testimony at the major Nuremberg trials through the media of cinematic footage in which he recounted certain of his experiences of atrocities at the Mauthausen camp. Although the bulk of the content of *Nazi Concentration Camps* is derived largely from 'raw' footage originally shot by army photographers, Taylor's cinematic evidence appears to be based upon footage he personally arranged to have filmed by his liberators, and which he took away as a personal 'memento'. Apparently, George Stevens arrived at Mauthausen within hours of its liberation to shoot additional footage of Taylor for the film. The OSS successfully recovered Taylor's private footage and incorporated parts of it into the final version of *Nazi Concentration Camps*. There is no sound in the film until Taylor makes his appearance giving oral testimony of different aspects of war criminality. However, since it records Jack Taylor's first-hand description of atrocities he witnessed whilst he was imprisoned at the camp, and his summation of the experiences of other inmates, which he insisted on having verified by at least one other person, his testimony can hardly be regarded as unduly second-hand or speculative. Taylor states on the film that:

> In October '44, I was the first Allied officer to drop onto Austria. I was captured December 1st, by the Gestapo, severely beaten, ah, even though I was in uniform, severely beaten, and, and, considered as a non-prisoner of war. I was taken to Vienna prison where I was held for four months. When the Russians neared Vienna, I was taken to this Mauthausen concentration lager [camp], an extermination camp, the worst in Germany, where we have been starving and, and beaten and killed, ah, fortunately, my turn hadn't come. Ah, two American officers at least have been executed here. Here is the insignia of one, a U.S. naval officer, and here is his dog tag. Here is the army officer, executed by gas in this lager [camp]. Ah . . . there were . . .
>
> [Question: 'How many ways did they execute them?']

88 Austrian concentration camp set up in March 1938. At first, the prisoners were political, but later Jews and Gypsies were also sent there. The number of prisoners was estimated at 199,404, of which 119,000 died. The largest national group there was the Poles. In May 1945, the camp was liberated by the Americans. For details the lives and memories of Austrian civilians living near the Mauthausen concentration camp, see G. Horwitz, *In the Shadow of Death* (New York: Tauris, 1990).

> Five or six ways: by gas, by shooting, by beating, that is beating with clubs, ah, by exposure, that is standing out in the snow, naked, for 48 hours and having cold water put on them, thrown on them in the middle of winter, starvation, dogs, and pushing over a hundred-foot cliff.[89]

Taylor's film testimony is presented against the grim background of Mauthausen camp, and contains graphic images of stacked emaciated corpses and barely living survivors. One remarkable part of his testimony states that 'I am Lt. (senior grade) Jack H. Taylor, U.S. Navy, from Hollywood, California' – and then adds: 'Believe it or not, this is the first time I have ever been in the movies.' Though this short sequence was the only description of the film's presentation in the actual trial transcript, a transcript of the film's narration was included in the volume titled 'Documents and Other Material in Evidence', which was appended to the trial transcript. See 30 *ibid* at 462–72.

Taylor's words have been recycled to some effect in recent years, as interest in the neglect of US personnel caught up in Nazi death camps has revived, following the end of the Cold War. Indeed, the film imagery was used in January 1997 in a press conference held by the US government as part of its efforts to compensate US victims of Nazi concentration camps.[90]

The immediate impact of screening the atrocity film

There are clear difficulties facing many of us today in attempting to imagine the level of shock caused by the first showing of this film upon those who were present in the courtroom over 50 years ago. This is because contemporary film audiences operate in a different cultural landscape in which movie footage of such horrors has become all too familiar. What we can do, however, is to discuss the accounts of those who were present at the original screening, including those who were responsible for keeping a formal record of the defendant's response to this evidence. Dr Henry Kellerman's oral testimony, preserved on the US Holocaust Museum's website, offers a striking commentary of the effects of one of these films upon the defendants:

> When we showed the film 'The Death Mills', which is a documentary we found showing some of the concentration camps and showing some of the scenes from the ghetto in Warsaw. We darkened the courtroom and had only lights shining on the faces of the 22 defendants. And I had opportunity to study the faces while that film was showing in all its

89 These images and Taylor's testimony have been mounted at http://www.jewishvirtuallibrary.org/jsource/Holocaust/mauthfilm.html.

90 http://www.justice.gov/opa/pr/1997/January97/029fcs.htm.

> brutality. And, it was amazing how they fell apart. [Hermann] Göring never looked at it, neither did [Rudolf] Hess. [Hjalmar] Schacht, who maintained all through the trial that he had nothing to do with the atrocities and so turned his back to the screen and crossed his arms in front of him, to indicate that he had, had been a absentee . . . during the Nazi period. [Hans] Frank, the 'Butcher of Poland,' broke into tears. So did [Fritz] Sauckel, who was the labor tsar . . . The only person who looked at the screen with obvious glee and pleasure was [Julius] Streicher who was the so-called Gauleiter [Nazi regional leader] in Bavaria Franconia, and who had been the editor and publisher of this filthy rag the 'Stuermer' [The Attacker], Stormtrooper you might call it. This was his show. He felt that he was vindicated completely by that picture.[91]

It is also worth quoting at length Dr Gilbert's record of the defendants' immediate reactions to these film sequences.[92] Gilbert and his colleague Kelly were 'posted at either end of the defendants' dock and observed the prisoners during the showing of this film'. Gilbert recorded his notes during the showing of the film 'at about 1–2 minute intervals'. Gilbert's extensive diary also recorded entries on the mood immediately before this film was shown:

> Afternoon Session: Göring, Ribbentrop, and Hess had a great laugh over the reading of Göring's telephone conversation with Ribbentrop on the day of Hitler's triumphant entry into Vienna, describing the whole thing as a lark, with birds twittering, etc.

Having set the scene, Gilbert then notes how the film caused a dramatic reversal in the atmosphere within the court, especially amongst the defendants:

> Then the hilarity in the dock suddenly stopped as Commander Donovan announced the showing of a documentary film on Nazi concentration camps as they were found by American troops . . . Schacht objects to being made to look at the film as I ask him to move over; turns away, folds arms, gazes into gallery . . . (Film starts). Frank nods at authentication at introduction of film . . . Fritzsche (who had not seen any part of film before) already looks pale and sits aghast as it starts with scenes of prisoners burned alive in a barn . . . Keitel wipes brow, takes off headphones . . . Hess glares at screen, looking like a ghoul with sunken eyes

91 http://www.ushmm.org/outreach/hkn015m.htm.

92 G. M. Gilbert, *Nuremberg Diary*, 45.

over the footlamp . . . Keitel puts on headphone, glares at screen out of the corner of his eye . . . von Neurath has head bowed, doesn't look . . . Funk covers his eyes, looks as he is in agony, shakes his head . . . Ribbentrop closes his eyes, looks away . . . Sauckel mops brow . . . Frank swallows hard, blinks eyes, trying to stifle tears . . . Fritzsche watches intensely with knitted brow, cramped at the end of his seat, evidently in agony . . . Göring keeps leaning on balustrade, not watching most of the time, looking droopy . . . Funk mumbles something under his breath . . . Streicher keeps watching, immobile except for an occasional squint . . . Funk now in tears, blows nose, wipes eyes, looks down . . . Frick shakes head at illustration of 'violent death' – Frank mutters 'Horrible!' . . . Rosenberg fidgets, peeks at screen, bows head, looks to see how others are reacting . . . Seyss-Inquart stoic throughout . . . Speer looks very sad, swallows hard . . . Defense attorneys are now muttering, 'for God's sake-terrible.' Raeder watches without budging . . . von Papen sits with hand over brow, looking down, has not looked at screen yet . . . Hess keeps looking bewildered . . . piles of dead are shown in a slave labor camp . . . von Schirach watching intensely, gasps, whispers to Sauckel . . . Funk crying now . . . Göring looks sad, leaning on elbow . . . Doenitz has head bowed, no longer watching . . . Sauckel shudders at picture of Buchenwald crematorium oven . . . as human skin lampshade is shown, Streicher says, 'I don't believe that' . . . Göring coughing . . . Attorneys gasping . . . Now Dachau . . . Schacht still not looking . . . Frank nods his head bitterly and says, 'Horrible!' . . . Rosenberg still fidgeting, leans forward, looks around, leans back, hangs head . . . Fritzsche, pale, biting lips, really seems in agony . . . Doenitz has head buried in his hands . . . Keitel now hanging head . . . Ribbentrop looks up at screen as British officer starts to speak, saying he has already buried 17,000 corpses . . . Frank biting his nails . . . Frick shakes his head incredulously at speech of female doctor describing treatment and experiments on female prisoners at Belsen . . . As Kramer is shown, Funk says with choking voice, 'The dirty swine!' . . . Ribbentrop sitting with pursed lips and blinking eyes, not looking at screen . . . Funk crying bitterly, claps hand over mouth as women's naked corpses are thrown into pit . . . Keitel and Ribbentrop look up at mention of tractor clearing corpses, see it, then hang their heads . . . Streicher shows signs of disturbance for first time . . . Film ends.

Another eye-witness account from an American prosecutor confirmed Gilbert's account:

Schacht and Fritzsche refused to look at the screen at all, and turned their heads away. All the rest seemed to have their eyes riveted to it. I wish every school child and adult could be made once a year on V.E-day to see

> this film and a few others at all the theatres in the U.S. to remind them that the Germans are dangerous.[93]

Telford Taylor, a senior Nuremberg prosecutor, had also recorded his recollections of the impact of the film, and his account broadly confirms the dramatic and highly incriminating impact of the film:

> the defendants were among the many who had not seen the film and the effect was stunning. The frightful condition of the living and the cascade of naked corpses pushed by bulldozers into an immense burial ditch were wrenching sights. Dr. Von der Lippe recorded that the film would rob its viewers of sleep and that he heard one of the defence counsel say it had become intolerable to sit in the same room with men like Kaltenbrunner and Frank.

Taylor also observed that: 'Schacht turned his back on the screen to show that he had no connection with such bestiality; Göring tried to brazen it out.' He recalls that the weaker defendants, such as Ribbentrop, Frank and Funk, appeared 'shattered', while others, although in better self-command, were still 'visibly depressed'.[94]

Airey Neave, a lawyer who assisted the British prosecutorial staff at Nuremberg, has also described the impact of the screening of the film in his memoirs.[95] He stated:

> as the lights went up, I looked at the dock. The defendants remained seated as if turned to stone. They were slow to rise when the judges filed out in disgusted silence. During the showing of the film the dock, as a measure of security was picked out by spotlights. Few of the defendants could bear to watch the whole film. Schacht, who had personal experience of a concentration camp, sat with his back to the screen . . . I cannot forget the sudden vision of those twisted faces, some like Funk and Fritsche with tears on their cheeks. I sometimes dream of it. I sought for any signs of true remorse and did not find them. These were crocodile tears. They wept for themselves, not for the dead. They feared for their own necks as they watched films of humble men and women executed by the S.S.[96]

Although all these accounts differ in some respect in their description of the defendants' reaction to *Nazi Concentration Camps*, what is clear is that the

93 Folder L. Felton, private letter, no date, Hoover Library, Felton Collection Ts Germany, F 236.

94 Taylor, 1992, *op cit*, 187. 95 Douglas, 1995, 25.

96 A. Neave, *On Trial in Nuremberg* (Boston, MA: Little, Brown & Co, 1979), 247.

film had a strong and lasting impact on those who witnessed it in the trials. Interestingly, for what it reveals about one of the purposes of the film, the prosecutors made an official record of its impact, which confirms the points already noted above.[97] Gilbert also recorded how the contents of this film appeared to knock the stuffing out of many of the defendants, even the swaggering Göring, whose earlier performances had been most effective in ridiculing the prosecution:

> After the showing of the film, Hess remarks, 'I don't believe it.' Göring whispers to him to keep quiet, his own cockiness quite gone. Streicher says something about 'perhaps in the last days.' Fritzsche retorts scornfully. 'Millions? In the last days? – No.' Otherwise there is a gloomy silence as the prisoners file out of the courtroom.[98]

This atrocities film has also been acknowledged by various of the Nuremberg prosecutors, such as Sprecher, to have made a most dramatic impact upon its immediate audience, and presumably upon the large media contingent covering the early stages of this trial.[99]

According to Gilbert, the powerful effect of this film continued to exert a profound influence upon the defendants, even though its implications varied from case to case. Under the sub-heading 'Evening In Jail' Gilbert's diary notes:

> We immediately went down to the cell block to talk to them individually. The first one was Fritzsche: 'No power in heaven or earth will erase this shame from my country! – not in generations not in centuries! –' Von Schirach seemed fairly well composed, but said, 'I don't know how Germans could do such things.' Frick made some feeble attempts at rationalization – 'I suppose the disruption of communications in the last few months – the bombing and confusion – I don't know.' Funk seemed depressed, and burst into tears as soon as we asked him how he was affected by the film. 'Horrible! Horrible!' he repeated in a choking voice. Streicher admitted the film was 'terrible' without any apparent feeling, . . . Speer showed no outward emotional effects, but said that he was the more resolved to acknowledge a collective responsibility of the Party leadership and absolve the German people of the guilt. Frank was extremely depressed and agitated. As soon as we mentioned the film, he began to cry in abject shame and rage. 'To think that we lived like kings and believed in that beast! – Don't let anybody tell you that they had no idea! . . .' Seyss-Inquart admitted: 'It gets you – But I can hold

97 Burton C. Andrus Collection, Colorado Springs, File 3.

98 Gilbert, *op cit*, 45–46.

99 See court TV interview *op cit*.

> out.' Still trembling with emotion, Doenitz said in half English and half in German, 'How can they accuse me of knowing of such things? They ask me why I didn't go to Himmler to check on the concentration camps. Why that's preposterous! He would have kicked me out as I would have kicked him out if he came to investigate the navy! . . .' We asked von Papen why he didn't watch the picture. 'I didn't want to see Germany's shame,' he admitted. Sauckel was completely unnerved . . . He stretched out his fingers and cried, wild-eyed, 'I'd choke myself with these hands if I thought I had the slightest thing to do with those murders! It is a shame! It is a disgrace for us and for our children – and for our children's children!' Schacht was burning with indignation. 'How dare they make me sit there with those *criminals* and watch a film on concentration camp atrocities! They know that I was an enemy of Hitler and ended up in a concentration camp myself! It is unforgivable!' Von Neurath was rather bewildered, didn't have much to say. Simply pointed out that he wasn't in power when all this went on. Raeder said that he had hardly even heard of concentration camps before. Just heard of three of them, when he made efforts to get some friends out. Jodl was calm, but evidently moved. 'It is shocking. Believe me – the shame of it all is that so many of the youth joined the Party out of idealistic motives.' Keitel was eating, having just returned from a conference with his defense attorney. He appeared to have forgotten the film until we mentioned it. He stopped eating and said with his month half full, 'It is terrible. When I see such things, I'm ashamed of being a German! – It was those dirty SS swine! . . . – I'll never be able to look people in the face again.' Hess seemed confused, kept mumbling, 'I don't understand – I don't understand.' Ribbentrop had a visible tremor of the hands, and looked utterly bewildered. 'Hitler couldn't even have looked at such a film himself. I don't understand. I don't even think that Himmler could have ordered such things. I don't understand.' Rosenberg was even more nervous than usual. 'It's an awful thing, even if the Russians did do the same thing – terrible – terrible – terrible . . . This just weakens our whole defense.[100]

Remarkably, this film appeared to exert a continuing effect upon the self-styled leader of the defendants, and prize showman, Göring:

> As for Göring, he was apparently disturbed because it had spoiled his show. 'It was such a good afternoon too, until they showed that film. They were reading my telephone conversations on the Austrian affair,

100 Gilbert, *op cit*, 46.

> and everybody was laughing with me. And then they showed that awful film, and it just spoiled everything.'[101]

Generally, the OSS's contribution to the prosecution case through their production and presentation of the concentration camp atrocity films has to be interpreted in terms of the particularly shocking content of the material presented. This cannot be dismissed as no more than an inevitably rhetorical effect of the cinematic medium itself.

It appears that the film created divisions amongst the defendants because some did not want to be associated with the 'criminals' who had committed such atrocities, or to admit that they had any prior knowledge or means of obtaining it. Also it would appear that Airey Neave's comments about the defendants only 'fearing for their own necks'[102] were justified, as Rosenberg stated the film 'just weakens our whole defense'.[103]

In addition to the film's impact upon the defendants, there is the wider issue of how it was perceived by the various lawyers, including the judges, and others within the Nuremberg Palace of Justice. Taylor recalls that the images in the film were very hard to stomach, it was literally sickening and many people had to be excused from the courtroom.[104] As already noted, one of the defence lawyers stated that, after watching the film, he found it intolerable to sit in the same room as some of the defendants, particularly Kaltenbrunner as the lead SS defendant.[105] The atrocity film has also been acknowledged by several of the Nuremberg prosecutors, such as Drexel Sprecher (who was formerly assigned to the OSS and had worked with James Donovan), to have made a most dramatic impact upon its most immediate audience. In an interview after the trial, Sprecher was asked: 'What was the atmosphere in the courtroom like when the concentration camp film was shown?' He replied that he had seen parts of the film before and so he was not particularly surprised by what he saw in the courtroom. However, the 'horrors of seeing the bodies stacked up and the ditches, and the movement of so many people onto trains and into concentration camps was a shocking thing to see'.

Sprecher also confirmed other eye-witness accounts when he noted that: 'it affected the audience very much'.[106] There is also clear evidence that the judges were shocked by what they saw in the film. For example, one news account filed from the trial states that the judges were so disturbed and shocked by the contents of the film that, after the film had ended, they forgot the normal protocols: 'the presiding judges retired without a word and without announcing, as usual, the time set for the next session'.[107]

101 Gilbert, *op cit*, 46–47. 102 Neave, 1979, *op cit*, 247. 103 Gilbert, *op cit*, 32.

104 Taylor, 1992, *op cit*, 247. 105 *Ibid.*

106 See Sprecher's interview available at: www.courttv.com/casefiles/nuremberg/sprecher.html.

107 'Atrocity Films in Court upset Nazis' Aplomb', *New York Herald Tribune*, 30 November 1945.

Furthermore, the judges referred to the OSS film evidence in their final judgment, which states: 'grim evidence of mass murders of Jews was also presented to the Tribunal in cinematography films, depicting the communal graves of hundreds of victims which were subsequently discovered by the Allies'.[108] The fact that these judges referred to the film in their judgment at all, particularly given the fact that it was only one amongst many thousands of pieces of evidence heard during the proceedings, and the fact that, at the time the judgment was composed in October 1946, nearly one year had elapsed from the original showing of the film on 29 November 1945, does suggest that *Nazi Concentration Camps* had a great impact, certainly with respect to determining the guilt of those defendants charged under Count Four with 'crimes against humanity'.

Given that senior OSS officials involved in the Nuremberg trials originally viewed these proceedings as part of a wider programme of Allied 're-education' designed to bring home to the German people the consequences of supporting Nazism, it is worth noting how the film was reported by the media. The original showing of the film was certainly covered extensively in the American newspapers the next day, and it was clear the reporters were shocked by what they had seen. For example, the headlines from these reports included 'War Crimes Court sees Horror Films',[109] 'Atrocity Films upset Nazis' Aplomb'[110] and 'Nazis on Trial see Horror Camp Film'.[111] The use of the words 'atrocity' and 'horror' indicate that, in the eyes of the journalists covering these trials, the court had witnessed such shocking images or almost unbelievable human destruction that they could have almost been viewing a fictitious horror film.

108 Judgment delivered on 30 September 1946, 493 – online at http://www.yale.edu/lawweb/avalon/imt/proc/09-30-46.html.

109 *New York Times*, 30 November 1945.

110 *New York Herald Tribune*, 30 November 1945.

111 *Washington Post*, 30 November 1945.

Chapter 7

Gathering and analysing the materials that became the R-Series of Nuremberg trial evidence

Nuremberg scholars are familiar with the major series of trial evidence known as the PS series, named after the contribution of Robert Storey's staff in the Paris Office ('PS' signifying 'Paris Storey'). The scholarship of the OSS and the Nuremberg trials contains little, if any, acknowledgement of the largely successful efforts of OSS's small group of research analysts, based in this agency's London Field Office, who staffed a Documentary Research Unit (DRU) from June 1945.[1] This section will review aspects of the work of this unit headed by First Lieutenant Walter Rothschild.[2] It will not discuss every aspect of the contents of the series. It will, however, discuss

1 To be fair, Jackson himself provided the following brief acknowledgement in his preface to a selection of Nuremberg documents, the red series: 'No work in a specialized field would be complete without its own occult paraphernalia, and the curious reader may desire an explanation of the strange wizardry behind the document classification symbols. The documents in the American series are classified under the cryptic categories of "L," "R," "PS," "EC," "ECH," "EC," and "C." The letter "L" was used as an abbreviation for "London," and designates those documents either obtained from American and British sources in London or processed in the London Office of the OCC, under the direction of Col. Murray C. Bernays and Col. Leonard Wheeler, Jr. The letter "R" stands for "Rothschild," and indicates the documents obtained through the screening activities of Lt. Walter Rothschild of the London branch of OSS. The origins of the "PS" symbol are more mysterious, but the letters are an abbreviation of the amalgam, "Paris-Storey." The "PS" symbol, accordingly, denotes those documents which, although obtained in Germany, were processed by Col. Storey's division of the OCC in Paris, as well as those documents later processed by the same division after headquarters were established in Nurnberg. The "EC" symbol stands for "Economic Case" and designates those documents which were obtained and processed by the Economic Section of OCC under Mr. Francis M. Shea, with field headquarters at Frankfurt. The "ECH" variant denotes those which were screened at Heidelberg. The letter "C," which is an abbreviation for "Crimes," indicates a collection of German Navy documents which were jointly processed by British and American teams, with Lt. Comdr. John Bracken representing the OCC.' (*Nazi Conspiracy & Aggression*, Vol. I, Preface, 14–15) available online at: http://www.nizkor.org/hweb/imt/nca/nca-01/nca-01-00-preface-03.html.

2 Many of the OSS staff were afforded notional military ranks as 'cover' for intelligence work, and to assist in the organisation's dealings with rank-conscious military officials.

in a reasonably full way the R-Series evidence concerning the Nazis' systematic destruction of European Jews.

The following summary of the content and deployment of the R-Series is highly selective. It concentrates mainly on those documents that the Nuremberg prosecutors made particularly effective use of, or – to a lesser extent – on documentation that, although not directly cited in the trial, nevertheless functioned to corroborate the contents of other materials presented as trial evidence. Thus, for present purposes, the practical significance of the R-Series depends on how the prosecutors actually made use of it either directly or indirectly as corroboration. Hence, the following analysis will directly cite and discuss those parts of the Nuremberg trials transcript where the prosecutors deployed these materials as part of their overall case.

One useful way to assess the significance of the R-Series is to ask the following question: how would our understanding of the nature and extent of Nazi atrocities stemming from the public record of the Nuremberg Tribunal be the poorer, if the material gathered and analysed by the OSS/R&A group had not been available to the Nuremberg prosecutors? Nuremberg prosecutors, including former OSS personnel, deployed documents from this series in a number of draft and final prosecution briefs.[3] Rothschild's group also supplied important details of the Nazis' persecution of the Christian churches,[4] which could then supplement other materials, including a draft R&A report written entirely in Washington.[5] In many cases, the prosecutors used material from the R-Series to establish the liability of a number of different individual and collective defendants (i.e. the 'criminal organisations'). In the case against Rudolf Hess (Hitler's former deputy), the charges against this defendant concerning his personal responsibility for war crimes and crimes against humanity rested largely on the contents of R-96.[6]

3 Draft briefs produced by Thomas Lambert and Lt Col. George Seay (OSS) used R-Series documents on pp. 38, 54, 40 41: Cornell Collection, *op cit*, Vol. 2, pt. 1/7.09.

4 See covering memo, Lt. Walter Rothschild Chief, Documentary Research Unit, to Col. M. Bernays, 'German Monists Organisation', 9 July 1945: Cornell Collection, *op cit*, Vol. 10/18.05. This was attached to a report published by Public Information Division (PID) of the British Foreign office in the PID/PW Series 15 dealing with the German Monists Organisation: 'This report might be useful in connection with the prosecution of religious organisations by the Nazi government.' There is a handwritten arrow '16 July to Commd'r Donovan' and 'hold for Neumann', presumably added by General Donovan himself.

5 See R&A 3114.4: Persecution of the Christian churches, draft for war crimes staff, 6 July 1945, Cornell Collection, *op cit*, Vol. 10/18.03; Lt. Carl E. Schorsche to Maj. William Coogan: 'R&A 3114.4: Persecution of the Christian church,' 10 July 1945. [Handwritten tick/note 'O'Malley']: *ibid*, Vol. 10/18.02.

6 Also cited as Exhibit Number GB-268. This concerns a letter from the Reich Minister of Justice to the Reich Minister and Chief of the Reich Chancellery on 17 April 1941, which deals with the introduction of penal laws against Poles and Jews in the incorporated Eastern

In order, however, not to create an exaggerated impression of the overall importance of the R-Series, it should be borne in mind that, at 589 dossiers, this documentation contributed only a minority of the evidence against any single defendant. Furthermore, evidence from the far larger PS-Series (4,021 documents), the details of which have already been analysed within the Nuremberg scholarship, contributed a far larger proportion of the overall trial evidence.[7] Most prosecution briefs contained a selection of evidence from each of the various series, with the PS-Series predominating. The remainder of this chapter will single out the most important themes from the R-Series (including material concerning the extermination of European Jews). These include: rebutting the argument that Nazi law authorised the actions of the Nuremberg defendants; demonstrating the nature and impact of genocidal policies in Eastern Europe; and exposing the non-voluntary nature of foreign labour recruitment.

It was important for prosecutors to anticipate and then overcome the extreme legalistic argument that law is essentially an expression of the will of the sovereign state. Hence, providing the government enacts rules in accordance with given constitutional protocols, then all the laws it passes are directly and absolutely binding upon all citizens irrespective of any moral considerations. It follows that it is not possible by reference to any 'higher law' or principles of justice, which were not recognised by Nazi regime, for the Nuremberg prosecutors to treat as a criminal act any deed which conforms to, or which is authorised by, such law. Nor can it be a crime to enact the laws of the Nazi state providing these are made in the constitutionally required manner within that regime.

The R-Series contains analysis of captured Nazi documentation that directly challenges this extreme defence argument. It includes material that indicates the extent to which the Nazis' initial seizure of power, which the leadership presented as a triumph for both the party and the German people, involved elements of deception. Hence, the standard positivist defence that individuals must follow the legally sanctioned rules of the state, irrespective of their blatant immorality, lacked credibility. This was particularly the case where the prosecutors could establish, by reference to R-Series materials, that the leadership of the Nazi Party had, through electoral fraud, disqualified themselves from being regarded as a legitimate sovereign government.

For instance, R-142 provides details of how the SA interfered with the secrecy and integrity of elections in order to identify, and then persecute, those who opposed them. Indeed, one report explained that:

territories. Hess plays a part in this insofar as the letter mentions that, in his capacity as the Deputy of the Fuehrer, he had proposed the discussion of the introduction of corporal punishment. See IMT 19, 384.

7 This is clear from the contents of NCA, *op cit.*

> The control was effected in the following way: some members of the election committee marked all the ballot papers with numbers. During the ballot itself, a voters' list was made up. The ballot-papers were handed out in numerical order, therefore it was possible afterwards with the aid of this list to find out the persons who cast 'No' – votes or invalid votes. One sample of these marked ballot-papers is enclosed. The marking was done on the back of the ballot-papers with skimmed milk . . .[8]

The British prosecutor Maxwell Fyfe deployed R-142 to demonstrate the complicity of different allegedly 'criminal organisations', including the Leadership Corps of the Nazi Party, the SS and SD, in acts of electoral fraud during the German plebiscites of 1936 and 1938. These organisations engaged in systematic violations of electoral law. Such violations involved drawing up reports on individuals whose support was questionable, and then monitoring how all individuals actually cast their vote during such supposedly 'secret ballots':

> In the Gau C[K]oblenz the Kreisgeschäftsführer of K[C]ochem, 'where supervisory control was ordered in several Ortsgruppen,' assured the SD that it was mostly women who voted 'no' or invalidly (R-142, USA-481).[9]

Prosecutors also deployed extracts from R-142 during their effective cross-examination of defence witnesses called by counsel for the SD, amongst whom its contents provoked some angry, if unconvincing, responses.[10] Jackson also cited this captured SD report during his important summing up to challenge the legality of the Nazis' rise to power:

> In these circumstances it is not surprising to find that there after, as the evidence such as the SD report on the conduct of the plebiscite at Kappel makes clear, the occasional votes of the people, always announced as triumphs for the Nazis, were conducted dishonestly (Document Number R-142).[11]

Whilst the extermination of European Jewry represented the most extreme instance of Nazi genocide addressed during the Nuremberg trials, the extermination of the Slavic population in Eastern Europe involved massive and systematic slaughter, whilst the persecution of the Christian churches also involved a brutal form of religious persecution. The R-Series includes internal documentation recording the harsh treatment meted out to

8 IMT 2, 107–8. 9 IMT 22,183–4. 10 IMT 19, 413. 11 IMT 9, 442.

the Ukrainian population as part of the brutal occupation policies enunciated by Party Chairman Martin Bormann and ultimately endorsed by the relevant government ministers within Berlin (albeit over the objections of many senior civil servants).[12] R-Series documentation clearly revealed that such repressive treatment included a number of genocidal measures. These included the discouragement of childbirth through contraception and abortion, the refusal to sanction the use of inoculation and other basic health services for Slavic groups within the occupied territories, and a rejection of any need to provide education beyond the lowest levels of numeracy and literacy sufficient to allow Slavs to work effectively for the Nazis as slave labourers.[13] R-Series documentation cited incriminating statements by responsible officials, including Commissioners Koch and Knuth, that 'any signs of intelligence' amongst subordinated populations must prompt summary executions. It also included related Nazi policy statements encouraging measures designed to create all forms of ethnic and racial tension to prevent any unified opposition emerging against Nazi occupation. As clear evidence of genocidal intent, such officials advocated that strategic cities, such as Kiev, 'ought to be depopulated through epidemics. Although it would be best if the superfluous part of the population starved to death.'[14] Related themes included frank admissions of the growing power of Himmler's SS to bypass other government departments and local commissioners. This evidence also demonstrated the overall supremacy (and hence legal accountability) of Nuremberg defendant Albert Speer, formerly in charge of Hitler's war economy, 'on all technical questions'.[15]

Related German documents included with the R-Series give precise details of the racist measures of genocide and ethnic purging Nazi officials used to confiscate the farms and factories and other real estate of different racially defined categories of Poles as part of wider attempts to 'Germanise' parts of the Polish population 'as rapidly as possible'. For example, this series contains detailed decrees that Himmler's office had issued regarding a policy of seeking to reclaim for Germany individuals resident in Poland from a wholly, or partly, German ethnic background who had become 'Polandised'. One of the potentially fatal sanctions such individuals faced for any non-compliance was detention in a concentration camp.[16] Today, such 'Germanisation' would be recognised as a form of genocide in that it undermined the basis for the survival of the Polish people as a distinct group and nation.[17]

12 See R-36 'Concerning Borman's letter', 19 August 1942, *Nazi Conspiracy and Aggression* (Red Series) (Hereafter NCA) Vol. 7, 52–59.

13 *Ibid*, 53, 58. 14 *Ibid*, 54. 15 *Ibid*, 57.

16 R-112: Brand, 'Racial Germans who do not apply for entry into the list for repatriation of German ethnic groups', NCA 7, 108–114.

17 SS-Brigadier Fuehrer General, 'Instructions for Internal Use on the Application of the Law Concerning the Property of Poles', 15 April 1941, NCA 7, 61–3, supported by specific

Another R-Series document is a plea from the Polish Central Committee to the regional Nazi administration drawing attention to the extreme conditions Polish workers faced whilst employed in Germany, including lack of nutrition, health services, adequate housing and child care services.[18] The prosecutor Thomas Dodd deployed extracts from this report most effectively to paint a vivid picture of the physical suffering inflicted upon all sectors of the Polish population by the Nazis' occupation and forced labour policies:

> MR. DODD: The conditions which were described . . . were not confined to the Krupp factories alone but existed throughout Germany; and we turn to a report of the Polish Main Committee made to the Administration of the General Government of Poland, Document Number R-103, Exhibit Number USA-204. This document is dated the 17th of May 1944 and describes the situation of the Polish workers in Germany, . . . it reads: 'The state of cleanliness of many overcrowded camp rooms is contrary to the most elementary requirements. Often there is no opportunity to obtain warm water for washing; therefore, the cleanest parents are unable to maintain even the most primitive standard of hygiene for their children or often even to wash their only set of underclothing. A consequence of this is the spreading of scabies which cannot be eradicated . . . We receive imploring letters from the camps of Eastern Workers and their prolific families beseeching us for food. The quantity and quality of camp rations mentioned therein – the so-called class T – is absolutely insufficient to compensate the energy spent in heavy work. Three and one half kilograms of bread weekly and a thin soup at lunchtime, cooked with kohlrabi or other vegetables without any meat or fat, with a meager addition of potatoes now and then, is a starvation ration for a heavy worker . . . When, on top of that, starvation is sometimes inflicted as punishment – for refusal to wear the badge "East", for example – the result is that workers faint at their work (Klosterteich Camp, Grunheim, Saxony). The consequence is complete exhaustion, an ailing state of health, and tuberculosis. The spreading of tuberculosis among the Polish factory workers is due to the deficient food rations meted out in the community camps which are insufficient to restore the energy spent in heavy work . . . The call for help which reaches us brings to light privation and hunger, severe stomach and intestinal trouble, especially in the case of children, resulting from the insufficiency of food

standard forms to authorise such confiscations of farms and factories, and statistical reports on the 'success' of such measures to date yielding a grand total of 955, 536 estates and just under 9 million hectares of land (63–65, 65–67, and R-91: SS-Brigade Leader Greifelt to Himmler, 23 February 1941, NCA 7, 68–70).

18 R-103: 'Situation of the Polish Workers in the Reich', NCA 7, 104–7.

> which does not take into consideration the needs of children. Proper medical treatment or care for the sick is not available in the mass camps . . . An indication of what these awful conditions may lead to is given by the fact that in the camps for eastern Workers ("Waldlust," Lauf, post office, Pegnitz) there are cases of 8-year-old, delicate, and undernourished children put to forced labor and perishing from such treatment . . . The fact that these bad conditions dangerously affect the state of health and the vitality of the workers is proved by the many cases of tuberculosis found in very young people returning from the Reich to the General Government as unfit for work. Their state of health is usually so bad that recovery is out of the question. The reason is that a state of exhaustion resulting from overwork and a starvation diet is not recognized as an ailment until the illness betrays itself by high fever and fainting spells. Although some hostels for unfit workers have been provided as a precautionary measure, one can only go there when recovery may no longer be expected (Neumarkt in Bavaria). Even there the incurables waste away slowly, and nothing is done even to alleviate the state of the sick by suitable food and medicines. There are children there with tuberculosis whose cure would not be hopeless and men in their prime who, if sent home in time to their families in rural districts, might still be able to recover . . . No less suffering is caused by the separation of families when wives and mothers of small children are away from their families and sent to the Reich for forced labor.'
>
> THE PRESIDENT: Is it a captured document?
>
> MR. DODD: It is a captured document, yes, Sir.[19]

Prosecutor Shawcross also relied upon another R-Series document to demonstrate the racist character of German occupation policies even within Western Europe, which verged upon the genocidal in the sense of attacking the long-term survival of particular ethnic groups deemed to be racially 'inferior':

> The method applied in Alsace was deportation. A captured report reads: 'The first expulsion action was carried out in Alsace in the period from July to December 1940 in the course of which 105,000 persons were either expelled or prevented from returning. They were in the main Jews, gypsies and other foreign racial elements, criminals, antisocial, and incurably insane persons, and in addition Frenchmen, and Francophiles. The patois-speaking population was combed out by these series of deportations in the same way as the other Alsatians.' (Document Number R-114). The report goes on to state that new deportations are being

19 IMT 3, 448–9.

> prepared and after reciting the categories affected, sums up the measures being taken: '. . . the problem of race has been given first consideration and this in such a manner that persons of racial value are to be deported to Germany proper and racially inferior persons to France.'[20]

Since this document also featured in Judge Parker's judgment summarising the most incriminating evidence presented during the trial, it is worthwhile to examine its contents more closely.[21] R-114 indicates that Gauleiter Wagner, of the German-occupied areas of Alsace, prepared plans and took measures leading to the expulsion and deportation of certain groups within the Alsatian civilian population. His plans called for the forcible expulsion of certain categories of so-called 'undesirable persons' as a means of punishment and compulsory Germanisation. Between July and December 1940 in the Alsace region, 105,000 persons were either expelled or prevented from returning. R-114 includes a memorandum, dated 4 August 1942, recording the details of a meeting of high SS and police officials that had been convened to receive the reports of the Gauleiter relating to the Alsatian evacuations. It states that the persons deported were mainly: 'Jews, Gypsies, and other foreign racial elements, criminals, asocial and incurably insane persons, as well as Frenchmen and Francophiles.' The Gauleiter stated that the Fuehrer had given him permission 'to cleanse Alsace of all foreign, sick, or unreliable elements', and that he highlighted the political necessity of further deportations. The memorandum further records that the SS and police officials present at the conference approved the Gauleiter's proposals for further evacuation.

Having cited R-114,[22] Shawcross then explicitly linked such policies of deportation and Germanisation to the Nazis' more obviously genocidal policies of sterilisation and extermination within Eastern Europe directed against individuals and groups not regarded as immediately useful to the Nazi war economy:

> Listen to Bormann's directives for the Eastern territory summarized by one of Rosenberg's subordinates. I quote: 'The Slavs are to work for us. Insofar as we do not need them, they may die. Therefore, compulsory vaccination and German health services are superfluous. The fertility of the Slavs is undesirable. They may use contraceptives or practice abortion; the more the better. Education is dangerous. It is enough if they can

20 IMT 19, 498.

21 IMT, Judgment, Judge Parker (no page numbers) but available online at http://www.yale.edu/lawweb/avalon/imt/proc/judwarcr.htm.

22 The prosecution used part of this dossier in other contexts including to demonstrate the complicity of the Nazi Party's Leadership Corps in war crimes. See IMT 4, 57.

> count up to a hundred. At best an education which produces useful stooges for us is admissible' (Document Number R-36).[23]

This document was cited as a particularly telling piece of evidence by Judge Parker in his contribution to the Tribunal's judgment.[24]

In setting out the economic case, which deeply implicated defendant Rosenberg, prosecutors Brudno argued that:

> I come now to the final phase of the case against the Defendant Rosenberg. We have seen how he aided the Nazi rise to power and directed the psychological preparation of the German people for waging of aggressive war. I will now offer proof of his responsibility for the planning and execution of War Crimes and Crimes against Humanity committed in the vast areas of the occupied East, which he administered for over 3 years. These areas included the Baltic States, White Ruthenia, the Ukraine, and the eastern portion of Poland . . .

Brudno then cited R-135: 'merely to illustrate the manner in which Rosenberg participated in the criminal activities conducted within his jurisdiction'. He then highlighted the casual brutality of 'harvesting' aspects of the bodies of victims of Nazi mass murder:

> I call your attention to the document numbered R-135, which was previously introduced as Exhibit Number USA-289. In this document the prison warden of Minsk reports that 516 German and Russian Jews had been killed, and called attention to the fact that valuable gold had been lost due to the failure to knock out the fillings of the victims' teeth before they were done away with. These activities took place in the prison at Minsk, a prison which . . . was directly under the supervision of the Ministry for the occupied east.[25]

Within the context of Nazi-occupied Eastern Europe, the theme of the Nazis' persecution of other religions, namely the Christian churches, also features within not only OSS-R&A reports but also with the evidence Rothschild's group procured and analysed. The prosecutors deployed R-Series materials in a particularly powerful manner during their case against the Leadership Corps as a 'criminal organisation'. Here prosecutor Storey had to establish the Leadership Corps' active participation embracing such measures as anti-Semitic activities and 'measures to subvert and undermine the Christian religion and persecute the Christian clergy'.[26] As part of this

23 IMT 19, 498–9. 24 IMT, Judgment, Judge Parker, *op cit.* 25 IMT 5, 62.
26 IMT 44, 47.

case, which highlighted the highly calculated policy of 'racheting up' levels of persecution of the Christian churches to the maximum possible, Storey stated:

> I now offer in evidence R-101(a) . . . there are several of those documents under R-101, and at the bottom you will notice they are labelled 'a,' 'b,' and 'c.' The first one is R-101(a), and I quote the first five paragraphs on Page 2 of the English translation: 'Enclosed is a list of church possessions which might be available for the accommodation of racial Germans. The list, which I beg you to return, is supplemented by correspondence and illustrated material pertinent to the subject. For political reasons, expropriation without indemnity of the entire property of the churches and religious orders will hardly be possible at this time. Expropriation with indemnity or in return for assignment of other lands and grounds will be even less possible. It is therefore suggested that the respective authorities of the orders be instructed that they make available the monasteries concerned for the accommodation of racial Germans and remove their own members to other less populous monasteries.' There is a marginal note opposite this paragraph that, translated, means 'very good.' 'The final expropriation of these properties thus placed at our disposal can then be carried out step by step in the course of time.'[27]

Storey then cited other aspects of Rothschild's dossier demonstrating the complex interweaving of different branches of the Nazi Party and German state that were involved in the persecution of the Christian churches. This, he suggested, was highly incriminating with respect to the SS defendants in particular, in that lines of complicity extended from Himmler's office down to the local level of the Nazi Party hierarchies:

> On 5 April 1940 the Security Police and Security Service SS sent a letter to the Reich Commissar for the consolidation of Germandom, enclosing a copy of the foregoing letter from Heydrich to Himmler of 21 February 1940, proposing the confiscation of Church properties. The letter of 5 April 1940 is included in the Document R-101(a), just introduced in evidence; and I quote from . . . Document R-101(a): 'The Reich Leader SS has agreed to the proposals made in the enclosed letter and has ordered the matter to be dealt with by collaboration between the Chief of the Security Police and Security Service and your office.' I now offer in evidence Document R-101(c), Exhibit USA-358. This is a letter dated July 30, 1941, written by an SS Standartenfuehrer whose signature is illegible, to the Reich Leader of the SS.[28]

27 IMT 3, 55. 28 IMT 4, 69.

Storey then extensively quoted from this document to illustrate how Nazi officials, including regional and local party leaders, had increasingly attacked the power and influence of the Christian churches by seizing control of church property without paying due compensation:

> The letter supplies further evidence of the participation of the Gauleiter in the seizure of church property. I quote from the first three paragraphs of the English translation of Document R-101(c), at the bottom of the page: 'With reference to the report of 30 May 1941, this office considers it its duty to call the Reich Leader's attention to the development which is taking place in the incorporated Eastern countries with regard to seizure and confiscation of church property. As soon as the Reich laws on expropriation became effective, the Reichsstatthalter and Gauleiter in the Reichsgau Wartheland adopted the practice of expropriating church real estate for use as dwellings and paying the appraised value into blocked accounts. Moreover, the East German Agricultural Administrations Limited reports that in the Warthegau all church-owned real estate is being claimed by the local Gau administration.'[29]

Storey then made fulsome reference to another document that was also included in the R-101 cluster of evidence bundled together that incriminated more senior Nazi officials, including the Chiefs of the Nazi Chancery and Party Main Office, and defendants Frick (Nazi Minister of the Interior) and Martin Bormann (Hitler's personal secretary). He suggested that forced expropriation was devised to deprive funding from the Christian churches:

> I next offer in evidence Document R-101(d), which immediately follows Exhibit Lumber USA-358 already in evidence. This is a letter from the Chief of Staff of the Main Office to Himmler, dated 30 March 1942, dealing with the confiscation of church property. The letter evidences the active participation of the Party Chancellery in the confiscation of religious property. In this letter the Chief of Staff, Main Office, reports to Himmler concerning the policy of the SS in suspending all payment of rent to monasteries and other church institutions whose property had been expropriated. The letter discusses a proposal made by the Reich Minister of the Interior, in which the Party Chancellery prominently participated, to the effect that the church institutions should be paid amounts corresponding to current mortgage charges on the premises without realizing any profit. The writer further suggests that such payments should never be made directly to the ecclesiastical institutions but rather should be made to the creditors of the institutions. I now quote

29 *Ibid.*

> from the fourth sentence on Page 3 of that document, the English translation, whereby such an arrangement would be in dine [sic] with 'the basic idea of the settlement originally worked out between the Party Chancellery and the Reich Minister of the Interior.' I understand the Reich Minister of Interior for 1933–1944 was the Defendant Frick. The Leadership Corps of the Nazi Party participated in the suppression of religious publications and interfered with free religious education. In a letter dated 27 September 1940 Reichsleiter and Deputy of the Fuehrer Bormann transmitted to the Defendant Rosenberg a photostatic copy of a letter from Gauleiter Florian dated 23 September 1940, which expresses the Gauleiter's intense disapproval, on Nazi ideological grounds, of a religious pamphlet entitled, *The Spirit and Soul of the Soldier*, written by a Major General Von Rabenau.[30]

In short, a close review of the content of the R-Series rebuts the suggestion that the OSS either ignored or downplayed the systematic extermination of civilians founded upon the perverse theories of the supremacy of a Aryan 'master race', and the rights of the German nation under Nazi leadership to dominate the whole of Europe. On the contrary, Rothschild's OSS unit provided highly incriminating documentation of the Nazis' genocidal policies in Eastern Europe and their incremental attack upon alternative ideologies, such as those embodied in the Christian churches.

Waging aggressive war and crimes committed against prisoners of war

An important element of the R-Series provided documentation relevant to traditional violations of the laws of war, that is, 'war crimes' in the traditional sense of breaches of established international rules and conventions regulating, for example, the treatment of captured troops. Controversially, the Allied prosecutors attached particular importance to this type of offence. As already noted, OSS personnel, including members of the Dupont, Dawes and Ginny missions, had been victims of such war crimes. A cluster of reports provided by the Rothschild group, R-110, addressed different aspects of the formal order removing POW status from captured aircrews, and which permitted the local populace to lynch such personnel. Document R-110 was captured by a combined British-American documents exploitation team, and then sent to the R&A London office from the Air Documents Research Centre in London. It consists of an original order signed by Himmler and dated 10 August 1943, stating that: 'It is not the task of the police to interfere in clashes between Germans and English and American terror fliers who have

30 *Ibid.*

bailed out.'[31] This order was transmitted in writing to all senior executive SS and police officers, and orally to their subordinate officers and to all Gauleiter. Justice Jackson cited these and other R-Series materials in his trial evidence regarding 'Crimes in the Conduct of War', arguing that there was an unprecedented quality to the Nazis' violation of established codes of laws that Germany had traditionally recognised as binding. Indeed, the fact that even those responsible for making this order recognised its illegal nature was clear from the stipulation that, outside of the leadership level, it had to be distributed orally so that there would be no written trace:

> Even the most warlike of peoples have recognized in the name of humanity some limitations on the savagery of warfare. Rules to that end have been embodied in international conventions to which Germany became a party . . . We will show by German documents that these rights were denied, that prisoners of war were given brutal treatment and often murdered. This was particularly true in the case of captured airmen, often my countrymen. It was ordered that captured English and American airmen should no longer be granted the status of prisoners of war. They were to be treated as criminals and the Army was ordered to refrain from protecting them against lynching by the populace (R-118). The Nazi Government, through its police and propaganda agencies, took pains to incite the civilian population to attack and kill airmen who crash landed. The order [R-110 quoted above] was transmitted on the same day by SS Obersturmbannführer Brand of Himmler's personal staff to all senior executive SS and Police officers, with these directions: 'I am sending you the enclosed order with the request that the Chief of the Regular Police and of the Security Police be informed. They are to make this instruction known to their subordinate officers verbally' (R-110).[32]

R-110 also demonstrates that Gestapo offices at Munich, Regensburg, Fuerth and Nuremberg had been screening prisoner of war camps in Bavaria for classes of prisoners of war to be sent to Dachau for liquidation by SS guards. These Gestapo offices had been criticised by the German High Command for their 'failure' to screen as effectively as the High Command desired. The prosecutor argued that, although such evidence had been sidestepped by defence lawyers:

31 R-153, SEA, 11 October 1945, cross-referencing R-13, R-19, R-110, R-117–119: Cornell Collection, Vol. 20, pt. 2.

32 IMT 2, 137. Incidentally, R-110 was also cited by Maxwell-Fyfe during the case against the Nazi Leadership Corps, and by Col. Storey for the same purpose. See IMT 22, 200 and IMT 4, 49–50.

> Yet it is one of the clearest cases of wilful premeditated murder of prisoners of war in violation of established international law. It is positive demonstration of the complete savagery of the responsible organizations with respect to the treatment of prisoners of war. It is Document Number R-178, Exhibit Number USA-910. The infamous Bullet Decree, under which the Gestapo sent recaptured officer prisoners of war to Mauthausen Concentration Camp for execution by SS guards, is additional proof of the criminal character of these organizations.[33]

American Prosecutor Dodd also extracted sections from R-124 to demonstrate breaches of the Geneva conventions regarding the use of Russian prisoners of war. This was particularly apparent with respect to breaches of Article 6 of the regulations annexed to the Hague Convention Number IV of 1907, which provides that: 'The State may utilize the labour of prisoners of war according to their rank and aptitude, officers excepted. The tasks shall not be excessive and shall have no connection with the operations of the war.' Dodd claimed that:

> In addition, the conspirators compelled prisoners of war to engage in operations of war against their own country and its allies. At a meeting of the Central Planning Board, again held on February 19, 1943, attended by the Defendant Speer and the Defendant Sauckel and Field Marshal Milch, the following conversation occurred and is recorded in our Document R-124 . . .: Sauckel: 'If any prisoners. are taken, they will be needed there.' Milch: 'We have made a request for an order that a certain percentage of men in the antiaircraft artillery must be Russians. Fifty thousand will be taken altogether, thirty thousand are already employed as gunners. It is an amusing thing that Russians must work the guns.'[34]

(This last statement was also cited by the Russian judge General Niktochenko in the Tribunal's judgment as a particularly incriminating piece of evidence.)[35]

Hartley Shawcross, the chief British prosecutor, also relied upon R-124 as demonstrating the casual attitude by senior officials, including Milch (effective Chief of the German Air Force) and Göring, towards obvious breaches of the Geneva Convention regarding the treatment of POWs. He argued that the policy reflected in R-124 was typical of a more general and casual disregard of long-established aspects of the law of war, and that this wider policy was reflected in the lack of any objections to such routine illegalities:

33 IMT 22, 258. 34 IMT 3, 456.

35 IMT, Judgment, *op cit*, General Niktochenko, Slave Labour: http://www.yale.edu/lawweb/avalon/imt/proc/judwarcr.htm.

> SIR HARTLEY SHAWCROSS: Under Article 31 of the Geneva Convention it might have been permissible to employ prisoners on certain work in connection with the raw materials of the armament industry. But the statement made by Milch at the Central Planning Board on the 16th of February 1943 in the presence of Speer and Sauckel had no legal justification at all. He said, if you will remember, and I quote: 'We have made the request that a certain percentage of men in our ack-ack artillery must be Russians. 50,000 will be taken altogether, 30,000 are already employed as gunners. This is an amusing thing that Russians must work the guns' (Document Number R-124). That was quite obviously flagrantly illegal. Nobody could have had the faintest doubt about it. The minutes record no protest whatever. It has not been suggested that Göring or any of the others who must have read the minutes and known what was going on, regarded this outrage by the effective head of the German Air Force as being in any way unusual.[36]

Once again, Jackson selected this body of evidence as especially relevant in his final summation of the most incriminating evidence on this aspect of the prosecution case:

> The third group of crimes was: Warfare in Disregard of International Law. It is unnecessary to labor this point on the facts . . . Also, we may take as established or admitted that the lawless conduct such as shooting British and American airmen, mistreatment of Western prisoners of war, forcing French prisoners of war into German war work, and other deliberate violations of the Hague and Geneva Conventions, did occur, and in obedience to highest levels of authority (R-110).[37]

Indeed, some of the most incriminating of the R-Series documentation took the form of internal German memorandum in which Germans complained about Nazi atrocities and breaches of international law regarding the selection of prisoners of war for execution. For example, R-178 contains detailed correspondence concerning a complaint by Major Meinel against Gestapo officers in Munich, Regensburg, Nuremberg, and Fürth. Meinel's allegation was that these officials were involved in the screening out and murdering of Russian prisoners of war.[38] This complaint was substantiated by other documents within the dossier.[39] One signed report states: 'The

36 IMT 19, 478. 37 IMT 2, 403. 38 IMT 20, 158.

39 These included a report from the Gestapo office in Munich which listed 18 camps surveyed by the Gestapo, and showing that a total of 3,088 Soviet prisoners of war had been considered, of which 410 were selected for execution at Dachau camp. This was on the basis that this group comprised: officials and officers, Jews, members of intelligentsia, fanatical Communists, agitators and others, runaways and the incurably sick. *Ibid.*

complaints of the High Command of the Armed Forces that the screening of the Russians had been carried out in a superficial manner must be most emphatically refuted.'[40]

Document G of the R-178 integrated dossier comprises a report from the Gestapo office in Munich complaining about the attitude and actions of Major Meinel who was alleged to have complained to the High Command of the Armed Forces. Document H of R-178b contains a statement that: 'Furthermore, I pointed out to Major Meinel that the work of the Gestapo Einsatzkommandos was done with the consent of the High Command of the Armed Forces, and according to rules which had been drafted in collaboration with the High Command of the Armed Forces' Organization of Prisoners of War.' Meinel, in giving his reply to the accusations made against him, had further incriminated the SS when he stated: 'When I mentioned that it weighed heavily on the officers' conscience to hand over the Russian prisoners, Regierungsrat Schimmel replied that the hearts of some of the SS men who were charged with executing prisoners were all but breaking.'[41] Document M comprises a notice that the regional Reich Commissioner for Defense was informed about these murders, and approved of them. Document T is a teletype from SS Obersturmbannführer Panziger Department IV (A) of the Gestapo office in Berlin, stating that:

> The prisoners of war who have been screened out will be transferred to the Buchenwald Concentration Camp owing to a decision arrived at in a conference with the High Command of the Armed Forces. Will you please inform the Higher SS and Police Leader today about this and also that Meinel is getting a different assignment.[42]

This evidence was particularly damaging for the defence lawyers who tried to insulate the military defendants from SS atrocities, as it clearly showed that members of the German High Command had agreed to the unlawful treatment of Allied prisoners.

The reaction of defence lawyers to the implications of R-178 was, from the perspective of the defendants as a whole, often counterproductive. Attempts by individual defence lawyers to discredit and challenge the contents of such R-documentation often involved recognition that the atrocities they reported in these bundles had taken place but that their clients were not wholly or solely responsible for their commission. The capacity of R-Series trial evidence to prompt this response is important. In deflecting or diluting responsibility away from one defendant, defence lawyers and their clients made statements that proved highly incriminating to other defendants or potential future defendants. For example, the lawyer for the High Command,

40 Document F, *ibid.* 41 *Ibid.* 42 IMT 20, 159.

which was prosecuted as a criminal organisation, attempted – with only limited success – to examine a witness in a manner that deflected liability for the killing of Russian POWs away from military officials to local Nazi party leaders (or 'Gauleiters'):

> DR. LATERNSER: Witness, you were shown the Document R-178. On Page 26 of this document, in the center of the page you will find that the Reich Commissioner for Defense in the defense areas agreed to the selection of the Russian prisoners of war and their murder. Then the prosecutor asked you just who this Reich Commissioner for Defense was at the time and you said that you did not know. Now I should like to ask you, who usually was the Reich Commissioner for Defense. Was not that the Gauleiter?
>
> BEST: Sometimes it was the Gauleiter and sometimes, if I remember correctly, they were senior officials, Oberprdsidenten and men of that kind; the ministers of the various states.
>
> DR. LATERNSER: The Reich Commissioners for Defense, therefore, were not military offices, purely military agencies under the OKH, is that right?
>
> BEST: No. As far as I remember – the organization at that time, the answer is 'no'.[43]

Defence counsel for the High Command, which was charged collectively as a 'criminal organisation', faced the difficulty that a number of the documents within the R-Series proved that the German Army had worked cooperatively with the SS with respect to the slaughter of civilians, often under the guise of 'anti-partisan actions'. For example, R-102[44] contains a report covering the activities, during October 1941, of the mobile killing-groups (or 'Einsatzgruppen') operating within the German-occupied territories of the Soviet Union. This states cynically that: 'Spontaneous demonstrations against Jewry followed by pogroms on the part of the population against the remaining Jews have not been recorded on account of the lack of adequate instructions.'[45] Telford Taylor, who prosecuted the ill-fated High Command case, claimed that these and other documents showed: 'that pacification and anti-partisan activities became mere code words for the extermination of Jews . . . the German Army received some similar policies and directives. It only remains to show that, in the field, the Army and the SS worked hand in glove.'[46] Taylor cited reports regarding the bloody suppression of the Warsaw ghetto before returning again to the much-cited dossier R-135 as evidence that most of the so-called 'partisans' the Nazi squads killed were in fact unarmed civilians:

43 IMT 20, 500. 44 Exhibit USA-470. 45 NCA 2, 382. 46 IMT 4, 462.

> To the same general effect is R-135, Exhibit USA-289, which is a report dated 5 June 1943 by the German General Commissioner for Minsk . . . describing an antipartisan operation in which 4,500 enemies were killed: 5,000 suspected partisans and 59 Germans. The cooperation by the German Army is shown in the following excerpt . . .: 'The figures mentioned above indicate that again a heavy destruction of the population must be expected. If only 492 rifles are taken from 4,500 enemy dead, this discrepancy shows that among these enemy dead were numerous peasants from the country. The battalion Dirlewanger especially has a reputation for destroying many human lives. Among the 5,000 people suspected of belonging to bands, there were numerous women and children.' The next paragraph shows again the participation of the Armed Forces personnel . . .[47]

Although the OSS did not have any particular expertise on military law, certainly not compared with that of the US Judge Advocate General's Department, Rothschild's DCU were still able to both procure and successfully analyse a number of documents relevant to the innovative charge of 'waging aggressive war'. For example, the R-Series reports included internal documentation of the General Staff of the German Army High Command regarding the 'top secret' plans for the invasion and seizure of Yugoslavia, codenamed 'Action 25', which clearly sought to exploit pre-existing ethnic tensions in the Balkan region.[48]

Other R-Series documents selected and deployed by the prosecution as evidence in the trials clarified the extent to which senior members of the German Army had been taken into Hitler's confidence during the military expansion of 1938–39. This was particularly the case concerning plans for the invasion of Poland and other breaches of international law, such as violations of various treaty obligations towards Slovakia.[49] This evidence helped with the wider task of attempting to prosecute the General Staff and High Command of the German Armed Forces as a 'criminal organisation' under Articles 9 to 11 of the Charter, an aspect of the case introduced and then presented by senior prosecutor Telford Taylor:

> COLONEL TELFORD TAYLOR: The Indictment seeks a declaration of criminality against six groups or organisations, and the last one listed in the Indictment is a group described as the General Staff and High

47 IMT, 4, 463.

48 R-95: von Brauchitsch, 'Deployment Instructions for Action 25', 30 March 1941, NCA 7, 70–72.

49 R-100: 'Information given to the Supreme Commander of the Army [Von Brauchitsch] by the Fuehrer on 25 March 1939', NCA, 7, 83–86.

> Command . . . The full flowering of German military strength came about through collaboration, collaboration between the Nazis on the one hand and the career leaders of the German Armed Forces, the professional soldiers, sailors, and airmen on the other. . . . But we will show that this group not only collaborated with Hitler and supported the essential Nazi objectives but we will show that they also furnished the one thing which was essential and basic to the success of the Nazi programme for Germany, and that thing was skill and experience in the development and use of armed might . . . Hitler, in short, attracted the generals to him with the glitter of conquest, and then succeeded in submerging them politically and, as the war proceeded, they became his tools. But if these military leaders became the tools of Nazism, it is not to be supposed that they were unwitting, or that they did not participate fully in many of the crimes which we will bring to the notice of the Tribunal. The willingness and, indeed, the eagerness of the German professional officer corps to become partners of the Nazis, will be fully developed. Your Lordship, there will be three principal parts to this presentation. There will be first a description of the composition and functioning of the General Staff and High Command group as defined in the Indictment; next, the evidence in support of the charges of criminality under Counts 1 and 2 of the Indictment; finally, the evidence in support of the charges under Counts 3 and 4. The members of the Tribunal should have before them three document books which have been given the designation CC . . . The second book contains documents in the C and L series, and the third book, in the PS and R-Series.[50]

Taylor then cited a number of the R-Series documents already discussed in an attempt to substantiate the questionable proposition that the entire German High Command constituted a single criminal organisation, akin to a criminal gang. Perhaps the most incriminating of these documents Taylor relied upon was R-150.[51] This indicates that, during the spring and summer of 1938, the German Air Force (or 'Luftwaffe') was engaged in war planning concerning the forthcoming military expansion of the Reich. This top-secret document, dated 2 June 1938, was issued by Air Group Command 3, and entitled 'Plan Study 1938, Instruction for Deployment and Combat, "Case Red" ', that is, action against the Western powers. For the prosecution, Alderman argued that:

> It is given significance by the considerable progress by this date of the planning for the attack on Czechoslovakia. I quote from the second

50 IMT 3, 305.

51 Also cited as USA Exhibit 82. Twenty-eight copies of this document were made, of which the one captured was number 16.

> paragraph on Page 3 of the English translation, referring to the various possibilities under which war with France may occur. You will note that they are all predicated on the assumption of a German-Czech conflict. 'France will either (a) interfere in the struggle between the Reich and Czechoslovakia in the course of Case Green, or (b) start hostilities simultaneously with Czechoslovakia. (c) It is possible but not likely that France will begin the fight while Czechoslovakia still remains aloof.' And then, reading down lower on the page under the heading 'Intention': 'Regardless of whether France enters the war as a result of Case Green or whether she makes the opening move of the war simultaneously with Czechoslovakia, in any case the mass of the German offensive formations will, in conjunction with the Army, first deliver the decisive blow against Czechoslovakia.' By mid-summer direct and detailed planning for Case Green was being carried out by the Luftwaffe. In early August, at the direction of the Luftwaffe General Staff, the German Air Attache in Prague reconnoitered the Freudenthal area of Czechoslovakia south of Upper Silesia for suitable landing grounds.[52]

In other words, this collection of documentation contradicted the defence claim that responsibility for planning for 'aggressive war', contrary to the Nuremberg Charter, was confined to Hitler and his foreign minister, Defendant Ribbentrop.

Ralph Albrecht, an OSS lawyer and expert in psychological warfare techniques who was seconded to the OCC, made effective use of R-140 to further incriminate the most senior of the Nuremberg defendants, Hermann Göring. He argued that this document substantiated the charge that Göring, who had special responsibility for the German Air Force, had played a major role in preparing Germany economically and militarily for the launching of an aggressive war in violation of international law:

> MR. ALBRECHT: May it please the Tribunal, two important conferences which have already been adverted to by the Prosecution show clearly how the Defendant Göring inspired and directed the preparation of the German economy for aggressive war. On the 8th of July 1938 he addressed a number of the leading German aircraft manufacturers and laid the groundwork for a vast increase in aircraft production. He stated that war with Czechoslovakia was imminent and boasted that the German Air Force was already superior in quality and quantity to the English. He said that: '. . . if Germany wins the war. Then she will be the greatest power in the world, dominating the world market, and Germany will be a rich nation. For this goal, risks must be taken . . .'

52 IMT 3, 12.

> That quotation, may it please the Court, is taken from Document R-140, Exhibit Number USA-10.[53]

The Tribunal's judgment on Göring certainly accepted as proven the case made by this aspect of the R-Series. The judges noted that this defendant was 'the planner and prime mover in the military and diplomatic preparation for war which Germany pursued'. The Tribunal's final judgment also appeared to endorse the remainder of the R-Series evidence regarding Göring's complicity in this form of war criminality.[54]

The British prosecutor, Sir Hartley Shawcross, deployed parts of the R-Series to rebut the defence argument that the Nazis' invasion of neutral Norway was justified by the threat that the Allies were about to invade this country. He deployed R-81 to demonstrate the complicity of Defendant Raeder, not least in relation to his decision to endorse this invasion even when it became clear that this was no longer a matter of national self-defence:

> Holland having been overrun, the course of the war soon showed that Germany's military aims and the interests of her strategy would be improved by further aggression. Norway and Denmark were invaded. No kind of excuse, then or now, has been put forward for the occupation of Denmark, but a strenuous attempt has been made in the course of this Trial to suggest that Norway was invaded only because the Germans believed that the Allies were about to take a similar step . . . It is true that in February 1940 Raeder pointed out to him that if England did occupy Norway the whole Swedish supply of ore to Germany would be endangered (Document Number D-881), but on the 26th of March he advised that the Russo-Finnish conflict having ceased, the danger of an Allied landing was no longer considered serious. Nonetheless he went on to suggest that the German invasion, for which all the directives had been issued, should take place at the next new moon, on the 7th of April (Document Number R-81).[55]

In other word, R-81 allowed the prosecutors to rebut Defendant Raeder's defence argument that the invasion of Norway was not itself an unlawful act.

Having examined in considerable detail the content and strategic deployment, largely to good effect, of elements of the R-Series (a project that largely falls within the scope of international criminal law scholarship broadly defined), it is now possible to discuss the specifically intelligence dimension.

53 IMT 4, 539.

54 IMT, Judgment: available online at: http://www.yale.edu/lawweb/avalon/imt/proc/judgoeri.htm.

55 IMT 19, 456–57.

That is, to examine how OSS officials gathered and analysed these materials, and how Rothschild's DRU was set up and deployed within the wider Nuremberg project.

Rothschild's work in gathering and organising the R-Series evidence

The scholarship of the OSS and the Nuremberg trials contains little, if any, acknowledgement of the largely successful efforts of OSS's small group of research analysts who staffed a documentary research unit (DRU).[56] As already noted, the DRU, based in the OSS's London Field Office, was headed by First Lt. Walter Rothschild.[57]

Unlike the majority of Jackson's staff recruited from outside OSS, Rothschild was no newcomer to questions relating to the details of the Nazi state and policy issues relating to how the Anglo-American authorities should, as part of their planned Civil Affairs programme, tackle immediate post-war issues regarding the distinctive personnel and institutions of Hitler's regime. On the contrary, during 1944 he was intensely involved in various Civil Affairs projects that demanded an in-depth knowledge of the Nazi state, its institutions, policies and leading personnel. One of these issues, which clearly overlapped with war crimes planning, concerned the status of German law under future Allied military government. If German law was to remain

56 To be fair, Jackson himself provided the following brief acknowledgement in his preface to a selection of Nuremberg documents, the red series: 'No work in a specialized field would be complete without its own occult paraphernalia, and the curious reader may desire an explanation of the strange wizardry behind the document classification symbols. The documents in the American series are classified under the cryptic categories of "L," "R," "PS," "EC," "ECH," "EC," and "C." The letter "L" was used as an abbreviation for "London," and designates those documents either obtained from American and British sources in London or processed in the London Office of the OCC, under the direction of Col. Murray C. Bernays and Col. Leonard Wheeler, Jr. The letter "R" stands for "Rothschild," and indicates the documents obtained through the screening activities of Lt. Walter Rothschild of the London branch of OSS. The origins of the "PS" symbol are more mysterious, but the letters are an abbreviation of the amalgam, "Paris-Storey." The "PS" symbol, accordingly, denotes those documents which, although obtained in Germany, were processed by Col. Storey's division of the OCC in Paris, as well as those documents later processed by the same division after headquarters were established in Nurnberg. The "EC" symbol stands for "Economic Case" and designates those documents which were obtained and processed by the Economic Section of OCC under Mr. Francis M. Shea, with field headquarters at Frankfurt. The "ECH" variant denotes those which were screened at Heidelberg. The letter "C," which is an abbreviation for "Crimes," indicates a collection of German Navy documents which were jointly processed by British and American teams, with Lt. Comdr. John Bracken representing the OCC.' (*Nazi Conspiracy & Aggression*, Vol. I, Preface, 14–15) available online at: http://www.nizkor.org/hweb/imt/nca/nca-01/nca-01-00-preface-03.html.

57 Many of the OSS staff were afforded notional military ranks as 'cover' for intelligence work, and to assist in the organisation's dealings with rank-conscious military officials.

intact, including the modifications made by the Nazi regime, then this could make it difficult to secure convictions from many of the acts and policies that involved war crimes and other atrocities. In the spring of 1944, Rothschild provided a detailed report to Franz Neumann, who headed Washington OSS-R&A's involvement in Civil Affairs planning and the production of various guides and handbooks, concerning the work completed by his 'Working Party' on German law. Controversially, at least as far as Neumann was concerned, Rothschild's group had recommended the use of German military tribunals to tackle crimes by German military personnel and resort to general 'catch all' clauses in proposed legislation abolishing offensive aspects of Nazi law.[58] Rothschild's report included statements regarding the need for a new constitutional and legal settlement to reinstate 'equal rights' and 'equality before the law', that is, to replace inherently racist laws, decrees and policies, which Neumann also found overly ambiguous as it allowed both a liberal and (following the influence of Jurist Carl Schmitt) an authoritarian judicial interpretation. Judges can interpret 'equal rights' (and analogous 'due process' provisions) to require both a formal procedural and a substantive version of equality.[59]

During the late spring of 1944, Rothschild had also been working on civil affairs related plans for 'the coordination of legislative functions between the Military Government and the Indigenous authorities'. As the title of the memorandum of the same name indicates, Rothschild sought to work out how, in practice, 'divided sovereignty' between Allied and German authorities could operate, and how possible disagreements regarding these two sources of law could be resolved. (Neumann objected rigorously to this paper as it was based on what he regarded as a false conception of sovereignty which ignored the fact that, within post-war Germany, Allied Military Government would be the only source of law and sovereignty.)[60] During the summer of 1944, Rothschild worked on a report, completed in first draft on 14 June 1944, containing detailed proposals for the 'Dissolution of the Nazi Party' and affiliated organisations.[61] This was a massive task given the permeation of German society by various Nazi or Nazi-affiliated institutions, which even made party membership obligatory for candidates for public office, co-opted the German Red Cross, and organised former independent trade unions into the Nazi Labour Front. Rothschild's work during late 1944 included

58 Neumann to Rothschild, 28 April 1944: NA, RG 226, Entry 146, Box 84, Folder 1236.

59 *Ibid.*

60 Neumann to Morse, Rothschild, Gilbert, Armstrong, undated but probably mid-May 1944, as it replies to Rothschild memorandum of 5 May 1944: NA, RG 226, Entry 146, Box 84, Folder 1236. Neumann recommended this report be withdrawn: *ibid.*

61 Neumann to Rothschild, 18 July 1944: NA, RG 226, Entry 146, Box 84, Folder 1236. Neumann received this report more favourably and made only a few proposed amendments to stiffen the measures on the Labour Front: *ibid.*

proposals for changing the criminal law of treason in post-war Germany to reflect the altered position of Allied occupation. Rothschild's analysis appears to assume that Allied Military Government will represent a 'foreign government' raising the possibility of Germans being charged under German laws against treason for cooperating with Allied officials. Neumann rejected Rothschild's analysis as it assumed that treason laws would continue to operate and that Allied Military Government was 'foreign' when in fact it was the sole sovereign power.[62] It also appears that Rothschild took an interest in materials secured by the OSS's Art Looting Investigation Unit, as original copies have been discovered amongst his papers.[63] In short, during 1944–45, Rothschild had built up considerable expertise, both independently and through his collaboration with OSS R&A's main expert on the organisation of the Nazi regime, Franz Neumann. This prior background, which included close cooperation with other Allied intelligence and military organisations, may explain why he and his London R&A staff were able to switch directly into war crimes documentary analysis without the period of acclimatisation which was required for most other branches of Jackson's organisation.

Details of Rothschild's DRU are sketchy in both the Nuremberg and OSS literature, consisting of only fragmentary references, many of which are worth quoting directly because they contradict the criticism that the OSS failed to honour the promises Donovan made when he first offered the services of the OSS to Justice Jackson. For example, during early August 1945, Neumann wrote an urgent memo from the London Field Office of OSS to Sherman Kent, the acting head of the OSS/R&A Branch presenting his 'First report on war crimes Europe', based upon 'extensive discussions with Commander Donovan, Colonel Murray Bernays, Colonel Wheeler, Colonel Amen, Alan Evans and Just Lunning'.[64] This report contrasts the quality and nature of the evidence-gathering and analysis work of the DRU with analogous work performed by other divisions of Jackson's organisation. Indeed, Neumann contrasts the fractious, confused and chaotic 'organisational setup' of Jackson's team based in London with the state of the organisation and work of the DRU. He claimed Bernays' operation based in London not only lacked a 'unified direction of research and collection of evidence' but also any clear chain of command and decision-making that integrates its rival sections. Neumann's report explained that Bernays had successfully appropriated new OSS staff from Washington, and that his section of the OCC was responsible for 'all documents in Great Britain'. It suggested that 'the Rothschild group' of the London OSS Field Office were acting as 'the counterpart of this organisation', that is, mirroring their work in document

62 Neumann to Rothschild, 25 November 1944: NA, RG 226, Entry 146, Box 84, Folder 1236.
63 http://www.rothschildarchive.org/ib/articles/AR2003.pdf
64 Neumann to Kent, 3 August 1945: NA, RG 226, Entry 45, Box 1.

procurement and analysis. Neumann's account is supported by an undated organisational chart for Jackson's pre-trial phase. This lists Lt. Rothschild and Allan Evans of the OSS's London Field Office as the distinctive 'second wing' of Colonel Bernays' 'Evidence Procurement' branch of the OCC.[65]

In a severe indictment of Bernays, Neumann remarks that *only* this OSS group 'is able to handle the documents and does so successfully'.[66] Rothschild also features in documentation related to the OSS's efforts to conduct research into the Nazis' persecution of the Christian churches. The OSS's extensive contacts with wider networks of Allied intelligence agencies and diplomatic sources also fed General Donovan with memoranda on religious persecution. For example, Walter Rothschild was the source of information from British Foreign Office sources on the 'German Monists Organisation', of potential use 'in connection with the prosecution of religious organisations by the Nazi government'.[67] There are also occasional references to the DRU in Justice Jackson's papers, the most important of which, a memo from Bernays, indicates the Rothschild was involved in discussions associated with the selection of the organisational defendants, particularly the amorphous German 'High Command':

> You will remember when we conferred with Lt. Rothschild about proposed groupings of defendants, we were very vague indeed about what the German General Staff really is and consists of.[68]

In short, it appears from the three fragmentary sources examined so far that the DRU worked semi-independently to supplement, in a comparatively successful manner, the evidence-gathering and analysis functions of Bernays' division of the OCC in London.

The single most complete, if somewhat partial, source on the institutional

65 This was supported by others including OSS's Whitney Harris, who had access to top secret OSS X2 (counter espionage) Branch documentation from his former colleagues in that branch, and Capt. Auchinchoss and OSS's Lt. Comdr. Bracken: 'Organization Chart', Jackson Papers, *op cit*, Box 106.

66 *Ibid.*

67 See Rothschild to Col. Bernays GSC: 'German Monists Organisation', 9 July 1945, Cornell Collection, Rare Books Room, Vol. 19, 18.05, which stated: '1. Attached is a report published by PID of the Foreign office in the PID/PW series 15 dealing with the German Monists Organisation'. Donovan's handwritten addition to Rothschild's memorandum indicated that he forwarded it on the 16 July to 'Commd'r James Donovan, Donovan's General Counsel', with the further order 'hold for Neumann', who was about to join the key European side of the OSS's war crimes project. '2. This report might be useful in connection with the prosecution of religious organisations by the Nazi government' [handwritten arrow 16 July to Commdr Donovan and 'hold for Neumann'].

68 Bernays to Donovan, 2 July 1945, Jackson Collection, University of Chicago.

processes through which the R-Series materials were gathered is a detailed report from early October that Rothschild made to, and at the request of, OSS's General Counsel and war crimes specialist, James B. Donovan.[69] As already noted, James Donovan was a senior member of Justice Jackson's US Chief of Counsel responsible for coordinating OSS's various contributions to the Nuremberg process, and with particular responsibility for the production of atrocity films and other 'visual evidence'. Rothchild's report from early October 1945, little more than a six weeks before the Nuremberg trial opened, is written not as a final report but rather as a summary of work to date. As such, Rothschild anticipated that the work of his DRU was to continue until Jackson terminated the phase of the forthcoming trial involving the preparation of documentary evidence. This implies that, despite some staff reductions during September 1945, this unit continued to operate after the general dissolution of the OSS at the start of October 1945. In other words, it became part of the OSS's successor organisation, the Strategic Services Unit of the US War Department (SSU). As of the start of October 1945, the DRU was a comparatively small organisation consisting of nine professional and four clerical staff, some of whom were on the budget of the General Counsel of OSS.[70]

Rothschild's report summarises the 'Contribution of the Documentary Research Unit to the Work of the U.S. Chief of Counsel'. It opens with a brief statement regarding the origins of this OSS unit, and the unique range of intelligence sources that it obtained. In the absence of the screening activity of Rothschild's unit, intelligence officials working for a variety of different Anglo-American military and air intelligence bodies would probably have processed documentation of particular interest to the Nuremberg prosecutors without ever realising that this was the case:

> The DRU was activated by R&A London on 10 June 1945 for the specific purpose of collecting and processing War crimes documents from sources in the UK. Mr. Allan Evans, Chief of R&A Branch, personally arranged that the DRU obtained access to all existing channels of documentary procurement which OSS had already established for other operations. In addition, General Donovan gave this Unit letters of introduction to several newly established document centers in London, notably to Gen. MacDonald of USSTAFF and through him to both CIOS and Air Intelligence. Contact was taken up with all these agencies and it was agreed that all documents of War Crimes interest should be submitted DRU for screening and processing in the interest of the Chief of Counsel.

69 Rothschild to James Donovan, 3 October 1945: Cornell Collection, Vol. 57.03; NA, RG 226, Entry 1, Box 2, Folder 7.

70 *Ibid.*

> The undersigned was appointed Chief of the Unit, several analysts from other R&A sections were assigned him; he was also authorized to employ German speaking legal experts to assist in this work.[71]

Rothschild's report emphasises that, when compared with the relatively slow start made by other sections of Justice Jackson's organisation during the mid-summer of 1945, the DRU 'hit the ground running', as it were. Indeed, by July 1945: 'DRU had already established all necessary contacts with document centers in the U.K.' This headstart impressed Colonel Bernays, whom Jackson had placed in charge of procurement of evidence. Bernays:

> approved all arrangements by DRU, and appointed the unit as his sole agent for the collecting and processing of documents in the U.K., with the sole exception of certain naval documents which were routed through a special channel.[72]

Rothschild noted that inter-agency collaboration was continued by Bernays' successor, Colonel Wheeler, so that: 'since its inception the DRU has been fulfilling functions which otherwise the U.S. Chief of Counsel would have had to carry through its own staff'.[73] In addition to the procurement and screening of German documents, the staff of DRU (most of whom had been analysing aspects of the Nazi regime throughout the war) assisted many of Jackson's staff through *ad hoc* consultancy on specific issues: 'With information and data on German government, administration and military organization.' Such assistance, which supplemented the assistance provided by Franz Neumann's specialists from Washington R&A Branch of OSS, would have been needed. This was because few of Jackson's senior staff possessed any grasp of the emergence and changing organisational structures of the Nazi regime and its internal policies. Even fewer could read German. The DRU also prepared 'a catalogue of all published laws and decrees signed by any one of the defendants in the period from January 1933 to May 1945'.[74] For reasons already mentioned, the Nuremberg prosecutors needed to establish not only that various Nazi laws and decrees were unlawful but also that the very act of enacting such measures was a criminal deed. In effect, Rothschild's report claims that, at an early stage, the DRU had already successfully carved out a vital niche for itself in the procurement of relevant documentation from a variety of different intelligence sources, and continued to service the requirements of Jackson's organisation once its core staff had moved to Nuremberg.

For present purposes, one of the most useful parts of this report lies in the details it provides of the wide-ranging Allied intelligence agencies that the DRU was able to draw upon in procuring and selecting materials for the OCC:

71 *Ibid.* 72 *Ibid.* 73 *Ibid.* 74 *Ibid.*

> Close contact is being maintained with the following Procurement centers in the U.K.: MIPS, London, the basic source for captured German documents; ADRC (Air Document Research Center) which is the overall source for air documents captured from the Germans and with whom a member of the DRU Staff is stationed permanently for screening purposes; ADI (K) and AI 12 – special US–British Air intelligence Agencies which obtain certain documents directly from *their* forward centers on the Continent; CIOS (now separated into the British BIOS and the American FIAT) who handle mostly technical documents. Material is obtained directly from them or through the British Document Center at Heddon House; U.S. Strategic Bombing Survey who collected a considerable number of German documents through their own field teams; EPS, a special agency formerly under G2 Shaef, interested mainly in documents on German Paramilitary organizations and the police; recently removed to Berlin as part of the Control Council.[75]

Securing this complex chain of inter-agency collaborations was particularly impressive given the notorious inability of intelligence agencies to cooperate with each other, even within a single nation. In addition, however, the DRU's document procurement and analysis activities served two distinct masters in the war crimes field: the War Crimes Branch of the Judge Advocate General Department (JAGD), responsible for non-international trials, as well as Jackson's OCC, which was established only to try the 'major war criminals'. An agreement was negotiated in August 1945 making the DRU the sole local channel for both these agencies, allowing an effective sharing of documentation relevant to both. In other words, the DRU acted as a joint sorting house for documentation obtained through Allied intelligence agencies located in the UK, the allowing materials originally gathered for the JAGD to be shared with the OCC and *vice versa*.

Amongst the most interesting sections of the Rothschild report is his summary of how individual documents were actually processed within a comprehensive screening, translation and analysis process. This reveals the manner in which the DRU employed various analytical categories formulated by internal OSS specialists, including Sheldon Glueck, a Harvard legal academic and war crimes specialist who was employed as a consultant to the OSS. Such screening preceded transmission to the OCC and, where appropriate, the JAGD:

> All documents are screened for anything or interest to the War Crimes prosecution and those found pertinent are translated into English. An analysis is then made on a form originally prepared by Prof. Glueck who

75 *Ibid.*

> based himself on the experiences of the DRU. At present, the DRU uses the official analysis form of the [OCC]. Thus covering all phases of document processing within the Unit and submitting all documents in final form to the U.S. Chief of Counsel. In the course of this operation, documents are also photostated.[76]

A central part of the process of analysing these documents was the adoption of a *thematic approach*. This approach brought together integrated dossiers stemming from different sources derived from various parts of the Nazi regime but which illustrated different aspects of a common topic relevant to the charges faced by the Nuremberg defendants. As Rothschild notes:

> It should be noted that these sets as a rule combine a number of individual documents on the same subject matter. Quite often, documents obtained from different sources were tied together in one dossier on a specific aspect of the case. For example, DRU submitted a set of documents on the German policy of killing US and British aircrews. The correspondence on the policy itself, conducted between the leading members of High Command of the German Armed forces, was connected with statements made by Göring at a meeting of his staff, with an order by Himmler to his police, with police orders on a lower level and finally with reports on actual killings sent out by local air force detachments. These several documents were analysed and presented to the US Chief of Counsel as integrated dossiers.[77]

Such dossiers were particularly helpful to the prosecutors who were drafting specific prosecution briefs in topics covered by the R-Series because they saved these lawyers considerable research. These integrated bundles were not cited as such in the prosecution briefs but were rather written up as if the hard-pressed prosecutors had personally assembled, analysed and cross-referenced all the relevant individual documents. In some cases, this allowed their draft briefs to appear to be the result of a far greater documentary research than was the case because a significant part of the cross-referencing work had already been accomplished by DRU officials.

As of the start of October 1945, Rothschild stated that: 'Over 140 sets of documents have been forwarded so far to the US Chief of Counsel, each one pertaining to one or several aspects of the case.' He also emphasised the *qualitative* aspects of the DRU's contribution, claiming that: 'Some of the documents obviously will be of paramount importance to the prosecution.' Rothschild's report cites the DRU's procurement from the American strategic bombing analysts (to which OSS had also contributed staff, including lawyers

76 *Ibid.* 77 *Ibid.*

who went on to become Nuremberg prosecutors such as Bernard Meltzer) of 71 volumes of Albert Speer's minutes of his meetings with Hitler and with German industrial leaders. Extracts of these minutes contained material implicating several of the Nuremberg defendants. Another document submitted by DRU, pertinent to the charge of 'waging aggressive war', was the overall 'masterplan' of the German Air Force prepared in May of 1938. This 'envisaged a major war against Britain, France and Russia to start in 1942 while the smaller countries, Czechoslovakia, Poland, Hungary and the Baltic States should have been annexed before that time'. Rothschild also claimed that: 'Another important document was an order by Keitel instructing the German armed forces to use terror methods against the civilian population in occupied territory.' He also highlighted how 'Several excellent documents were obtained from EDS out of Himmler's private files.' Rothschild finished his report by attaching a copy of a commendation of the work of the Unit received from Colonel M. C. Bernays.

A close survey of the relevant OSS literature, much of which has been declassified or otherwise made public only during the last decade, suggests that the contributions of the DRU were well regarded by senior OSS war crimes staff who relocated from Washington to continental Europe during July 1945. One would expect Rothschild to present a positive view of his unit's work. This positive impression was, however, also shared by Franz Neumann. Neumann, at this time First Chief of the OSS's War Crimes Research Unit, reported most positively on Rothschild's work. As already noted, Neumann contrasted the positive qualities of this unit with the chaotic state of affairs prevailing in other sections of Jackson's organisation at that vital time in preparing for the Nuremberg trials.[78]

Conclusion

The material examined and discussed in this section contradicts the criticism that OSS officials failed to honour General Donovan's early promises concerning the ability of this organisation to gather and analyse pertinent instances of actual and potential evidence. It has demonstrated that the evidence gathered and integrated into 598 thematic dossiers played an important role in helping establish key parts of the prosecution case. This conclusion is supported by the fact that, in a number of cases, R-Series documents were singled out as especially compelling not only by Jackson's summary of the prosecution case but also within the Tribunal's final judgment.

78 Neumann to Kent, 3 August 1945: NA, RG 226, Entry 45, Box 1.

Chapter 8

General Donovan's contribution to the Nuremberg trials

> In the early stages of the case, General Donovan was personally very helpful.
>
> (Justice Jackson, US Chief Nuremberg Prosecutor, to President Truman, 1 December, 1945)

> General Donovan had contributed a great deal to the early stages of the trial preparation because of his work with the OSS, which he headed during World War II. Donovan made available all the evidence which had been accumulated by his staff.
>
> (Gerhart, Justice Jackson's biographer, 359)

> Great enterprises attract illustrious people and often lead to fierce personal quarrels. The Jackson–Donovan conflict involved differences about both policy and procedure, but one must wonder what additional benefits might have accrued to the prosecution if these two great men could have composed their differences.
>
> (Drexel Sprecher, Nuremberg Prosecutor, 170)

> I never had any feeling that anyone had trapped me into the thing [the Chief Prosecutor's collaboration with Donovan's OSS] but I was in the trap.
>
> (R. H. Jackson)[1]

Introduction

General William Donovan, a former New York State prosecutor and successful Wall Street lawyer,[2] was the sole wartime Director of the Office of

1 Oral History Project, University of Chicago Law School, Jackson Collection.

2 William Joseph Donovan was born in Buffalo, New York State, in January 1883. He was a college football player (where he earned the nickname 'Wild Bill') at Columbia University, from where he graduated in 1905. In 1912, he established, and led, a New York State National Guard cavalry troop that served in the 1916 Pancho Villa campaign on the Mexican

Strategic Services (OSS) – the American wartime intelligence organisation. This organisation was formally abolished in October 1945 but then reconstituted as the CIA in 1947 but without Donovan as its director. This chapter discusses some of the factors that explain the emergence of inter-agency collaboration between Donovan's OSS and Justice Jackson. Jackson, a former US Supreme Court Judge, was appointed Chief of Counsel for the US Nuremberg prosecution body, the Office of Chief Counsel (OCC). This chapter then describes in some detail the different types of support with which Donovan was able to provide Jackson, including specialist war crimes staff, logistical provisions and assistance in both domestic and international negotiations. The final sections examine the nature, sources and implications of the growing tension between Jackson and Donovan, his ostensible or 'presumed' deputy.[3] In other words, the aim is to describe – and as far as possible explain – the emergence of close cooperation between Donovan and other members of the OSS and senior war crimes prosecutors employed by Jackson's organisation. A second aim is to explain the factors behind the eventual breakdown of this cooperation at its most senior level; that is, the rupture of the Donovan–Jackson relationship.

Before this chapter examines the details of the formation of the immediate post-war relationship between Donovan and Justice Jackson, and thereby the OSS and the US Nuremberg prosecutors, it is necessary to clarify the earlier and repeated attempts by Donovan to carve out a role for his agency within proposed war crimes trials. It is vital to see how these were largely frustrated during the last two years of the war, largely because – as an intelligence organisation – the OSS lacked any policy-making role. Such clarification is important because it help explain, at least in part, why Jackson – who had no prior background in working in areas related to Nazi war crimes – had

border. During the First World War Donovan served in France with the US Army's 165 Infantry (69th New York) Regiment. For his military service, he was awarded the Medal of Honor (America's highest valour award), for leading a successful assault. He not only reached the rank of Colonel by the end of the war but also earned the Distinguished Service Cross, and three 'purple hearts'. From 1918 he served as the US Attorney for the Western District of New York and was later promoted to Assistant US Attorney General, 1924–29. From 1929 to 41, Donovan practised law in New York and was Republican nominee for Governor of New York in 1932. Before American involvement in the Second World War, he acted as an emissary for Navy Secretary Frank Knox and President Roosevelt, during which time he travelled to Britain and elsewhere in Europe. In July 1941, he was appointed by Roosevelt as Coordinator of Information (COI), a position which made him the first overall chief of the US intelligence community. He was re-appointed by Roosevelt as Director of the Office of Strategic Services (OSS, successor to the COI) in June 1942, a post he held until October 1945, when the OSS was disbanded. For additional biographical information, see: http://en.wikipedia.org/ wiki/William_J._Donovan.

3 During an interview, one former Nuremberg prosecutor, Henry King, described Donovan as Jackson's 'presumed deputy': http://www.roberthjackson.org/Man/theman2-6-3/.

every good reason to initiate collaboration with Donovan and his organisation, and why Donovan, for his own reasons, promptly accepted the type of inter-agency collaboration offered by Jackson.

There are a number of factors that we can identify which, to a greater or lesser extent, explain Donovan's interest in extending his organisation's involvement in war crimes issues into the immediate post-war period. These factors include institutional expansionism, a strategy for securing the post-war survival of at least certain branches of the OSS. Later in this chapter, we will discuss aspects of Donovan's dispute with Jackson that indicate that the OSS Director also had personal ambitions to play a starring role in the Nuremberg trials. These ambitions included conducting a pre-scripted cross-examination of Göring and Schacht. Their evidence would be provided effectively for the prosecution, and – Donovan hoped – secured as part of private deals resembling a plea-bargain arrangement. The plan was that such dramatic trial evidence would effectively not only incriminate other defendants but also discredit the entire regime in which they played a leading role.

Donovan's attempts to secure a leading role for the OSS

Donovan had taken an interest in war crimes issues almost from the start of the COI/OSS, which continued throughout the war. An inspection of the archival record of Donovan's own office files reveals that, as early as a series of memorandum from the summer of 1942, the OSS Director had taken a significant interest in war crimes issues. These included an analysis of the difficulties posed by trials of the Japanese, as well as German soldiers, and their military and political leaders. For example, in a memorandum of 17 August 1942, Donovan stated the need:

> That we examine into the set-up and the methods of the special mission which was set up by the British in the last war to inquire into the atrocities of the Germans. Profiting by the experience I wish you would discuss among yourselves the possibility of setting up a fact finding board that would inquire into this whole matter of Japanese atrocities and treatment of prisoners. In addition to obtaining statements from all those who have been imprisoned, prepare a report and draw such conclusions as the facts indicate, including a finding whether or not this treatment of the prisoners is a policy of the higher command or was the result of the action of independent commanders.[4]

4 Donovan to Com. Vanderbilt: NA, RG 226, M1642, Roll 121.

In other words, Donovan was interested in learning the historical lessons of the previous World War in order to address war crimes issues that could arise in the immediate post-war context, particularly the legally complex issue of allocating different degrees of criminal responsibility for those who issue and receive orders to commit war crimes.

At the end of October 1943, President Roosevelt asked Donovan whether, and to what extent, the question of war crimes trials had been looked into at the OSS.[5] In response, Donovan immediately sent him a memorandum prepared in the OSS and referred to the fact that a list of proposed German war criminals, and thus potential defendants, was already being processed.[6]

At this time, Donovan formulated initial plans for the selection of defendants consistent with the vague generalities contained in existing policy statements issued by the Allied leadership, which are discussed below. This was a topic that had long exercised Donovan and his senior officials. The OSS's role as an intelligence agency monitoring the actions and intentions of the Nazi military, political, economic and administrative leadership meant that, from its inception, this organisation inevitably gathered considerable material that was relevant to the identification and ranking of potential war crimes defendants. Certainly, the OSS regarded the preparation of lists of possible war criminals as falling within its remit if only by default. For example, an internal memorandum sent to Donovan and the OSS Supporting Committee on 17 September 1942 argued that the OSS needed *to begin* to formulate a list of alleged Nazi war criminals and circulate this to other potentially interested US agencies. President Roosevelt never gave OSS formal responsibility for identifying and selecting appropriate defendants in proposed war crimes trials from the Axis powers in general (including Italy and Japan), this task being reserved to a future decision within the immediate post-war period. Nevertheless, Donovan took on this task partly to keep up with the analysis of the OSS's British counterparts in Special Operations Executive (SOE). Equally importantly, the OSS had strategic reasons for avoiding the institutional embarrassment of having this agency's *own* spies, agents and double-agents within Germany, including those working within the Gestapo (Hans Gisevius) and Foreign Ministry ('George Wood'), featuring on the 'wanted list' of other Allied agencies, such as the US Army's Counter Intelligence Corps. Taylor wrote:

> David Bowes-Lyon has asked if we have or are in the process of preparing a list of Nazi War Criminals in Allied Countries in accordance with the President's statement about trials after the war. Bowes-Lyon is under

5 On this see Roosevelt Library, PSF/Subject, Box 167, correspondence from 25, 27 and 29 October 1943.

6 *Ibid.*

> the impression that SOE is compiling such a list in England and supposes that we might want to do the same thing here. His feeling is – and this corresponds to my own – that such a list is important chiefly for negative reasons, that is, to prevent irresponsible persons from compiling and eventually publishing lists which would probably include the names of choice British and American agents.[7]

It appears that only limited progress on drawing up such a list took place during the next 12 months. However, by 15 October 1943, there is documentary evidence of further developments. Donovan's office files from this period contain a memo sent to him on 15 October 1943 from the Polish ambassador ['L' ambassadeur de Pologne']. From this it is clear that Donovan's early thinking and plans included the idea of selecting a number of leading Nazis, such as Göring and Himmler, for a 'summary' form of justice, particularly those responsible for the indiscriminate extermination of both Christian and Jewish civilians. This memo states:

> I find it difficult to give you a comprehensive list of all the Nazi leaders responsible for war crimes who should be brought to justice in the summary way we discussed . . . Furthermore, I am sending you a list of those in Poland and drawing your special attention to it, considering that Poland has been chosen by the Nazis as the country which they are out to destroy completely and where they are quite openly exterminating the nation and the Christian and Jewish Poles indiscriminately.[8]

Donovan's files from this period also contain a memorandum from the Secretariat (C. H. Bane) to Dr Rogers, noting that Donovan was personally pro-active in ordering that such a list of potential defendants should be established:

> The Director's [Donovan's] reaction to the attached document was that it 'might go to the Planning Staff with the thought of preparing a list of German officers who should be punished'. Accordingly, I am sending the material to you.[9]

This memo included an interesting attachment which identified a number of leading Nazis as potential defendants in future war crimes trials:

7 Edmond L. Taylor (OSS psychological warfare specialist) to Donovan, October 1942: NA, RG 226, M1642, Roll 121.

8 Donovan to Polish Ambassador, 15 October 1943: NA, RG 226, M1642, Roll 121.

9 Bane to Rogers, 25 October 1943: NA, RG 226, M1642, Roll 121.

> MEMBERS OF HITLER'S CABINET . . .
> LEY – Labor Minister, Chief for slave labor measures;
> FUNK – Economic, Reichsbank Chief (successor of Schacht).
> GOVERNORS OF THE VARIOUS COUNTRIES
> . . . HANS FRANK – POLAND . . .

These and other individuals eventually featured amongst those selected as major war criminals at the first Nuremberg trials.

There is other evidence suggesting that, during the second half of 1943, and partly as a result of Donovan's personal interests, the Central European Section of R&A section was regularly involved in monthly discussions concerning who should be ultimately identified and prosecuted as a Nazi war criminal. These discussions were supplemented by a formal OSS/R&A report on this topic. For example, there is an internal OSS memo dated 1 November 1943 on Lt. Comdr. Hinks' memorandum on 'Trial on War Criminals', which includes the following important remarks:

> There follow the essential points of my conversation with Mr. Holborn of R& A, in regard of the preparation of a list of war criminals: . . . As far the United States is concerned, the State Dept. has adopted a definite view in regard to the trial of war criminals and considerable work has been done in this subject, in conjunction with the Justice Dept . . . For your information, Mr. Holborn told me that this subject comes up regularly about once a month. He has, within recent weeks, sent the General a memorandum on the subject under Dr. Langer's name and has also produced a report entitled, 'Trial of War Criminals and the Armed Forces'.[10]

Donovan's office files also suggest that considerable internal discussion had been generated by the question of where responsibility for drawing up and maintaining lists of Nazi war criminals should lie. The OSS planning group suggested that 'a panel of R&A men [should be called] and discuss this problem'.[11]

Donovan's files indicate that the OSS had drawn up a proposed list of alleged war criminals that had been discussed at an internal 'German Panel' meeting of 29 October 1943. Initially, Donovan was only willing to develop this area of investigation further under the leadership of the R&A Central European Section's Hajo Holborn, if this project could be carried out in conjunction with other government agencies:

10 Richard Helms to Robert B. McLeod, 1 November 1943: NA, RG 226, M1642, Roll 121.

11 Hinks to McLeod: 'Trial of War Criminals', 27 October 1943: 'General Donovan has suggested that we might prepare a list of war criminals': NA, RG 226, M1642, Roll 121.

> It was suggested that Dr. Hajo Holborn would be the best person to provide the necessary information . . . In the light of the facts, it would not appear to be advisable for R&A to undertake any independent investigation unless requested by the State Dept. or the Inter-Allied Investigation Commission.[12]

I have found no evidence that, despite Donovan's personal willingness to develop OSS involvement in such an inter-agency project regarding war crimes trial planning, the necessary degree of inter-agency collaboration was ever forthcoming from these branches of government, whose cooperation was vital to its success.[13] By September 1944, however, the OSS leadership appeared to have decided to push forward even without support from other agencies. Hence, the Central European Section of the R&A Branch revised and extended lists of prominent individuals in the Third Reich who could, at a later date, be formally charged as war criminals. This more detailed list related names to specific functions, activities and responsibilities.[14] Once again, many of those who featured on this revised R&A list were eventually tried at Nuremberg.

The wartime efforts of the OSS to carve out a role with respect to future war crimes prosecution was not confined to drawing up possible lists of Nazi defendants. It is worth examining an important memorandum Donovan sent to President Roosevelt as early as 1943.[15] This document indicates that, by the autumn of 1943, Donovan was making detailed plans for the extradition of listed Nazi war criminals. This planning took place during a period when elsewhere little thought had been devoted to the institutional implications of these issues.[16] In this memo, which is in effect a covering letter, Donovan argued that Roosevelt should mobilise other branches of the US government, including the US State Department, by holding a convention:

> You will recall that you asked me certain questions about the possibility for the trial of war criminals. I enclose a proposal, prepared by our Planning Group, which I sent to the State Dept. some months ago, which would have the United Nations conclude a convention for the extradition of Axis war criminals . . . I have prepared a partial list of present German

12 McLeod to Hinks: 'Listing of war criminals', 2 November 1943: NA, RG 226, M1642, Roll 121.

13 Later we will review James Donovan's downbeat assessment of the failures of such wartime inter-agency cooperation, which he presented to Jackson in May 1945.

14 OSS/R&A 2577.2: 'Problems concerning the treatment of war criminals: list of potential war criminals under proposed Allied policy Directives', 30 September 1944.

15 Donovan to Roosevelt, 25 October 1943: NA, RG 226, M1642, Roll 121.

16 *Ibid.*

> officials in that class of criminals, and will see whether other names might be included.[17]

Donovan's memo also sought to anticipate possible defence arguments in subsequent war crimes trials. In particular, it aimed to rebut the positivist argument that Nazi defendants who had committed even the worst atrocities were still acting in a manner that, in a technical sense, was authorised by prevailing German law. The proposed counter-argument from OSS was that German positive law formulated during the Nazi era must, following a decision by the Permanent Court of International Justice at the Hague, be considered 'legally invalid' by international law. Any positive German law authorising atrocities against civilians and others should be treated not only as contrary to established principles of natural law but also inconsistent with the German constitution:

> NAZI CRIMINALS
>
> Introduction
>
> No German could be held responsible for any act committed at the order or with the backing of the German Government if the German legal system were held to be valid. In that case, the individual executing a specific act, can easily invoke the justification of positive German law which is so flexible that it will cover any action backed the authority of state or party. It must then be stressed that the basic tenets of the German legal system are not only morally reprehensible but are legally invalid. This may be proven by the Advisory Opinion of December 4, 1935 rendered by the Permanent Court of International Justice at The Hague. The Danzig Free State had, by a statute of September 1, 1935, imitated the Nazi penal code which allowed punishment even where no statute declared an action punishable if an action is 'deserving of punishment according to the healthy racial feeling'. The permanent Court declared such penal provision incompatible with the civil liberties guaranteed in the Danzig Constitution. We should take the view that the basic principles of Natural law are valid everywhere and cannot be suspended by positive laws . . . We must, therefore, demand from all members of this court and from all representatives of the public prosecutor's office that they are first politicians, and only then judges and not vice versa.[18]

Roosevelt, for his part, forwarded the OSS memorandum to the US Secretary of State; and also asked him about the 'present status of the war crime trials'.[19] It appears that little came of Donovan's would-be initiative, however.

17 *Ibid.* 18 Deutsches Recht, 1939, 485, *ibid.* 19 Bigman, 1995, *op cit*, 197.

By January 1944, the OSS were engaged in producing their own analysis of war crimes issues raised by the text of the Moscow Declaration of 1 November 1943, which had been issued by the Allied leadership. The fact that the R&A Branch had completed a report on the outstanding problems with the Moscow Declaration, which had not been acted upon by the senior policy-makers of the Joint Chief of Staffs who first commissioned it,[20] possibly added to the frustration of Donovan's attempts to prepare the OSS for a major post-war role in this area.[21] Bigman has provided the best available analysis (drawing on German-language as well as US archival sources) of the immediate institutional context surrounding the reaction to the Moscow Declaration:

> After this declaration, the retribution for war crimes could certainly be considered as a declared war aim of the Allies, yet, as with most other war aims, this lacked concrete ideas or even plans for its realisation.[22]

On 6 October 1944, Donovan presented to McCloy, who was second only to Stimson within the US War Department, the just completed R&A Branch report titled 'Problems Concerning War Criminals' (R&A 2577). This was accompanied by a somewhat exaggerated (and ultimately counterproductive) covering note from Donovan stating that this 'was the story' on the war crimes question.[23] The head of the R&A Branch, William L. Langer, took measures to ensure a wide distribution for this report within OSS, with a copy sent direct from Langer to Donovan,[24] who – in turn – took the report sufficiently seriously to forward another copy to John McCloy, Assistant Secretary of War.[25]

It appears that Donovan's personal views on how best Nazi war criminals should be tried was influenced, to some extent, by his OSS–R&A Branch colleague, Franz Neumann (OSS's leading analyst specialising in Nazi Germany). Donovan's policy position during the war was consistent not only with the earlier R&A reports supervised by Neumann's Central European Section of OSS–R&A, but also with both Neumann's own private opinion about the strategic advantages for post-war democratic reconstruction of having the Nazi regime convicted by German courts for violations of German law. Following the arguments of Neumann's R&A sub-section, Donovan's own plan at this time at least was to have OSS oversee trials held by anti-Nazi Germans according to traditional German criminal law. The rationale for

20 See R&A 1482: 'The Statement of Atrocities of the Moscow Tripartite Conference, December 10, 1943'; see also R&A 113.33, Political Intelligence Report No. 33, section 1.3.

21 R&A Report, 1482.

22 Bigman, 1995, *op cit*, 196.

23 B. Smith, 1982, *op cit*, 58.

24 Memo, 30 September 1944: NA 226, M1642, roll 121.

25 Memo, 3 October 1944: NA, RG 226, M1642, roll 121.

this was that this would ensure that there could be no question of the trials being discredited as mere victor's justice, or critiques made of the imposition and backdating of newly created offences (a critique which later haunted the legal validity of the Nuremberg trials).[26]

One internal OSS memo to Donovan from Franz Neumann dated May 1945 (but reflecting earlier exchanges between these two men) indicates that Donovan had previously broached the subject with Neumann of OSS's institutional involvement in war crimes prosecution issues, and that Neumann himself was anxious to influence the OSS Director's own approach. Neumann, who had been appointed Acting Chief of R&A's Central European Section, sent a memo on 4 May 1945 direct to General Donovan entitled 'War Criminals'. He introduced his three main arguments by reference to specifically political factors:

> Pursuant to the conversation which we had some time ago concerning the trial of war criminals. I take the liberty of stressing certain political aspects of the problem which tend to be overlooked.[27]

Neumann's first point was designed to combat the possibility of extra-judicial executions of war criminals by implying that this would mean that the policy of the US would display less respect for the rule of law than Stalin's Soviet Union:

> Mr. Justice Jackson, in a statement made before his appointment, seemed to stress his preference for a disposal of Nazi leaders accused of political crimes by non-judicial procedure – that is, by straight execution without trial. Without arguing the merits of this statement, I should like to point out that this is not the Russian point of view. Trainin's book and a pamphlet by D. N. Pritt, K. C., M.P. (Communist Party follower) makes it clear that the USSR and the Communists desire trials not only for violation of the rules of warfare but also for the breaking of the peace. There are indications that influential circles in GB are likely to oppose such trials for fear that during them British appeasement policy toward Germany may be exposed. This is brought out dramatically in the book by Cassius: 'The Trial of Mussolini' (London 1943).[28]

Neumann's second argument to Donovan was designed to combat the possibility that, given the prevailing state of international law, internal atrocities committed by the Third Reich against its own citizens would escape war

26 F. von Schlabrendorff, *The Secret War Against Hitler* (Oxford/Boulder: Westview Press, 1994), 259–61.

27 Neumann to Donovan, 4 May 1945: NA, RG 226, M1642, Roll 121.

28 *Ibid.*

crimes trials. This obvious injustice could arise if undue weight was given to the legalistic argument that such atrocities committed by Germans on their fellow nationals (including members of Neumann's own family) were not genuine war crimes since they did not occur between those legally defined as 'combatants':

> No mention has yet been made of how to deal with crimes committed by Germans against Germans, although Mr Grew committed the US to the punishment of such offenses. The problem will loom large in Germany and Austria, but as yet no provision has been made to meet it by the occupation authorities.[29]

Neumann's final point was that the division of responsibilities between Allied and municipal courts was primarily a *political*, rather than a purely legal, issue:

> This leads to the final problem that of a division of labour between Allied and international tribunals on the one hand and German courts on the other. It can hardly be assumed that Allied and international tribunals will be able to deal with more than an insignificant number of crimes and criminals (I consider even 5,000 an insignificant number). It is a political question whether and to what extent reconstituted German courts should be allowed to deal with the much larger number of crimes and criminals not handled by us.[30]

Neumann finished this somewhat direct approach to his ultimate superior within the OSS, one that bypassed at least three separate layers of intermediary authorities within this organisational hierarchy, in a cautious – even defensive – manner: 'I bring these political problems respectfully to your attention so that you may communicate them at your discretion to the proper persons.'

On 15 December 1944, Donovan committed his organisation to cooperation with the War Crimes Division of JAG (Legal Department) of the US Army.[31] The OSS agreed to cooperate in the gathering of evidence for future trials and to prepare lists of potential defendants.[32] Following this initiative from the OSS Director, James Donovan, and R&A Chief, William Langer, also became especially pro-active on the war crimes question. This was particularly the case during the winter of 1944–45, when Allied victory in Europe

29 *Ibid.* 30 *Ibid.*

31 T. Taylor, *The Anatomy of the Nuremberg Trials: A Personal Memoir* (New York: Knopf, 1992), 47.

32 Donovan to List S, 15 December 1944: NA, RG 226, Entry 190, Box 536, Folder 124.

was appearing increasingly likely. James Donovan wrote a letter to the JAG War Crimes Office on 20 January 1945, requesting advice on whether the OSS:

> [S]hould make positive plans for the gathering of information and evidence pertaining to war crimes committed against nationals other than those specified in the directive referred to, and as to the ultimate use of all information furnished by your office.[33]

At the start of 1945, Donovan's own efforts included making high-profile representations to have an American judge of his choice, Justice Douglas of the Supreme Court, act as a US observer on Soviet war crimes trials of Nazis taking place during the winter of 1944–45.[34] Donovan's office files from the late winter of 1944–45 show that he was willing to intervene personally to ensure that any inter-agency liaisons or internal OSS projects in this field, which were always at risk of being dissipated as a mere subset of other joint projects with, for example, the War Crimes Office, were instead highly centralised and coordinated under James Donovan.[35] In March 1945, after discussion with the President's close adviser Harry Hopkins, Donovan sent a memorandum to Vice-President Truman suggesting that the 'German people themselves' should 'undertake to bring to trial and punish certain war criminals under pre-1933 German laws'.[36] Summing up the wartime efforts of the OSS Director's work in this area prior to Jackson's appointment in May 1945, Taylor notes:

> Although there was a certain volatility in Donovan's thinking on the subject, it nevertheless is clear that his interest was genuine, for early in April he directed the OSS General Counsel, Lt James Donovan: 'to get us a top-flight staff on war crimes' which were 'something on which we must be prepared at once.'[37]

33 Cited, or paraphrased, in an internal memorandum 24 January 1945 Memorandum from Melvin Purvis, War Crimes Office to Lt. James B. Donovan: 'Scope of War Crimes Information Desired and Intended Ultimate Use Thereof'. NA, RG 226, Director's Office Files M1642, Roll 121.

34 Cheston to Steeinius, 12 January 1945 (seeking to have a formal request made through US State Department channels), Director's Files: NA, RG 226, M1642, Roll 121, Frame 659.

35 See memorandum from Donovan to Colonel Doering, 10 February 1945: '1. Amplifying my memorandum of 15 December 1944 on this subject, I want to make it clear that until further notice you and the General Counsel are to serve as our sole direct liaison with all agencies on all war crimes matters, except as you may specifically direct. Our contribution in this field is to be a co-ordinated one and, whatever working liaison may be finally established, I want control centralised now until further notice': NA, RG 226, M1642, Roll 121.

36 Taylor, 1992, *op cit*, 47.

37 *Ibid*.

On the other hand, the OSS was never a policy-making institution. Whilst the war itself was still raging, the efforts of Donovan to play a key role in responding to, and further pressing for clarification of, the practical implications of Allied war crimes policy was largely frustrated by the hopelessly vague generalisations of the Allied leaders. For example, questions concerning the ultimate fate of Nazi war criminals had already been addressed in two major international agreements. The first was the resolution signed in St James's Palace, London, which included a commitment by Allied governments and governments in exile to: 'Place amongst them the principle of war mass punishment, through the channel of organized justice, of those guilty and responsible for their crimes, whether they have ordered them, perpetrated them, or in any way participated in them.'[38]

In addition, the US government had to take note of various presidential statements issued during the war. President Roosevelt's statement of 21 August 1942 included the following commitment:

> The United Nations are going to win this war. When victory has been achieved, it is the purpose of the Government of the United States, as I know it is the purpose of each of the United Nations, to make appropriate use of the information and evidence in respect of these barbaric crimes of the invaders, in Europe and in Asia. It seems only fair that they should have this warning that the time will come that they shall have to stand in courts of law in the very countries which they are now oppressing and answer for their acts.[39]

Further statements were made by the US President on 7 and 12 October 1942. These included the following commitments:

> It is not the intention of this Government or of the governments associated with us to resort to mass reprisals. It is our intention that just and sure punishment shall be meted out to the ringleaders responsible for the organized murder of thousands of innocent persons and the commission of atrocities which have violated every tenet of the Christian faith. (7 October).
>
> The United Nations have decided to establish the identity of those Nazi leaders who are responsible for the innumerable acts of savagery. As each of those criminal deeds is committed it is being carefully investigated; and the evidence is being relentlessly piled up for the future purposes of justice. We have made it entirely clear that the United Nations seek no mass reprisals against the populations of Germany and Japan. But the ringleaders and their brutal henchmen must be named,

38 Taylor, 1992, *op cit*, 25–26.

39 *Ibid*, 26.

> and apprehended, and tried in accordance with the judicial processes of criminal law. (12 October).[40]

It is clear even from a casual reading of these largely rhetorical gestures that there was little clarity concerning the type of trial, the specific offences with which defendants could be charged, or the criteria for the selection of defendants. Hence, Donovan's willingness to devote OSS resources to detailed war crimes trials planning had been frustrated because of this lack of specific detail.

In short, largely as a result of Donovan's promptings and personal support, the OSS leadership, particularly within the R&A Branch, devoted regular attention to a series of interrelated war crimes trials planning tasks. These included developing the implications of existing Allied policy statements, identifying potential defendants on the basis of these implications and anticipating possible arguments that such defendants could seek to reply upon. In addition, OSS officials analysed not only extradition issues but also the wider political programme of de-Nazification (itself developed partly by Neumann's colleagues as part of Allied Civil Affairs preparations for future Allied military government) to which planned war crimes trials could contribute an integral part. Finally, these officials studied the implications of creating a division of labour between international tribunal on the one hand, and local German-staffed courts on the other. Taken together, both the depth and breadth of this analysis placed Donovan's organisation at the forefront of those US agencies with potential responsibility for war crimes trials planning.

The next section will explore the question of whether, once the European war ended in May 1945, the opportunity of joining forces with Jackson's newly created organisation provided Donovan with the opportunity, if he handled negotiations appropriately, to translate detailed wartime analysis into practical action. It will examine the emergence of the Donovan–Jackson relationship as, perhaps, the two most senior architects of the Nuremberg war crimes trials project.

The courting and honeymoon phases

During President Harry Truman's first days in office, on 12 April 1945, he asked Supreme Court Justice Robert Jackson to serve as Chief US Prosecutor for the proposed war crimes trials, an appointment formally confirmed on 2 May 1945 with the grand title of 'US Chief of Counsel for the Prosecution of Nazi War Criminals'. In a memorandum to Truman delivered on 29 April, Jackson anticipated that:

40 *Ibid.*

> Time . . . will not permit the setting up of new organisations to dig up evidence but we will need the liberal and prompt co-operation from Army and Navy intelligence, FBI, OSS, and all other organisations in getting it together.[41]

Hence, even before his appointment was formalised, Jackson anticipated that he would need to make considerable use of the expertise of the OSS and other US intelligence organisations.

For his part, Donovan had previously contacted Jackson personally, congratulating him on his appointment and offering any institutional assistance that the OSS could provide with respect to this agency's accumulated materials. Probably spurred by Neumann's memo of the previous day, Donovan wrote to Jackson on 5 May 1945, informing him that:

> We have done certain work in the war crimes field, at the request of the War Crimes Office in the Office of the Judge Advocate General. I have asked our General Counsel, who has been directing our agency's contribution, to co-operate with you in any manner which you deem advisable.[42]

Jackson appointed Donovan within the first two weeks of the creation of his own new organisation, the Office of the Chief of Counsel (hereafter OCC).[43] Jackson gave the OSS Director the role of his senior aide, an offer Donovan accepted verbally on 12 May 1945, with this proposal formally approved by President Roosevelt three days later. The terms of the agreement were not however finalised until 7 June by means of a letter from Jackson to Donovan. This stated:

> I wish therefore to confirm my understanding with you and the General Counsel of OSS that we shall rely upon your agency to assist us in all aspects in preparing for the prosecution of the major European Axis criminals. This includes the collection, evaluation and presentation of evidence of all types (including photographic), with such assistance from other Departments and agencies of the Government as may be required.[44]

Donovan's appointment as senior aide lacked any precise remit, although Donovan himself clearly viewed his position as second only to Jackson.

41 Cited in E. C. Gerhart, *America's Advocate: Robert H. Jackson* (New York: Bobbs-Merrill, 1958), 310.

42 *Ibid*; Taylor, *op cit*, 46–47.

43 Jackson Diary, *op cit*, 12 and 15 May 1945.

44 Jackson to Donovan: NA, RG 226, M1642, Roll 121.

Taylor recalls that: 'Soon General Donovan was being referred to as Jackson's First Deputy [although] the hierarchical relation between the General on the one hand, and Shea and Alderman on the other was never clarified.'[45] With respect to administrative – as distinct from strategic – matters, Donovan was given an ambiguous decision-making role in the absence of Jackson, when Francis Shea appears to be designated as *de facto* deputy in charge of the overall organisation with full authorisation to take all necessary actions on Jackson's behalf.[46] Had Donovan been acting as sole *de facto* deputy to Jackson, then this would have been his role. Jackson and Donovan appointed James Donovan to the role of Liaison Officer between OCC and OSS.

Is it even appropriate to refer to a 'honeymoon period' in the Donovan–Jackson relationship? Could it be the case that it was precisely a range of differences in their backgrounds and values, rather than interpersonal affinities, which helped ensure an extended period of cooperation between Jackson and Donovan? Commentators have noted the possibility of difficulties in the Jackson–Donovan partnership, certain of which stemmed from biographical, as well as political, factors. Taylor for example recalls that 'the personal ties between Jackson and Donovan were never strong and they gave way shortly before the trials began'.[47] Some of these factors could be anticipated to lead to sharp differences with Jackson over the style, tactics and overall strategy for the proposed trials. For example, having surveyed the recently released collection of Donovan's papers, located at Cornell Law School, from his period as a Nuremberg prosecutor, Dennis Smith notes some important biographical differences potentially relevant to their subsequent relationship within the Nuremberg process:

> Donovan played an important part in the International Military Tribunal proceedings in his role as special assistant to the U.S. chief of counsel, Supreme Court justice Robert H. Jackson. Both men grew up in upstate New York, Jackson in Frewsburg and Donovan in Buffalo. Jackson attended the Albany Law School for a year and would become the last member of the Supreme Court to gain admission to the bar by reading law in a law office instead of through graduation from law school. Donovan graduated from the Columbia Law School and, despite an undistinguished academic record, became a prominent attorney in New York City. In World War I he earned the Congressional Medal of Honor and many other decorations. Most importantly, however, he was the founding director of the Office of Strategic Services – the precursor of the Central Intelligence Agency – and thus offered valuable intelligence

45 Taylor, *op cit*, 47.
46 'Assignments for London phase of the work', 28 June 1945, Jackson Papers, *op cit*, Box 106.
47 Taylor, *op cit*, 47.

> to Jackson as the Allies gathered evidence to construct their case against the German war criminals. Jackson and Donovan were acutely aware of the historical moment of the Nuremberg process . . .[48]

In other words, having qualified 'the hard way', Jackson's path to a prominent position in law was very different from that of Donovan's, and lacked the element of privilege associated with graduation from an elite American law school.

Donovan was a New York State Republican, and therefore not only a political rival of Jackson but also represented many of the conservative values that Jackson found personally objectionable. Indeed, Conot notes that:

> Although the two men were on 'Bob' and 'Bill' terms, they had been lifetime political opponents in New York State. Donovan had once run for Governor on a Republican ticket, was a supporter of Thomas Dewey, and, as a cosmopolitan, big business Wall Street lawyer, represented all that was anathema to the Democratic, small-town upstate Jackson.[49]

It followed that Donovan and his OSS colleagues could well have been beginning their relationship with Jackson and his senior staff with a considerable handicap. In other words, neither party to the Jackson–Donovan relationship could rely on personal friendships or shared political affiliations granting them any special position or privileges.

Donovan and other OSS prosecutors could only overcome this possible handicap by demonstrating to both Jackson and his senior loyalist group that securing the continued cooperation of the talents and expertise of a wide range of OSS officials was indispensable to the successful realisation of Jackson's own programme. Because, unlike other senior colleagues amongst the US prosecutors, Donovan and other OSS officials seconded to the OCC could not rely upon personal loyalty from Jackson, their services were vulnerable to being dispensed with. This was particularly true once the diverse roles played by different branches of the OSS, which, for the most part, were heavily weighted towards gathering and analysing prosecution evidence, rather than actual trial advocacy, became less vital. Given the General's political background and wartime experience of bitter inter-agency conflict with the FBI, as well as with US Army's military intelligence (G-2), it is unlikely that he was naïve about this vulnerability.[50]

Furthermore, the terms of the wide-ranging support offered by Donovan held attractions to both sides. At this early stage in trial preparation, starting from mid-May, Jackson urgently needed a wide range of resources that

48 1998, *op cit*, 1. 49 Conot, *op cit*, 150. 50 This is discussed below.

the OSS alone was able to provide.[51] There is little doubt that, whatever Donovan's underlying motivations and agenda, he committed relevant parts of the OSS to meeting Jackson's requirements. Indeed, Taylor credits Donovan's 'collaboration' with Jackson with 'laying the groundwork for the war crimes trials'.[52] If the personal backgrounds and political affiliations created potential for instant conflict between Donovan and Jackson, then to what extent, if at all, did this actually take place during the opening months of trial preparation? Certainly, during the period leading up to the first Nuremberg trials in November 1945, a remarkably constructive relationship existed between staff seconded to form part of Donovan's OSS war crimes staff and other elements of Jackson's organisation. It appears that, from May to late July 1945 at least (the time Donovan left for the Far East on OSS business), interpersonal relations between Jackson and the OSS Director remained positive, if not personally close. As previously discussed, both men had their own reasons to ensure that their mutually beneficial relationship worked well.

It is appropriate to refer to the period from May through to October as a honeymoon period in the OSS–OCC relationship, even though this was, as already discussed, very much a marriage of convenience, rather than mutual affection. The course of inter-agency cooperation between Jackson and Donovan, each of whom was a forceful leader of their respective organisation, contained potential for interpersonal – as well as institutional – conflict, particularly over trial strategy. However, and as already discussed, during the early months of this collaboration, both leaders shared a common interest in making considerable efforts to satisfy the immediate interests and priorities of the other. During this honeymoon phase, Donovan appears to have gone to considerable pains to 'cultivate' OSS's relationship with Jackson. For example, he arranged for senior OSS officials to greet and offer Jackson lavish open-ended hospitality,[53] air transport and additional secretarial and administrative assistance during Jackson's various sorties throughout continental Europe.[54] For his part, during mid-October Jackson took Donovan into his confidence on various professional issues relating to the organisation of the trials, and even the behind the scene intrigues concerning the selection of Judge Biddle as one of the two American Tribunal members, and not as

51 Conot, *op cit*, 15. 52 Taylor, 1992, *op cit*, 354–55.

53 Jackson Diary, *op cit*, 7 July 1945.

54 *Ibid*, 23, 25, 29 May 1945 (met at Paris by OSS colonel, travelled in Donovan's personal aircraft). Also entries for 8 July (use of OSS offices and other facilities in Austria for meetings with OSS agents from Hungary). The fact that OSS headquarters in Germany was located in the very champagne factory that Ribbentrop had worked for the provision of free refreshment for Jackson: *ibid*, 26 and 27 May and 7 July 1945.

overall President, as he had hoped.[55] Jackson, as already noted, detested Biddle.[56]

In a rare display of deference to the greater relevant experience and expertise of OSS officials, Jackson insisted at their 15 May meeting that: 'he had men on the team who knew more about the materials available and the problems to be faced'. Hence, Donovan must 'feel entirely free to tell me frankly if he thought I was headed wrong'.[57] On the same day, General Donovan, James Donovan and Jackson met at Jackson's office to share information and strategic thinking regarding the nature and scope of the OSS's future contribution to the OCC.

As Sprecher, a Nuremberg prosecutor who personally assisted Donovan at Nuremberg, has recalled, the OSS Chief brought much personal, as well as organisational, expertise to the OCC. Such expertise, possessed not only by Donovan personally but also by various espionage specialists and OSS informants and double-agents, was certainly required by the founding members of the original OCC, who lacked the necessary factual and legal background:

> As the Chief of America's principal wartime intelligence agency, Bill Donovan had considerable knowledge of developments in Nazi Germany and in German-occupied Europe. OSS had been involved in a number of ways. Under Allen Dulles the OSS office in Switzerland had assisted a number of refugees from Nazi Germany who had knowledge of Nazi crimes [particularly Hans Gisevius and von Schlabrendorff].[58] Of more significance to the Nuremberg Trial, the OSS Research and Analysis Branch had produced in-depth studies of the inner workings of the Nazi regime. These were of great value in providing instructions and orientation to Jackson's staff.[59]

Indeed, the ability of Donovan's OSS to meet vital gaps in Jackson's organisational resources and capabilities perhaps explains the uncharacteristic degree of deference each leader showed to the other at the start of their relationship. Jackson's own account of his reasoning for recruiting Donovan

55 Persico, 1994, *op cit*, 61, 76.

56 Taylor, *op cit*, 123, who notes that Jackson and Donovan supported the British judge Lord Lawrence for the presidency of the IMT.

57 Jackson Oral History Project, Columbia University, JXO 1202, 1213.

58 Donovan made extensive use of Fabian Von Schlabrendorff, who was a German lawyer. During his early years as a student at the University of Berlin, he was the leader of a small anti-Nazi group. He was arrested for his involvement in the 20 July 1944 assassination attempt on Hitler and was imprisoned at various concentration camps including Sachsenhausen, Flossenbürg, Dachau and Innsbruck.

59 Sprecher, 1998, *op cit*, 167.

contains a ready acknowledgement that his newly formed office still had much to learn from the prior background and expertise of OSS staff in the war crimes field, including that accumulated by Donovan personally:

> This I consider to be due him for the foresight, energy and skill which has been shown by him and his department in organising this work. Without these efforts we would be in very bad shape. Also if he is identified with it, it commits the entire O.S.S. organisation to our assistance and, in view of the size and diversity and geographical coverage by his staff, this would be very important ... I told him it was my judgement it would not need him full time in the preliminary work because he already had much background in it that the rest of us did not.[60]

Both men appeared to suppress any doubts they had concerning the personality and policies of the other. Certainly, Donovan did not at this stage highlight his opposition to any trial of German military leaders as a group of 'conspirators', or his preference for trials according to traditional German law, rather than retrospectively created and applied international law. During the first weeks and months of their collaboration, relations between the leadership of the two agencies appeared to be generally cooperative, if not personally close. Donovan and Jackson may well have appreciated that each needed the services of the other in order to realise their own goals. Donovan was not slow to exploit his new-found relationship with Jackson to boost one of his key interests, the preservation of the OSS into a peacetime central intelligence organisation. In agreeing to assist Jackson, Donovan acquired an ally, who might be prevailed upon to plead Donovan's case for a reconstituted post-war centralised intelligence agency with the US President. Having a US Supreme Court judge support the continuation of the OSS in face-to-face meetings with the President was certainly an attractive option for Donovan. Jackson duly obliged in a personal conference with the President on 1 June 1945,[61] during which the three men discussed now best to proceed with various defendants under US or British control, such as Hans Frank, former Governor of Poland.[62] Jackson also supported Donovan's cause in his contribution to extended meetings between himself and Donovan and senior officials from the State Department, whom Jackson found to be 'amazingly uninformed as to the intelligence service in foreign countries'.[63] Jackson further canvassed President Truman on the OSS's behalf in subsequent meetings, stressing that his experience of preparing an international war crimes trial had confirmed the:

60 Jackson Diary, *op cit*, 11 May 1945. 61 *Ibid*, 1 June 1945.
62 *Ibid*, 16 June 1945. 63 *Ibid*, 13 June 1945.

> importance of getting political intelligence as well as merely military intelligence out of foreign counties, using our own case as an example, and also the importance that the reports not pass through some department for screening which would have a special interest in slanting the information.[64]

During this meeting with Truman, the US President confirmed a joint proposal that OSS should:

> send copies of all confidential cables to me [i.e., Jackson] at the same time as they are sent to the President so that I could advise him as to any special situations arising. He approved this arrangement.[65]

With reference to the various types of assistance that stemmed from the relationship between Donovan and Jackson, Taylor's memoir notes:

> The two men, old acquaintances but not close friends, had collaborated with little friction during the early months of their war crimes association. Jackson had benefited greatly from the personnel, facilities, and contacts provided by OSS, and there is no reason to question the good faith of Donovan's support.[66]

Unfortunately for present purposes, Taylor does not analyse each of these different types of support or provide a range of examples. This is a gap in the Nuremberg literature that the remainder of this chapter seeks to fill. On the face of it, the opening weeks of the Donovan–Jackson relationship appeared to have opened on a positive note as one of common respect bolstered – if not entirely motivated – by mutual and institutional self-interest.

To ensure smooth administrative coordination between the OSS and OCC, Donovan entrusted his namesake, James Donovan, to work closely with Jackson. The OSS Director instructed James Donovan to take a positive and optimistic attitude towards future work with Jackson, and to both anticipate and then oblige Jackson's various requests as far as possible. Hence, this OSS senior lawyer even promised Jackson to have a dry run of the case against Göring prepared within six weeks.[67]

During their first meeting on 7 May, James Donovan followed Donovan's instructions fully. He filled Jackson in on the fragmentation of administrative agencies who could, and perhaps should, have been tackling war crimes trials

64 *Ibid*, 16 June 1945, recording that Truman agreed with Jackson on this point.

65 *Ibid*. 66 Taylor, 1992, *op cit*, 147.

67 Jackson Diary, *op cit*, 14–15 May 1945. The report was supplemented by multiple copies of a large chart: R&A 3152.

planning and preparation issues. He also offered a detailed, if discouraging, assessment of their relative abilities based upon the past experiences of the OSS Director and more recently his own office. These agencies ranged from a special office in the Army's JAG department, which had itself been frustrated and allowed to degenerate into an 'orphan organisation', to the War Department's small scale policy unit – consisting only of Colonel Bernays and two other officials mainly concerned with war crimes against American military personnel. Jackson accepted James Donovan's analysis of the limited prospects of receiving significant help from Navy sources, other than regarding 'particular instances of unlawful conduct toward navy personnel'.[68]

The OSS General Counsel also gave Jackson an equally downbeat assessment of the likelihood of receiving support from the US State Department, whose relevant official was not only already overburdened with work but was also subject to the competing political imperatives of his superiors. He also informed Jackson that interest in war crimes issues within the Justice Department had 'somewhat waned' of late, and that the UN War Crimes Commission had been allocated no investigative staff whatsoever. It was, therefore, largely dependent upon newspaper cuttings and any information sent to them by the OSS.

James Donovan told Jackson that OSS had both the organisational resources and expertise to provide considerable assistance. However, it would be a mistake to expect this organisation to magically conjure up completed trial briefs supported by comprehensive dossiers of incriminating evidence against individual defendants who had yet to be officially listed as such, for criminal offences that had still to be decided upon or even formulated. Indeed, as already noted, Donovan's attempt to take the initiative in this field from 1943 onwards had largely been frustrated by the lack of clear and specific Anglo-American wartime policy on post-war trials of war criminals. There was not even an official list of potential defendants, other than the OSS's own unsolicited suggestions. The wartime Allied leadership had spoken of peacetime war crimes trials only in vague generalities, and – despite the OSS Director's pressure – delayed taking any institutional steps to fulfilling these grand promises of peacetime retribution, a point that applied even to the Judge Advocate General's legal office within the US Army.[69]

James Donovan made it clear that Jackson would find that progress on building up individual cases against alleged Nazi war criminals within the US Navy was in little better shape than the Army's efforts to date. Even the US State Department had little practical enthusiasm for holding international trials, particularly if these prejudiced the government's standing with neutral countries. However, after strategically lowering expectations, he promised that the OSS could and would help Jackson remedy this major deficit by

68 *Ibid*, 7 May 1945. 69 *Ibid*.

devoting much of its considerable resources to this issue, and at their opening meeting on 7 May, handed over a sample of various OSS–R&A reports on war crimes issues that Neumann's team had already prepared from the summer of 1944 onwards.[70] Jackson read over these reports during the next three of four days, and recorded that 'Donovan's studies from OSS are very complete and encouraging', by which he must have meant the three full-length R&A reports prepared by the CES during 1944.[71]

Jackson's reaction to James Donovan's downbeat and disappointing briefing on the preparedness of agencies other than the OSS, and the state of concrete evidence suitable for criminal prosecutions, was the realistic judgement that 'our case will have to be built from the ground up'.[72]

During this initial meeting, James Donovan carried out the instructions of the OSS Director. He made a pitch for the superiority of OSS analysis of trial strategy. Part of this involved making various criticisms of the so-called 'Bernays plan' (formulated by Murray Bernays). This had been circulating in various drafts during the previous months, and had strongly influenced Jackson's early thinking on trial strategy. This plan had, James Donovan claimed, failed to make proper use of: 'the good deal of material', including various R&A reports, which had been previously sent to Bernays' section.[73] These materials had included a strong critique of the undifferentiated and simplistic character of Bernays' early version of the 'criminal conspiracy model', designed to characterise Nazi domestic atrocities as calculated steps to realise Hitler's single and all-encompassing master plan.

Jackson's private record, which has been declassified only since 1984, indicates that his first contact with OSS specialists, including in one sense the OSS Director himself, created a positive impression regarding both their abilities, their current institutional state of preparedness compared with other relevant agencies, and willingness to lend much needed support. James Donovan was a sensible choice for the OSS Director to appoint to this liaison position because, as Taylor notes: 'James Donovan made an excellent impression on Jackson and joined the inner circle of his advisers.'[74]

Jackson certainly felt that he had good reason to learn whatever lessons the OSS could teach his office. As early as 7 May 1945, Jackson:

> Talked with General Donovan of OSS by phone . . . [who] promised full co-operation, and arranged with James Donovan counsel for O.S.S, for an interview later today to get a view on what O.S.S has and to get arrangements for orientating it with our theory of the case . . . he [JD] came at 4 o'clock saying that General Donovan had told him to talk to me very frankly and he did. He gave the most intelligent survey of the

70 *Ibid.* 71 *Ibid*, 11 May 1945. 72 *Ibid.* 73 *Ibid.*
74 Taylor, 1992, *op cit*, 47.

> whole field that I have yet had. It adds up to the proposition that in view of the size of the promises, mighty little had been done towards their fulfilment.[75]

It is clear from the context that James Donovan was giving voice to a generalised sense of the OSS's frustration that had, albeit in coded terms, also been expressed in earlier R&A war crimes reports from Neumann's sub-section. As already noted, the source of the frustration was that the Allied leadership's grand promises of retribution, made on numerous occasions during the course of the war, had been neither developed nor acted upon in a concrete and practical way.

By early May 1945, Jackson had formulated a tentative strategy for the forthcoming months that was broadly consistent with General Donovan and James Donovan's critical analysis of the state of preparedness of Washington-based government agencies. Jackson acknowledged that, almost from the start of his project, Donovan's organisation was one of only three executive bodies that had provided real help: 'the only real help we have is from the war department and OSS, together with some from Justice'.[76]

Under the Donovan–Jackson arrangement, which was copied to the R&A Branch, OSS agreed to collect and analyse the evidence 'for half the case in the early planning'.[77] Neumann was selected as one of the 'top-flight staff on war crimes' to take charge of the OSS's war crimes research under the overall administrative supervision of James Donovan.[78] However, it soon became clear to Jackson that, however valuable the prior OSS–R&A reports were, there still remained an urgent need to prepare, from the ground up, highly detailed briefs suitable for trial purposes. Now that the war was over, the data contained in these reports needed to be enriched with greater factual information from captured German records. The latter contained sufficient evidence directly to connect the actions of responsible Nazi leaders with the specific criminal offences with which they were soon to be formally charged and prosecuted. It was not until August 1945 that the offences were actually formulated by means of an international agreement signed in London, the Nuremberg Charter.[79] For this reason, it was understandable that the OSS had been unable to prepare such prosecution briefs to date.

During May and June, Donovan gave war crimes research 'top priority'

75 Jackson Diary, *op cit*, 7 May 1945. 76 *Ibid.* 77 Smith, 1983 *op cit*, 249 n. 3.

78 Taylor, 1992 *op cit*, 47.

79 This legal agreement mandated the prosecution of war criminals by the International Military Tribunal (IMT). The agreement was signed by representatives of the US, Great Britain, France and the Soviet Union, and it set out the constitution, jurisdiction and functions of the IMT. Nothing in this agreement prejudiced the provisions established by the earlier Moscow Declaration concerning the return of war criminals to the countries where they committed their crimes for local trials by national courts.

within OSS, including for officials located in field offices across Europe and the Far East.[80] As a result, during the next months: 'this work . . . would command higher priority from the two units concerned [CES-R&A and the International Law Unit] than other work now on the docket'.[81] Jackson's memo to Donovan, 8 June 1945, suggests that Jackson was willing to reimburse OSS for the additional financial burdens that its liaison was creating, even though his Executive Order from the US President positively required all agencies to lend such support:

> Referring to my letter dated 7 June 1945, I wish to confirm our further agreement that requests that any expenses incurred by the OSS which are directly attributable to requests from me in connection with the preparation of the United States prosecution of the major Axis War Criminals, will be reimbursed out of the funds to be made available to me, upon your proper submission of vouchers, in amounts approved by the Bureau of the Budget.[82]

In short, Donovan's prioritisation of war crimes issues led to a series of internal developments within OSS. For instance, during the third week of May 1945, Neumann and Phoebe Morrison (who headed R&A's International Law Unit) participated in discussions with 'James Donovan and representatives from Justice Jackson's office'. Neumann and Morrison had prepared and circulated a seven-page document entitled 'The Trial of German War Criminals' for 'Discussion at the Chiefs' Committee Meeting'. This gave a provisional indication of the possible contributions of OSS–R&A, together with a range of topics falling outside its remit.[83] Prior to the meeting with Jackson's representatives, this document had been discussed internally within OSS with William Langer, head of the R&A Branch and Sherman Kent, head of this branch's Europe Africa Division. During such discussion, war crimes research was recognised as appropriate for both the remit and specific expertise of R&A–CES staff.[84] The OSS also established other contacts with senior members of Jackson's staff.[85] Donovan's prioritisation of war crimes issues prompted the involvement of senior level officials, and generally indicates the seriousness with which the OSS leadership were addressing war crimes issues, including evidence gathering and trial preparation more generally.

80 James Donovan to Edward J. Glavin, 24 May 1945: NA RG 226, M1642, Roll 121.
81 See Hartshorne to Kent, 22 May 1945: NA, RG 226, Entry 1, Box 2, Folder 6.
82 NA, RG 226, M1642, Roll 121.
83 'The Trial of German War Criminals', 21 May 1945: NA, RG 226, Entry 1, Box 2, Folder 6.
84 See Hartshorne to Kent, 22 May 1945: NA, RG 226, Entry 1, Box 2, Folder 6.
85 'Progress Report' documentation entitled 'Europe-Africa Division', May 1945, NA RG 226, Entry 42, Box 1.

Irrespective of various internal controversies within OSS regarding the implications of giving priority to war crimes work, which were not revealed to Jackson, from late May 1945 Donovan continued to supply Jackson's new organisation with considerable logistical and administrative support.[86] This included the provision, through Colonel Amin, of office accommodation for Jackson's growing numbers of European staff in both Paris and London, which contained at least two dozen OSS officials.[87] In both locations, the OSS made available formerly OSS-controlled buildings. The majority of those originally assigned to Jackson's team, including researchers, lawyers and even stenographers, either came from OSS, or had direct associations with, and continuing loyalties to, this agency.

Recruiting Donovan's OSS personnel

Taylor is surely correct to emphasise the great benefits with respect to the recruitment of specialist personnel that Jackson derived in a direct way from bringing Donovan into his organisation as his deputy. It should be recalled that, at the start, Jackson's prosecution office initially comprised only four key individuals recruited, not on the basis of their knowledge of, or prior background in, international criminal law, nor for their expertise on the details and organisation of Nazi war crimes. Instead, Jackson selected his core staff on the basis that these were lawyers Jackson already knew personally and trusted, particularly Francis Shea[88] and Sidney Alderman,[89] a point emphasised by his employment of his own son, William Jackson.[90] Jackson had to resist political pressure from the Democratic Party chairman to appoint 'hack lawyers as a political payoff', and similar pressure from Jewish lobby groups.[91] As Persico notes:

> Jackson's resources at this point were undeniably thin: a six-page master plan, a secretary, his son and a friend as aides, and a potential executive officer in Murray Bernays. Bernays impressed him, but Jackson was disappointed by the rest of the War Department. The departmental staff

86 The OSS provided Jackson with considerable assistance with the duplication of documentation. See, for example, Jackson Diary, *op cit*, 7 July 1945.

87 See memo 15 June 1945, Donovan to Jackson, confirming that Amen has 'moved into 7 Rue de Presbourg, which is reasonably ready for the complete occupancy, plus 1,000 square feet OSS building'. NA, RG 226, M1642, Roll 121.

88 Shea had recently served as a former Assistant Attorney General under Jackson.

89 Alderman was a senior Washington Attorney, and general counsel for the Southern Railway Company.

90 On the appointment of Jackson's core staff: NA, RG 107, 'War Crimes', 16 May 1945, War Department Files, 000.5; Conot, *op cit*, 15, describing Shea and Alderman as the 'two longtime Washington friends' around whom Jackson assembled his staff.

91 Persico, 1994, *op cit*, 26.

> had collected only sketchy data on scattered atrocities thus far, hardly the quality of evidence that forms the life's blood of any successful prosecution.[92]

This Jackson-loyalist group was eventually expanded from Shea and Alderman to include: Colonel Robert G. Storey, who would become Director of the Documentation Division and Executive Trial Counsel; Colonel John Harlan Amen, a Brooklyn prosecutor who would become Director of the Interrogation Division; Colonel Telford Taylor, a former deputy of Jackson's in the Department of Justice[93] and Thomas J. Dodd, a future US Senator.

By selecting these particular staff, Jackson signalled from the start that he valued prior friendship and personal loyalty at least as highly as specialist qualifications or relevant expertise. This was a point that Murray Bernays, who – in conjunction with OSS specialist Dr Franz Neumann[94] – helped formulate Jackson's original trial strategy centred around a large-scale criminal conspiracy charge, was later to discover to his cost. Both Neumann and Bernays later became marginalised. In short, Jackson's initial recruitment policies meant that his small team lacked the necessary expertise within both international criminal law and the type and range of offences committed by the Nazi regime. Donovan presumably realised that Jackson's recruitment strategy had created a vacuum, which more appropriately qualified OSS staff, many of whom retained their first loyalty to the OSS Director personally, could more than adequately fill.

There is evidence that, for his part, Jackson appreciated the urgency of his need to recruit a variety of different categories of OSS staff. Jackson's motivations for approaching Donovan with a view not only to setting up inter-agency collaboration but also recruiting him personally included a considerable measure of institutional self-interest. Persico notes that, within weeks of his appointment, Jackson realised that his chronic 'staffing problems' resulting from his initial hiring policies could be resolved, almost at a stroke, providing he was willing to broker a deal with the OSS

92 *Ibid*, 27.

93 Taylor had also previously worked with Jackson and also lacked any background in either international law or Nazi war crimes, having joined Jackson's OCC from an earlier period as an US army intelligence officer based at Bletchley Park, England, involved in Anglo-American liaison work over intercepted German communications.

94 On Neumann's role, which was to later culminate as First Chief of the War Crimes Research Unit for the OCC, see Hulme and Salter, *op cit*. Neumann supplied Donovan and other senior prosecutors with initial drafts of the indictments of most, if not all, of the individual defendants. He also pressed to have the political leadership of the party as defined by an internal decree of 1 December 1936 indicted as a criminal organisation: see Neumann to Jackson, Indictment of Organisations, 14 September 1945: Cornell Collection, Vol. 19/62.02.

Director sufficient to bring Donovan and elements of his OSS staff fully on board:

> And then Senator Alben Barkley tipped him off to where the gold lay. The key was a proud man, a power in his own right, and wooing him could be tricky, Barkley warned. Jackson was prepared to chance it. He buzzed Elsie Douglas and told her to ring up the Office of Strategic Services on Q street and arrange a lunch date for him with . . . Donovan . . . Jackson came to Donovan like a man hungry for a crust of bread. Fifteen minutes into their meeting, Donovan seemed to have spread a banquet before him.[95]

Donovan offered Jackson considerable help. Donovan actively promoted the benefits that Jackson could expect to receive from his close cooperation with the OSS. This included his ability to make available incriminating evidence, including trial witnesses, from his links with Soviet Intelligence (NKVD), members of the German opposition and even OSS Gestapo double-agents who might not otherwise be available to Jackson.[96]

Furthermore, as an integral part of their routine intelligence gathering and analysis, OSS officials, he claimed, had gathered considerable know-how in the policies, command responsibilities and actions of the leading Nuremberg defendants. In addition to specialist research analysts, Donovan could provide staff capable of offering a wide range of logistical support. At its peak of operations in 1945, the OSS employed some 13,000 individuals workers (8,500 men and 4,500 women), of whom about 60 per cent served overseas. Most were on active duty in the armed forces, with civilians comprising one-quarter of the total. As Persico notes:

> The OSS, Donovan explained, had field operations throughout Europe. His people had been tracking potential war criminals since 1942 and had accumulated substantial dossiers. Furthermore he had every imaginable specialist within his ranks: scientists, linguists, even architects who could build Jackson a courthouse if need be. Best of all, he had attracted some of America's brightest young lawyers into the OSS. Depending on the demands of the war in the Pacific, he could make many of these people available to Jackson . . . Donovan not only had an organisation in place, but knew how to open doors throughout Washington and the military. If Jackson had Donovan at his side, the battle of preparation, recruitment, and organisation would be half won.[97]

95 Persico, 1994, *op cit*, 27. 96 Jackson Diary, *op cit*, 15 May 1945.

97 Persico, 1994, *op cit*, 27–28. Persico based his research on this point partly on interviews with Jackson's son.

Later we will discuss Donovan's ability to exploit his domestic and international contacts. Amongst the OSS specialists, whose expertise as support staff Donovan offered to Jackson, were a large number of experts in the deployment of truth drugs, psychology, public relations, film production and visual presentation more generally.[98]

An arrangement for the OSS to make an extensive contribution to Jackson's staff was agreed initially in a telephone conversation between Jackson and Donovan at the start of May. This was followed up by a formal letter of agreement between Jackson and Donovan, which was brokered partly by James Donovan, indicating that the Chief US Prosecutor was intent on mobilising existing personnel resources within various US government agencies. It is worth re-examining the letter of agreement in terms of staffing implications:

> I have determined that it would be in the best interests of the government to have all existing facilities used in the preparation of the prosecution and to create new facilities only when absolutely necessary. I wish therefore to confirm my understanding with you and the General Counsel of OSS that we shall rely upon your agency to assist us in all respects in preparing for the prosecution of the major European Axis criminals. This includes the collection, evaluation, integration and presentation of evidence of all types (including photographic).[99]

The creation and formalisation of the relationship between Jackson's prosecution office and that of OSS, was not, as one might expect, that of the OSS intelligence officials having to quickly build up a body of expertise to service Jackson's requirements. On the contrary, it was staff largely from OSS's Central European Section of the Research and Analysis (R&A) Branch, rather than Jackson's employees, who brought to this new project over two years of prior experience of developing an analysis of the political, strategic and international law aspects of prosecuting Nazi war criminals.[100]

Hence, within weeks of his appointment, Jackson had come to appreciate

98 B. Smith, *Reaching Judgement at Nuremberg* (New York: Basic Books, 1977), 41. Jackson resisted Donovan's suggestions for the use of OSS truth drugs on any of the Nuremberg defendants, even Hess who was widely suspected of faking amnesia. Gill to [Andrus] 20 October 1945, Jackson Papers, *op cit*, Box 107: 'Psychiatry and Personality Studies of Nazi Leaders'. See Cave-Brown, *op cit*, 744–45, who notes: 'according to Donovan's papers on the subject, Jackson gave his approval for the use of the [truth] drug. A doctor who had been involved in the program was asked to join Donovan's party [to Nuremberg]. . . . Donovan realised the dangers too, and when the party set off for Germany, the name of the doctor was not on the list', *ibid*, 751–2.

99 Jackson to Donovan, 7 June 1945: NA, RG 226, Entry 1, Box 2, Folder 7; also at NA, RG 226, Director's Files, M1642, Roll 121.

100 Katz, 1989, *op cit*, 49–51.

that the OSS war crimes staff were, on the evidence he had sampled to date, at least as well prepared for the extensive work of gathering evidence and trial preparation as any other branch of the US government. Taylor confirms that it was OSS's relevant expertise, rather than any particular affinities for General Donovan, that was a vital factor here when he notes that: 'Sorely pressed for staff and general logistical support, Jackson jumped at the offer.'[101]

An agreement to establish inter-agency collaboration was formalised on 5 May 1945.[102] However, this initial contact was not particularly significant with respect to Donovan's own *personal* position because, as already noted, the terms of Jackson's appointment by President Truman *positively required* the OSS and other Washington agencies to lend whatever cooperation they could. Indeed, it was Jackson's positive view of the OSS's prior strategic analysis, commitments and resources that motivated him to phone Donovan on 12 May and offer him the position of his senior aide and *de facto* deputy on the 'trial staff'. Meanwhile, President Truman confirmed Donovan's appointment as Jackson's special assistant in a telephone call on 15 May, followed up by a formal letter of appointment within days. Jackson's initial approach seeking to recruit the General personally resorted to flattery, claiming his approach was recognition of the 'foresight, energy and skill' that his organisation had already demonstrated with respect to war crimes issues.[103] This rhetorical flourish was not entirely inaccurate because, as already noted, Donovan had repeatedly attempted to carve a niche out for the OSS on war crimes trials issues.

It is likely that both Jackson and Donovan were aware that their own personal relationship would need careful handling. At the time of his personal recruitment to the OCC as Jackson's senior aide, Donovan even made it clear that he recognised Jackson as 'captain of the team'. This surely represented a positive gesture to reassure Jackson, who was ten years younger than Donovan, that the former OSS Director would not attempt to usurp his role.[104] Such reassurance was supported by the terms of a formal OSS–OCC agreement between Jackson and Donovan in mid-May 1945. It was further bolstered by Donovan instructing his subordinates within the OSS to take positive steps to supply the OCC with much-needed trial evidence of both documentary and testimonial types. As Bradley Smith notes:

> Even prior to the 18 May meeting [which had confirmed the victory of the pro-trial lobby within Washington] tentative arrangements were

101 *Ibid*, 47.

102 NA, RG 107, 'Assistant Secretary of War', 000.5, War Crimes File May–Dec 1945, Box 16; Jackson to Donovan, 7 June 1945 (re IPOG 10): NA, RG 218, CCS 000.5 War Crimes, Sec. 4, Box 3.

103 Jackson Diaries, *op cit*, 11 May 1945.

104 *Ibid*, 15 May 1945.

> made for the OSS to aid in providing documentary material to the chief of counsel's office, and . . . a formal agreement was concluded between Jackson and William Donovan . . . whereby the latter agreed to give Jackson assistance 'in all respects'. By 9 May, the first steps had been taken to establish a special interrogation team that could garner evidence from captured officials of the Third Reich, such as Schacht, von Papen, and Field Marshal von Rundstedt.[105]

Over the next months, and with Donovan's active encouragement, senior OSS officials rapidly proceeded to develop every aspect of the formal Donovan–Jackson agreement, discussed above. This included exploiting pre-existing contacts to obtain the secondment of senior legal staff from the JAG department, such as Comdr. John O'Malley.[106] Furthermore, on occasions Donovan positively supported Jackson when his administrative guidance was questioned in staff meetings, with statements such as those who were discontented with their assignments could 'take the next flight home'. Taylor recalls that such a severe management attitude was 'ill-calculated to sooth the dissidents'.[107] However, for present purposes, this public display of strong personal support for Jackson's authority is interesting, as it contrasts with his latter role as a focal point for staff dissent.

It is clear then that the origins of the Jackson–Donovan collaboration were based largely upon a perceived mutual self-interest, the shared view that each organisation had much to gain and little to lose from entering into a close institutional relationship with the other. Certainly, Jackson would have known that Donovan had 'on tap' as it were a series of ready established contacts with all manner of US military and civilian organisations whose cooperation was required, as well as a range of both political and international contacts.[108] Potentially, at least, Donovan's domestic contacts, which included close links with US naval intelligence and the British SOE and – to a lesser extent – M16, could not only shortcut possible delays but also open up sources of trial evidence that might otherwise not be so readily available. Although a Republican, Donovan enjoyed a personal relationship with Democrat President Roosevelt, dating from the time when they were both studying law together. He was also particularly close to both presidential adviser Harry Hopkins, and Frank Knox, the newly appointed Secretary for the US Navy and the owner of the influential *Chicago Daily News*. Donovan was also on good terms with another senior presidential adviser who had specific responsibility for war crimes policy,

105 B. Smith, 1981, *op cit*, 232–3.

106 See Kent to Langer, 2 August 1945, 2: NA, RG 226, Entry 1, Box 2, Folder 7.

107 Taylor, *op cit*, 78.

108 The latter are discussed under a separate heading below.

Samuel Rosenman.[109] As already noted, Donovan had also developed close professional relationships with British military, political and intelligence leaders during his visits of inspection between 1940 and 1941.[110]

Appointing Schlabrendorff to this personal staff opened up for Donovan access to family members of those who had been persecuted and killed by the Nazi regime, some of whom, such as Frau Struenck (whose husband was executed as part of the repression following the 20 July assassination attempt on Hitler), were summoned to appear at Nuremberg as potential witnesses.[111] Hans Gisevius, who was an OSS double-agent, supplied Donovan with a detailed account of the 'events leading up to Putsch [attempted coup] of 20 July', and the link between the two men was subject to challenge in the trial itself.[112] This challenge stemmed from Gisevius's role as a 'star prosecution witness' who later was to inflict considerable damage upon Göring's defence case and general credibility amongst fellow defendants.[113]

The flow of OSS staff and support

Jackson was surely correct when he recognised that Donovan was able to supply his office with ample well-qualified legal, research analysts, specialist

109 It was to Rosenman to whom the results had to be forwarded of later diplomatic discussions negotiating the London Agreement under which the trials were to proceed. The friendly tone between Donovan and Rosenman is clear, for example, from a letter from Donovan to Rosenman, 14 July 1945: 'attaching a copy of the draft London agreement as it stood before I left . . . I believe it will be approved with very little change. I hope that you might be able to see me during the coming week, and I'll telephone you to see if we can make a date.' War crimes file, Rosenman Papers, Harry S. Truman Presidential Museum and Library, Nuremberg Collection.

110 Danchev, *op cit*, 20–23.

111 Cable to Donovan, Amzon 1883, presumably 5 or 6 November (no date) 1945. This noted that the witness was a close personal friend of Admiral Canaris, was well known to Schlabrendorff and: 'should be of great assistance to you on war crimes matters . . . will have her report to your office for instructions.' Donovan or one of his assistants wrote on this telegram: 'hold . . . until you have talked to Gaevernitz' [Dulles' German-American assistant]. Donovan Collection: 53.082. Her statement 'An den Allierten Militaergerichtshof,' is also contained at this location.

112 Cornell Collection, Vol. 93. This included details of the opposition's contacts with OSS intermediaries (*ibid*, 13–14). See Nuremberg transcript 3 June 1946, IMT 15, 286 regarding applications from the Defendants Hess and Frank to put an interrogatory to General Donovan regarding the relationship between the witness Gisevius and the United States Office of Strategic Services.

113 Sprecher records how defence counsel attempted to highlight Gisevius's contacts with the OSS in order to discreit his damaging testimony: 'Upon further examination Dr. Seidl asked Gisevius if he had ever been active in the intelligence service of a foreign power. Gisevius answered "At no time." He also stated that he had not received funds from any power at war with Germany. He did admit that "he had friendly and political contacts with several members" of the Office of Strategic Service (OSS).' 1999, *op cit*, 918.

academic consultants and support staff to fill the vacuum created by his initial recruitment policies. Jackson's diary confirms his recognition that, long before his appointment and the final decision to hold formal legal trials, Donovan had actively sought to make an early start on war crimes issues which included recruiting a range of legal staff qualified in international law (Phoebe Morrison, Raphael Lemkin[114] and Sheldon Glueck), and had – as discussed above – been frustrated. Donovan had recruited such staff in anticipation of OSS playing a key role in wartime planning for post-war trials. The problem for Donovan's strategy had been a lack of any clear and specific policy guidance from Washington policy-makers sufficient to allow these legal staff to develop detailed plans and trial strategies to implement these policies:

> Long ago, General Donovan desired to begin work on the war criminals project but was unable to get definite targets to shoot at. The fact is that it was dealt with by top officials only in terms of naïve generality, and Donovan's outfit was not a policy-making one. The subject is one in which policy extends to detail. Glueck, a consultant, has written a book on war criminals. O.S.S assembled a considerable group of experts on all subjects including international law.[115]

Although Jackson was unimpressed with one of these 'legal experts' (Glueck who had made unwelcome attacks upon his legal opinions whilst Attorney General), Jackson noted that 'it is plain that O.S.S. has given extensive and intelligent attention to the problem'. In the same cable, Jackson pressed the OSS to transfer to his office the services of Raphael Lemkin (whose seminal analysis first formulated the concept 'genocide' and decisively shaped post-war United Nations declarations on this topic). Donovan approved the reassignment of this war crimes consultant.[116] Lemkin's secondment to the OCC was needed to help prepare 'an evidentiary case study drawn from material in his book and additional material he has secured since his publication . . . and develop his book's analysis further'. Lemkin eventually contributed 'a very large amount of evidence of atrocities in Poland'.[117]

At this time, Jackson also instructed Taylor that: 'the staff should continue

114 Lemkin was already well known as the author of *Axis Rule in Occupied Europe: Laws of Occupation, Analysis of Government, Proposals for Redress* (Washington: Carnegie Endowment for International Peace, 1944). Lemkin first coined the term 'genocide' in this work.

115 Jackson diary, *ibid*, 7 May 1945.

116 Lemkin also helped prepare the 1948 Genocide Convention. See Conot, 1983, *op cit*, 11, 391–95.

117 See point 7, 'Polish Atrocities', Notes of a Staff Meeting, 31 August 1945, 2, Jackson Papers, *op cit*, Box 110.

in close contact with OSS regarding their interrogation of Rausschning [a prominent German witness] and send details of his testimony ASAP'.[118]

Previously, I suggested that Donovan's involvement stemmed partly from a combination of institutional and perhaps personal interests. Donovan, it appears, was willing to adopt an equally instrumental view of where his own organisation's particular interests lay in connection with the Nuremberg project. Donovan was adept at exploiting Jackson's shortage of suitable staff to the advantage of the OSS. Earlier accounts have, in a very general way, noted the benefits for Jackson of involving Donovan as a senior aide able to mobilise the extensive resources of OSS. Taylor, for example, referring to the inter-agency cooperation between Jackson's office and Donovan's OSS, recalls that: 'It was a relationship which greatly benefited the Nuremberg project in terms of staff and equipment.'[119] Such generalisations, however, require far more detailed analysis of the specific details. This analysis is set out in a latter section of this book. During the first weeks and months of their liaison, relations concerning staffing between Jackson and Donovan were cooperative.

On 16 June, Donovan submitted to Jackson a detailed proposal for an organisation framework consisting of a series of sub-groups, which assigned key strategic and coordinating positions to existing or former OSS staff. Donovan's plan assigned to himself the role of both Jackson's 'Deputy in all respects' and a leading member of 'the trial group'. It also allotted OSS Lt. Gordon Dean to Jackson's 'secretariat',[120] James Donovan, OSS's General Counsel and chief lawyer to an Executive Committee of a Strategic Board and trial group. Colonel Storey was given a central role in both the trial team and responsibility for heading the 'Preparation Staff responsible for facts and law'. Under Storey's command was a 'Documentation Staff' of scholars and specialists drawn largely from the expertise of the OSS Research and Analysis Branch to evaluate and synthesise the documentary evidence. They were directed by Chandler Morse, head of the R&A Branch's London field office. Storey was also helped by OSS's Drexel Sprecher, with James Donovan approving this assignment.[121] OSS's Comdr. Ralph Albrecht, a formidable New York international lawyer, was also included in the high-level Prosecution Review Board.[122] Jackson's first organisational framework reveals that he

118 *Ibid.* 119 1992, *op cit*, 47.

120 Jackson went on to credit Dean with the idea of publishing sections of the Nuremberg prosecutors' evidence as a permanent record. See *Nazi Conspiracy & Aggression* (Washington: US Government Printers, 1946), Vol. I, Preface (Part 4 of 4): 'Mention must first be made of Mr. Gordon Dean, who was responsible in large part for the conception of this undertaking.'

121 Sprecher, 1998, *op cit*, 54.

122 As already noted, Jackson was even being willing to reimburse the OSS for the additional financial burdens that its staff reassignments were creating, even though the relevant Executive Order from President Roosevelt *required* all agencies to grant such support. See Donovan to Jackson, 16 June 1945: NA, RG 226, M1642, Roll 121.

accepted nearly all of Donovan's suggestions. As a result, he granted OSS officials – long accustomed to accepting the General's desires as direct military orders – a number of strategically important functions within the Nuremberg prosecutors office. Later, other OSS officials, including Daniel Margolies,[123] Lt. Col. Murray Gurfein,[124] Marvin Flisser and Whitney Harris,[125] and Dr Henry Kellermann[126] bolstered Jackson's middle-order legal staff assigned to Nuremberg, and each went on to make a significant contribution. A similar point can be made regarding the input of James Donovan.[127]

The contributions of those OSS and former OSS lawyers that Donovan provided to the Nuremberg prosecutors has remained one of the few unexamined aspects of this much-researched landmark trial. Only the OSS literature has mentioned in passing the previously unacknowledged OSS background of a surprisingly high proportion of the senior staff, including both trial lawyers and preparatory 'research and analysis' staff, which Jackson employed as 'his' prosecutors.[128] In certain cases,[129] Jackson knew of, and indeed specifically sought, current or former OSS staff. In other instances, however, there is little evidence that Donovan ever disclosed their OSS and related intelligence background.[130]

The valuable memoirs of Drexel Sprecher and Telford Taylor,[131] and shorter published recollections of Whitney Harris, suggest that Donovan did not even disclose such information to other former OSS officials employed by Jackson's office, who had worked in different sections of this organisation without being aware that they shared a common employer.[132] Many OSS officials, even those not directly engaged in 'operations' were 'celled up'. That is, they were given a 'cover' of various military ranks and titles,[133] and required not to reveal their status as OSS intelligence officials other than on a

123 Taylor, 1992, *op cit*, 217.

124 *Ibid*, 82, 137, 146, 185, 265, 387.

125 *Ibid*, 172, 216, 246, 508, 608–9, 610–11, 625.

126 Kellermann received a Doctor of Law (J.D.) degree from the University of Berlin in 1937, and had emigrated to the US in the same year. In 1945, the OSS assigned him to prepare pre-trial briefs for the International Military Tribunal held in Nuremberg. He also interrogated a number of witnesses and defendants: Katz, 1989, *op cit*, 11, 51; http://www.ushmm.org/outreach/smwcrime.htm.

127 James Donovan both coordinated OSS–OCC liaison, and later took charge of the film evidence at Nuremberg. See Twist, *op cit*; Taylor, 1992, *op cit*, 47, 49, 56, 79, 86, 98, 138, 186, 200.

128 P.K. O'Donnell, *Operatives, Spies and Saboteurs: The Unknown Story of the Men and Women of World War II's OSS* (NY: Free Press, 2004), who notes, without further elaboration, that: 'OSS played a major role in the Nuremberg war crimes trial.' *Ibid*, 307.

129 Such as James Donovan, Robert Gill and General Donovan himself.

130 Such as Bernard Meltzer, Drexel Sprecher, Murray Gurfein and Ralph Albrecht.

131 See Taylor, 1992, *op cit*; Sprecher, *op cit*.

132 Whilst it is impossible to prove a negative, evidence for this contention is provided in the final section.

133 M. Warner, *The Office of Strategic Services: America's First Intelligence Agency* (Washington: CIA publications, 2000).

'need to know' basis. Hence, at OSS post-war reunions even close friends discovered, for the first time, that each had been working for the same organisation during the war.[134] For example, James Donovan, OSS's 'General Counsel' (i.e., senior legal official), was eventually titled as 'Commander Donovan' (having secured several dramatic promotions whilst working as a Nuremberg prosecutor). Even the official record of the US prosecution team, written after the expiry of any conceivable military reason justifying anonymity, still maintains the fiction that James Donovan and other OSS officials were US Navy or Army personnel unconnected with intelligence matters.

Given these complexities, it is not surprising that nearly all the major historical accounts of the Nuremberg trials have been misled by such devices into significantly *underestimating* the proportion of Jackson's senior and middle-ranking staff that Donovan made available to the OCC. Donovan provided Jackson with able trial lawyers to prepare some of the major briefs, such as Whitney Harris, Ralph Albrecht, Bernard Meltzer and Drexel Sprecher. In addition to legal staff, OSS informants and academic consultants, Donovan approved the relocation of a considerable number of technical staff, ranging from translators, reprographic specialists, film-makers and other 'presentational' experts, and secretarial staff. As Sprecher recalls:

> In helping Jackson's operation get underway, OSS had furnished large numbers of support personnel . . . and supplied both equipment and funds for compensating large numbers of personnel.[135]

In short, between May and July 1945, the General 'muscled in' on Jackson's organisational structure by capturing key posts for a range of OSS employees, and supplied a sufficient range of specialist personnel to make the continuation of Jackson's project almost inconceivable without his organisational assistance.

In early June 1945, Donovan decided that there was a need to relocate the 'top staff' still at Washington to Paris and London as soon as possible.[136] Jackson reconfigured his organisational structures on a number of occasions, in which different prosecutors were promoted, moved sideways or demoted in seniority within the overall hierarchy. Throughout these organisational upheavals, Donovan was consistently and publicly ranked second only to Jackson. The OSS Director's seniority was also expressed in his ability at this stage at least, to largely determine the nature of his own assignments. Donovan's seniority as second only to Jackson was respected not only within internal OSS charts but also in the formalities of Jackson's internal memorandum. When announcing his senior staff in various press releases

134 C. Ford, *Donovan of OSS* (Boston: Little Brown, 1970), 309.

135 Sprecher, *op cit*, 167.

136 Jackson Diary, *op cit*, 7 June 1945.

and other public documentation, Jackson cited Donovan as the highest-ranking member of his organisation.[137] By late July, Donovan's tactics of securing key positions for OSS loyalists, combined with his extensive efforts to anticipate and meet Jackson's needs, meant that he had become a vital person within Jackson's senior staff, playing 'a key role under Jackson'.[138]

This support with respect to staffing was supplemented by the recruitment of additional OSS staff, including Colonel Robert Gill, who had 'come over at Donovan's request'. Gill had previously been in charge of handling intelligence material supplied by POWs, and had acquired useful information about the mental disposition and physical state of proposed defendants, such as Herman Göring's drug addiction. Jackson gave Gill the post of 'executive officer' within Europe, where 'his knowledge of the ways around Europe' were deemed highly valuable.[139] As head of a document-gathering division (not officially titled as such at this stage), Gill mobilised a significant number of former OSS colleagues, including Marvin Flisser, Chief of the Field Branch, and Daniel Margolies, a former OSS Secret Intelligence Branch official and trained lawyer who had run a network of agents inside Nazi Germany.[140] Gill would have had access to many other OSS agents employed across Europe who were charged with interrogation and other forms of evidence-gathering for the proposed trials.[141] Gill, who was further promoted to Brigadier General, was partly responsible for negotiating the introduction of IBM's simultaneous translation system, which greatly reduced the delays that would otherwise have resulted from every document and statement

137 See, for example, Jackson's press release 28 May 1945, Jackson Papers, *op cit*, Box 95.

138 Persico, 1994, *op cit*, 45.

139 Jackson Diary, *op cit*, 14 June and 10 July 1945. Gill's appointment as 'executive officer on the continent' was only formalised at a meeting with both Jackson and General Donovan on 10 July 1945.

140 Gerhart, *op cit*, 335; www.osssociety.org/pdfs/Spring%202001.PDF (on Flisser's role); and Gaskin, *op cit*, 4–5 (re Margolies). Margolies had been part of the labour section of OSS–SI, and claimed to have been selected by Donovan in June 1945 to work in Paris and then Frankfurt with six female German assistants on captured German Army records (Oberkammando). Until August, he was mainly responsible for selecting documents capable of being used as evidence in the trial, and then – after a short period in the document division working once again on German Army files – he was relocated to Nuremberg. Here, his much-needed German language and investigative skills were deployed in the interrogation sections under Colonel Amen: *ibid*, 5.

141 It appears that the OSS retained a number of European staff in preparation for the Nuremberg trials. See the obituary to Carl Buehler III, who had been stationed in Italy and Austria, through the end of the war, and assigned to assist in the preparation of materials for these trials, see 'Obituary', *Chicago Tribune*, 16 August 1998. See also the obituary for Adolph Schmidt, *Pittsburgh Post-Gazette*, 19 December 2000, giving details of Lieutenant Colonel Schmidt's service with OSS in both the African and European theatres, which included locating and collecting a number of records that were subsequently used in the Nuremberg trials.

having to be translated from, say, English into German and then into both French and Russian.[142] Another Donovan loyalist was his namesake, James Donovan, who also secured rapid promotion within the OCC.

During May 1945, Donovan successfully proposed that film specialists from the OSS Presentation Branch could usefully gather and present both still and movie photographic evidence of Nazi atrocities. Donovan created a special unit was under the command of navy captain John Ford, the well-known Hollywood director, in order to gather photographs and film depicting the Nazi war crimes.[143] In addition to Sprecher, other former insiders including Jackson's senior aide and ultimate successor Telford Taylor, have argued that, during the summer of 1945, the OSS's wide-ranging collaboration with, and support for, Jackson's new organisation was largely responsible for enabling the trials to take place.[144]

Donovan may have realised that, irrespective of the new formal organisational hierarchy and protocols within the OCC, many of these staff had no personal attachment to Jackson and every reason to continue their habit of taking orders directly from their former OSS Director, who attracted strong bonds of loyalty.[145] One obvious example of this was the consternation caused late one night when James Donovan was overheard reporting back to the OSS Director on the telephone in a manner which made it clear that he continued to see himself as engaged on an OSS project, rather than an OCC assignment.[146] In short, Donovan was adept at exploiting Jackson's lack of experienced staff, and actively intervened to ensure that OSS staff occupied key positions. Indeed, once Jackson had come to appreciate the importance of the actual and potential contribution of OSS staff for the successful completion of his project, he then became vulnerable to threats from Donovan to withdraw his support if Jackson refused OSS requests. For example, by early June, Donovan felt secure that he had made himself and OSS seconded staff sufficiently vital to Jackson's project to threaten to withdraw OSS cooperation when James Donovan appeared to have been passed over for membership of Jackson's 'advance party' to Europe.[147] On 11 June, Donovan threatened to withdraw OSS cooperation because James Donovan had been personally slighted by his comparative 'neglect' within Shea's allocation of staff functions. Jackson's response to this threat was conciliatory.[148] Jackson even accepted personal fault for failing to 'assign definite tasks to each person

142 Whitney Harris, 1954, *op cit*, 27.

143 Ultimately over 12 million still photographs and 10 million feet of film were found and then produced into a 3½ hour presentation entitled *The Nazi Plan*. The film was submitted as evidence and formed part of the official proceedings of the Tribunal. It has also become the basis for *Nuremberg: Its Lesson for Today*, the official US documentary about the trial.

144 Taylor, 1992, *op cit*, 354–55.

145 This is discussed more fully below.

146 Taylor, *op cit*, 79.

147 Jackson Diary, *op cit*, 6 June 1945.

148 *Ibid*, 11 June 1945.

and hold them to it', and attributed part of the remaining difficulties to Shea's 'lack of tact'. Jackson's conciliatory approach to Donovan's threat, which was explained over lunchtime meeting with the 'two Donovans', appeared to 'smooth out' their 'ruffled feathers'.[149]

As we will see in more detail letter, there was a sense in which the OSS's cooperation remained conditional and contingent upon this organisation's leader having his own specific demands met. In this sense, the much-needed staffing resources provided by Donovan were double-edged. Indeed, to mix metaphors, they were capable of acting as the cheese in a concealed mousetrap.

Members of staff that Donovan had transferred to the OCC could, on occasions, generate complaints. Jackson was later faced by complaints about Shea's tactlessness from Professor Glueck, OSS's specialist consultant on 'penological aspects' of war crimes, and the author of a major legal work on this topic. Ironically, Glueck was complaining not only about Shea, but about now having to 'take orders' from James Donovan, who a few years previously had been one of his law students.[150] Before being transferred to the European side of Jackson's project, Glueck made specific proposals concerned with how best to 'corral the evidence', which he presented to a staff conference.[151] Glueck also strongly advocated the psychiatric examination of the leading defendants, which did in fact take place at Nuremberg itself under Dr Gilbert and others. Under pressure from Donovan, Jackson ordered Shea to 'make amends' to Glueck, and various other members of the overall prosecution staff whom Shea had slighted.[152] Hence, one possible 'downside' of the inter-agency collaboration with OSS staff was a degree of interpersonal tensions derived from personal vanities, male ego and pride. Furthermore, many of Donovan's seconded staff could be expected to remain personally loyal to him and other fellow OSS officials. This meant that Donovan, rather than Jackson, was sometimes regarded as the person to whom such complaints should be taken because he still represented their champion and OSS leader.

By the time the OSS was dissolved at the start of October 1945, Donovan's organisation had supplied a considerable proportion of Jackson's technical, logistical and legal staff based at Nuremberg. James Donovan's Special Projects sub-section included 37 OSS staff, whilst the Field Photographic Branch, responsible for film evidence, comprised 26 such individuals. The figures for other branches were: R&A 8; Presentation (which produced large-scale charts of different aspects of the Nazi regime's chain of command) 10; Secret Intelligence 12; X-2 Counter-intelligence (responsible partly for preparing the case against Kaltenbrunner under Whitney Harris) 7; and reproduction 4. The grand total of civilian (38) and military (66) was 104 staff.

149 *Ibid*, 13 June 1945. 150 *Ibid*, 14 June 1945. 151 *Ibid*, 21 June 1945.
152 *Ibid*.

This figure supported 21 military and 13 civilian OSS staff engaged in war crimes work in Washington.[153] At this time, October 1945, Jackson's senior aides considered that they needed all these staff and were reluctant to agree to their return or redeployment.[154] Jackson himself sought to retain all these staff based at Washington, Paris and London as well as Nuremberg at least until the trials themselves started, at which time he could perhaps afford to lose some as part of a wider reorganisation.[155]

Providing evidence from Dulles' OSS contacts within the German opposition

At the end of May 1945, Donovan accompanied Jackson to Frankfurt where he 'got his first real view of the destruction which had been visited upon Germany'.[156] Both men then met with Allen Dulles and Colonel Robert Gill; the latter was later to become Jackson's executive officer in Europe. The two men then returned to London and made arrangements for creating a French office for Jackson's new organisation in a former OSS base in Paris.

During the war Donovan, largely through Allen Dulles, had made extensive contacts with members of the German anti-Nazi opposition from both the political left and conservative right, many of whom became victims of Nazi atrocities and reprisals. As Schlabrendorff notes:

> During the war, one of the many tasks of Donovan's office [OSS] was to keep up clandestine contacts with the German resistance. After the war, I became acquainted with him and we met a number of times.[157]

One important prosecution resource that Donovan made available to Jackson from the start of their liaison were individuals within the Nazi hierarchy who had operated as secret agents for the OSS, obtaining and transmitting classified information for the OSS prosecutors. The Cornell collection has an early memorandum in which the OSS were proudly announcing the relevance of Gisevius as both a witness and a source of incriminating evidence (which he in fact went on to present to the Nuremberg Tribunal on 8–9 April and 10 May 1946).[158] Donovan's organisation encouraged Gisevius to write an extensive account of his experiences within the Gestapo, as a prominent member of the anti-Nazi German opposition and informant for the OSS. By

153 Cutter to Jackson, 9 October 1945: Director's Files: NA, RG 226, M1642, Roll 110, Frames 172–74.

154 *Ibid* (reporting on the view of Colonel Street that Jackson could not afford to release any of these OSS staff).

155 Gill to Cutter, 16 October 1945: Director's Files: NA, RG 226, M1642, Roll 113, Frames 265–66.

156 Gerhart, *op cit*, 312. 157 *Ibid*, 261. 158 Salter, 2004, *op cit*, 841–54

fleshing out the details of the work carried out by the OSS lawyers, research analysts, academic consultants and agents, materials in the Cornell collection also draw much-needed attention to the wider issues raised by Donovan's willingness to cooperate so extensively with Jackson's organisation. Such anti-Nazi Germans could represent not only important sources of information regarding incriminating documentation but also act as possible trial witness for the prosecution. The credibility of German witnesses amongst the domestic German population at large might help to legitimise the overall trial process within Germany by offsetting the impression of mere 'victor's justice'. Donovan personally interrogated Otto Skorzeny, Hitler's favourite paratrooper, who had led the mission to 'rescue' Mussolini from Allied hands.[159] Donovan discussed another such prominent German witness with Jackson during their first formal meeting following his appointment in mid-May 1945.[160] Referring to the OSS's contacts with the German resistance to Hitler, Jackson recorded that:

> For example, it has a witness now in Switzerland who was one of the original organisers of the Gestapo and remained in through the early purges and down to the time of the rise of Himmler. He would be available as a witness. Many other leaders of similar character are in their possession. All of these he [General Donovan] put at our disposal. Many other leaders of similar character are in their possession. All of these he put at our service.[161]

Donovan was dangling the bait supplied by Allen Dulles, his Chief of Station in Bern, Switzerland, and later to become Director of Central Intelligence from 1953 to 1962. Bern was the heart of not only espionage activities within Europe but also the centre of Swiss banking and German gold transfer activity, which included highly questionable transfers of gold derived from concentration camp victims.[162]

159 W. Stevenson, *The Bormann Brotherhood: A New Investigation of the Escape and Survival of Nazi War Criminals* (New York: Harcourt, 1973), 116–17.

160 Jackson's Diary, *op cit*, 15 May 1945. 161 *Ibid.*

162 The authors of the recent report on the 'Safehaven project' note: 'Dulles had extensive pre-war ties to European banking circles, Dulles spent his tenure in Bern constructing an "Old-Boy" network of sources that extended throughout neutral and Axis-occupied Europe. It was an astonishingly successful system, ideally suited to his situation in neutral Switzerland and well-conceived to gain access to European government and business circles. For example, Dulles counted among his close personal friends no less than Thomas B. McKittrick, President of the Bank for International Settlements (BIS) in Basel. McKittrick also was an OSS source who provided Dulles with "comfortable access" to the thinking of the bankers most responsible for moving German assets throughout Europe. Among other kinds of information, McKittrick kept Dulles informed of the comings and goings of Reichsbank Vice President Emil Puhl, the architect of the German gold transfer

During his first visit to occupied Germany, Jackson later made personal contact over lunch and dinner with Dulles. Dulles, and the fruits of his espionage activities, appeared to have made a positive impression upon Jackson. Given the importance of one of these witnesses Donovan had previously promised and ultimately supplied, it is worth citing Jackson's impression in full:

> Allen Dulles has maintained an O.S.S. post in Switzerland and it is a most valuable one for us. He has:
>
> a. A witness ready to testify who was one of the founders of the Gestapo, knows its early history, its transformation etc.,
> b. A witness who for several years has forwarded us telegrams and reports right out of the German Foreign Office . . .
> c. Count Ciano's Diary.[163] Eda, daughter of Mussolini . . . strapped five volumes of the diary about her body when she escaped from Italy to Switzerland. She became bitter at her father when he refused to save Ciano from the German firing squad. . . . After long negotiations, Dulles personally got the diaries. It contains much said to be damaging to Ribbentrop. [Hitler's Foreign Minister] . . .
>
> Dulles also has a complete roster with photographs of the whole SS as of about 2 years ago. What a God send if it proves true.[164]

Jackson then set Ben Kaplan the task of studying the contents of the Ciano Diaries.[165]

arrangements. Other well-placed sources available to Dulles in high European financial circles included: Dr. Eduard Waetjen, Abwehr agent, member of the German resistance, and commercial adviser to the German Consul-General from February 15, 1945; Maurice Villars, General Director of the Zürich Electro-Bank; and Swedish economist and Economic Adviser to the BIS, Dr. Per Jacobsson, who was close to the extensive Japanese diplomatic and business circles in Switzerland. In 1945, Jacobsson provided information that helped to scuttle a Japanese attempt to buy vitally needed ball-bearings in Sweden and later served with Maurice Villars as a mediator in Japanese peace feelers put forward in Switzerland . . . such contacts were clearly important.' See sub-section G. 'The Office of Strategic Services and Project Safehaven' forming part of the 'Preliminary Study on US and Allied Efforts to recover and Restore Gold and other assets Stolen or Hidden by Germany During World War, 11 May 1997, co-ordinated by Stuart E. Eizenstat, prepared by William Z. Slany, the Historian Department of State.

163 This record by Count Galeazzo Ciano was later published as *The Ciano Diaries* (New York: Doubleday, 1946). See M. Salter and L. Charlesworth, 'The Ciano Diaries at the Nuremberg Trial', (2006) 4(1) *Journal International Criminal Justice* 103–27; L. Charlesworth and M. Salter, 'Ensuring The After-Life Of The Ciano Diaries: Allen Dulles's Provision Of Nuremberg Trial Evidence' (2006) 21(4) *Intelligence and National Security* 568–603.

164 Jackson Diary, *op cit*, 27 May 1945.

165 *Ibid*, 13 June 1945.

Schlabrendorff, together with OSS double-agent Hans Gisevius, Fritz Kolbe, aka 'George Wood' (who had supplied Dulles with over 1600 secret and top secret readings of Nazi diplomatic traffic), and a previously imprisoned Lutherian minister, were debriefed at OSS HQ at Wiesbaden, Germany. These members of the anti-Nazi German opposition were debriefed by Jackson, Donovan, Dulles and Colonel David K. Bruce (also from OSS)[166] for a full afternoon. During this debriefing, Schlabrendorff claimed to have personally seen orders for the killing of US parachutists.[167] Jackson himself recorded that:

> Allen Dulles arrived from Switzerland with four Nazi refugees who are probable witnesses and assistance in the case. We spend the afternoon interrogating two of them. One [Schlabrendorff] was a lawyer whose brother in law had been a general and the lawyer had been attached to the Army as a legal adviser. He had seen orders to dispatch American paratroopers and had discussed various orders with high military personnel . . . he had been a refugee whose life had been saved by Dulles and was very helpful outlining the parts of the military personnel in war crimes. The other witness [Gisevius] had been active politically in anti-Nazi movements and was engaged in the attempt on Hitler's life of July 20th 1944. The two men . . . had been close to the highest political figures in Germany . . . Present and participating in the examination were RHJ, Gen. Donovan, Amen, Bruce, Monoghan, Dulles, and an aid of Dulles who acted as interpreter. We interrogated the other witness who had been employed in the German Foreign Office and who had for some years furnished documents out of that office to Dulles in Switzerland. He gave us in great detail the part of different Foreign Office characters in the activities he considered criminal. All of these witnesses were anti-Nazi but not anti-German.[168]

This opposition network, which had itself engaged in a measure of war crimes trials planning through its prominent jurists, such as Fabian von

166 The role being played at Nuremberg by Col. David Bruce is not clear. He is mentioned by William Jackson, son of Justice Jackson, as leaving London, after having accompanied the Jacksons, Allen Dulles and General Donovan on a 'Grand tour of the continent' (including the OSS HQ in the Henkel Champagne plant at Wiesbaden, Frankfurt and Nuremberg) for America on 12 July 1945: see letter from William Jackson to his mother, 12 July 1945, Jackson Papers, *op cit*, Box 2. Bruce headed London OSS field office between 1942 and 44, returning to OSS Washington to chair the OSS's planning group in autumn 1944, before returning to Europe in the summer of 1945, see *OSS Against the Reich, the WW II Diaries of Colonel David K. E. Bruce*, Nelson D. Lankford (ed.) (Ohio: Kent State University Press, 1991), 203.

167 Jackson Diary, *op cit*, 7 July, 1945; Jackson to Irene, 12 July 1945, Jackson Papers, *op cit*, Box 2; Gerhart, *op cit*, 333–34.

168 Jackson's Diary, *op cit*, 7 July 1945.

Schlabrendorff (a former German Army lawyer), was uniquely placed to supply affidavits and produce useful witnesses. Its members were also able to provide Jackson's officials, few of whom understood German, considerable logistical support as trustworthy analysts and translators. This was a resource exploited by Donovan personally, as he took Schlabrendorff on to his personal staff at Nuremberg, and charged him with providing a constructive critical analysis of the adequacy of the draft indictment against the various Nuremberg defendants.[169] Writing from Jackson's perspective, Gerhart notes that these men were 'two important witnesses' who provided 'vital additional evidence'.[170] Gerhart recognises the importance of Gisevius and Schlabrendorff, when he notes that their debriefing yielded 'additional vital evidence in two important interviews'. Apparently, 'members of Jackson's staff were amazed at the stories these men told', not least by the fact that two former German lawyers had been so heavily involved in plots to kill Hitler and overturn the Nazi regime.[171]

Correspondence from Jackson's son and personal assistant, William Jackson, records that:

> Our mission was the collection of evidence and interviewing of witnesses etc., we got into an interesting collection of German underground people including one gent who had made several unsuccessful and one partially successful attempt on Hitler's life.[172]

In short, Donovan made available to Jackson the insights and personal experiences of key members of the anti-German opposition, two of whom, Gisevius and Schlabrendorff, were later to play important roles. Gisevius was to become a devastatingly effective star witness, for the prosecution, whereas Schlabrendorff helped Donovan as a senior personal aide.[173]

In addition, whilst at Nuremberg Donovan had contacts with a number of other anti-Nazi Germans, some of whom, such as journalist Paul Scheffer, he

169 Fabian von Schlabrendorff, *op cit*, 259–61.

170 Gerhart, *op cit*, 334: 'Gisevius was a towering blond man who had been on the inside of the German Gestapo, and who had plotted with others against Hitler's life.' *Ibid.*

171 Gerhart, *op cit*, 334: 'Lawyers, whatever else the public may think of them, are not generally regarded as cloak and dagger assassins.' Gerhart also records that Jackson's private secretary, Elsie Douglas, noted: 'For the first time in my life I had been face to face with men who risked their lives from day to day to take the lives of other men . . . It dawned on me that politics and life in Germany had been different. Men lived from day to day and knew not what to expect when darkness fell. They must have been thankful each morning that they had not been arrested during the night, as was the custom of the Gestapo. At once the cruelty and cold-bloodedness of the hard and bitter competition of Europe struck home to me.' *Ibid*, n. 3, 507–08.

172 See letter from William Jackson to his mother, 12 July 1945, Jackson Papers, *op cit*, Box 2.

173 Salter, 2004, *op cit*.

had personally assisted in having released from US custody as an 'enemy alien' by testifying to his anti-Nazi credentials. Donovan sought to find a role for Scheffer in anticipating possible defence arguments that the Nazi defendants might choose to deploy, and as a source of information on the pre-war involvement of elements of the German Army with the Nazi Party.[174]

Donovan's assistance with the geo-politics of international negotiations

Perhaps the most important contribution the OSS Director made during the early honeymoon phase of OSS–OCC relations related to the international relations aspect. Donovan had developed positive contacts with the British, French and Soviet governments, as well as with the Vatican and its vast network of information – facilitated by Donovan's status as a prominent Irish-Catholic.

Certainly Donovan's extensive foreign and diplomatic contacts helped open many doors for Jackson on the international stage. On 28 May 1945, when Jackson made his first exploratory trip to Britain, he had good reason to include Donovan on this trip. As Sprecher notes: 'When Jackson made his first exploratory trip to Europe in May 1945, he promptly accepted Donovan's offer to accompany him so he could take advantage of Donovan's extensive wartime connections.'[175] One purpose of this trip during May was to examine the 'considerable part of our evidence' assembled in London by the OSS and other bodies, such as the UN War Crimes Commission. This evidence was now available to the OSS's London R&A field office, which had further cultivated its relations with another important source of potential trial evidence, British navy intelligence officials. At this important meeting with British officials, Jackson requested that Donovan accompany him, presumably because of the General's extensive connections developed through negotiating a series of intelligence and operational agreements with America's wartime allies. The operation branches of the OSS (including Special Operations) were largely modelled upon the British 'Special Operations Executive' (SOE). During his wartime liaison with various British authorities, Donovan had established particularly good working relations with leading British political, legal, diplomatic and intelligence officials, some

174 See the correspondence between Donovan and Paul Scheffer at 12.228 and 62.02, Cornell Collection, *op cit*. On Donovan's assistance to Scheffer, see declassified FBI files available online at http://foia.fbi.gov/donovan/donovan1c.pdf, and http://colley.co.uk/garethjones/scheffer/fbi2.htm.

175 Sprecher, *op cit*, 167. This included a visit to London on 26 June in which Jackson and Donovan departed Washington to meet with his Allied counterparts in London to discuss legal proceedings against Nazi officials.

of whom had cultivated Donovan to help exert pressure on President Roosevelt to enter the war.[176]

On accepting the offer of appointment to Jackson's staff, Donovan also offered to carry out war crimes related 'instructions' in Europe during his forthcoming visit on OSS business during the third week of May.[177] Jackson requested Donovan to carry out the first major survey of possible trial evidence on continental Europe. This survey included the further exploitation of the General's diplomatic contacts with the Soviets, with whom Donovan had shared wartime intelligence,[178] and access to captured security force documentation:

> I asked him to undertake to interview . . . some of the higher level criminals such as Göring with a view to finding full information as to what he knew of Russian preparations for the war or what he considers induced them to make war on Russia, together with any information as to their chemical or other inventions useful hereafter, and any information that might be useful if we should put him on the stand as a witness or any positions he might be taking in defence. I also asked him to . . . get any captured documents, particularly of a political character, and have them processed. Also to get any information that might be available to the organisation [OSS] through the foreign office of Britain or other governments, and to look the field over so as to be able to advise us as to our procedures when we go to Europe.[179]

With these instructions, Donovan left for London and promised to keep in touch with Jackson through OSS's secure communication network. Donovan's intelligence background meant that he was able to alert Jackson

176 A. Danchev, *Establishing the Anglo-American Alliance: The Second World War Diaries of Brigadier Dykes* (London: Brasseys, 1990). In 1941, Dykes, British Secretary of the Combined Chief of Staff Committee in Washington, had been given the task of escorting Donovan around British military and intelligence facilities in the Mediterranean region, including Greece, Spain, Portugal, Bulgaria, Yugoslavia, Albania, Turkey, Palestine, Iraq and Egypt, in order to impress on him (and indirectly Roosevelt) the mutual benefits of America providing greater military support to the British war effort. During this 'pre-war' period for Donovan, he was introduced to high-ranking diplomats, generals, European royalty and political leaders, and acquainted himself with the military and political developments taking place. One British source, noted: 'The Prime Minister has directed that every facility should be afforded to Colonel Donovan, who has been taken fully in our confidence.' 1608, FO to Lampson, 24 December 1940, FO371/24263, PRO/NA; Troy, *op cit*, 36–41; Smith, 1983, *op cit*, 40–54.

177 Jackson Diary, *op cit*, 12 May 1945. Donovan was scheduled to leave for Europe on Thursday 17 May.

178 B. F. Smith, *Sharing Secrets with Stalin: How the Allies Trade Intelligence: 1941–1945* (New York: Diane Publishing Company, 1998).

179 Jackson's Diary, *op cit*, 15 May 1945.

to be careful when discussing matters with the British because the Russians 'had the code of the British Foreign Office' and this could prove embarrassing during the build-up to the trials.[180] On 29 May, Donovan and Bill Whitney joined forces with Jackson to conduct rather disorganised and *ad hoc* negotiations with the British Attorney General, Sir David Maxwell Fyfe, who had just been appointed to head the British prosecutors, as well as officials representing the British Treasury and Foreign Office. In these negotiations, Donovan lent powerful support to Jackson's position that there was a need for declaratory judgments against key Nazi organisations, and for a later four power conference to set up the organisational and legal basis for the proposed trials.

In June 1945, Donovan made an early visit to London on Jackson's behalf, meeting with senior government officials responsible for war crimes issues, including the British War Crimes Executive.[181] Furthermore, the OSS Director was, it seems, providing personal support for Jackson as the latter was negotiating various detailed aspects of the planned trials. These included the role of psychiatric examination of each defendant, and decisions over the method of killing those sentenced to death, arguing for hanging, not execution by firing squad (as hanging was deemed highly dishonouring to military defendants).[182]

Documentation from OCC planning meetings, as well as from later prosecution sources from the spring 1946, confirms how important the Vatican became as a source of documentation of Nazi atrocities for the Nuremberg prosecutors.[183] Indeed, following their meeting with the Pope, Jackson reported back that:

> The justice found unexpected cooperation on the part of the Vatican. He is very much interested and has followed war crimes in great detail. He furnished the Jackson material in English. These are most generally concerned with Committees 2 and 3. The Justice will let Tardini, the Papal Secretary of State, know what else we want. The Vatican showed some caution, as is natural, but really talked with great candour.[184]

Although a strict legalist in his public statements, Jackson was far from naïve in his recognition of the inevitable interaction between geo-political and

180 *Ibid*, 16–17 May, 1945.

181 DAG(a) unsigned memo on a meeting with General Donovan, 9 June 1945: London PRO/NA, LCO.2/2980, 'Attorney General's committee and British War Crimes Executive', 453ff.

182 Kelley to Andrus, 25 October 1945, Burton C. Andrus Collection, Colorado, USA; cf. 'Psychiatric Investigation of Defendants', Jackson Papers, *op cit*, Box 107.

183 'Re Documents furnished by the Vatican on Persecution of the Churches, used at Nuremberg', February 1946, Jackson Papers, *op cit*, Box 111.

184 Minutes of Meeting, 31 August 1945: Jackson Papers, *op cit*, Box 110.

strictly legal aspects of his task. His diary contains references to many official and semi-official meetings with influential American politicians and government officials during which Jackson floated and exchanged views on the various strategic and geo-political issues that were at stake.[185] Jackson defended his planned trial against accusations that there was no law adequate to the Nazi atrocities, that a trial would provide an opportunity for further Nazi propaganda and that the defendants should therefore be executed.[186]

Concerning the specifically political and geo-political aspects of the case, Jackson often preferred to confer with the two Donovans rather than his other trial lawyers. These aspects included Jackson's opposition to penal labour reparations and the possible impression that the forthcoming trial might be 'conducted merely to provide victims for it'. They discussed Allied relations with neutral countries and the ambiguous role and orientation towards legality of the Soviet Union, and the danger that an apparently 'anti-German' trial might have the effect of 'driving into Russian hands the German population'.[187] For his part, Donovan stressed the importance of arranging the trial in a manner that would have the effect of 'impressing the German people with their own failure'. In one private planning meeting with Jackson, Donovan:

> [E]xplained the ramifications of his own organisation, its contacts with the Russian secret service with which it has maintained satisfactory exchanges [and] with the British Foreign Office. It has also had a contact with a substantial German underground.[188]

Clearly, and from the start, both the OSS leadership and Jackson viewed the trial as mediated by both geo-political and legalistic considerations. With Donovan's support, Jackson – rather that the US State (that is, Foreign Affairs) Department – played the leading role in negotiating the procedures of the proposed international military tribunal with the Russian, French and British governments. This entailed addressing formidable diplomatic as well as strictly legal issues, particularly regarding contacts with senior officials from the Soviet Union.[189] The legal elements were intended to serve – or at least not contradict – some of the ideological aims of the geo-political aspects, particularly the formidable task of post-war democratic reconstruction along Western lines. Clearly, the shadow of what was to become the Cold War was already beginning to exert an impact, and Donovan, who was in receipt of current secret intelligence on the intentions of foreign powers, was able to advise Jackson over how best to handle these aspects. Donovan's influence over Jackson with respect to taking a firm line with the Soviet

185 See Jackson Diary, *op cit*, 18, 26–27 May 1945. 186 *Ibid*, 16 May 1945.
187 *Ibid*, 15 May 1945. 188 *Ibid*. 189 *Ibid*, 14 June 1945.

representatives within the international negotiations regarding the proposed trials was noted, with some disquiet, by British officials such as Patrick Dean, who complained on 1 July that:

> Jackson, inspired by General Donovan, appears to be thinking that we should now try to reach agreement to set up four courts, each under the presidency of one of the four parties concerned, to handle these trials, and that in this way we should avoid being drawn into a trial which is too Soviet a character . . . General Donovan, who clearly does not like the Russians much, is attracted by the idea of running the Courts without Soviet participation.[190]

The Anglo-American relationship within the Nuremberg process was assisted by the efforts and personal contacts of Bill Whitney, an OSS official and former New York lawyer whose services Donovan made available to Jackson.[191] At the start of their cooperation in May 1945, Jackson recorded that Donovan 'offered to put Whitney onto his staff and use him in London and thought he would be very helpful there with a little instruction. This is likely to be a very helpful move in getting us oriented in London.'[192] Whitney had formerly headed the OSS-London Field Office.[193] More important for present purposes, however, was the fact that, in addition to his legal experience in America, he was also a well-connected member of the English bar and British legal establishment more generally. Donovan used Whitney to help prepare the diplomatic ground with both the British Attorney General and Lord Chancellor's Department.[194] Gerhart notes that: 'Mr Whitney's familiarity with London, his acquaintance with the British Bar and the knowledge he had of both the British and the American legal systems made him a very valuable asset.'[195] Whitney was also helpful in the face-to-face international Church House negotiations between the American, Russian, French and British delegations in London on Friday 13 July 1945 in exercising a moderating impact upon Jackson.[196] Whitney's influence and greater personal knowledge of British establishment sensitivities may explain why

190 Dean to Foreign Office, 1 July 1945, quoted in Taylor, *op cit*, 60.

191 Taylor, 1992, *op cit*, 53.

192 Jackson Diary, *op cit*, 15 May 1945.

193 B. Smith, 1983, *op cit*, 88–89; Sprecher, 1998, *op cit*, 59.

194 Jackson Diary, *op cit*, 28 May 1945. The OSS employed Whitney and 'a small staff' in London for the purposes of liaison with their British counterparts.

195 Gerhart, *op cit*, 322.

196 Taylor, *op cit*, 62 (quoting Shea's diary). Whitney, according to Taylor, dropped out of the scene by the end of July 1945: *ibid* 68. However, Sprecher recalls that Whitney was still active, with Jackson sending him Sprecher's own draft prosecution brief on the Nazis' destruction of the German Trade Unions during mid-August 1945: Sprecher, 1998, *op cit*, 59, citing NA: RG 128, Box 43, Folder 230 (Labor).

Jackson deferred to Donovan's suggestions, cabled from London, regarding arrangements for conducting formal diplomatic negotiations with the British authorities, including the Foreign Office.

Donovan contributed his negotiating expertise with senior British legal and Foreign Office authorities, including David Maxwell Fyfe (British Attorney General and later senior Nuremberg prosecutor), Sir Thomas Barnes (Treasury Solicitor) and Lord Simon (Lord Chancellor), as well as the UN War Crimes Commission. Donovan was, for example, pro-active in encouraging the British authorities to include Hess, former deputy to Hitler, amongst the proposed list of defendants for the first international trials.[197] In early June 1945, Jackson recognised the importance of Donovan's role in another part of his report to the President:

> Since a considerable part of our evidence has been assembled in London, I went there on May 28 with General Donovan to arrange for its examination, and to confer with the United Nations War Crimes Commission and with officials of the British Government responsible for the prosecution of war criminals. We had extended conferences with the newly appointed Attorney General, the Lord Chancellor, the Foreign Secretary, the Treasury Solicitor, and others. On May 29, Prime Minister Churchill announced in the House of Commons that Attorney General Sir David Maxwell Fyfe had been appointed to represent the United Kingdom in the prosecution. Following this announcement, members of my staff and I held extended conferences with the Attorney General and his staff.[198]

These negotiations were, by all accounts, important in winning over the previously reluctant British political and legal leadership to the cause of holding a four-party international trial broadly along the lines that Donovan and Jackson sought.[199] As Gerhart notes:

> The British press took a keen interest in these preliminaries and helped create sentiment in favour of the trials. After meeting with British representatives, Justice Jackson issued a statement to the British press that there were no substantial difference of opinion between the American and British war crimes authorities.[200]

197 'Note on conversation with General Donovan, 9 June 1945: Lord Chancellor's Office (LCO) 2/2980/x/j.7320; Dean to Maxwell Fyfe, 19 June 1945: LCO, 2/2980/x/j.7320.

198 United States Report to the President from Justice Robert H. Jackson, Chief of Counsel for the United States in the Prosecution of Axis War Criminals, 7 June 1945: originally published in (1945) 39 *American Journal of International Law* 178 (Supp); available at: http://www.roberthjackson.org/documents/060745/.

199 Gerhart, *op cit*, 312.

200 *Ibid.*

The question of which Nazis merited prosecution was discussed initially with the British authorities on 29 May, namely with David Maxwell Fyfe, who later went on to become a Nuremberg prosecutor within the British delegation. At this meeting within the House of Lords, Jackson's negotiating team consisted only of himself, Donovan and the OSS's Bill Whitney, with Donovan arguing for a far wider list than the initial one drawn up by the British, which named only Göring as a definite candidate, with question marks against Hess and von Papen.[201] One result of Donovan's 'diplomatic' interventions was that the British agreed to Donovan's request that both Hess and von Papen be added to the list of Nuremberg defendants already proposed by the British. During these negotiations, Donovan helped further widen the original list of defendants to include a new provisional list consisting of Robert Ley,[202] Alfred Rosenberg[203] the Hungarian regent, Nicolas von Horthy,[204] and von Papen.[205] Donovan succeeded in having Hess's name included in this list of defendants in June 1945 and then in later debates. This was despite widespread misgivings over this potential defendant's apparent mental state. The OSS Director insisted that: 'He should be brought to trial as a major war criminal, and if he were to put forward the plea of unfitness he should be examined by a body of medical men and, if found unfit to plead, sent to Broadmoor.'[206] With Jackson, Donovan successfully resisted British suggestions that flogging be included amongst the penalties.[207]

In short, Jackson appears to have given Donovan considerable responsibility for developing these early liaisons with the British, possibly out of deference to the OSS's pre-existing formal and interpersonal contacts with senior officials in London, which Jackson lacked.[208] This delegation of negotiating responsibilities to Donovan may have been one of Jackson's better decisions. Certainly, Donovan appears to have been comparatively successful in exerting pressure in favour of the American model of an international war crimes trial and trial strategy, rather than Winston Churchill's notorious desire to practise summary execution. It was also successful in revising the British Foreign Office's reluctance to share captured German documents with the other three Allies.[209] As Sprecher recalls: 'In London Bill Donovan had

201 Jackson Memo, 'Meeting at House of Lords May 29 1945 2.30 pm', Jackson Papers, *op cit*, Box 95.

202 Chief of the Nazi Labour Front.

203 Chief Nazi ideologist.

204 Whose father Donovan has previously interrogated.

205 Former German Foreign Minister prior to Ribbentrop.

206 DAG(a) unsigned memo on a meeting with General Donovan, 9 June 1945: PRO/NA, LCO.2/2980, 'Attorney General's committee and British War Crimes Executive', 453ff.

207 Minutes of Meeting on 29 May, PRO file, LCO, 2/2980; Jackson Diary, *op cit*, 29 May 1945; Jackson Memo, 'Meeting at the House of Lords', *op cit*.

208 Jackson Diary, *op cit*, 11 June 1945.

209 Sprecher, 1998, *op cit*, 16; Taylor, 1992, *op cit*, 46–48, 53, 56, 60, 61, 68, 78–79.

protested vigorously and with some success against the restraints of the British Foreign Office in sharing captured German documents with the other three Allies.'[210]

The General's positive relationship with British authorities was important to Jackson because the British, who still recalled the humiliating and farcical results of the Leipzig trials of 1919–21 held after the First World War, had long opposed the very idea of holding post-war trials. Jackson tended to include Donovan as a key member of his negotiating team. Such negotiations with senior British officials, including the Attorney General, Lord Chancellor and Sir Anthony Eden, took place both formally and over dinner at Claridges Hotel.[211] During their contacts with such senior legal figures, Jackson and Donovan worked effectively together in securing British support for the details of the Americans' 'theory and method of procedure'.[212] Apparently, the result of such teamwork was 'utmost cordiality in welcome and readiness to co-operate'.[213]

Jackson's formal 'Report to the President on Atrocities and War Crimes; June 7, 1945', summarising the achievements of the early part of his mission, credits Donovan for contributing to the establishment and development of military and international relations, which were already bearing fruit in terms of the provision of evidence suitable for trial purposes:

> The officials of other countries were most anxious to help. For example, the French brought to General Donovan and me in Paris evidence that civilians in Germany had beaten to death with wrenches three American airmen. They had obtained from the German Burgomeister identification of the killers, had taken them into custody, and offered to deliver them to our forces. The sum of these conferences is that the British are taking steps parallel with our own to clear the military and localised cases for immediate trial, and to effect a complete interchange of evidence and a co-ordination of planning and preparation of the case by the British and American representatives. Despite the fact that the prosecution of the major war criminals involves problems of no mean dimensions, I am able to report that no substantial differences exist between the United Kingdom representatives and ourselves, and that

210 Sprecher, 1998, *op cit*, 167.

211 See the 'top secret' minutes of a formal meeting on 29 May 1945 at the House of Lords between Jackson, Donovan and Whitney on the US side, and the British Attorney General (Maxwell Fyfe), Solicitor General, Treasury Solicitor and other officials, Jackson Papers, *op cit*, Box 95.

212 See also the minutes of Jackson and Donovan's formal meeting with the British at the House of Lords, 29 May 1945, Jackson Papers, *op cit*, Box 95.

213 Jackson Diary, *op cit*, 28 May 1945.

> minor differences have adjusted easily as one or the other of us advanced the better reasons for his view.[214]

Indeed, during these negotiations with the British authorities, Jackson appears to have agreed with Donovan's suggestions for the use of certain Nazi leaders of 'weak and low character' as highly useful prosecution witnesses, whose contributions could perhaps bring the proposed trial to a speedier conclusion than would otherwise be the case.[215] (Later sections will show how Jackson later reversed his position on the legitimacy of Donovan's plans to deploy such German witnesses as prosecution assets.) On 9 June 1945, Donovan also discussed with the British authorities the possibility of holding 'a series of trials by the same court on the same indictment' of groups of Nazi defendants, such as, presumably, industrialists, leading civil servants and doctors implicated in atrocities.[216] This suggestion was to later take root in the second round of American-led trials against middle-ranking Nazi defendants known as the Nuremberg 'Subsequent Proceedings'.

At this time, Donovan's relationship with the British officials did not, however, preclude a number of frank and forceful exchanges. Indeed, he felt sufficiently confident in the strength of his pre-existing relations with British officials to suggest that they had been 'somewhat exclusive' in the handling of possible defendants in their custody, and that their list of proposed suspects unduly excluded specific individuals.

Under pressure from Donovan, the British legal authorities also agreed to Jackson's proposed additions of high-ranking officials within the Nazi Party and government. The newly appointed British Attorney General also agreed to remedy Donovan's complaints about 'exclusivity' and to 'make it his business' to mobilise and coordinate various government agencies involved in war crimes issues.[217]

Throughout the pre-trial negotiations, Donovan's prior wartime experience of dealing with the Russian authorities, who were not generally prone to cooperation, would have proved helpful, as the Americans and the Russians were often predisposed to take contrary positions on most major issues. Donovan also assisted Jackson when the two men held a meeting at the end of May with the Russian ambassador to England, Gusev, to inform the Soviet authorities of the state of Anglo-American negotiations. Both men pressed the Soviets to appoint their own chief prosecutors as soon as possible, whilst emphasising that any delays on the Soviets' part would not be allowed

214 United States Department of State Bulletin. Washington, DC: Government Printing Office, 7 June 1945.

215 'Minutes of a meeting of May 29, 1945', 2: PRO/NA, LCO /x/j/ 7320.

216 'Note of a conversation with General Donovan', 9 June 1945: LCO, 2/2980/x/j/7320.

217 See the minutes of a formal meeting at the House of Lords, 29 May, Jackson Papers, *op cit*, Box 95.

to hold up the progress of the Anglo-Americans.[218] Despite this 'blunt posture', Donovan and Jackson were warmly received, possibly because of the good wartime liaison between the OSS and the Russians. Jackson thought that it was likely that their conversation was being secretly recorded.[219] Donovan was later invited to give speeches to conference dinners arranged with the Russian delegation.

Donovan also accompanied Jackson to pre-trial meetings with senior French government officials and diplomats, during which both men sought to influence the appointment of the French judges in favour of those who were 'broad-minded and non-technical'. Such judges, he hoped, would be more amenable to the retrospective inventions of new offences of 'crimes against the peace' and 'crimes against humanity' which Jackson was seeking to have included in new primary legislation authorising the trials themselves.[220]

When planning his negotiating team for the forthcoming four power international conference in July, Jackson selected himself, Donovan, Bernays and his son William to represent US interests.[221] On 18 June 1945, Donovan was one of Jackson's senior staff who departed from the US to begin these negotiations with the British, French, and Russians in London. Donovan met initially with Sir Basil Newton, of the Foreign Office, on 21 and 24 June to exchange information on the proposed location of the trials. Donovan, and other senior staff,[222] participated in the opening rounds of these four power negotiations.[223] The General and Jackson were involved in eve of conference discussions with the French officials, and the same two men also liaised with the US ambassador.[224] It is likely that Donovan's positive contacts developed during the war would have helped smooth Jackson's path in the build up to, and conduct of, difficult international relations between British, French and Russian delegations. Donovan's contacts and negotiating skills were useful to Jackson in the four power negotiations for the creation of the legal framework for the Nuremberg Tribunal, the protracted haggling over the wording of the relevant offences that were eventually agreed in the London Agreement and Charter of August 1945. The Charter, effectively a founding statute of new international criminal law, provided the formal legal basis for the Nuremberg trials.[225] By the time the London conference began, the war in

218 Jackson Diary, *op cit*, 30 May 1945; Taylor, *op cit*, 53.

219 Jackson Diary *op cit*, 30 May 1945.

220 *Ibid*, 10 July 1945.

221 *Ibid*, 21 June 1945.

222 Murray Bernays, Alderman and Shea, Whitney, James Donovan, Dean and Jackson's son, William.

223 Gerhart, *op cit*, 324.

224 *Ibid*, 29 June and 5 July 1945.

225 *Ibid*, 28 May 1945. The Foreign Ministers set up the International Conference on Military Trials (ICMT) to be held beginning in June in London. The other representatives to the ICMT were, from the Soviets, General I. T. Nikitchenko of the Soviet Supreme Court and Professor A. N. Trainin, who had written a book about Nazi leaders' culpability for the

Europe was over. Hitler and most of the highest-ranking Nazis – excepting Hermann Göring – were confirmed dead, greatly relieving worries that a trial would simply become a vehicle for propaganda. General and James Donovan both contributed to the vital early stages of these international negotiations in London.[226] The beginning of the Cold War rift began to show up at the conference. Influenced by the recent negative experiences of OSS officials in the newly 'liberated' Eastern Europe, Donovan heavily influenced Jackson to privately distrust the intentions and actions of the Soviets.[227]

In mid-July, Donovan also assisted Jackson to orient himself to the needs, procedures and expectations of senior American military and administrative officials based in occupied Germany whose cooperation was vital to the preparation of the case. This included accompanying Jackson to important meetings with General Lucius Clay and Ambassador Robert Murphy in the Farben Building, where the issue of the location of the proposed four power international trials continued to be discussed.[228] This was politically sensitive for Donovan. Many of his OSS subordinates had, in the previous year, accumulated a series of extremely negative experiences of Soviet actions and intentions, particularly in newly 'liberated' Eastern Europe. Although politically to the left of Donovan, Jackson was perhaps influenced by the OSS Director's hard-line stance that the trials most certainly should not take place in the Soviet zone of Allied occupied Germany, such as Berlin, as the Soviets were strongly pressing for. Donovan's pressure may have been one factor in influencing the decision to inspect the facilities available in the American-controlled zone of Nuremberg in southern Germany. Donovan certainly accompanied Jackson on his subsequent visit to this grim war-torn city, which still carried with it the stink of rotting corpses buried under the rubble of bombed buildings. As Persico notes, in July 1945:

> He [Jackson] travelled in a Dakota transport with his son, Bill, and . . . Donovan, whose OSS personnel always met them with useful information wherever they landed. By July 7, they had checked out Wiesbaden

crime of aggressive war, the implications of which the OSS–R&A Branch had extensively analysed. The French authorities sent Judge Robert Falco of the highest court in France, and Professor André Gros, an authority on international law. The British representatives were the Lord Chancellor, Lord Simon, and the Attorney General, Sir David Maxwell Fyfe. Halfway through the conference, Churchill's coalition was defeated in elections, so the new representatives became Lord Jowitt and Sir Hartley Shawcross, but for the sake of simplicity the new government kept Maxwell Fyfe as the official British liaison.

226 Sprecher, 1998, *op cit*, 167. This includes a visit to London on 26 June in which Jackson and Donovan departed Washington to meet with their Allied counterparts in London to discuss legal proceedings against Nazi officials.

227 A. Tusa and J. Tusa, *The Nuremberg Trial* (New York: Atheneum, 1983), 78.

228 These discussions took place on 8 July: Taylor, *op cit*, 61.

> [where OSS had established a major base in a former Champagne Factory building], Frankfurt and Munich.[229]

In short, Jackson included Donovan in his party visiting different possible locations for the planned trials, including the Nuremberg Palace of Justice.[230]

During July 1945, Donovan continued to assist Jackson on continental Europe. He travelled with him to Salzburg in the American-controlled zone of Austria, and then on to Paris on 10 July. In Paris, Donovan and Jackson decided upon the division of responsibilities between Story (analysis of documentation), Amen (interrogation) and Gill (evidence-gathering in continental Europe). Donovan then returned with Jackson to London to resume the four power international negotiations over the legal and organisational basis of the proposed trials with the French, British and Soviet delegates. Donovan was entrusted to select, obtain and bring back secret State Department documents vital to the case during his visit to Washington in the middle of this month. Indeed, Jackson noted to the undersecretary of state that Donovan could be fully entrusted with this task of selecting the most important documents because 'of his experience here'.[231] Jackson also reported that 'General Donovan is good enough to carry to you the draft of agreement between the Four Powers.'[232] As far as Jackson was concerned, then, Donovan still represented a trusted intermediary even with the most senior members of the American government. This suggests that, at least until he departed Europe in the third week of July to deal with OSS affairs in the Far East,[233] Jackson still included Donovan as one of his most important and valuable senior colleagues.

In short, there is evidence that the positive nature of Donovan's contacts with the British and, to a lesser extent, with both the Soviets and Vatican authorities, assisted Jackson's task of establishing the legal, diplomatic and institutional basis for the planned Nuremberg trials.

Donovan's assistance with American organisations

Of necessity, during the Second World War the General had developed working relations with senior military figures, under whose command specific OSS attachments, including Special Forces commando groups, worked. As an

229 Jackson to Irene, 'Friday Eve' [6 July 1945], Jackson Papers, *op cit*, Box 2; Jackson Diary, *op cit*, 7 July 1945; Persico, 1994, *op cit*, 37.

230 *Ibid*, 40; Oral History/JXO, *op cit*, 1300. Jackson recommended Nuremberg following his team's visit on 7 July 1945.

231 Jackson to Grew, 12 July 1945: Jackson Papers, *op cit*, Box 111 (letter one).

232 *Ibid* (letter two).

233 The relevant literature gives different dates but Jackson Diary suggests that Donovan was on route to China by 27 July: *op cit*, 27 July 1945.

ambitious head of a newly created and expansionist intelligence organisation, Donovan had to rapidly acquire knowledge of which buttons to press to open which particular doors in the intelligence, diplomatic and military hierarchies. It is arguable that Donovan's experience not only with the various branches of the US military but also government and intelligence bodies was equally important for Jackson's task. In other words, the knowledge and expertise gained in working closely with different branches of the Allied armed forces and intelligence bodies proved particularly valuable in Donovan's new role as Jackson's deputy. In the domestic context, where rivalries between institutions could be as bitterly fought as disputes between nations, Donovan drew upon his long experience of Washington political machinations. He was, therefore, able to supply Jackson with a stream of strategic advice about how best to identify, anticipate and avoid the various pitfalls that could lie ahead of the prosecution. In order to identify and gather relevant documentation and witnesses, Jackson and Donovan had to secure cooperative relations with Generals Eisenhower, Smith, Clay, Betts and others. Jackson and his non-OSS staff lacked prior experience in the curious and opaque workings of British and American military authorities. Donovan, by contrast, had a military as well as legal background even prior to his appointment as OSS Director. Hence, Jackson shrewdly brought Donovan along to other meetings with a series of high-level military officers in Germany. These included meetings with General Clay, which aimed to smooth the path of the prosecutors' project. For example, Donovan negotiated the possibility of trial appeal provisions and ensured access of Jackson's interrogators to the US Army's I. G. Farben inquiry.[234] During May 1945, Donovan was particularly concerned to avoid prompting political and media criticism of undue delay that was likely to place 'a great deal of heat' upon the prosecutors. Jackson accepted his suggested strategy for deflecting such pressure by expediting: 'the trial by normal military tribunals of a number of cases which were violations of ordinary laws of war and the sort of things military tribunals ordinarily clean up very promptly'.[235]

Towards the end of May 1945, Donovan joined forces with Jackson during the latter's visit to continental Europe to survey and gather trial evidence, including that available from the trials of lesser war criminals before Allied military tribunals which were currently under way. Donovan joined Jackson in Paris, where the two men engaged in 'a series of war crime review conferences with American and French army officers'.[236] During this trip, Donovan

234 United States Report to the President from Justice Robert H. Jackson, Chief of Counsel for the United States in the Prosecution of Axis War Criminals, June 7, 1945: originally published in (1945) 39 *American Journal of International Law* 178 (Supp.); available at: http://www.roberthjackson.org/documents/060745/.

235 Jackson Diary, *op cit*, 17 May 1945.

236 Gerhart, *op cit*, 311.

assisted Jackson in putting pressure on US Army and Navy lawyers to get their best cases prepared for domestic or Military Commission trial as soon as possible, even if sentencing had to be delayed to ensure that possible witnesses at the international trials were not hanged prematurely.[237] As Gerhart implies, Donovan's contribution was particularly important because: 'Jackson's background was one of civilian not military justice.'[238] Jackson's own Report to the President noted Donovan's contribution in negotiating with a range of military, political, diplomatic and former French resistance officials now holding governmental posts, with whom Donovan had previously established working relations in his capacity as OSS Director:

> I flew to Paris and Frankfort and conferred with Generals Eisenhower, Smith, Clay, and Betts, among others, and arranged to have a representative on hand to clear questions of conflict in any particular case. We also arranged an exchange of evidence between my staff and the Theater Judge Advocate's staff. . . . Cases such as this are not infrequent. Under the arrangements perfected, the military authorities are enabled to move in cases of this class without delay. Some are already under way; some by now have been tried and verdicts rendered. Some concentration camp cases are also soon to go on trial.[239]

OSS logistic support, such as the provision of mass microfilming facilities for 340 tons of documentary evidence from the German Foreign Office, would – on occasions – form part of various logjams and possible disputes with the US military authorities. Hence, Donovan's presence at meetings with senior members of the US armed forces was, on occasions, important for technical, as well as strategic reasons.[240]

Given his relations with senior American military officials, the General was also in a strong position to request and receive 'special executive assignments' from staff formally employed by other agencies responsible for aspects of war crimes issues. These included James O'Malley, Officer-in-Charge of the Division of the US Army-Navy War Crimes Office,[241] and members of the Judge Advocate General's office assigned to the Europe, which had previously been a 'customer' of OSS's war crimes research. Donovan was even able to provide Jackson's organisation with the services of a specialist in providing accommodation and catering, Captain John Vonetes. Vonetes

237 Jackson Diary, *op cit*, 17 May 1945. 238 *Ibid.*

239 United States Report to the President from Justice Robert H. Jackson, Chief of Counsel for the United States in the Prosecution of Axis War Criminals, June 7, 1945: originally published in (1945) 39 *American Journal of International Law* 178 (Supp.); available at: http://www.roberthjackson.org/documents/060745/.

240 Jackson Diary, *op cit*, 8 July 1945, regarding meetings with Clay and Robert Murphy.

241 *New York Times*, 24 December 2000, section 1.

mobilised his own contacts to secure approximately 100 units of accommodation within bomb-damaged Nuremberg, some very grand, for Jackson's senior staff. He also provided the prosecutors with lavish food and entertainment, particularly when Jackson and Donovan were entertaining senior prosecutors from the other Allied delegations.[242] At this time, that is early to mid-July 1945, Donovan's status was perhaps at its peak.

Indeed, within internal OCC correspondence, Murray Bernays praised the role played by the London base of OSS in securing the only measure of support from various British intelligence and military agencies that Jackson's advance party had been able to obtain.[243] Jackson corroborates this point in a cable forwarded to OSS, where he notes how:

> [T]he mission is already settled and prepared to move ahead, largely because of the fine co-operation of the UK case and London OSS . . . It is urgent that OSS (to whom a separate cable is being sent on this subject forward its studies to us as soon as possible even if they are not in final draft form, so that we may use [it] to influence the British attitude [which was disinclined to] 'push the political and economic case'.[244]

On the other hand, Jackson probably appreciated that there were limits to the doors that Donovan could open for him within the complex hierarchy of American government organisations with whom the Nuremberg prosecutors needed to liaise. During the war, Donovan's organisation had developed notoriously bad relations with not only the US Army's Military Intelligence Division (G-2), but also with the FBI.[245] If any question arose over securing cooperation from these particular sources of trial evidence and background data on atrocities, potential defendants and witnesses, then any personal intervention from Donovan on Jackson's behalf could have proved counterproductive.

In short, Donovan exploited his personal and institutional contacts with key figures within the US armed forces in order to facilitate aspects of the Nuremberg project. Whilst Donovan's association with Jackson's organisation was not universally beneficial in securing inter-agency cooperation, it is more than probable that Jackson was right to continue to exploit the OSS Director's contacts and to recognise the benefits that accrued from this during the vital trial preparation stage.

242 Persico, *op cit*, 46.
243 Bernays to Cutter, 9 July, 'May thru File', NA, RG 107, 'war crimes' 000.5, Box 16.
244 Memo to Telford Taylor's office of 30 June 1945: NA, ASW 00.5, 'War Crimes'.
245 Cave-Brown, *op cit*, 821–22; Bradley Smith, 1983 *op cit*, 57–58, 340–46, 357–58.

The provision of documentation

Over and above Donovan's personal resources, as an organisation, the OSS supplied Jackson's staff with extensive documentation. This was drawn not only from its own internal files, including comprehensive biographical data on likely defendants and witnesses, but also information it had received from both British and American intelligence organisations. For example, Donovan personally received a copy of the Seventh Army 'Report on Dachau', the notorious concentration camp: 'a part of which was written by Second Lieutenants Meyerhoff and Glazier of the R&A Branch who are assigned to this unit'.[246] Persico recalls one of many examples of the support that stemmed from Donovan's prioritisation of war crimes investigation:

> In mid-June, Storey received an urgent telephone call from an OSS ensign named English. The naval officer, in the unfathomable ways of the OSS, had been sent to scour Eastern Europe for Documents. He was calling he said, because he had come across something that might interest Storey. A German nobleman . . . had offered to reveal the hiding place of all of Rosenberg's files . . . Storey ordered Ensign English to fly the crates to Paris, and four days later a C-47 touched down at Orly field bearing three thousand pounds of the Nazis' meticulously recorded past, dating back to 1922.[247]

Although in this context it is not possible to drawn a clear-cut distinction between Donovan the individual and the OSS as an institution, this wider institutional provision of evidence will be discussed in the next chapter.

Donovan had the ability, which he used, to summon documentary evidence from OSS sources independent of Jackson's organisation. His appointment of Gill, Flisser and other OSS staff, for example, to coordinate and analyse information on war crimes and potential war crimes defendants obtained from various OSS continental field offices represented a major contribution. Donovan's own Nuremberg files contain a large amount of documentation that does not form part of the record of the OCC, and which reflects his own personal evidence-gathering activity. For instance, the Cornell Collection includes extensive details of the trial and the conviction of Quisling, the former fascist puppet leader of German-occupied Norway. The quantity of documentation, which includes a private English translation of the large trial transcript, is less surprising given that Donovan's organisation played a major role in securing evidence from the Rosenberg files. This evidence was taken, via OSS agent Brogden, to the Norwegian prosecutors. It helped break

246 Richard Crosby, Major AUS Commanding, to Donovan, 22 June 1945: NA, RG 226, M1642, Roll 121.

247 Persico, 1984, *op cit*, 42.

down one of Quisling's main defence arguments that he had not been party to the decision of the Germans' to invade Norway. Donovan's copy contains annotations suggesting that he was privately mining evidence presented at this earlier trial for use against the German military officials, such as Doenitz and Jodl, and was anxious to learn any lessons from how the Norwegians had both organised and secured this conviction as a treason trial, without resort to newly created, and retrospectively applied, international law, which underpinned Jackson's trial strategy.

In addition, and acting independently of the OCC, Donovan issued numerous orders to OSS Secret Intelligence and Counter-intelligence (X-2) Branch officials based in Germany and Austria to gather various affidavits, witness statements and to conduct interrogations of likely witnesses.[248] Once again, the Cornell Collection provides ample evidence of the fruits of his activities in this area.[249] A similar point applies to the memoirs of former OSS Secret Intelligence and R&A officials based in Germany and continental Europe more generally, such as William Casey,[250] and Stuart Hughes.[251]

Other forms of support provided by Donovan

Donovan provided Jackson and other OCC prosecutors with other forms of support, including with respect to the selection of judicial personnel and assistance with the preparation of evidence of the Nazis' complicity with religious persecution. We have already discussed the OSS Director's interventions to try to secure French judges who would adopt a broad, rather than narrowly legalistic, approach to their task. In addition, during the mid-summer of 1945, Donovan was also contributing as a prosecutor to the constitutionally fraught issue of the selection of judges for the proposed trials. The very procedures, personnel and other institutional arrangements necessary to hold the first ever international war crimes trial had to be invented through negotiation. Furthermore, Jackson's office was the party taking the lead in setting up these negotiations. Hence, it was always likely that both Jackson and Donovan would, as the two most senior US officials within the OCC, play a part in questions of judicial recruitment.

248 For a sample of such interrogations with a wide variety of witnesses and potential defendants, including German generals, see Cornell Collection, *op cit*, 6.03–6.18, 7.19–22, 8.02, 8.17, 10.02, 10.10, 10.11, 10.08, 11.09.

249 For example, sub-division 10 of this collection includes numerous examples of Donovan's personal attempts to gather evidence on the complicities of members of the German High Command from non-Nazi sections of the German Army from a series of German generals including Walther von Brauchitsch, Erich von Manstein, Franz Halder, Walter Warlimont and Siegfried Westphal.

250 W. Casey, *The Secret War Against Hitler* (Washington: Regnery, 1988), 218.

251 S. Hughes, *Gentleman Rebel* (New York: Ticknor and Fields, 1990), 169–70.

Of course, it is possible on constitutional grounds to criticise Donovan and Jackson for making such interventions. Indeed, the very idea of allowing prosecutors to select the judicial personnel hearing their case would be both legally and constitutionally problematic in a domestic context as a violation of conventional expectations of due process. However, the Nuremberg trial did not have the benefit of a pre-existing institutional system of international criminal justice, including an established and independently appointed judiciary. Telford Taylor raised in a staff meeting the 'question as to the policy regarding the prosecutors having a direct hand in picking the judges'. Jackson, however: 'recognised the difficulty but did not see how he could avoid having a hand in it'.[252]

Donovan, acting as Jackson's deputy, was in fact heavily involved in a pro-active way in conducting negotiations with senior army lawyers regarding the selection of judges for the proposed war crimes trials. For example, Donovan's office files contain memorandum from General Weir (Assistant Judge Advocate General) on the topic of 'Suggested personnel for assignment as American member or members of the international Court for Trial of major German war criminals'.[253] Donovan had personally asked John M. Weir 'for a list of individuals from whom the American member and alternate for the big court could be picked'. Weir was defending the proposition that 'as the court was supposed to be a military court, I considered that the American member should be a military man. I am still of that opinion, so my list starts with military men.' Weir's reaction to Donovan's request was not altogether insensitive to questions of judicial objectivity in that he had previously argued against selecting individuals whose wartime experiences may have been particularly prejudicial with respect to German defendants:

> The European countries, especially England and Russia, are inclined to detail very high-ranking officers on any international court, board or commission. The increase rank may be accomplished by a temporary promotion for the period of the trial . . . I doubt the desirability of detailing on the court any officer who was in combat command on the European front.[254]

Later, Jackson used Donovan's ability to exert behind the scenes pressure upon the British authorities to have the British judge, Lord Shawcross,

252 Minutes of Meeting, 31 August 1945, Jackson Papers, *op cit*, Box 110.

253 John M. Weir, Assistant Judge Advocate General to Commander Donovan: 'Suggested personnel for assignment as American member or members of the international court for trial of major German war criminals', 14 August 1945. NA, RG 226, M1642, Roll 120.

254 Weir to Donovan, 26 July 1945: NA, RG 226, M1642, Roll 120.

appointed President of the IMT rather than the unctuous American Judge Parker. As already noted, Jackson disliked Parker intensely.[255]

Donovan involved R&A specialists such as Franz Neumann and part-time consultants to gather and analyse evidence of religious persecution. Through his extensive intelligence contacts with members of the German opposition to Hitler, Donovan employed the expert services of Fabian von Schlabrendorff, who had experienced Nazi persecution at first hand.[256] One of Schlabrendorff's many memoranda to Donovan addressed the 'Relationship of the German churches to Hitler'.[257] This memorandum emphasised that senior members of the Catholic Church had resisted Hitler's policies by insisting – through their priests – on the essentially 'unchristian character' of National Socialism. Schlabrendorff recalled that 'quite a number of the lower clerics ended up in prison or in a concentration camp', and that Delp, a leading Jesuit who was ultimately executed by the Gestapo, 'participated in the conspiracy that led to 20 July' (i.e., the failed assassination attempt on Hitler).

Donovan's extensive contacts with wider networks of Allied intelligence agencies and diplomatic sources also fed Donovan with additional evidence of religious persecution. For example, Lt. Walter Rothschild, Chief of the OSS–R&A Documentary Research Unit, a specialist section working out of the agency's London field station, supplied information from British Foreign Office sources on the 'German Monist Organisations', of potential use 'in connection with the prosecution of religious organisations by the Nazi government'.[258] Donovan's handwritten addition to Rothschild's memorandum indicated that he forwarded it on 16 July to James Donovan, with the further order 'hold for Neumann'. Neumann was about to join the key European side of the OSS's war crimes project.[259]

Donovan's long-range interventions: July–September 1945

Donovan's relocation to the Far East did not mean that he was totally out of touch with issues and controversies involving OSS staff within the

255 *Ibid*, 8 October 1945.

256 Fabian von Schlabrendorff was a lawyer and first lieutenant in the reserves. During his early years as a student at the University of Berlin he was the leader of a small anti-Nazi group. He was arrested for his involvement in the 20 July 1944 assassination attempt on Hitler and served time at various concentration camps, including Sachsenhausen, Flossenbürg, Dachau and Innsbruck. He was released in early May 1945 by US forces.

257 From 'Memorandum to General Donovan', 4 October 1945: Cornell Collection, Vol. 10, 18:04.

258 See Memorandum from Rothschild to Col. M. Bernays GSC, German Monist Organisation, 9 July 1945, Cornell Collection, Vol. 10, 18.05.

259 R&A Report 3114.4 (draft for war crimes staff, dated 6 July 1945: Cornell Collection, Vol. 10, 18.02).

Nuremberg trial preparations. For example, in August 1945, Donovan had to intervene personally to resolve a measure of conflict between Neumann, who had been appointed chief of OSS war crimes research, and James Donovan, who – as the General Counsel of OSS – regarded himself as the coordinator of *all aspects* of OSS war crimes work. There is some evidence that, despite his influence upon General Donovan, Neumann may, in some respects, have overplayed his hand in insisting upon receiving an unprecedented form of autonomy within Jackson's organisation, a privilege denied even to the most senior figures within it. For example, James Donovan soon became able to 'rein in' Neumann's free-wheeling operation that had antagonised Jackson's section chiefs, at least to some extent. General Donovan issued an internal OSS memorandum entitled 'Responsibility for Work in Connection with War Crimes', ordering that 'all war crimes activities undertaken by OSS shall be under the direction of the General Counsel'.[260] It further ordered that all personnel 'shall retain their basic branch assignment', and that James Donovan must in the future give prior approval to any future staff re-assignments. It is possible, but by no means certain, that this memo represented a direct response to Neumann's successful negotiations to establish a large measure of operational autonomy, and earlier reluctance to accept unconditionally direct orders from James Donovan.

Furthermore, in a outgoing cable, classified initially as 'top secret' and addressed to '109 [General Donovan] & 535 only', Bill Whitney,[261] reported on 14 August 1945 that Neumann had now been specifically instructed by Jackson to return to London. This stemmed from a combined attack upon Neumann from Amen, Storey and Gill, who clearly resented Neumann's ability to reject their demands that his team be assigned exclusively to one of their sections. These three senior members of Jackson's office 'developed strong complaints . . . against OSS men travelling on continent without prior clearance with them'. Although Whitney records that 'Justice Jackson showed extremely friendly and appreciative attitude generally towards OSS contribution', he had drawn the line at Neumann's free-wheeling operation:

> Jackson gave firm direction that no-one is to employ his name on [the] continent without first reporting to Gill and being approved by him to fit into the work either under Storey or under Amen. Justice Jackson has himself taken [the] initiative [and has] sent [a] cable instructing Neumann [to] return to London because Neumann is not to conduct interrogation

260 Donovan to List S, 27 August 1945 (OSS 77572): NA, RG 226, Entry 1, Box 2, Folder 7.

261 As already discussed, Whitney was an OSS lawyer who was also a member of the British bar and who possessed extensive connections in the legal establishment of that country: Gerhart, *op cit*, 322.

> but is to act in [an] advisory capacity explaining [OSS and other] studies etc. . . . OSS interests best served by neither initiating from present any objectives whatsoever under Justice Jackson's name except those specifically approved by him. His attitude is that OSS did excellent work of laying foundation and that there is still room for valuable OSS contribution provided that it is strictly within [the] above policy.[262]

This cable provoked agent 535 (presumably Neumann himself) to take issue with these allegations, and attempted disciplining measures. The defensive response, which was addressed to 'Whitney alone', was that:

> Location of Neumann specifically cleared with Jackson, who asked that he go to Paris and then recommend where he could make most effective contribution. Storey was informed . . . Jackson program outlined by you is exactly what we had in mind from [the] outset . . . I know nothing which had been done which is not within purview of his original general directives to us, which we have carried out by giving all possible assistance.[263]

For present purposes, this dispute is interesting insofar as it reveals that, having used the resources of Donovan's organisation to lay the foundations for and generally build up a formidable organisation that dwarfed that of the British, French and Russia counterparts, Jackson's position in relation to Donovan had become far stronger. The threats to dissolve the OSS throughout the late summer of 1945 further weakened Donovan's position, presumably also in Jackson's eyes. The above exchange suggests that, by mid-August, Jackson considered himself in a position to treat Donovan and his OSS staff as less indispensable than was previously the case. This was particularly true during the late summer of 1945, when the preparation of the case was moving towards the preparation of legal trial briefs against individual defendants based on extensive captured documentation that, with the help of OSS officials and those from other agencies, Jackson had already acquired. This view of his enhanced position in relation to Donovan and the OSS meant that Jackson could effectively assert his authority over Neumann and subordinate his group of specialists into the pre-existing hierarchy of section heads as their specialist consultants, despite Neumann's reluctance.

On the question of the selection of defendants, there is evidence that, from mid-July to October 1945, the influence of OSS senior officials and others had waned in the absence of General Donovan. It appears that Jackson adopted a surprisingly 'flexible' (some would say cavalier) attitude to the task

262 Outgoing Cable 46529, 14 August 1945: Jackson Papers, *op cit*, Box 111.

263 Incoming Cable from '535', No. 39079, 15 August 1945, Jackson Papers, *op cit*, Box 111.

of selecting defendants, claiming in a staff meeting at the end of August 1945 that:

> [T]his present list [of defendants] is only window dressing. The people at Potsdam got put on the spot and they made the commitment to publish the list before September 1 without consulting us. The Justice will feel no embarrassment about adding other defendants more adequately to represent the criminal organisations.[264]

Incidentally, had Jackson expanded the list of SS defendants as promised at this point, then surely Karl Wolff would have been included to supplement Kaltenbrunner.

On the other hand, Taylor's important memoir records some of the unfortunate effects of Jackson failing to make best use of some of the OSS's expertise on the defendants, not least the expertise of General Donovan and Franz Neumann, both of whom had specialist knowledge of the structure and hierarchy of the Third Reich. Taylor records how Neumann's undisputed expertise of the empirical aspect of Nazi war crimes was not always used to its best effect during the rushed process of actually *selecting* defendants for formal indictment a few months prior to the opening of the first major trial:

> Jackson involved his staff in drafting the indictment, but for some reason ignored them in the defendant-selection process. He and Aldermann were fine lawyers, but neither was an expert on the structure and hierarchy of the Third Reich . . . Neither I nor . . . any of my friends and contemporaries on Jackson's staff were consulted . . . Late in August, hearing rumours of what was afoot, I enlisted Franz Neumann's aid and circulated a memorandum on defendant selection in which I suggested some criteria.[265]

Their joint approach was, however, also largely ignored by Jackson for what may have been internal political reasons. According to Taylor, the result was that serious deficiencies occurred in the preparation of the cases against the industrialists Gustav and Krupp, 'which had serious and continuing consequences'.[266] Taylor attributes the blunders associated with the prosecution of Krupp partly due to pressure on the legal teams having to rush the completion of unfamiliar work, and as a result of:

> Jackson's and Shawcross's failures to organise their staffs so that the informational resources of men like Passant and Franz Neumann would

264 Taylor 1992, *op cit*, 90. 265 *Ibid.* 266 *Ibid.*

> be adequately considered when the chief prosecutors made the final decisions.[267]

Of course, this rebuff to Taylor and Neumann did not mean that OSS lacked any degree of influence on strategic decision-making over who should be selected for the first major trials because, as already noted, Donovan certainly had exerted influence during joint negotiations between himself and Jackson and other Allied prosecutors, particularly the British, whom he persuaded to widen their original list of merely ten defendants to include Hess, Streicher and others.

By late September, Donovan had returned from the Far East and was engaged in the winding down of the OSS consequent upon Truman's decision to abolish the organisation by 1 October 1945. This involved the R&A Branch being hived off to the State Department and other branches either abolished or merged into a scaled-down 'Strategic Services Unit' (SSU) of the US War Department. Such reconfiguration did not bring to an end the contribution of current and former OSS staff within the Nuremberg project however. Indeed, as Dunlop notes:

> One of Donovan's last acts as director of the OSS was to send a memorandum to all OSS men who were working on war crimes investigations to continue their activities under the direction of the general counsel [James Donovan]. At the end of September he flew to Germany to take up his duties as . . . prosecutor.[268]

For his part, James Donovan regarded the dissolution of the OSS as 'almost a paper change', since his war crimes work with approximately 130 OSS staff engaged in various capacities would continue almost as before.[269] Donovan initially flew to OSS HQ in Berlin near Wansee Lake, consulted with 'his still loyal OSS men' before viewing harrowing concentration camp film footage, intended for use as trial evidence, whose production James Donovan had been supervising.[270] After only a few days, Donovan flew to Nuremberg to take up residence there in a 'suburban house . . . under heavy army guard', with his own set of offices in the Palace of Justice directly across from those of Jackson.[271] This implied that he was still being recognised as the latter's effective deputy or at least co-deputy.

In short, it is appropriate to refer to a honeymoon period of cooperation between Jackson and Donovan and their subordinate staff providing one does not ignore the clear fact that, at one level at least, this inter-agency relationship more closely resembled the instrumental and mutually beneficial

267 *Ibid*, 117. 268 Dunlop, *op cit*, 479. 269 *Ibid*. 270 *Ibid*.
271 *Ibid*, 180.

nature of a 'marriage of convenience' than something more personal. In addition to supplying over 130 staff for Jackson's organisation who were fully seconded and at least formally under Jackson's control, Donovan ordered his senior staff within Europe to give high priority to cooperating with Jackson in the search for documentary evidence and conducting interrogations. It might be an exaggeration to say that Donovan's various forms of assistance to Jackson was indispensable. However, our review of the available source material concerning Donovan's support regarding his exploitation of domestic and international contacts, the provision of not only extensive logistical and staffing support but also documentary evidence, suggests that it is difficult to challenge the conclusion of Telford Taylor. Taylor's first-hand experience suggested that Donovan's assistance helped lay the very foundations for these trials.[272]

The honeymoon ends in desertion: Donovan departs and plays away

After a relatively promising start between May and late July 1945, it appears that the relationship between Donovan and Jackson became increasingly strained, particularly during the autumn and winter of 1945. Indeed, in his later contribution to an oral history, Jackson recalled that, with respect to his collaboration with the OSS: 'I never had any feeling that anyone had trapped me into the thing but I was in the trap.'[273] Perhaps he only realised later that Donovan had his own agenda to exploit the trials for the sake of his personal and institutional interests. Jackson may have recognised only belatedly that securing key positions for OSS staff loyal to the OSS Director from which pressure could be exerted was one of Donovan's strategies to realise such interests. Indeed, during July, there is some evidence that OSS officials from various branches of this organisation overplayed their hand when seeking to exploit the trials to continue their wartime skills in black propaganda against the Nazis. These officials pressed Jackson to accept a rumour campaign of new revelations of atrocities and the deployment of a pre-trial film, *Crime and Punishment*, which was extremely prejudicial to the defendants. Jackson strongly rebuffed this propaganda initiative.[274]

The standard accounts of the Nuremberg trials attribute the rift between Jackson and Donovan to the period after the latter's return from OSS affairs in China 1945, and the fact that he had 'absented himself' from the frantic 'coal face' of trial preparation since late July 1945. Certainly it is true that,

272 Taylor, 1992 *op cit*, 354–55.

273 R. H. Jackson, Oral History Project, University of Chicago Law School, Jackson Collection.

274 Memo for Jackson, 12 July 1945: 'OSS proposals for propaganda', and Jackson to Donovan: NA, RG 238, Main Office Files, Box 213.

after contributing to the successful four power negotiations in London which, on 8 August 1945, culminated in the London Agreement and Nuremberg Charter, Donovan 'was absent from Jackson's staff for over one month', not returning to Nuremberg until 14 September by one account,[275] and early October according to another.[276]

However, the present author's research suggests that the final rift between Donovan and Jackson once he returned from China was prefigured by a number of earlier confrontations that had at least partly soured the honeymoon phase. During the mid-summer of 1945 Jackson's behaviour also gave Donovan grounds for criticism, at least in his opinion. Jackson, who had little prior experience of running a large-scale organisation, complained to Donovan in mid-July about the 'administrative burdens' that their liaison was creating for him, particularly regarding personnel and financial matters. The tone of a memorandum from Donovan to Jackson indicates that, on occasions, their exchanges could be forceful and blunt, even during this comparatively early phase of their relationship. Donovan, in turn, was clearly not shy of offering gratuitous and high-handed advice to Jackson about the administrative and financial 'facts of life' involved in running a public agency. Donovan adopted a tone not common in the dealings between deputies and their superiors within prosecution organisations when he stated:

> Relative to your letter of 11 July 1945, concerning the fiscal arrangements between OSS and your office of chief of counsel (which your letter of 8 July confirmed), I thought that this matter was entirely settled. You are right in stating that if under the procedure already established OSS cannot give you the kind of service you require without involving you into burdensome administrative details, then you should obtain personnel from Departments that could assume the obligation. . . . It seems to me, however, that the Congress will wish to know just how money has been spent in order to determine how appropriations should be made. . . . Insofar as the OSS is concerned, it is required only that you should designate one person on your staff (I thought this had been done) as a certifying officer whose duty it will be to accept obligations in your name against your appropriation. Of course, you understand that salaries and expenses of OSS military and naval personnel working for you are not charged to you . . . In any case it will be necessary for you to have a definite allotment from the President's emergency fund or some similar source – otherwise you will be a mendicant, dependent for life upon other agencies who can hinder you if they so desire, and you will be in the position of receiving only the benefit of a diversion of funds appropriated by the Congress for a different purpose . . . There is no escape from

275 Sprecher, 1998, *op cit*, 167.

276 Dunlop, *op cit*, 480.

> some degree of administration; but this can be delegated by you to some other member of your staff. I think the plan under which we are working imposes the minimum of that burden.[277]

There is evidence from Jackson's diary that signs of tension with Donovan had arisen somewhat earlier than the existing literature suggests, which typically locates the emergence of the conflict to the period beginning early November 1945. Jackson's diary indicates that, during mid-July, Jackson records a 'long conference' with James Donovan, who was forced to account for some of the General's more erratic personal behaviour, including attempts to recruit staff in areas that Jackson did not consider to be the responsibility of the OSS.[278] As the next section will discuss, these disputes represented little more than minor spats compared with the friction which emerged and intensified during the autumn of 1945 following Donovan's return from the Far East.

The irretrievable breakdown

In order to understand the later and more intense phase of difficulties between Donovan and Jackson, it is first necessary to appreciate the background context, which included the dissolution of the OSS by President Truman on 20 September 1945 (taking effect from 1 October).[279] Previously, in the autumn of 1944, Donovan had presented a memorandum to Roosevelt addressing the continuation of the OSS after the war. Following various protests, Roosevelt, who was a political friend and supporter of Donovan, postponed any such plans. In April 1945, when this plan was being revived, Roosevelt died, and was replaced by President Truman, who was far from being supportive of the continuation of the OSS.

At this time, Donovan received an internal memorandum from William Langer (Chief of R&A) attempting to make a case for preserving the R&A Branch intact notwithstanding threats to the survival of other branches of OSS during the immediate post-hostilities period.[280] In the course of this argument, Langer bemoans the effect of the existing uncertainties upon staff morale and retention. He notes that, notwithstanding the end of the war within Europe, the R&A Branch was currently 'busier than it ever has been':

277 Donovan to Jackson, 12 July, Donovan Office Files: NA, RG 226, M1642, Roll 121.

278 Jackson Diary, *op cit*, 15–18 July.

279 This removed Donovan and appointed his former Assistant Director, General John McGruder, to head a new scaled-down organisation, the Strategic Services Unit of the War Department. For a copy, see Directors Files: NA RG 226, M.1642, Roll 120, Frame 0851.

280 Langer to Donovan, 11 June 1945: NA, RG 226, Entry 1, Box 2, Folder 23.

> In the European field, we have a huge amount of work to do for the Reparations Commission and for the War Crimes Commission, but these are, of course, *ad hoc* assignments which cannot possibly be long-lived.[281]

As Bradley Smith notes, the exploitation by the OSS leadership of the war crimes issue for ulterior motives may have been overly optimistic. Ironically, it was precisely the very importance of preparing for war crimes trials that prevented such work from bringing additional kudos to OSS sufficient to justify its continued existence as an intelligence agency within a post-hostilities context:

> At this point, however, there was little that the harried Donovan could do beyond approving R&A's own efforts to go into such postwar activities as that of war crimes prosecution with 'the purpose of strengthening its basic program' rather than simply continuing to be of service to other government agencies . . .[282]

As previously noted, on 20 September 1945, the OSS was abolished by Presidential Executive Order. Its component parts were then absorbed by different various agencies in the Washington bureaucracy.[283] The net effect was that Donovan's power-base had been unceremoniously removed. Once Donovan's ambitions to take charge of the peacetime intelligence agency he had been advocating were frustrated by President Truman, he began to covet Jackson's own role, at least for the planned 'subsequent proceedings' at Nuremberg against middle-ranking Nazi defendants.[284]

In turn, this meant that Donovan's personal role at Nuremberg became the sole focus of his energies and the self-assertion of his strong ego. Donovan was unwilling to be subordinated to the role of a cog in a larger machine controlled by others who he saw as his juniors. Conot's book on the Nuremberg trials, for example, suggests that: 'Donovan, having made the OSS manpower available to Jackson and facilitated the gathering of evidence, had expected to play a role in the trial second only to the Justice's.'[285] Dan Kiley, the OSS's

281 *Ibid.* 282 B. Smith, 1983, *op cit*, 386, 289.

283 The R&A Branch was absorbed by the State Department's 'Interim Research and Intelligence Service'. The secret intelligence (SI) and counter-intelligence (X-2) sections were absorbed into the War Department as the 'Strategic Services Unit' (SSU), with James Donovan working, without enthusiasm, for this new agency. In fact, the subsequent history can be interpreted as confirming Donovan's claims that the US required a modified version of OSS even in peacetime. For example, as early as 22 January 1946, President Truman had to create a temporary Central Intelligence Group (CIG) as a body for the coordination of intelligence activities at the national level, with espionage transferred from the War Department to the newly created CIA in 1947. These developments effectively reversed the rationale given for the abolition of the OSS.

284 Taylor, 1992, *op cit*, 273. 285 Conot, *op cit*, 150.

Chief of Design,[286] confirms this when he recalls from his personal contribution to the OSS's collaboration that: 'He [Donovan] was a great trial lawyer, and he wanted a big part in it.'[287] On the other hand, it would be unwise to overstate the significance of this egotistic element. As Taylor recalls:

> [T]here is no apparent reason to question the good faith of Donovan's support or to believe he was any more self-seeking than the rest of us, as we all naturally hoped that outstanding performance in a unique and noteworthy cause would bring both private satisfaction and public credit.[288]

In short, one of the factors that prompted the disagreement with Jackson was the removal of Donovan's wartime institutional power-base. This meant that his former part-time work with Jackson suddenly became his main chance to express and assert himself on a high profile public stage. Persico has broadly supported this interpretation of the psychological factors at play in Donovan's increasingly assertive stance against Jackson:

> Nuremberg had become an emotional life raft for General Donovan. True, Donovan had returned from his long stay in the Far East to most positions of power at the trials already staked out, and after an uncomfortable dinner at Jackson's home, he was well aware that his honeymoon with the chief prosecutor was over . . . Harry Truman viewed a post-war OSS as an incipient American Gestapo, and had virtually killed off the intelligence agency that was Donovan's reason for being. The General's restless energies now sought a new outlet at the Palace of Justice . . .[289]

Hence, on his return from the Far East in mid-September 1945, followed by a delayed return to the OCC base in Nuremberg only a month before the trial was due to start, Donovan appeared to be increasingly determined to impose his own will upon the trial proceedings more generally. He delayed his return to Germany to the first week of October. This meant that he had taken no part in the drafting of the crucial indictment,[290] and hence the established trial strategy. Donovan's interventions took place in a context where he must have known that insisting on the superiority of his preferred approach would place him on a collision course with the direction in which Jackson was increasingly taking the official US prosecution strategy. Jackson apparently

286 Following the resignation of Eero Saarinen immediately after the end of the Second World War.

287 H. Gaskin, *Eyewitness to Nuremberg* (London: Arms and Armour, 1998), 20.

288 Taylor, *op cit*, 147.

289 Persico, 1994, *op cit*, 119.

290 Taylor, *op cit*, 147.

'resented the fact that Donovan had absented himself during the preparatory work'.[291] There is, however, no evidence that Donovan clashed with Jackson immediately on his return to Nuremberg as part of a deliberate power play. On the contrary, the two men dined together in early October, and successfully conspired to derail plans to have Francis Biddle appointed President of the IMT.[292] Also, on 8 November 1945, Jackson obtained Donovan's assistance, in the company of several psychiatrists, to probe the defendant Hess's apparent display of amnesia, which turned out to be at least partially feigned. Donovan had experience of deploying the services of psychiatrists and psychologists within the OSS. Their strategy was to show Hess certain newsreels, which Donovan, James Donovan and OSS film specialists had been preparing for use as trial evidence. These showed Hess in his former position as Hitler's deputy at the '1934 Party Day in Nuremberg'. The aim was to gauge his reaction. Hess, however, continued to feign lack of any recollection of his past role.[293]

On the other hand, there is some evidence, based on interviews with former OSS staff working with Donovan at Nuremberg, that Donovan was voicing increasing doubts over Jackson's perceived redirection of the prosecution case in his absence. Dunlop interviewed Adolph Schmidt, who undertook various investigative tasks for Donovan from his OSS/SSU Berlin HQ. Schmidt recalled that the former OSS Director was practising his German language skills so that he could play a leading role in the trial room as 'prosecuting attorney', even though this would involve a possible conflict with Jackson's preferred approach:

> [Schmidt to Donovan] 'You are going to do it in German? [Donovan] 'I am going to do it all in German so the men in the box know just why they are being tried. We'll be the laughing stock of the legal profession if we don't show that this war has been criminally conducted.' . . . [Donovan] 'Jackson is saying that Hitler and his men lost the war, shoot them . . . This won't do. Otherwise if we lost a future war, our politicians could be shot too.'[294]

In Donovan's absence, Jackson had grown more accustomed to making decisions without consultation with Donovan, and had asserted direct personal control over the OCC.

Undoubtedly, Jackson's own handling of Donovan's position contributed to the breakdown of their relationship. Instead of meeting personally with Donovan to discuss the possible roles he sought in the trial, he delegated this task to Robert Storey (whom Persico describes as 'an OSS veteran').[295]

291 Conot, *op cit*, 150. 292 Persico, 1994, *op cit*, 76. 293 Gerhart, *op cit*, 358.
294 Dunlop, *op cit*, 480. 295 Persico, 1994, *op cit*, 120.

Donovan regarded Jackson's deployment of a subordinate as an intermediary as a deliberate and ungrateful snub to his standing, and immediately threatened to resign.[296] Jackson's reply in writing, itself not a particularly diplomatic response, claimed that he had assumed Donovan wished to work with witnesses and that this would prove difficult given his stated plans to return to the US in January 1946. This appeased Donovan sufficient for him to remain on staff.[297] However, by mid-November at the latest, it became clear that it was Robert Storey, rather than Donovan, who was entrusted with the work of acting as Jackson's deputy. This was confirmed by Jackson's decision to appointed Storey to chair the newly created 'Planning Committee of the Panel of Trial Counsel' responsible for deciding 'any and all policy matters concerning the trial plan for presenting the U.S. case'. Although Jackson appointed Donovan a member of this committee, his name was – probably for the first time – listed mid-way down the membership. This probably represented a symbolic indication of his demotion within the OCC hierarchy, in that his name had typically been listed as second only to Jackson in earlier official documentation.[298]

Gerhart emphasises the presence of subjective and personal dimension to the final breach between Jackson and Donovan, in that the question of whose trial strategy was to prevail rapidly turned into a battle of wills between these two strong and determined men, with neither willing to compromise:

> Justice Jackson debated the issue with General Donovan at great length. Each was determined in his own view . . . Both men discussed the issue with Robert G. Storey. Donovan would not yield. Neither would Jackson. The break finally came.[299]

Gerhart then quotes a personal communication from Storey:

> I was present when the break came and Justice Jackson said to General Donovan, in effect: 'Bill, you may be right, and I think I am right, but it so happens I have the responsibility and I am going to run this case according to my best judgement. I highly respect you, personally and officially, but its an honest difference of opinion.' General Donovan replied in substance: 'Bob, you may be right but I believe you are wrong. If that is your final decision, I shall return to the States and withdraw from the prosecution'.[300]

296 *Ibid*; Sprecher, 1998, *op cit*, 168. 297 Sprecher, 1999, *op cit*, 168.

298 'Special Memorandum No. 10: Plan for presenting documents and briefs in support of United States case in Chief', 14 November, 1945: Jackson Papers, *op cit*, Box 111.

299 Storey to Gerhart, 4 November 1953, cited in Gerhart, *op cit*, 359.

300 Gerhart, *op cit*, 359.

Although these statements regarding the subjective and interpersonal dimensions are helpful, it is still necessary to explore the factors behind this aspect of the dispute in greater depth. In addition to interpersonal factors and any power bid that Donovan may also have been making behind the scenes, the dispute between Donovan and Jackson centred around six major points of contention, not all of which were obvious to lower-ranking prosecutors at the time:[301]

- Donovan's refusal to accept the OCC institutional organisation and his creation of an organisation within the OCC.
- Donovan's insistence that his staff alone possessed an adequate prior background in the economic policies of Hitler's regime, and the linkage between German business interests and the Nazi Party, to prepare the 'economic case'.
- The OCC's decision to prosecute the German High Command as a distinct 'criminal organisation' for which proof of membership alone was to be sufficient for conviction.
- Jackson's increasingly firm view, which hardened considerably over the period in which Donovan was away, that each of the defendants could and should be prosecuted on the basis of documentary, rather than oral, testimony.
- Jackson's refusal to consider making private deals with defendants such as Schacht and Göring, which would have culminated in these defendants giving evidence useful to the prosecution and highly damaging to the other defendants.
- Donovan's contacts with a German lawyer, Leverkühn.

Each of these six areas of controversy will, for purposes of analysis, now be examined in turn. We need, however, to bear in mind that these points of friction were in fact largely taking place at the same time. Hence, from the perspective of both men caught up in an escalating and increasingly bitter controversy, it is likely that tensions in any one of these five areas was likely to intrude into how each of them regarded their other areas of dispute.

Excluding Donovan and the OSS lawyers from the economic case

Taylor's memoir recalls that Jackson's exclusion of Donovan from the economic case 'caused friction between Jackson and General Donovan'.[302] What, however, was covered by this phrase? According to Meltzer, a former OSS Nuremberg prosecutor who worked on the economic case:

301 Sprecher, 1998, *op cit*, 166.

302 Taylor, *op cit*, 80.

> The economic case included, first, crimes against peace by defendants who had financed the building of – or who had built – the German war machine, with knowledge of Germany's aggressive purposes. The case also encompassed war crimes and crimes against humanity resulting from the systematic plundering and pillaging of occupied territories, and the deportation and exploitation of millions of slave laborers.[303]

At the trial itself, Meltzer presented the case against Walther Funk, who had served the Nazi regime as economics minister under Göring, and as president of the Reichsbank:

> Funk had headed the bank when it became a storehouse of the gold fillings, jewelry, eyeglass frames, and other valuables stripped from the corpses of concentration-camp victims.[304]

Donovan appears to have been interested in taking the lead on the economic case and in the relationship between Nazi industrial policies, rearmament and the 'preparation for aggressive war'. Indeed, Donovan had already told one of the staff that he would have 'full charge' of the economic case. Donovan had been privately preparing the ground for this bid for the economic case. This probably explains why there is a surprisingly large number of OSS and other intelligence documents, including OSS biographical records, contained with Donovan's Cornell Collection relating to the actions, policies and collaboration of major industrialists, banks and financiers.[305] These include I. G. Farben, a company that both financed and then materially benefited from its relationship to the Third Reich.[306]

303 B. Meltzer, 'The Crime of Silence', *University of Chicago Magazine*, February 1996: http://magazine.uchicago.edu/9602/9602Meltzer.html. Meltzer: 'coordinated and reviewed the work of a group of lawyers, who assembled the evidence and prepared trial briefs on the various aspects of the economics case'. He was also involved in the pre-trial interrogations of several German leaders, including Hermann Göring: 'Of the defendants I met face to face, I found Göring the most interesting and the most diabolical,' Meltzer says. 'Intellectually quick, verbally nimble, and always wily. He often sensed the ultimate purpose of a question as soon as it was put', *ibid.*

304 *Ibid.*

305 'The Acquiring of Totalitarian Control in Germany: Economic; and the Economic Planning and Mobilization for Aggressive War', Edgar Bodenhiemer, Cornell Collection, 13.05; 'Basic Facts for a History of German War and Armaments Economy', G. R. Thomas, *ibid*, 13.12; 'The Reich Ministry of Armament and War Production (Speer Ministry)', *ibid*, 13.13; L. T. Crowley, 'Germany's Economic Base for Aggression', *ibid*, 13.14; Dr W. Vocke '. . . the responsibility of former Reichsbank Directors . . .', *ibid*, 13.15; 'Economic Planning and Mobilization for Aggressive War', *ibid*, 62.03; 'subject: Briefs Prepared by Economic Section (Frankfurt),' *ibid*, 61.06.

306 J. Purcell and A. Sacks, 'Preliminary Report: Concealment of Ownership of Some I.G. Farben Selling Companies', *ibid*, 13.18.

His Nuremberg files indicate that Donovan took a particular interest in material relevant to the proposed 'economic case' against the industrialists and bankers who both financed Hitler's regime and profited enormously from it. For example, he was organising material on economic dimensions, including the actions and policies of leading German industrialists, from the OSS biographical records branch.[307] There are biographical reports containing material that could also be used against Göring's massive appropriation of German industrial concerns.[308] Evidence from General Georg Thomas implicated an industrial group composed of Thyssen, Kirdorf, the banker von Schroeder and Krupp von Bohle.[309] Associated issues related to the economic exploitation of forced labour, in which both defendants Speer and Saukel were implicated by Thomas for 'crimes against humanity', and the 'looting' of Jewish assets.[310] Thomas also supplied Donovan with a detailed analysis of 'Basic facts for a history of German war and Armaments economy', which placed many of the events that could form the basis of the economic case in an appropriate historical context.[311]

Donovan's interests was not merely personal. Indeed, he had good reason to believe that he personally, with the support of various R&A and other OSS specialists, was more than well qualified to take charge of the economic case. He felt qualified to make a case linking German industrialists and financiers to Nazi expansionism, the abuse of slave labour and concentration camp inmates, and ultimately to war crimes. Yet Donovan's attempt to secure for himself and former OSS colleagues the key economic case against leading Nazi industrialists and financiers by bringing into the prosecution team OSS specialists, such as Dickinson, proved particularly controversial for Jackson.[312] Donovan had apparently groomed Dickinson to take administrative charge of the economic case. This was rebuffed when James Donovan told him over

307 Donovan's file include OSS biographical reports on, for example, Walter Rohland, a leading industrialist in coal and steel industries, and overall head of the 'Steel Trust' cartel. Rohland was a policy-maker within the Nazi economic policies, including the administration of various German businesses making, for example, tanks for the Ministry of Armament and War production. He was also director of numerous companies benefiting directly from the Nazis' rise to power. Cornell Collection, *op cit*, Vol. 17, 53.062.

308 See, for example, the OSS biographical report on Hellmuth Rohnert, one of most powerful men in 'Göring Combine', and a director of numerous metal, battery, electricity, power and manufacturing and other companies. Rohnert worked with the Nazis' administration of German 'National Group industry'. The OSS report stated that he was directly involved in 'determining and executing Nazi economic policies'. Cornell Collection, *op cit*, Vol. 17, 53.06253.063.

309 Cornell Collection, *op cit*, Vol. 2, 6.6.

310 See 'The influence of central organisation on development and activities of the war economy organisation', 38: extracts from Nuremberg document PS 2353: Cornell Collection, *op cit*, Vol. 2: 6.14.

311 Cornell Collection, *op cit*, Vol. 7, pt. 2, 13.12.

312 Jackson Diary, *op cit*, 16 July 1945.

the phone on 19 July that overall charge of that aspect of the case had been handed over to Shea so that there was no longer any point in pushing Dickinson for that role. James Donovan also reported that Jackson had told him that he would not embarrass the OSS Director by emphasising this rebuff and expected him to act in a similarly discreet way.[313]

Jackson's rejection of Donovan's bid for the leadership of the economic case may have been more annoying to the OSS Director than Jackson appreciated. Certainly, Donovan was aware that it was well known within US government circles that the OSS had developed considerable experience in economic questions within Nazi Germany. This expertise had been appreciated certainly by the State, Military Intelligence and Treasury Departments, each of whom had commissioned reports from the OSS. Indeed, within US government circles, Donovan's organisation had become the obvious source of expertise on the close relationship between certain industrialists and the Nazi Party.

OSS officials had, of course, already intensively studied German industrial and commercial developments. OSS–R&A specialists had been extensively involved in studying the organisation and operation of the German war economy, including the hiding of looted assets,[314] and studies of the behaviour of German cartels within insurance, banking and heavy industries.[315] Neumann's group had closely studied German economic controls and control agencies, including those relating to administration of foreign workers by the German Labour Front, and the concentration of capital.[316] These economic aspects of Nazi rule had to be analysed not only as a key part of identifying sabotage and espionage targets, but also as part of the OSS–R&A's anticipated role in preparing for post-war occupation government and de-Nazification of Germany and Austria. Part of the de-Nazification programme, as envisaged by OSS specialists such as Neumann, involved severing the connections between certain German industrial cartels or 'trusts' and right-wing political movements, not least by breaking up the cartels themselves.[317]

It could be argued that Neumann's background as a former trade union lawyer and Labour Court judge equipped this senior OSS research analyst to take charge of empirical research and to help prepare materials on the Nazis' exploitation of labour generally. Neumann's group had produced a series of

313 Taylor, *op cit*, 79.

314 OSS–R&A officials had cooperated with the Safehaven Project addressing economic aspects of Nazi rule including cartels and the suppression of trade unionism. See Director's Files: NA, RG 226, M1642, Roll 108, Frames 1213, 1221.

315 Progress report document entitled Europe-Africa Division, May 1945, 2: NA RG 226, Entry 42, Box 1.

316 Neumann to Morse and Evans (London R&A): 12 December 1944: NA, RG 226, Entry 146, Box 84, Folder 1236.

317 Katz, *op cit*, 45–49, 84–88.

studies on topics that they were particularly keen to draw to Justice Jackson's notice, either directly or through James Donovan. These included detailed accounts of 'German economic preparation abroad', and activities of '65 leading industrialists'.[318] Neumann was concerned that, notwithstanding his own expertise in the collusion of German industrialists with Nazi war criminality and his supervision of the related 'Eisenberg project', Jackson could remove his OSS–R&A team from playing any leading role in the preparation of the economic case.[319]

Jackson's exclusion of the Neumann group, whose expertise could have served as a spearhead for Donovan to present dramatic trial evidence, took place in early August 1945. A memorandum from an informal staff meeting involving Telford Taylor, Alderman, Benjamin Kaplan and Deinard, presented Jackson with the following request:

> [I]t is felt that Neumann and . . . Kellermann, Marcuse and Eisenberg . . . who have assisted him hitherto should be put full-time on the staff of the Chief of Counsel and that they should be assigned to Colonel Kaplan on the aspect of the case which he is preparing.[320]

This meant that it was planned that Neumann's team were to be explicitly excluded from the economic case, and instead assigned to Colonel Kaplan's small team consisting of Farr, Johnston and Murray, which had to address the criminal organisations charges, including the case against the SS and Gestapo.[321] The reason for Donovan's exclusion in favour of Jackson's long-standing friend Francis Shea, which Jackson announced to a staff meeting on 12 July, probably contained a distinctly political element, given the reluctance of the British to approve of any connection between colonialism and war criminality. Hence, Neumann was willing to contest Shea's assignment, which he notes was the only specific one made to date, directly with Jackson, without seeking prior approval. Donovan and Neumann's opposition to Shea's control of the economic case, and the OSS's marginalisation of one of the topics this intelligence agency was most suited to contribute was, however, entirely unsuccessful. In fact, Jackson resisted any attempt to reassert

318 See Memorandum of James Donovan to Justice Jackson, 29 July 1945, LOC, Jackson Papers, Box 101, in which Donovan presented the only existing copy of the R&A–CES report, 'German Economic Preparation Abroad', with a curious request that it be returned for reproduction and distribution to Jackson's senior staff.

319 Neumann to Kent, 3 August 1945: NA, RG226, Entry 1, Box 2, Folder 7: 'Francis Shea has been put in charge of economic aspects of the prosecution. I hope you have discussed the EISENBERG project with him . . . You will find in a memorandum that I transmitted today to Mr. Justice Jackson an expression of my views in regard to this aspect of the case.' *Ibid.*

320 See Memorandum for Mr Justice Jackson, 1945 August 15, LOC/Jackson Papers, Box 107.

321 *Ibid.*

the jurisdiction of the OSS's major expertise in the politically sensitive 'economic aspect' of war crimes – including the responsibilities of leading German industrialists. It may have become apparent to Jackson that the interests of Neumann's group included a distinctly left-wing agenda. This involved not merely removing the leading personnel of the Nazi regime and prosecuting them but also replacing those socio-economic structures that, they claimed, first enabled such individuals to seize and retain power. Put crudely, Neumann's studies implied the need for the reform of capitalist economics which strikes at the roots of German fascism by eliminating the economic foundations of the anti-democratic policy of German big industry.[322] This was not an approach favoured by either Jackson or the British authorities, who – as an imperialist power – were particularly sensitive on this point.

Amongst the American team of Nuremberg prosecutors, it was the OSS contingent who possessed the greatest specialists in the role of industrialists in the Nazi era, including Franz Neumann's team of research analysts who had prepared extensive civil affairs guides on related topics of the German economy.[323] These specialists had studied the role of the Nazi regime in maintaining economic/political controls in occupied Europe and had experts, including Franz Neumann, on the connections between political repression and economic controls.[324] The OSS–R&A Branch had produced several wartime reports on economic and financial controls in occupied Europe (R&A 2500.15), which document in enormous detail how Nazi repression and military occupation was supported by an array of economic controls.[325] Other such reports detail the sources of funding that the Nazi movement and its predecessors, and which might still be available from industrialists and financiers in the post-war years for a worrying fascist revival (R&A

322 Herbert Marcuse, Preface to *Franz L. Neumann, The Democratic And Authoritarian State* (Boston: Little Brown, 1957), viii.

323 Neumann was a leading academic authority, and author of a widely recognised study of the relationship between the Nazi Party, German industrialists and other groups that comprised the interdependent power elites of Nazi Germany. See F. Neumann, *Behemoth* (Oxford: Oxford University Press, 1942/1944).

324 'German Economic Penetration Abroad', 2 June 1945: NA, RG 226, Entry 116, Microfilm Publication 1642, Reel 108. See also L-104 and L-7: OSS, 'The Technical and Economic Troops in Occupied Europe', 1943 and 1944: NA, RG 153, entry 135, Box 1 and 4. These boxes also contain the some of the results of the OSS's contribution to the civil affairs guides and handbooks prepared for the US army occupation forces; George to Donovan, 'RE Rebuilding of German Economic, Political, and Military Power Positions Abroad by the Evasion of Allied Controls over the Exit of German Assets and Personnel from Germany (SAFEHAVEN)', (nd), but context places it in April–June 1945: NA, RG 226, Entry 116, Microfilm Publication 1642, Reel 108.

325 R&A 2500.15: 'German Military Government over Europe: Economic Controls in Occupied Europe.' This 155-page report was sent to Donovan at Nuremberg: Cornell Collection, 20.03.

1934.1). OSS-X-2 (counter-intelligence) Branch had cooperated with OSS–R&A officials to investigate the connections between German corporations and repressive controls in Nazi-occupied Europe. Hence, during his dispute with Jackson, over whom he was to take charge of the economic case, Donovan had some reason to claim special expertise in this field meriting recognition in the allocation of responsibilities for trial preparation.

This claim to expertise was not confined to his subordinates. With Neumann's assistance, Donovan had previously given evidence in person concerning economic aspects of Nazi aggression before the US Senate's Kilgore Committee.[326] Furthermore, the OSS War Crimes Unit also composed a report for the OSS Director's presentation on 13 June to the Kilgore Committee on 'Nazi Methods of Economic Warfare', and 'The Economic Base for German Aggression and National Security'.[327] Neumann, who had recently been promoted to Acting Chief of the CES following his successful work on Civil Affairs Guides, was specifically commissioned by Donovan to prepare a briefing paper to assist this presentation.[328] This presentation was aimed to focus upon the OSS's 'current and projected activities to eliminate the German economic base for further aggression'.[329] In this important note from mid-May 1945, which summarises progress on financial and political aspects of war crimes research to date, Neumann identifies the following four studies as having 'already been issued or will be issued shortly'. The two most relevant to Donovan's claim for leadership over the economic case were described by Neumann as:

> [R&A] 2500.15 Economic and Financial Controls in Occupied Europe (as an information paper). This study contains a wealth of information on what Nazi-Germany did in establishing its economic and financial

326 See memorandum from Neumann, Acting Chief, Central European Section, to Donovan via Mr Richard Hartshorne, Acting Chief, R&A, 'Request of the Kilgore Senate Committee', lists studies under way or planned, 15 May 1945, letter from H. M. Kilgore, Chairman, US Senate Committee on Military Affairs, Subcommittee on War Mobilization, to Donovan, including attached list of subcommittee members, 9 May 1945; Langer to Cheston, 'Statement for Kilgore Committee', attached draft statement for committee, 9 May 1945: Director's Office, Miscellaneous memos to Donovan: NA, RG 226, Entry 1, Box 2, Folder 23. See also 'Kilgore Committee' Folder: NA, RG 226, Entry 146, Box 38, Folder 518.

327 See R&A Branch 'Monthly Progress Report', May 1945, 9: NA RG 226, Entry 42, Box 1, and memorandum from Senator Kilgore to William Donovan, 9 May 1945: NA RG 226, Entry 1, Box 2, Folder 23. Other witnesses include Francis Biddle, US Attorney General (soon to be appointed as a judge to the Nuremberg IMT), Hans Morgenthau, Secretary to the Treasury (and a strong opponent of war crimes trials) and Major General Hilldring, Director of the Civil Affairs Division of the US War Department.

328 Neumann (Acting Chief, Central European Section) to Donovan, 15 May 1945: Request of the Kilgore Senate Committee: NA, RG 226, M1642, Roll 108.

329 Memorandum from Senator Kilgore to William Donovan, 9 May 1945, 2: NA, RG 226, Entry 1, Box 2, Folder 23.

> domination over occupied Europe. The first draft of the study is finished; it will be issued in the near future.
>
> In cooperation with X-2, there have been prepared a series of insurance studies showing the corporate ties of German insurance with foreign insurance and the control of foreign insurance by German insurance corporations. Several such studies have been issued.[330]

In Neumann's memorandum to General Donovan, Neumann also identifies four further 'Planned Studies' that were also of relevance to the Kilgore Committee's investigations. The following three of these were directly relevant to the economic case:

> For Mr. Justice Jackson, the Central European Section has undertaken to prepare the following study: Plans of the Nazi Party to Establish Their Domination in Germany, Europe, and Ultimately Over the World . . . Though it is primarily a political analysis, it will nevertheless deal with economic techniques by which domination was achieved or planned to be achieved.
>
> Also for Mr. Justice Jackson, we are preparing a study, 'The Principal Organisations of Nazi Germany Involved in the Commission of War Crimes.' Though this study is primarily a political one, it will nevertheless deal with certain German economic organisations (like the National Economic Chamber and its affiliated German Chambers of Commerce Abroad, the National Groups, the German dominated European cartels, etc.).
>
> The R&A branch is fully cooperating with the Safe Haven project. Cooperation is primarily with the Dept. of State and secondarily with FEA.[331]

The last point, regarding the full cooperation of OSS–R&A and the Safehaven

330 The other two studies were described as [R&A]1934.2, 'The Pattern of Illegal Anti-Democratic Activity in Germany After the Last War: The Free Corps'. This project describes the internal attempts of aggressionists groups in Germany, especially the Free Corps, to re-establish German militarism, and defines the backers. And, secondly, [R&A] 1934.1, 'The Clandestine Nazi-movement in Post-War Germany'. This study describes the likely trend of the post-Nazi movement and outlines the support which this movement is likely to receive internally and externally.

331 *Ibid.* The fourth was a 'series of studies dealing with the European ramifications of German Nazism. The first part of the study, R&A No. 2832, entitled Ramifications of German Nazism in Sweden, Switzerland, Spain and Portugal, is in preparation. This study aims at showing the connections which the Nazi Party maintained in the neutral states with 'indigenous fascist and semi-fascist groups'. *Ibid.*

project investigating looted Nazi economic assets is particularly interesting. From the spring of 1945 at least, the involvement of OSS officials within the Safehaven project was sufficiently extensive to prompt a more formal treatment within the OSS hierarchy. A memorandum from the Acting Director of Strategic Services, Edward Buxton, called upon the OSS to 'make a substantial contribution to this program'. Hence, station chiefs were instructed to report on the status of Safehaven operations in their area. Furthermore, Donovan authorised the creation of an Economic Intelligence Collection Unit (Econic) in Washington under John A. Mowinckel, reporting directly to Donovan's office. This unit both monitored and integrated Safehaven reporting into its own detailed reports on specific topics. These included a large report at the request of the State Department on the activities of the Swiss firm Johann Wehrli & Co, AG (Wehrlibank), a private Swiss banking house with global interests then under investigation by the Justice Department for its role in transferring private German assets overseas.[332] Indeed, it has become topical, given the current interest in the role played by this project in seeking to investigate assets looted by the Nazis from their victims. This topic has even witnessed recent litigation in 1996.[333] During this action, a memorandum from Allen Dulles, OSS Chief in Berne, to Donovan, was cited during a class action against three Swiss banks brought on 21 October 1996 by former 'slave laborers'. The plaintiffs alleged that these banks had 'conspired to launder and conceal Nazi assets in violation of Swiss federal banking laws and international neutrality agreements'.[334] When Dulles informed Donovan of the results of talks over concealed assets, the OSS Director had sent a memo to Roosevelt, relaying the Bern report:

> Weber is personally friendly with Puhl. By the terms of this arrangement, it is possible for the Reichsbank, within the framework of their previous

332 Circular Memorandum for All Strategic Services Officers and Chiefs from Acting D/SS (Acting Director of Strategic Services), 16 April 1945: NA, RG 226, Entry 116, Microfilm Publication 1642, Reel 108; RG 226, Entry 183, Box 21, 'Wehrli combine', (nd). For analysis, see sub-section G. 'The Office of Strategic Services and Project Safehaven' forming part of the 'Preliminary Study on US and Allied Efforts to recover and Restore Gold and other assets Stolen or Hidden by Germany During World War, 11 May 1997, co-ordinated by Stuart E. Eizenstat, prepared by William Z. Slany, the Historian Department of State: http://www.ess.uwe.ac.uk/documents/two.htm; More generally, see http://www.archives.gov/research/holocaust/records-and-research/documenting-nazi-plunder-of-european-art.html.

333 See, http://www.courttv.com/legaldocs/misc/naziswiss.html, citing US District Court for the Eastern District Of New York, 1996, Jacob Friedman, Lewis Salton, Elizabeth Trilling-Grotch, Charles Sonabend, and David Boruchowicz, on behalf of themselves and all others similarly situated, v. Union Bank Of Switzerland, Swiss Bank Corporation, and Credit Suisse (defendants in a class action).

334 The following extract of an OSS memorandum is taken from the court transcript: 'At the end of May, Reichsbank official Emil Puhl met with Swiss National Bank Chairman Ernst Weber to discuss blocked credits.'

> gold transactions, to sell gold for Swiss francs in accordance with a monthly quota. This quota amounts to approximately 6,000 kilograms of gold, worth approximately 30,000,000–40,000,000 Swiss francs. If it should become necessary, Weber stated, he was ready to take even more gold than the amount fixed in the monthly quota. Under the fairly broad arrangement thus reached, it will be possible to exchange Swiss francs just as before for the foreign exchange of 3rd countries . . . The effects of this smuggling and the outlook for the following six months are still as good as they were before. It is possible for us to anticipate that for the last half of the current year, as in the initial half, Germany will receive an additional 3,000,000 Swiss francs worth of ball bearings through the means I have reported above. Moreover, the ball bearings in question are the kind which Germany requires most and on which deliveries are needed as quickly as possible.[335]

What is interesting here is that the expertise of OSS officials in economic aspects of Nazi rule, including the exploitation of banking and financial sectors, has recently been recognised by contemporary lawyers.

During his memorandum to Donovan, Neumann also made a strong case for a future study of the role of the holding company as a legal device employed to exert control over foreign companies in neutral countries, and thereby indirectly support Nazi aggression.

Furthermore, in this context for Donovan it must surely have appeared contradictory that OSS–R&A officials were, in the Planning Memorandum of mid-May 1945, entrusted by Jackson to develop the 'common plan' conspiracy part of the case showing a plan to achieve European and ultimately world domination. This included demonstrating 'the economic techniques by which domination was achieved or planned to be achieved'. Yet, with respect to the economic case, they were regarded as unable to address the economic aspect of that plan.[336]

In attempting to gain control of the economic case, Donovan was seeking to by-pass Shea's jurisdiction. Internal OCC documentation appears to suggest that Jackson's only concession to Donovan's demands in this area was, in mid-November 1945, to allow a former OSS official, Lt. Colonel Murray Gurfein, to take responsibility for presenting 'economic aspects of the conspiracy'.[337] Gurfein was regarded as 'an experienced prosecutor and interrogator', who strengthened Shea's team considerably.[338] Otherwise,

335 Donovan to Roosevelt, 7 October 1944, relaying report from Dulles: NA, RG 226, M1642, Roll 30.

336 Neumann to Donovan, 15 May 1945, *op cit*.

337 Special Memorandum No. 10: Plan for presenting documents and briefs in support of United States case in Chief', 14 November 1956: Jackson Papers, *op cit*, Box 111.

338 Taylor, *op cit*, 82.

Jackson resisted pressure from Donovan and Neumann, and allotted this aspect of the case to Shea. In turn, Shea's team prepared their case in full control of isolation from the other trial lawyers, presumably because of its extremely politically sensitive aspects. Donovan continued to work to his own agenda. He deployed his personal staff to conduct interviews with captured German military officials involved in developing a 'war economy', such as General Georg Thomas.[339]

With respect to the OSS Director's actions in this area, James Donovan was placed in a difficult position. In one sense, he was subject to competing authorities. However, even he had to accept in public that the General's behaviour with respect to the attempt to bypass Shea (who had been personally appointed to this position by Jackson), and attempting to substitute his own expert, Dickinson, was particularly shameful. Given the perceived importance of placating Shea, Jackson stood firm on this issue, perhaps knowing that Donovan was soon to leave for the Far East in any event. Hence, Jackson nipped in the bud the General's plan for taking over the economic case by publicly supporting Shea and sacking Dickinson, 'who could not work for me in any capacity'.[340] On 26 July, Jackson records with some pleasure that officially Dickinson's removal was being explained away in Washington as due to his ill-health, and – in an interesting choice of military terminology – noted that: 'that battle [with Donovan] appears to have been won by a surrender in the first round'.[341] It appears from Jackson's diary that the General took this setback without much complaint, and had even settled the dispute over financial reimbursement to the OCC in a manner that suited Jackson.[342] In short, whilst in June 1945 Jackson felt sufficiently insecure as to back down to Donovan's threats with respect to Shea's staff allocations, by July Jackson was no longer willing to repeat this climbdown with respect to OSS demands to take over the economic case from Shea.

All things considered, Donovan appeared to other senior prosecutors such as Telford Taylor to be working according to *his own* specific agenda, and in a

339 See 'Interrogation of General Georg R. Thomas by Captain Nordon', Cornell Collection, 6.12; and associated files, *ibid*, 6.13; Thomas, 'The Influence of Central Organization on Development and Activities of the War Economy Organization'; 'War and Armament Economic Measures from Entry into Austria (1938 till Mobilization 1939)'; 'Execution of the Economic Mobilization', *ibid*, 6.14; Thomas, 'Staff Evidence Analysis: Two drafts of General Thomas entitled "Fundaments for a History of the German War and Armament Economy" ', *ibid*, 6.15.

340 Jackson Diary, *op cit*, 26 July 1945.

341 *Ibid.*

342 *Ibid*, 27 July 1945: 'We arrived at Bovington and were met by General Donovan. He had remained over on his trip to China. He reported generally on our situation at Washington, said that Dickinson was no longer working, and that he had made an arrangement with the Budget by which it had recognised the legality of all OSS expenditures on our behalf and that therefore no reimbursement need be considered. As he was leaving [for China?] at one o'clock on Saturday morning, we did not have long together.'

provocative manner that represented a significant challenge to Jackson's overall authority:

> The general had certainly not been acting like a team member . . . He summoned Bernard Meltzer, of Shea's staff asked him what the economic group's 'best' pieces of evidence was and then called for Meltzer's opinion on how the presentation of the American case should be divided among the senior lawyers – a question which Meltzer (then a naval lieutenant, junior grade) could not have answered with either propriety or adequate knowledge.[343]

Taylor's account summarises only partly Meltzer's own recollection sent to him as a letter in December 1982. This fuller account notes that Donovan sent for Meltzer only when Shea, his chief, 'was absent from Nuremberg', so that Meltzer was 'acting for him in relation to the group working on the briefs concerning "economic crimes" '. Meltzer recalled that Donovan was, he believed, interested in hearing details about 'the most sensational' piece of evidence this group had acquired. Donovan persisted in pressing Meltzer on this question at this meeting, asking him to 'shoot from the hip', but Meltzer did not apparently feel able to oblige his former OSS Director.[344] Later Donovan secured access to a draft of the economic case by some other route.[345]

Meltzer then states that:

> The General then took another tack: He asked me how I thought the American case should be divided. I thought that he was asking about a division among himself, Frank Shea, and other high-ranking personnel.

Apparently, Donovan's attempt to lure him into such highly contentious discussions, which could have been an attempt to test his loyalties as a former OSS subordinate, was not successful, as Meltzer claimed lack of relevant knowledge.[346]

Taylor's quotation suggests that he was unaware of Bernard Meltzer's background as a former OSS official involved in analysing the implications of bomb damage. Had Taylor been aware of this, it is unlikely that he would have been surprised that Donovan would expect former OSS staff to retain an element of loyalty to this organisation's sole leader.

There was one particularly remarkable implication of Jackson's refusal to allow Donovan (and his personal and former OSS staff) to take charge of, or

343 Taylor, 1992, *op cit*, 180.

344 Meltzer to Taylor, 23 December 1982: Telford Taylor Papers, Law Library, Columbia University Law School, New York, NY: Folder TTP-CLS, Correspondence, 20–1–2–18.

345 'Preliminary Brief on "The Economic Case" ', Lt. O. H. Korican: Cornell Collection, 13.06.

346 Meltzer to Taylor, 23 December 1982, Telford Taylor Papers, *op cit*.

even contribute to, the economic case. This was that it became necessary to remove OSS staff from specifically economic dimensions of elements of the overall case to which they had already been allocated under 'Part IV (E) Economic Planning for Aggressive War'. Hence, the contributions of former OSS staff to the Nazis' suppression of 'Labor Unions' had to be shunted aside, despite their obvious centrality to such economic planning.[347] This reversed the earlier commitment Jackson had made: 'the subject [persecution of trade unions] belongs more to the economic case and to the preparation of aggressive war rather than to Committees 2 and 3 under the guise of crimes against humanity'.[348] In other words, Jackson's opposition to the attempts by Donovan and Neumann to secure for themselves leadership of the preparation of the economic case was such that he was even willing to distort the organisation of the pre-trial preparation of the overall case by creating artificial distinctions.

In short, Donovan, with Neumann's support, attempted to argue that OSS staff, expertise and other resources meant that they should play the lead role in preparing the economic case linking Nazi war crimes to the actions and policies of German industrial cartels, banks and financiers. Despite having a powerful case in one respect, Jackson's need to remain loyal to Shea during pre-trial preparation, combined with pressure from the British authorities, meant that Jackson successfully resisted this pressure. It is possible that the implicitly left-wing implications of Neumann's analysis of the linkages between Nazi war criminality and German industrialists was a contributory factor here.

Prosecuting the German General Staff and the High Command

Donovan certainly supported the idea of prosecuting senior military officers for their involvement in specific war crimes. Indeed, he was particularly anxious to secure the testimony of Waffen-SS officers serving in Eastern Europe who could offer testimony on the responsibilities of specific members of the German High Command for some of the worst Nazi atrocities committed against civilians and, perhaps, Soviet prisoners of war.[349] The collection

347 'Legal Staff Organisation', undated, Jackson Papers, *op cit*, Box 111, which refers to 'Economic Planning and Mobilisation for Aggressive War (except Labor Unions'), and then lists a series of topics under this heading, all of which overlapped with OSS expertise, not least the 'Use of German Business Organisations', a particular specialism of Neumann.

348 Minutes of Meeting, 31 August 1945: Jackson Papers, *op cit*, 110.

349 See Broggan to Col. Black, 23 November 1945, reporting that Donovan was seeking to interrogate Maj. Gen. Ernst A. Road [Rode], Waffen-SS leader of 19th Lithuanian Division regarding the High Command case. Donovan wanted to be phoned immediately, even whilst at home, if this source became available (work and home number handwritten by

at Cornell Law School includes 16 documents[350] authorising killing of Russian prisoners of war and Polish inmates within German concentration camps, mentioning specific SIPO, SD, RSHA and camp commanders.[351] His files also include OSS Biographical Records documentation on Jodl's responsibilities for the 'total war' and atrocities on the Eastern front.[352]

Despite his work to establish the *individual* responsibility for war crimes of specific high-ranking military leaders, he rejected Jackson's plan to superimpose a *collective* form of organisational liability. This, he believed, was based on little more than belonging to an amorphous military group. Persico, for instance, recognises that Donovan's increasing scepticism and desire to limit the wide-ranging focus of Jackson's prosecution strategy came to a head partly over the prosecution of former German generals as members of the High Command, indicted as a 'criminal organisation'. As a former highly decorated military officer in the First World War – who had apparently killed surrendering German prisoners whenever there was no practical alternative – this element of Jackson's trial strategy may have struck a particularly raw nerve with Donovan.[353]

The OSS Director's objections to prosecuting the High Command were that the use of criminal organisation charges against senior military officers, as if they were a criminal syndicate, was an abuse of procedure.[354] Donovan first raised his disagreement with Jackson when the two men met in Berlin in the second week of October 1945.[355] It was, Donovan argued, one thing

Broggan?). Donovan was gathering a series of earlier US Army Counter-intelligence Corp reports on Rode, reporting that his evidence was considered reliable, and summarising his account of the final days of the Third Reich, the reaction to the OSS's Operation Sunrise, lines of military command, Rode's relationship with Himmler and Kaltenbrunner. Rode also supplied his interrogators with a 'personality list' of Waffen-SS officers. Cornell Collection, *op cit*, Vol. 17, 53.061.

350 Nine from 1941, seven from 1944.

351 1165-PS: Cornell Collection, *op cit*: Vol. 20, Pt. 3.

352 This report noted that: 'Jodl . . . [was] responsible for the planning of the German campaign in the USSR, and for many of the inhuman actions committed by the German army during the occupation of Soviet territory. On the other hand, he has also been mentioned as disagreeing with Hitler on basic principles of military strategy in the East.' Cornell Collection, *op cit*, Vol. 15, Pt. 1, 37.03.

353 Cave-Brown claims that: 'He did, however, have a strong opinion about the German General Staff and the corps of officers, both of which had been declared criminal organisations. Donovan thought this indictment wrong, for he subscribed to the view that, except where there was evidence of criminal actions in contravention of the Geneva Convention, these organisations were comprised of officers who had obeyed the orders of their government, as he had obeyed the orders of his, right or wrong: perhaps in this he was influenced by the execution by the Micks [nickname for an Irish-American regiment] of Prisoners at the Ourcq in 1918, when, had Germany won the war, he might have been arraigned for war crimes.' *Op cit*, 744.

354 Conot, *op cit*, 150.

355 Taylor, *op cit*, 240.

to prosecute individual military leaders for their personal responsibility for specific crimes, quite another to convict them of membership of a 'criminal organisation' solely on the basis of their position and function.[356] Donovan's final letter to Jackson frankly summarised his beliefs regarding the prosecution of the High Command as a criminal organisation:

> When in Berlin [early October] you first showed me the Indictment I said it was unbecoming to our country to use such a device as there employed against the General Staff. I still think so. The young British officer [Calvocoressi] who prepared it told me he was not very proud of the job. I urged a revision so that such members who were participants be charged individually and not by position or function.[357]

Donovan then reminded Jackson that he had argued for the prosecution of senior German Army officers where there were grounds for, and evidence of, individual guilt, and had defended this position in face-to-face discussions with senior American officers during earlier meetings on continental Europe. However, the use of criminal organisation charges was a greater abuse of the democratic values of legality and the rule of law than 'executing the guilty ones' on political grounds.[358]

For Donovan, it was dishonest to ignore the fact that the High Command included a good proportion of officers who were actively opposing Nazism, many of whom, such as Admiral Canaris, former head of German military intelligence, had paid the ultimate price for their opposition and plots to depose Hitler.[359] Indeed, Donovan would have known that, through Dulles' contacts with the German opposition, the OSS had actively encouraged and supported members of the German High Command in their opposition to Hitler.[360] He argued that to punish such individuals for membership alone risked discrediting the legal and moral basis of the prosecution case, noting 'it is repugnant to me that there should be any pretext as we find in the trial today for the defendants to assert that the prosecution is unfair'.[361] Conot suggests that Donovan challenged this policy in various meetings with Jackson, including a frank face-to-face encounter:

356 Conot, *op cit*, 150.

357 Donovan to Jackson, 27 November 1945: quoted in Taylor, *op cit*, 147.

358 *Ibid.* 359 Conot, *op cit*, 150.

360 Apparently, Donovan had contacts with head of German Army Military Intelligence, Admiral Canaris. In the summer of 1943, Donovan met Canaris met secretly with Stuart Menzies, Chief of British Intelligence at Santander, Spain. Canaris presented Menzies and Donovan with his peace plan: a ceasefire in the West, Hitler to be eliminated or handed over, and continuation of the War in the East. Although Donovan and Menzies supported this, President Roosevelt flatly declined any further negotiations: http://www.canaris.dk/new_page_3.htm.

361 *Ibid.*

> He [Donovan] favored prosecuting individuals in the military. And he certainly favored prosecuting organisations like the SS and the Gestapo. Membership alone would be sufficient to convict those people of war crimes. But to convict top-ranking generals and admirals simply because they were top-ranking? . . . Hang a general because he had committed a crime, Donovan said, not because he was a general. Jackson replied that he was going ahead with the prosecution of the High Command anyway.[362]

It appears that this element at least of the Donovan–Jackson dispute remained comparatively private, as Taylor, who was preparing the case, 'knew nothing of this rift over the organization charge against the General Staff'.[363] The matter did not get aired during staff meetings that both Taylor and Donovan personally attended.[364] However, Taylor recalls that Donovan summoned him to his office once to suggest that a distinction should be made between German Army field commanders, who 'were only doing their duty', and the staff officers at Hitler's military HQ.[365] Taylor left this meeting with the 'suspicion that he had been in touch with some of the field commanders'. Taylor sensed that Donovan had the hope of 'getting them to testify against the two army defendants, Generalfeldmarschall Keitel and General Jodl, who were both in the second of Donovan's categories'.[366]

Taylor's suspicions were well founded. At this time, Donovan was cultivating various German generals, and he supplied a certain amount of the information he had gathered to Jackson.[367] The Cornell Collection files provide considerable documentary evidence of the various ways in which the General attempted to undermine any solidarity between the military High Command defendants. They contain numerous documents confirming what Telford Taylor merely suspected: that Donovan was seeking to 'turn' one group of former officers, who had served as military leaders in the field, against a far smaller sub-group of their immediate superiors, such as the defendant Keitel, who had personally formulated military policy in conjunction with Hitler. Donovan's reluctance to support criminal organisation charges with respect to the German High Command may have been influenced by the following statements from Georg Thomas's diary:

> The General Staff of the Army (with the exception of certain individuals was, under its chiefs Beck and Halder, never a place where agitation for war was conducted. On the contrary, it always tried through professional objectivity to prevent a war. The office of Admiral Canaris and my own

362 Persico, *op cit*, 120. 363 Taylor, *op cit*, 147. 364 *Ibid*, 147–48.
365 *Ibid*, 148. 366 *Ibid*.
367 For copies of Donovan's contacts, see 'Donovan File' Jackson Papers, *op cit*, Box 2.

office within the OKW, have always fought against war. It would therefore be a mistake to put the General Staff of the Army or the OKW in their entirety on an equal footing with criminal organisations of the party.[368]

Donovan's files include other papers from General Thomas including a document entitled 'Concerning the question of guilt', which highlighted the real dilemmas facing individuals in positions of authority, such as Thomas and Schacht, who opposed Hitler's policies. This document gives an insider's perspective on how Hitler transformed and politicised the German Army through rapid promotions, punishment, indoctrination, playing various sides off against each other, nepotistic appointments and rapid promotion of Nazi-minded officers. Thomas blames not the whole General Staff as an institution but rather the actions and policies of specific individuals, particularly Göring, Blomberg Reichanau and Milch: 'These men bear the guilt for the introduction of Nazism into the Armed services, and for the circumstances which make the Armed services partly guilty for the crimes of this war.'[369]

In addition, Sprecher's memoir recalls that, during mid-October, he assisted Donovan in preparing for the interrogation of another German general: General Warlimont. He did so partly by helping translate for Donovan parts of a German military manual. This stated that a German soldier could refuse to obey an order if he believes he is being forced to commit a crime. Such documentation represented a vital piece of evidence to rebut standard defence arguments that military perpetrators of war crimes had no choice but to obey superior orders.[370]

As Donovan gathered more evidence from his own German sources, it appears that his own rejection of the criminal organisation charge strengthened. Indeed, Donovan appears to have developed a personal animosity to those preparing this aspect of the case. Taylor also recalls that: 'He asked [Peter] Calvocoressi to his office, but treated him with manifest hostility, probably because of Peter's connection with the General Staff Indictment.'[371] Taylor is clearly basing his comment on first-hand experience since Jackson had allotted Taylor and Peter Calvocoressi (a former British intelligence official), together with Berthoud and Becker, to prepare the High Command case, comprising more than 40 briefs, against an artificially constructed 'organisation', the German Staff and High Command of the German Armed

368 See 'The influence of central organisation on development and activities of the war economy organisation', 38: extracts from Nuremberg document PS 2353: *Cornell Collection* Vol. 2: 6.14.

369 *Cornell Collection*, Vol. 2, 6.6.

370 Sprecher, 1998, *op cit*, 168, citing memorandum between Sprecher and Donovan of 15 and 17 October 1945.

371 Taylor, *op cit*, 180.

Forces. Taylor had connections with a variety of Allied intelligence agencies including OSS, with whose R&A Branch he had worked closely during the summer of 1945.

OSS historians have argued that this policy dispute was central to Donovan's conflict with Jackson, and that it intensified once Jackson refused to advise President Truman to oppose the indictment of the General Staff.[372] For his part, Jackson clearly acknowledged this dispute over the prosecution of the High Command in his letter to Donovan of 27 November. This noted that he understood that Donovan had 'expressed complete disagreement with the indictment of the General Staff and the High Command'. Jackson complained that, if Donovan's work with German military witnesses reflected this dissident view, then it was entirely 'at odds with the policy of the case as settled by the indictment'. Insofar as Donovan was continuing to pursue his alternative policy in defiance of that of Jackson, the result could be 'serious embarrassment'.[373]

In short, both Donovan and Jackson recognised that they were heading for a collision with respect to the prosecution of the German High Command as a criminal organisation. Jackson rejected Donovan's claim that not only was such a prosecution on the basis of membership alone unjustified, it would result in brave members of the anti-Nazi German opposition whom OSS had actively assisted being wrongly labelled as 'war criminals'.

The merits of witness or documentary evidence

The 'Jackson Center' note that one of the key elements of the Jackson–Donovan dispute of late October and November 1945 related to their differences over which types of evidence should predominate within the trials:

> During this time, the debate between General Donovan and Justice Jackson came to a climax. Jackson wanted the trial to be based on documents, while Donovan believed enemy witnesses were necessary for a successful trial. Donovan, who was one of Jackson's chief staff members, would not relent, leaving Nuremberg by the end of the month, only a few days into the trial.[374]

This organisation also recorded the recollections of surviving prosecutors on this dispute, including that of Henry King, a supporter of Jackson's documentary approach, who has noted:

372 Cave-Brown, *op cit*, 744. 373 Jackson to Donovan, 27 November 1945, *op cit*.
374 http://www.roberthjackson.org/International_Law/time_capsule/.

> In the evidentiary phase of the Nuremberg trials Jackson's approach offered fairness to the defendants. Jackson wanted the primary Nuremberg case against the Nazis to be substantiated by their own documents, with less reliance on the testimony of witnesses. This approach precipitated a critical dispute with William J. Donovan, his presumed deputy, who wanted the case to be based on greater use of witnesses . . . It was Jackson's view that Nuremberg would have greater historic credibility if the Nuremberg cases were based on the defendants' own documents. Ultimately the defendants at Nuremberg convicted themselves through Jackson's approach. This approach also fortified the credibility and historic significance of the trial. It also meant that where there was no documentary support for a conviction, the defendant had to be acquitted – as in fact was the case with three defendants. In its decision, the Nuremberg Court commented that the case against the defendants rests largely on documents of their own making.[375]

Writing from within an international law tradition of scholarship, Wald has noted:

> Indeed there was debate originally whether any live witnesses would be used at all in the major Nuremberg trials. Jackson's preference was to rely on documentary evidence alone. Another aide, William 'Wild Bill' Donovan, the famed Office of Strategic Services (OSS) leader, fell out with Jackson over this very issue. Donovan wished to present the Nuremberg judges with warm breathing witnesses to incredibly horrible events. It should be noted here that the Charter of the Nuremberg Tribunal specifically authorized it to consider the reports of national State commissions which held public hearings and took live testimony involving atrocities in their respective countries. In the proceedings before the Nuremberg Tribunal, only ninety-four live witnesses (in addition to nineteen of the defendants) eventually testified.[376]

This explanation of one key element of the Jackson–Donovan dispute has been generally confirmed by other researchers, including Gerhart's well-informed bibliography of Jackson. Gerhart identifies some additional strands to the dispute regarding the perceived dangers of witnesses damaging aspects of the prosecution case in a way that would be impossible if the same points where proved through the use of authenticated documents:

375 http://www.roberthjackson.org/Man/theman2-6-3/.

376 P. M. Wald, 'To "Establish Incredible Events by Credible Evidence": The Use of Affidavit Testimony in Yugoslavia War Crimes Tribunal Proceedings' (2001) 42 *Harvard International Law Journal* 535 at 538–39.

> There arose in the early stages of preparation for the trial a great controversy as to whether the United States case should be established by the testimony of witnesses, by the use of documents, or by a combination of both. General Donovan argued earnestly that the American case should be proved through the testimony of witnesses. Justice Jackson believed it was too risky to use enemy witnesses, for regardless of how favourable their previous testimony, on cross-examination a great deal of unfavourable testimony could result. It was argued [by Donovan] that the case would be colorless without witnesses. Jackson, however, firmly resolved that it would be mainly a documentary case.[377]

These accounts are useful as generalisations but it is necessary to qualify certain details regarding how both Jackson and Donovan handled this element of their dispute.

Jackson, it appears, played a careful game of delaying the threatened confrontation with Donovan over this matter until a time of his own choosing. During October, Jackson appears to have left open any decision as to who would be in charge of the trial presentation of any particular part of the case, such that, at this time, Donovan would have had little reason to think that he was to be excluded. As late as 5 November, Donovan was still being listed as the most senior 'trial counsel'.[378]

On the other hand, at this time, Jackson seemed to be keeping his options open by claiming to a staff meeting that the relevant documents had to be prepared in such a way that 'any good trial lawyer could pick up the trial briefs and go ahead with the presentation of the case on the particular sections'.[379] This implied that those who had devoted themselves to the preparation of trial briefs, whether through documentation analysis or the preparation of witness testimony, could no longer assume that their past labours automatically guaranteed them the more glamorous role of presenting that evidence in open court before the international media. Jackson also warned staff, but perhaps Donovan in particular, that they could not treat any defendants or witnesses as their private property, not least because of the demands for access from the other three national prosecution organisations: 'The French and Russians cannot be excluded from interrogations indefinitely, but that the Russians should produce their prisoners before they should be permitted to do any interrogating.'[380]

Certain undated OCC documentation from this period would, perhaps, have given Donovan reasonable grounds for believing that Jackson intended

377 Gerhart, *op cit*, 359. 378 Taylor, *op cit*, 146.

379 Notes of Staff Meeting/Pre-trial Planning, 19 October 1945: Jackson Papers, *op cit*, Box 110.

380 *Ibid.*

to allocate him a key role with respect to certain high-profile witnesses. For example, a document entitled 'Plan for Presenting documents and briefs' lists General Donovan, together with Amen, Alderman and Dodd, as the key members of OCC responsible for 'Oral Testimony of Witnesses' (with Donovan listed first in deference to his rank). The same document indicates that Jackson had yet to harden his position on the use of such witnesses, as in the opening statement that this plan:

> Does not include oral testimony of witnesses which may be used at any time during the documentary case. Col Amen, Mr Alderman, Mr Dodd and others have made recommendations based on interrogations of witnesses. Other studies by General Donovan are underway.[381]

Donovan's advocacy of elements of Neumann's approach and perhaps that of his own personal staff, drawn from members of Dulles' group of German anti-Nazis, supported the idea of turning the contradictions contained in the Nazis' own defence statements against them. Their plan was to allow these defendants the opportunity effectively to condemn themselves and others from their own mouths.[382] Donovan regularly insisted that the case needed 'an affirmative human aspect', deploying German as well as foreign witnesses.[383] Colonel Amen, the head of the Interrogation Division, broadly supported greater use of witnesses. Additional high-level support came from Telford Taylor, whose paper on the 'order of proof and related subjects' stated:

> More important, however, I see no reason to resign ourselves to spending four or five dreary days doing nothing but putting in documents. It has seemed to me that the introduction of documents is not an independent process (and a boring one it would surely be) but rather that the documents will be introduced while other, and, we hope, more interesting things are going on. Either there will be a witness on the stand, and the document will be introduced in the course of his interrogation, or a member of the prosecution staff will be on his feet in front of the court explaining or arguing a portion of the case and pointing out the significance of documents or testimony . . . The general tone of . . . the memorandum suggests that we will present our case largely by reading from documents. For the reasons given above and in my memorandum on this same general subject of 3 November, I disagree.[384]

381 'Plan for Presenting documents and briefs', Jackson Papers, *op cit*, Box 111.

382 This is clear from the R&A Report 3110, 18 July 1945: 'Leadership Principle and Criminal Responsibility', revised for Jackson: NA, RG 238, Entry 52f, Box 28.

383 Conot, *op cit*, 150.

384 Taylor to Jackson and Board of Review: 'Order of Proof and Related Subjects', 3 November 1945: Jackson Papers, *op cit*, Box 111.

If anything, Taylor's position on the importance of testimonial evidence appeared to strengthen with the increasingly firm stand taken by Donovan.[385]

By contrast, Jackson, who lacked any recent experience of cross-examination within criminal trials – preferred to rely upon documentary evidence. Together with Robert Storey, Jackson increasingly insisted that the written prosecution briefs had to be composed in such a way that they were 'self-proving', including 'just as little talk and as many documents as possible'.[386] Such reliance appeared sensible to Jackson and others, partly because it saved considerable time by reducing extended periods of cross-examination whose course was not always predictable.[387] Jackson had become increasingly impressed with the quality and implications of captured German documentation, and less in need to curry favour with Donovan's trial strategy focused upon the provision of dramatic witness testimony of German witnesses, including former OSS double-agents such as Han Gisevius.

In order to counter Jackson's position on the self-sufficiency of documentary proof, Donovan attempted to gather considerable evidence from potential 'live' witnesses. In particular, he sought out those non-Nazi German officials who held positions of traditional authority, which would normally command credibility amongst the German population at large, such as senior military figures. Such oral testimony could, he believed, serve the wider political purpose of the trials, which included assistance in de-Nazification programmes, by having a particularly instructive rhetorical effect upon both the judges and the wider public. Here, it is important to recall that both Jackson and Donovan were acutely aware of the wider political objectives of the forthcoming trial, including its role in assisting democratic reconstruction, and drawing a line under the Nazi era. As Taylor recalls:

> The friction between Donovan and Jackson early in November had not diminished Donovan's belief that the prosecution should call witnesses, and most of his activities continued to be directed to that end. He was privately seeking prominent German witnesses who would testify against one or more of the defendants. These included defendants who would testify against other defendants, and it was this feature of his actions which led Jackson to lower the boom.[388]

Donovan, who was still a member of a senior planning committee for the trials, the Board of Review, began to press his alternative approach both with

385 Cf 'Proposed Plan of Trial Organisation', # 5, 16 October 1945 (where Taylor appears agnostic): Jackson Papers, *op cit*, Box 111.

386 Storey's report of Jackson's directive, 29 October 1945, quoted in Taylor, *op cit*, 146.

387 I am indebted to a telephone interview with Drexel Sprecher on 5 May 1998 for this important point.

388 Taylor, *op cit*, 180.

Robert Storey at various meetings during October and – more forcefully – November 1945.[389] As Taylor recalls:

> During the first half of November there were several joint meetings of the Trial Panel, and later of the Planning Committee, during which there was acrimonious discussion of such trial questions as the use of witnesses, the value of 'self-proving briefs', and the scheduling of the various portions of the American prosecution's case. General Donovan, Alderman, and I all thought the idea of briefs in which the documents would 'prove' the case without supporting argument was absurd, and that we should not back away from the use of witnesses. On November 5 there was a particularly sharp set-to, during which Donovan denounced the whole basis of Storey's planning as 'foolish'.[390]

Alderman also wrote in his diary that this confrontation was 'extraordinary' and 'left me with a very painful impression of the whole situation'.[391] Seven days later, Taylor recalls that: 'There was another unpleasant flare up, and it was during these weeks that the relations between Jackson and Donovan became so badly strained that soon thereafter they reached breaking point.'[392] In planning meetings, Donovan insisted that the immediate priority for the prosecutors should be to select the key witnesses and then to decide who was to examine and cross-examine them during the trial. Jackson publicly rejected this as founded on an incorrect premise regarding his preferred trial strategy. He argued that Donovan needed to acquaint himself better with the powerful documentary evidence that had, partly as a result of the collaboration of OSS officials, been flooding into the prosecution office.[393] Jackson asked an aide to summarise a number of the most legally incriminating documents. These included German documents relating to medical killings, which could, unaided by any witness testimony, more than adequately establish the criminal liabilities of certain defendants for crimes against humanity. Jackson also suggested that Donovan viewed for himself extracts from Hans Frank's diaries, Rosenberg Papers (which OSS's Lt. English had discovered), and dozens of other similarly powerful examples.

Donovan rejected the implications of Jackson's claims. He insisted instead that his consultation with media representatives found that they would find a prosecution based on documents alone extremely dull and lacking human interest. Hence, one unfortunate result of the prosecutors adhering to Jackson's exclusively documentary approach would be that media coverage of the trial – and hence its educational and political functions – would die out

389 Sprecher, 1998, *op cit*, 168.
390 Taylor, *op cit*, 146–47.
391 Quoted in Taylor, *op cit*, 147.
392 Taylor, *op cit*, 147.
393 Persico, 1994, *op cit*, 91.

almost at once. What was needed, Donovan claimed, was flesh and blood witnesses testifying to their experience of the nature and impact of Nazi criminality.[394]

Jackson did not like having his policy challenged publicly at planning meetings by his senior aide. Hence, he sought to end the relevant meeting early, and tackle the issues in a private way over dinner with Donovan. Donovan was not, however, so easily placated. Instead, he remained insistent that the forthcoming trial was unprecedented and would involve 'the greatest morality tale ever told'. The educational and public relations aspects of the trial required a human interest dimension. In turn, this was best supplied by the moving testimony of German witnesses who had personally suffered under the Nazis, such as members of Dulles' opposition group, including Gisevius.

Jackson replied by giving additional reasons why he remained convinced of the comparative advantages of a prosecution case founded on German documents: 'Documents unlike witnesses do not have faulty memories or commit perjury.'[395] Whilst his documentary approach may create criticism in the short term, Jackson insisted that it remained the best way of ensuring that a credible and permanent record is generated of Nazi atrocities, and to make sure that Nazi leaders would be convicted by means of their own words.

Persico claims that Jackson's position concealed certain ulterior motives at play during this face-to-face confrontation over dinner:

> As Jackson watched Donovan's car pull away, he accepted that he had probably alienated the general. Still he was certain he was on the right track. What he did not admit was that it was a long time since he had examined a witness in court. The documentary approach, along with its inherent superiority, seemed far less daunting.[396]

Apparently, Jackson's position hardened the more it was challenged, and he ended up by taking an even more extreme view than Storey, Chief of the Documents Division, who of course had every reason to seek to prioritise the type of evidence for which he had been responsible.[397] In fact, Jackson began to insist that the prosecution should 'put on no witnesses we could reasonably avoid'.

Donovan, however, remained undaunted by Jackson's increasingly uncompromising stance and refusal to accept his own counter-arguments in favour of witness testimony and the 'development' of such testimony in advance through private arrangements.[398] Hence, he continued to identify certain witnesses with whom he could enter into private discussions. The result, which may have been deliberate, was to generate a degree of personal authority, control and power with respect to the future deployment in court

394 *Ibid*, 92. 395 *Ibid*. 396 *Ibid*. 397 Taylor, *op cit*, 148. 398 *Ibid*.

of 'his' witnesses, virtually ensuring that he would have to be entrusted with their dramatic cross-examination.

It appears that, during the first week of November, Donovan had become increasingly frustrated with Jackson's continued rejection of his insistence on the importance of witness testimony. Given his own expression of contempt for Jackson's reliance upon 'self-proving' written briefs, he could hardly accept any role in the presentation of evidence without making a humiliating retraction, which he was not willing to do. As a result, Jackson's increasingly militant position must have appeared a deliberate attempt to reassert his authority over Donovan backed up by the threat of totally excluding him from any role in the trial itself. Certainly, on 7 November, this undercurrent of tension blew up in a full-scale confrontation when Jackson asked Storey to contact Donovan to enquire what role the former OSS Director sought in the trials. Taylor interprets Jackson's decision to use a lower-ranking intermediary for this purpose as possibly a deliberate provocation: 'Considering that Storey had become the main source of Donovan's discontent, that Donovan outranked Storey and was nearly a decade older than Jackson, and that Jackson was much indebted to Donovan for material support, Jackson's manner of raising the question was either a deliberate provocation or extraordinarily tactless.'[399]

Donovan was, as Taylor recalls, 'understandably angry' by this personal snub, and responded by a letter. This began by stating:

> To prevent misunderstanding, let me tell you of my talk with Bob Storey today. He said that he came to ask me what part I wanted to take in the trial. I replied that you not he should ask that question. However today I could only conclude that you took this means of cancelling our original arrangement [Donovan as Jackson's deputy and senior trial counsel] and of indicating that you considered that you saw no place for me. I am sorry you did not take a different means for telling me. I told Storey that you had the rights – as you had the responsibility – to prepare and try the case as you wanted, and to make your decision without asking my opinion. Accordingly – I will finish up the various matters I am doing which should be complete early in December . . . I shall be here until this time is complete.[400]

Donovan, whose expression of indignation may – in some measure – have been strategically staged to pressurise Jackson into altering his position on witness testimony, received a prompt reply from the Justice the following day. This claimed that there had been a misunderstanding. He had not intended to have his use of Storey as an intermediary 'to convey to you that you should

399 *Ibid.* 400 Quoted in *ibid*, 148–49.

take no part but was to learn your judgement and preferences before I make any assignments'.[401] In other words, he was merely consulting with the General so that his preferences could be taken into account when he later decided upon the division of staff responsibilities. Jackson's letter to Donovan also stated that he recognised that: 'He did not think highly of reliance upon captured documents . . . and would not be interested in the documentary aspect of the case.' Hence:

> I anticipated that you would prefer to work with live witnesses or cross-examination of defendants or defense witnesses. But it is not likely that the defense part of the case will be reached until after the first of the year . . . If you are of the opinion that the trial as it is now shaping up does not present a place of interest to you, I shall understand and accept your decision. But I do not want you to reach that conclusion on any misunderstanding of the motives either of myself or Colonel Storey.[402]

Although Jackson's wording was, in one sense, conciliatory, he remained entirely firm on his decision to rely upon captured documents, even in the face of Donovan's threat to resign or to consider himself wrongfully dismissed. Jackson's reply carefully refused to bow to Donovan's pressure and instead put the ball back into Donovan's court.

Both sides to this dispute knew that Donovan had previously indicated that he wanted to leave Nuremberg for the US early in the New Year to resume his legal practice. This demand placed pressure on Jackson to accept Donovan's alternative strategy almost from the start of the trials. Hence, strictly speaking, Jackson's request for this information did not, in itself, mean that he had no further use for Donovan, always providing that the former OSS Director was willing to stay longer at Nuremberg. Another condition, however, was that Donovan must become willing to work within, and contribute constructively to, the Justice's documentary approach. In effect, this demanded Donovan's complete surrender. The fact that Donovan responded in the way he did is revealing. Arguably, it suggests that his continued involvement remained conditional upon Jackson climbing down, and allowing Donovan to engage in precisely the type of dramatic cross-examination of prominent German witnesses during November and December 1945 for which he had been preparing almost from the start of his involvement.

It appears that one of Jackson's strategic responses to Donovan's challenge regarding witnesses was to refuse to be pressurised into making decisions dictated by Donovan's own time-scale, which included a demand to make his contribution during November and December. Hence, Jackson delayed any decision on the selection of prosecution witnesses. Indeed,

401 *Ibid.* 402 *Ibid.*

Jackson even made the use of witnesses dependent upon prosecutors complying with various procedures, including the production of written affidavits recording the details of proposed testimony. Certainly, this is one interpretation of the following statement within an internal planning document dated 14 November 1945:

> Witnesses: Responsibility of the Interrogation Division for interrogation of defendants and for preparation of testimony of witnesses continues, except where specific assignments of particular witnesses are made to other members of staff. The testimony of proposed witnesses must, with all possible speed, be reduced to affidavit form and submitted. Decision as to the use of each witness at the trial will be made, subject to approval by the four Chief Prosecutors, when his testimony is in this form. An assignment of the counsel to examine a witness at the trial will be made in connection with the decision as to whether such witness will be used.[403]

Taylor's memoir is helpful in adding further support to the view that, during November 1945, the month in which the trials opened,[404] Donovan was pressing hard to have witness testimony from the German generals with whom Donovan himself had been working. Taylor provides additional detail based, in part, on his own experiences at Nuremberg:

> My suspicion that Donovan was trying to turn some of the German generals into witnesses against Keitel and Jodl was sound. He had been in touch with what he called the 'Brauchitsch Group' and had secured Jackson's permission to allow it to submit a statement on behalf of the German Army. Dated November 19, 1945, it was signed by Field Marshal Walter von Brauchitsch (Commander in Chief of the German Army, 1938–41), Field Marshal Erich von Manstein (perhaps the ablest German field commander of World War II), General Franz Halder (Chief of the Army General Staff 1938–42), and two generals of lesser rank. Their document proved worthless for Donovan's purpose, as he himself saw, since it pointed the finger of blame for Germany's sorry state at Hitler and away from the army, and attributed no individual responsibility to Keitel or Jodl.[405]

Useful as it is, Taylor's account now needs to be supplemented with the additional information contained in Donovan's own Nuremberg files forming the Cornell Collection. Dennis Smith's review of Donovan's Cornell

403 'Special Memorandum No. 10', 14 November, Jackson Papers, *op cit*.

404 More precisely, on 20 November 20 1945 at the Palace of Justice in Nuremberg, Germany.

405 Taylor, 1992, *op cit*, 180.

Archive has provided details of previously unknown aspects of this aspect of the OSS Director's work with German generals, including Donovan's sustained interest in introducing into the Nuremberg process remarkable evidence taken from another German general:

> A sense of . . . urgency is revealed in a terse response to an assistant's typed note, also among the Donovan Papers: 'General Donovan: These are the copies of the excerpts of the Thomas diary, as far as it went. J.E.S.' Donovan replies: 'Get some more.' The person referred to is Georg R. Thomas, a German general of the infantry who was arrested by the Gestapo in 1944 before being captured by the Allies.[406]

The dramatic, and to a prosecutor potentially appealing nature of Thomas's testimony is clear from the following extract of an extended handwritten statement, entitled 'Concerning the Question of Guilt', that Donovan obtained, in which Thomas stated:

> The terrible indictment which the Allied Court has made against the war criminals of the period of the Nazi regime, against its political and military organizations, and indirectly thereby against the whole German people, must cause each thinking person to ask this question: How was it possible that a nation which gave to the world a Kant, Goethe, Lessing, Bach and Beethoven, trusted and obeyed such a regime for twelve years? History will pass a terrible judgment over the past twelve years of the German people because even after the present feelings of hatred, vengeance and egotism will have made room for greater objectivity, and when the German people will no longer heap upon itself self-accusations and denunciations, in order to prove its political change of heart, the one thought will remain as a sad recognition: How could a whole nation follow the mad teachings of this man? It is therefore absolutely essential that men who have proven themselves opponents of this regime, and who are able out of their personal experience to contribute to an elucidation of the question of the failure of the German people, say everything openly which might serve to disentangle this German question.[407]

Taylor records one particularly unpleasant expression of the growing bitterness and frustration that Donovan had built up with Jackson's insistence on relying mostly upon dry documentary evidence. Donovan was not above

406 Dennis Smith, 1999, *op cit*, 2.

407 See also Georg Thomas, 'Basic Facts for a History of German War and Armaments Economy,' Georg R. Thomas, Cornell Collection, 13.12; 'The Reich Ministry of Armament and War Production (Speer Ministry)', *ibid*, 13.13.

taking his frustrations out on other members of Jackson's team, even those in poor health:

> Alderman was not a strong person physically or emotionally. He was very tired, and Jackson sent him home for a long rest. At Orly Airport he ran into General Donovan, who sublimated his Nuremberg frustrations by a sneering reference to Alderman's total reliance upon documents. Sidney did not return to Nuremberg until mid-January of 1946.[408]

In his letter to Donovan on 26 November 1945, Jackson recognised that his official policy on the self-sufficiency of documentary evidence represented one of 'fundamental differences in viewpoint about the case' which separated them. In this letter, he complained that Donovan had, in effect, been pursuing an alternative agenda with 'his' witnesses, the results of which he had improperly withheld from his fellow prosecutors:[409]

> During your long absence from the case, my own confidence grew with the study of the documents analyses that our case could safely rest wholly on documents, and that witnesses need be used, if at all, only incidentally. With this you disagreed and proposed more reliance on oral testimony. I was and am willing to consider use of any witness only when he has made a complete written statement of what his testimony is. This I have from some proposed witnesses but none from any you have been working with. The planning board advise that they have nothing except oral statements from you.[410]

Jackson took an uncompromising line when he argued that: 'I am going to try this case by indisputable documentary proof.'[411]

There is some evidence that Jackson's uncompromising stance with Donovan may have been deployed specifically to bring matters to a head with this determined rival and, in effect, force a showdown that Donovan could not win. Hence, once Jackson had effectively forced Donovan's resignation, it became possible to modify his earlier stance. During a recent interview, Drexel Sprecher recalls that during the trial process Jackson was eventually forced to modify his initial stance of seeking to rely mainly upon documentary evidence, to a strategy closer to that espoused by Donovan:

> QUESTION: Do you, do you think the U.S. case was too reliant upon documents?
>
> SPRECHER: No. I don't think that the U.S. case was too reliant upon

408 Taylor, 1992, *op cit*, 199. 409 *Op cit*. 410 *Op cit*.
411 Persico, 1994, *op cit*, 119–21.

> documents. I think that at first, Jackson probably wanted to use documents and have very few witnesses. But he was persuaded that he ought to have at least several. And so we had several very good prosecution witnesses.
>
> QUESTION: And, and why was he persuaded to have witnesses? What were the arguments?
>
> SPRECHER: I think one of the main things was to get a break in the trial. And just avoid the constant repetition of things about documents. And that the live witnesses kind of brought the whole thing to life in a way that the documents did not.[412]

Furthermore, the use of oral testimony by German victims of the Nazis also helped off-set the attitude that Nuremberg represented little more than 'victor's justice':

> QUESTION: What was the attitude of the German people toward the trial?
>
> SPRECHER: I think . . . there was a set of different attitudes, in that they changed as the trial went on. At the beginning, I think a lot of the Germans felt this is just the victors over the vanquished kind of thing. But when they began to see that there were not only defense counsel, but that the German witnesses were testifying about what they had experienced, which showed crimes by the Nazi regime, then I think there tended to be a great change and a great more receptivity to listening to what was going on at the trial, both by radio and through the newspapers.[413]

Hence, there is some evidence supporting the view that Donovan's strategy concerning oral testimony was superior in both strictly legal and wider democratic-political terms, and that Jackson's uncompromising line during November 1945 was motivated at least partly by his need to repel Donovan's challenge to his leadership of the US prosecutors.

Donovan's plea-bargaining proposals for Schacht and Göring

A major disagreement between Jackson and Donovan concerned their difference in judgement regarding the merits of Donovan's alleged negotiations with the defendants Hjalmar Schacht and Hermann Göring in which they

412 Interview with Drexel Sprecher: http://www.courttv.com/archive/casefiles/nuremberg/sprecher.html.

413 *Ibid.*

would give state's evidence in return for specific concessions.[414] Jackson was later to flatly reject Donovan's actions in this area.[415] However, the increasingly forceful tone of the exchange of memos and verbal exchanges in high-level planning meetings indicates that a discernible battle of wills was taking place between two determined and often uncompromising individuals, both of whom had grown accustomed to exercise firm institutional leadership within their respective spheres. Donovan's tendency from October onwards to engage in freelance interrogation of German witnesses without consultation with John Amen,[416] to whom Jackson had assigned the role of chief of interrogations, caused Amen to complain bitterly that the General was trespassing into his own zone of special responsibilities.[417] Such complaints meant, in effect, having to either placate Amen at Donovan's expense, or concede to Donovan, and thereby risk alienating Amen. As Persico notes, Jackson's reaction to this 'painful dilemma' was to chose the first option: 'He knew all too well his debt to Donovan. Yet he resented the General's interference and disapproved of the direction in which Donovan wanted to take the trial.'[418]

Jackson may, perhaps, have become suspicious of the OSS's involvement in unofficial promises of legal immunity following his review of Karl Wolff's interrogation reports. It has been claimed that, notwithstanding Donovan's more 'flexible' attitude to such arrangements than Jackson's, the OSS Director rejected point blank an approach from Kaltenbrunner at Nuremberg. Kaltenbrunner had sought some form of privileged treatment in return for handing over to the American intelligence authorities control over one group of his former 'stay behind' agents in Soviet-controlled Eastern Europe, including the Balkans.[419] Jackson's growing commitment to a purely, or largely, documentary approach to the forthcoming trials was, by contrast, based partly on apparently valid legal grounds. That is, his firm rejection of organising the trial in such a way to create the impression that the prosecution had, in effect, bought favourable witness testimony, which was, therefore, tainted. Certainly, Donovan at this stage was directing staff to interrogate other potential 'live' witnesses.[420] This reflected his fundamental disagreement with Jackson concerning what he regarded as the obvious advantages of

414 Sprecher claims: 'The conflict culminated around a disagreement concerning Donovan's interrogation of leading German officials, including the Nuremberg Defendant Hjalmar Schacht.' Sprecher, 1998, *op cit*, 166.

415 *Ibid.* 416 Amen had been a Brooklyn prosecutor.

417 Persico, 1994, *op cit*, 119. 418 *Ibid*, 119–120. 419 *Ibid*, 752.

420 Andor C. Klay (original Hungarian name was Sziklay), retired State Department employee, wrote in the Hungarian-American newspaper *Amerikai Magyar Népszava* on 18 February 1994, that under the direction of General Donovan of the OSS he interviewed the Hungarian Admiral Horthy on two occasions. Once in Weilheim, another time in the Oberursel (near Frankfurt) interrogation centre. See Admiral Miklós Horthy: Memoirs: http://victorian.fortunecity.com/wooton/34/horthy/22.html. N. 23. Horthy was Governor or Regent of

deploying a strategy of divide and rule, in which senior German officials and civilians within the Nazi regime would testify against each other. Such testimony would very publicly discredit the regime, particularly in the eyes of the German population.

On the other hand, there is evidence that, although Jackson was to retrospectively criticise Donovan's attempted plea-bargaining negotiations as entirely improper, and out of line with Jackson's own policy from the start, this represented a strategic and self-serving exaggeration. Indeed, it appears that during their negotiations with the British authorities at the end of May 1945, Jackson supported Donovan's view that certain Nazis could be turned around as effective witnesses for the prosecution.[421] Furthermore, at a staff meeting in mid-October, Jackson appeared willing to entertain his staff trading concessions in return for admissions of liability from the Nuremberg defendants, including presumably evidence incriminating other defendants, even when this took place in the absence of their lawyers:

> With respect to the interrogation of defendants after the serving of the Indictment on them (probably today), there may be three courses: First they may want to tell their full story; second they may talk after their counsel are present; or third, they may be willing to make some agreement in return for receiving copies of documents to be used against them. They may not obtain counsel for ten days or so. The Justice approved Colonel Amen's suggestion to call the defendants in and offer them a choice on the record as to whether they desire to talk.[422]

Whilst this could hardly be taken as a ringing endorsement of any privately negotiated deals for charges or evidence to be dropped in return for giving evidence useful for the prosecution, it did represent a step in that direction.

Having set the scene, it is now both possible and timely to discuss the details of Donovan's attempts to negotiate private deals with first Schacht and then Göring. During November, Donovan attended interrogations of both Schacht and of Göring.[423] In this respect, he was able to draw upon the

Hungary. On 19 March 1944, Nazi troops occupied Hungary. Horthy was forced to stay on as a figurehead. In August 1944, he removed the Nazi puppet government and appointed a new cabinet to seek an armistice. With a preliminary armistice agreement signed in Moscow, he attempted to enforce it on 15 October, but overwhelming German forces, supporting a strong Hungarian Nazi movement, thwarted it. Arrested by the Gestapo, Horthy and his family was taken to Germany. After the war he served as a *witness* at the Nuremberg Trials.

421 'Minutes of a meeting of May 29, 1945', p.2: PRO/NA, LCO/x/j/7320.

422 Staff Meeting Minutes, 19 October, Jackson Papers, *op cit*, Box 110.

423 For copies of the Schacht letters and Donovan's replies, see 'Donovan File' Jackson Papers, *op cit*, Box 2.

cooperation of former OSS subordinates: Commander Ralph G. Albrecht and Colonel Murray Gurfein, both of whom had legitimate reasons to interrogate Schacht. Donovan also deployed von Schabrendorff to assess Schacht's answers to questions and the case against him.[424] Gurfein was helping prepare the politically sensitive 'economic case' but under Shea's direction. He therefore had every reason to interrogate Hitler's former Finance Minister. Gurfein was responsible for contributing to the prosecution's case for the 'individual responsibility' of Göring. Donovan was, as Conot notes, 'well acquainted' with these former OSS officials, and he:

> [A]ccompanied both Gurfein and Albrecht . . . to interrogations. The OSS chief had the knack, born of a man skilled in intelligence gathering, of projecting a sympathetic air. Schacht, who had ultimately joined the July 20 conspiracy [to kill Hitler], was anxious to divorce himself from his co-defendants, and refused to participate in any overall defense plan to justify the regime or exonerate the other defendants. He wished to testify . . . so long as he was able to act the part of the German Nationalist, and not appear to be a handmaiden of the prosecution.[425]

Schacht sought to make direct contact with a member of the prosecution suspected of being particularly sympathetic to the idea of a plea-bargaining deal.[426] Indeed, Donovan's plea-bargaining initiative had been prompted by Schacht's ingratiating letter to Donovan dated 14 November 1945. This clearly sought to flatter Donovan and play to his pride:[427]

> I am among the few people who have watched and gone through the frightful events of the last twelve years in Germany and with open eyes. Thanks to my official position I think I know more of the background of Hitler's policy than many others. I welcome the installation of the International Military Tribunal, the competence of which nobody can doubt . . . I do it the more willingly as the trial will prove that I am in no way guilty of any crime or any immorality . . . I would therefore be very grateful, if an officer of your high standing, of your experience and wisdom and of your well known international reputation would be willing to look into a brief summary of the underlying reasons and conditions of the dreadful Nazi regime, as I have as I experienced them. . . . I would prefer to submit such [a] summary to a man of your judgement

424 Schlabrendorff to Donovan, 'Evaluation of Schacht, Cornell Collection', *op cit*, 48.08; Schlabrendorff, 'Subject: Trial Brief on Dr. Hjalmar Schacht', *ibid*, 48.08.

425 Conot, *op cit*, 151.

426 Bradley Smith, 1977, *op cit*, 270.

427 Cited in Persico, 1994, *op cit*, 119; Conot, *op cit*, 151–52; Bradley Smith, 1977, *op cit*, 270–71.

> and capacity than to any of the lawyers or defense counsel which can appear before courts.[428]

Donovan, who – following his marginalisation by Jackson had been given few responsibilities[429] – grasped this apparent opportunity of putting Schacht on the stand to testify against the other defendants. Donovan deployed his own staff to investigate aspects of the Schacht case.[430] They obtained additional material suggesting a rather different and more complex situation than that contained in Jackson's indictment. This material showed that he had opposed Hitler from 1937 onwards, and – as early as 1935 – had even supplied confidential information to the American embassy in Berlin warning the Americans of Hitler's military intentions.[431] Georg Thomas, one of the anti-Nazi generals whom Donovan was cultivating, revealed that had been arrested and detained in Flossenbürg and Dachau concentration camps, during which time he had shared a cell with Schacht, and thereby became personally acquainted with this defendant. Thomas's interrogation and diary entries supplied Donovan with further details of Schacht's role after 1937, emphasising that this defendant was never a party member and had even strongly opposed Göring's influence within the government. This documentation suggests that, from 1937, Schacht had increased his opposition to a wide range of Hitler's policies on the Jews, the persecution of churches, the education of youth, 'financial manipulation' the 'muzzling' of the law and Hitler's breaches of agreements with foreign countries.[432] Donovan's files contain a number of other documents providing additional information on Schacht and the latter's unsigned memo on 'The financing of the Armament programme'.[433] These reports from his own staff and sources confirmed Donovan's suspicion that, despite his early support for Hitler, Schacht was more suitable as a prosecution witness than as a defendant in a major war crimes trial.

428 Schacht to Donovan, 14 November 1945: Enclosure in Jackson to Truman, 1 December 1945, 12-1045 State Department II; also cited partly in Persico, 1994, *op cit*, 119; Conot, *op cit*, 151–52.

429 On an organisational chart of 14 September the day Donovan returned, the general was listed as merely one of three associate counsel but without any specific position or division within the overall organisation. Sprecher, 1999, *op cit*, 167.

430 See the extensive collection of documentation at Cornell Collection, *op cit*, 48.02–48.09.

431 See 'Affidavit from S. R. Fuller, following request Lt. Col. Griggs', 8 October 1945, copy of enclosure B of your confidential memorandum to the President Roosevelt, dated 11 October 1935, swearing it is a true account of his conversation with Dr Hjalmar Schacht on 23 September 1935: Cornell Collection, *op cit*, Vol. 2, 6.17.

432 See 'Summary' and then transcript of the Interrogation of General Georg R. Thomas, 9 November 1945, Cornell Collection, *op cit*, Vol. 2: 6.12; 'Thoughts and Events', Georg Thomas diary, 1–32 tr. 12 November 1945, with covering memo from JES and handwritten reply from Donovan stating: 'Get some more.' Cornell Collection, *op cit*, Vol. 2: 6.13.

433 1168-PS: Vol. 20, Pt. 3, Cornell Collection, *op cit*, Vol. 20, Pt. 3.

Against this background, Donovan discussed with his former OSS subordinate Murray Gurfein the possibilities that were opened up by Schacht's letter, and both agreed that 'Schacht would make a useful and dramatic witness.'[434] As Persico notes: 'Donovan, a seasoned courtroom lawyer, could smell a defendant willing to turn state's evidence a mile off. If he could get Schacht on the stand testifying against the others, that would be a major breakthrough.'[435] However, Donovan would have appreciated that his belief in providing dramatic witness testimony, in which the former leaders of Nazi Germany would publicly discredit one another, clashed with Jackson's overall view. In particular, it contradicted Jackson's increasing insistence that, as already noted, the case should be made almost entirely on the basis of evidence contained in captured German documentation. Donovan therefore needed to draw upon his rhetorical skills in an effort to win over Jackson to his scheme.

In response to Schacht's letter, which not surprisingly he took to represent an overture from a potentially cooperative witness, the General sent a memorandum to Jackson on the same day. This reminded Jackson that there had been previous indications of this defendant's possible willingness to cooperate with the prosecution, and that Donovan had apprised Jackson of these. The OSS Director argued that the time had now come to make a decision as to how the prosecution should respond to the opportunities provided by such offers of cooperation. Donovan's carefully drafted letter appeared to balance the factors for and against entering into a mutually beneficial arrangement with this defendant, whilst also taking a severe view of Schacht's overall conduct:

> I have carefully gone over the briefs and proofs on the Schacht matter . . . Schacht made possible the rearmament project. It was his support in financial matters that strengthened Hitler's position. Aided by influences and what he should have known about Hitler's character, we may have enough to hold him for aggressive war. There is strong argument in this.[436]

Donovan's memorandum went on to highlight a number of points that, he claimed, lessened or mitigated Schacht's guilt, some of which were well known but others were extremely sensitive diplomatically. These countervailing factors included the fact that this defendant had maintained cooperative relations with the American embassy in Berlin (through Donald Heath), and, through these and other contacts with the OSS, via its double-agent Hans Gisevius,[437] had given the Allies prior notice of the German attack on

434 Conot, *op cit*, 152. 435 Sprecher, 1998, *op cit*, 167.

436 Donovan to Jackson, 14 November 1945: Enclosure in Jackson to Truman, 1 December 1945, 12-1045 State Department II.

437 Bradley Smith, 1977, *op cit*, 271.

Russia.[438] The OSS had passed on all information Schacht had provided to the relevant Allied authorities.[439]

Donovan then wrote that: 'Schacht claims that Roosevelt sent him a message that he would be needed after the war. He worked with the resistance movement and finally found himself in a Gestapo prison and then in a concentration camp.'[440] This claim represented an elaboration of one aspect of the talks that Schacht had engaged in with Sumner Wells, a prominent American diplomat in 1940.[441] Donovan maintained that Schacht had supported the resistance movement, something which had led to both his breach with Hitler and to his final detention in a concentration camp. Furthermore, the evidence regarding aggressive war was not straightforward or unambiguous. This was because this defendant had attempted to divert Hitler from open warfare in favour of the acquisition of colonies, and when this failed, attempted to cut off finance for the military build-up to war.[442]

Donovan would have appreciated that, if Jackson believed Schacht's accounts of the wartime cooperation he had, at considerable personal risk, provided to the OSS and the US State Department, then the continuation of his trial in a straightforward manner without any previous plea-bargaining arrangement could prove counterproductive. Donovan added:

> In view of all this I return to the suggestion that consideration be given to the possibility of giving him the opportunity to fight his way out by actual testimony only dealing with the facts. He could strengthen the case considerably and without promises he could be given the chance in the direct case to state his position. As I have already told you there have come certain suggestions that he would like to talk with me. If anything develops I will let you know.[443]

Although carefully disguised rhetorically, Donovan was, in effect, recommending that 'Schacht be turned around and made into a prosecution witness'.[444]

Jackson, by contrast, was not receptive to Donovan's recommendations

438 'Memorandum for: General Donovan', M. I. Gurfein/Donald Heath, Cornell Collection, 48.09.

439 Bradley Smith, 1977, *op cit*, 271.

440 Donovan to Jackson, 14 November 1945: Enclosure in Jackson to Truman, 1 December 1945, 12-1045 State Department II.

441 Bradley Smith, 1977, *op cit*, 271.

442 *Ibid.*

443 Taylor, 1992, *op cit*, 181; cf. Sprecher, 1998, *op cit*, 168. Later, in 1948, following Schacht's conviction, Drexel Sprecher was to receive a hand-written letter from him requesting a reference that he had given cooperation in giving truthful information at Nuremberg. Sprecher supplied this and this defendant was released from confinement shortly after this. Sprecher, 1998, *op cit*, 210.

444 Bradley Smith, 1977, *op cit*, 271.

because he regarded Schacht as one of the most implicated of the defendants as he had helped paved the way for Hitler's early seizure and consolidation of power, and provided economic policies that largely financed military preparations for planned war.[445] Ten days after Schacht's approach, Donovan acted to help prepare the ground for the implementation of his own proposals concerning such plea-bargaining.

Donovan was not easily deterred by what he regarded as a most promising offer rich in possibilities for advancing his own position. As Smith notes: 'Donovan was too experienced a lawyer and had spent too much time as head of the OSS to be led in blind however.'[446] Hence, he sent Jackson a memorandum discussing the general use of witnesses that noted that he had informed Schacht's counsel that his client could not be seen until defendant Schacht 'made clear what exactly he was prepared to do'.[447] Jackson resented the General's interference in his established trial strategy, and disapproved of the direction in which Donovan wanted to take the trial.[448] Hence, on 26 November, Jackson brought matters to a head in a long memorandum, which also tackled other areas of disagreement.[449] In this document, Jackson firmly rejected Donovan's plans for using Schacht as a prosecution witness:

> Then too, we do not see alike about the defendants such as Schacht. I do not think he will help us convict anyone we do not already have convicted on the documents. And if he did, I do not think we should give him any advantage for doing so. In short, I do not think we can afford to negotiate with any of these defendants or their counsel.[450]

Jackson effectively sabotaged Donovan's plans by stating that he would not assign to him any role in the examination or cross-examination of Schacht or any other witnesses whatsoever.[451]

Donovan's proposals for effectively allowing Schacht to benefit from a behind the scenes deal with the American prosecutors were contrary to the strictly legalistic line taken by Jackson. However, this proposal was dwarfed

445 Jackson Oral History Project, *op cit*, 345.

446 Bradley Smith, 1977, *op cit*, 271–72.

447 Donovan to Jackson, 24 November: Enclosure in Jackson to Truman, 1 December 1945, 12-1045 State Department II.

448 Persico, 1994, *op cit*, 120.

449 Jackson to Donovan, 26 November 1945: Truman Museum and Library, Nuremberg Collection: http://www.trumanlibrary.org.

450 *Ibid.* Jackson extended his critique of such private deals, 'bargains' or 'negotiations' in another section of this letter, which we shall discuss later in connection with the General's contacts with Göring.

451 Donovan's contacts with Schacht were briefly at issue in the trial itself regarding the fate of correspondence between this defendant and Göring. See Nuremberg transcript 5 March 46/IMT, 8, 544: 'the letter [of Schacht] was last seen by Schacht in the possession of one Von Schlaberndorff, who worked with General Donovan, but who is no longer here'.

in significance when compared to Donovan's suggested deal with Göring, Hitler's one-time deputy and potential successor. Donovan's recently released Nuremberg files at Cornell University include extensive handwritten and signed reports documenting the General's interrogation of Göring. Donovan was monitoring the material which Göring's defence lawyer was seeking to obtain, presumably to offset the risk of being ambushed in court by material that the trial lawyers were not aware of and had no effective reply to.[452] Donovan's interest may have been based on his desire to undertake the prestigious role of cross-examining Göring personally. It would have been clear to Donovan that the cross-examination of Göring was likely to become one of the most dramatic aspects of the entire trial. Hence, his personal interest in playing this role. These new materials provide evidence that Göring's reputation as the most defiant of the Nuremberg defendants is unjustified. It is now clear that this defendant had been willing to cooperate with Donovan's plans to have the former deputy to Hitler 'sell out' his fellow defendants during trial testimony conducted by Donovan himself. There is some evidence that Göring's reputation as the most defiant of the Nuremberg defendants, who – on many occasions – outwitted his prosecutors, could be damaged. This would have occurred if Göring's willingness to enter into private deals with Donovan, which included 'selling out' a number of his fellow defendants, had been better appreciated. It will be shown below that is was only Jackson's rejection and defeat of Donovan's alternative trial strategy – rather than Göring's enduring loyalty to Hitler and his other defendants – which meant that he was effectively forced to resort to his 'plan B', a defiant plan to 'go down fighting'.

According to Dunlop, Donovan:

> [S]pent ten days alone interrogating him . . . One day he confronted Göring with details of his looting [based on studies by the OSS Art Looting investigators and presumably others], He had intended to open a new museum to house the art, according to the report: 'Either in Berlin or at Counhall in which a railroad was to be built from Berlin to bring tourists'. Time and again Donovan accused Göring of kindling the Reichstag fire that had given Hitler the excuse to crack down on the political left and strengthen his hold on the levers of power.

When interrogating Göring, Donovan would have had in front of him the OSS–R&A 'dry run' trial brief on this defendant, prepared over the early

452 See Roger Barett JAGD to Donovan, 13 November, 1945. This reports on a list of documents examined by Göring's lawyer, Dr Stahmar, noting that he examined one British file not on the American list: UK 62 'Note from Secret Files: 23.1.42' indicating Hitler's 'determination to remove all Jews from Europe'. Cornell Collection, *op cit*, Vol. 18, 60.12.

summer, which contained various dossiers of his role in looting and other crimes. Despite his pressure, Donovan could not extract a confession regarding the Reichstag fire.[453] According to Dunlop, the former OSS chief then began to offer Göring the outlines of a deal to help him secure what was, probably, his best available option: 'You are walking on the edge of the grave,' Donovan told Göring, 'and the question is only how you will go in, whether your people will learn that you were a man to be respected for what you did for Hitler or to be despised.'[454]

For reasons already noted, Donovan's pursuit of his own alternative trial strategy with Göring was entirely at variance with Jackson's preferences. Donovan's Nuremberg files contain numerous memoranda regarding Göring both to and from Donovan, particularly from his own OSS personal staff, such as Captain Otto Norden and von Schlabrendorff. Indeed, Schlabrendorff appears to have played an especially important support role in Donovan's work with Göring. Dunlop notes that this 'OSS resistance leader' was called in to assist in the preparation of lines of questioning.[455]

These newly available materials cast new light on Taylor's claim that the General, who was older and at least as experienced in many of the pertinent issues as Jackson, was, with respect to Göring at least, largely working according to his own agenda, which included an alternative trial strategy much more attuned to political objectives of de-Nazification through a public discrediting of former Nazi leaders. Dunlop notes that:

> Donovan considered it critical to shorten the trial as much as possible. He was of the opinion that if Göring would assume responsibility as the representative of Hitler for most of the war crimes, his conviction, sentencing and execution would be quick. Other top Nazis could then be tried, but the rank and file could be turned over to German courts. Donovan believed that if the Germans themselves tried the Nazis, they would share the responsibility for their condemnation and would help atone for their nation's crimes against humanity. Moreover it seemed to Donovan that the trials should not be conducted under Anglo-Saxon law but under German law, which the Nazis had violated. Only then would the German people as a whole share in the world's revulsion for the Nazis and prevent the rise of another Hitler in the future. Could Schlabrendorff suggest how he might talk Göring into a deal? After all, the Nazi knew full well that his execution was already a certainty.[456]

Göring may have heard from Schacht that, as a former senior intelligence official, Donovan was 'open to offers'.[457] According to Taylor's memoir,

453 Dunlop, *op cit*, 481. 454 *Ibid.* 455 *Ibid.* 456 *Ibid.*
457 Persico, 1994, *op cit*, 119.

Göring had also 'sensed that Donovan was approachable'.[458] It appears that Göring: 'sent Donovan word that, for a price, he was willing to testify against Ribbentrop, Kaltenbrunner, Schacht and Speer and ... Streicher'.[459] In response, Donovan discussed with Göring's lawyer, Dr Stahmer, his client's view about giving testimony for the prosecution. Göring was willing to give prosecution evidence but only in return that 'he be given an honourable death before a firing squad instead of a shameful death at the end of a rope'.[460] These negotiations also became known among the defence lawyers. Another source, the diary of Dr Victor von der Lippe, assistant to Dr Walter Siemers (the defence lawyers of Raeder) notes:

> Among the American prosecutors General Donovan . . . played a special role. The relations between Donovan and the Chief Prosecutor were strained. From an apparently well-informed source it was heard that Donovan had a very different plan for the trial than Jackson. He had the intention of making Göring, the second man in the Third Reich, a privileged witness for the prosecution, and giving him opportunity . . . to save his head. Göring, in conversation with Donovan, accepted this plan.[461]

In this way, Donovan began to pursue his alternative strategy with Göring. This is clear from an interrogation report in which Göring agreed to reveal certain details regarding the improper dismissal of Generalfeldmarschall von Blomberg and General Werner von Fritsche in 1938 only if this could be conducted in private with Donovan. This interview took place on 6 November 1945, in the presence only of an interpreter. Göring requested Donovan that certain aspects 'be kept a secret', thereby creating a conspiratorial quality to the Göring–Donovan relationship.[462] The next day, Donovan sent Jackson a curt letter setting out in detail his own alternative trial strategy, which represented a direct challenge to Jackson's project, and even perhaps his authority.

Jackson replied in kind on 8 November 1945, largely rejecting Donovan's strategy. Undaunted, and clearly viewing Göring as his own special witness, Donovan defied Jackson by instructing the military official in charge of the detention of the defendants, Colonel Andrus, that no others were in future to be permitted to interrogate this defendant.[463] This created problems for

458 Taylor, 1992, *op cit*, 181.

459 Persico, 1994, *op cit*, 119. All these defendants had crossed him through the years, with 'Streicher maligning his manhood', *ibid.*

460 *Ibid.* 461 23 November entry, quoted in Taylor, 1992, *op cit*, 181–82.

462 Pre-trial interrogation of Göring, 6 November 1945: NA, RG 238, Microfilm M.1270, Roll 6.

463 Cf. CSDIC/CMF/X reports on Göring, June–July 1945, with letters from General Donovan to James Donovan, warning him to limit access to the prisoners severely: NA, RG 153 Judge-Advocate General, Internal Affairs Division, Box 1534.

Jackson as clearly members of the other delegations demanded access rights to this key defendant as part of their own preparation of the overall case. Jackson then overturned Donovan's instruction, reaffirming the former position, and informed Donovan of this in a letter.[464]

Following an overture from the former Reich Marshal, Donovan decided in mid-November that a protracted confrontation with the wily Göring was not desirable.[465] Donovan agreed with Göring that the latter 'would answer a questionnaire made up by the prosecution, and once the questions and answers had been agreed to by both sides, he would take the stand and give his testimony in open court'.[466] In effect, Donovan was seeking to turn Göring into a prosecution witness against his fellow defendants. Indeed, Donovan attempted to sell his proposal for this virtual plea-bargaining arrangement to Jackson, as an arrangement that, he suggested, fell short of a private 'deal' or 'negotiated bargain', which Jackson had expressly ruled out. Indeed, Donovan claimed that his plan was broadly consistent with the agreed policy of not allowing any defendant to testify who had not previously incriminated others in writing.[467] Indeed, Donovan claimed that, during his interrogations, Göring had already provided such incriminating evidence 'against certain of the defendants'.[468] Donovan suggested that his proposals regarding Göring offered an important way forward in that 'a confession from the last sane leader of the gang' could amount to the best 'practical means of bringing home to the German people the guilt of these men'.[469] According to Persico, the attraction for Donovan of a private plea-bargaining deal with Göring was clear: 'Donovan could envision it all: Schacht testifying against Göring, Göring against Speer, Speer against Saukel. What a spectacle: the Nazi leaders consuming each other before the world.'[470] Donovan insisted that if the prosecution could place Göring and Schacht on the stand and get a public confession from them, then that would make a more convincing case in the eyes of the German public and elsewhere than Jackson's preferred approach.

Another alternative and even more radical scenario that Donovan now envisaged was to have Göring 'assume all responsibility for what had happened in the Third Reich, so that Göring alone would be indicted, as the representative of Hitler'.[471] According to Schlabrendorff, who was personally involved in Donovan's scheming:

464 Jackson to Donovan, 'Interrogation of Witnesses', 14 November 1945: Burton Andrus C. Collection, Colorado Springs, US.

465 Bradley Smith, 1977, *op cit*, 175.

466 *Ibid.*

467 Donovan to Jackson, 27 November 1945, enclosure in Jackson to Truman, 1 December 1945, 12-1045 State Department II.

468 *Ibid*, Donovan to Jackson, 24 November 1945.

469 *Ibid*, Donovan to Jackson, 27 November 1945.

470 Persico, *op cit*, 119.

471 Schlabrendorff, *op cit*, 262–63. For no doubt incomplete copies of Donovan's contacts with Göring, see 'Donovan File', Jackson Papers, *op cit*, Box 2.

> In this, the trial would have been over in the shortest possible time, with the conviction, sentencing and execution of Göring by the Allies. The rest of the defendants could then have been turned over to a duly appointed German court, consisting of German jurists with anti-Nazi records. . . . When Donovan asked me what I thought about the chances of persuading Göring to assume all responsibility for the policies of the Third Reich and plead guilty, I advised him to wear full uniform with all the medals he had ever received for that visit to Göring in prison. I also urged him to appeal to whatever was left of Göring's sense of officers' honour, making it plain at the same time that his life was forfeit in any case.[472]

According to this account, Donovan was receptive to Schlabrendorff's advice. Donovan followed it with, from his point of view, quite encouraging results. However, these were promptly ruined by Jackson's outright rejection of Donovan's alternative strategy:

> I was not mistaken in my appraisal of Göring. After returning from his visit in Göring's cell, Donovan informed me that the latter was willing to cooperate. The Allies, however, most certainly were not, as Donovan found out when he submitted his plan to Chief Prosecutor Jackson. The idea of seeing their carefully prepared mammoth trial going down the drain did not at all appeal to the Allied officials, who were looking forward to months in the spotlight while the case against the accused was being presented to the world.[473]

In a recent interview with Ned Putzell, a former colleague of Donovan's pre-firm law and his senior OSS aide at Nuremberg, stated that Göring had, in the final months of the war, been acting as an OSS informant. Donovan was able to approach and offer concessions to Göring on that basis, which reflected this defendant's disillusionment with Nazi fanaticism:

> Through Donovan, I came to examine Göring during the preparations for the Nuremberg trials . . . A lot of high-ranking Americans believed his heart had not really been in the Nazi cause. Before Hitler killed himself, Göring was already giving vital information to us which I passed on to the president. What was Göring like? I asked Putzell. 'Oh, he could be very charming indeed.' This was a view shared by Hartley Shawcross on the British side, who recollects that Göring repeatedly winked at him during examination. 'Then, again, he might have been acting,' Putzell continues. When I questioned Göring, the plan was to find out whether he had been a truly dedicated Nazi. I don't think he was. Hitler had

472 Schlabrendorff, *op cit*, 262–63. 473 *Ibid*, 263.

> suspected him of disloyalty and other Germans told us that Göring was not a strong supporter.[474]

Later, we shall see that Putzell claimed that Donovan and Göring actually won at least one aspect of their respective battles with Jackson over Göring's treatment at Nuremberg.

Not surprisingly, Donovan's unauthorised dealings with Göring (and Schacht) clashed with Jackson's own ideas, and hence contributed to a growing rift between the two senior prosecutors. On or around 24 November, Jackson sent a stern note to Donovan and other senior staff instructing that:

> No agreement shall be made with any defense council on behalf of this office for the use by the United States of any defendant as a witness except on written authorization. It will be the general policy that no defendant will be used as a witness for the prosecution who does not in advance make a written and signed statement incriminating other defendants against whom other evidence is deemed weak or insufficient to establish guilt.[475]

This conflict over plea-bargaining came into the open in a face-to-face meeting between Donovan and Jackson on 25 November, in which Donovan was told, 'I don't want any deals', because this was an international proceeding tackling profound moral issues. Any conviction based on testimony secured through promises of favourable treatment would be tainted.[476] Donovan's response was to continue to press Jackson in a memorandum to authorise a deal with Göring and Schacht in which both would provide useful testimony. He reminded the Chief Prosecutor that he had already supplied him with copies of letters from these defendants to him, and that he had refused to see Schacht 'until he made it clear what he was prepared to do'. He also emphasised to Jackson that 'Göring has offered to testify before the tribunal' and 'in interviews with him he has already incriminated certain of the defendants'.[477] Donovan stated that he did not want to press Jackson for a decision on the proposed deal with Göring until he had received 'a full written question and answer statement containing the necessary safeguards usually surrounding a confession'. To obtain this, Donovan suggested that Jackson instruct Göring to be made available from Sunday 25 November as required: 'It is not my wish to see him except with his own counsel, who is anxious that I continue to see him. This is damn hard work and if he is to be ready the present momentum must not be lost.'[478]

474 P. Wyatt, 'The quality of mercy', *Spectator*, 1 February 2003.
475 Quoted in Taylor, *op cit*, 183. 476 Quoted in Persico, 1994, *op cit*, 120.
477 Donovan to Jackson, 24 November, quoted in Taylor, *op cit*, 183. 478 *Ibid.*

Donovan also insisted that any documentary evidence produced by the victorious allies would not be sufficient to convince the various audiences for this trial, particularly the German one, that the defendants are guilty. Instead, this required verbal evidence from the former German leaders themselves, particularly Göring.

Up until this point, 25 November, Jackson had stalled with respect to Donovan's proposals for making deals with Göring and Schacht. However, the combination of points of contention prompted the Chief Prosecutor to bring matters to a head by excluding Donovan from participation in the trial.[479] Jackson sent a memo on 26 November that rejected Donovan's proposals for the use of Schacht and Göring as cooperative witnesses outright.[480] Instead, Jackson insisted that, since he had overall responsibility for trial strategy, he would rely largely on 'indisputable documentary proof' produced at the time by the relevant German authorities.[481]

Jackson may also have feared that granting Donovan's requests could open the floodgates for many others. For example, at this time, Jackson was also facing a related proposal to cut a deal with defendant Albert Speer. Speer had offered to trade his technical information on the organisation of a war economy and armaments manufacture, which could prove useful to the Anglo-Americans in the event of a new war with the Soviets, for a period of imprisonment rather than the death sentence. Jackson's firm rebuttal of Donovan's brokerage of deals with selected defendants had not yet filtered down to the prisoners themselves it seemed, and Jackson did not follow up on Speer's request, the implications of which were that this one-time German leader might have been spared a trial.[482]

Informal contacts with Leverkühn and Lahousen

Donovan and Dulles' contacts with the German opposition included individuals with links to Admiral Wilhelm Canaris's Abwehr, which had become one of the focal points for anti-Nazi opposition. As Conot notes with respect to a cooperative prosecution witness, Major General Erwin Lahousen,[483] one of Donovan's opposite numbers in German military intelligence: 'As such

479 Taylor, *op cit*, 184.

480 This is discussed in more detail in the next section.

481 *Ibid*; JXO, *op cit*, 1386–87; Gerhart, *op cit*; Storey, *op cit*, 98; Cave-Brown, *op cit*, 744; Conot, *op cit*, 150–51; Harris, *op cit*, xxxvi.

482 B. Smith, *op cit*, 221; Persico, *op cit*, 121; cf. 'Speer Interrogation', 2 November 1945: NA, RG 238.

483 Lahousen, an Austrian, was to become the first witness for the prosecution at the Nuremberg trials, giving damning evidence against Ribbentrop. He had been head of the second bureau of the German Intelligence Service from 1939 to 1943. Like many senior officers in Canaris's organisation, Lahousen was anti-Nazi and had participated in an aborted pre-war plot to assassinate Hitler.

his name had become familiar to . . . Donovan all the more so because a number of high ranking Abwehr officers had been at the nexus of the opposition to Hitler.'[484] Donovan exploited contacts within German military intelligence, including the German lawyer with connections to the intelligence world, Paul Leverkühn, from Hamburg. During the war, Leverkühn was sent by Canaris to Instanbul, where apparently he made contact with Allied officials. At Nuremberg, Leverkühn had befriended Lahousen, and was used by Donovan as an insider source of evidence regarding defendant von Papen. Leverkühn painted a slightly different impression of this defendant in his five-page signed account he had prepared for Donovan.[485] Leverkühn also maintained that von Papen had defied von Ribbentrop by making other contacts with Americans in an effort to establish peace contacts with the Allies. This report claimed that the Gestapo objected to von Papen's devout Catholicism, and that this defendant had also been embroiled in disputes with Himmler.[486] Donovan had become acquainted with Leverkühn 'several years prior to the war'.[487] Taylor notes that: 'As head of the OSS, Donovan must have known of Leverkühn's Abwehr [military intelligence] activities, and after the war brought him to Nuremberg as a consultant.'[488]

Donovan may well have had prior information on Lahousen and certainly took an interest in him as a potential witness. Although still classified as an enemy prisoner of war, Lahousen was provided with accommodation in the guest house reserved for prosecution witnesses, the same billets that Donovan had provided for Leverkühn.[489] Donovan's Nuremberg files contain a number of copies of interrogations of Lahousen by Colonel Amen and others, possibly indicating that Donovan and his own German consultant von Schlabrendorff were taking a personal interest in cultivating this particular witness.[490]

Although Donovan had requested, and Jackson granted, permission for Donovan to consult with Leverkühn, Jackson accused Donovan of abusing this limited authorisation.[491] Jackson discovered that, on 22 November, Donovan had, through Leverkühn, invited Lahousen to be his dinner guest at his Nuremberg accommodation, even though the General himself was not present for most of the evening.[492] Instead, OSS lawyer Ralph Albrecht was present, together with four women, and apparently there was little or no

484 Conot, *op cit*, 149–50.

485 Leverkühn suggested that Donovan should make contact with Baron von Lersner, a diplomat, and gain other information from Miss Rose, von Papen's secretary of ten years, including his instruction that Leverkühn himself should make contact with Donovan at Turkey.

486 Cornell Collection, *op cit*, Vol. 15, Pt. 2, 43.04.

487 Taylor, *op cit*, 182.

488 *Ibid.*

489 *Ibid.*

490 Cornell Collection, *op cit*, Vol. 16, 11–14, 39.02, 53.034, 61.01

491 Schlabrendorff, *op cit*, 263.

492 Sprecher, 1998, *op cit*, 168.

prosecution business discussed, other than Albrecht asking Lahousen a few questions regarding his former intelligence chief.[493] Lahousen had accepted this offer even though it clashed with a prior arrangement with Richard Sonnenfeldt, one of Colonel Amen's staff.

Lahousen accepted this invitation only after Leverkühn had promised to 'straighten out' the potential snub to Sonnenfeldt.[494] Amen, who of course was in overall charge of the Interrogation Division, had previously questioned Lahousen with Leverkühn acting as his intermediary. Amen was annoyed at Donovan's behaviour regarding these two Germans, and complained strongly to Jackson. Taylor recalls that:

> Innocuous the occasion may have been, but Amen was enraged that Sonnefeldt's appointment with Lahousen had been trumped and suspected that Donovan was trying to steal his star witness. He sharply cross-examined the unhappy Lahousen, who was far from well, and then complained to Jackson.[495]

Sprecher recalls that: 'Clearly Amen saw Donovan as a free-wheeling competitor in dealing with witnesses both before and during the trial.'[496]

Jackson accepted Amen's complaints concerning Donovan. Indeed, perhaps he even exploited these for his purposes in order to seize an opportunity to publicly reprimand Donovan. Four days after the start of the trials, Jackson issued an order prohibiting entertainment of, and negotiations with, all Nazi prisoners. This, as Sprecher notes: 'Appeared to be aimed directly at Donovan.'[497] Dennis Smith's analysis of Donovan's Nuremberg files provides additional details of Donovan's reaction to Jackson's barely veiled and public rebuke, to which the former OSS Director reacted with characteristic defiance:

> The relationship between Jackson and Donovan was not an easy one . . . Jackson, however, did not yield on the question of negotiating with the defendants or their counsel for testimony. Partly in response to Donovan's efforts in that direction . . . Jackson addressed a memorandum to Donovan and other senior staff lawyers that detailed in no uncertain terms the ground rules for dealing with the prisoners of war. This memorandum is among the Donovan Papers now at the Cornell Law Library. A pencilled check next to his name on the list of recipients indicates that it is Donovan's own copy. Under the heading 'Matters which I think may cause criticism and confusion in reference to high-ranking prisoners of war require that the following instructions will be observed,' point two,

493 Taylor, *op cit*, 182 494 *Ibid.* 495 *Ibid*, 183.
496 Sprecher, 1998, *op cit*, 169. 497 *Ibid.*

which has been underlined, reads: 'No social entertaining of any prisoner of war shall be undertaken or permitted by any member of this staff.' In the right-hand margin next to it is a cartoon figure with a smiling face.[498]

Although useful as far as it goes, it remains necessary to supplement Smith's account of Donovan's defiance. It was on 24 November that Jackson sent his memo containing an implicit reprimand to Donovan copied to all senior staff, stating that he was issuing a series of orders regarding, as Smith notes, matters which 'may cause criticism and confusion in reference to high-ranking prisoners'. These included three rules that:[499]

1) No person . . . shall be billeted or reside with any such prisoners of war;
2) [prohibiting entertainment as quoted immediately above by Smith]; and,
3) Such witnesses shall be interrogated, communicated with or interviewed on behalf of this office only be persons authorised in writing to do so.[500]

In other words, Donovan was rebuked for providing prosecution billets for Lahousen and Leverkühn, providing Lahousen with entertainment and, thirdly, for conducting interrogations outside of Amen's directions.

The substance of Jackson's complaint, clarified in a later letter to Donovan personally, was that the former OSS Director had interfered with accepted divisions of responsibility within the OCC by deploying Leverkühn as an intermediary with potential trial witnesses: 'with whom Amen [in charge of all interrogations] had been working under my instruction'.[501] Jackson's objection stemmed partly from his related position on the inappropriateness of being seen to make deals with defendants, their counsel or those who might be indirectly working with them.

Jackson later set out his perception of events in personal correspondence with Donovan on 26 November. In this he stated that: 'I disapprove the use being made of the German lawyer Leverkühn. You told me you were consulting with him and to that I saw no objection.' However, Jackson then pointed out that it was only two days previously that he had learned that Leverkühn 'is living in the house with some of our prisoners of war witnesses with whom Amen has been working under my instructions'. He emphasised that Amen had complained that one of 'his' witnesses, Lahousen, had missed: 'an

498 Dennis Smith, 1999, *op cit*, 1–2499 Taylor, 1992, *op cit*, 182.

500 *Ibid*. The original, which Donovan appears to have annotated on rule 2, is contained in the Cornell Collection.

501 Jackson to Donovan, 26 November, *op cit*.

appointment to complete his written statement', which Leverkühn 'had assumed to set aside' in favour of attendance at a social evening at Donovan's billet.[502] Jackson claimed that this snub to Amen was also an affront to his own authority, especially given that he had never met Leverkühn, let alone employed or otherwise delegated any authority to him. Jackson accused Donovan of entrusting part of his own responsibility as a leading Nazi war crimes prosecutor to a German national whose own interests did not necessarily coincide with those of the Allied prosecutors. According to Jackson:

> From what little I can learn, he was mixed up badly with the Nazis and is not a man who should be trusted with knowledge of our case. His relationship with some of the defendants may not be disinterested. I do not think he should consort with our witnesses and be possessed of information which comes from such association as to what we are doing, trying to prove, etc. Leverkühn must get out of these billets and out of Nuremberg. His presence will cause trouble as sure as night follows day.[503]

Jackson was, at this point, responding to Donovan's challenge head on by reasserting his personal authority by simply issuing orders which would make it clear to the former OSS Director and others who were challenging him that he remained firmly in control and would fight off all contenders by sheer force of his organisational position as Chief Prosecutor. Since Donovan had grown accustomed to commanding a large organisation and having his wishes taken as direct orders for others to obey, it was clear that he was not likely to back down. Hence, during the end of November and early December the various bones of contention were coming to a head. Since neither man was willing to subordinate his own preferred strategy to that of the other, an acrimonious breakdown was fast emerging.

In short, it is possible to identify five points on which Donovan challenged Jackson's authority: the prosecution of the German High Command; the exclusion of the OSS from the economic case; the use of an exclusively documentary approach; the rejection of Donovan's proposals to negotiate plea-bargain type arrangements with defendants Schacht and Göring; and, finally, Jackson's refusal to countenance Donovan's use of Leverkühn as an informant and intermediary within the witness house.

An acrimonious divorce

It appears that each of these elements of dispute discussed immediately above contributed in its own way to the final irretrievable break up of the Jackson–

502 *Ibid.* 503 *Ibid.*

Donovan relationship. Taylor recalls that Donovan personally resented Truman's abolition of the OSS on 20 September 1945, and 'when Donovan rejoined Jackson early in October, he was undoubtedly in a sensitive and unhappy mood'.[504] Taylor's memoir also notes that one of the consequences of the abolition of the OSS was that 'he no longer had the logistic or organizational clout which had theretofore made him so useful to Jackson'.[505] Jackson's controversial General Memorandum No. 5 on 'Trial Organisation', dated 22 October, created a Board of Review chaired by Storey, who was clearly being favoured over Shea, Alderman and of course Donovan. Donovan was not even listed as a member of this new body, which included OSS lawyers such as Ralph Albrecht. Instead, the former OSS Director was initially listed in an earlier draft as one of its 'consultants' (a position he later rejected). Apparently, however, Jackson had not at this stage decided (or at least not made public) any decision to exclude Donovan. Indeed, in private conversation with Shea, Jackson stated that 'a part of the case had to be given to General Donovan to try'.[506]

Additional factors on Donovan's side may have included the influence of members of Donovan's personal staff. In addition to various psychological and interpersonal factors, it is possible that, as he devoted himself full-time to trial preparations and a detailed study of the lengthy indictment finalised in early October, Donovan became increasingly aware of the major flaws in Jackson's trial strategy and administration. Certainly, one of Donovan's expert German consultants and a member of his personal staff, Fabian von Schlabrendorff, frankly expressed his considerable scepticism with the largely retrospective legal basis of the trial (which, for many, perversely duplicated the worse excesses of the Nazis' abuse of legality). He also criticised both Jackson's 'skill' as an administrator and the adequacy of the draft indictment:[507]

> Our way of dealing with the top leaders of the Third Reich would . . . have differed markedly from the way the victorious Allies handled the problem after the war. It was my opinion then . . . that the trials at the International Tribunal would one day be considered a great political mistake, at least by the Western Powers . . . My conviction in this case stems not from any hindsight. On the contrary, I was given the opportunity to express my opinion even before the trials began through my acquaintance with . . . Donovan . . . As the preparation for the trials progressed, Donovan began to have doubts about them. Knowing that I was a jurist, and familiar with my role within the anti-Hitler resistance,

504 Taylor, *op cit*, 148. 505 *Ibid.* 506 Francis Shea's Diary, quoted in *ibid*, 139.

507 Fabian von Schlabrendorff, 1994, *op cit*, 259–61. On 6 October 1945, the Chief Prosecutors had published their joint statement of indictment.

> he wanted to get my professional opinion and asked me to come to Nuremberg to look at the draft of the indictment . . . I accepted that invitation, and spent some time carefully studying the lengthy draft Donovan gave to me. After going over the entire document word by word, I set down my professional opinion rejecting the entire indictment on four counts: 1) It used retrospective law . . . 2) The indictment was based on Anglo-Saxon trial law . . . 3) The accusations dealt exclusively with offenses against *Allied* citizens . . . 4) The accusers were also the judges . . . After reading my memorandum on the draft, Donovan was more than ever convinced that he had been right in questioning the wisdom of the trials. He began to search for ways of shortening and limiting the proceedings as much as possible.[508]

Taylor's memoir also recalls a growing pattern of tension over a series of issues, including the preparation of the High Command and economic cases, and the policy of regarding witness testimony.[509] However, of the factors previously examined it was, perhaps, Donovan's plans for the deployment of Göring and Schacht as cooperative witnesses that represented the most serious challenge to Jackson's largely documentary approach. Therefore, it is not surprising that this element provided the spark which ignited the explosion between these two men. It is possible that, if we take the various points already discussed together, Donovan was in effect making a sustained bid to challenge and even ultimately displace Jackson from his leadership role in determining prosecution strategy.

Donovan had made no secret of his opinion that the case required more administrative control, intellectual direction, and cohesiveness. Indeed, Sprecher's memoir provides a clear example of Donovan relying upon the personal loyalty of former OSS officials seconded to the OCC in ways that were, strictly speaking, improper, and were perhaps consistent with the actions of someone who had become almost a leader of internal dissent within the OCC:

> When I first met General Donovan in Nuremberg . . . he asked me if I could obtain for him translations of the different oaths by which Party members, government officials, and soldiers pledged loyalty to Adolph Hitler. I was delighted to perform this service although I was not assigned to work for General Donovan and, strictly speaking, he should have requested Colonel Storey, my Chief in the Documentation Division,

508 *Ibid*, 262.

509 Colonel Telford Taylor went onto present the prosecution case against the German High Command on 4 January 1946 in an impressive manner that led to his appointment as lead prosecutor in later Nuremberg trials or 'Subsequent Proceedings'.

> if I could perform this service for him. Within a day or so I sent Donovan a memorandum with the translations he requested. At Donovan's request I also gathered some notes for him which were taken from the German military manual . . . for his use in interrogating General Walter Warlimont, former Deputy Chief of the Armed Forces Operations Staff . . . I was greatly pleased with the minor assistance I provided Donovan . . .[510]

The first two weeks of the trial witnessed the 'final rupture' between Jackson and Donovan. For his part, Jackson's letter of 26 November, replying to Donovan's earlier challenge, brought the entire range of issues discussed above to a head. Jackson frankly acknowledged that Donovan had opposed the key parts of his trial strategy, and – in his work with Göring and other witnesses – had refused, unlike other prosecutors, to provide a detailed written account of the testimony they were willing to provide. In that way, Donovan had adopted an attitude of defiance by pursuing a policy of turning Göring, for example, into a prosecution witness in return for some concession, a plea-bargaining policy which Jackson had every reason to reject as improper. Jackson claimed that there had emerged fundamental differences between their view of the place of witness testimony and the legitimacy of deals with defendants and witnesses. Hence, he could not trust Donovan to play the very public starring role he had long envisaged for himself as cross-examiner of Göring, Schacht and others:

> Obviously if the work you are doing with witnesses or with such a defendant as Göring reflects this attitude, it is at odds with the policy of the case as settled in the indictment and may result in serious embarrassment . . . In short, I do not think that we can afford to negotiate with any of these defendants or their counsel for testimony. We have interrogated them extensively and I would put some parts of some interrogations in evidence, but I would not put one of the defendants on the stand as our witness. To use one of them ourselves will create the impression that there was some kind of bargain about his testimony, opening the door to that defendant to plead for leniency on the ground that he was 'helpful' and may give a background for claims that promises were made to that effect. My view is, therefore, that we should prove our case against these defendants with no use of them as witnesses. I have instructed our own Dr Kempner that we will have no negotiations on such matters, either with defendants or their counsel, despite the fact that one of them approached him with an offer to testify. I know that 'turning of state's

510 Sprecher, 1998, *op cit*, 167–68, citing a memorandum Sprecher to Donovan of 15 October 1945.

> evidence' would be dramatic and sensational – but I think it better for the reputation of our case that each defendant do any confessing on his own behalf not on ours.[511]

Donovan's formal request to further question Göring in preparation for his planned dramatic cross-examination of this defendant was rejected out of hand, with Jackson curtly telling the former OSS Director that: 'I won't be able to use you in any position of prominence when the trial begins. We just don't see eye to eye.'[512] Jackson closed the letter by stating: 'Frankly Bill, your views and mine appear to be so far apart that I do not consider it possible to assign to you examination or cross-examination of witnesses. Therefore I did not respond to your request for access to Göring.'[513]

In effect, Jackson's letter slammed the door shut on Donovan being able to play any meaningful role in the trials. This uncompromising stance derailed the goals that the former OSS Director had been working towards at least since his return from the Far East in mid-September.

Donovan did not take his marginalisation well. The following day, he replied with his own memorandum attempting to rebut Jackson's criticisms on a point-by-point basis. Donovan claimed that several of Jackson's conclusions were based on misunderstandings of both his actions and intentions. With respect to Leverkühn, he insisted that both Amen and Jackson had already been told 'all I know about him'. And that both had previously stated that he 'would be useful and he has been'. Donovan repeated his view that Jackson was at fault for discounting out of hand evidence of the positive value that securing a public confession and incriminating testimony from Göring could exert upon both the trial and its historical significance.[514] He insisted:

> It is true that I have frequently told you squarely and honestly that (1) the case needed centralised administrative control. (2) that there was a lack of intellectual direction. (3) that it was not handled as an entity (4) that because it was a lawsuit plus something else it needed an affirmative human aspect with German as well as foreign witnesses. I never knew that there was disagreement on these points. As I told you several weeks ago I am leaving within a few days. Time will not be concerned with our opinions – right or wrong.[515]

511 Jackson to Donovan, 26 November 1945: Truman Museum and Library, Nuremberg Collection: http://www.trumanlibrary.org.

512 This letter together with the others is contained in a bundle of correspondence Jackson sent to Truman in December 1945 to cover himself from the fallout from his dispute with Donovan: Jackson to Truman, 1 December 1945, Jackson Papers, *op cit*, Box 101.

513 *Ibid.* 514 *Ibid*, cf. Sprecher, 1998, *op cit*, 169.

515 Donovan to Jackson, 26 November 1945, in Jackson to Truman, 1 December, *op cit*.

At the end of November, just after the trial had opened, Donovan began to pay farewell visits. He further intrigued against Jackson, even over dinner with one of the American judges, Francis Biddle. He complained that the opening days of the trial which had been based on the recitation of documents had, as he had warned, been flat and lacked human interest.[516] Donovan argued, once again, that Göring should now be introduced as a witness to face questioning to reinvigorate proceedings and presumably be cross-examined by Donovan himself in line with the private discussions.[517] He further complained that one reason why the prosecution case was incoherent was that Jackson had proved himself to be a poor administrator, and that he had raised these issues personally with Jackson but had been unreasonably rebuffed.[518] Biddle recalled that: '[He] is eager to get Jackson to put on Göring, who he thinks would come through.'[519]

The British and American press reported Donovan's departure, with the British media, which had become critical of the American contribution to date, siding mainly with Donovan.[520] Apparently, Donovan began to use his contacts with the American media to start a campaign against Jackson, particularly with respect to his policy concerning the High Command case. He encouraged hostile media coverage that cited the outrage of unnamed American military officers regarding Jackson's plan to establish guilt only by reference to membership of the German High Command. Such coverage began to appear from 26 November 1945, even within the influential *New York Times*. This coverage presented Donovan's arguments against Jackson as reflecting widespread military opinion. Taylor notes that: 'Comparable attacks in other periodicals, some referring by name to General Donovan, subsequently appeared.'[521]

Neither man had an interest in publicising the details of their personal dispute. Donovan may not have wanted it known that he had been sacked, whilst Jackson had no interest in making public the presence of dissension within his organisation.[522] According to Sprecher, once again:

> Donovan decided to leave Nuremberg. He did so quietly, . . . So far as I have learned, neither Jackson not Donovan spoke publicly about their falling out. When I asked Jim Donovan why General Donovan had left, he replied he had important work to do in winding down OSS. Otherwise Jim Donovan was tight-lipped about a matter of which he clearly had additional knowledge.[523]

516 Taylor, *op cit*, 185. 517 Persico, 1994, *op cit*, 121. 518 *Ibid.*

519 Biddle Letter, 28 November 1945: University of Syracuse, New York, George Arents Research Library, Francis Biddle Collection, Box 14, trial documents.

520 Taylor, *op cit*, 238 521 *Ibid*, 185. 522 Taylor, *op cit*, 185.

523 Sprecher, 1998, *op cit*, 169.

Whilst Donovan witnessed the first days of the trials, and left Nuremberg shortly after Jackson's opening statement, Sprecher recalls: 'At the time the nature of the conflict was unclear to most of us junior prosecutors.' During Jackson's opening speech to the IMT, Donovan sat 'near the head of the prosecution table'. This continued to give the impression to less senior colleagues, such as Sprecher, that: 'I had every expectation that Donovan, among other things, would interrogate some of the German officials he had been questioning. Junior members of staff often know little of what goes on amongst their superiors.'[524]

Schlabrendorff has provided a graphic account of the upshot of final face-to-face confrontation between Donovan and Jackson, and Donovan's attempt to extract revenge by encouraging OSS-affiliated staff to leave Nuremberg:

> When I next saw Donovan, he was shaking with anger and frustration after what had evidently been a stormy session with . . . Jackson. He told me that he was resigning from his post as deputy prosecutor because he did not want to be in any way connected with the coming trials; he had become thoroughly convinced that they were legally and politically unsound. He also suggested it would be wise for me to get out of Nuremberg at once – advice I took no time in following.[525]

Donovan also encouraged OSS loyalists amongst the potential trial lawyers, such as Murray Gurfein, to leave Nuremberg just at the trials were opening, which a number did.[526]

Whether in fact Donovan resigned on a point of principle – as he claimed – or had been effectively dismissed for blatant defiance and subversion of Jackson's trial strategy, is open to dispute. This question is complicated by the fact that the memoirs of the parties and contemporary correspondence do not clarify the precise timing and sequence of events. What is certain is that on 26 November, Jackson's memo effectively marginalised, and in this sense dismissed, Donovan. Jackson claimed he could not risk Donovan hijacking the presentation of trial evidence in a way that would prove impossible for him to recover from. Instead, he was to entrust this role to others, including Amen, with whom Donovan was in dispute but who had respected Jackson's own official policy:

> Now the question as between you and John Amen as to which shall examine and cross-examine defendants and witnesses is not simply a personal one, or one of military rank. He has been for months at work with these defendants and witnesses. So far as I know, John has worked

524 *Ibid*, 170. 525 Schlabrendorff, *op cit*, 263 526 Taylor, *op cit*, 185, 387.

> fully in accord with my view of the policy of the case. You and I both know that the slant of counsel who examine and cross-examine a witness often determines the whole slant and effect of his testimony. Once an adverse attitude is developed at the bar by an associate, it will be almost impossible for me to alter it.[527]

Realising that he had been defeated, Donovan attended the reading of the indictment, assisted Jackson only briefly by countermanding a military order restricting Jackson's movements, and left Germany in early December. He took with him a collection of documents, some of which form part of his newly discovered collection at Cornell Law School.[528] Despite the considerable support Donovan had provided to Jackson, he therefore played no role in the presentation of trial evidence. As Gerhart notes: 'Donovan returned to the United States. Although he had been selected by Jackson as one of the top trial lawyers, he never made an appearance before the International Military Tribunal.'[529]

During early 1946, Donovan also concealed his Nuremberg war crimes files by having these hidden away in the back of his law firm's vaults. Here they remained undiscovered for over 50 years, possibly to the detriment of continuing prosecution work. On the other hand, from the point of view of historians, this at least preserved the Nuremberg collection from the vagaries of the CIA's selective and phased declassification programmes, which continues to affect all other OSS records relating to war crimes issues. His removal and concealment of this collection represents both one episode within the wider drama of Donovan's fraught involvement within the Nuremberg process, and part of a wider tendency to entrench the OSS's legacy.[530]

Donovan threatened to subvert and discredit Jackson's management of the case in the eyes of senior government officials in Washington by deploying the services of a public relations firm. On 1 December 1945, Justice Jackson

527 Jackson to Donovan, 26 November, *op cit*.

528 JXO *op cit*, 1366–67; Persico, *op cit*, 134.

529 Gerhart, *op cit*, 359.

530 Donovan was particularly concerned to rule the legacy of his wartime agency, even from beyond the grave, by encouraging a series of official and semi-official historical projects both recording the positive achievements of his embattled agency, and identifying the lessons that a sympathetic historical reconstruction of its legacy could hold for its various successor agencies, such as the CIA and US Army's Special Forces. Donovan succeeded in prompting a genre of celebratory writings on the emergence and legacy of the OSS, and hence the origins of the CIA, that continued long after his death. Donovan's decision to misappropriate this collection may be explained in part by this wider motivation to exercise 'information-control' over the post-war interpretation of his agency's legacy. Donovan's own place in history depended, in part, on his ability to protect this legacy from the threat of its oblivion, or hostile reinterpretation, by those rival government institutions, such as the US State Department, that had already swallowed up surviving aspects of the OSS.

sought to protect himself from the resulting hostile media coverage and wider repercussions stemming, according to Taylor, from 'Donovan's political and military eminence'[531] by sending copies of their correspondence directly to President Truman.[532] He explained to Truman that the source of the conflict lay in Donovan's over-inflated ego and unwillingness to contribute to a team effort unless he was made captain of that team: 'When I asked him to work with me, I was repeatedly told that he would not work in second place to anybody . . . But he was the head of the OSS and I needed what help that organisation could give.'[533] Jackson further argued that Donovan's absence over the crucial summer months had meant that he had become 'entirely out of touch' with how the case was developing, and implied that the General's alternative strategy was also out of step with how Jackson and the remainder of the latter's senior colleagues were approaching their tasks. Hence, the morale of such staff had improved following Donovan's decision to depart: 'except a few of his organisation members whom I could do without if necessary'.[534] Allegedly 'since he came back, his ideas and mine of handling the case were far apart. They were so far apart that I had to tell him that I would not put him on the floor to conduct any part of the case.'[535] Jackson insisted that his decision to dismiss Donovan was not a mistake.[536] Truman forwarded Jackson's memo to the State Department with the terse comment that it was 'self-explanatory'.[537] In private correspondence, with his wife, Jackson noted that if Donovan or his friends 'want to ruin him, let them keep on talking, I have enough in writing to take care of him. Have sent it all to the President. But it will all probably all die out in a few days – I stay and he moves on; so why worry.'[538] Three weeks later, Jackson wrote again bitterly complaining that Donovan had been sabotaging his work: 'He was a skunk . . . Too long to particularise, but I simply could not let him take part in a case he was sabotaging. If he ever starts anything, God help him.'[539]

During the second half of December 1945, Jackson placed Donovan under indirect pressure to return official documentation that he, Bill Whitney, Shelden Glueck (OSS academic consultant)[540] and Murray Bernays had allegedly taken away with them, including incomplete sets of UN War Crimes Commission files. Jackson sent a note to Sheldon Glueck, advising him that:

> General Donovan and Murray Bernays have received sharp complaint from United Nations War Crimes Commission, London, that Prof.

531 Taylor, *op cit*, 185.
532 Jackson to Truman, 1 December 1945, Jackson Papers, Box 101.
533 *Ibid.*
534 *Ibid.*
535 *Ibid.*
536 *Ibid.*
537 Taylor, *op cit*, 185.
538 Jackson to Irene, 20 December 1945, Jackson Papers, Box 2.
539 *Ibid*, 6 January, 1946.
540 On Glueck's role, see Hagan and Greer, 'Making War Criminal' (2002) 30 *Criminology* 231–64.

> Glueck has turned over to Harvard Law Library incomplete set of Commissions Minutes and documents and the Library has asked Sweet and Maxwell Law Publishers to secure missing numbers . . . there will be serious repercussions from passing them on . . . They make the same request with reference to sets furnished [by] my office for use of General Donovan and Colonel Bernays. The international character of the War Crimes Commission makes this matter of more than ordinary serious concern . . .[541]

Jackson discovered that Donovan was set to return from Paris to the US in mid-December, and he had an official from the US Army attempt to 'secure' any UNWCC documents he was taking away with him before he left Europe, but this message arrived too late. However, Donovan's office was contacted and 'request submitted'.[542] The tone of Jackson's telegram expressed continuing annoyance and even appeared to imply that Donovan had stolen secret state documents.[543] Jackson may well have been exploiting this issue to further embarrass Donovan and other OSS staff who had left with him, particularly given that he personally sent the memos on a technical matter that surely could have been safely delegated to an administrative subordinate. Certainly, Captain Norden, Donovan's senior administrative aide at Nuremberg, replied in defensive and somewhat less than frank terms that:

> I as aide to Gen. Donovan had charge of his files at Nuremberg. Gen. Donovan on his departure instructed me to return all documents and interrogations being studied by him to the respective sections and certain specific papers to Col. Storey. I acted accordingly . . . Whitney had charge of all papers turned over by the commission and all such papers were delivered by Whitney to Bernays in July and August. I shipped all the General's personal papers to the States, but I am not aware of any documents other than General Donovan's handwritten notes in those papers.[544]

The last sentence is blatantly untrue, as the Cornell Collection contains many hundreds of official OCC documents in addition to Donovan's personal handwritten notes.

541 OCC, Nuremberg to War Department, 12 December 1945: NA, RG 238, Entry 52F, Folder 18-MC-IN.

542 WARCOS to Jackson, 13 December: NA, RG 238, Entry 52F, Folder 18-MC-OUT.

543 'Jackson gravely concerned over secret documents, property United Nations War Crimes Commission London in possession of General Donovan for use in preparation of the Nuremberg case and desires immediate return by General.' WARCOS to OCC from Griggs, WCL 28777, 12 December 1945: NA, RG 238, Entry 52F, Folder 18-MC-OUT.

544 OCC (Paris) to War Dep't, 15 December 1945: NA, RG 238, Entry 52F, Folder 18-MC-IN.

Amongst the summaries that Jackson received of newspaper coverage of the trials was a brief report that 'Gen. Donovan returned to the US and declined any statement to the press'.[545] Jackson received a letter in March 1946 warning him that Donovan was seeking a public relations specialist to discredit Jackson's management of the trials.[546] It is possible that immediately after the trials had concluded, Donovan intervened indirectly once more through remaining OSS staff to ensure that Göring was in fact rewarded for his earlier cooperation with Donovan. In the interview with Putzell, his former senior OSS aide at Nuremberg quoted earlier, it was stated:

> But he was condemned, nonetheless, I retorted. Putzell nods 'Yes, but Donovan secretly decided, with the agreement of the British contingent, to let him die by cyanide. Göring had been very co-operative with us and he genuinely did seem deserving of some sort of mercy.' How did they get hold of the cyanide? I was surprised by the answer. 'Everyone in active service in the OSS was given a cyanide pill in case they were captured by the Germans and tortured. So we had quite a few on us.' Putzell and a colleague handed one tablet to Göring. How did he react? Putzell laughs gutturally. 'I think he was glad to have it. It was better than being hanged.' Much better as it turned out. Some of the hangings were botched horribly.[547]

Whilst there is little independent confirmation of the claim that it was the OSS which had provided the cyanide, this interview with one of Donovan's senior aides at Nuremberg does provide additional support to the view that Donovan was negotiating with Göring, that the latter had proved cooperative and may even have received some element of reward. James Donovan continued to write to the former OSS Director after he departed the trials and remarked, perhaps maliciously, on certain academic criticisms of the legal basis of the trials, and pointed out press reports on the embarrassment that Jackson had suffered at the hands of Göring during the latter's cross-examination. Given that General Donovan had sought this role for himself, presumably his junior namesake would have thought that he would have received some delayed satisfaction at the public humiliation that Jackson suffered on that occasion.[548]

545 WARCOS to Dean for Jackson for info from Griggs, WCL 30401, 18 December 1945: NA, RG 238, Entry 52F, Folder 18-MC-OUT.

546 Horsky to Jackson: now only listed in note as 'Papers desired RHJ Files' in Jackson Papers, *op cit*, Box 2.

547 Wyatt, *op cit*.

548 James Donovan to William Donovan, 4 June 1946: James Donovan Papers, Hoover Institute.

Was either leader proved right?

Smith argues that Jackson's approach, which prevailed notwithstanding the objections of Donovan and others, was ultimately vindicated by the final judgment of the IMT itself. He quotes the following extract from this judgment delivered on 1 October 1946:

> Much of the evidence presented to the Tribunal on behalf of the Prosecution was documentary evidence, captured by the Allied Armies in German army headquarters, Government buildings, and elsewhere. Some of the documents were found in salt mines, buried in the ground, hidden behind false walls and in other places. The case, therefore, against the defendants rests in large measure on documents of their own making, the authenticity of which has not been challenged except in one or two cases.[549]

This interpretation also receives strong support from the memoirs of Telford Taylor. Taylor seeks to exonerate Justice Jackson from any suggestion that he drove away Donovan, his senior deputy; and that Donovan's proposal to enter into negotiations with Schacht and Göring was clearly superior to Jackson's reliance upon documentary evidence:

> In my opinion Jackson was quite right [to claim he had to dismiss Donovan] . . . Although I was in general agreement with Donovan's view that the American case should include witnesses, his proposals with regard to Göring and Schacht were ill conceived and dangerous. Each of the two would gladly have seen the other boiled in oil, and if called by the prosecution would have tried to strip the other of whatever shreds of credibility he still retained. Efforts to tie them down to prepared question-and-answer statements would have collapsed under the pressure of cross-examination, and reliance on prior undertakings by Göring would have been about as sensible as entering into a no-first-strike treaty with a cobra.[550]

While there is clearly some merit in Taylor's concerns, this position underestimates the extent to which the reward for cooperating with the prosecution remained conditional upon compliance with the prior undertakings, and that neither Schacht nor Göring would have had any self-interest in departing from the prepared script controlled by the prosecution. Furthermore, even if they had showed signs of behaving as Taylor predicted, then, as prosecution witnesses, they could simply have been instructed by Jackson to cease giving evidence. On the basis of their actual performances

549 5 IMT, 1946, 163. 550 Taylor, 1992, *op cit*, 186.

at Nuremberg, which were forceful, it is unlikely that either man would have been crushed by defence counsel cross-examination, particularly given that the German lawyers were not trained in this particular common law skill.

Taylor has, however, provided additional moral and political objections to Donovan's proposals regarding Göring in particular, which perhaps have greater force:

> But the issue lay deeper than the hatred between Göring and Schacht. With Hitler, Himmler and Goebbels dead, Göring was the surviving leader and symbol of Nazism. To put him forward as the man who could tell the truth about the Third Reich and lay bare the guilt of its leaders, as Donovan appeared to expect, was nothing short of ludicrous. To his fellow defendants and everyone else Göring had made it clear that his aim was to defend the record of the Nazi years and discredit the trial, to the best of his ability. 'To set a thief to catch a thief' may be a useful tactic for a district attorney fighting gangland. But summoning Göring to speak, in any other role than that of an accused murderer being given the opportunity to defend himself, could have no place in an avowedly idealistic proceeding dedicated to the future peace of the world and the advancement of international human rights.[551]

Yet again there are possible counter-arguments. Göring was surely as well placed as any surviving Nazi leader to reveal the inner workings of Hitler's regime. Furthermore, whilst it is true that Göring did defend the regime in his trial testimony, this was very much his plan B. There is no reason to believe that, as an immoral cynic, he would not have come through with equal force for the prosecution. What is more, the prosecution of Ribbentrop relied heavily on the posthumous testimony of another fascist leader, the brutally frank and highly incriminating diaries of Count Ciano, Mussolini's son-in-law and Foreign Minister. The prosecutors had no moral compunction in relying upon this testimony of a committed fascist, and accepting that even a fascist can record their experiences of fascism in a credible manner.

Taylor's interpretation has been accepted as fact by legal commentators. For example, Douglas states:

> Jackson in particular favored the use of captured documentary evidence, material he considered 'harder'; and less vulnerable to being discredited by defense attorneys practiced at the art of tendentious cross-examination. Prosecution counsel William Donovan's vehement argument that a greater reliance upon eyewitness testimony would have provided the trial

551 Taylor, *op cit*, 186.

with 'an affirmative human aspect' led to his unceremonious removal from the prosecution team after the first week of the trial.[552]

Douglas does not appear to appreciate that the German lawyers representing the defendants were experienced only in civil law regimes, where criminal trials do not entail the cross-examination of witnesses. By contrast, the US and British prosecutors, whose experience stemmed from common law legal systems, were highly experienced in the techniques and strategies of cross-examination. Hence, one of the so-called 'objections' to Donovan's position should be reinterpreted as an effort to exploit a real weakness amongst the defendants. Furthermore, it could equally be argued that Donovan's proposals for adopting a trial strategy which combined testimonial and documentary evidence was never in fact attempted, and that there is little reason to believe that it would not have been equally successful.[553]

Gerhart has provided a more balanced assessment of the relative arguments, noting that: 'There is little doubt that the trial would have been more glamorous had the Donovan view prevailed.' Yet he ultimately sides with Jackson on the basis that Donovan's alternative strategy would have resulted in a 'weaker case', not only with respect to the trial proceedings but also regarding the creation of an authentic, permanent and indisputable record generated by German officials confronting the German people with the grim and tragic consequences of their popular endorsement of Nazism.[554] On the other hand, with respect to the *specifically political* objectives of the trial, particularly the concerted indictment of an entire system of racist ideology and repressive governance from the very mouths of its former leaders, Donovan's proposals may have proved even more successful particularly in capturing the attention of the German media and, more importantly, the German population. This suggestion, of course, can only be speculation, given that the only approach that the prosecution team implemented was that proposed by Jackson.

Neither of the two men ever put on record their side of the conflict, with Jackson glossing over the dispute in his various writings on the trials. However, Schlabrendorff has recalled that Donovan remained bitter over Jackson's treatment of his alternative plan for years afterwards: 'Years later in New York, Donovan told me that he was more than ever convinced that history would justify his decision to walk out on the Nuremberg trials.'[555] Schlabrendorff clearly supported this view, and pointed to the various problems of delay, and the farce of having Russian prosecutors blame the

552 See L. Douglas, 'Film as Witness: Screening Nazi Concentration Camps Before the Nuremberg Tribunal' (1995) 105 *Yale Law Journal*. 449–50, 451, n. 10; based partly on Taylor, 1992, *op cit*, 146–49.

553 See Bradley Smith, 1978, *op cit*, 175–76, 285, where Smith supports Donovan's plans over those of Jackson.

554 Gerhart, *op cit*, 359–60.

555 Schlabrendorff, *op cit*, 264.

Nazis for the Katyn Forest massacre of captured Polish soldiers which their own officers had, in fact, committed – a contradiction that Donovan had previously warned Jackson about.

Although the General was present at Nuremberg only for the first three weeks of the trial, the transcript of the trial itself indicates aspects of his contribution that do not appear to have been noticed within either the OSS or Nuremberg scholarship to date. First, there is evidence from the proceedings of 5 March 1946 that Donovan, together with von Schlabrendorff and Murray Gurfein,[556] was gathering correspondence from Schacht. This was material that Schacht's defence lawyer, Dr Rix, was anxious to introduce into evidence:

> DR. RIX: Before the recess, I was about to tell the Tribunal, as to Number 2 of the list of documents, that in my presentation I would confine myself to really important and quite short quotations, after having made them available to the Prosecution in our document book . . . I now turn to Number 3, Subparagraph (a), which is the Schacht memorandum to Hitler of 3 May 1935 concerning the legal rights of Jews, dissolution of the Gestapo, *et cetera*. May I again ask the Prosecution to see to it as far as possible that this document, which has not been introduced so far, be procured together with Document 1168-PS, which at the time of Schacht's interrogation by Colonel Gurfein was produced. As I heard yesterday, the document has not yet been found, but perhaps Colonel Gurfein, who has already gone back, can assist us in this matter. These two documents are very important, as they constitute parts of a Schacht memorandum which can be understood and appreciated only in its entirety. Furthermore, here is a letter addressed by Schacht to General Field Marshal Von Blomberg. It deals with restriction of armaments, *et cetera*, and its relevancy is, I think, obvious . . . Then there is the letter written by Schacht to Göring in November 1942. Göring's answer was to dismiss Schacht for defeatism, or rather in consequence of this letter Schacht was dismissed for defeatism. A further consequence of this letter was that Göring excluded him from the Prussian State Council. A copy of this letter was last seen by Schacht in the possession of one Von Schlaberndorff, who worked with General Donovan, but who is no longer here. Where Schlabrendorff is now, I do not know. May I ask the Prosecution to assist us also in this matter. Furthermore, there is a telegram of January 1943 from Göring to Schacht, excluding him from the State Council.[557]

Towards the latter half of the trial in June 1946, General Donovan's role in securing anti-Nazi witnesses also became contentious in relation to the

556 As already noted, Gurfein was a former OSS official.

557 8 IMT, Tuesday 5 March 1946, am session, 555–56.

damaging evidence supplied against Göring and others by the former OSS intelligence source Hans Gisevius.

> SIR DAVID MAXWELL FYFE: 'The next applications from the Defendants Hess and Frank to put an interrogatory to General Donovan. If I may put the objection quite shortly, that raises the same point as the application on 2 May 1946 for Mr. Patterson of the United States War Department. The objection of the Prosecution is the same as I made on that occasion, that when you are cross-examining a witness as to credibility you are bound by his answer, and should not, in the opinion of the Prosecution, be allowed to call evidence to contradict him. So it is on exactly the same point, the relationship between the witness Gisevius and the United States Office of Strategic Services.[558]

This objection was accepted by the IMT.[559] However, the Gisevius/OSS relationship remained controversial, at least as far as a number of the Nuremberg defence lawyers were concerned. For example, Dr Seidl, defence counsel for defendants Hans Frank and Rudolf Hess, sought to impugn Gisevius's testimony because of his status as a 'traitor' to the German state based upon his assistance to the OSS, the intelligence service of a foreign state with whom his nation was at war. As the following extract makes clear, Seidel insisted the credibility of Gisevius's testimony depended in part upon his integrity as a person. This, in turn, could only be established by means of an interrogatory with General Donovan, with whose organisation Gisevius had enjoyed a long-standing relationship:

> THE PRESIDENT: And with reference to Hess and Frank, as to Gisevius's evidence, Dr. Seidl, do you wish to say anything about that?
>
> DR. SEIDL: Mr. President, the application regarding the obtaining of official information from the Minister of War was made for the sole purpose of obtaining evidence as to the credibility of the witness Gisevius. Afterwards I made another application to examine Secretary of War Patterson by means of an interrogatory dealing with the same subject. On the following day I made an application to examine the Chief of the OSS, General Donovan, also by means of an interrogatory. I think that this new application is in the hands of the Tribunal. I have made this further application only because the first named witness, Patterson, was Minister of War for only a comparatively short period, and because it seemed helpful to have the chief of that organization himself as an additional witness ... The Tribunal does not appear to be bound by any

558 15 IMT, 3 June 1946, 286. 559 *Ibid*, 8 June 1946, 41.

> particular rules in dealing with the question of additional witnesses in connection with the credibility of other witnesses . . .
>
> THE PRESIDENT: One moment, Dr. Seidl. Do the questions which you wish to put with reference to the witness Gisevius relate solely to credibility?
>
> DR. SEIDL: In my written application I have already said that as far as I am concerned, it is not a question of whether in certain circumstances the witness Gisevius was guilty of an action which from the German legal standpoint might constitute the crime of treason. I only put that question in connection with the examination of the credibility of the witness before the Tribunal.
>
> THE PRESIDENT: That is what I thought.[560]

These various attempts to discredit the damning evidence of one of Donovan's double-agents by emphasising his 'traitorous' connection with the OSS were rejected by the judges. As a result, Donovan was not required to provide evidence at the request of the defence counsel. This surely would have been the final indignity for the former OSS Director.

Conclusion

Donovan's wartime role meant that his increasingly conflictual relationship with Jackson can – at one level – be interpreted as a case study of more general tensions and contradictions that can arise from this remarkable form of institutional collaboration between official bodies with contrasting roles and governed by different institutional imperatives.[561] In other words, it may be fruitful to consider the positive and negative dimensions of the Jackson–Donovan relationship as raising, in microcosm, a series of issues that could be of wider significance regarding other examples of cooperation between war crimes prosecutors and senior intelligence officials.

560 *Ibid*, 11 May, 1946, 330–31.

561 These more general contradictions have been analysed in detail in I. Bryan and M. Salter, 'War crimes prosecutors and intelligence agencies: The case for assessing their collaboration' (2001) 16 *Intelligence and National Security* 93–120; M. Salter, 'The Prosecution of Nazi War Criminals and the OSS: The Need for a New Research Agenda' (2002) 2 *Journal of Intelligence History* 77–119.

Summation: taking stock

What are the implications of the various points and arguments discussed and advanced in this book? One must surely be the importance of researchers placing the *ad hoc* and occasional immunity deals for a small number of Nazi war crimes suspects in the context of a far more extensive history of the active contributions of other intelligence officials. Failure to appreciate this wider context risks misrepresenting the exception as the norm. This misrepresentation could, in turn, create the false impression that historical research had taught the lesson that prosecutors should avoid *any* inter-agency collaboration with intelligence officials agencies because the latter will only exploit such liaisons to subvert legality.

The implications of this conclusion are significant. With respect to the legal response to many cases of atrocities, such as those that were committed in former Yugoslavia, we must give credit to civilian and military intelligence agencies for playing a vital role in gathering evidence through electronic intercepts, agents and satellite surveillance that would not otherwise have been available to the prosecutors. Yet, we must also recognise the possibility of there being a 'down side' to allowing such close collaboration.[1] Given that Wolff gained legal immunity at least partly through Dulles' direct interventions within the Nuremberg process, then this and related cases must be considered as a major breach of one of the key liberal principles supposedly underpinning the entire Nuremberg and related war crimes trials: the need to reinstate and consistently apply a liberal conception of the rule of law following a period of extended state lawlessness and dictatorship.

On the other hand, it is possible to adopt a more challenging and broadly 'realist' understanding of the character of sovereign power. This insists upon the priority of the political realm over that of law. The implications of adopting this realist view are to put in question the vanities of liberal constitutional expectations regarding the 'normality' of 'rule of law', defined as the supremacy of legality over sovereign state power. If we follow this line of

1 Bryan and Salter, *op cit*; Salter, 2002, *op cit*.

interpretation, then the issues highlighted by the Wolff case would need to be reframed somewhat differently. The agenda would have to switch away from predictable displays of moral outrage at how US intelligence officials subverted legality (understood as liberal 'due process', rule-governed decision making and 'corrective justice') with respect to those who ordered or otherwise participated in acts of genocide.

Instead, we would need to adopt a more coldly analytical, socio-legal concern with the empirical details of how, that is, through what practices, different types of institutional dynamics and exchanges can open up, and then sustain, various zones of lawlessness with impunity. Immunity deals for war criminals that take place within these law-free zones can certainly be interpreted as the 'exception' (albeit in the merely quantitative sense of the term). However, it must also be recognised that their very 'exceptionality' (in the founding qualitative sense) implicitly determines, from the start and throughout, the de-politicised dreamscape of constitutional 'normality'. Yet this is a spurious 'normality' infatuated with its own deluded expectations of the legal process as reflecting a constitutionally authorised, law-governed and law-centred form of state power within a government lacking substantial sovereignty.

A third, less challenging but perhaps more politically 'responsible' reaction would be for researchers and others to accept that immunity deals for war criminals brokered by intelligence agencies contradict traditional standards and widely prevailing expectations regarding the rule of law. One could then explore, through the methods of 'immanent criticism' associated with the Frankfurt School of Critical Theory (associated with Neumann, Marcuse and Adorno), the nature, sources and implications of these various contradictions internal to the liberal-democratic world view. For instance, one could discuss the contradiction between liberal principles of equal treatment for all, and actual cases where intelligence agencies granted privileged treatment in pursuit of their own agendas with respect to alleged Nazi war criminals. Such immanent criticism would remain resolutely agnostic as to the ultimate theoretical and moral validity of these liberal constitutional expectations themselves. However, those who adopt such a stance would thereby lay themselves open to the charge of being incapable of establishing, through a combination of theoretical argumentation and empirical research, a clear order of rank between competing theoretical assumptions as to the relationship between law and society. Such an abdication of choice is, of course, far from neutral; it is an endorsement of a classic neo-liberal idea that every perspective must be given an 'equal chance' in the manipulated market place of ideas.

The present, largely empirical, study cannot claim to have resolved the question of which of these possible reactions to legal immunity deals, defined as historically exceptional at least with respect to the Nuremberg trials, merits endorsement. My suspicion is that we must, for reasons already discussed, discard the mainstream reaction of one-sided and partisan outrage at the existence of such deals. Instead, the choice between the realist and immanently critical approaches sketched above cannot be decided upon until a debate is instituted between these two very different modes of defining and then analysing the dilemmas within this field. It is possible that such a debate may be inclusive, and yet result in one of these approaches becoming constructively modified to provide a more adequate theoretical starting point for future empirical analysis of declassified archival materials. This, of course, is renewed speculation.

Bibliography

Aarons, John and Mark Loftus. *The Secret War Against the Jews* (NY: St. Martin's Press, 1994).

Alderman, Sidney. 'The London Negotiations for War Crimes Prosecutions' in Jackson Papers, *op cit*, Box 112, 18, 50–51 (published later in *Negotiating with the Russians* (NY: World Peace Foundation, 1951).

Bigman, M. *Amerikanische Geheimdienstanalysen über Deutschland 1942–1949* (Studien zur Zeitgeschichte, München, 1995).

Bower, Tom. *Blind Eye to Murder. Britain, America and the Purging of Nazi Germany - A Pledge Betrayed* (2nd edition, London: Warner Books, 1995).

Breitman, Richard. *Himmler, The Architect of Genocide* (London: Grafton, 1992).

——. 'New Sources in the Holocaust in Italy', 16:3, *Holocaust and Genocide Studies*, 2002, 404

Breitman, Richard, *et al. US Intelligence and the Nazis* (Washington: IWG-US National Archives, 2004).

Bryan, Ian and Michael Salter. 'War Crimes Prosecutor and Intelligence agencies: The case for assessing their collaboration, 16, *Intelligence and National Security* (2001) 93–120.

Case Karl Wolff (No. 580), Rüter-Ehlermann/ Rüter/ Bauer/ Bracher: Justiz und NS-Verbrechen. Sammlung deutscher Strafurteile wegen nationalsozialistischer Tötungsverbrechen 1945–1999, Amsterdam 1971, Vol. 20 (12.4.1964-20.3.1965), 380–504.

Casey, William. *The Secret War against Hitler* (Washington, DC: Regnery, 1988).

Cave Brown, A. *The Last Hero, Wild Bill Donovan* (NY: Times Books, 1982).

Chalou, George C. (ed.). *The Secrets War: The Office of Strategic Services in World War II* (Washington, DC: National Archives, 1992).

Conot, Robert. *Justice at Nuremberg,* (NY: Harper and Row, 1983).

Danchev, Alex. *Establishing the Anglo-American Alliance: The Second World War Diaries of Brigadier Dykes* (London: Brasseys, 1990).

Dollmann, Eugen. *Call Me Coward* (London: Kimber and Co, 1956).

——. *The Interpreter* (London: Hutchinson, 1967).

Douglas, Laurence. 'Film as Witness', *Yale Law Jnl* (1995) 450–51.

Dulles, Allen. *The Secret Surrender* (NY: Harper and Row, 1966).

Allen Dulles' Papers, Mudd Library, Princeton University, New Jersey, USA.

Dunlop, Richard. *Donovan – America's Master Spy* (NY: Rand McNally & Co, 1982).

Gaskin, Hilary. *Eyewitness to Nuremberg* (London: Arms and Armour, 1998).

Gerhart, Eugene C. *America's Advocate*: *Robert H. Jackson* (NY: Bobbs-Merrill, 1958).

Gilbert, Gerald M. *Nuremberg Diary* (New York: Signet, 1947).

Gilbert, Martin. *The Holocaust: The Jewish Tragedy* (London: Fontana, 1987).

Goda, N. 'Manhunts: The Official Search for Notorious Nazis', in *Breitman et al,* 2004, ch.15.

Harris, Whitney. *Tyranny on Trial* (Dallas: Southern Methodist Univ. Press, 1954).

Hersch, B. *The Old Boys* (NY: Macmillan, 1992).

Hilberg, Raul. *The Destruction of the European Jews* (New Haven: Yale University Press, 2003).

Hoehn, Hans. *The Order of the Death's Head* (London: Penguin, 2000).

Höttl, Wilhelm. *The Secret Service* (NY: Praeger, 1954).

——. *The Secret Front: The Story of Nazi Political Espionage* (London: Weidenfeld & Nicholson, 1953).

Hulme, Claire and Michael Salter. 'The Persecution of Religion as a War Crime: The OSS' Response within the Nuremberg Trials Process', 3 *Rutgers Jnl of Law and Religion* (2001). http://www.camlaw.rutgers.edu/publications/law-religion/v3n1.htm.

Jackson Papers, Manuscript Division, Library of Congress, Washington D.C: Jackson Diaries at Box 95.

Katz, Barry. *Foreign Intelligence, Research and Analysis in the Office of Strategic Services, 1942–1945* (Cambridge, MA: Harvard University Press, 1989).

Kellerman, H. 'Settling accounts – the Nuremberg Trials', *Leo Baeck Yearbook*, Vol. XLII (1997) 337–55, 346.

Kiley, Dan. 'Architect of Palace of Justice Renovations', in *Witnesses to Nuremberg*, eds. B. M. Stave and M. Palmer, with L. Frank (NY: Twain, 1998), 15–38.

Judgement of Nuremberg: *1946* (London: HMSO, 1999).

Koehl, Robert. *The Black Corps* (Madison: University of Wisconsin Press, 1983).

Lamb, Richard. *War in Italy 1943–1945: A Brutal Story* (NY: St. Martins, 1994).

Lang, Jochen von [co-author: Claus Sibyll]. *Der Adjutant. Karl Wolff: Der Mann zwischen Hitler und Himmler* 1985; Frankfurt/M., Berlin: Ullstein, 1989 (all quotations are based on private translations carried out by Anja Becker, but soon to be published in English translation).

Linklater, Magnus, Isabel Hilton and Neal Ascherson. *The Fourth Reich* (London: Hodder and Stoughton, 1984).

Lingen, Kersin von and Michael Salter. 'Contrasting Strategies within the War Crimes Trials of Kesselring and Wolff', 25 *Liverpool Law Review* (2005) 225-266.

Mangold, Tom. *Cold Warrior: James Jesus Angleton* (London: Simon and Schuster, 1991).

Moseley, R. *Mussolini's Shadow: The Double Life of Count Galeazzo Ciano* (Cambridge, MA: Yale University Press, 1999).

Naftali, Timothy. 'Artifice: James Angleton and X-2 Operations in Europe', in Chalou, 1992 *op cit.*

——. 'CIA and Eichmann's Associates', in R. Breitman *et al, US Intelligence and the Nazis*, 2004.

Neave, Airey. *On Trial In Nuremberg* (Boston: Little Brown, 1979).

Niethammer, Lutz. *Das Mitläuferfabrik: Die Entnazifizierung am Beispiel Bayern* (Berlin: Verlag, 1982).

Persico, Joseph. *Penetrating the Reich* (NY: Viking Press, 1978).

——. *The Lives and Secrets of William Casey: From the OSS to the CIA* (NY: Viking/Penguin, 1990)

——. *Nuremberg: Infamy on Trial* (NY: Viking/Penguin, 1994).

Petersen, N. 'From Hitler's Doorstep' in Chalou, 1992.

——. *From Hitler's Doorstep: The Wartime Intelligence Reports of Allen Dulles* (Pennsylvania: Pennsylvania State University Press, 1996).

Grose, Peter. *Gentleman Spy: The Life of Allen Dulles* (Boston: Houghton Mifflin & Co., 1994).

Reitlinger, Gerald. *The Final Solution* (London: Valentine, Mitchel & Co, 1953).

Reynolds, Michael. *The Devil's Adjutant* (Spellmount: Staplehurst, Kent, 2002).

Salter, Michael. 'The prosecution of Nazi War criminals and the OSS: The need for a new research agenda', 2 *The Journal of Intelligence History*, (2002), 77–119.

——. 'Unsettling Accounts: Methodological Issues Within the Reconstruction of the Role of a U.S Intelligence Agency Within the Nuremberg Trials', 56 *Current Legal Issues* (2003) 275–305.

——. 'Intelligence Agencies And War Crimes Prosecution: Allen Dulles' Involvement In Witness Testimony At Nuremberg', 2 *Journal of International Criminal Justice* (2004), 826–854.

Salter, Michael and Lorie Charlesworth. 'Prosecuting and Defending Diplomats as War Criminals: Ribbentrop and the Nuremberg Trials', 27 *Liverpool Law Review* (2006) 67–96.

——. 'The Ciano Diaries at the Nuremberg Trial', *Journal International Criminal Justice* 2006 4(1), 103–127.

——. 'Ensuring The After-Life Of The Ciano Diaries: Allen Dulles' Provision Of Nuremberg Trial Evidence', *Intelligence and National Security*, 2006 in press.

Salter, Michael and Maggi Eastwood. 'Negotiating Nolle Prosequi at Nuremberg: The Case of Captain Zimmer', 3 *Journal of International Criminal Justice*, (2005), 649–665.

Salter, Michael and Suzanne Ost. 'War Crimes and Legal Immunities: The Complicities of Waffen-SS General Karl Wolff in Nazi medical experiments' (2003) 4 *Rutgers Jnl of Law and Religion*: www.lawandreligion.

Schlabrendorff, Fabian von. *The Secret War Against Hitler* (Oxford: Boulder/Westview Press, 1994)

Sereny, Gitta. *Albert Speer: His Battle with the Truth* (London: Macmillan, 1995).

Simpson, Christopher. *Blowback: America's Recruitment of Nazis and Its Effects on the Cold War* (NY: Collier Books, 1988).

——. *The Splendid Blond Beast: Money, Law and Genocide in the Twentieth Century* (Maine Monroe: Common Courage Press, 1995).

Smith, Bradley. *Reaching Judgement at Nuremberg* (NY: Basic Books, 1977).

——. *The American Road to Nuremberg*: *The Documentary Record 1944–1945* (Stanford: Hoover Institution Press, 1982).

——. *The Shadow Warriors. OSS and the Origins of the CIA* (NY: Basic Books, 1983).

Smith, B. F. and E. Agarossi. *Operation Sunrise: The Secret Surrender* (NY: Basic Books, 1979).

Smith, D. 'The Legacy of Nuremberg: Sustaining Human Rights', 25 *Cornell L.F.* 3, 4 (1999)

Sprecher, Drexel. *Inside the Nuremberg Trial: A Prosecutor's Comprehensive Account: Vols. 1 and 2,* (Lanham, MD: University Press of America, 1998).

Storey, Robert. *Final Judgement: Pearl Habor to Nuremberg* (San Antonio: Naylor Co., 1968).

Taylor, Telford. *The Anatomy of the Nuremberg Trials: A Personal Memoir* (NY: Knopf, 1992).

Trevelyan, Robert. *Rome 1944: The Battle for the Eternal City* (London: Book Club Associates, 1981).

Trial of War Criminals before the Nuremberg Military Tribunal Under Control Council No.10, ('TWC') Washington: U.S. Government Printing Office, 1953).

Tusa, Ann and John Tusa. *The Nuremberg Trial* (NY: Atheneum, 1983).

Winks, Robin. *Cloak and Gown, Scholars in the Secret War, 1939-1961* (NY: Morrow, 1987).

Wehner, Wolfgang. '15 Jahre Zuchthaus für Wolff,' *Süddeutsche Zeitung*, 1 October 1964, 1, 9–10.

Wolfe, Robert, IWG Historian. 'Analysis of the Investigative Records Repository (IRR) File of Klaus Barbie *(Alias Klaus Altmann, Klaus Becker, Heinz Becker, Klaus Behrens, Heinz Behrens, Klaus Spier, Ernst Holzer)*', September 19, 2001: http://www.archives.gov/iwg/research-papers/barbie-irr-file.html

——. 'Coddling a Nazi Turncoat' in Breitman *et al* 2004 *op cit.*

Appendix: Abbreviations

CCC	Churchill College Cambridge (Donovan Papers)
CIA	Central Intelligence Agency
CIC	US Army's Counter Intelligence Corp
CIG	Central Intelligence Group (pre-CIA)
CSDIC	Combined Services Detailed Interrogation Centre
G2	US Army Military Intelligence Division.
ICTY	International Criminal Tribunal for the former Yugoslavia
ICTR	International Criminal Tribunal for Rwanda
JAG	Judge Advocate General (US Army legal branch)
NA	US National Archives, Modern Military Archives II, College Park, Washington DC, USA
OCC	Office of Chief of Counsel, Nuremberg prosecutors office
ODEUM	Vatican's Order of the Sovereign Order of Malta
OSS	Office of Strategic Services
PRO	Public Records Office, Kew, London (renamed National Archives towards the end of this project)
RG	Record Group (for NA)
RSHA	The security police division of Himmler's SS [Reichssicherheitshauptamt]
SA	Paramilitary Nazi 'Brown shirts'
SD	Political Intelligence branch of the SS (Sonder-Dienst).
SSU	Strategic Services Unit
SIM	Italian Military Intelligence organisation
UNWCC	United Nations War Crimes Commission

Index

www.ingramcontent.com/pod-product-compliance
Ingram Content Group UK Ltd.
Pitfield, Milton Keynes, MK11 3LW, UK
UKHW022006180926
475701UK00003B/223
* 9 7 8 1 9 0 4 3 8 5 8 0 6 *